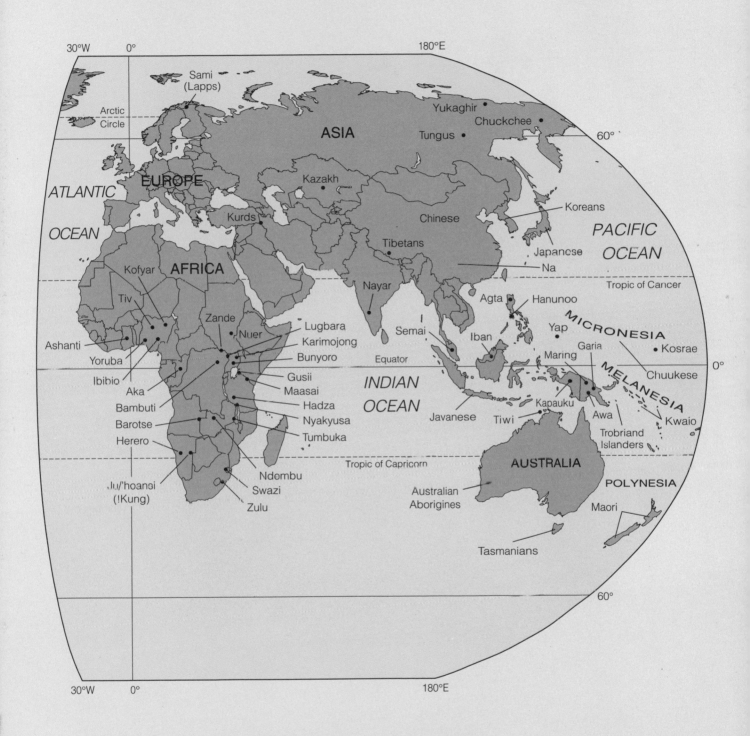

www.wadsworth.com

www.wadsworth.com is the World Wide Web site for Thomson Wadsworth and is your direct source to dozens of online resources.

At www.wadsworth.com you can find out about supplements, demonstration software, and student resources. You can also send e-mail to many of our authors and preview new publications and exciting new technologies.

www.wadsworth.com
Changing the way the world learns®

Seventh Edition

HUMANITY

An Introduction to Cultural Anthropology

James Peoples
Ohio Wesleyan University

Garrick Bailey
University of Tulsa

THOMSON
™
WADSWORTH

Australia • Canada • Mexico • Singapore • Spain
United Kingdom • United States

Senior Acquisitions Editor: *Lin Marshall*
Assistant Editor: *Nicole Root*
Editorial Assistant: *Kelly McMahon*
Technology Project Manager: *Dee Dee Zobian*
Marketing Manager: *Lori Grebe Cook*
Marketing Assistant: *Teresa Jessen*
Senior Project Manager, Marketing Communications:
  Linda Yip
Project Manager, Editorial Production: *Catherine Morris*
Art Director: *Maria Epes*
Print Buyer: *Rebecca Cross*
Permissions Editor: *Sarah Harkrader*

Production Service: *Vicki Moran, Publishing
  Support Services*
Compositor: *Graphic World*
Text Designer: *Ellen Pettengell*
Photo Researcher: *Stephen Forsling*
Copy Editor: *Diane Ersepke*
Illustrator: *Lotus Art*
Cover Designer: *Belinda Fernandez*
Cover Image: *Kurt Mauer Photography*
Text and Cover Printer: *R. R. Donnelley/Willard*

Printed in the United States of America
1 2 3 4 5 6 7 09 08 07 06 05

For more information about our products, contact us at:
Thomson Learning Academic Resource Center
1-800-423-0563
For permission to use material from this text or product, submit a request online at http://www.thomsonrights.com. Any additional questions about permissions can be submitted by e-mail to thomsonrights@thomson.com.

Library of Congress Control Number: 2005920355

Student Edition: ISBN 0-534-64643-3
Instructor's Edition: ISBN 0-495-00406-5

Thomson Higher Education
10 Davis Drive
Belmont, CA 94002-3098
USA

Asia (including India)
Thomson Learning
5 Shenton Way
#01-01 UIC Building
Singapore 068808

Australia/New Zealand
Thomson Learning Australia
102 Dodds Street
Southbank, Victoria 3006
Australia

Canada
Thomson Nelson
1120 Birchmount Road
Toronto, Ontario M1K 5G4
Canada

UK/Europe/Middle East/Africa
Thomson Learning
High Holborn House
50–51 Bedford Road
London WC1R 4LR
United Kingdom

Latin America
Thomson Learning
Seneca, 53
Colonia Polanco
11560 Mexico
D.F. Mexico

Spain (including Portugal)
Thomson Paraninfo
Calle Magallanes, 25
28015 Madrid, Spain

BRIEF CONTENTS

Chapter 1 THE STUDY OF HUMANITY 1

Part I HUMANITY, CULTURE, AND LANGUAGE 20

Chapter 2 CULTURE 20
Chapter 3 CULTURE AND LANGUAGE 41

Part II THEORIES AND METHODS OF CULTURAL ANTHROPOLOGY 63

Chapter 4 THE DEVELOPMENT OF ANTHROPOLOGICAL THOUGHT 63
Chapter 5 METHODS OF INVESTIGATION 87

Part III THE DIVERSITY OF CULTURES 104

Chapter 6 ADAPTATION: ENVIRONMENT AND CULTURES 104
Chapter 7 EXCHANGE IN ECONOMIC SYSTEMS 131
Chapter 8 MARRIAGES AND FAMILIES 150
Chapter 9 KINSHIP AND DESCENT 172
Chapter 10 ENCULTURATION AND THE LIFE CYCLE 192
Chapter 11 GENDER IN COMPARATIVE PERSPECTIVE 212
Chapter 12 THE ORGANIZATION OF POLITICAL LIFE 239
Chapter 13 SOCIAL INEQUALITY AND STRATIFICATION 259
Chapter 14 RELIGION AND WORLDVIEW 280
Chapter 15 ART AND THE AESTHETIC 306

Part IV ANTHROPOLOGY IN THE GLOBAL COMMUNITY 328

Chapter 16 GLOBALIZATION 328
Chapter 17 ETHNICITY AND ETHNIC CONFLICT 354
Chapter 18 WORLD PROBLEMS AND THE PRACTICE OF ANTHROPOLOGY 378

CONTENTS

Preface xiii

About the Authors xix

Chapter 1
THE STUDY OF HUMANITY 1
Subfields of Anthropology 2

Archaeology 2

Concept review: Primary Interests of the Five Subfields of Anthropology 3

Biological/Physical Anthropology 4

Cultural Anthropology 5

A closer look: Five Million Years of Humanity 6

Anthropological Linguistics 10

Applied Anthropology 10

Cultural Anthropology Today 12

Understanding Human Cultures:
Anthropological Approaches 13

Holistic Perspective 14

Comparative Perspective 14

Relativistic Perspective 14

The Value of Anthropology 16

Summary 17

Key Terms 18

InfoTrac College Edition Terms 18

Suggested Readings 18

Part I
HUMANITY, CULTURE, AND LANGUAGE 20

Chapter 2
CULTURE 20
Introducing Culture 21

Defining Culture 22

Shared . . . 22

. . . Socially Learned . . . 23

. . . Knowledge . . . 25

. . . and Patterns of Behavior 25

Cultural Knowledge 26

Norms 26

Values 26

Symbols 27

Classifications and Constructions of Reality 29

A closer look: The Cultural Construction of Race 30

Worldviews 32

Culture and Human Life 32

Concept review: Components of Cultural Knowledge 33

Cultural Knowledge and Individual Behavior 34

Is Behavior Determined by Culture? 34

Why Does Behavior Vary? 35

Biology and Cultural Differences 36

Summary 39

Key Terms 39

InfoTrac College Edition Terms 40

Suggested Readings 40

Chapter 3
CULTURE AND LANGUAGE 41
Humanity and Language 42

Five Properties of Language 43

Multimedia Potential 43

Discreteness 44

Arbitrariness 44

Productivity 44

Displacement 44

How Language Works 45

Sound Systems 46

Concept review: Some Differences Between Consonant Phonemes in English 47

Variations in Sound Systems 47
Words and Meanings 49

A closer look: Indian Givers 50

Nonverbal Communication 51

Language and Culture 52

Language as a Reflection of Culture 52
Language and Worldview 54

Social Uses of Speech 56

Globalization: Globalization and Language 57

Summary 60

Key Terms 61

InfoTrac College Edition Terms 61

Suggested Readings 62

Part II
THEORIES AND METHODS
OF CULTURAL ANTHROPOLOGY 63

Chapter 4
THE DEVELOPMENT
OF ANTHROPOLOGICAL THOUGHT 63

Nineteenth Century: Origins 64

Early Twentieth Century: Development 67

American Historical Particularism (ca. 1900–1940) 67
British Functionalism (ca. 1920–1950) 70

Mid-Century Evolutionary Approaches (ca. 1940–1970) 71

Anthropological Thought Today: Divisions 72

A closer look: Things or Texts? 73

Concept review: Overview of the Scientific and Humanistic Approaches in Cultural Anthropology 74

Scientific Orientations 74

Sociobiology and Evolutionary Psychology 74
Cultural Materialism 76

Humanistic Orientations 77

Interpretive Anthropology 79
Postmodernism 80

Either/Or? 81

Why Can't All Those Anthropologists Agree? 82

Summary 84

Key Terms 85

InfoTrac College Edition Terms 85

Suggested Readings 85

Chapter 5
METHODS OF INVESTIGATION 87

Ethnographic Methods 88

Ethnographic Fieldwork 88
Problems and Issues in Field Research 90

Globalization: Who Owns Culture? 91

Fieldwork as a Rite of Passage 94
Ethnohistory 95

A closer look: Marshall Sahlins, Gananath Obeyesekere, and Captain James Cook 96

Comparative Methods 96

Cross-Cultural Comparisons 96
Controlled Historical Comparisons 99

Concept review: Methods of Investigation 101

Summary 101

Key Terms 102

InfoTrac College Edition Terms 102

Suggested Readings 102

Part III
THE DIVERSITY OF CULTURES 104

Chapter 6
ADAPTATION: ENVIRONMENT
AND CULTURES 104

Understanding Human Adaptation 105

Foraging 107

Foraging and Culture 107

Globalization: Globalization and the Making of Indianness 112

Domestication 113

Advantages of Domestication 113

A closer look: Domesticates in the Old and New Worlds 114

Horticulture 116

Varieties of Horticulture 116
Cultural Consequences of Horticulture 117

Intensive Agriculture 118

Varieties of Intensive Agriculture 119
Cultural Consequences of Intensive Agriculture 120

Pastoralism 123

Herding Environments 123
The Karimojong: An Example from East Africa 125

Adaptation and Culture 126

Concept review: Major Forms of Adaptation
and Their Cultural Consequences 127

Summary 127

Key Terms 128

InfoTrac College Edition Terms 128

Suggested Readings 129

Chapter 7
EXCHANGE IN ECONOMIC SYSTEMS 131

Concept review: Three Forms of Exchange
in Economic Systems 133

Reciprocity 133

Generalized Reciprocity 133

Balanced Reciprocity 134

A closer look: "Insulting the Meat" Among the !Kung 135

Negative Reciprocity 136

Reciprocity and Social Distance 137

Redistribution 138

Market Exchange 139

Money 140

On Market Economies 142

Globalization: Globalization and Markets 144

Peasant Marketplaces 146

Summary 148

Key Terms 148

InfoTrac College Edition Terms 149

Suggested Readings 149

Chapter 8
MARRIAGES AND FAMILIES 150

Some Definitions 151

Concept review: Terms for Groups Formed
on the Basis of Kinship Relationships 152

Marriage 152

Functions of Marriage 154
Two Unusual Forms 155

Marriage in Comparative Perspective 156

Marriage Rules 157
How Many Spouses? 157
Marriage Alliances 160
Marital Exchanges 161

Kinship Diagrams 163

A closer look: Marriage and the Culture Wars 164

Postmarital Residence Patterns 164

Influences on Residence Patterns 165
Residence and Households 166

Family and Household Forms 167

Two-Generation Households 167
Extended Households 167

Summary 169

Key Terms 170

InfoTrac College Edition Terms 170

Suggested Readings 170

Chapter 9
KINSHIP AND DESCENT 172

Why Study Kinship? 173

Cultural Variations in Kinship 173

Unilineal Descent 174

Concept review: Forms of Descent 175

Unilineal Descent Groups 177
Descent Groups in Action 178
Avunculocality Revisited 181

Cognatic Descent 181

Cognatic Descent in Polynesia 182

Bilateral Kinship 183

Influences on Kinship Systems 183

Classifying Relatives: Kinship Terminologies 184

Cultural Construction of Kinship 185
Varieties of Kinship Terminology 185
Why Do Terminologies Differ? 187

Summary 189

Key Terms 190

InfoTrac College Edition Terms 190

Suggested Readings 191

Chapter 10
ENCULTURATION AND
THE LIFE CYCLE 192

Growing Up 193

Diversity in Child Care 193

Two African Examples 194

Aka 194
Gusii 196
Implications for Modern Parents 199

Life Cycle 200

Concept review: Some Variations in the Life Cycle 201

Infancy 201

Childhood and Adolescence 202

Initiation Rites 204

Male Initiation Rituals: A New Guinea Example 204

Female Initiation Rituals: Mescalero Apache 206

Adulthood 206

Old Age 208

Summary 210

Key Terms 210

InfoTrac College Edition Terms 210

Suggested Readings 210

Chapter 11

GENDER IN COMPARATIVE PERSPECTIVE 212

Cultural Construction of Gender 213

Sex and Gender 213

The Hua of Papua New Guinea 214

Gender Crossing and Multiple Gender Identities 217

Cross-Gender Occupation or Work Roles 219

Transvestism 220

Associations with Spiritual Powers 220

Same-Sex Relations 220

The Sexual Division of Labor 221

Understanding Major Patterns 222

Concept review: Factors Affecting the Major Patterns in the Sexual Division of Labor 225

Understanding Variability 227

Gender Stratification 228

Universal Subordination? 229

Influences on Gender Stratification 232

Gender Stratification in Industrial Societies 235

Summary 236

Key Terms 237

InfoTrac College Edition Terms 237

Suggested Readings 237

Chapter 12

THE ORGANIZATION OF POLITICAL LIFE 239

Forms of Political Organization 240

Bands 240

Concept review: Political Organization 241

Tribes 242

Chiefdoms 244

States 244

Social Control and Law 246

Social Control 246

Globalization: The Global Economy and the Future of the Nation-State 247

Law 249

Legal Systems 249

Self-Help Systems 249

Court Systems 252

A closer look: Murder Among the Cheyenne 253

Concept review: Legal Systems 255

Summary 256

Key Terms 256

InfoTrac College Edition Terms 257

Suggested Readings 257

Chapter 13

SOCIAL INEQUALITY AND STRATIFICATION 259

Systems of Equality and Inequality 260

Egalitarian Societies 260

Concept review: Systems of Equality and Inequality 261

Ranked Societies 261

Stratified Societies 262

Castes in Traditional India 263

Classes in Industrial Societies: The United States 265

Maintaining Inequality 268

Globalization: Globalization and Inequality 269

Ideologies 271

American Secular Ideologies 272

Theories of Inequality 273

Functionalist Theory 273

Conflict Theory 274

Who Benefits? 275

A closer look: Rewards and Security 276

Summary 277

Key Terms 278

InfoTrac College Edition Terms 278

Suggested Readings 278

Chapter 14

RELIGION AND WORLDVIEW 280

Defining Religion 281

Beliefs About Supernatural Powers 281

Myths and Worldviews 281

Rituals and Symbols 282

Theories of Religion 283

Intellectual/Cognitive Approaches 285

Psychological Approaches 286

Sociological Approaches 287

Supernatural Explanations of Misfortune 289

Sorcery 289

Witchcraft 290

Interpretations of Sorcery and Witchcraft 291

Varieties of Religious Organization 292

Concept review: Varieties of Religious Organization 294

Individualistic Cults 294

Shamanism 295

Communal Cults 297

Ecclesiastical Cults 298

Revitalization Movements 300

Melanesian Cargo Cults 300

Native American Movements 301

Summary 303

Key Terms 304

InfoTrac College Edition Terms 304

Suggested Readings 304

Chapter 15

ART AND THE AESTHETIC 306

The Pervasiveness of Art 307

Forms of Artistic Expression 309

Body Arts 309

Visual Arts 312

A closer look: Understanding Osage Art 313

Performance Arts 317

Concept review: Forms of Artistic Expression 319

Art and Culture 319

Secular and Religious Art 319

Art and Gender 321

Social Functions of Art 322

Globalization: The Arts of Traditional Peoples
and the Global Economy 323

Summary 325

Key Terms 325

InfoTrac College Edition Terms 326

Suggested Readings 326

Part IV

ANTHROPOLOGY IN THE GLOBAL COMMUNITY 328

Chapter 16

GLOBALIZATION 328

Globalization 329

The Development of Global Trade 329

European Expansion 329

The World and the Industrial Revolution 335

The Emergence of the Global Economy 338

A closer look: Islamic Banking 341

Globalization: The Continuing Process 342

Globalization: Religion and Politics: Globalization
and the Rise of "Fundamentalism" 343

Population Growth and Inequalities
in the Global Economy 346

Consequences of Globalization
and the Global Economy 350

Summary 351

Key Terms 352

InfoTrac College Edition Terms 352

Suggested Readings 352

Chapter 17

ETHNICITY AND ETHNIC CONFLICT 354

Ethnic Groups 355

Situational Nature of Ethnic Identity 355

Attributes of Ethnic Groups 356

Fluidity of Ethnic Groups 358

Types of Ethnic Groups 358

Concept review: Levels of Ethnic Identity 359

The Problem of Stateless Nationalities 360

Globalization: A Clash of Civilizations? 361

A closer look: Ethnic and Religious Differences
in Iraq 364

Resolving Ethnic Conflict 368

Homogenization 368
Segregation 370
Accommodation 370
Resolution 371

Concept review: Responses to Ethnic Differences 372

Summary 375

Key Terms 375

InfoTrac College Edition Terms 375

Suggested Readings 376

Chapter 18

WORLD PROBLEMS AND THE PRACTICE OF ANTHROPOLOGY 378

Applied Anthropology 379

Population Growth 380

Anthropological Perspectives on Population Growth 380
Costs and Benefits of Children in North America 380
Costs and Benefits of Children in the LDCs 382

World Hunger 384

Scarcity or Inequality? 384
Is Technology Transfer the Answer? 386
Agricultural Alternatives 388

Anthropologists as Advocates 389

Indigenous Peoples Today 389

A closer look: Indigenous Rights and Wild Rice 390

Vanishing Knowledge 393
Medicines We Have Learned 394
Adaptive Wisdom 395
Cultural Alternatives 397

Globalization: Globalization and the Question of Development 398

Summary 399

Key Terms 400

InfoTrac College Edition Terms 400

Suggested Readings 400

Glossary 402

Notes 408

Bibliography 413

Photo Credits 427

Peoples and Cultures Index 428

Name Index 433

Subject Index 434

BOXES
A closer look
Five Million Years of Humanity 6

The Cultural Construction of Race 30

Indian Givers 50

Things or Texts? 73

Marshall Sahlins, Gananath Obeyesekere, and Captain James Cook 96

Domesticates in the Old and New Worlds 114

"Insulting the Meat" Among the !Kung 135

Marriage and the Culture Wars 164

Murder Among the Cheyenne 253

Rewards and Security 276

Understanding Osage Art 313

Islamic Banking 341

Ethnic and Religious Differences in Iraq 364

Indigenous Rights and Wild Rice 390

Globalization
Globalization and Language 57

Who Owns Culture? 91

Globalization and the Making of Indianness 112

Globalization and Markets 144

The Global Economy and the Future of the Nation-State 247

Globalization and Inequality 269

The Arts of Traditional Peoples and the Global Economy 323

Religion and Politics: Globalization and the Rise of "Fundamentalism" 343

A Clash of Civilizations? 361

Globalization and the Question of Development 398

PREFACE

In 1985, when we first agreed to write a textbook that introduces undergraduates to cultural anthropology, we settled on the rather ambitious title *Humanity*. We felt that this all-encompassing title accurately captures the most distinctive feature of the field: of all disciplines in the social sciences, anthropology alone studies all the world's peoples. One or another kind of anthropologist looks at peoples who live on all continents and at peoples who lived in the prehistoric past, the historic past, and the present day.

Cultural anthropology—the main subject of this book—describes and tries to explain or interpret the fascinating cultural variability of the world's diverse peoples. In *Humanity*, we try to convey to students the life-enriching as well as the educational value of discovering this variability. In the process of discovery, we hope our readers will experience a change in their attitudes about other cultures and about humanity in general. We also hope our readers will reconsider their own identities as individuals, as cultural beings, and as members of an increasingly worldwide human community. Toward this end, we include material that will teach students new ways of looking at some of the problems that afflict the world in the twenty-first century, particularly those involving globalization and ethnic conflicts, and recent issues involving marriage, population growth, hunger, and the survival of indigenous cultures. Lastly, we want students to grasp the full significance of the oldest anthropological lesson of all: that their own values, worldviews, and behaviors are a product of their upbringing in a particular human group rather than universal among all rational persons.

The previous (sixth) edition was completed just after the 2001 attacks on the World Trade Center and the Pentagon. Events of the past three years suggest that September 11th may have been a historical watershed. As we write, the United States is actively involved in wars in Iraq and Afghanistan. Attacks from Islamic extremists have occurred in Indonesia, Pakistan, the Philippines, Russia, Spain, and Morocco. For the moment at least, isolated regional or local conflicts are eclipsed by a growing global conflict between Western and Islamic peoples. These conflicts and the continuing threat of terrorist attacks lead some to believe that peoples of different ethnicities and religions can never live together in peace and security. Some think that military might offers the best chance to protect their nations from suicide bombers and, even more ominously, from attacks using nuclear or biological weapons.

In the short term, wars and other conflicts separate the antagonists from one another. Yet, overall, the world's regions now interact more frequently and intensively than ever before, and it is hard to imagine that this tendency is reversible. The main reasons for this increasing interdependence of peoples and nations include the increasing integration of the global economy, growing international migration, educational exchanges between countries and regions, the availability of the Internet, the worldwide spread of consumer culture and popular media, and new forms of conflict and cooperation between the world's nations. Words like *multiculturalism* and *multinationalism* have become familiar to most people in just the past couple of decades. Anthropology has much to say about these changes. Just as importantly, anthropology helps us become more aware of how our own lives are affected by such changes.

Changes in the Seventh Edition

Since the first edition of *Humanity* in 1988, the nations of our planet have become literally and figuratively more connected. More than ever, people who live in one place are able to affect other people who live half a world away through the complex connections captured by the word *globalization*. Outsourcing by corporations based in the United States and Europe is resulting in unprecedented transfers of capital, technology, and jobs, most recently to China and India. Directly or indirectly, globalization is producing social, cultural, political, and economic consequences that are remolding the lives of all the world's peoples. This edition again integrates globalization into the text of each chapter and continues to include inserts that discuss dimensions of globalization such as language, market exchanges, inequality, art, and migration.

The major organizational change is the relocation of material on enculturation and the life cycle, which has been moved from Chapter 4 to Chapter 10, thanks to the helpful feedback from reviewers. The one chapter that was new to the previous edition, titled "Art and the Aesthetic," is retained and revised.

In all chapters, we again rewrote the text to streamline certain discussions, update factual material, and reflect recent changes in the field's emphases. In most chapters, numerical data have been updated with the most recently available statistics. As before, all chapters have brief introductions that preview the contents and make the chapter material more relevant and engaging.

For instructors who taught from previous editions of *Humanity,* the following chapter-by-chapter overview of the primary revisions for the seventh edition will be helpful.

Chapter 1 again introduces the five subfields and anthropological perspectives on the human species. The section on biological anthropology is relocated and contains new discussion of the uses of gene sequencing in paleoanthropology. The "A Closer Look" box on human biological evolution contains the latest (2004) available findings and interpretations. The discussion of relativism again distinguishes methodological and moral relavism, using the example of female genital mutilation. Certain professional specializations are eliminated as key terms, although the coverage of the specializations is the same.

Chapter 2 (culture) retains the distinction between behavioral patterns and cultural knowledge, although the section "Cultural Knowledge and Individual Behavior" is revised. The cultural construction of reality receives more emphasis and is now illustrated by an insert on the cultural construction of race.

In Chapter 3 (language) we condensed the subsections on phonology and morphology and deleted the section "Language and Classifications of Reality." This allowed the expansion of the section on nonverbal communication and inclusion of new examples from Japanese and Korean cultures. "A Closer Look" provides some new place names derived from Native American languages.

Chapter 4 (theory) benefits from a slight reduction in the length of the first three sections to make room for substantial new material on modern theoretical orientations. We distinguish the scientific and the humanistic approaches used by modern theorists, eliminating the phrase "idealist approaches." Scientific approaches are illustrated by entirely new discussion of sociobiology (evolutionary psychology) and cultural materialism. Humanistic approaches are exemplified by interpretive anthropology and an expanded coverage of postmodernism.

Chapter 5 (methods) is updated and the part on professional ethics expanded. The globalization box, now titled "Who Owns Culture?" is rewritten to focus on conflicts over the control of cultural images and the issue of indigenous intellectual property rights.

In Chapter 6 (adaptation) some information is updated and the wording is streamlined. We continue to cover hunting and gathering, cultivation, and pastoralism in a single chapter. In addition to the major adaptations themselves, we place most emphasis on their main effects on cultural systems to set the stage for analysis in later chapters.

Chapter 7 (exchange) now begins with a fieldwork anecdote illustrating the difference between market transactions and exchanges organized by reciprocity. We added a brief discussion of the symbolic dimensions of material exchanges. The globalization box, covering the internationalization of markets, contains new material on China.

Chapter 8 (marriages and families) is substantially revised. It contains entirely new coverage of fictive kinship, matrifocal families, and ambilocal residence. Alongside the Tiwi and Nayar, new information on the Na of south China illustrates the difficulties of defining *marriage.* The discussion of arranged marriages now includes information that we hope will help overcome ethnocentric opinions. There is new coverage of "dowry deaths" in South Asia. Finally, "A Closer Look" now discusses anthropological insights on the proposed U.S. constitutional amendment to prohibit legally recognized marriage between gays.

In Chapter 9 (kinship, descent, and terminology) we made few changes other than to clarify the distinction between kinship and descent and to redraw the figure on Omaha kinship terminology.

Chapter 10 (formerly Chapter 4, on enculturation and life cycles) is partially rewritten to reflect its new location. There is increased emphasis on the relevance of comparative material on child care to the constraints on parents in modern societies. New examples include Chuuk (Micronesia) and East Asia, discussed in the context of adulthood and old age.

Rather than trying to be comprehensive, Chapter 11 (gender) still focuses on four topics: cultural construction, multiple gender identities, sexual division of labor, and gender stratification. There is new discussion on the possible influence of the reproductive roles of women and men as a contributing factor to the sexual division of labor. We retained all material dealing with the relevance of anthropological studies for the understanding of gender relations in North American societies.

Chapter 12 (politics and law) is shortened. The globalization box, "The Global Economy and the Future of Nation-State," is moved from Chapter 16 and modified to better suit the context of this chapter.

In Chapter 13 (inequality and stratification), we updated statistical data on the distribution of annual income and wealth (net worth) in North America. In several places, we hint at the relationship between global inequality and international terrorism.

Chapter 14 (religion) retains the addition of the anthropomorphic approach made in the previous edition. Additional material on shamanism is new to this edition, including Zuni and South Korea as examples and discussion of whether shamans are somehow different from other individuals.

The most significant change in Chapter 15 (art) is the deletion of the box "A Native View of Maori Art" and the creation of a new box, "Understanding Osage Art." The new box focuses on the use of religious symbolism in art.

In Chapter 16 (globalization) the text and the closer look box "Islamic Banking" are updated. A new globalization box titled "Religion and Politics: Globalization and the Rise of 'Fundamentalism'" appears. From news stories, we tend to think that fundamentalism is unique to Islam, but this box discusses the emergence of Christian fundamentalism and Hindu extremism as powerful political forces in the United States and India.

Chapter 17 (ethnicity and ethnic conflict) is reduced in length. We deleted the closer look box "The Collapse of the Soviet Union," replacing it with a more timely box, "Ethnic and Religious Differences in Iraq." The box "A Clash of Civilizations?" is retained, since Samuel Huntington's work now seems more relevant than ever.

In Chapter 18 (world problems and the practice of anthropology) we deleted the El Salvador case as our main example of the inequality explanation of world hunger, replacing it with a discussion of the Irish potato famine. We also added a new box titled "Indigenous Rights and Wild Rice," discussing how biotechnology companies and genetically altered rice threaten the traditional wild rice used by the Anishinaabe (Chippewa/Ojibwa) of Minnesota and Wisconsin.

Of course, the glossary, notes, and bibliography are revised to reflect the preceding textual changes. There are a dozen or so new key terms, but a nearly equal number are deleted, for we continue to believe that the main findings of anthropology are more important than mastery of several hundred vocabulary words. As in previous editions, we cite the works consulted for each chapter at the end of the book as a way to keep readers' attention focused on the content. Wherever possible, we attempt to give full credit to the scholars whose theoretical ideas or ethnographic information we use by integrating their names into the chapters themselves.

Pedagogical Features

A difficult problem in introductory texts is balancing the conceptual and theoretical material with ethnographic cases and examples. Our general rule is that all ethnographic examples illustrate some particular idea, theory, concept, or relationship. Most examples are relatively brief, varying from a sentence or two to a full paragraph. In some cases, however, discussion extends to a full page or more. We hope that the examples help bring the theories and concepts to life.

The seventh edition retains most of the closer look boxes, which appear in almost all chapters. Concept reviews, appearing in every chapter, condense concepts and distinctions into a form that emphasizes key differences in just a few words. Most are in tabular format.

As in earlier editions, every chapter concludes with suggested readings. For most chapters, we have replaced some of the older books with more recent ones. Approximately one-third of the photographs are new to this edition.

In addition to these general pedagogical aids, *Humanity* includes several features intended to help students retain information and enhance learning. These include:

- A concise preview of each chapter
- Boldfaced key terms, listed in order of appearance at the end of each chapter
- Boxed features, including globalization boxes
- Point-by-point summaries at the end of each chapter
- Maps on the inside of the front and back covers, showing national boundaries and the locations of the various peoples and cultures that receive significant discussion in the book
- A glossary at the end of the book that succinctly defines each key term
- Photos, with the caption tying the illustration directly to the text discussion
- Three indexes: peoples and cultures index, names (of scholars/authors mentioned or cited), and subjects

Acknowledgments

Over the seven editions of *Humanity*, the comments of reviewers have greatly improved the book. In this edition, we thank the following scholars for their critiques of the sixth edition and their suggestions for improvement:

Laura Anderson, University of Oklahoma
Thomas Durbin, California State University, Stanislaus
Karen Field, Washburn University

Debra Guatelli-Steinberg, The Ohio State University

Zibin Guo, University of Tennessee at Chattanooga

Francisca James-Hernandez, Pima Community College

Patricia Johnson, Pennsylvania State University

Timothy J. Knickerbocker, Central College

David Lumsden, York University

Mike Simonton, Northern Kentucky University

Christina Taylor Beard-Moose, Suffolk County Community College

Adam Wetsman, Rio Hondo College

In addition to the formal reviewers, Jim thanks his colleagues in the Sociology/Anthropology Department at Ohio Wesleyan. Matt Peoples made great suggestions for the revisions to Chapter 3. Deborah was tolerant of my long hours at nights and on weekends.

Supplements

Humanity: An Introduction to Cultural Anthropology, Seventh Edition, is accompanied by a wide array of supplements prepared for both instructors and students to create the best learning environment inside and outside the classroom. All of the continuing supplements have been thoroughly revised, enlarged, and updated. In addition, there are several supplements new to this edition. Especially noteworthy are those that use the Internet.

Supplements for Instructors

Online Instructor's Manual with Test Bank. Prepared by Bruce P. Wheatley of the University of Alabama at Birmingham, this online supplement offers the instructor chapter summaries, lecture suggestions, and discussion questions to facilitate in-class discussion; film/video resources; and Internet and InfoTrac College Edition exercises for each chapter. The test bank consists of 25 to 30 multiple-choice and 10 to 15 true/false questions with answers and page references, as well as 5 to 10 short answer/essay questions. A concise user guide for Info-Trac College Edition is provided as well.

***ExamView* Computerized and Online Testing.** Create, deliver, and customize tests and study guides (both print and online) in minutes with this easy-to-use assessment and tutorial system. *ExamView* offers both a *Quick Test Wizard* and an *Online Test Wizard* that guide you step-by-step throughout the process of creating tests. Its unique "WYSIWYG" capability allows you to see the test you

are creating on the screen exactly as it will print or be displayed online. Using *ExamView*'s complete word processing capabilities, you can enter an unlimited number of new questions or edit existing questions.

Wadsworth's Cultural Anthropology Transparency Acetates 2006. A set of four-color acetates from Wadsworth's Cultural Anthropology texts is available to help you prepare lecture presentations.

Multimedia Manager for Anthropology: A Microsoft PowerPoint Link Tool 2006 CD-ROM. This *2006 CD-ROM* contains digital media and PowerPoint presentations for all of Wadsworth's 2006 introductory anthropology texts, placing images, lectures, and video clips at your fingertips. Start with the preassembled Power-Point Presentations, which include chapter outlines and key terms. Then easily add video and images from Wadsworth's anthropology texts—all included on the CD-ROM. You can also add your own lecture notes and images to create a custom-made lecture presentation. The new Wadsworth Multimedia Manager also includes exciting new Lecture Launchers from field research around the world, supported by Earthwatch Institute.

Wadsworth Anthropology Video Library. Qualified adopters may select full-length videos from an extensive library of offerings drawn from excellent educational video sources such as Films for the Humanities and Sciences.

Case Studies in Cultural Anthropology

George D. Spindler, Series Editor

Since its inception in 1960, the Spindler series has influenced the teaching of countless undergraduate and graduate students of anthropology. Now, Thomson Wadsworth offers you a selection of over 60 classic and contemporary ethnographies in this series, representing geographic and topical diversity. Newer case studies focus on culture change and culture continuity, reflecting the globalization of the world and treating students to firsthand accounts of the interface between formerly separate ethnic groups and their strategies for survival. Students come to grasp more fully the enormity of the changes they see in the world around them.

Case Studies on Contemporary Social Issues

John A. Young, Series Editor

This series explores how anthropology is used today in understanding and addressing problems faced by human societies around the world. Each case study in this new and acclaimed series examines an issue of socially recognized importance in the historical, geographical, and cultural context of a particular region of the world, and includes comparative analysis that highlights not only the local effects of globalization but also the global dimensions of the issue. The authors in this series write with a readable narrative style as they explain, sometimes illustrating from personal experience, how their work has implications for advocacy, community action, and policy formation.

Learn more about these series by visiting the Case Studies page on the Thomson Wadsworth Anthropology Resource Center http://anthropology.wadsworth.com

About the Authors

James Peoples received a B.A. from the University of California, Santa Cruz, and a Ph.D. from the University of California, Davis. Within the field of cultural anthropology, his research interests include cultural evolution, human ecology, and cultures of the Pacific. In addition to coauthoring *Humanity,* he is the author of *Island in Trust,* a book that describes the findings of his fieldwork on a Micronesian island. He has published numerous articles in professional journals, dealing with Micronesian economies and development, human adaptation, and the evolution of culture. Peoples has taught at the University of California, Davis, and at the University of Tulsa. He joined the Sociology/Anthropology Department at Ohio Wesleyan University in 1988. In addition to offering undergraduate classes in his primary research areas, he teaches "Native American Societies of the Southwest" and "Cultures of East Asia." Peoples's latest interest is in the Korean peninsula, to which he hopes to return soon.

Garrick Bailey received his B.A. in history from the University of Oklahoma and his M.A. and Ph.D. in anthropology from the University of Oregon. His research interests include ethnohistory, cultural evolution, and ethnicity and conflict, with a primary focus on the native peoples of North America. His publications include *Navajo: The Reservation Years* (with Roberta Bailey), *Changes in Osage Social Organization 1673–1906, The Osage and the Invisible World,* and *Art of the Osage* (with Dan Swan, John Nunley, and Sean Standingbear). He has been a Senior Fellow in Anthropology at the Smithsonian Institution in Washington and a Weatherhead Resident Scholar at the School of American Research in Santa Fe. Actively engaged in contemporary American Indian issues, he has served as a member of the Indian Health Advisory Committee, Department of Health, Education, and Welfare; and as a member of the Glen Canyon Environmental Review Committee, National Research Council. He is currently a member of the Native American Graves Protection and Repatriation Act (NAGPRA) Review Committee. He has taught anthropology at the University of Tulsa since 1968.

Chapter One

THE STUDY OF HUMANITY

Subfields of Anthropology

Archaeology

Biological/Physical Anthropology

Cultural Anthropology

Anthropological Linguistics

Applied Anthropology

Cultural Anthropology Today

**Understanding Human Cultures:
Anthropological Approaches**

Holistic Perspective

Comparative Perspective

Relativistic Perspective

The Value of Anthropology

© James L. Stanfield/National Geographic Society

Cultural anthropologists conduct field research among the world's diverse peoples. Here anthropologist Dawn Chatty talks to a man from the Harsous people of the Middle Eastern nation of Oman.

WHAT MAKES HUMANS DIFFERENT from other animals? Is there such a thing as "human nature" and, if so, what is it like? How and why do human groups differ, both biologically and culturally? Why have human cultures changed so much in the last 10,000 years? How are people who live in industrialized, urbanized nations different from "traditional" or "indigenous" peoples? These are a few of the questions investigated by **anthropology,** the academic discipline that studies all humanity.

ALMOST EVERYTHING about people interests anthropologists. We want to know when, where, and how the human species originated and why we evolved into what we are today. Anthropologists try to explain the many differences between the world's cultures, such as why the people in one culture believe they get sick because the souls of witches devour their livers, whereas the people in another hold that illness results from tarantulas flinging tiny magical darts into their bodies. We want to know why many Canadians and Australians like beef, which devout Hindus and Buddhists refuse to eat. We are interested in why some

New Guineans often engorge themselves with the meat of pigs, which is the same animal flesh that some Middle Eastern religions hold to be unclean. In short, anthropologists of one kind or another are liable to investigate almost everything about human beings: our evolution, our genes, our emotions, our intellects, our art styles, our behaviors, our languages, and our religions.

ANTHROPOLOGISTS, THEN, study a lot of different things about humanity. In fact, it is commonly said that the distinguishing characteristic of anthropology—the feature that makes it different from the many other fields that also include people as their subject matter—is its broad scope. A good way to emphasize this broad scope is to say that anthropologists are interested in *all* human beings—whether living or dead, Asian or African or European—and that they are interested in many different *aspects* of humans, including their technologies, family lives, political systems, religions, and languages. No place or time is too remote to escape the anthropologist's notice. No dimension of humankind, from skin color to dress customs, falls outside the anthropologist's interest.

Subfields of Anthropology

Because anthropology is such a broad discipline, no single anthropologist can master the entire field. Therefore, modern anthropologists specialize in one of five principal subfields: archaeology, biological (or physical) anthropology, cultural anthropology, anthropological linguistics, or applied anthropology. (The Concept Review summarizes the primary interests of each of the five subfields.) Anthropology is even more complicated than this fivefold division implies because each subfield is in turn divided into several areas of study. Although cultural anthropology is the primary subject of this book, a brief look at the other subfields helps to understand the whole discipline.

Archaeology

The word *anthropology* often calls to mind an archaeologist digging in the earth. **Archaeology** is the investigation of the human past by excavating and analyzing material remains. Because it researches the many ways human life has changed over the centuries and millennia, archaeology has much in common with history. It differs, however, in its methods and, to some extent, its goals. Modern archaeology is usually divided into two major kinds of studies: prehistoric and historic.

Prehistoric archaeology is the study of ancient, preliterate cultures—those that never kept written records of their activities, customs, and beliefs. Although prehistoric peoples lacked writing, some information about their way of life can be recovered from the tools, pottery, ornaments, bones, plant pollen, charcoal, and other materials they left behind, in or on the ground. Through careful excavation and laboratory analysis of such material remains, prehistoric archaeologists reconstruct the way people lived in ancient times and trace how human cultures have changed over centuries and even over millennia. Contrary to the impression given by much North American media, the main goal of digging a particular site is not to recover valuable treasures and other artifacts, but to see how people of a particular place lived long ago. Indeed, research conducted by prehistorians provides our main source of information about how people lived before the development of writing.

Over decades of field research and laboratory analysis, prehistoric archaeologists have learned that all human populations once lived by hunting wild animals and gathering wild plants. Agriculture did not exist anywhere until around 10,000 years ago, when some peoples of the Middle East began planting wheat and barley—for the first time, humans transformed certain wild plants into *crops*. Somewhat later, peoples of southern China, southeast Asia, and west Africa domesticated other plants. On the other side of the world, in what we now call the Americas, different plants were brought under human control in southern Mexico and western South America. Surprisingly, most available evidence suggests that these six regions where agriculture developed were independent—meaning that the people of one region domesticated plants on their own, rather than learning the idea of agriculture from other peoples. Similarly, civilization (living in cities)

		Anthropology		
Archaeology	**Physical/ Biological**	**Cultural**	**Anthropological Linguistics**	**Applied**
Changes in human cultures over very long time spans by excavating sites, to reconstruct human prehistory and supplement written historical documents	Biological evolution of *Homo sapiens;* physical variation among human populations; comparisons of human anatomy and behavior with other primate species	Differences and similarities in contemporary and historically recent diverse cultures, investigated through intensive fieldwork and careful comparisons	General relation between language and culture; role of language and speaking in cultural and social life of specific peoples; how language shapes cognition and thought	Applications of anthropological skills, knowledge, concepts, and methods to the solution of real-world problems

developed in several different regions independently, beginning about 5,000 years ago.

To learn about people of the past who lived in literate societies, historians use written materials such as diaries, letters, land records, newspapers, and tax collection documents. The growing field of **historic archaeology** supplements such written materials by excavations of houses, stores, plantations, factories, and other historic structures. For example, the cover story of the April 16, 2001, issue of *Time* magazine was "What Jesus Saw: Jerusalem Then and Now." Historic archaeologists worked with other scholars to reconstruct life in ancient Jerusalem, providing hard data on living conditions and other topics lacking in written accounts.

Many archaeologists today are employed not in universities but in museums, public agencies, and for-profit corporations. Museums offer jobs as curators of artifacts and as researchers. State highway departments employ archaeologists to conduct surveys of proposed new routes in order to locate and excavate archaeological sites that

© Robert Brenner/Photo Edit

▲ Prehistoric archaeologists investigate the remote past by the careful excavation of material remains.

will be destroyed. The U.S. Forest Service and National Park Service hire archaeologists to find sites on public lands so that the appropriate parties can make decisions about the preservation of cultural materials. Those who work in the growing field of *cultural resource management* locate sites of prehistoric and historic significance, evaluate their importance, and make recommendations about total or partial preservation. Since the passage of the National Historic Preservation Act in 1966, private corporations and government bodies that wish to construct factories, buildings, parking lots, shopping malls, and other structures must file a report on how the construction will affect historical remains and on the steps taken to preserve them. Because of this law, the business of *contract archaeology* has boomed in the United States. Firms engaged in contract archaeology bid competitively for the privilege of locating, excavating, and reporting on sites affected or destroyed by construction. Hundreds of (mostly small) contract archaeology companies exist, providing jobs for thousands of archaeologists and students.

Biological/Physical Anthropology

Biological (also called **physical**) **anthropology** is concerned with the anatomy and behavior of monkeys and apes, the physical variations between different human populations, and the biological evolution of the human species. As its name and these subjects indicate, biological anthropology is closely related to the biological and zoological sciences in its goals and methods.

The specialization of **primatology** studies the evolution, anatomy, adaptation, and social behavior of primates, the taxonomic order to which humans belong. Research on the behavior of group-living monkeys and apes has added significantly to the scientific understanding of many aspects of human behavior, including tool use, sexuality, parenting, cooperation, male–female differences, and intergroup conflict and aggression. Field studies of African chimpanzees and gorillas, the two apes genetically most similar to the human species, have been especially fruitful sources of hypotheses and knowledge.

For example, in the 1960s the famous British primatologist Jane Goodall observed tool making among African chimpanzees. Chimpanzees modified sticks to fit into holes in termite mounds. When termite soldiers attacked the intruding objects, the chimps withdrew the probes and licked off the tasty insects. Goodall observed adult chimps teaching their young how to probe for termites, showing that humanity's closest animal relatives have at least a semblance of cultural tradition. Chimpanzee groups also wave tree branches in aggressive displays against other groups and wad up leaves to use as sponges to soak up drinking water. Chimps use heavy rounded stones as hammers against flat stones to crack open the hard shells of nuts and even leave the tools under nut trees for future use. These and other observations changed our understanding of human–animal differences, for prior to such studies making tools was widely considered to be one of the things humans could do that other animals could not.

Another type of biological anthropologist studies how and why human populations vary physically due to hereditary, genetic factors. This subfield is **human variation.** All humanity belongs to a single species,

© Michael K. Nichols/National Geographic Society

▲ Field studies by primatologists overturned some earlier notions about human uniqueness, such as the idea that humans are the only species to use and make tools. Here a young chimpanzee inserts a twig into a termite mound to probe for the nourishing insects.

which taxonomists refer to as *Homo sapiens sapiens.* One of the most important findings of anthropology is that the physical/genetic similarities among the world's peoples far outweigh the differences. Indeed, many anthropologists today believe that the term *race* has little biological meaning, no matter how much importance people attach to visible physical differences in their cultural ideas and beliefs (discussed in Chapter 2).

Nonetheless, peoples whose homelands are in Africa, Asia, Europe, Australia, the Pacific islands, and the Americas were once more isolated from one another than they are today. During this separation they evolved differences in overall body and facial form, height, skin color, blood chemistry, and other genetically determined features. Anthropologists who specialize in human variation measure and try to explain the differences and similarities among the world's peoples in such physical characteristics.

Another important goal of physical anthropology is to understand how and why the human species evolved from prehuman, apelike ancestors. The specialization that investigates human biological evolution is known as **paleoanthropology.** Over decades of searching for fossils and carrying out meticulous laboratory studies, paleoanthropologists have reconstructed the history of how humans evolved anatomically.

Since the late 1970s, paleoanthropologists have a new method for investigating human evolution. Scientists in the field of molecular genetics are able to sequence DNA—the genetic material by which hereditary traits are transmitted between generations. By comparing DNA sequences, geneticists can estimate how closely different species are related. The more similar the DNA between two or more species, the less time has elapsed since their divergence from a common ancestor. Studies comparing the genetic sequences of African apes with humans show that humans share 97.7 percent of their DNA with gorillas and 98.7 percent with chimpanzees and bonobos (also known as pygmy chimpanzees).

Through analyzing fossils, comparing DNA sequences, and other methods, the outlines of human evolution are becoming clear. Most scholars agree that the evolutionary line leading to modern humans split from those leading to modern African apes (chimpanzees and gorillas) around five to six million years ago. (See the feature A Closer Look for an overview of basic facts and the latest findings on human biological evolution.)

Most physical anthropologists work in universities or museums as teachers, researchers, writers, and curators. But many people trained in biological anthropology also apply their knowledge of human anatomy to solve prob-

lems. For instance, specialists in **forensic anthropology** work for or consult with law enforcement and other agencies, where they help identify human skeletal remains. Among their contributions are determining the age, sex, height, and other physical characteristics of crime or accident victims. Forensic anthropologists gather evidence from bones about old injuries or diseases, which are then compared with medical histories to identify victims. For example, forensic anthropologist Clyde Snow disinterred the bones of some of the northern Iraqi Kurds killed by Saddam Hussein's government in the late 1980s. In the 1990s, teams of forensic anthropologists exhumed remains from graves in Bolivia, Guatemala, El Salvador, and Haiti to identify victims of political assassination and determine the causes of their deaths.

Cultural Anthropology

Cultural anthropology (also called **social anthropology, sociocultural anthropology,** and **ethnology**) is the study of contemporary and historically recent human societies and cultures. As its name suggests, the main focus of this subfield is culture—the customs and beliefs of some human group (the concept of culture is discussed at length in Chapter 2).

As we'll see in future chapters, cultural anthropologists study an enormous number of specific subjects, far too many to even be listed here. But some of their overall objectives are:

- studying firsthand and reporting about the ways of living of particular human groups
- comparing diverse cultures in the search for general principles that might explain human ways of living
- trying to understand how various dimensions of human life—economics, family life, religion, art, communication, and so forth—relate to one another in particular cultures and in cultures generally
- understanding the causes and consequences of cultural change
- enhancing public understanding and appreciation of cultural differences and multicultural diversity.

This last objective is especially important in the contemporary world, in which individuals with diverse cultural backgrounds regularly come into contact with one another in our emerging global society.

To some people, ethnological studies seem a bit esoteric—"interesting," they are likely to say, "but of little practical value." Most anthropologists disagree. We think that what we learn by our descriptions, comparison, and analyses of cultures helps to improve the human

In his 1871 book *The Descent of Man,* the British naturalist Charles Darwin proposed that humans and African apes (including chimpanzees and gorillas) are closely related. Noting the anatomical similarities between humans and apes, Darwin argued that humans must have evolved from an apelike ancestor over eons of time. In his day, there was little evidence in the form of fossils that linked ape to human, but Darwin realized that the many physical similarities between humans, chimps, and gorillas can only be explained by a common biological ancestry.

By the early 1900s, most scientists accepted Darwin's general theory of biological evolution as well as his specific hypothesis about the close relationship between humans and apes. But where was the physical evidence in the form of fossils—where was the "missing link" that was supposed to prove that humans have apelike ancestors? Before answering such questions, we first describe briefly how scientists classify living organisms using the methods of taxonomy.

Even in Darwin's day, taxonomists recognized the similarity between African apes and humans. Both are classified in the same taxonomic superfamily (Hominoidea), though in different families (Pongidae for apes, Hominidae for humans). Below the family level, modern humans are classified in the genus *Homo,* in the species *sapiens,* and in the subspecies *sapiens.* Thus you and I are *Homo sapiens sapiens;* the common chimpanzee is *Pan troglodytes;* the mountain gorilla is *Gorilla gorilla.* Generally, the criterion used to decide whether two very similar animals are in the same species is whether they mate and produce fertile offspring under natural conditions. All humans can do so.

Assigning an extinct animal known only from fossils to a species, or even to a genus, is often difficult. In human evolution, there are many ambiguities and uncertainties, many of which center around issues of whether a particular fossil is or is not a direct ancestor of humans: For example, was this fossil a hominid and, if so, was it a *Homo* and, if so, to which species did it belong? These uncertainties are inherent in the fossil record; they are not, as some believe, "proof" that those who study human evolution are "just speculating."

Missing Links and Other Misconceptions

Throughout the twentieth century, an enormous amount of evidence accumulated about the biological evolution of modern humans from an apelike ancestor over several millions of years. Despite this evidence, many misconceptions remain about human evolution. A good way to introduce the topic of human evolution is to correct a few of them.

1. Scientists have still not found the missing link. The term *missing link* refers to a fossil that is intermediate between ape and human, combining some ape features with some human fea-

tures. In Darwin's day, no such half-and-half fossil had yet been discovered. Contrary to what some people still believe, in fact the first missing link was discovered in South Africa back in the 1920s. Named *Australopithecus africanus,* its skull was much like that of an ape, but it walked bipedally (on two legs rather than four). Future discoveries showed that its pelvis, legs, and feet were much like those of modern humans. Later, literally thousands of such fossils were found, representing hundreds of individuals; East Africa alone has yielded more than 300 hominid fossils. Today there are numerous "links," and debate centers largely on how fossils are related to one another and on which particular remains are directly ancestral to humans.

2. People evolved from chimpanzees or gorillas. Although these two African apes are indeed our closest relatives in the primate family, humans did not evolve from them. Rather, modern humans and modern apes share a common ancestor that lived in Africa sometime between about five and eight million years ago. Metaphorically speaking, the living apes are our cousins, not our evolutionary grandparents. Your ancestors were not chimpanzees.

3. The main difference between apes and humans is brain size and intelligence. Certainly, the size of the brain does differentiate people and apes—a chimpanzee's cranial capacity averages around 400 cubic centimeters, a gorilla's around 500, and a human's around 1,300. And people are, in many ways, "smarter" than apes—humans use more sophisticated tools, speak complex languages, solve abstract problems, drastically modify their environments, and so forth. But the first change that began to differentiate the evolutionary line leading to modern apes from that leading to modern humans was not brain size, but the form of locomotion—human ancestors walked on two legs millions of years before brains increased notably in size. Thus, evolutionarily speaking, it was bipedalism that set humanity on a different evolutionary path from modern apes. In fact, when biological anthropologists judge whether a disputable fossil fragment is or is not a hominid, their main criterion is whether it regularly walked on two legs, not the size of its brain.

4. People are the only primate to make tools. Until the mid-twentieth century, scholars sometimes said that tool use distinguished people from other primates. But other scholars recognized that many other animals also use objects as tools (e.g., sea otters use stones to break open abalone shells to get at the meat inside). Then some scholars claimed that humans are the only creatures to actually manufacture tools, meaning that only humans modify a natural object (a stone, a stick) into a particular shape to make it more useful. This too proved to be a misconception when in the 1960s Jane Goodall observed chimpanzees

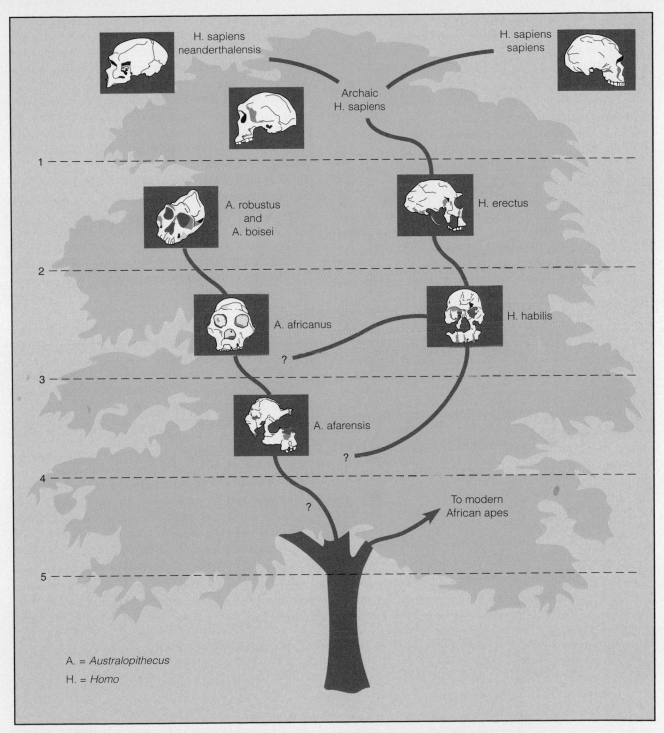

▲ **Figure 1.1** Common ancestors of modern apes and humans, dating between five and one million years ago.

modifying sticks to make termite probes and using leaves to soak up water from hollow trees. So tool making is not a uniquely human trait, although of course only humans are capable of taking technology to its more complex forms.

5. Neandertal man is our immediate ancestor. In 1856, quarry workers accidentally unearthed some bones from a "cave man" in Germany's Neander Valley. At the time, no one realized their significance, and there was debate about whether they came from a deformed European with a projecting face or even whether they were human at all. Later, fossils were found in both Europe and western Asia, along with convincing evidence that Neandertals made stone tools, hunted large mammals, built shelters, used fire, and buried their dead. By the mid-twentieth century, many scientists thought that Neandertal was our direct ancestor. (Perhaps it was comforting to think that modern humans evolved in Europe or in the Middle East.) By the late twentieth century, though, both fossil evidence and DNA comparisons demonstrated fairly clearly that *Homo neandertalensis* is not a direct human ancestor but an offshoot that lived around 130,000 to 35,000 years ago. It is likely that fully modern humanity (*Homo sapiens sapiens*) first evolved in Africa within the last 200,000 years, then spread over the rest of the Earth, replacing any other hominids that might still have existed in Europe and Asia, including Neandertal populations.

6. Humans are the most advanced or most evolved species. Actually, phrases like *most evolved* have little objective meaning in modern evolutionary science. Biologists and physical anthropologists speak of *differences* between species (such as between monkeys and apes and between apes and humans), but to speak of one species being more advanced than another involves value judgments. We can only say that humans and apes evolved differently, depending on the specific kinds of pressures they encountered in their history, but we should not say that humans are more evolved.

7. Human evolution is just a theory, not supported by hard evidence and indisputable fact. See misconception number 1. Notice, though, that few "facts" are indisputable in science because future research may change scientific opinions. Indeed, in recent years scientific views on human evolution have undergone quite a revolution.

Most importantly, until the 1970s most scholars thought that human evolution was essentially *linear;* that is, one hominid species arose from its ancestor, which quickly became extinct, perhaps because it could not compete. Linear evolution means that only one or, at most, two hominid species lived at the same time. In this view, there was an evolutionary line leading from an apelike creature through various transitional forms (the "links" that used to be "missing") to modern humans.

So into the 1970s most researchers thought that two million years ago there were only two hominids alive, found only in Africa. Both were members of the genus called *Australopithecus,* which at the time seemed to be the probable link between extinct apes and modern humans. The chimpanzee-sized *Australopithecus africanus* was mainly a meat-eater and eventually evolved into modern humans. The somewhat larger *Australopithecus robustus* was mainly a vegetarian and an evolutionary dead end that left no modern descendants. Both were considered hominids because both were bipedal. *Australopithecus africanus* was sometimes known as the "killer ape" because it was a predator, so killing animals for food was one of the things that began to differentiate hominids from pongids. Or so most paleoanthropologists believed.

Today it is fairly well established that the human family tree is not linear, but has *multiple branches;* that is, several species of early hominids coexisted (see Figure 1.1). This means that one species evolved into two or more new species, which then coexisted for a long time. Perhaps the first hominid, living between about three and four million years ago, was *Australopithecus afarensis* (also known as Lucy, discovered in the 1970s). Lucy is most simply described as a creature with an apelike head and humanlike limbs. In 2001, researchers announced a possibly new hominid species from Kenya living 3.5 million years ago, about the same time as Lucy, but with smaller molars and a flatter face. Either one of these could have been the earliest hominid. There could have been even earlier species: in 2004, several teeth were discovered in Ethiopia that might have come from a very humanlike ancestor. If future analysis supports this find, it pushes the date of the earliest hominid back to nearly six million years ago.

By about two million years ago, most contemporary researchers think, there were four or five hominids living: *Aus-*

condition. We believe that our studies of other cultures will help us to understand our own way of life. And, as we shall see later, specific studies carried out by cultural anthropologists have helped solve practical problems in real human communities.

To do research and collect information about particular cultures, ethnologists conduct **fieldwork.** Fieldworkers ordinarily move into the community under study so that they can live in close contact with the people. If practical, they communicate in the local language.

tralopithecus africanus, Australopithecus robustus, Australopithecus boisei, Homo habilis, and possibly *Homo rudolfensis* (whether the latter is a different species from *habilis* is disputable). The three australopithecine species eventually died out, leaving no modern descendants. *Homo habilis* (probably the first to make chopping tools out of stone) evolved into *Homo erectus* around 1.8 million years ago.

Homo erectus is the first hominid known to have left Africa and is found as far away from Africa as Indonesia (when first discovered, it was called Java Man) and China (Peking Man). Although its brain size averaged only around 900 cubic centimeters, *Homo erectus* was almost as tall as modern people with a low forehead and a large but recognizably human face. This early form of humanity made sharp stone tools, butchered animals, and used and probably controlled fire.

In Africa, some local populations of *Homo erectus* evolved into archaic *Homo sapiens* by 200,000 years ago, and probably earlier. (*Archaic* is used to emphasize that there was great variety in the earliest *Homo sapiens* populations, with *Homo sapiens neanderthalensis* probably arising out of one form.) In the next 100,000 years, some of these people left Africa and migrated into Europe and throughout Asia, bringing a modern human body type, technology, language, and culture with them. If there were any local populations of *Homo erectus* left in eastern and southeastern Asia, they were replaced by *Homo sapiens sapiens*. By 12,000 years ago, human beings had migrated to every land mass on Earth except Antarctica and the remote islands of the Pacific.

What Does All This Have to Do with Us?

What relevance does the evolutionary history of humanity hold for modern humanity—for humans as we are today? If evolution is accepted, then the characteristics of a living species are a product of the forces that shaped it in its past. So the way modern people are—human nature, as some call it—might be more understandable if we can reconstruct our evolutionary past. For instance, many popular writers have claimed that humans are naturally aggressive, either because evolving into predators made us fierce or because our ancestors competed over resources so that early hominids had to fight to defend their territories. As evidence

for their views, such writers cite research that allegedly showed that australophithecines were "killer apes," that *Homo erectus* ate their own kind, that Neandertals made weapons used in violent encounters, and so forth. If modern humans are prone to violence and warfare, evolution made us this way, some claim. Implicit in the argument is that violence and warfare are so difficult to control because they are part of our genetic heritage.

Such arguments are not necessarily wrong, but the evidence about human evolution is subject to many interpretations. That humans evolved from apelike ancestors is practically indisputable, but researchers differ on details of the process. For example: Which early hominid is *the* earliest? Were the australopithecines our ancestors or just an evolutionary branch that died out? Did *Homo sapiens sapiens* originate only in Africa, migrate from there, and eventually displace hominids in other regions? There is no generally accepted answer to such questions. Particular biological anthropologists have their own opinions and publish them. Then others support or attempt to refute them based on their views of what the evidence shows or, sometimes, based on their own biases or previous statements. If the interpretations of human *physical* evolution are contentious, then think about the uncertainties involved in trying to reconstruct the *behavior* (e.g., aggression) of an ancestor.

Some people, of course, do not accept evolution at all, and they especially do not accept the notion that humans evolved from any other so-called lower form of life. Those few who bother to read the scientific literature on human evolution misinterpret the many disagreements and contentious issues. "See," such skeptics often say, "those evolutionists can't even agree among themselves. Why should we believe them when they don't even believe one another?" But, fundamentally, evolutionists *do* believe one another. They disagree only on specific details and particular issues; they do not disagree on the fact that humans and apes shared a common ancestor some millions of years ago. Scholarly disagreement indicates that scholars are considering evidence and coming to different conclusions. It does not mean that the scholars are making things up. Indeed, it means something very obvious: Bones do not speak for themselves.

Sources: Begun (2004); Haile-Selassie et al. (2004); Jurmain et al. (2000); Wood (2002); Wood and Richmond (2002)

Daily interaction with the members of a community provides anthropologists with firsthand experiences that yield insights and information that could not be gained in any other way. Fieldworkers usually report the findings of their research in books or scholarly journals,

where they are available to other scholars and to the general public. A written account of how a single human population lives is called an **ethnography** (which means "writing about a people"). We have more to say about fieldwork in Chapter 5.

© Reuters/Corbis

▲ Forensic anthropologists work with governments and international organizations to identify human skeletal remains and to help determine the causes of death. These forensic specialists are examining remains in El Salvador.

Anthropological Linguistics

Defined as the study of human language, linguistics is a field all its own, existing as a separate discipline from anthropology. Linguists describe and analyze the sound patterns and combinations, words, meanings, and sentence structures of human languages. As discussed in Chapter 3, language has some amazing properties, and the fact that humans are able to learn and use language at all is truly remarkable.

Language interests anthropologists for several reasons. For one thing, the ability to communicate complex messages with great efficiency may be the most important capability of humans that makes us different from primates and other animals. Certainly our ability to speak is a key factor in humanity's evolutionary success.

Cultural anthropologists are interested in language because of how the language and culture of a people affect each other. The subfield of **anthropological linguistics** is concerned with the complex relations between language and other aspects of human behavior and thought. For example, anthropological linguists are interested in how language is used in various social contexts: What style of speech must one use with people of high status? Does the particular language we learned while growing up have any important effects on how we view the world or how we think and feel?

Applied Anthropology

In the past, most professional anthropologists spent their careers in some form of educational institution, either in colleges and universities or in museums. Today, hundreds of anthropologists hold full-time positions that allow them to apply their expertise in governmental agencies, nonprofit groups, private corporations, and international bodies. Hundreds of others make their living

▲ In her laboratory, paleoanthropologist Meave Leakey compares two possible ancestors of modern humans. After decades of fieldwork and laboratory measurements, the outlines of humanity's biological evolution are becoming clear.

as consultants to such organizations and institutions. These institutions and organizations employ anthropologists because they believe that people trained in the discipline will help them in problem solving. In recognition of the growth of noneducational employment opportunities, the American Anthropological Association (the professional organization of anthropologists) officially recognizes **applied anthropology** as a separate subfield. Since about 1990, roughly half of those earning an anthropology Ph.D. have acquired jobs in some federal, state, or local governmental agency or in the private sector.

We discuss some of the ways applied anthropologists have contributed to the alleviation of human problems in later chapters. For now, a few examples will illustrate some of the work they do.

Medical anthropology is one of the fastest growing specializations. Medical anthropologists investigate the complex interactions among human health, nutrition, social environment, and cultural beliefs and practices. Because the transmission of viruses and bacteria is greatly affected by people's diets, sanitation, sexual habits, and other behaviors, one role of medical anthropologists is to work with epidemiologists to identify cultural practices that affect the spread of disease. Different cultures have different ideas about the causes and symptoms of disease, how best to treat illnesses, the abilities of traditional healers and doctors, and the importance of community involvement in the healing process. By studying how a human community perceives such things, medical anthropologists can provide information to hospitals and agencies that helps them deliver health care services more effectively.

Development anthropology is another area in which cultural anthropologists apply their expertise to the solution of practical human problems, usually in the Third World. Working both as full-time employees and as consultants, development anthropologists provide information about communities that helps agencies adapt projects to local conditions and needs. Examples of agencies and institutions that employ development anthropologists include the U.S. Agency for International Development, the Rockefeller and Ford Foundations, the World Bank, and the United Nations Development Program. One important role of the anthropologist in such institutions is to provide policymakers with knowledge of local-level ecological and cultural conditions, so that projects will avoid unanticipated problems and minimize negative impacts.

Educational anthropology offers jobs in public agencies and private institutions. Some roles of educational anthropologists include advising in bilingual education, conducting detailed observations of classroom interactions, training personnel in multicultural issues, and adapting teaching styles to local customs and needs. Many modern nations, including those of Europe and the Americas, are becoming more diverse due to international migration. As a response to this trend, an increasingly important role for educational anthropologists working in North America is helping professional educators understand the learning styles and behavior of children from various ethnic and national backgrounds.

Private companies sometimes employ cultural anthropologists full time or as consultants, creating a professional opportunity often called *corporate anthropology*. As globalization erodes barriers to international commerce, people of different cultural heritages increasingly conduct business and buy and sell one another's products.

© Markus Matzel/Peter Arnold

© Brian Vikander/Corbis

▲ One message anthropologists teach their students is understanding and appreciating the diversity of the world's many cultures. As interaction among peoples increases, the lesson of cross-cultural understanding becomes ever more important.

In recent decades, the dramatic growth of overseas business activities has encouraged North American companies to hire professionals who can advise executives and sales staff on what to expect and how to speak and act when they conduct business in other countries. Because of their training as acute observers and listeners, anthropologists are employed in the private sector in many other capacities as well: They watch how employees interact with one another, analyze how workers understand the capabilities of office machines, study how the attitudes and style of managers affect worker performance, and perform a variety of other information-gathering and analysis tasks.

As these examples show, anthropologists apply their knowledge and skills to the solution of practical human problems in many ways. Speaking broadly, cultural anthropologists are valuable to governments, international agencies, companies, and other organizations because they are trained to do two things very well: first, to observe, record, and analyze human behavior in very diverse settings; and, second, to look for and understand the cultural assumptions, values, and beliefs that underlie that behavior.

Cultural Anthropology Today

As our brief summary of the five subdisciplines confirms, anthropology is indeed a diverse field. Even by itself, cultural anthropology—the main subject of this text—is enormously broad, for modern fieldworkers live among and study human communities from all parts of the world, from the mountains of Tibet to the deserts of the American Southwest, from the streets of Chicago to the plains of East Africa.

In the popular imagination, fieldworkers go to far-off places to study "native" peoples. Except for some common but mistaken stereotypes about "natives," this image was reasonably accurate until the 1970s. Until then, ethnology differed from sociology and other disciplines that studied living peoples mainly by the kinds of cultures we studied. Cultural anthropologists focused on small-scale, non-Western, preindustrial, subsistence-oriented cultures, whereas sociologists tended to study large Euro-American, industrial, money-and-market countries. Not too long ago, many cultural anthropologists sought untouched tribal cultures to study because living among the "primitives" usually enhanced one's reputation. In a few cases, a "new tribe" was "discovered" by an anthropologist, or more often by someone else, with exaggerated media coverage. Of course, the people usually turned out not to be previously unknown after all.

Today all this has changed. You are about as likely to find an anthropological fieldworker studying a Canadian medical clinic as a New Guinea village. A few subjects of recent studies in modern settings include American bodybuilders, the cultural significance of Elvis, British witches' covens, Appalachian towns, New Jersey fraternities, courts of law, the decline of the middle class, the U.S. Congress, and family life in the Silicon Valley. In the early twenty-first century, anthropologists have published professional articles with titles such as "The Virtual Nuclear Weapons Laboratory in the New World Order." As these examples illustrate, cultural anthropologists are increasingly working "here at home" rather than far away.

Some studies done in the anthropologist's own country are of recent immigrant communities. North America—sometimes said to be the continent of immigrants—includes people of diverse origins, as we all know. Some immigrants become largely or partly assimilated: over a period of decades or generations they adopt many of the customs and beliefs of the so-called mainstream. In other cases, though, there is considerable cultural continuity with the past—immigrants continue their language, cuisine, family relations, wedding and funeral customs, and other practices and beliefs. For example, the United States government relocated thousands of Hmong, a people of highland southeast Asia, into the Central Valley of California. Even after two or three decades of living in the United States, many immigrant Hmong still speak little English, bring large numbers of relatives to live with them in houses other Americans consider "single-family" dwellings, use their traditional methods of curing, and occasionally eat animals that Americans define as pets.

Even many of those who work "far away" now conduct fieldwork in more than one place. This is largely because of the effects of **globalization**—the intermixing and migrations of peoples with diverse homelands, the multinational reach of communications media, the movement of production and services to overseas locales, the increase in international travel and tourism, and so forth. If an anthropologist wants to study "a people" and "their culture" in the world today, it is increasingly informative to study them in all the places on our planet where they now live.

So the boundaries between cultural anthropology and other disciplines (especially sociology) are much less clear-cut than they were even a few years ago. Most ethnological fieldwork, however, still occurs in relatively small communities (on the order of a few hundred to a few thousand) where the researcher can interact directly with people and experience their lives firsthand. More than any other single factor, the intense fieldwork experience distinguishes cultural anthropology from other disciplines concerned with humankind. Also, cultural anthropology remains far more comparative and global in its scope and interests than the other social sciences and humanities. Even today, ethnologists are far more likely to conduct research in a country other than their own than are sociologists or psychologists.

Cultural anthropology overlaps greatly with other fields. Almost all ethnologists specialize in a particular world *region* (such as West Africa, China, the Pacific islands, or Latin America) where they do fieldwork. Someone who specializes in a geographic region will read the works of historians, sociologists, novelists, and political scientists who have written about the region. Sociocultural anthropologists also specialize in particular *subjects* (such as political structures, childhood maturation, legal systems, or art). To increase their knowledge of such subjects, anthropologists become familiar with the work of geographers, political scientists, psychologists, and artists or art historians—disciplines that have made some particular dimension of human life their subject area.

For such reasons, cultural anthropologists regularly study subjects that "belong to" other disciplines. This point is nicely illustrated by anthropological research interests in such areas as ethnomusicology, ethnopoetics, ethnobotany, and ethnolinguistics. (Here's an at least half-true general principle: Any subject can be made into a subject for anthropological research by prefixing it with "ethno.") Cultural anthropology thus cuts across many disciplines, encompassing many of the subjects that other scholars consider their special province—law, religion, economics, literature, music, and so on.

Understanding Human Cultures: Anthropological Approaches

Because cultural anthropologists study many of the same kinds of things as other scholars, obviously it is not *what* they study that makes their field distinct. The main difference between anthropology and other social sciences and humanities is not so much in the *kinds* of subjects we investigate as in the *approaches* we take to studying human life. We believe it is important that cultures and communities be studied holistically, comparatively, and relativistically. Because it is these perspectives as much as anything else that make cultural anthropology distinctive, they need to be introduced.

Holistic Perspective

To study a subject holistically is to attempt to understand all the factors that influence it and to interpret it in the context of all those factors. The **holistic perspective** means that no single aspect of a human culture can be understood unless its relations to other aspects of the culture are explored. Holism requires, for example, that a fieldworker studying the rituals of a people must investigate how those rituals are influenced by the people's family life, economic forces, political leadership, relationships between the sexes, and a host of other factors. The attempt to holistically understand a community's customs, beliefs, values, and so forth is one reason ethnographic fieldwork takes so much time and involves close contact with people.

Taken literally, a holistic understanding of a people's customs and beliefs is probably not possible because of the complexity of human societies. But cultural anthropologists have learned that ignoring the interrelations between language, religion, art, economy, family, and other dimensions of life results in distortions and misunderstandings. The essence of the holistic perspective may be stated fairly simply: *Look for connections and interrelations between things, and try to understand parts in the context of the whole.*

Comparative Perspective

As we have already seen, until the 1970s anthropologists focused mainly on non-Western peoples, many of whom thought and acted quite differently from the citizens of their own (usually European or North American) nation. Anthropologists soon learned that the ideas and concepts that applied to their own societies often did not apply to those of other peoples, whose cultural traditions were vastly different. They learned, for example, to mistrust the claims put forth by French scholars about human nature when the only humans these scholars had ever met lived in western Europe!

More than most people, anthropologists are aware of the enormous diversity of the world's cultures. This diversity means that any general theories or ideas scholars might have about humans—about human nature, sexuality, warfare, family relationships, and so on—must take into account information from a wide range of societies. In other words, general theoretical ideas about humans or human societies or cultures must be tested from a **comparative perspective.**

The main reason why anthropologists insist on comparison is simple: Unless we compare and contrast cultures, we have no way of discovering whether some customs or belief is unique to one culture (e.g., your own), or is found among only certain cultures, or is universal among all cultures. And unless we know whether a custom or belief is found in one, in only some, or in all cultures, we cannot investigate why it exists. Many people mistakenly think that the customs and beliefs familiar to them exist among people everywhere, which is usually not the case. Anthropologists know that the cultural ideas and practices of people living in different times and places are far too diverse for any general theory to be accepted until it has been tested in a wide range of human groups. The comparative perspective that anthropologists use to investigate their ideas may be stated as: *Generalizations about humans are likely to be mistaken unless they take the full range of cultural diversity into account.*

Relativistic Perspective

Fundamentally, **cultural relativism** means that no culture—taken as a whole—is inherently superior or inferior to any other. Anthropologists adopt this perspective because concepts such as superiority require judgments about the relative worthiness of behaviors, beliefs, and other characteristics of a culture. But such judgments are usually rooted in one's values, which, by and large, depend on the culture in which one was raised. (If you think there are universal standards for judging cultures, you may be right. However, aside from such actions as homicide, people don't agree on what they are.)

To see why a relativistic approach to studying cultures is important, contrast cultural relativism with **ethnocentrism.** Ethnocentrism is the belief that the moral standards, manners, attitudes, and so forth of one's own culture are superior to those of other cultures. Most people are ethnocentric, and a *certain degree* of ethnocentrism is probably essential if people are to experience the sense of belonging necessary for contentment and if their culture is to persist. Mild ethnocentrism—meaning that people hold certain values dear but don't insist that everyone else hold and live by those values—is unobjectionable and inevitable. It is to be expected of humans who, after all, generally become committed to their values while growing up. But extreme ethnocentrism—in which people believe their values are the only correct ones and that all people everywhere should be judged by how closely they live up to those values—leads to attitudes and behaviors of intolerance that are anathema to cultural anthropology.

Clearly, ethnocentric attitudes are detrimental to objectivity, and ethnographic fieldworkers should avoid evaluating the behavior of other people according to the standards of their own culture. Like the holistic and comparative perspectives, the essential point of cultural relativism may be stated simply: *In studying another culture, do not evaluate the behavior of its members by the standards and values of your own culture.*

Unfortunately, many people misunderstand the word *relativism*. To anthropologists, relativism is a *methodological principle* that refers to an attitude that is essential for maximum objectivity and understanding when studying a people whose way of life differs from their own. As a methodological principle, relativism recognizes that behavior viewed as morally wrong (or sinful) in one society may not be wrong or sinful in another. Unqualified condemnations of the actions or beliefs of some group of people have no place in anthropological research or in anthropological writings.

In nonanthropological settings, the term *relativism* is commonly used in another way. *Moral relativism* (or relativism as a *moral principle*) means there are no absolute, universal standards by which to evaluate actions in terms such as right and wrong or good and bad. Some people blame moral relativism for a host of social problems. For example, perhaps you have heard that society's acceptance of extramarital sex or tolerance for homosexuality erodes family values and increases divorce rates, or that the failure of public schools to teach traditional values and morality leads to delinquency and violence, or that the lack of attention given to religious teachings is responsible for high crime rates. Recently, fearing the societal consequences of legalizing stable relationships between gay persons, the legislatures of a number of states have passed "defense of marriage acts" that define marriage as a relation between a man and a woman. Such arguments and policies imply that there *are* absolute standards and clear rules about right and wrong or moral and immoral behavior. But moral relativism *taken to its extreme* says that there are few such standards or rules.

Newcomers to anthropology often confuse the two meanings of relativism, mistakenly believing that anthropologists promote both kinds of relativism. Most anthropologists certainly are methodological relativists, but far fewer are moral relativists. Anthropologists are as likely as anyone to consider oppression, slavery, murder, slander, and so forth as morally objectionable. The September 11, 2001, terrorist attack on the United States is viewed with as much horror by anthropologists as by most other people, although most of us seek to understand the historical background and cultural context that led to it rather than interpreting it simply as the incarnation of evil.

However, the issue of relativism is not as simple in practice as the distinction between methodology and morality implies. An example will illustrate. Most people have heard of the custom generally called *female circumcision* or *female genital mutilation*. The practice is widespread—but not even close to universal—in some regions of northern Africa. It varies in severity, ranging from removal of the clitoris to stitching shut the labia until marriage. Cultural beliefs about the reasons for the custom also vary, but most often focus on controlling unmarried female sexuality and raising a woman's desirability as a marriage partner. Further complicating the issue is that in many places a majority of older women support the custom (so it is not unambiguously an issue of male control or oppression of women). Often a woman herself considers it a symbol of her femininity and of her and her family's honor.

How should an anthropologist consider this custom? Do we think of it as just another age-old tradition—like eating with your fingers, or women going about barebreasted, or men covering their genitals with nothing but penis sheaths—that varies from people to people but is *inherently* neither right nor wrong? Surely not: This custom causes pain, exposes people to the danger of infection and other complications, and is applied only to women because of their gender. In most cases, it is forced upon a girl around a certain age even if she objects. Because of its pain, danger, selectivity, and social enforcement, female circumcision is not comparable to customs surrounding food and home decoration, which vary from people to people but are generally "harmless."

Then, is female genital mutilation a form of oppression? And if so, by whom? Can culture itself oppress people? If it is oppression, does the anthropologist simply record it, place it in its local cultural context, compare the cultures that practice it with other cultures that do not, develop an idea about its meaning and why it occurs, and then leave it alone? That is what many anthropologists believe we should do *as anthropologists*. Others disagree, believing instead that we should speak out against such practices, both as anthropologists and as human beings.

But exactly what counts as "such practices"? Does female footbinding in nineteenth-century China count? Would tightly binding the waists of women in nineteenth-century Europe count? In North America, how are twenty-first-century breast augmentation or reduction, hip and thigh liposuction, face lifts, and nose jobs different from female circumcision? Is it that they seem to be voluntary? Then, if a North African woman consents to her circumcision, does her consent make the custom okay by us? And if a young North American woman feels constrained by the ideals of beauty as defined by the culture in which she grew up, is her liposuction or breast augmentation truly voluntary? And why is so little said about the removal of the foreskin of most American male infants, who have absolutely no choice when their genitals are mutilated?

Such answers are not at all obvious, which is our main point. Most anthropologists would probably be satisfied with the following solution. Relativism as a methodological principle is essential to anthropological research, for it facilitates fieldwork and leads to greater objectivity. Moral relativism is a separate matter and depends largely on one's values. When an anthropologist encounters customs (such as female circumcision) that rather clearly cause harm, then the matter becomes complex because it is difficult to remain morally neutral. In such cases, we need to examine the custom very closely to place it in its cultural context; perhaps the "harm" is necessary given the way the people live. We also need to consider comparable practices (such as breast augmentation) that might have a similar character or function within our own culture. After doing so, we might note that "we" sometimes do similar things as "them"—though we have trouble recognizing the similarity because it involves "us"— so that we need to examine ourselves when we condemn others. Of course, such a view does not resolve the essential problem of cultural relativism (just how "relativistic" should we be?), but at least it reminds us that all human groups believe and do things that some other human groups find abhorrent.

The Value of Anthropology

What insights does anthropology offer about humanity? What is the value of the information that anthropologists have gathered about the past and present of humankind? In future chapters we look further at how anthropological research contributes to the solution of human problems. For now, we note some of the most general insights and contributions.

First, anthropology helps us understand the biological, technological, and cultural development of humanity over long time spans. Most of the reliable information available about human biological evolution, prehistoric cultures, and non-Western peoples resulted from anthropological research. This information has become part of our general storehouse of knowledge. Because it is recorded in textbooks and taught in schools, we easily forget that someone had to discover these facts and interpret their significance. For example, only in the late nineteenth century did most scientists accept that people are

related to apes, and only in the late twentieth century did the closeness of this relation become apparent.

Anthropology has contributed more than just data and facts. Concepts first developed or popularized by anthropologists have been incorporated into the thinking of millions of people. To illustrate, in this chapter we have used the term *culture,* confidently assuming our readers know the word and its significance. You may not know that the scientific meaning of this word, as used in the phrase *Japanese culture,* is not very old. Well into the nineteenth century, people did not fully understand the importance of the distinction between a people's culture (the *learned* beliefs and habits that made them distinctive) and their biological makeup (their *inherited* physical characteristics). Patterns of acting, thinking, and feeling often were thought to be rooted in a group's genetic makeup.

For example, because there are obvious differences in the physical appearance of various peoples, many believed that physical differences accounted for differences in beliefs and habits as well. In other words, differences that we now know are caused largely or entirely by learning and upbringing were confused with differences caused by biological inheritance. Early-twentieth-century anthropologists such as Franz Boas, Alfred Kroeber, and Ruth Benedict marshaled empirical evidence showing that race and culture are independent of each other. As this example shows, anthropologists have in fact contributed much to our understanding of the human condition, although most people are not aware of these contributions.

Another value of anthropology is that it teaches the importance of understanding and appreciating cultural diversity. Anthropology urges its students not to be ethnocentric in their attitudes toward other peoples. Cultural relativism is not only important to the objectivity of fieldworkers but also one of the main lessons anthropology offers to the general public. Mutual toleration and understanding among the world's peoples is increasingly important in this era of world travel, international migration, multinational businesses, globalization, and conflicts based on ethnic or religious differences. The world's problems will not be solved simply by eliminating ethnocentrism. But a relativistic outlook on cultural differences might help to alleviate some of the prejudices, misunderstandings, interethnic conflicts, and outright racism that continues to afflict so many people on all continents.

A related point is that anthropology helps people to avoid some of the miscommunication and misunderstandings that commonly arise when people from different parts of the world interact with one another. As we shall see in future chapters, our upbringing in a particular culture influences us in subtle ways. For instance, English people know how to interpret one another's actions on the basis of speech styles or body language, but these cues do not necessarily mean the same thing to people from different cultures. A Canadian salesperson selling products in Turkey may wonder why her host will not cut the small talk and get down to business, whereas the Turk can't figure out why the visitor thinks they can do business before they have become better acquainted. An Anglo-American trying to appear self-confident in his dealings with a Latin American may instead come across as arrogant or egotistical. A middle manager from a German firm may be unintentionally offensive when he places the business card of his Korean or Japanese counterpart in his pocket without carefully studying it. Anthropology teaches people to be aware of and sensitive to cultural differences—people's actions may not mean what we take them to mean, and much misunderstanding can be avoided by taking cultural differences into account in our dealings with other people.

Finally, because of its insistence on studying humanity from a comparative perspective, anthropology helps us to understand our own individual lives. By encouraging you to compare and contrast yourself and your ways of thinking, feeling, and acting with those of people living in other times and places, anthropology helps you see new things about yourself. How does your life compare to the lives of other people around the world? What assumptions do you unconsciously make about the world and other people? Do people in other cultures share the same kinds of problems, hopes, motivations, and feelings as you do? Or are individuals raised in other societies completely different? How does the overall quality of your existence—your sense of well-being and happiness, your self-image, your emotional life, your feeling that life is meaningful—compare with that of people who live elsewhere? Anthropology offers the chance to compare yourself to other peoples who live in different circumstances. By studying others, we gain new perspectives on ourselves.

Summary

1. Defined as the study of humanity, anthropology differs from other disciplines in the social sciences and humanities primarily because of its broad scope. The field as a whole is concerned with all human beings of the past and present, living at all levels of technological development. Anthropology is also interested in all aspects of humanity: biology, language, technology, art, religion, and all other dimensions of human life.

2. Individual anthropologists of today usually specialize in one of five subdisciplines. Archaeology uses the material remains of prehistoric and historic peoples to investigate the past, focusing on the long-term technological and social changes that occurred in particular regions of the world. Biological/physical anthropology studies the biological dimensions of human beings, including nonhuman primates, the physical variations between contemporary peoples, and human evolution. Cultural anthropology, or ethnology, is concerned with the social and cultural life of contemporary and historically recent human societies. By conducting fieldwork in various human communities and describing their findings in ethnographies, cultural anthropologists contribute to the understanding of cultural diversity and to making the general public more aware and tolerant of cultural differences. Anthropological linguistics studies language, concentrating on the interrelations between language and other elements of culture. Finally, applied anthropology uses the concepts, methods, and theories of anthropology to solve real-world problems in such areas as health, development, business, and education.

3. Until around 1970 cultural anthropology (the main subject of this text) concentrated on cultures that are popularly known as "tribal," "indigenous," or "preindustrial." This is not as true today, when anthropologists often do their research in the urbanized, industrialized nations of the developed world. It is increasingly difficult to distinguish ethnology from the kindred discipline of sociology. However, firsthand, extended fieldwork in villages or relatively small towns or neighborhoods continues to be a hallmark of cultural anthropology. Also, ethnologists are far more comparative and global in their interests and research than other social scientists.

4. Cultural anthropologists approach the study of other cultures from three main perspectives. Holism is the attempt to discover and investigate the interrelations between the customs and beliefs of a particular society. The comparative perspective means that any attempt to understand humanity or explain cultures or behaviors must include information from a wide range of human ways of life, for anthropologists have learned that most customs and beliefs are products of cultural tradition and social environment, rather than of a universal human nature. In practicing cultural relativism, fieldworkers try to understand people's behaviors on their own terms, not those of the anthropologist's own culture. This requires that anthropologists avoid being ethnocentric in their research, for each people have their own history and values. Most anthropologists consider themselves to be methodological relativists, but moral relativism is a separate, though related, matter.

5. Anthropology has practical value in the modern world. Only anthropology allows us to see the development of human biology and culture over long time spans. Most of the knowledge we have about human evolution, prehistoric populations, and modern tribal societies was discovered by anthropologists. Early anthropologists were instrumental in popularizing the concept of culture and in showing that cultural differences are not caused by racial differences. The value of inculcating understanding and tolerance among citizens of different nations is another practical lesson of anthropology, one that is increasingly important as the economics of the world become more interdependent and as international terrorism makes the consequences of international misunderstanding more serious. The information that ethnographers have collected about alternative ways of being human allows us to become more self-aware.

Key Terms

anthropology
archaeology
prehistoric archaeology
historic archaeology
biological/physical
    anthropology
primatology
human variation

paleoanthropology
forensic anthropology
cultural anthropology
    (social anthropology,
    sociocultural anthro-
    pology, ethnology)
fieldwork
ethnography

anthropological linguistics
applied anthropology
globalization
holistic perspective
comparative perspective
cultural relativism
ethnocentrism

InfoTrac College Edition Terms

origin of civilization
chimpanzee behavior

human evolution
relativism

female genital mutilation

Suggested Readings

The following books are among the best introductions to the subdisciplines of anthropology:

Agar, Michael. *Language Shock: Understanding the Culture of Conversation.* New York: William Morrow, 1994.

Written in an informal style, this book is a readable first look at anthropological ideas about the relationship between language and culture.

Ervin, Alexander M. *Applied Anthropology: Tools and Perspectives for Contemporary Practice.* Boston: Allyn and Bacon, 2000.

Thorough introduction to applied anthropology. Covers ethics, roles of anthropologists in policy formation and program assessment, and specific methods.

Fagan, Brian. *People of the Earth: An Introduction to World Prehistory.* 11th ed. New York: Pearson, 2003.

Comprehensive textbook, written for undergraduates, covering the prehistory of all continents.

Jurmain, Robert, Harry Nelson, Lynn Kilgore, and Wendy Trevathan. *Essentials of Physical Anthropology.* 5th ed. Belmont, Calif.: Wadsworth, 2003.

A relatively brief introduction to primatology, human evolution, and genetic and physical variation among human populations.

Peterson, Dale, and Karl Amman. *Eating Apes.* Berkeley: University of California Press, 2003.

Despite humanity's close relationship to African apes, their very existence is seriously endangered by human predation and other human impacts. This book tells the tragedy in narrative form.

Renfrew, Colin, and Paul Bahn. *Archaeology: Theories, Methods, and Practice*. 3rd ed. London: Thames and Hudson, 2000.

Comprehensive yet user-friendly textbook focusing on the methods archaeologists use to investigate the past.

The following ethnographies are excellent for introducing the ways of life of various peoples around the world. All are highly readable.

Farrer, Claire R. *Thunder Rides a Black Horse: Mescalero Apaches and the Mythic Present*. 2nd ed. Prospect Heights, Ill.: Waveland, 1996.

Concise account of ethnographer's experience with the modern Apache. Focuses on girls' puberty ceremonies, interweaving Apache culture into the account.

Kraybill, Donald B. *The Puzzles of Amish Life*. Intercourse, Penn.: Good Books, 1990.

Focuses on how the Amish of Lancaster County, Pennsylvania, have maintained intact communities and their values by selectively using modern technologies.

Shostak, Marjorie. *Nisa: The Life and Words of a !Kung Woman*. New York: Vintage, 1983.

A readable biographical account of a woman of the !Kung (formerly called the Bushmen), a hunting and gathering people of the Kalahari desert in southern Africa.

Turnbull, Colin. *The Forest People*. New York: Simon & Schuster, 1962.

A sympathetic ethnography about the traditional culture of the BaMbuti pygmies of the African rain forest.

Ward, Martha C. *Nest in the Wind*. Prospect Heights, Ill.: Waveland, 1989.

A delightful account of a fieldworker's experiences and difficulties on a tropical Pacific island.

Companion Website for This Book

The Wadsworth Anthropology Resource Center
http://anthropology.wadsworth.com

The companion website that accompanies *Humanity: An Introduction to Cultural Anthropology,* Sixth Edition, includes a rich array of material, including online anthropological video clips, to help you in the study of cultural anthropology and the specific topics covered in this chapter. Begin by clicking on Student Resources. Next, click on Cultural Anthropology, and then on the cover image for this book. You have now arrived at the Student Resources home page and have the option of choosing one of several chapter resources.

Applying Anthropology. Begin your study of cultural anthropology by clicking on Applying Anthropology. Here you will find useful information on careers, graduate school programs in applied anthropology, and internships you might wish to pursue. You will also find real-world examples of working anthropologists applying the skills and methods of anthropology to help solve serious world problems.

Research Online. Click here to find a wealth of Web links that will facilitate your study of anthropology. Divided into different fields of study, specific websites are starting points for Internet research. You will be guided to rich anthropology websites that will help you prepare for class, complete course assignments, and actually do research on the Web.

InfoTrac College Edition Exercises. From the pull-down menu, select the chapter you are presently studying. Select InfoTrac College Edition Exercises from the list of resources. These exercises utilize InfoTrac College Edition's vast database of articles and help you explore the numerous uses of the search word, *culture.*

Study Aids for This Chapter. Improve your knowledge of key terms by using flash cards and study the learning objectives. Take the practice quiz, receive your results, and email them to your instructor. Access these resources from the chapter and resource pull-down menus.

Chapter Two

CULTURE

Introducing Culture

Defining Culture

Shared . . .

. . . Socially Learned . . .

. . . Knowledge . . .

. . . and Patterns of Behavior

Cultural Knowledge

Norms

Values

Symbols

Classifications and Constructions of Reality

Worldviews

Culture and Human Life

Cultural Knowledge and Individual Behavior

Is Behavior Determined by Culture?

Why Does Behavior Vary?

Biology and Cultural Differences

© D. H. Hessell/Stock Boston

Culture is the shared and learned ways of thinking, feeling, and acting found among a human society or other group. These people in Seoul, South Korea, are honoring the birthday of Buddha with prayers and gifts.

MANY PEOPLE USE THE WORD *culture* practically every day. For example, you may think you increase your "appreciation of culture" by going to a symphony or an art gallery. Perhaps you have heard someone complain about the "popular culture" of TV sitcoms, action movies, computer games, tongue and body piercings, soap operas, and rap music. Maybe you yourself use peoples' speech style or personal tastes as a basis for thinking that some individuals are more "cultured" than others because of their ethnic identity, social class, or where they went to school.

TAKEN IN CONTEXT, these ways of using the word *culture* are fine. But anthropologists define and use the term in different way; we want people to appreciate the full significance of culture for our understanding of humanity. In the anthropological conception, the distinction between "high culture" and "low culture" is largely meaningless, and it is impossible for one group of people to "have more culture" than another group.

IN THIS CHAPTER, we discuss the anthropological conception of culture. After giving the word a fairly precise definition, we cover some of its main elements, introducing some terms along the way. We then discuss why culture is so important to the human species. Finally, we explain the modern anthropological view of how cultural differences and physical/biological differences between human populations are related.

Introducing Culture

The Englishman E. B. Tylor was one of the founders of the field that was later to become cultural anthropology. In 1871, Tylor wrote a book titled *Primitive Culture,* in which he pulled together much of the information available about the native peoples of other lands (that is, places other than Europe). The book begins with a definition that many consider the earliest modern conception of culture: culture is "that complex whole which includes knowledge, belief, art, morals, law, customs, and any other capabilities and habits acquired by man as a member of society." Notice that this definition is very broad, including almost everything about a particular people's overall way of life, from their "knowledge" to their "habits." Notice also that culture is something individuals acquire as "a member of society," meaning that people obtain their culture from growing up and living among a particular group.

Since Tylor's day, anthropologists have defined culture in hundreds of ways, although the main elements of Tylor's original conception of culture are still with us. Practically all modern definitions share certain key features. Anthropologists agree that culture

- is learned from others in the process of growing up in a particular human society or group
- is widely shared by the members of that society or group
- is responsible for most of the differences in ways of thinking and behaving that exist between human societies or groups
- is so essential in completing the psychological and social development of individuals that a "cultureless" individual would not be considered normal by other people

Culture, in brief, is learned, shared, largely responsible for group-level differences, and necessary to make individuals into complete persons.

Cultural anthropologists often use the term *culture* when they want to emphasize the unique or most distinctive aspects of a people's customs and beliefs. When we speak of Japanese culture, for example, we usually mean whatever beliefs and customs the Japanese people share that make them different from other people. How Japanese think and act differs in some ways from how North Americans, Iranians, Chinese, and Indians think and act, and the phrase *Japanese culture* concisely emphasizes these differences. So to speak of the culture of a people is to call attention to all the things that make that people distinctive from others and, hence, that make that people unique in some respects.

Notice that there are some things that anthropologists do *not* mean when we use the word *culture*. We do not mean that Japanese culture is better or worse than, say, French or Indian culture. We mean only that the three differ in certain identifiable ways. Anthropologists also do not mean that Japanese, French, or Indian culture is unchanging. We mean only that they remain in some ways distinct despite the changes they have experienced over the years. Above all, anthropologists do not mean that Japanese, French, or Indian cultures are different because of the physical (biological) differences between the three peoples. We mean only that Japanese, French, and Indian children are exposed to different ways of thinking and acting as they grow up, so that they *become* Japanese, French, or Indian because of their upbringing in different social environments.

How do cultures differ? In what ways do they vary? As a first look, we can say that cultures vary in their ways of thinking and ways of behaving. *Ways of thinking* means what goes on inside people's heads: how they perceive the world around them, how they feel about particular people and events, what they desire and fear, and so forth. *Ways of behaving* refers to how people commonly act: how they conduct themselves around parents and spouses, how they carry out ceremonies, what they do when they are angry or sad, and so forth. Obviously, thought and behavior are connected. How we act depends, in part, on how and what we think. In turn, the ways we think depend, in part, on how people around us behave.

Although ways of thinking and behaving are related, it is important to distinguish between them. To do so, anthropologists often distinguish *mental* components and *behavioral* components of culture.

Culture's mental components include all the knowledge and information about the world and society that children learn while growing up. These include attitudes about family, friends, enemies, and other people; notions of right and wrong (morality); conceptions about the proper roles of males and females; ideas about appropriate dress, hygiene, and personal ornamentation; rules about manners and etiquette; beliefs about the supernatural; standards for sexual activity; notions about the best or proper way to live (values); and perceptions of the world. The list could, of course, be greatly expanded to include all other knowledge that the members of a society or other group have learned from previous generations. All these kinds of knowledge largely determine how members of a culture think.

In this book, we use the phrase **cultural knowledge** to refer to the attitudes, ideas, beliefs, conceptions, rules, values, standards, perceptions, and other information stored in people's heads. To avoid repetition, we use the terms *beliefs* and *ideas* as synonyms for *knowledge*.

For now, there are two key points about cultural knowledge. First, ideas and beliefs are learned as a consequence of being born into and growing up among a particular group. This means that any information that people genetically inherit (such as "instincts") is not—by definition—part of culture because it is not learned. Second, individuals do not invent culture. Rather, the members of any given generation are carriers of the cultural ideas and beliefs they have learned from previous generations and will pass along, perhaps with some modifications, to future generations. Some people, of course, have more influence on their culture than do others, but even very important people who are viewed as innovators are building on the cultural knowledge their group has learned from previous generations.

As for the behavioral components of culture, they include all the things people regularly do, or how they habitually act. As the terms *regularly* and *habitually* imply, members of the same culture generally adopt similar behaviors in similar situations (for example, in church, on the job, at a wedding or funeral, visiting a friend). Anthropologists are usually more interested in these regularities and habits—in what most people do most of the time when they are in similar situations—than in the behavior of individuals. We are most concerned with **patterns of behavior.** To avoid repetition, we will use the terms *behavior(s)* and *action(s)* as synonyms for *behavioral patterns,* but *pattern, habitual,* and *regular* are always implicit.

Although we distinguish between the mental and the behavioral components of culture, the two are closely related and profoundly affect each other. To emphasize these interconnections, we speak of **cultural integration,** meaning that the various elements of culture fit together in a more or less coherent way. Stated differently, cultural integration means that the various parts of culture are mutually interdependent. We use the phrase *cultural system* when we wish to emphasize the integration of culture.

Defining Culture

The concept of culture is so important that it is useful to have a formal definition of the term:

> The **culture** of a group consists of shared, socially learned knowledge and patterns of behavior.

For convenience, we discuss each major component of this definition separately.

Shared . . .

By definition, culture is *collective*—it is shared by some group of people. "Shared by some group of people" is deliberately vague because the "group" that "shares" culture depends largely on our interests. The people who share a common cultural tradition may be quite numerous and geographically dispersed, as illustrated by the phrases *Western culture* and *African culture.* Although we use such phrases whenever we want to emphasize differences between Africans and Westerners, the peoples to whom they refer are so diverse that the term *group* has little meaning. At the other extreme, the group that shares a common culture may be small. Some Pacific islands or Amazonian tribes, for instance, have only a couple hundred members, yet the people speak a unique language and have distinct customs and beliefs.

Despite these and other complexities, when we say people *share culture* we usually mean at least one of two things. First, the people are capable of communicating and interacting with one another without serious misunderstanding and without needing to explain what their behavior means. Second, people share a **cultural identity:** they recognize themselves and their culture's traditions as distinct from other people and other traditions. Thus, not all Africans (or Westerners, or Native Americans) share culture by the first criterion, although in the modern era they do by the second.

People who share a common culture often live in the same **society,** a territorially defined population most of

© Steve Raymer/Corbis

▲ By definition culture is shared by some human group, but the "group" may be very small or very large and inclusive. As this photo of Malaysian Muslims praying illustrates, when we speak of "Islamic culture" we are not speaking of a particular society, but of the culture of those people around the world who practice Islam.

whose members speak the same language and share a sense of common identity relative to other societies. The identification of a cultural tradition with a single society is sometimes convenient because it allows us to use phrases like *American culture* and *Indian culture.* Societies and cultures, however, do not always share the same physical territory. For example, we usually think of a modern nation as a single society, yet many cultural groupings, identities, and traditions (subcultures) coexist within the boundaries of most modern nations.

. . . Socially Learned . . .

Individuals acquire their culture in the process of growing up in a society or some other kind of group. The process by which infants and children learn the culture of those around them is called **enculturation** or **socialization.** Learning one's culture, of course, happens as a normal part of childhood. To say that culture

is learned from others seems obvious, but it has several important implications that are not so obvious.

To say that culture is *learned* is to emphasize that culture is not acquired genetically, that is, by means of biological reproduction. A people's culture does not grow out of their gene pool or biological makeup, but is something the people born into that group acquire while growing up among other members. Africans, East Asians, Europeans, and Native Americans do not differ in their cultures because they differ in their genes—they do not differ *culturally* because they differ *biologically.* Any human infant is perfectly capable of learning the culture of any human group or biological population, just as any child can learn the language of whatever group that child is born into. To state the main point in a few words: *Cultural differences and biological differences are largely independent of one another.*

To say that culture is *socially* learned is to emphasize that people do not learn culture primarily by trial and error learning. The main way children learn culture is by observation, imitation, communication, and inference, and not by trial and error. One important way in which humans differ in degree, though not in kind, from other primates is the ability to learn by imitating and communicating with other humans. When you were an infant, you did not learn what is good to eat primarily by trying out a variety of things that might have been edible, then rejecting things that were not edible. Rather, other people taught you what is and is not defined as food. If you are a North American or European, you probably view some animals (cattle, fish) as food and others that are equally edible (horses, dogs) as not food. You did not discover this on your own, by repeated trials and errors, but by learning from others what is edible, good tasting, and nourishing. This social learning spared you a lot of the costs (and possible stomach ache and danger) of learning on your own by trial and error.

Think about the enormous advantages of humanity's reliance on social learning rather than simple trial and error learning. First, anything that one individual learns can be communicated to others in a group, who thus take advantage of someone else's experience. If you develop a new tool and share your knowledge, other members of your community can also use it.

Second, the culture that any generation acquires is passed to the next generation, which transmits it to the third generation, and so on to future generations. Thus any new knowledge acquired by one generation is poten-

tially available to future generations (though some of it is lost or replaced with each generation). By this process of repeated social learning over many generations, knowledge accumulates. Because of this accumulation, people alive today live largely off the knowledge acquired and transmitted by previous generations. In modern societies, certain kinds of knowledge are transmitted through formal education in schools and colleges, as well as from informal teaching by parents, relatives, and community members.

Third, because culture is socially learned, human groups are capable of changing their ideas and behaviors very rapidly. Genetic change (biological evolution) in a population is slow because it relies on biological reproduction. In contrast, no genetic change and no biological evolution have to occur for the knowledge and actions of a human population to be utterly transformed. Furthermore, your genetic makeup is more or less fixed at conception. But in the course of your life, your ideas and actions are likely to change dramatically. By the time you are 50, you will probably resemble your parents a lot more biologically than you will culturally.

In sum, culture is learned, not inborn, which means that cultural differences cannot be explained by biological/ genetic differences between groups of people. And the fact that culture is *socially* learned gives humanity some big advantages over other animals: innovations can spread, knowledge can accumulate, and peoples' ideas and actions can change rapidly.

▶ As children such as these Solomon Islanders grow up, they learn appropriate ways of thinking, feeling, and acting. This process of social learning is known as enculturation or socialization.

© Michael McCoy/Photo Researchers, Inc.

. . . Knowledge . . .

When anthropologists use the phrase *cultural knowledge,* we do not mean that a people's beliefs, perceptions, rules, standards, and so forth are true in an objective or absolute sense. In our professional role, anthropologists do not judge the accuracy or worthiness of a group's knowledge. We simply recognize that the knowledge of any cultural group differs to a greater or lesser degree from the knowledge of any other group; in fact, such differences are one of the things we attempt to describe and understand. What is most important about cultural knowledge is not its truth value, but that

- the members of a culture share enough knowledge to be capable of behaving in ways that are meaningful and acceptable to others so that they can avoid frequent misunderstandings and the need to explain what they are doing
- the knowledge guides behavior such that the people can survive, reproduce, and transmit their culture

In a few words, cultural knowledge must lead to behavior that is meaningful to others and adaptive to the natural and social environment. We consider some of this knowledge in the next section.

. . . and Patterns of Behavior

Human behavior varies from culture to culture, as you have heard. But even individuals who are brought up in the same culture differ in their behaviors. The behavior of individuals varies for several reasons. First, individuals have different *social identities:* males and females, old and young, rich and poor, family X and family Y, and so forth. Actions appropriate for people with one identity may not be appropriate for others. Second, the behavior of individuals varies with *context and situation:* a woman acts differently depending on whether she is interacting with her husband, child, priest, or employee. Third, each human individual is in some ways a *unique* human individual: even when brought up in the same society, we all differ in our emotional responses, appetites, interpretations of events, reactions to stimuli, and so forth. Finally, cultural standards for and expectations of behavior are often *ambiguous,* a point covered in more detail later in this chapter. For these and other reasons, it is a mistake to think of behavior as uniform within the same culture.

Despite such complexities, within a single cultural grouping there are behavioral regularities or patterns. For instance, if you were to visit an Amazonian rain forest and encounter people known as the Yąnomamö, you might be shocked by some of their actions. By most cultures' standards, the Yąnomamö are unusually demanding and aggressive. Slight insults often lead to violent responses. Quarreling men may duel one another in a chest-pounding contest, during which they take turns beating one another on the chest, alternating one blow at a time. More serious quarrels sometimes call for clubs, with which men bash one another on the head. Fathers sometimes encourage their sons to strike them (and anyone else) by teasing and goading, all the while praising the child for his fierceness.

If, on the other hand, you visited the Semai, a people of Malaysia, you might be surprised at how seldom they express anger and hostility. Indeed, you might find them *too* docile. One adult should never strike another—"Suppose he hit you back?" they ask. With this attitude toward violence, murder is nonexistent or extremely rare—so rare, in fact, that there are no penalties for it. The Semai seldom hit their children—"How would you feel if he or she died?" they ask. When children misbehave, the worst physical punishment they receive is a pinch on the cheek or a pat on the hand. Ethnographer Robert Dentan suggests one reason for the nonviolence of the Semai: Children are so seldom exposed to physical punishment that when they grow up they have an exaggerated impression of the effects of violence.

The contrasting behavioral responses of Yąnomamö and Semai people illustrate an important characteristic of most human behavior: its social nature. Humans are supremely social animals. We seldom do anything alone, and even when we are alone we rely unconsciously on our cultural upbringing to provide us with the knowledge of what to do and how to act. Relationships between people are therefore enormously important in all cultures. Anthropologists pay special heed to the regularities and patterning of these social relationships, including such things as how family members interact, how females and males relate to one another, how political leaders deal with subordinates, and so forth.

Borrowing a term from theatrical performances, the concept of **role** is useful to describe and analyze interactions and relationships in the context of a group. Individuals are often said to have a role or to play a role in some group. Roles usually carry names or labels such as *mother* in a family, *student* in a classroom, *accountant* in a company, and *headman* of a Yąnomamö village. Attached to roles are the group's *expectations* about what people who hold the role should do. Learning to be a member of a group includes learning its expectations. Expectations include rights and duties. The *rights* (or privileges) I have according to my role include the benefits the group members agree I should receive as a member. My *duties* (or obligations), according to my role, include other group members' expectations of me.

Rights and duties are usually *reciprocal:* my right over you is your duty to me, and vice versa. My duties to the group as a whole are the group's rights over me, and vice versa. If I adequately perform my duties to the group, other members reward me, just as I reward them for their own role performance. By occupying and performing a role in a group, I behave in ways that others find valuable, and I hope that some of my own wants and needs will be fulfilled. Conversely, failure to live up to the group's expectations of role performance is likely to bring some sort of informal or formal punishment. Among Yąnomamö, young men who refuse to stand up for themselves by fighting are ridiculed and may never amount to anything. The shared knowledge of roles and expectations is partly responsible for patterns of behavior.

Although defining culture as shared and socially learned knowledge and behavior seems pretty inclusive, some things most people commonly think are part of culture are not seen as part of culture by many anthropologists. For example, many anthropologists would not see architecture and art objects such as paintings and sculptures as part of a people's culture. They are, rather, physical representations and material manifestations of cultural knowledge. They are products or expressions of culture rather than parts of culture. Thus art expresses a culture's values, ideals of beauty, conflicts, worldviews, and so forth. Houses and public buildings are products of various aspects of culture such as family life, sexual practices, political organization, religious beliefs, and economic activity.

Similar considerations apply to other kinds of physical objects and material things. For example, tools are physical manifestations of the ideas of their human makers and users, who have a mental template that determines the form of the tool. Even writing is not seen as "part of" culture by many anthropologists. Rather, writing is a means of storing knowledge, transmitting information, and—in the case of fiction—telling stories that are meaningful in the culture.

Cultural Knowledge

As we have seen, cultural knowledge includes a people's beliefs, attitudes, rules, assumptions about the world, and other mental phenomena. In this section we discuss five elements of cultural knowledge: norms, values, symbols, classifications of reality, and worldviews. We cover these five elements because they are among the most important components of cultural knowledge and because their anthropological meaning goes beyond that of everyday speech.

Norms

Norms are shared ideals (or rules) about how people ought to act in certain situations, or about how particular people should act toward particular other people. The emphasis here is on the words *ideal, rule, ought,* and *should.* To say that norms exist does not mean everyone follows them all the time; indeed, some norms are violated with great regularity. Rather than referring to behavior itself, *norm* implies that (1) there is widespread agreement that people ought to adhere to certain standards of behavior, (2) other people judge the behavior of a person according to how closely it adheres to those standards, and (3) people who repeatedly fail to follow the standards face some kind of negative reaction from other members of the group. Notice that we are able to make collective judgments about someone's personal morality or character because we share common norms. Notice also that shared expectations about how roles should be performed are one kind of norm.

Sometimes people feel that norms are irrational or arbitrary rules that stifle their creativity or keep them from doing what they want for no good reason. People may believe that some norms about proper conduct are confining, such as norms about how to dress correctly for special occasions, or about when and to whom we must give gifts, or about fulfilling familial obligations, or about when to have sex. But in fact, norms are quite useful to us as individuals. It is mainly because we agree on norms that we know how to behave toward others and that we have expectations about how others should behave toward us.

For example, when you enter a roomful of strangers at a party, you are somewhat uncertain about how to act. But everyone knows how to go about getting acquainted in your cultural tradition, so soon you are introducing yourself, shaking hands, and asking the other guests what they do, what they are studying, and so forth. Here, and in many other cases in everyday life, norms are not experienced as oppressive. They serve as useful instructions on how to do something in such a way that others know what you are doing and accept your actions as "normal."

Values

Values consist of a people's beliefs about the way of life that is desirable for themselves and their society. Values have profound, although partly unconscious, effects on people's behavior. The goals we pursue, as well as our more general ideas about the good life, are influenced by the values of the culture into which we happen to have been born or raised. Values affect our motivations and thus influence the reasons we do what we do. Values are also critical to the maintenance of culture as a whole because they represent the qualities that people believe are essential to continuing their way of life. It is useful to think of values as providing the ultimate standards that people believe must be upheld under practically all circumstances. People may be deeply attached to some of their values and, under certain circumstances, be prepared to sacrifice their lives for them.

An excellent example of how values provide ultimate standards is the American emphasis on certain rights of individuals, as embodied in the Bill of Rights to the Constitution. No matter how much some Americans hate what the press prints, despise what the conservatives or the liberals stand for, or feel about the pro-lifers or pro-choicers, few believe that unpopular organizations or speech should be suppressed, so long as they do not engage in or advocate violence. Freedom of the press, speech, and religion; the rule of law rather than of individual leaders; the rights of persons accused of a crime: these and other ultimate standards supersede private interests and opinions.

Although people may cherish their values, it is easy to overemphasize their importance. For one thing, to uphold one value sometimes leads us to neglect others (e.g., career enhancement versus family life, personal integrity versus success in a course). For another, how we rank the relative importance of values varies from time to time and circumstance to circumstance. Finally, our fears and personal interests can lead us to ignore values in pursuing some other goal (e.g., we value the rights of war prisoners but they can be ignored due to threats from possible future terrorists).

Symbols

A **symbol** is something (like an object or an action) that represents, connotes, or calls to mind something else. Just as we learn norms and values during socialization, so do we learn the meanings that people in our group attach to symbols. And just as norms and values affect patterns of behavior, so do the understandings people share of the meanings of symbols. In fact, unless individuals agree that certain actions communicate certain meanings, social interaction would be far more difficult than it usually is. Our common understandings of the meanings of actions allow us to interact with one another without the need to explain our intentions, or to state explicitly what we are doing and why.

For the most part, the understandings that the members of a culture share about the meanings of actions and objects are unconscious. We can speak to inquiring strangers about our values and explain to them why we believe they are important. But it is nearly impossible to tell someone why a wink, a tone of voice, a way of wearing jewelry, a particular gesture, a way of walking, a style of dress, or a particular facial expression carries the meaning it does rather than some other meaning. We "just know." "Everyone knows," for such things are common knowledge and maybe even common sense.

Two important properties of symbols are that their meanings are arbitrary and conventional. *Arbitrary* in this context means that there are no inherent qualities in the symbol that leads a human group to attribute one meaning to it rather than some other meaning. Thus, the wink of an eye that often means "just kidding" in some cultures is—literally—meaningless in other cultures. *Conventional* refers to the fact that the meanings exist only because people implicitly agree they exist. Thus, at an intersection, a red light means "stop," but only because all drivers agree that it does.

Words provide a familiar example of the arbitrary and conventional nature of symbols. In English the word for a certain kind of large animal is *horse,* but in Spanish the same animal is called *caballo,* in German *pferd,* in Arabic *hisanun,* in French *cheval,* and so on for other languages. There is nothing about the animal itself that makes one of these words better than the others. The meaning "horse" is conveyed equally well by any of the words, which is another way of saying that the meaning is arbitrary and conventional.

The shared understandings that allow people to correctly interpret the meanings of behaviors are enormously important parts of cultural knowledge. Because you assume that the people you interact with share your understandings, in most situations you know how to act so as not to be misunderstood. Culture, in other words, includes common understandings of how to interact with one another appropriately (i.e., according to shared expectations) and meaningfully (i.e., in such a way that other people usually are able to interpret our intentions).

To most North Americans, for example, the meanings of actions such as nodding the head to show agreement or affirmation, walking hand in hand in public, and embracing a friend or relative seem commonsensical or even natural. Yet these and most other social behaviors result from social learning and do not mean the same thing everywhere.

Nonverbal communication provides a fine example of these understandings. When you interact with someone face to face, the two of you are engaged in a

▲ When we interact with one another, we communicate meanings by our facial expressions, body language, and even how much space we maintain between one another. By North American standards, these Moroccan men probably are standing too close together.

continual giving and receiving of messages communicated by both speech and actions. Spoken messages are intentionally (consciously) sent and received. Other messages—including body language, facial expressions, hand gestures, touching, and the use of physical space—are communicated by nonverbal behavior, much of which is unconscious. Nonverbal messages emphasize, supplement, or complement spoken messages. We are not always conscious of what we are communicating nonverbally, and sometimes our body language even contradicts what we are saying. (Is this how your mother could tell when you were lying?)

The general point is that cultural knowledge conditions social behavior in ways people do not always recognize consciously—at least until someone's behavior violates our understandings. Furthermore, many gestures and other body movements with well-known meanings in one culture have no meaning, or have different meanings, in another. On a Micronesian island studied by one of the

authors, people may answer "yes" or show agreement by a sharp intake of breath (a "gasp") or by simply raising the eyebrows. One may also answer "yes" by the grunting sound ("uh uh") that carries exactly the opposite meaning to North Americans. Pointing out a direction is done with the nose, not the finger. You would signal "I don't know" or "I'm not sure" by wrinkling your nose, rather than by shrugging your shoulders. It is rude to walk between two people engaged in conversation; if possible, you walk around them; if not, you say the equivalent of "please excuse me," wait for permission, and then bend at your waist while passing between them.

Aside from showing the social usefulness of shared understandings of symbolic behavior, these examples of personal space and gestures illustrate one way misunderstandings occur when individuals with different cultural upbringings interact. Raised in different cultures where spacing and gestures carry different meanings, individuals (mis)interpret the actions of others based on their own culture's understandings, often seeing the others as rude, unfriendly, insensitive, overly familiar, and so forth. Arabs and Iranians often stand "too close" for the Canadian and American comfort zone. In South Korea, it is common to see two young females holding hands or with their arms around each other while walking, but their touching symbolizes nothing about their sexual orientation. Japanese are less likely than North Americans to express definite opinions or preferences. To Americans, this often comes across as uncertainty, tentativeness, or even dishonesty, whereas the Japanese view it as politeness. The common American tendency to be informal and friendly is viewed as inappropriate in Japan and many other cultural settings, where feelings of warmth and closeness are confined to narrow circles, or where outward manifestations of emotions are held in check.

In a world where the globalization of trade and international travel are commonplace, it is worth knowing that much of what you "know" is not known to members of other cultural traditions, just as what they "know" may be unfamiliar to you. Think before you take offense at their actions. And think before you give it.

Classifications and Constructions of Reality

The members of a cultural tradition share ideas of what kinds of things and people exist. They have similar **classifications of reality,** meaning that people generally agree on how nature, objects, groups, individuals, and other phenomena should be divided into categories. Another phrase for this is the **cultural construction of reality:** from the multitude of differences and similarities that exist in some phenomena, a culture recognizes (constructs) only some features as relevant in making distinctions. The cultural construction of reality implies that different peoples do not perceive the human and natural worlds in the same ways.

For instance, all cultures recognize kinship relationships, but they classify relatives in diverse ways. Whether someone is or is not your "blood" relative, and if so what kind of relative, might seem to depend largely on how they are related to you biologically. In one sense, this is correct. But how you conceive of your relatives, and how you place relatives into named categories like *uncle* and *cousin* is not determined strictly by how they are related to you biologically. English speakers think of the sisters of both our mother and our father as a single kind of relative, and we call them by the same kinship term, *aunt.* But in some cultural traditions the sister of your mother

is considered one kind of relative and the sister of your father a different kind, and you would call each by a separate kinship term.

Thus, people of different cultural traditions vary in the way they conceive of their societies as divided up into kinds of people. The phrase *kinds of people* also applies to how the members of a culture classify one another into categories loosely referred to as *racial.* Probably most people think of the members of one race as physically more similar to one another than they are to members of different races—thus, the "white race" and the "black race" are physically distinct. In fact, though, most anthropologists agree that race is culturally constructed rather than biologically given (see A Closer Look).

The same applies to the way people classify the natural world. Cultural knowledge provides not only the categories by which we classify kinds of people but also categories by which plants, animals, phases of the moon, seasonal changes, and other natural phenomena are classified. The way people classify the things in their natural environment both affects and is affected by how they relate to that environment.

For example, on the island of Mindoro in the Philippines lives a people known as the Hanunóo, who grow most of their food by a method called shifting cultivation. This method involves farming a plot for one or two years, abandoning it for a number of years until it has recovered its potential to yield a crop, and then replanting it. The Hanunóo judge whether a plot they abandoned some years previously has recovered enough for replanting by the quantity and kind of natural vegetation that has recolonized the plot. The need to assess the degree of readiness of a plot for recultivation has led the Hanunóo to develop an extremely complex classification of the plants found in their habitat. They are able to identify more than 1,600 kinds of plants, which exceeds by more than 400 the number of species that a botanist would distinguish.

Which classification is right, that of the Hanunóo or that of the botanist? Both. The point is not that the Hanunóo are right and the botanist wrong, or vice versa. Rather, the botanist uses one set of criteria to decide whether two individual plants belong to the same kind, and these criteria have been adopted because scientists find them useful. The Hanunóo use a different set of criteria that, over the course of many generations, they have developed for their specific needs.

The cultural construction of the environment influences the way a people perceives the natural world. It also influences how a people defines and uses natural resources (which, therefore, are not entirely natural). Plants and animals are classified not just into various kinds but

Race remains one of the most explosive topics of our time. It weighs heavily on political decisions, as illustrated by the outcome of the Florida vote in the American presidential elections of 2000. Politically liberal Americans think that affirmative action policies based in part on race are necessary to redress centuries of discrimination against "racial minorities." Conservatives counter by arguing that "race-based" hiring and admissions practices deny equal opportunity to qualified white people, many of whom come from socioeconomic backgrounds that are just as deprived as those of many minorities. Pollsters emphasize the "racial divide" that distinguishes "blacks" from "whites" on various social issues. Some Anglo college students dread the sight of Chinese or Japanese Americans in their classes, fearing they are likely to be curve-busters.

Most people who debate such public issues assume that race is an objective, natural category into which particular individuals with their clearly visible physical characteristics can be placed. If you can't say what race you are, it is probably because you are of "mixed race." We can observe the racial differences between humans by visiting almost any large city in North America, where members of different races mingle. Race seems real. Race even seems obvious.

Most anthropologists disagree. They argue that race is not, in fact, an objective and natural category, but a cultural classification of people based on perceptions and distinctions that arise more from culture than from biology. Race, they believe, is a cultural construct rather than a biological reality. What does this mean, and why do most anthropologists believe it? There are several main reasons.

First, genetic studies show that the genetic variation within a given race far exceeds the variation between races. Two randomly chosen individuals within the same racial category are about as likely to be as different from one another in their total genetic makeup as are two individuals of different races. So, genetically, races are not discrete populations. This is because fully modern humans—*Homo sapiens*—evolved only within the last 200,000 or so years, so that significant genetic divergences have not had very long to occur.

Second, most of the differences between individuals that we attribute to race are only skin deep. We focus on certain visible physical traits when we place individuals in racial categories: skin color, details of facial features, hair characteristics, and so forth. Were we to look beyond observable traits, we would find that if other (invisible or less visible) traits were used, different racial categories would often result. For example, a racial clas-

sification of the world's people based on blood groups (ABO, rH, and other factors) would yield a different classification than one based on skin color. The same applies to a racial classification based on the shape of teeth or jaws, or on the ability to digest lactose (a milk enzyme). In short, the traits we use to define races lead to one kind of racial classification, but a different classification would be made were we to use other traits. We define some traits as relevant, whereas others are unrecognized (unperceived) or irrelevant.

Third, just how many races are there? Most older people raised in North America would say three, which used to be called Mongoloid, Negroid, and Caucasoid. This threefold classification of humanity is based on the history of contacts between Europeans and certain peoples of Africa and Asia. But why only three? The so-called pygmies of central Africa are quite different physically from their Bantu neighbors, as are the once-widespread Khoisan peoples of southern Africa. The indigenous peoples of New Guinea, Australia, and surrounding islands are quite different not only from many of their neighbors, but from some of the Africans whom they outwardly resemble in their skin coloration. Many people of southern Asia have skin as dark as some Africans, although in some other physical characteristics they resemble Europeans. Shall we also call these groups separate races?

Along the same lines, different cultures sometimes develop different racial classifications of people. In Brazil, there are a multitude of terms that refer to people of different physical types. Based on his fieldwork, Conrad Kottak reported that in a single village in northeastern Brazil, 40 different terms were used in a racial classification! To non-Japanese, Japan appears to be a racially homogeneous country. Yet many Japanese recognize and emphasize the differences between native Japanese and descendants of immigrants from Korea. Some Japanese are prejudiced against the Burakamin, the modern descendants of groups whose ancestors are believed to have engaged in low-level occupations. Yet Burakamin are so indistinguishable physically that some Japanese still investigate the past of potential spouses to be sure they are not Burakamin.

Fourth, racial classifications change over time even within the same cultural tradition. In the Americas, people who are today considered to be indistinguishable racially once were widely viewed as members of different races. When large numbers of Irish immigrated to the Americas after the potato blight struck Ireland in the mid-nineteenth century, they were considered a race by many white Americans whose ancestors had lived here somewhat longer. Jews were also seen by many as a distinct racial group. Such distinctions sound silly today—to most North Americans, at any rate. (How silly will present-day racial divisions seem in the next century?)

The difficulty of determining how many races there are, the fact that different cultures disagree on the number and definition of races, and the varying ways that race has been viewed historically—all should make us suspicious that races are objectively definable biological groupings.

Does all this mean that some anthropologists deny that there are important physical differences between populations whose ancestors originated in different continents? No. What they deny is that these differences cluster in such a way that they produce discrete biological categories of people (i.e., races). Individual human beings differ from one another physically in a multitude of visible and invisible ways. If races—as North Americans typically define them—are real biological entities, then people of African ancestry would share a wide variety of traits whereas people of European ancestry would share a wide variety of *different* traits. But once we add traits that are less visible than skin coloration, hair texture, and the like, we find that the people we identify as "the same race" are less and less like one another and more and more like people we identify as "different races." Add to this point the fact that the physical features used to identify a person as a representative of some race (e.g., skin coloration) are continuously variable, so that one cannot say where "brown skin" becomes "white skin." We can see that although physical differences are real, our use of physical differences to classify people into discrete races is a cultural construction.

For these and other reasons, most anthropologists agree that race is more of a cultural construction than a biological reality. Indeed, the American Anthropological Association recommends eliminating the word *race* from the 2010 American census.

What does it matter? So long as people can—if not today, then someday in the future—avoid viewing some "races" as inferior to others, why is it so important that we recognize that races are culturally constructed?

It might matter a great deal, given the past and current realities of racial divisions. Racial terms (e.g., *brown, black, white*) carry connotations, making it very difficult for most people to use such terms in a neutral manner. Once a culture has classified people into kinds or types, it is difficult to avoid ranking the types according to some measure of quality, goodness, or talent. Familiar qualities include intelligence, work ethic, athletic abil-

ity, and musical talent. Some people believe that Asians are smart and work hard, whereas African Americans are better natural athletes and more musically talented. From such seemingly innocent stereotypes, we too easily conclude that it is natural talent that puts many Asians near the top of their class, and some African Americans near the bottom academically. Books such as *The Bell Curve* (1994) argue that genetically based intellectual abilities explain much of the differential success of different "races" in America today. Such arguments are moot if race is indeed a cultural construction.

There is another reason to view race as culturally constructed: Doing so helps to avoid confusing "race" with other kinds of differences that have nothing to do with physical differences. Most North Americans do not distinguish—at least not consistently—differences due to "race" from differences due to language, national origin, or cultural background. The latter differences, of course, are based on culture and/or language, not on physical characteristics. Too easily, race is confused with ethnicity. For example, many people view Native American and Hispanic as the same kind of identity as race. But Hispanics may be black or white or brown or any other color, and many people who identify themselves as Native American based on their origins and culture are indistinguishable physically from Americans with European ancestry.

Lastly, race is currently a part of the way people identify themselves to one another. It is an important part of an individual's social identity, meaning that another person's perception of you is affected by your assumed membership in some racial category. Such an identity often carries with it a great degree of "racial pride." Racial pride is often a positive force in the lives of people who have suffered the effects of prejudice and discrimination, as older African Americans who were part of the 1960s Black Power movement will appreciate. Yet racial pride cuts both ways, as people who are familiar with the beliefs and activities of the Aryan Nation and other such groups dedicated to maintaining "racial purity" know. Although race may be a source of pride, it is also a major—perhaps *the* major—source of conflict and division in many of the world's nations. Political leaders and opinion shapers in the popular media can and do manipulate the opinions of one "race" about other "races" to further their own political and social agendas. Depending on your own "racial" identity and values, it may be either comforting or disconcerting to realize that race is a cultural construction and therefore a division of our own making.

also into various categories of usefulness. Because members of different cultural traditions may perceive nature in different ways, what one group considers *food* is not necessarily defined as *food* by another group. For example, Muslims and Orthodox Jews consider pork unclean. Traditional Hindus refuse to consume the flesh of cattle, their sacred animal. The fact that a given animal or plant is edible does not mean that people *consider* it edible (or else more North Americans would eat dogs, as do many East and Southeast Asians, and horses, as do many French).

Even a people's conception of time is, in part, culturally constructed. Consider the units of time used by most of us in the modern world: seconds, minutes, hours, days, weeks, months, years, decades, centuries, millennia. Of these, only days, months, and years are in any sense "natural," meaning that they are based on natural occurrences (sunrises, moon phases, seasonal changes). Even these natural occurrences do not correspond with our cultural units: Days do not run from sunrise to sunrise but begin at midnight; months no longer reflect lunar phases; new years begin in January rather than at solstices or equinoxes. The other units by which we divide the passage of time are culturally defined, meaning that although we have instruments to record them precisely, they exist only because we agree they exist.

Finally, people of different cultures differ in their beliefs about the kinds of things that do and do not exist. For instance, some people believe that individuals they consider witches use malevolent supernatural powers to harm others. Traditional Navajo believe that witches can change themselves into wolves, bears, and other animals. The Tukano people of the Bolivian rain forest think that a spirit of the forest controls the animals they depend on for meat. So a Tukano shaman periodically makes a supernatural visit to the abode of the forest spirit. He promises to magically kill a certain number of humans and to send their souls to the forest spirit in return for the spirit's releasing the animals so the hunters can find game.

In sum, not only do different cultures classify objective reality in different ways, they also differ on what reality *is:* one culture's definition of reality may not be the same as that of another culture.

Worldviews

The **worldview** of a people is the way they interpret reality and events, including their images of themselves and how they relate to the world around them. Worldviews are affected by cultural constructions of reality, which we have just discussed. But worldviews include more than just the way a culture carves up people and na-

ture. People have opinions about the nature of the cosmos and how they fit into it. All cultures include beliefs about spiritual souls and include more beliefs about what happens to souls after bodies are lifeless. People have ideas about the meaning of human existence: how we were put on Earth, who or what put us here, and why. They have notions of evil, where it comes from, why it sometimes happens to good people, and how it can be combated. They have beliefs about what supernatural powers or beings are like, what they can do for (or to) people, and how people can worship or control them. Everywhere we find myths and legends about the origins of living things, objects, and customs. (We have more to say about such topics in Chapter 14.)

These examples all seem to be based in a group's religion. But it is important not to confuse worldview and religion, and especially not to think that *religion* and *worldview* are synonymous. Although religious beliefs do influence the worldview of a people, cultural traditions vary in aspects of worldview that we do not ordinarily think of as religious.

For instance, the way people view their place in nature is part of their worldview: Do they see themselves as the masters and conquerors of nature, or as living in harmony with natural forces? The way people view themselves and other people is part of their worldview: Do they see themselves, as many human groups do, as the only true human beings, and all others as essentially animals? Or do they see their way of life as one among many equally human but different ways of life? Most modern scientists share a similar worldview: They believe that all things and events in the universe have natural causes that we can discover through certain formal procedures of observation, experimentation, and systematic logic.

The Concept Review summarizes the five major components of cultural knowledge in just a few words.

Culture and Human Life

Anthropologists believe that culture is absolutely essential to humans and to human life as it is usually lived—in association with other people, or in social groups.

As those who study animal behavior know, living in social groups does not require culture. Many species of termites, bees, ants, and other social insects live in quite complex groups, yet they have no culture. Gorillas, chimpanzees, baboons, macaques, and most other primates are also group-living animals. Primatologists have shown that chimpanzees learn to use and make simple tools, share food, communicate fairly precise messages, have

Component	Definition	Example
Norms	Standards of propriety and appropriateness	Expected behaviors at weddings and in classrooms
Values	Beliefs about what is worthwhile	Individual rights
Symbols	Objects and behaviors with conventional meanings	Meanings of nonverbal behavior
Classifications	Divisions of reality into categories and subcategories	Kinds of persons and natural phenomena
Worldviews	Interpretations of events and experiences	Origin of good and evil

intergroup conflicts in which animals are killed, and form relationships in which two individuals who are physically weaker cooperate to overpower a stronger animal. Yet few anthropologists claim that chimpanzee groups have culture in the same sense as all human groups do. (Some use the term *protoculture* to emphasize that many animal behaviors are socially learned rather than instinctive.) If other group-living social animals cooperate, communicate, and survive without culture, why do people need culture at all?

The main reason boils down to the following: The culture of the society or other group into which people are born or raised provides the knowledge (information) they need to survive in their natural environments and to participate in the life of groups. This knowledge, which infants begin to socially learn soon after birth, is necessary because humans do not come into the world equipped with a detailed set of behavioral instructions inherited genetically from their parents. Rather, people are born with a *propensity to learn the knowledge and behaviors of the group they were born into from observation, interaction, and communication with members of that group.*

Culture is necessary for human existence in at least three specific ways:

1. Culture provides the knowledge needed to adapt to our surroundings—to harness resources from the natural environment and to solve problems of living in a particular place. It gives people the skills they need to produce the tools, shelter, clothing, and other objects they use to survive. As they grow up, children socially learn skills for tracking game, gathering wild plants, making gardens, herding livestock, or finding a job, depending on how people make their living in a particular society. Because most human populations have lived in the same environment for many generations, if not centuries, the current generation is usually wise to take advantage of the adaptive wisdom learned and

passed down by its cultural ancestors. Culture is so important to a human group's ability to survive in a particular place and time that some anthropologists believe that adaptation is the most essential purpose of culture itself (others disagree, however, as discussed in Chapter 4).

2. Culture is the basis for our social life. It provides ready-made norms, values, expectations, attitudes, symbols, and other knowledge that individuals use to communicate, cooperate with one another, live in families and other kinds of groups, relate to members of their own and the opposite sex, and establish political and legal systems. As they grow up, people learn what actions are and are not acceptable, how to win friends, who relatives are, how and whom to court and marry, when to show glee or grief, and so forth.

3. Culture affects our views of reality. It provides the mental framework by which people perceive, interpret, analyze, and explain events in the world around them. The culture we acquire while growing up in a given group provides a filter or screen that affects how we perceive the world through our senses. Some objects "out there" in the world are sensed, others are not. Some events are important, others can be ignored. During socialization, people learn the categories, symbols, worldviews, and other knowledge that filter their perceptions of reality and give meaning to things and events. Growing up in a given culture thus leads people to develop shared understandings of the world (keep in mind that "shared understandings" do not imply Truth).

In sum, culture is essential to human life as we experience it because it provides us with the means to adapt to our surroundings, form relationships in organized groups, and interpret reality. Adaptation, organization, interpretation—these are three of the main reasons culture is essential to a normal human existence. In later chapters we look at some of the diverse ways in which various cultures have equipped their members to adapt to their environment, organize their groups, and understand their world.

Cultural Knowledge and Individual Behavior

How are the shared ideas and beliefs of a group of people related to the behavior of individuals? This question is important not only for studying other cultures but also for how people think about their own lives and how they relate to society.

Is Behavior Determined by Culture?

Some believe that culture largely determines or dictates behavior, a view known as **cultural determinism.** If strictly and literally true, then personal freedom is an illusion, as is the exercise of free will. We only *think* we are free and have free will, when culture is pulling our strings.

Many anthropologists of the past (and a few in the present) believed that culture is, in effect, all powerful in the lives of individual human beings. They viewed culture as existing independently of individuals, who were treated merely as culture's carriers and transmitters. Culture is, as some anthropologists said, a superorganism. Others claimed that "culture follows its own laws," implying that people themselves have little ability to alter the course of the future of their society and culture.

Yet most people do not experience their culture as all powerful. Although it *could* be true that your mind is mainly a vessel that carries your culture, you probably think there is a lot more to you than that. Most modern anthropologists agree, and they reject notions of extreme cultural determinism. Culture does shape individuals, but it is also shaped by individuals. In fact, any one way of conceptualizing the relationship between knowledge and behavior is simplistic, for knowledge and actions are related in many ways.

For example, some actions are habitual—some of the time, people do what they have always done in similar situations. Much of our behavior is habitual in this sense. Living with other people would be a lot more difficult if we had to treat each interaction as a new one and decide anew what to do every time we found ourselves in a given situation. But many other actions are not habitual, so people often have to make choices among alternative actions.

There are other situations in which knowledge provides rules or instructions that tell individuals what to do: how to act toward friends, coworkers, and mothers-in-law; how to perform their roles acceptably; how to worship; and so forth. Likewise, there are cultural standards for how to have weddings, how to settle quarrels, and so forth. Those "deviants" who do not follow the rules of their culture are usually brought back into conformity, ostracized, or eliminated. In such situations, the normative dimensions of culture are critical: Norms tell us how to do things; usually we do them in these ways; when we do we receive rewards: when we don't we are punished.

Again, this view applies to some of our actions, but notice that cultural knowledge consists of far more than just rules or instructions. It consists of values that provide only rough and sometimes conflicting guidelines for behavior. It includes shared constructions of reality and worldviews, which certainly influence our actions, but only indirectly (by affecting how we perceive and interpret the world) rather than directly (as instructions). Finally, cultural knowledge includes attitudes, understandings of symbols, and other kinds of ideas and beliefs that affect how people act, but not in the same way as rules do. The effects of these and other mental components of culture are too subtle and complex to think of them as rules or instructions.

Even when a culture's rules provide detailed instructions—as they sometimes do—the actions of individuals are not preprogrammed. People usually have some leeway to choose between alternative courses of action. In their everyday lives most people do not blindly follow their culture's "dictates." They plan, calculate, weigh alternatives, and make decisions. For those actions that are important in their own lives or in the lives of others they care about, they think ahead and consider the possible benefits and costs before they act. In deciding how best to approach the relation between knowledge and behavior, we must take into account people's ability to think ahead, plan, and choose.

One way to do this is to realize that formulating plans and making choices are thinking processes, involving both rational and emotional faculties. Therefore they occur within the existing framework of cultural knowledge. Planning and choosing involves at least the following procedures: deciding on one's goals (or ends); determining the resources (or means) available to acquire these goals; considering which specific actions are likely to be most effective; calculating the relative costs (in time and/or resources) and benefits (rewards) of these alternative actions; and, finally, choosing between alternative behaviors.

Cultural knowledge affects every step of this choice-making process. Norms force individuals to take into account how others are likely to react to their behavior. Values affect the goals that people have and help prevent them from acting in ways that infringe on the rights of others. Choices are affected by the existing cultural constructions of people and things, worldviews, and individuals' anticipation of how others will interpret the meaning of their actions. We can see how important cultural knowledge is when people choose: It affects goals, perceptions of resources, availability of means, relative weighting of costs and benefits, and so on. So important is the effect of cultural knowledge on individual decisions that one influential anthropologist long ago defined culture itself as "standards for deciding what is, . . . what can be, . . . how one feels about it, . . . what to do about it, . . . and how to go about doing it" (Goodenough 1961, 552).

So one important way cultural knowledge affects actions is by its profound influences on choices individuals make about what to do in various situations. Another way to say this is that cultural knowledge supplies "boundaries" for behavior. Speaking metaphorically, culture draws the lines that behavior usually does not cross, meaning that it determines which behaviors are likely to be proper or acceptable or understandable to others. Within these boundaries, people are free to choose between alternative actions. Most people do not violate these cultural boundaries because they believe in the moral correctness of norms and values, because they fear negative reactions from others, or because doing so would involve actions that others might misinterpret.

Why Does Behavior Vary?

The complexity of the relationship between knowledge and actions is one reason why the distinction between knowledge and behavior is so important. Shared cultural knowledge profoundly affects individual actions, but for the most part it does not determine them in detail. In fact, ideas and beliefs sometimes do not predict behavior very well. We cannot always say what someone will do in a given situation, even when cultural expectations are fairly clear. There are several major reasons why the actions of individuals vary and often depart from expectations.

The most obvious reason is that no two individuals have exactly the same life experiences, even though they are brought up in the same cultural setting. A related reason is that no two individuals (except identical twins) have the same genetic makeup, and our genes affect how we react to our life experiences. Different life experiences and biological uniqueness make individuals different (to greater or lesser degrees, of course) in their reactions and actions.

Other reasons are more subtle. Norms and values are not always consistent and do not always provide unam-

biguous guidelines for behavior. Generally, you should not tell someone a lie, but frequently a small lie is necessary to preserve a personal relationship or to avoid hurting someone's feelings. Here small lies are told to avoid greater harms. Often, too, small lies are so useful to achieve our personal goals that our private interests take precedence.

In many situations, pursuing one worthwhile goal or upholding one value conflicts with pursuing another goal or upholding another value, so that people must choose between them. Most North Americans believe in the work ethic, value success and getting ahead on the job, and want to be good mothers and fathers. They hold these beliefs, values, and goals simultaneously. But jobs and career advancement too often detract from the time we devote to the pursuit of "family values," so we must decide how to allocate our time and energy between activities that are all culturally defined as worthwhile.

Also people find ways to justify (both to themselves and to others) violations of norms and accepted moral standards when such norms and standards conflict with their interests. You might rationalize stealing from your employer if you think you are underpaid. Your boss might rationalize working you overtime for not much extra pay because he is pressured from his own boss. Your company might lay off its workers and move its operations overseas because it must operate in a "highly competitive global environment." Your classmates might rationalize cheating on a test because the instructor is boring, the textbook is unclear, and the course is all B.S. anyway.

Finally, people receive contradictory messages about what actions are proper and morally right. Sometimes ideal models for behavior are contradicted by the messages and models people receive from the actions of their parents, relatives, friends, political leaders, and the media. We generally agree that adultery and violence are wrong, for example, but we gain the impression from many sources that they are common and almost to be expected. Parents want us to uphold their standards of sexual morality, but when we watch TV videos and halftime shows at the Superbowl we are exposed to a different set of values.

We chose the preceding examples because they are familiar to most readers. But the main point of the examples is this: All cultures have abstract public values and publicly acknowledged norms that distinguish right from wrong, appropriate from inappropriate, and so forth. But all real people recognize that real-world situations are complicated. Real-life individuals have personal goals to pursue and sometimes yield to temptation. People have to choose between values and norms that at least sometimes and in some circumstances are in conflict.

In sum, all humans and all groups must periodically deal with the complicated conflicts between private interests and public duties. The actions of individuals are often an uneasy compromise between the two. Human behavior is indeed embedded in a context of cultural knowledge, but its relation to this context is complex and variable.

Biology and Cultural Differences

In many ways, humans are like other mammals: We must regulate our body temperatures, balance our energy and liquid intake and expenditures, and so forth. But, as you know by now, anthropologists say that humans are special mammals because we rely so heavily on culture for our survival and sense of well-being. How, then, are biology and culture related?

Although we cannot discuss this issue in depth, it is necessary to address one important dimension of this relationship—that between group-level biological differences and cultural differences. Do biological/genetic/ physical differences between groups of people have anything to do with the cultural differences between them? To rephrase the question so that its full implications are apparent: Is there any correlation between cultures and human physical forms, or races, as they are usually called? (See A Closer Look for why the whole concept of race is problematic.)

Before the twentieth century many people believed that the physical differences between groups of people explained differences in how they thought, felt, and behaved. That is, many people believed that "racial" differences partly or largely accounted for differences in culture. According to this notion, now called **biological determinism,** cultural differences have a biological basis, meaning that groups of people differ in how they think, feel, and act because they differ in their innate biological makeup.

Biological determinism is potentially a convenient theory of what makes groups of people different from one another in their beliefs and actions. It is simple to understand and can be a politically useful idea, especially when combined with ethnocentric attitudes about the superiority of one's own culture. If French or English culture is superior to African or Native American culture, then it must be because the French or English are innately superior biologically to Africans or Native Americans (it is obvious how so-called inborn differences in intelligence are brought into such opinions). Colonial rule, the expropriation of land and other resources, slavery,

forced labor, genocides and attempted genocides, and other practices could be and were justified by the idea that groups of people differed in their customs and beliefs because of their physical differences.

With few exceptions, modern ethnologists reject biological determinism. We believe that the physical differences between human populations do not cause cultural differences. The diverse cultures of Africa did not and do not differ from the cultures of Europe, Asia, or the Americas because the peoples of these continents differ biologically. Nor do the cultures of different ethnic groups within a modern nation differ because these ethnic groups differ physically: African Americans, Euro Americans, and Asian Americans do not differ in their beliefs and actions because of their different genetic makeup.

To claim that physical differences are irrelevant as causes for cultural differences might seem like a sweeping overgeneralization. Certainly, it is difficult to prove. But this claim is based on evidence, most of which is quite familiar. Consider the following three unquestionable facts.

- Individuals of any physical type are equally capable of learning any culture. For instance, the North American continent now contains people whose biological ancestors came from all parts of the world. Yet modern-day African, Chinese, Indian, Irish, and Italian Americans have far more in common in their thoughts and actions than any of them have in common with the peoples of their ancestral homelands. Indeed, many members of these groups have been assimilated with and are culturally indistinguishable from citizens with English or German or French ancestry.

- An enormous range of cultural diversity was and is found on all continents and regions of the world. Despite the physical similarities between them, Native Americans were enormously diverse culturally when the people of Europe learned of their existence after 1492. Most West Africans are biologically similar, yet they are divided into dozens of different cultural groupings. The same disjunction between physical characteristics and cultural diversity applies to people of North Asia, South Asia, Europe, and other regions. Far too much diversity occurs within populations who are biologically similar for biological differences to be a significant cause of cultural variation.

- Dramatically different cultural systems succeed one another in time within the same biological population and indeed within the same society. Cultures can and regularly do undergo vast changes within a single hu-

© Jeff Greenberg/The Image Works

▲ Race and culture vary independently of one another, because members of different "racial" categories can share the same culture. This multiethnic crowd in Miami Beach is watching a performance.

man generation; these changes cannot be due to genetic changes in the population, which usually take many generations to be noticeable.

Because of these and other kinds of evidence, most cultural anthropologists feel justified in reaching the following conclusion: Physical (including "racial") differences between human populations are largely irrelevant in explaining the cultural differences between them. This means that if we want to explain the differences between the Kikuyu culture of East Africa and the Chinese culture of East Asia, we should largely ignore the physical and genetic differences between the Kikuyu and the Chinese. We might argue that differences in the Kikuyu and Chinese natural environment, technology, and history make their cultures different. But for the most part we ignore the possibility that genetic differences between groups explain cultural differences between groups.

So most cultural anthropologists strongly oppose biological determinist notions. In fact, in the early decades of the twentieth century some anthropologists, such as

Franz Boas, fought such ideas by marshaling evidence that—to state the point simply—culture is not determined by race.

None of this should be taken to mean that biological factors are irrelevant for culture. Human beings have physiological needs and biological imperatives just like other animals. Food, water, shelter, and the like are necessary to sustain life. Sexual activity is pleasurable for its own sake as well as necessary for reproduction. People become sick and may die from disease, so coping with the effects of viruses, bacteria, and other microorganisms is a biological necessity. Finally, no human society will survive unless its females give birth and its members effectively nurture and enculturate their children. To persist over many generations, all groups develop means of meeting these biological needs and coping with these environmental problems; those that have failed to do so are no longer around.

Because humans are both cultural and biological beings, much of what we do is oriented around the satisfaction of biological needs for food, shelter, reproduction, disease avoidance, and so forth. Such imperatives must be dealt with in all societies. It is partly because of these universal problems that anthropologists have discovered **cultural universals,** or elements that exist in all known human societies.

Some cultural universals are obvious because they are requirements for long-term survival in a species that relies on social learning, material technology, and group living. Such universals include tools, shelter, methods of communication, patterns of cooperation used in acquiring food and other essential resources, ways of teaching children, and so forth. There is no great mystery about why all human groups have such things.

Other cultural universals are not so obvious. They do not seem necessary for the physical survival of individuals or groups, but they are nonetheless present in all cultural traditions. Among these are ways of assigning tasks and roles according to age, gender, and skill; prohibitions on sexual relationships (incest taboos) between certain kinds of relatives; organized ways of sharing and exchanging goods; games, sports, or other kinds of recreational activities; beliefs about supernatural powers and rituals that are used to communicate with and influence them; decorative arts; singing and other forms of music; ways of classifying various kinds of relatives into social categories; customary ways of handling the dead and expressing grief; myths, legends, and folklore; and rites of passage that ceremonially recognize the movement of people through certain stages of life.

More elements found in all cultures could be listed. But our point is that all human cultures share certain characteristics whose universal existence is not obviously explained by the fact that they are necessary for short- or long-term survival. The very existence of such cultural universals suggests that the human genetic makeup limits the forms that culture can take.

Perhaps there is an inborn biological basis for sexual rules, religion, play, kinship, art, and other cultural uni-

© Bruce Connolly/Corbis

▲ It is not clear if music helps in survival or performs other kinds of essential functions for societies and cultures, it nonetheless is a cultural universal. These Chinese are skilled drummers.

versals precisely because they *are* universal. Yet the precise forms that these and other universal elements take vary from culture to culture. For instance, all human societies have beliefs about the supernatural (religion), but the nature of these beliefs varies enormously among cultures, as seen in Chapter 14. Likewise, people in all societies keep track of their family and kinship relationships, but they do so in a wide variety of ways, as documented in Chapters 8 and 9. Male/female differences are important among peoples, but in highly diverse ways, as shown in Chapter 11. Most of the rest of this book deals with these and other cultural variations.

Summary

1. In anthropology the term *culture* usually refers to the whole way of life of some society or group. To describe and analyze culture we distinguish between its mental and behavioral components, or between cultural knowledge and patterns of behavior. Culture is defined as the shared, socially learned knowledge and behavioral patterns characteristic of some group of people. The term *group* may refer to an entire society, an ethnic group, or a subculture, depending on the context of the discussion.

2. Culture is socially learned, meaning that each generation learns their culture from communicating and interacting with previous generations, a process called enculturation or socialization. Culture can also be transmitted from one group or individual to another. These properties give humanity certain major advantages and are largely responsible for our success as a species.

3. Cultural knowledge is not true in any objective sense, but it must at least allow a society to persist in its environment and must enable people to interact appropriately and meaningfully. Cultural knowledge has many components, some of which are norms, values, common understandings of the meanings of symbols, classifications and constructions of reality, and worldviews. Because these and other components of cultural knowledge are products of social learning—not

inborn—we must learn them during enculturation, although they may seem natural or commonsensical.

4. People often say that cultural knowledge determines the actions of individuals, but this view is simplistic. Cultural ideas and beliefs serve as more than just rules or instructions for actions. A more useful and realistic view sees cultural knowledge as affecting the choices people make about how to act in particular situations. Cultural knowledge limits and influences behavior but does not determine it in great detail, for people's actions are usually not programmed by their culture.

5. Biological determinism is the notion that the culture of a human population derives in part from biological or "racial" factors. If true, then biological differences are relevant in explaining cultural differences between human groups. This idea is rejected by nearly all ethnologists, who consider the biological differences between groups largely irrelevant as explanations for cultural differences. The shared biological heritage of the human species, however, certainly does affect culture, because how people meet biologically given needs is reflected in their culture. The existence of cultural universals also suggests that the shared genetic heritage of all humanity affects the kinds of cultures that are possible in the human species.

Key Terms

cultural knowledge
patterns of behavior
cultural integration
culture
cultural identity
society

enculturation
  (socialization)
roles
norms
values
symbols

classifications of reality
  (cultural constructions
  of reality)
worldview
cultural determinism
biological determinism
cultural universals

⚲ InfoTrac College Edition Terms

cultural misunderstanding
(also cross-cultural
misunderstanding)

race and intelligence
cultural construction of
race

social darwinism
race in Brazil

Suggested Readings

Brown, Donald E. *Human Universals.* New York:
McGraw-Hill, 1991.

A description and analysis of cultural universals.

Cronk, Lee. *That Complex Whole: Culture and the Evolution of Human Behavior.* Boulder, Colo.: Westview,
1999.

*A readable yet sophisticated book addressing the relation-
ship between culture, biology, and human nature. Author's
views are controversial.*

Hooker, John. *Working Across Cultures.* Stanford: Stanford University Press, 2003.

*Applies the anthropological concept of culture to issues of
conducting business in other countries, including Mexico,
Northern Europe, India, China, Turkey, and Zimbabwe.*

Middleton, DeWight R. *The Challenge of Human Diversity: Mirrors, Bridges, and Chasms.* Prospect
Heights, Ill.: Waveland, 1998.

*Brief discussion of anthropological concepts used to de-
scribe and understand cultural diversity. Includes examples of interactions between people of different cultural
backgrounds.*

Spradley, James, and David W. McCurdy, eds. *Conformity and Conflict: Readings in Cultural Anthropology.* 11th ed. Boston: Allyn and Bacon, 2003.

Collection of interesting essays for introductory students.

Companion Website for This Book

The Wadsworth Anthropology Resource Center
http://anthropology.wadsworth.com

The companion website that accompanies *Humanity: An
Introduction to Cultural Anthropology,* Sixth Edition, includes a rich array of material, including online anthropological video clips, to help you in the study of cultural
anthropology and the specific topics covered in this chapter. Begin by clicking on Student Resources. Next, click
on Cultural Anthropology, and then on the cover image
for this book. You have now arrived at the Student Resources home page and have the option of choosing one
of several chapter resources.

Applying Anthropology. Begin your study of cultural
anthropology by clicking on Applying Anthropology.
Here you will find useful information on careers, graduate school programs in applied anthropology, and internships you might wish to pursue. You will also find real-
world examples of working anthropologists applying the
skills and methods of anthropology to help solve serious
world problems.

Research Online. Click here to find a wealth of Web
links that will facilitate your study of anthropology. Divided into different fields of study, specific websites are
starting points for Internet research. You will be guided to
rich anthropology websites that will help you prepare for
class, complete course assignments, and actually do research on the Web.

⚲ **InfoTrac College Edition Exercises.** From the
pull-down menu, select the chapter you are presently studying. Select InfoTrac College Edition Exercises from the list of resources. These exercises utilize
InfoTrac College Edition's vast database of articles and
help you explore the numerous uses of the search word,
culture.

Study Aids for This Chapter. Improve your knowledge
of key terms by using flash cards and study the learning
objectives. Take the practice quiz, receive your results,
and email them to your instructor. Access these resources
from the chapter and resource pull-down menus.

Chapter Three

CULTURE AND LANGUAGE

Humanity and Language

Five Properties of Language

  Multimedia Potential

  Discreteness

  Arbitrariness

  Productivity

  Displacement

How Language Works

  Sound Systems

  Variations in Sound Systems

  Words and Meanings

  Nonverbal Communication

Language and Culture

  Language as a Reflection of Culture

  Language and Worldview

Social Uses of Speech

© Pablo Corral V/Corbis

Symbolic language is one of humanity's most remarkable capabilities. In speaking, gesturing, and using physical space, these women from Ecuador communicate both verbally and nonverbally.

A S CHILDREN GROW UP, THEY SOCIALLY LEARN the sounds, words, meanings, and grammatical rules needed to send and receive complex messages. Language is the shared knowledge of these elements and rules. Along with our heavy dependence on culture, the ability to communicate complex, precise information is the main mental capability that distinguishes humans from other animals.

WE BEGIN this chapter by discussing briefly a few of the many reasons why language is so remarkable. Then we describe some features of language that make it more sophisticated than the communication systems of other animals. We show how people send and receive messages by following unconscious rules for combining sounds and words in ways that other people who know the language recognize as meaningful. People also communicate by nonverbal means, including through bodily movements and spatial relationships. We shall see that cultures vary in how they interpret these elements of communication, although some expressions and movements seem to carry similar meanings universally. Finally, we discuss how language is related to certain aspects of culture and how speaking is itself a culturally conditioned behavior.

Humanity and Language

Although we talk to one another every day, we seldom consider how remarkable it is that we can do so. Yet the ability to speak and comprehend the messages of language requires knowledge of an enormous number of linguistic elements and rules. Language and culture together are critical to the development of human individuals—unless we learn them, our psychological and social development is incomplete. In all probability, without them we would be unable to think, as the word *think* is generally understood, because language and culture provide our minds with most of the concepts and terms for thought itself. Thus the workings of the human mind depend crucially on the knowledge of some language.

The importance of language for human life is further revealed by several points. First, *Homo sapiens* is the only animal capable of speech. Other animals—including honeybees, social species of ants and termites, some whales and dolphins, gorillas, and chimpanzees—are capable of impressive feats of communication, but only humans have language in a fully developed form. In 2004, scientists reported that a border collie correctly retrieved over 200 objects called out by its master, including items the names of which its master had not intentionally taught it. With the aid of intensive training from humans, chimpanzees and gorillas can learn to use sign language or to manipulate symbols standing for words and concepts into sentences. With no human interference, one chimp taught sign language to another and they used it to send messages to one another. Despite these feats, no great ape is capable of responding to this simple request: "Tell me what you plan to do tomorrow."

In fact, language is so critical to humanity that it helped to shape our biological evolution. This includes, of course, the speech regions of our brain, but it also includes our vocal tract. The human *vocal tract* consists of the lungs, trachea, mouth, and nasal passages. This part

▲ Successful attempts have been made to teach sign language to a few chimpanzees and gorillas. These apes have learned signs for things, actions, and even emotional states, and can combine these signs into meaningful sentences. However, they are not capable of mastering language in its fully developed forms.

of our anatomy is biologically evolved for speech for it is a remarkable resonating chamber. Distinctive vowel sounds are made by raising and lowering the tongue or parts of the tongue. This modifies the shape of the mouth and hence produces sounds of different wavelengths, which our ears recognize as different sounds (compare where your tongue is for the vowels in *sit* and *set,* and in *teeth* and *tooth*). Most consonants are produced by interrupting the flow of air through the mouth. The initial sound of the word *tap* is formed by bringing the tip of the tongue into contact with the alveolar ridge just behind the teeth, then releasing the contact suddenly. You change *tap* to *sap* by blowing air through your mouth while almost, but not quite, touching the tip of your tongue to your alveolar ridge, thus making the initial sound into a brief hissing noise. You do all this unconsciously and with astounding speed and precision. The other vowels and consonants of English and other languages are made by articulating various parts of the vocal tract in different ways. Each sound is possible because the chamber formed by the mouth, throat, and nasal passages, and the muscles of the tongue and lips, are biologically evolved to allow us to produce them. There is a good reason why chimpanzees cannot speak human words: Their vocal tract is not evolved to do so. Yet, with training, any human can utter the sounds found in any language.

Second, language makes it possible for people to communicate and think about abstract concepts, as well as about concrete persons, places, things, actions, and events. Among these abstractions are *truth, evil, god, masculinity, wealth, values, humanity, zero, law, democracy, jihad, universal, space,* and *hatred.* Humans all understand abstractions such as these. Indeed, without the ability to conceptualize such abstractions, culture as we experience it could not exist. And our everyday behavior is greatly affected by abstract ideas such as *friend* and *enemy, food* and *poison, beautiful* and *ugly, play* and *work.*

Third, the social learning by which children acquire culture would be impossible without language. Language makes it possible for the knowledge in one person's mind to be transmitted into the mind of another person. During enculturation, we learn not just "facts" and "lessons" about the world. We hear (or read) stories and myths, whose lessons are only implicit. The worldview of a culture is communicated (and perhaps even shaped) by language.

Finally, language allows humanity to enjoy the benefits of the most complete and precise form of communication in any animal. We can communicate incredibly detailed information about past, present, and future events. In fact, we can learn about events that happened far away and long ago and speculate about events that could possibly happen tomorrow but probably won't. We can tell lies. We can discuss plans, contingencies, and possible courses of action, based on our expectations about what might happen in the future. All these are things humans do so routinely we consider them ordinary.

In brief, language is powerful. It makes abstract thought possible. It allows the relatively quick and easy transmission of information from one individual (and generation) to another. It allows the communication of complex and precise messages, including speculations and lies.

Five Properties of Language

We can best understand the power of language by describing some of the properties that distinguish it from the communication abilities of other animals. Back in 1960, linguist Charles Hockett identified 13 features shared by all human languages. Only 5 of the 13 are important for our purposes.

Multimedia Potential

Messages use some medium for their transmission from sender to recipient. For example, writing is the medium in which the messages of this book are transmitted. When you speak, the medium for your message is speech, transmitted to the ears of your listeners by sound waves. Gestures and bodily movements are communications media, which are received by the sense of sight rather than hearing. Messages can also be transmitted through other media, including touch and even chemicals, whose odors carry meaning for animals such as ants and dogs.

Unlike most other ways of communicating, language has *multimedia potential,* meaning that linguistic messages can be transmitted through a variety of media. The original medium for language, of course, was speech. But once the ancient Sumerians, Egyptians, Chinese, and Mesoamericans found it useful to keep records of taxes, labor, oracles, the passage of time (through calendars), and the conquests of their rulers, the medium of writing developed. Over several centuries, writing techniques spread to other regions such as the Greek islands, South Asia, Japan, Korea, and western Europe. American Sign Language is a medium for the hearing impaired. Even touching and the resulting nerve signals can be a medium for language. Helen Keller, both blind and deaf, communicated and received linguistic messages by touch. Morse code, signing, and the Internet are all possible because of language's multimedia potential.

Discreteness

When we speak we combine discrete units according to shared and conventional rules. Knowing how to speak a language means knowing both the units and the rules for combining them. Thus words are composed of discrete units of sound (e.g., *j, u, m, p*) that are combined to communicate a meaning (*jump*). Sentences are composed of discrete units of meanings (words) that are combined according to rules to communicate a message.

Alphabets are possible because of the property called *discreteness*. In alphabetic writing, people combine the letters of their alphabet to form words. The letters of the English alphabet symbolize discrete sounds, and originally each sound was pronounced in a similar way in all the words in which it appeared. For example, the letter *t* appears in *student, textbook, eat,* and *today,* and so does the sound we symbolize as *t* in the English alphabet. The same applies to all other letters in an alphabet.

In English writing, most letters no longer represent a single sound. The letter *a,* for example, is pronounced differently in the words *act, father, warden, assume,* and *nature.* The same is true for other letters that represent English vowels. Some single sounds in English are rendered in spelling as two letters, such as *th, ou,* and the *gh* in *rough.* Why does the spelling English now uses for certain words not reflect the way these words are pronounced? Basically, because changes in spelling have lagged behind changes in pronunciation since the invention of the printing press.

By themselves, most sounds carry no meaning: The three English sounds in the word *cat,* for example, are meaningless when pronounced by themselves. But by combining this limited number of sounds in different ways, words are formed, and words do communicate meanings. Thus, the three sounds in *cat* can be put together in different sequences to form the words *act* and *tack.* Words, then, are composed of sound combinations that have recognized, conventional meanings in a speech community.

Just as all languages use a small number of sounds to make a large number of words, words are combined according to the grammatical rules of the language to convey the complex messages carried by sentences. By mastering their language's words and their meanings, and the rules for combining words into sentences, speakers and listeners can send and receive messages of great complexity with amazing precision (e.g., "From the basket of apples on your left, hand me the reddest one on the bottom.").

Discrete sounds are sometimes said to be the building blocks of language. By recombining them in different sequences and numbers, an infinite number of words can be pronounced (although most languages have only thousands of words).

Arbitrariness

The relationship between the strings of sounds that make up words and the meanings these words communicate is *arbitrary,* which means that words are symbols (see Chapter 2). When children learn to speak and understand verbal messages, they learn the combinations of sounds that are permissible according to the rules of their language. For instance, in English, *mp, nt,* and *ld* are all possible combinations, but *pm, tn,* and *dl* are not (although these combinations are used by other languages). Children also learn to match certain sound combinations (words) with their meanings. By the age of 1, most children have learned the meanings of dozens of words. They have mastered many words that refer to objects (*ball*), animals (*doggie*), people (*mama*), sensory experiences (*hot*), qualities (*blue, hard*), actions (*eat, run*), commands (*no, come here*), emotions (*love*), and so forth. The child learns to associate meanings with words, even though the specific sound combinations that convey these various meanings have no inherent relation to the things themselves. Thus the feelings aroused by "I love you" in English are also aroused by "Te amo" in Spanish, although the sounds of the message are different.

Because the relation between meanings and words or sentences is arbitrary, our ability to communicate linguistic messages is based entirely on conventions shared by the sender and receiver of a message. When we learn a language, we master these conventions about meanings, just as we strive to master pronunciations and other things.

Productivity

Productivity refers to a speaker's ability to create totally novel sentences and to a listener's ability to comprehend them. Productivity means that a language's finite number of words can be combined into an infinite number of meaningful sentences. The sentences are meaningful because the speaker and listener know what each word means individually and the rules by which they may be combined to convey messages. The amazing thing is that individuals are not consciously aware of their knowledge of these rules, although they routinely apply them each time they speak and hear. For example, unless you are trained in linguistics, you probably do not know that you form an English plural by adding one of *two* sounds (either –z or –s) to the end of a noun.

Displacement

Displacement refers to our ability to talk about objects, people, things, and events that are remote in time and space. Language has this property because it uses symbols (words, sentences) to transmit meanings, so things and people do not have to be immediately visible for us to communicate about them. We can discuss someone who is out of sight because the symbols of language (in this case, a name) call that person to mind, allowing us to think about him or her. We can speculate about the future because, although its events may never happen, our language has symbols that stand for future time, and more symbols that allow us to form a mental image of possible events. We can learn about events that happened before we were born, such as the Reagan presidency and the wars in Korea and Vietnam.

Displacement makes it possible for us to talk about things that may not even exist, such as goblins, ghosts, and ghouls. We can even give these imaginary things detailed characteristics in our mind's eye, although our real eyes have never seen them. We can tell one another stories about things that never happened, and thus create myths, folklore, and literature. People can learn of events remote from them in space, such as World Trade Organization talks in Cancún, fighting in Afghanistan and Iraq, explorations of Mars, and civil unrest in Chechnya. Political leaders can be misled themselves or can mislead citizens about weapons of mass destruction and terrorist "connections" in faraway places. Much that is familiar in human life depends on this important property of language.

Together, multimedia potential, discreteness, arbitrariness, productivity, and displacement make language the most precise and complete system of communication known among living things. Because of them, you understand the following lie perfectly although you've never read or heard it before: "Last Tuesday at 7:02 P.M., Denzel Washington chased my neighbor's dog around the yard and bit her ear."

How Language Works

As children learn the language of their community, they master an enormous amount of information about sounds, sound combinations, meanings, and rules. Linguistic units (sounds, words) and the rules for combining them make up the total system of linguistic knowledge called a **grammar.** *Grammar* refers to all the knowledge shared by those who are able to speak and understand a given language: what sounds occur, rules for combining them into sequences, meanings that are conveyed by these sequences, and how sentences are constructed by stringing words together according to precise rules.

Grammatical knowledge is *unconscious:* those who share a language cannot verbalize the nature of the knowledge that allows them to communicate with one another. It also is *intuitive:* speaking and understanding are automatic, and we ordinarily do not need to think long and hard about how to speak or understand linguistic messages.

This scientific use of *grammar* differs from the everyday use of the term. In everyday speech we judge people partly on the basis of whether we consider their grammar proper. In the United States there are several dialects, or regional variants, of English. One, called *Standard American English* (SAE)—the dialect we usually hear in the national news media—is culturally considered as the most "correct." Other dialects, especially those spoken by many African Americans and by southern or Appalachian whites, are looked down on by many of those whose dialect is SAE.

But there is no such thing as superior and inferior dialects (or languages) *in the linguistic sense.* That is, each language, and each dialect, is equally capable of serving as a vehicle for communicating the messages its speakers need to send and receive. So long as a person successfully communicates, there is no such thing as "bad grammar," or people who "don't know proper grammar." The exchange of messages

Merle: I ain't got no shoes.

Pearl: I ain't got none either.

is perfectly good English—to members of certain subcultures who speak one English dialect. So long as speakers communicate their intended meaning to listeners, then the words they use or the ways they construct their sentences are as valid linguistically as any other.

The evaluations we make of someone else's grammar or overall style of speech, then, are cultural evaluations. Culturally, people consider some dialects as more correct and/or sophisticated than others. But if the history of the United States had been different, some other dialect of American English might have become standard, and the sentences

Jennifer: I have no shoes.

Christopher: Nor do I.

might have become a cultural marker by which one segment of the population judges another as unsophisticated.

This point is so important that it is worth rephrasing. Many languages are not uniform but have variations based on region, socioeconomic class, ethnicity, or some other difference between groups of people. Such variations in the grammar of a single language are called **dialects.** The speakers of a language or dialect share a complete knowledge of its grammar. For example, the grammar used by some African Americans differs slightly from that of SAE. But a linguist would never describe the differences between the two dialects in terms of relative superiority because each dialect is capable of conveying the same messages.

In contrast, when some speakers of SAE label African American, Appalachian, or southern dialects as substandard English, they are basing their judgments on their own assumptions about the relative correctness of dialects. But this judgment is entirely *cultural. Linguistically,* all languages and all dialects work as well as others, meaning that all languages and all dialects have equal ability to communicate the messages their speakers need to send and receive.

With this point about the relativity of languages and dialects in mind, here we discuss two aspects of grammar: (1) sounds and their patterning, and (2) sound combinations and their meanings. (A third field studies the rules for combining words into sentences, but this complicated subject is outside the scope of this book.)

Sound Systems

Every time we speak, our vocal tract emits a string of sounds. The sounds of a language, together with the way these sounds occur in regular and consistent patterns, make up the *phonological system* of the language. The study of sound systems is called **phonology.**

The particular sounds that the speakers of a language recognize as distinct from other sounds are called **phonemes.** Phonemes are individual sounds that make a difference in the meanings of words. Linguists use slash marks / / to show that a particular sound is a phoneme in a given language. Thus, a few English consonants are / f /, / t /, / b /, / n /, / z /, and / l /. Some English vowels are / a /, / i / (pronounced "ee"), / o /, and / u /. In linguistic jargon, words consist of a string of phonemes.

For example, the word *brought* consists of four phonemes: / b /, / r /, / ɔ /, and / t /. If you substitute any other phoneme for one of the phonemes, you either change the word into another word (e.g., *bright,* in which a different vowel sound, / ay /, is substituted for / ɔ /) or make it unintelligible (e.g., *blought* or *broughk*). Notice that writing the word *brought* using the phonemes (the sounds that speakers recognize as distinctive) is not identical to how we ordinarily spell the word.

Languages have different phonemes, and various languages' phonological systems are patterned differently. This means that languages recognize and distinguish between sounds based on different sound qualities, and that each language has its own logic and consistency in making these distinctions.

As an example of the patterning of the phonological system of one language, compare three phonemes of English: / b /, / p /, and / v /. The phoneme / b / appears in *boy, probation,* and *flab.* It is made by putting the lips together and then releasing them while making a slight vibration with the vocal cords. The phoneme / p / appears in *pat, approach,* and *example.* We make the / p / sound the same way as / b /, except that we do not vibrate our vocal cords. / v / appears in *vibration, every,* and *love.* You pronounce it similarly to / b /, but your lower lip touches your upper teeth and you blow through the narrow slit created while vibrating your vocal cords. (Go ahead: try it.)

You can hear the vibration of your vocal cords in / b / and / v / by placing your hands over your ears while saying the word *bat* or *vat* slowly and listening for a slight buzz during the pronunciation of / b / and / v /. This buzz is the sound your vocal cords make when your lungs force air through them while they are constricted, or tightened, until they are nearly in contact with one another. All sounds in which the vocal cords vibrate are called *voiced.* Examples of other voiced consonants in English are / d /, / z /, / g /, and / ǰ / (/ ǰ / is the first and last sound in *judge*).

Now place your hands over your ears while saying the word *pat.* You will not hear a buzz during the pronunciation of / p /. This is because your vocal cords are completely open, so the flow of air from your lungs is unimpeded and no buzzy sound is created. All sounds in which the vocal cords are open, so that their vibration does not contribute to the sound, are called *voiceless.* Other voiceless phonemes in English are / t /, / s /, / k /, and / č / (/ č / is the first and last sound in *church*).

The only difference between *bat* and *pat* is this first sound, and the significant difference between the sounds / b / and / p / is that the vocal cords vibrate during / b / but are open during / p /. Stated technically, the only difference between the two phonemes is that / b / is voiced, whereas / p / is voiceless. As for / v /, you change *pat* or *bat* to *vat* by softly touching your lower lip to your upper teeth and expelling air while vibrating your vocal cords.

We discussed these three English phonemes in some detail to make a general point: Our mutual understanding of words is based on our shared ability to hear distinctions between their sounds and to recognize these distinctions as significant. If the difference between / b /, / p /, and / v / was not significant, we would not recognize any difference between words that differ only in these sounds—*pat, vat,* and *bat* would have the same meaning and therefore would be the same word.

There are many other differences between phonemes, of course. A few such differences are summarized in the

Some Differences Between Consonant Phonemes in English

Basis of Difference	Description of Difference	Contrasting Sounds and Words
Voicing	Whether vocal cords vibrate	/ t /, / d / ant, and; tear, dare / s /, / z / sip, zip; ass, as / f /, / v / feel, veal; leaf, leave
Articulation point	Location of tongue	/ g /, / b / guy, buy; fig, fib / r /, / l / ram, lamb; steer, steal
Nasalization	Whether air flows through nose	/ b /, / m / by, my; bomb, mom / d /, / n / dough, no; nod, non
Interruption of air flow	Whether flow of air is completely stopped for an instant or is constricted in its flow	/ t /, / s / tea, see; night, nice / d /, / z / do, zoo; died, dies

Concept Review. If you pay close attention to what happens to the parts of your mouth and to the flow of air as you pronounce the example words, you will detect differences you probably never knew existed.

Variations in Sound Systems

We have just put into words what every speaker of English unconsciously and intuitively knows: that we detect the difference between sounds such as / t /, / d /, and / f /, and that we recognize this difference as significant. Can't speakers of other languages hear this difference? And doesn't everyone recognize this difference as significant?

No. There are a great many languages in which sounds that differ only slightly in pronunciation (e.g., voiced or voiceless) are not recognized as different sounds. For such languages, such sounds are not separate phonemes and speakers may not even be able to hear the difference between them. If you speak Spanish, you may know that / v / and / b / are not recognized as distinctive sounds, so native Spanish speakers at first have difficulties hearing *vat* and *bat*, or *very* and *berry* as different words. Japanese makes no distinctions between the English phonemes / l / and / r /. In Korean, whether a consonant like / t / is stressed (written as / tt / by linguists) matters for the meaning of a word. On the island of Kosrae, Micronesia, the distinctions between the sounds / t / and / d /, / p / and / b /, and / k / and / g / make no difference in meaning. It is as if English-speaking people made no distinction between *tan* and *dan,* between *pig* and *big,* and between *cot* and *got.* In English, / k / and / g / are different phonemes; in Kosraen, they are alternative ways of pronouncing the same phoneme.

So differences between sounds that are meaningful in one language's phonological system do not always make a difference in meaning in another's. Conversely, one language may recognize distinctions between similar sounds that the speakers of another language do not detect. For example, we have referred to the English phoneme / p / as if it is always pronounced the same way. In fact, we use two pronunciations for / p /, depending on the sounds around it. Consider the words *pit* and *spit.* You might think that the only difference between the two is the sound / s /. If so, you are wrong. The / p / in *pit* is followed by a short puff of air (called aspiration) between it and the vowel; the / p / in *pit* is said to be *aspirated.* The / p / in *spit* is not followed by such a puff; it is *unaspirated.* (You cannot hear this difference, but you may be able to feel it: Put your hand immediately in front of your mouth while saying the two words, and you may feel the aspiration after the / p / in *pit,* but not after the / p / in *spit.*)

In many languages this minor (to English speakers) difference in pronunciation matters for the meanings of words. In Thai, for example, / p / and / pʰ / (the ʰ stands for aspiration) are separate phonemes, which means that those who speak Thai detect the difference between many aspirated and unaspirated sounds and recognize it as changing the meaning of many words. This is seen in the following Thai words:

paa forest	*pʰaa* to split
tam to pound	*tʰam* to do
kat to bite	*kʰat* to interrupt

Note that a difference in sound that is nearly inaudible to a speaker of English changes the meanings of the paired Thai words just listed. Hindi, the language spoken

47

© Michael S. Yamashita/Corbis

▲ Languages do not recognize the same differences in phonemes as making a difference in the meanings of words. These Japanese farm women do not distinguish between / r / and / l /, whereas English speakers do not distinguish between / t / and / tʰ /.

by many Asian Indians, also recognizes the differences between aspirated and unaspirated sounds.

One of the most interesting ways languages differ in their phonological systems is the way the pitch of the voice is used to convey meaning. (The *pitch* of a voice depends on how fast the vocal cords vibrate: The higher the frequency of vibration, the higher the pitch of the voice.) English speakers use pitch to convey different meanings, as you can see by contrasting the following sentences:

She went to class.
She went to class?

The first statement is turned into a question by altering the pitch of the voice. In the question, the pitch rises with the word *class*.

Speakers of English use pitch changes over the whole sentence to communicate a message; that is, the voice pitch falls or rises mainly between words, rather than within a word. There are many other languages in which

a high, medium, or low pitch used within an individual word, or even in a syllable, changes the fundamental meaning of the word.

Languages in which the pitch (or tone) with which a word is said (or changes in the voice pitch during its pronunciation) affects the meaning of a word are known as **tone languages.** Tone languages are widespread in Africa and in southeastern and eastern Asia. Chinese, Thai, Burmese, and Vietnamese are all tone languages (Japanese and Korean, incidentally, are not), which is why they have a musical quality to ears accustomed to English. As an example of how pitch can affect meaning, consider these words from Nupe, an African tone language:

bá (high tone) to be sour
bā (mid tone) to cut
bà (low tone) to count

Here, whether the two phonemes in *ba* are pronounced with a high, mid, or low tone changes their meaning. Be-

▲ In tone languages, the voice pitch a speaker uses when speaking a word, or changes in the pitch within a word, makes a difference in the meaning of the word. Vietnamese is only one of many tone languages.

cause the tone with which a word is pronounced changes its meaning, the pitch of the voice is a kind of phoneme in tone languages. It has the same effect as adding / s / in front of the English word *pot,* which totally alters its meaning to *spot.*

Words and Meanings

Words are combinations of phonemes to which people attach conventional meanings. Any language contains a finite number of words, each matched to one or more meanings. The total inventory of words in a language is called its **lexicon.**

Of all linguistic elements, words are the most easily transmissible across different languages. When groups who speak different languages come into contact, one or both groups often incorporate some of the "foreign" words into their lexicon. Incorporation is especially likely to happen if one language's words have no counterparts in the lexicon of the other, as is commonly the case for many nouns. Because of the way the world trading and political system has developed in the last five centuries, English words have spread widely into other languages. Japanese and Korean have incorporated hundreds of English words, many from the realm of technology and commodities. In France the use of English words became such a hot political issue that the government recently outlawed the "importation" of further English words.

But, lest English speakers become too proud, it should be noted that English (a Germanic language) itself has, over the centuries, adopted words from the Romance languages (which originated from Latin), as anyone who has studied French, Spanish, Portuguese, Italian, or other Romance languages knows. Less well known is the fact that the early English colonists who settled in the Americas adopted lots of words from Native Americans—words that are now incorporated into the English lexicon (see A Closer Look).

Morphology is the study of meaningful sound sequences and the rules by which they are formed. In studying meanings, morphologists need a more precise concept than *word.* To see why, ask yourself if you know the meaning of the following sound sequences, none of which qualifies as a word:

un	ed
pre	s
non	ing
anti	ist

You do, of course, recognize these sound sequences. Those in the first column are prefixes, which change the meaning of certain words when placed before them. Those in the second column are suffixes, which alter a word's meaning when they follow the word.

Sound sequences such as these are "detachable" from particular words. Take the words *art* and *novel,* for example. Adding the suffix *-ist* to these words creates new words meaning "a person who creates art" or "one who writes novels." That *-ist* has a similar meaning whenever it is attached to other words is shown by the made-up word *crim;* you don't know what this word means, but by adding *-ist* to it, you instantly know that a *crimist* is "a person who crims."

To analyze such compound words and their meanings, linguists have a concept that includes prefixes and

The first European settlers of eastern North America came from the British Isles. With the exception of French-speaking Quebec and parts of the American Southwest, most citizens of Canada and the United States speak English as their native language. Few of us know about the influence of the original native languages of North America—those spoken by American Indians—on the English vocabulary. Many familiar English words, phrases, and place names are derived from one or another Native American language.

The earliest Spanish and Portuguese explorers were surprised at how many of the plants and animals in the "New World" (North and South America and the Caribbean) were unknown to them. A few animals, such as deer and wolves, were enough like familiar European fauna that European words were applied to them. Others, however, had no European counterparts. Terms taken from North American Indian languages were adopted for many of these, including *cougar, caribou, moose, raccoon, chipmunk, opossum, skunk,* and *chigger.* Other "English" terms for animals are taken from the languages of South American peoples: *condor, piranha, tapir, toucan, jaguar, alpaca, vicuña,* and *llama.* Plants, too, were unfamiliar, and Native American words were adopted for *saguaro, yucca, mesquite, persimmon, hickory,* and *pecan,* to name only some of the most common derivatives.

As we shall see in Chapter 6, Indians of the Americas were the first to domesticate numerous food plants that now have worldwide importance. All the following crop names have Native American origins: *squash, maize, hominy, avocado, tapioca* (also called *manioc* and *cassava,* both words also taken from native languages), *pawpaw, succotash, tomato,* and *potato.* Indian words for natural features other than plants and animals also were adopted by European immigrants: *bayou, muskeg, savanna, pampas, hurricane, chinook.* Terms in various Native American languages for clothing, housing, and other material objects have made it into English: *igloo, teepee, wigwam, moccasin, parka, poncho, toboggan, husky, canoe, kayak,* and *tomahawk. Caucus* and *powwow,* for meetings, are two other English words with native origins.

People everywhere name geographical locations. The earliest European settlers often named American places to honor important people in their home countries—for example,

Charleston, Albuquerque, Columbus, Carolina, and Virginia (the latter named after the supposed condition of England's Queen Elizabeth I). Other American place names are derived from European geography—Nova Scotia (new Scotland), New Hampshire, Maine (a province in France), and, of course, New York and New England.

Native American peoples had their own names for places and landscape features, and often these names were the ones that endured and appear on modern maps. River names with Indian origins include Mississippi, Ohio, Yukon, Missouri, Arkansas, Wabash, Potomac, Klamath, Minnesota, and Mohawk, to mention just a few of the most familiar. The lakes called Huron, Ontario, Michigan, Oneida, Tahoe, and Slave have Indian names, as do hundreds of other bodies of water in Canada and the United States. Whole states are named after Indian peoples such as the Illini, Massachuset, Ute, Kansa, and Dakota, whereas names of other states and provinces are derived from native words, such as Manitoba, Ontario, Saskatchewan, Texas, Oklahoma, Ohio, Minnesota, Iowa, and Nebraska. A few large cities with names derived from Indian languages are Tuscaloosa, Tallahassee, Natchez, Tulsa, Cheyenne, Miami, Chicago, Saskatoon, Ottawa, and Omaha. Seattle was named after a particular Indian leader, Seal'th, of the West Coast. Finally, the names of two whole countries on the North American continent have Indian roots: *kanata* (Canada) is an Iroquoian word meaning village (although it now is applied to a much larger community), whereas the area formerly known as New Spain took a name meaning "the place of the Mexica" (another name for the Aztecs) after winning its independence in 1823.

Aside from the inherent interest in the historical fact that many words in the English vocabulary have Indian origins, the adoption of words is a reminder of another, wider point: The culture of those of us who live in the modern world is the product of interaction among disparate peoples. In the past five centuries, increasing contact among the major regions of the planet has led to the spread of cultural beliefs and ideas. Like our languages, our cultural traditions have multiple origins. We shall discuss some of these connections and their impacts in later chapters.

Sources: Nestor (2003); Weatherford (1991)

---

suffixes such as *uni-, -ing, -ly.* Any sequence of phonemes that carries meaning is known as a **morpheme.** There are two kinds of morphemes in all languages. **Free morphemes** are any morphemes that can stand alone as words; for example, *type, walk, woman, establish.* **Bound morphemes** are attached to free morphemes to modify their meanings in predictable ways;

for example, *dis-, bi-, -er, -ly.* Thus, by adding suffixes to the example free morphemes, we get

typist	typed	typing
walked	walking	walks
womanly	womanhood	womanish
established	establishment	establishes

Both prefixes and suffixes—which in English are the two kinds of bound morphemes—can be attached to a free morpheme to change its meaning, as shown in the following examples:

desire	desirable	undesirable
excuse	excusable	inexcusably
possible	impossible	impossibility
health	healthful	unhealthy
complete	incomplete	uncompleted

Just as phonemes are a language's minimal units of sound, morphemes are the minimal units of meaning. Thus, we cannot break down the free morphemes *friend, possible, man,* or *run* into any smaller unit that carries meaning. Nor can we break down the bound morphemes *non-, -ish, -able,* or *tri-* into any smaller units and still have them mean anything in English.

People learn how to make new compound words by applying a rule of compound-word formation, not by learning each compound word separately. For instance, take the English rule for forming a plural noun from a singular noun. It can be done by adding the bound morpheme / z /, as in *beads, apples, colors, eggs.* (Incidentally, / z / represents one of only a few cases in English in which a phoneme is also a morpheme. When used as a bound morpheme at the end of a noun, / z / usually carries the meaning "more than one.") Children learn the rule for plural formation at an early age, but it takes them a while longer to learn the many exceptions. Adults think it cute when children apply the morphological rules of English consistently to all words, saying "childs," "mans," "foots," "mouses," for plurals and using "goed," "runned," "bringed," and "doed" to make a present-tense verb into a past-tense verb.

Nonverbal Communication

People send and receive messages using more than just sounds, words, and sentences. Facial expressions are enormously important in conveying a speaker's emotions and intentions. We routinely send both conscious (intentional) and unconscious (implicit) messages by how we move our bodies or parts of our bodies. *Kinesics* studies the role of bodily motions in communication. We can convey feelings and other emotions and messages by touching another person.

Some nonverbal facial expressions and bodily movements convey the same messages among all peoples, so presumably they have a biological basis. Pleasure, sadness, anger, puzzlement, and some other emotional responses are shown by similar facial expressions everywhere, so

▲ In the process of interacting with parents and other adults, children learn the rules for forming morphemes out of sounds and the meanings people in their community attach to these morphemes.

they convey similar meanings universally. Notice, though, that facial expressions can be used to deceive, as with phony smiles and feigned anger. Also, frequently a given facial expression is normatively appropriate (as in greeting someone), so the expression occurs regardless of the actual internal emotional state of the person.

We communicate nonverbally, often unconsciously, by means of spatial relationships, meaning how closely people who are interacting space themselves apart when standing or sitting or walking. *Proxemics* studies the meanings conveyed by space and distance. Edward Hall, who pioneered the field of proxemics with his books *The Silent Language* and *The Hidden Dimension,* noted that in the United States people communicate messages by how far apart they stand or sit while interacting. There is intimate distance (up to about 18 inches), personal distance (more than 2 feet to 4 feet), and social distance (over 4 feet), the latter applying mainly to formal situations. (Try violating these conventions by standing a bit too close to an acquaintance; just be sure to do so in an area where the person can back away from you.) It is usually offensive or a sign of aggression "to get in someone's face," as illustrated by barroom quarrels and player–umpire altercations.

Like speech, most forms of nonverbal communication are symbolic: A particular bodily motion or distance does not inherently convey a certain message, but does so only because of conventions, or common understandings. Because much nonverbal communication is arbitrary and conventional, there is great potential for misunderstanding when people do not share understandings about nonverbal messages—that is, when people have learned different conventions. Probably the potential for misunderstanding is even greater with nonverbal messages than for spoken language. In speaking to a "foreigner," both of you generally know that you don't understand the other's language, so at least both of you are aware of your ignorance. But with nonverbal messages both of you are more likely to think you do understand, so one or both of you might give or take offense when none is intended.

Miscommunication is especially likely with touching, the unspoken rules for which vary greatly from people to people and even from individual to individual. On one Micronesian island, married, engaged, or romantically involved couples never walk hand in hand, although close friends of the same sex frequently do so (carrying no implication of sexual preference). Public hugging, even in greeting or to say goodbye, is seldom seen; according to cultural norms, handshakes are sufficient. Touching someone on the head—including what North Americans consider an affectionate rub or friendly pat—is offensive. Imagine the snickers (which in part covered embarrassment) when a visiting Anglo couple were seen kissing.

Some scholars who study nonverbal communication distinguish "low touch" and "high touch" cultures. Such dichotomies are usually simplistic, but it is true that cultures vary greatly in how they define situations in which touching is normatively desirable or appropriate. There is often an implicit power dimension to physical contact as well: High status people are much more likely to affectionately touch subordinates than the reverse—affectionate (or "faked affectionate") touching symbolizes familiarity, and touching by lower status individuals is often seen as "too familiar."

Similar ideas apply to the use of space. Again, the possibilities for miscommunication are great when people with different cultural upbringings interact. Sometimes Middle Easterners or Latin Americans stand too close for North Americans' comfort. Simply becoming aware that cultural norms about body motions, touching, distance, and so forth differ from people to people can help us all avoid taking offense when none is intended. In a world where international migration, tourism, global business, and other forms of intercultural contact are exploding, awareness of such differences is both personally useful and socially valuable.

▲ People communicate nonverbally in a variety of ways, including body language, touch, and spatial proximity. This woman at a market in Lebanon seems to be using all three forms of nonverbal communication simultaneously.

Language and Culture

A major interest of anthropological linguists is how the culture a group of people share is related to the language they speak. This topic is potentially very technical, so here we focus on only two areas in which language and culture might be most closely tied together. First, many parts of language reflect the social relationships between individuals and the cultural importance people attach to different things or categories. Second, some scholars have suggested that language powerfully shapes a people's perception of reality and even their entire worldview. We discuss these possible interconnections in the remainder of this section.

Language as a Reflection of Culture

Anthropological fieldworkers try to learn the language of the community they work with. Obviously, speaking in the local language facilitates interaction and may help create relations of trust. But fieldworkers also know that learning language helps fieldworkers understand the local culture. This is because many aspects of the language a people speak reflect their culture.

For instance, a complex lexicon tends to develop around things that are especially important to a community. People assign names or labels to those objects, qualities, and actions about which they frequently communicate. You can see how vocabulary reflects a people's need to communicate about certain subjects by considering different subcultural and occupational categories in North American society. Take automobile or carpentry tools, for example. A professional mechanic or carpenter identifies hundreds of kinds of tools; the Saturday-afternoon home mechanic or handy spouse identifies perhaps several dozen; and the rest of us don't know what a feeler gauge or miter saw looks like. Numerous other examples could be cited, of course, but there are no surprises here.

However, not all specialized vocabularies are developed just to meet the need of the members of some group to converse easily or precisely about things that matter to them. They also serve as status markers for professions and other groups. Lawyers speak "legalese" only partly because they need to make fine distinctions between points of law that are obscure to the rest of us. Legalese is a secret—as well as a specialized—vocabulary. Entry into the select group of attorneys depends in part on mastery of an esoteric vocabulary with all its nuances. And it is helpful to the profession that the general population cannot understand real estate agreements and other contracts written by attorneys. Most of us are compelled to pay for the special knowledge of an attorney to interpret important documents.

You might have noticed that college professors, when acting out their professional roles, sometimes use esoteric words, complex sentence constructions, and "sophisticated" speech styles. (Even textbook authors sometimes do the same thing with their word choices and writing styles.) This is partly to increase the precision of communication, but it also serves to distinguish them from other people with less (or different forms of) formal education.

Members of various ethnic and "racial" categories may have their own ways of pronouncing words or styles of speaking. In part, dialects based on ethnic identity are learned at a young age from family and friends. But there may be more to speaking a dialect than speaking the way you learned while growing up. In Canada and the United States, many African and Hispanic Americans adopt a speech style as a symbol of pride in their identity. To show they are cool, some young Anglos adopt phrases they hear from the media or from persons with African or Hispanic heritages. Hip-hop and rap have become mainstreamed because of their use of language as well as rhythm.

In sum, in a diverse society, occupational, ethnic, and other kinds of groups develop vocabularies and speech styles to facilitate communication, to help ensure the continuation of their privileges and rewards, to mark themselves off from everyone else, to symbolize cultural and racial pride, and so on. What about differences *between* whole languages, spoken by members of *different* cultures? Similar ideas apply. To understand them, the concept of **semantic domain** is useful. A semantic domain is a set of words that belongs to an inclusive class. For example, *chair, table, ottoman,* and *china cabinet* belong to the semantic domain of "furniture." "Color" is another semantic domain, with members such as *violet, red,* and *yellow.*

Semantic domains typically have a hierarchical structure, meaning that they have several levels of inclusiveness. For instance, two colors the English language distinguishes can be further broken down:

Blue	Green
aqua	kelly
sky	mint
royal	forest
teal	lime

We divide the semantic domain of color into specific colors (e.g., blue, green), each of which in turn is divided into kinds of blue or green, and—for some of us—into even more specific "shades of forest green."

In a similar way, different languages vary in the semantic domains they identify, in how finely they carve up these domains, and in how they make distinctions between different members of a domain. Some differences are obvious. For instance, tropical lowland peoples are not likely to have the semantic domains we call "snow" or "ice" in their native language, whereas some Arctic peoples have an elaborate vocabulary about snow and ice conditions. Further, the degree to which some semantic domain has a multilevel hierarchical structure depends on the importance of the objects or actions in people's lives: Island, coastal, or riverine people dependent on fish are likely to have many categories and subcategories of aquatic life, fishing methods, and flood and tide stages, for instance. Can we go beyond such fairly obvious statements?

For some domains we can. There are some things or qualities that seem to be "natural domains," meaning that the differences between their elements seem natural and obvious. In fact, they seem to be inherent in the things themselves. We therefore might expect that people everywhere would carve up these domains in similar ways. For instance, the wavelength and amount of light reflected from an object determines its color, so color is an inherent (natural) quality of a thing. Surely anyone can recognize that blue and green are different colors. Likewise, biological kinship is a natural relationship, in the sense that who an infant's parents are determines who will and will not be the baby's genetic relatives. It seems obvious that aunts and uncles are fundamentally different kinds of relatives from parents.

Although blue and green are objectively different colors, and aunts are objectively different relatives from mothers, not all peoples recognize these differences and make them culturally significant. The semantic domains of color and relatives are in fact divided differently by different cultures, and these divisions are not at all self-evident.

The domain of relatives is an excellent example of how members of different cultural traditions divide an apparently natural domain according to different principles. Because we return to this subject in a later chapter, here we want only to show that different cultures do not in fact make the same distinctions between relatives as we do; that is, the way relatives are culturally distinguished is variable.

Consider the relatives that English-speaking people call *aunt, first cousin,* and *brother.* An aunt is a sister of your mother or father; a first cousin is a child of any of your aunts and uncles; and a brother is a male child of your parents. These individuals are all biologically related to you differently, so you place them in different categories and call them by different terms.

But notice that other distinctions are possible that you do not recognize as distinctions and are not reflected in the kinship lexicon of English. All your aunts are not related to you in the same way: One is the sister of your mother, one is the sister of your father. Why not recognize this difference by giving them each their own terms? Similarly, your first cousins could be subdivided into finer categories and given special terms, such as terms meaning *child of my father's sister, child of my mother's brother,* and so on. And since we distinguish most other categories of relatives by whether they are male or female (e.g., brother versus sister, aunt versus uncle), why does sex not matter for any of our cousins?

How do we know that the way a people divide the domain of relatives into different categories is cultural rather than natural? Because different cultures divide the domain in different ways. People in many societies, for instance, call their mother's sister by one term and their father's sister by another term (although we collapse both into one term, *aunt*). It is also common for people to distinguish between the children of their father's sister and their father's brother, calling the first by a term we translate as "cousin," the second by the same term as they use for their own brothers and sisters. Even stranger—if you think that relatives are a purely natural category—are peoples who call the daughters of their maternal uncles by the term *mother* (just like their "real mother"), but not the daughters of their paternal uncles, for whom they use the term *sister.* (These various ways of categorizing kin, by the way, are not random, for such labels are related to other aspects of a people's kinship system—see Chapter 9.) Obviously, the way various peoples divide the seemingly "natural domain" of biological relatives is not the same the world over.

The same applies to color, our other example. Brent Berlin and Paul Kay found diversity in color terms among various human populations. Some had only two terms for, roughly, "light" and "dark." Others had terms for other wavelengths of the color spectrum, which, however, do not always translate neatly as our words *red, blue, green,* and so forth. This does not mean that members of other cultural traditions are unable to detect differences between what we call, for example, *green* and *yellow.* It means that any differences they perceive are not linguistically encoded, presumably because they do not need to communicate precise information about colors.

Other examples could be cited, but the overall point is clear. Cultures divide up the world differently, forming different categories and classifications of natural and social reality out of the objective properties of things. The implications of this point are more important than you might think. If you know a word for something—an object, a kind of person, an emotion, a natural feature of the landscape—you tend to think it is real. To our perceptions, it appears as a "thing." These kinds of "things" *are* real, in one sense (the word refers to *something,* even if only to emotions or abstractions). But this reality might differ for someone who speaks a language that reflects a different culture. You may think you know what is meant by *democracy* or *the rule of law,* but do other peoples mean the same thing?

Language and Worldview

As just discussed, many aspects of a language reflect the culture of the people who speak it. Could the converse also be true? Is it possible that knowing a given language predisposes its speakers to view the world in certain ways? Could it be that the categories and rules of their language condition people's perceptions of reality and perhaps even their worldview?

Language could shape perceptions and worldviews both by its lexicon and by the way it leads people to communicate about subjects such as space and time. Any language's lexicon assigns labels to only certain things, qualities, and actions. It is easy to see how this might encourage people to perceive the real world selectively. For instance, as we grow up, we learn that some plants are "trees." So we come to think of *tree* as a real thing, although there are so many kinds of trees that there is no necessary reason to collapse all this arboreal variety into a single label. But we might perceive the plants our language calls *trees* as more similar than do people who speak a language that makes finer distinctions between these plants.

Further, language might force people to communicate about time, space, relations between individuals and between people and nature, and so forth in a certain kind of way. Potentially, this constraint on the way people must speak to be understood by others can shape their views of what the world is like.

The idea that language influences the perceptions and thought patterns of those who speak it, and thus conditions their worldview, is known as the **Sapir-Whorf hypothesis,** after two anthropological linguists who proposed it. One of the most widely quoted of all anthropological passages is Edward Sapir's statement, originally written in 1929:

> [Language] powerfully conditions all our thinking about social problems and processes. Human beings do not live in the objective world alone, nor alone in the world of social activity as ordinarily understood but are very much at the mercy of the particular language which has become the medium of expression for their society. . . . The fact of the matter is that the "real world" is to a large extent unconsciously built up on the language habits of the group. . . . The worlds in which different societies live are distinct worlds, not merely the same world with different labels attached. (Sapir 1964, 68–69)

Sapir and Whorf believed that language helps define the worldview of its speakers. It does so, in part, by providing labels for certain kinds of phenomena (things, concepts, qualities, and actions), which different languages define according to different criteria. Some phenomena are therefore made easier to think about than others. The attributes that define them as different from other, similar things become more important than other attributes. So the lexicon of our language provides a filter that biases our perceptions.

But the Sapir-Whorf hypothesis is subtler than this. In the 1930s and 1940s, Benjamin Whorf suggested that language conditions a people's conceptions of time and space. He noted that English encourages its speakers to think about time using metaphors derived from space (e.g., "a long time" and "a long distance"), although time is not really "long" or "short" in the same sense as distance. Also, English-speaking people talk about units of time using the same concepts with which they talk about numbers of objects (e.g., "four days" and "four apples"), although it is possible to see four objects at once but not four units of time. Finally, English-speaking people classify events by when they occurred: those that have happened, those that are happening, and those that will happen.

Because they share a different language, however, the Native American Hopi speak about time and events differently, Whorf believed. With no tenses exactly equivalent to our past, present, and future and no way to express time in terms of spatial metaphors, Hopi speak of events as continuously unfolding, rather than happening in so many days or weeks. Whorf argued that the Hopi language led the Hopi people into a different perception of the passage of time.

The units of time sequence of the English language are a good example of the issue. Units appearing on calendars—days, months, and years—are time units that are based on natural cycles (though months are not precisely based on lunar phases). But decades, centuries, and millennia are linguistic categories with no natural basis. Units used on watches—seconds, minutes, and hours—are purely linguistic units as well. How much is the perception of the passage of time affected by such arbitrary divisions imposed on our minds by language? Do the time units of calendars and watches "create" our views of time?

What shall we make of the Sapir-Whorf hypothesis? Certainly, none of us as individuals creates the labels our language assigns to reality, nor do we create the constraints our grammar places on the way we talk about time and space. We must adhere to certain rules if we are to be understood. Surely this necessity biases our perceptions *to some degree*. The question is, how much? More precisely, how important is language as opposed to other influences on perceptions and views of reality?

Although intriguing, the Sapir-Whorf hypothesis is not widely accepted today, for several reasons. First, if a language greatly shapes the way its speakers perceive and think about the world, then we would expect a people's worldview to change only at a rate roughly comparable to the rate at which their language changes. Yet there is no doubt that worldviews are capable of changing much more rapidly than language. How else can we explain the fact that the English language has changed little in the past 150 years compared with the dramatic alteration in the worldviews of most speakers of English? How else can we explain the spread of religious traditions such as Islam and Christianity out of their original linguistic homes among people with enormously diverse languages? (This is not to suggest that these traditions have remained unchanged as they diffused.)

Second, if language strongly conditions perceptions, thought patterns, and entire worldviews, we should find that the speakers of languages with a common ancestor show marked cultural similarities. More precisely, we would expect to find the cultural similarities between speakers of related languages to be consistently greater than the cultural similarities between speakers of languages that are less closely related. Sometimes we do find this. But we often do not.

Third, billions of people alive today are bilingual or multilingual. In Europe, North America, and some nations of Africa and southeast Asia, many children routinely learn two languages while growing up. Yet there is no evidence that they perceive reality in different ways while speaking one or the other language. The globalization insert contains more information on the extinction of languages and multilingualism.

Also, many differences in languages that would seem to affect perceptions and views of reality do not, in fact, seem to do so. A familiar example is that in some languages nouns are classified as either "feminine" or "masculine." As children learn these languages, they learn that different nouns require different articles (as opposed to the English articles *a* and *the*, which are gender neutral) and that adjectives acquire different endings depending on whether they refer to nouns that are masculine or feminine. The Romance languages (including Spanish, French, Italian, Romanian, and Portuguese) classify objects in this way, whereas English does not. The Sapir-Whorf hypothesis seems to imply that the speakers of Romance languages somehow view gender as a more significant distinction than do speakers of other languages: Every time people speak, they use gendered terms, which should reinforce the significance of gender in their minds. But there is no evidence that speakers of Romance languages have more "gendered" views of reality than do speakers of English or other languages that do not classify nouns as feminine or masculine.

For these and other reasons, the Sapir-Whorf hypothesis is not highly regarded by most scholars today. But future research may uncover unexpected effects of language on perception and, perhaps, on worldviews.

Social Uses of Speech

During enculturation, humans learn how to communicate and how to act appropriately in given social situations. They learn that different situations require different verbal and nonverbal behavior, for how one speaks and acts varies with whom one is addressing, who else is present, and the overall situation in which the interaction is occurring.

To speak appropriately, people must take the total context into account. First, they must know the various situations, or social scenes, of their culture: which are solemn, which are celebrations, which are formal versus informal, which are argumentative, and so on. Cultural knowledge includes knowing how to alter one's total (including verbal) behavior to fit these situations. Second, individuals must recognize the kinds of interactions they are expected to have with others toward whom they have particular relations: Should they act lovingly, jokingly, contemptuously, or respectfully and deferentially toward someone else? Cultural knowledge thus also includes knowing how to act (including how to speak) toward others with whom an individual has relations of certain kinds.

These two elements—the particular situation and the specific individuals who are parties to the interaction—make up the *social context* of verbal and nonverbal behavior. The field of **sociolinguistics** investigates how speech behavior is affected by cultural factors, especially by the social context.

How the speech of the parties to a social interaction reveals and reinforces the nature of their relationship is seen clearly by terms of address. In some parts of the United States, unless instructed otherwise, Americans usually address those of higher social rank with a term of respect followed by the last name (e.g., Dr. Smith or Ms. Jones). Those with higher rank are more likely to address those with lower rank by their first name, or even by their last name used alone. This nonreciprocal use of address terms often not only expresses a social inequality, it also reinforces it each time the individuals address each other.

Spanish speakers have a similar understanding with polite address terms such as *Don* or *Señora*. They also have to choose between two words for *you:* the formal (*usted*) versus informal (*tú*). *Tú* is used between occupants of certain statuses, such as between intimate friends and relatives and to address children. In parts of Latin America, the informal *tú* is also a marker of rank, used by landlords, officials, and some employers toward their tenants, subordinates, servants, and employees. Here the fact that a social subordinate uses *usted* with a higher-ranking

The migration of peoples is one of the most important phenomena of humanity's past. When people move to a new region, they carry lots of "baggage"—not just their possessions, but also their genes, cultures, and languages. Until several hundred years ago migration was the main way languages spread to new regions. For instance, when one people of China (who call themselves Han) developed a politically complex form of culture around 3,500 years ago, they began to conquer their neighbors to the south and west and many Han migrated to new regions. By about 1,000 years ago they occupied most of the country we now call China. Their language (known as Mandarin) spread with them, displacing other peoples and their languages or assimilating them culturally and linguistically as they conquered them politically. Still, even today, China's 1.3 billion people speak dozens of languages, including Cantonese, Hunanese, Tibetan, and many others.

In the past 500 or so years, large-scale migrations have continued. Indeed, the largest-scale migrations in history are the ones that brought the bodies, cultures, and languages of western Europeans to the Americas, which to the Europeans was a New World. A great many of the several hundred indigenous languages of North and South America disappeared between the 1500s and the 1900s, as the people who spoke them either died out or became linguistically assimilated into whichever European ethnic group came into political and economic dominance. Today, the vast majority of people who live in the Americas speak English, Spanish, Portuguese, or French. Most of those who speak some indigenous Native American language also speak one of these four languages as a second language.

On a global level, no one knows how many languages spoken a few hundred years ago are extinct today. A recent estimate is that between 4,000 and 9,000 languages have disappeared since the fifteenth century. The United Nations estimates that roughly half of the remaining languages are endangered. In some cases, as among Native North Americans and the Australian aborigines, the main reason for linguistic extinction was the biological extinction of the speakers from disease and violence. In other cases, although the people whose ancestors once spoke their own language are alive today, the languages have died as the groups became assimilated culturally and linguistically into their nation's majority.

To see how a language can wither away over several generations, consider the languages of immigrants. A percentage of second and third generations of immigrants may continue to know the language of their ancestral land, but after that few descendants are likely to speak it. Once a language is no longer spoken in the home, it takes an effort to learn it, and over time fewer and fewer children will do so. If children are exposed only to the majority language in formal school settings as well as in their peer group relations, the chances that they will learn the language of their ancestry dwindles. Only if there is an entire community of speakers—who use the language among themselves, who serve as linguistic models for young children, and who reward youngsters for speaking it well—is a language likely to survive. In present-day North America, the Amish are one such community, as are various big-city "Chinatowns," "Koreatowns," and numerous Latino communities. In the future, there may be many more such American linguistic communities, such as the Hmong (refugees from southeast Asia who were resettled in the United States in the 1980s) and South Asians (in Silicon Valley, California).

The Summer Institute of Linguistics, located in Monterey, California, publishes *Ethnologue,* a rich source of information on the world's languages. According to *Ethnologue,* there are about 6,800 languages in existence today, of which 4,500 are spoken only in Asia and Africa. One 2001 study notes that the vast continent of Asia—which contains two-fifths of the earth's land surface and three-fifths of its people—still contains thousands of languages, but most are very localized and more than half of Asia's languages have fewer than 10,000 speakers. In Africa, where humanity began and where our species probably acquired the capacity for language, 116 languages are nearly gone. In Canada and the United States around 260 indigenous (Native American) languages are still spoken. This sounds like a respectable number, but 160 of them are no longer being learned by children, so most of them will be extinct within a few decades. In Brazil, where there were once probably hundreds of indigenous languages, at least 42 are extinct and 18 others are endangered. And, according to *Ethnologue,* more than 140 languages once spoken by Australian aborigines are nearly gone—many have fewer than a dozen speakers, almost all elderly people.

In the last half of the twentieth century, *globalization* became increasingly important in the withering of languages. Globalization is the process by which the nations of the world are increasingly integrated into a single system. Globalization has many dimensions: economic (in trade and production), political (in international organizations), and "cultural" (here in the narrow sense, as in films, music, sports, and other forms of entertainment). We consider some of these in later chapters.

There is a linguistic dimension to globalization as well. When companies from two nations trade, either they need to use translators or someone has to learn the language of their counterparts. When videotapes are rented by people on remote Pacific islands or in the mountain villages of Southeast Asia, people are exposed to new languages. Globalization thus promotes the success of a few languages—namely, those used on the global arena. Over time, communication in one of these languages becomes more and more useful. If, at the same time, the linguistic community that once sustained the local language is disintegrating, the language may become endangered.

Contrary to most English speakers' linguistic chauvinism, today Mandarin has more native speakers than any other language, around 900 million. But English is now the language most widely used in worldwide commerce, the international mass media, and globally popular culture. More than any other single language, English is learned as a second language in diverse countries from Japan to Mexico. In fact, more people now speak English as their second language (about 350 million) than as their first language (about 320 million). In places like South Asia and the Pacific, where there are many hundreds of localized indigenous languages, English is usually the *lingua franca*—the language that people learn as their second language so that they can communicate widely with one another. And English nouns are commonly used for modern objects and technology.

That English is so widely spoken as a second language is a result of the history of colonialism and the twentieth-century economic and political dominance of the United States in world affairs. It is certainly not because English is a superior language nor because it is easy to learn as a second language. Some countries known for their strong national identity resent the influx of English words—notably France, which actually has laws against the use of certain English words.

Can you say *Llanfairpwllgwyngyllgogerychwyrndrobwllllantysiliogogogoch*? If you are Welsh and proud of it, you probably can. It is the name of a town in northern Wales (in Great Britain) of about 3,400 people. The name describes the location of the town: "The Church of St. Mary in the hollow of white hazel near the rapid whirlpool by the Church of St. Tysilio of the red cave." Being able to pronounce the name has become a linguistic symbol of ethnic pride among young Welsh, because for decades the Welsh language looked as if it were going to be replaced by English. In 1991, the British census revealed that there were only half the number of Welsh speakers as in 1911, and most of these were elderly people. But schools in Wales now require the Welsh language to be taught and the ability to pronounce the word correctly symbolizes the linguistic revival.

As the examples of French and Welsh suggest, the desire to preserve the language of one's native land is a mark of national or ethnic identity. Speaking a particular language can do more than send the messages encoded in the words and sentences. With the spread of globalization, speaking a native tongue can tell people that you are proud to be who you are. In Europe many people learn several languages, because languages are emphasized in schools and because so many Europeans travel widely on their continent. Such multilingualism is almost certainly a positive force in the world. Perhaps more American school districts should realize that learning "foreign languages" is not a costly luxury in the world we now live in.

Critical Thinking Questions

1. Sometimes breakdowns in communication lead to misunderstandings and conflicts between individuals and nations. Given this fact, is the development of a single language that would reduce miscommunication necessarily a bad thing? Or is breakdown in communication really an important reason for conflicts, compared to other reasons?

2. Whether the widespread use of English as a second language will endanger other languages is debatable, because language can be a major source of ethnic or national identity and pride. Under what future circumstances is English likely to rise to worldwide dominance?

Sources: Sampat (2001); Ethnologue website (http://www.sil.org/ethnologue/ethnologue.html); *The Columbus Dispatch* (August 26, 2001)

person, while the latter uses *tú,* symbolizes and reinforces the social differences between them.

Speech style and habits depend on status and rank in other ways. For example, there used to be greater differences between the speech of men and women in North America than there are today. Because of their fear of being considered "unladylike," women were less likely to use profanity, at least in public. Men, likewise, were expected to avoid using profanity in the presence of women so they would not "offend the ladies." Certain words were regarded as more appropriate for women's use than men's, such as *charming, adorable,* and *lovely.* Today, largely as a consequence of the women's movement and the popular media, there are fewer differences between women's and men's vocabularies.

Other cultures exhibit customs in speech behavior with which most English-speaking people are unfamiliar. Here are a few examples:

- Some languages accentuate the difference between the sexes far more than English does. In languages such as Gros Ventre (of the northeastern United States) and Yukaghir (of northeastern Asia), men and women pronounced certain phonemes differently. In Yana, an ex-

◄ Japanese honorifics include rules about formality and politeness, many of which are related to the relative status of the individuals interacting.

© Nick Clements/FPG/Getty Images

tinct language spoken by a people who formerly lived in northern California, many words had two pronunciations, one used by men and one by women. In a few languages, the vocabularies of men and women differ, with men using one word for something and women using quite a different word. In a language spoken by the Carib, who formerly inhabited the West Indies, the vocabularies of men and women differed so much that early European explorers claimed (mistakenly) that the sexes spoke different languages. In many languages, the speech of the sexes differs in other respects, such as the degree of forcefulness of their speech, the degree to which they avoid confrontational speech, and the tone of voice.

- In parts of Polynesia and Micronesia there used to be a special *respect language,* with which common people had to address members of the noble class. On some islands this was much more than a difference in speech style because different words were used. Often there were severe penalties for commoners who erred in addressing a noble.
- On the Indonesian island of Java, there are distinct "levels" of speech, involving different pronouns, suffixes, and words. A speaker must choose between the three levels—plain, more elegant, and most elegant. The speech style the parties to the interaction use depends on their relative rank and on their degree of familiarity with one another. In choosing which style to use with a specific person, a Javanese communicates not only the message of the sentence but also information about the quality of the relationship. Accordingly, changes in the relationship between two individuals are accompanied by changes in speech style.
- In Japanese, a complicated set of contextual norms (called *honorifics*) governs the degree of formality and politeness people normally use to show respect to those of higher social position. For instance, verbs and personal pronouns have several alternative forms that speakers must choose between in addressing others. The main determinant of which forms are used is the relative status of the parties. One form of the verb is used when the speaker is of higher status than the listener, another form when the two are of roughly equal status, and yet another when the speaker is a social inferior. Women, who to some extent even today are considered "beneath" men, often address men with the honorific verb forms that symbolically express the superiority of the addressee. Similarly, Japanese use different forms of personal pronouns (*I, you*), to reflect the relative status of the parties. In fact, when a social superior is addressing an inferior, he or she often does not use the pronoun *I* as a self-reference but refers to

his or her status relative to the person being addressed. For instance, a teacher says to a student, "Look at teacher" instead of "Look at me"; a father says to his son, "Listen to father" instead of "Listen to me"; and so forth. Reciprocally, one usually does not use the pronoun *you* with one of higher status but replaces it with a term denoting the superior's social position. This yields sentences like "What would teacher like me to do next?" and "Would father like me to visit?" Confused foreigners trying to learn the subtleties of Japanese speech etiquette are usually advised to use the honorific forms to avoid giving offense unintentionally. Korean has a similar set of speech norms.

- All societies have customs of taboo, meaning that some behavior is prohibited for religious reasons or because it is culturally regarded as immoral, improper, or offensive. It is fairly common to find taboos applied to language: Some words cannot be uttered by certain people. For instance, the Yąnomamö of the Venezuelan rain forest have a custom known as *name taboo*. It is an insult to utter the names of important people and of deceased relatives in the presence of their living kinfolk. So the Yąnomamö use names such as "toenail of sloth" or "whisker of howler monkey" for people, so that when the person dies they will not have to watch their language so closely. Other name taboos are enforced only against specific individuals. Among the Zulu of southern Africa, for example, a woman was once forbidden to use the name of her husband's father or any of his brothers.

As the preceding examples show, speech is affected by the social context, including how situations are culturally defined and the particular individuals who are engaged in speaking and listening. Norms partly explain why people's use of language varies with context—you are not expected to act and speak the same way at a party as you do in church or at work, for instance, and you know intuitively and unconsciously how to adjust your behavior to these various social scenes.

The choice of speech style, words, and phrases is governed by more than just norms, however. People have personal goals, and speaking in a certain way can help them get what they want. In everyday life we strive to present the image of ourselves that we want someone else to perceive. The opinions that employers, friends, lovers and hoped-for lovers, coworkers, roommates, and even parents have of us depend partly on how we speak—our use of certain words and avoidance of others, the degree of formality of our style, whether we try to hide or to accentuate regional dialects, and so forth. In short, how we speak is an important part of what social scientists call our *presentation of self*. It is part of how we try to control other people's opinions of us. Like the jewelry we wear and where we wear it, how we sit, stand, and walk, and how we comb our hair or shave our head, the way we speak is part of the way we tell others what kind of a person we are. Almost without knowing it, we adjust our speech style, mannerisms, and body language to manage the impressions other people have of us.

We noted early in this chapter that language is composed of symbols that convey conventional meanings. We can now add that the very act of speaking is itself symbolic in another way. Just as the morphemes of language communicate meaning, so do the multitude of ways in which we can say them. Like the clothes we wear, the foods we eat, and the cars we drive, the way we speak is part of the way we present ourselves to the world. Others will interpret not only our words and sentences but also our style of speech and body language. If we can adjust our style and body language, we can to some extent control the implicit messages we communicate about ourselves. (In modern times, if you have enough money you can buy the instruction of professional specialists to correct your bad speech and habits and improve your self-presentation.) The act of speaking, then, conveys messages beyond the meanings of the words and sentences themselves; consciously or unconsciously, every time we speak we tell the world who we are.

Summary

1. Along with culture, language is the most important mental characteristic of humanity that distinguishes us from other animals. Five properties of language that differentiate it from other systems of communication are its multimedia potential; the fact that it is composed of discrete units (sounds, words) that are combined in different sequences to convey different meanings; its reliance on the shared, conventional understanding of arbitrary and meaningful symbols; the ability of people to intuitively and unconsciously combine the sounds and words of language creatively to send an infinite number of messages; and the fact that language allows humans to communicate about things, events, and persons remote in time and space.

2. *Grammar* refers to the elements of language and the rules for how these elements can be combined to form an infinite number of meaningful sentences. Grammatical knowledge is enormously complex, yet it is both unconscious and intuitive. Linguists divide the study of language into several fields, including phonology, morphology, and syntax.

3. Phonology is the study of the sounds and sound patterns of language. Only some of the sounds humans are able to make with their vocal tracts are recognized by any specific language. The features of sounds that speakers recognize as significant—that is, as making a difference in the meanings of words in which they occur—vary from language to language. The sounds that speakers recognize as distinct from other sounds are called the phonemes of the language. Among many other differences, languages vary in the way they use voice pitch to convey meanings, as illustrated by tone languages.

4. Morphology studies meaningful sound sequences and the rules by which they are formed. Any sequence of phonemes that conveys a standardized meaning is a morpheme. Free morphemes can stand alone as meaningful sequences, whereas bound morphemes are not used alone but are attached to free morphemes during speech. When people learn a language, they learn its free and bound morphemes and their meanings along with the rules by which bound morphemes can be attached to free morphemes.

5. Some aspects of language, particularly lexicon, reflect the cultural importance of subjects, people, objects, and natural phenomena. The need to converse easily about some subject leads to the elaboration of semantic domains connected to the subject, as seen in the domain of color. In other domains, such as relatives, anthropologists have discovered surprising diversity in how various peoples divide kin into kinds and give them different labels according to different principles.

6. The Sapir-Whorf hypothesis claimed that the language a people speak predisposes them to see the world in a certain way by shaping their perceptions of reality. The lexicon of a language might influence perceptions by leading its speakers unconsciously to filter out certain objective properties of reality in favor of other properties. The conventions of language also might force individuals to talk about subjects such as time and space in a certain way if they are to be understood. Although language does, in some ways and to some degree, shape perceptions and worldviews, the notion that language shapes perceptions and thought processes to a significant degree is not highly regarded by most modern scholars.

7. Sociolinguistics is the study of how speech is influenced by cultural factors, including culturally defined contexts and situations, the goals of the speaker, the presence of other parties, and so forth. Speech can be used in subtle ways to mark differences in rank and status, as between ethnic groups, classes, and males and females. Because speech is part of the way we present ourselves to others, control of the way we speak is one way we influence how others perceive us.

Key Terms

grammar	lexicon	bound morpheme
dialects	morphology	semantic domain
phonology	morpheme	Sapir-Whorf hypothesis
phonemes	free morpheme	sociolinguistics
tone languages		

InfoTrac College Edition Terms

chimpanzee language	kinesics (also proxemics,	English language
indigenous language	body language)	globalization
Native American language	linguistic relativity	

Suggested Readings

Agar, Michael. *Language Shock: Understanding the Culture of Conversation.* New York: William Morrow and Company, 1994.

Enjoyable description and analysis of the uses of language in society. Full of illustrative personal stories and anecdotes.

Crystal, David. *English as a Global Language.* 2nd ed. Cambridge University Press, 2003.

Discusses the rise of English in the global arena, with a discussion of future possibilities.

Fromkin, Victoria, Robert Rodman, and Nina Hyams. *An Introduction to Language.* 7th ed. New York: Heinle, 2002.

Excellent and witty beginning textbook, readily understandable, with many examples.

Lakoff, Robin. *The Language War.* Berkeley: University of California, 2000.

An influential linguist shows how language is used in political conflicts and intrigues.

Salzmann, Zdenek. *Language, Culture, and Society: An Introduction to Linguistic Anthropology.* 2nd ed. Boulder, Colo.: Westview Press, 1998.

An introductory text, describing language as a system of communication as well as how language use is affected by social context, nonverbal communication, and other interconnections between language and culture.

Companion Website for This Book

The Wadsworth Anthropology Resource Center
http://anthropology.wadsworth.com

The companion website that accompanies *Humanity: An Introduction to Cultural Anthropology,* Sixth Edition, includes a rich array of material, including online anthropological video clips, to help you in the study of cultural anthropology and the specific topics covered in this chapter. Begin by clicking on Student Resources. Next, click on Cultural Anthropology, and then on the cover image for this book. You have now arrived at the Student Resources home page and have the option of choosing one of several chapter resources.

Applying Anthropology. Begin your study of cultural anthropology by clicking on Applying Anthropology. Here you will find useful information on careers, graduate school programs in applied anthropology, and internships you might wish to pursue. You will also find real-world examples of working anthropologists applying the skills and methods of anthropology to help solve serious world problems.

Research Online. Click here to find a wealth of Web links that will facilitate your study of anthropology. Divided into different fields of study, specific websites are starting points for Internet research. You will be guided to rich anthropology websites that will help you prepare for class, complete course assignments, and actually do research on the Web.

InfoTrac College Edition Exercises. From the pull-down menu, select the chapter you are presently studying. Select InfoTrac College Edition Exercises from the list of resources. These exercises utilize InfoTrac College Edition's vast database of articles and help you explore the numerous uses of the search word, *culture.*

Study Aids for This Chapter. Improve your knowledge of key terms by using flash cards and study the learning objectives. Take the practice quiz, receive your results, and email them to your instructor. Access these resources from the chapter and resource pull-down menus.

Chapter Four

THE DEVELOPMENT OF ANTHROPOLOGICAL THOUGHT

Nineteenth Century: Origins

Early Twentieth Century: Development

American Historical Particularism (ca. 1900–1940)

British Functionalism (ca. 1920–1950)

Mid-Century Evolutionary Approaches (ca. 1940–1970)

Anthropological Thought Today: Divisions

Scientific Orientations

Sociobiology and Evolutionary Psychology

Cultural Materialism

Humanistic Orientations

Interpretive Anthropology

Postmodernism

Either/Or?

Why Can't All Those Anthropologists Agree?

© Paul Chesley/Stone/Getty Images

As a separate academic discipline, anthropology arose in the nineteenth century out of the contact between people who lived in different regions of the world and had diverse cultural traditions. These Buddhists live in Thailand.

A S A DISTINCT FIELD OF STUDY, anthropology was born in the 1800s out of the contact between western Europeans and peoples of other lands—the two Americas, Africa, the Middle East, Asia, and the islands of the Pacific Ocean. As Western intellectuals in the centuries after Christopher Columbus's voyages struggled to understand people who felt, thought, and acted differently from themselves, they did so in terms of their own conceptions of the world. Most European scholars who wrote two or three centuries ago shared a worldview that could not readily account for other forms of human existence. Their perceptions and interpretations of other peoples were, from a modern perspective, mistaken both factually and conceptually—especially because at that time the modern notion of *culture* had not yet developed. But by the mid-1800s, some Western intellectuals began to think about the peoples and cultures of other continents in new ways: They explained humanity and our diverse ways of living in terms of natural processes, not divine creation. Out of their attempts to classify and make sense of human biological and cultural diversity, the field of anthropology arose.

WE BEGIN this chapter by describing some of the historical factors that contributed to the rise of anthropology in the late 1800s. Next, we introduce some nineteenth-century ideas about humanity and discuss why later scholars either rejected or modified them. As we briefly trace the development of anthropological thought in the twentieth century, we focus on how each successive approach contributed to the formation of anthropology today.

CONTEMPORARY ETHNOLOGISTS agree on certain issues, but there are major divisions and disagreements in the field. One such division is between those who view the study of culture as a scientific, explanatory enterprise and those who see it as a humanistic, interpretive endeavor. We end our discussion by covering some of the reasons anthropologists disagree on so many fundamental issues.

Nineteenth Century: Origins

The discipline we now call anthropology originated as a separate field of scholarly study in the late nineteenth century. By then, most of the world's major geographic regions were known to the Western world and many regions had been colonized by one or another European power. During more than three centuries of contact, various Western traders, missionaries, and colonists had written hundreds of descriptions about the beliefs and customs of the native peoples of the Americas, Africa, Asia, and the islands of the Pacific Ocean. Who were all these people? How were they related to the more "civilized" people of the West? How could European intellectuals make sense of them and their "savage" ways of life?

Europeans also uncovered evidence of earlier cultures in their own continent, in the form of what we now call archaeological sites. In the 1800s tools made from stone were discovered in the earth, in clear association with extinct mammals. In Germany's Neander Valley, a partial skeleton of a humanlike creature was unearthed. Who made those ancient, prehistoric stone tools? Were they manufactured by the ancestors of modern-day Europeans? Were the Neander bones human and, if so, what did they mean?

Answers to these and many other questions about living "primitive" and ancient "prehistoric" peoples varied, but until the mid-1800s the Judeo-Christian worldview provided the framework for most interpretations. Perhaps the "savages" of other lands were the degenerated descendants of Noah's errant son, Ham. Or maybe they were remnants of one of the lost tribes of Israel. Possibly, the Neander bones and prehistoric artifacts were buried in the ground by the Devil to undermine believers' faith. Whatever the specific explanation, the customs and be-

liefs of distant, unfamiliar peoples generally were interpreted in terms of the biblical account of world creation and human history.

As the nineteenth century progressed, new theories about the Earth and about life itself emerged. In geology, James Hutton and Charles Lyell amassed evidence showing that the Earth was many millions of years old (today we know it is even older—around 6 billion years), rather than the few thousands of years suggested by the Scriptures. In biology, Charles Darwin's 1859 book *On the Origin of Species* revolutionized theories about life. Rather than each plant and animal having been separately made by a Creator and reproducing "after its own kind," Darwin proposed that one species emerged out of another. The great variety of plant and animal life can be explained by a gradual, and entirely natural, process of transformation and diversification.

There was great resistance in scholarly as well as religious circles to Darwin's theory of evolution. But by the closing decade of the nineteenth century, it was apparent that evolution explained so much about life that most scholars accepted it. In an 1871 book, Darwin noted the physical similarities between apes and humans, arguing that the similarities showed that humans likely were descended from African apes. Discoveries in Africa in the 1920s confirmed his hypothesis, establishing the field of paleoanthropology as a legitimate science (see A Closer Look in Chapter 1 for the most recent findings).

As well as offering an explanation of biological evolution and the origin of species, Darwin's ideas also influenced how intellectuals viewed human cultural existence. The concept of evolution suggested that the history of life was progressive: "Lower" and simpler forms gave rise to "higher" and more complex forms. Competition—"survival of the fittest," as it came to be

◄ Painting by Raphael showing the expulsion of Eve and Adam from Paradise. Well into the nineteenth century, the biblical account of history provided the dominant framework explaining the existence of "natives" in other lands and the nature of their culture.

called—was the force that powered this progress. In the fossil record, it was possible to find evidence of the evolutionary "stages" through which successively higher forms of life developed.

Many thought that the same notions applied to human ways of life. Evolution and progress provided the ideas that suggested how the "savages" of other lands were related to one another, to the early residents of Europe who left behind those prehistoric stone tools, and to Western civilization itself. Just as life itself had passed through earlier and simpler forms, so had humankind's various ways of life—*cultures,* we call them today. Those prehistoric Europeans who manufactured stone tools had lived in the early stages of cultural development. Likewise, the various "primitives" of Africa, the Americas, Asia, and the Pacific had not evolved very far culturally—certainly not as far as Westerners. By studying these peoples and comparing their customs, scholars thought they could reconstruct the stages of *cultural* progress.

Discovering such stages was the main goal of anthropology in the nineteenth century. Western ethnologists tried to use written accounts of the customs and beliefs of other peoples to reconstruct how human culture had progressed on its long road to what they thought was the pinnacle of human cultural achievement: Western civilization. They believed that Polynesians, Africans, Indians, and various "natives" of other continents were not simply living in the Devil's iron grip. Rather, in light of the concept of evolution, nineteenth-century intellectuals reasoned that such peoples were "undeveloped." Their thought processes were superstitious (not yet scientific), their technologies were primitive, their manners rude, their morals unenlightened. They were—in a word—precivilized. Therefore, to trace human progress, scholars must study the ancient ancestors of civilization: surviving "primitive" cultures.

To do so, nineteenth-century anthropologists devised an approach that today is known as **unilineal evolution.** The contents of their voluminous writings are detailed and complex. But once we understand their assumption that cultural evolution proceeded from simple to complex, with the West at the pinnacle, the basics of unilineal evolution can be stated fairly simply, as follows. First, compile the hundreds of accounts of other cultures written by explorers, settlers, missionaries, traders, and other (mainly Western) observers. Next, compare all these cultures to determine which were the simplest, the next most simple, . . . to the most complex. Then develop a classification of the cultures into a series of stages of increasingly complex evolution, labeling these stages according to where they fit in humankind's progress out of our "rude beginnings." For example, in his 1877 work *Ancient Society* the American Louis Henry Morgan applied the terms *savagery, barbarism,* and *civilization* to levels of cultural development. If information comes in about a new culture, place that culture in its appropriate classificatory stage; for example, the Iroquois of North America belong in the stage of "barbarism." Finally, come up with an explanation for why people living at one stage developed into the next stage; for example, Morgan thought that the invention of pottery propelled some savages into barbarism, whereas some barbarians were launched into civilization once they invented writing.

Using these procedures, all cultures can be arranged in a sequence of progressive stages. The "simplest" cultures found on Earth today are the surviving representatives of the earliest stages of cultural evolution, so they are like living fossils. Further, those prehistoric artifacts from Europe and other continents provide additional evidence of humanity's rude beginnings, for the ancient ("stone age") ancestors of modern-day Europeans were precivilized.

The concept of stages could account for why cultures differed: People with different customs and beliefs represent different stages of cultural development. Do you want to know why the Fijians of the Pacific have different customs from the aboriginal peoples of Australia? The basic answer is that the Australians were arrested in their development at the stage of savagery, whereas the Fijians had progressed all the way into barbarism. Do we want to know how the very earliest humans lived? Then we should study the surviving representatives of savagery, such as the Australian aborigines or the Polynesians. Are you curious about the immediate ancestors of civilized folk? Examine cultures such as the Iroquois or Fijians, who are living representatives of the barbarism stage, which was the immediate precursor of the stage of civilization.

As an example of this approach, consider E. B. Tylor, whose 1871 book *Primitive Culture* investigated the origins and development of religious beliefs. Tylor argued that religions had passed through three stages, called *animism*, *polytheism*, and *monotheism*.

The earliest stage, animism, is the belief that natural phenomena have spiritual components—rocks, mountains, plants, and animals have a kind of spiritual essence, like a soul. Out of such beliefs, early humans evolved the belief that the world contains innumerable supernatural beings such as ghosts, demons, mountain gods, and nature spirits.

How can the origin of these animistic beliefs be explained? Tylor argued that ancient peoples sought to explain their experiences. Two questions puzzled them: First, what is the difference between a live person and a dead person? Early humans reasoned (falsely but logically, given their prescientific mentality) that living people have a spiritual essence—a soul—that gives life to the physical body and that causes death when it leaves. Second, what is the origin of the images seen in dreams, trances, and visions? Ancient folk concluded that the things they see in their dreams and fantasies actually do exist and are not the products of their imaginations and hallucinations. By this logic, the fact that people sometimes see their deceased relatives in dreams must mean that their souls live on after the death of the body they inhabited. As such beings proliferated, Tylor reasoned, eventually the world was viewed as full of spirits. The earliest religions were therefore animistic, which was the first stage of human religion.

At a later stage of cultural evolution, some peoples elevated some of the spirits to a higher position than others. As they took on more prominence in the belief system, they ultimately became gods of the sun, moon, rain, sky, earth, animals, war, agriculture, and so forth. This is the next stage of religion, *polytheism*—belief in many gods.

Eventually, one god acquired dominance over the others, the rest became viewed as false gods, and the final stage of religion, *monotheism*—one god—was born. Religion thus had simple origins in peoples' attempts to explain their experiences, and it evolved into its final form (note that monotheism is the religion of most Westerners) over many centuries. Or so Tylor argued.

From a modern perspective, the unilineal evolutionists were mistaken, as we shall see. But in their comparisons and classifications, they did help establish one of the important hallmarks of anthropology: the comparative perspective (see Chapter 1). Further, they had faith that the application of scientific methods and reasoning would lead to the discovery of the natural laws that governed the development of human culture. The "history of mankind is part and parcel of the history of nature, . . . our thoughts, wills, and actions accord with laws as definite as those which govern the motion of waves, the combinations of acids and bases, and the growth of plants and animals," wrote Tylor (1871, 2). Just as sciences like physics and biology were explaining natural phenomena, nineteenth-century ethnologists believed they were discovering the principles that governed cultural systems. Later anthropologists were not sure that they had gotten these "laws of culture" right. In fact, many anthropologists of today question whether there are any such laws at all and whether a science of culture is even possible. Still, the search for the general causes of cultural differences and of regularities in culture change remains an interest of many—not all—modern scholars.

Another legacy of the nineteenth century is the establishment of anthropology as a separate academic discipline. Scholarly fields that investigate aspects of humankind had long been represented in European and American universities as departments or schools of religion, theology, art, philosophy, classics, history, anatomy, medicine, and so forth. But a discipline whose focus was the physical and cultural diversity of humanity was not established until the last decades of the 1800s. In the United States, the first anthropology course was taught in 1879 at the University of Rochester. In 1886, the first anthropology department was founded at the University of Pennsylvania. It was followed near the turn of the century by university departments at Columbia, Harvard, Chicago, and California (Berkeley).

Early Twentieth Century: Development

Nineteenth-century anthropologists established the study of other cultures as a legitimate subject for scholarly research and university education. It was clear that to understand humanity, we must take the great diversity of the world's cultures into account and compare cultures systematically. But by the beginning of the twentieth century, anthropologists on both sides of the Atlantic began to challenge both the methods and the conclusions of the unilineal evolutionists.

American Historical Particularism (ca. 1900–1940)

In the United States, an approach known as **historical particularism** developed. It was "historical" because its main goal was to uncover the *past* influences on a given culture that shaped its present form. It was "particularistic" because it emphasized that each people, and each culture, has its own *unique* past. Because each culture has its own particular history, each must be studied on its own terms. More than anyone else, American anthropologist Franz Boas formulated this way of studying and analyzing culture, and his ideas revolutionized the field.

Studying each culture "on its own terms" was not what the unilineal evolutionists did. In making their comparisons and formulating their stages, they had imposed their own "terms" (e.g., complexity, progress) on other cultures. Take the notion of complexity, for example. In technology, most people *might* agree that spears as hunting weapons are simpler than bows and arrows, which in turn are simpler than guns and bullets. But what can *complex* mean when applied to other customs and beliefs, like those about marriage, political organization, or religion?

▲ Often considered the "father of American anthropology," Franz Boas challenged the unilineal evolutionists' concept of stages. In doing so, he made many lasting contributions, including popularizing the notion of cultural relativism and marshalling evidence that cultural differences and biological differences are largely independent of one another.

Does it have any objective meaning to say that animism is "simpler" than monotheism? Boas realized that such features are merely *different* from culture to culture. By any *objective* criterion, one form of marriage or religion does not represent "progress" over another. The stages of the nineteenth-century evolutionists derived from ethnocentric assumptions, Boas thought. They placed their own cultural existence at the top of the evolutionary ladder, then invented/labeled the "earlier stages," slotted particular cultures into their preconceived classifications, and felt they were discovering the laws of cultural development using the methods of science.

These points seemed to mean that the unilineal evolutionists were wrong: Cultures do not develop along a single series of progressive stages, culminating in nineteenth-century European civilization. Instead, each culture changes along its own path, depending on the particular influences that affect it. To understand a culture, therefore, we must study it *individually,* not as a representative of some hypothetical stage, which Boas thought existed only in the minds of the evolutionists. Anthropologists must free themselves from preconceived ideas and assumptions and give up speculative schemes of evolution and ethnocentric definitions of progress.

Accompanying Boas's call for less speculation was his demand for more facts. Anthropologists simply did not know enough about human cultural differences to generalize, he felt. What was most urgently needed in his day was more information, which Boas thought could only be obtained from firsthand fieldwork. Anthropologists themselves needed to go out and gather knowledge about other cultures, rather than relying on incomplete and biased accounts written by untrained and often casual observers. Firsthand fieldwork, too, was rare for scholars in the nineteenth century. The unilineal evolutionists have been called "armchair anthropologists" because (with the notable exception of Lewis Morgan) they carried out all their research in their offices, using documentary sources of varying reliability.

Boas was scornful of abstract theories developed in the comfort of an armchair. He believed that to understand another culture, one must have the familiarity that can only come from long personal experience with it. Anthropologists must therefore immerse themselves in the study of other peoples. They must try to experience their customs and understand their beliefs from an insider's perspective, rather than speculate wildly about cultural progress on a grand scale. And Boas took his own advice. He conducted extensive fieldwork among two Native American peoples, the Eskimo (Inuit) and the Kwakiutl, and he sent his many students out to do research on other cultures far from home. The work done on the Polynesian island of Samoa by one of Boas's students, Margaret Mead, became enormously influential in the 1920s and 1930s after the publication of her 1928 classic *Coming of Age in Samoa.*

Two other benefits would follow from lengthy, firsthand fieldwork. First, the traditional customs, beliefs, and languages of many of the world's peoples were already gone due to diseases, genocide, assimilation, and other forces. Surviving cultures and languages were disappearing or changing rapidly. Boas believed it was the duty of anthropologists to record disappearing traditions before they were gone forever. Many students of Boas did their

fieldwork among Native American peoples, whose cultures they believed were especially endangered.

Second, Boas felt that the main need of the infant field of anthropology was more factual information about other cultures, collected by unbiased fieldworkers. Facts ("data") about a given culture should be collected without preconceived notions, for preconceptions lead to inaccuracies. Fieldworkers can only become unbiased by approaching their studies relativistically (see Chapter 1)— not judging another culture's morality by their own moral codes, nor evaluating the overall worth of a culture by their own standards of worthiness. More than any other single figure, Boas imparted to anthropology the doctrine of cultural relativism, which requires studying another culture on its own terms. He also did as much as anyone to show that biological differences and cultural differences are largely independent of one another; that is, the culture a human group shares is entirely learned, not explained by their genetic heritage (see Chapter 2).

In sum, historical particularism made several enduring contributions to modern anthropology: (1) it discredited the overly speculative schemes of the unilineal evolutionists; (2) it insisted that fieldwork is the primary means of acquiring reliable information; (3) it imparted the idea that cultural relativism as a methodological principle is essential for maximum understanding of another culture; and (4) it demonstrated and popularized the notion that cultural differences and biological differences have little to do with one another. These contributions helped to shape modern cultural anthropology.

Historical particularism spawned several intellectual offspring in the first half of the twentieth century, all of which shared its emphasis on cultural uniqueness and relativism. Some anthropologists began to study how cultural elements ("traits") were transmitted ("diffused") from one people or region to another. These **diffusionists** tried to deduce the origin and historical spread of traits and complexes of traits by analyzing the present distribution of those traits and trait complexes.

Another offspring of historical particularism is **configurationalism.** One of Boas's students was Ruth Benedict, whose 1934 book *Patterns of Culture* was influential. Benedict argued that, from the vast array of humanly possible cultures, each particular culture develops only a limited number of "patterns" or "configurations" that dominate the thinking and responses of its members. Each culture develops a distinctive set of feelings and motivations that orients the thoughts and behaviors of its members. (Note the emphasis on cultural uniqueness.) These configurations give each culture a distinctive style, and the thoughts and actions of its members reflect its configurations. Behavior that one people considered crazy or abnormal would be acceptable and maybe even ideal among another people. (Note the emphasis on cultural relativism.)

For example, Benedict wrote that the Kwakiutl of the northwest coast of North America are individualistic, competitive, intemperate, and egoistic. This cultural configuration affects Kwakiutl customs. They stage ceremonies known as *potlatches* in which one kin group gives away enormous quantities of goods to another. The aim is to shame the rival group because if the rival is unable to return the presentations on certain occasions, its members suffer a loss of prestige. In fact, to avoid losing prestige the recipient group is obliged to return gifts of even greater value. Over time the presentations might snowball until the members of one group, in their ceaseless quest for prestige, are materially impoverished (or so Benedict imagined). The whole complex of behaviors connected to the potlatch reflects the cultural configuration of the Kwakiutl—the Kwakiutl are so caught up by the prestige motivation that groups impoverish themselves to achieve this goal. Benedict used the term *Dionysian* to describe the Kwakiutl, after the Greek god known for his drinking, partying, and other excesses.

Benedict contrasted the Kwakiutl configuration to the Zuni of the North American Southwest. Zuni control their emotions, she claimed. They are moderate, modest, stoical, orderly, and restrained in their behavior. They do not boast or attempt to rise above their fellows but are social and cooperative. This "Apollonian" cultural theme, as Benedict called it, penetrates all of Zuni life. Unlike a Kwakiutl leader, a Zuni man does not seek status; indeed, a leadership role practically has to be forced on him. So, according to Benedict, each culture has its unique patterns and themes, which makes it possible for a person that culture A labels a megalomaniac to be culture B's ideal person.

Although modern anthropologists agree that different cultures emphasize different themes or patterns, most think that Benedict overemphasized the effect of culture on the thoughts, feelings, and actions of its members. It is misleading to characterize cultures in simple terms, such as that Kwakiutl are Dionysian (given to excesses), whereas Zuni are Apollonian (moderate in all things). To do so easily leads one people to develop stereotypes about the "personality" or "character" of another people. For example, some Americans say the Japanese have "authoritarian" personalities because they seem to submit to the authority of their bosses and to be more devoted to their companies than some other people. In most such opinions, one's own culture is assumed to be the standard, and

▲ Margaret Mead was Franz Boas's most famous student. She conducted fieldwork in several regions, including in Bali (shown here), and helped to popularize anthropological ideas about the importance of learning and anthropological findings about cultural variability.

others are judged using it as a reference point. Thus Italians are "excitable" to North American perceptions because they seem to be so enthusiastic about love, food, and family. Similarly, according to common American stereotypical labels, French are ethnocentric, Irish have fiery tempers, Swiss are humorless, and Swedes are sensual. But "the" Zuni, "the" Irish, and "the" members of other human communities are not simple products of their culture's "configurations." Rather, the personality and character of the members of a culture are highly variable.

Historical particularism greatly changed the way anthropologists thought about culture and conducted research, but it has limitations. Think about the claim that each culture is unique—like no other. Certainly, if differences between cultures are what we are most interested in, we can always find them. Once we've found them, we can go on to claim that no two cultures are alike. So at some level, the claim that "each culture is unique" is correct. So also is the claim that no two individuals brought up within the same culture are exactly alike. Yet they *are* alike in some ways. So, *in some ways,* no culture is like any other. But also, *in some ways,* a given culture does have things in common with some other cultures. More generally speaking, there are similarities as well as differences between ways of life. Historical particularists tended to overlook the similarities and to neglect the investigation of factors that might explain them.

Consider also the claim that, because each culture is the unique product of its particular past, one cannot generalize about the causes of cultural differences. To say (as did most particularists) that adaptation to the environment is most important in culture X, art styles in Y, values in Z, and so forth, is to say little more than that everything is related to most everything else. The holistic perspective (Chapter 1) tells us that culture is "integrated." It is also possible, however, that some influences are more important than other influences in all or most human populations—for example, it is possible that environmental adaptation is *generally* more important than art or values in causing a people to live the way they do. Interrelationships do not imply that every factor has equal weight as a causal influence.

By the 1940s, the interests of many American anthropologists returned to discovering the general principles of human cultural existence. Meanwhile, another way of studying human diversity developed in Europe.

British Functionalism (ca. 1920–1950)

Around the same time that historical particularism dominated American anthropology, quite a different approach was popular in Great Britain. The basic tenet of **functionalism** was that the cultural features of a people should be explained by the functions they perform. By *functions,* British anthropologists meant how existing ideas and actions contribute to the well-being of individuals and/or to the persistence of the whole group or society.

A leading British functionalist was Bronislaw Malinowski. Malinowski believed that the whole purpose (function) of culture is to serve human biological and psychological needs. These basic, biologically given needs include nutrition, reproduction, shelter, protection from enemies, and maintenance of bodily health. As social animals, people also need affection and emotional security. Unlike other animals, we humans have few inborn drives or instincts that provide behavioral instructions for how to meet our needs. Instead we have culture, which provides the learned behaviors, cooperative patterns, and social institutions (e.g., families, political associations) that make need fulfillment possible. Some parts of culture (e.g., food, tools used in production) meet our needs directly. Other parts (e.g., family life, educational practices) raise and enculturate new generations of group members. Still other cultural features (e.g., religious practices, art) instill adherence to the common norms and values that make group cooperation possible. These latter features also function to fulfill needs, but they do so indirectly, by helping the society persist over many generations and encouraging individuals to conform.

Malinowski thus considered the biological needs of individuals as the starting point for explaining culture. It is hard to argue with the point that culture meets human needs—although it's worth mentioning that living in a given time and place (e.g., modern Los Angeles) also creates additional perceived "needs." But notice that, *by themselves,* the biological needs of individuals cannot explain why cultures *differ.* All humans everywhere have much the same kinds of biological needs, yet peoples vary in the types of cultures they develop to fulfill these needs. Why do different peoples living in different times, places, and circumstances meet their needs in so many different ways? For example, some people satisfy their nutritional need for protein by eating beef, whereas others—such as many devout Hindus and Buddhists—not only refuse to consume cattle flesh but maintain a vegetarian diet. So the *common human need for protein* cannot explain the *diverse cultural ways* in which protein is acquired. To generalize the point: The basic needs of humans are the same everywhere and can be satisfied in so many different ways that they cannot explain cultural variation. At the least, differences in the natural environment in which people live must be taken into account to explain cultural differences.

Another influential British functionalist was A. R. Radcliffe-Brown. Radcliffe-Brown was most concerned with how diverse human groups and societies are organized, which is often called *social structure.* He assumed that societies are *systemic,* meaning that they have a tendency toward stability or *equilibrium.* To live in a society, then, is to live in a *social system,* the various parts of which tend to be in balance.

Radcliffe-Brown argued that the primary function of different elements of culture is to keep the entire social system in a steady state, or to maintain social equilibrium. He used an analogy to make his point. Society is like a living organism, with individual people analogous to cells and groups of people analogous to organs. In a biological life form, cells and organs are parts of a whole. Each has a function to perform to keep the entire organism alive and reproducing. We study the physiology of the organism by analyzing how all its complementary parts work together to keep the body alive.

Analogously, for Radcliffe-Brown, the functions of the various parts of a social and cultural system are to maintain the entire "social body." The parts of the system (institutions, as he called them) ordinarily function harmoniously to maintain the entire society or "to keep the system going." Occasionally, something will disrupt the state of equilibrium, but all societies have social mechanisms (e.g., behavioral norms, means of social control) that regulate disruptions and return the social system to a steady state. When we study a social and cultural system, we need to uncover the functions that different institutions perform and how they relate to one another.

But is the organic analogy valid? Most contemporary scholars say no. Unlike cells, individual human beings have minds and wills of their own, independent of the requirements of the social system. Also, the emphasis on steady states and equilibrium as the normal condition of society is misguided, many feel. Change—whether at slower or faster rates—is the *normal* social and cultural condition, yet functionalism failed to produce an adequate theory of how and why change occurs. Conflict—violent and otherwise—and disagreements between individuals and groups are also widespread in human communities. We need an approach that explains how and why conflict occurs, not just how it is reduced and regulated.

Despite these shortcomings, Radcliffe-Brown's emphasis on how the different aspects of culture relate to one another had an enduring impact on how anthropologists study culture today. More than previous approaches, functionalism emphasized the integration of culture: Parts (economy, religion, family, etc.) cannot be understood in isolation from each other or from the whole system. By their insistence that societies are integrated systems, the British functionalists strengthened the holistic perspective.

Like the American historical particularists, the British functionalists emphasized the necessity for anthropologists to conduct firsthand fieldwork. Malinowski, especially, is famous because of his ethnographic writings about the Trobriand Islanders of the western Pacific. Not only is fieldwork the best means of obtaining reliable information about a people, it is also a necessary part of the training of anthropologists, Malinowski believed. We cannot claim to understand people, nor their diverse cultures, until we have immersed ourselves in the experience of some culture other than our own. Malinowski thought the main objective of fieldwork is to see the culture as an insider to the culture sees it. In an often quoted passage from his famous 1922 ethnography *Argonauts of the Western Pacific,* Malinowski wrote:

> [T]he final goal, of which an Ethnographer [*sic*] should never lose sight . . . is, briefly, to grasp the native's point of view, his relation to life, to realise *his* vision of *his* world. (1922, 25)

Finally, Malinowski thought it essential that fieldworkers take a holistic view of the culture of the communities they study and live in. In his words:

> [T]he whole area of tribal culture *in all of its aspects* has to be gone over in research. . . . An Ethnographer who sets out to study only religion, or only technology, or only social organization cuts out an artificial field of inquiry, and he will be seriously handicapped in his work. (1922, 11; italics in original)

Although he said it differently, clearly Malinowski was urging fieldworkers to study the interrelationships between the various elements of a culture.

Because of the work of early-twentieth-century anthropologists like Boas and Malinowski, the fieldwork experience is today an important part of the graduate training of almost all anthropologists. And both relativism and holism are perspectives that most modern fieldworkers regard as necessary for objectivity and understanding. In fact, many contemporary anthropologists half-jokingly refer to fieldwork as their *rite of passage.* More than other aspects of their training, fieldwork transforms the anthropologist as a person, giving individual anthropologists a different perspective on themselves and their own culture.

Mid-Century Evolutionary Approaches (ca. 1940–1970)

We saw that Boas's attack nearly demolished the armchair speculations of the unilineal evolutionists. But one can study a subject without making the same mistakes nineteenth-century intellectuals made. Beginning around 1940, a few anthropologists renewed the study of cultural evolution shorn, they believed, of the invalid assumptions of the unilineal evolutionists. Two such American anthropologists were Leslie White and Julian Steward, whose ideas greatly influenced modern thought.

Leslie White believed that the unilineal evolutionists had been right about some things. First, some cultural features have, in fact, "developed" and "improved" over the centuries, namely, the technologies available for harnessing natural resources. In the realm of technology (tools and techniques for extracting energy and useful materials from the environment), progress did occur in (pre)history. White even proposed a reasonably objective way to measure technological evolution: Since the main function of technology is to capture the energy available from the environment, those technologies that capture the most energy per person are more evolved.

Second, White argued that cultures have, in fact, grown more complex over the centuries. The civilized Egyptians did have a more complex culture than the nomadic Inuit. He thought that nonethnocentric definitions of cultural complexity are possible: Societies with more people and territory, more occupational specialization, more functional differentiation, and more inequality can be defined as "more complex." By these criteria, for example, most hunting-gathering cultures such as the Inuit are "simple," whereas ancient civilizations such as those of the Egyptians, the Chinese, and the Inca are complex.

Technological progress and cultural evolution are related. In a few words: As technology becomes more productive, societies become larger and more complex. For this reason, White is sometimes called a *technological determinist,* meaning that he believed the technology available to a people has enormous impacts on other aspects of their culture. For instance, hunter-gatherers who exploit wild resources must live in small groups and remain mobile according to season. They tend to have little property, to share food and other products, and to have weak leaders. But people with an agricultural technology are generally more sedentary, live in large villages, accumulate wealth, and develop powerful leaders.

White's contemporary, Julian Steward, agreed that technology is an important part of culture, helping to shape many other aspects of a people's way of life. But Steward felt that the local environment is also an important influence on culture. Tools, after all, must be applied to the resources available in the environment to produce food and other necessities. The abundance, seasonal availability, and spatial variability of resources affect how people apply their technology and what and how much they produce. Steward argued that environment and technology together determine the basic form of *adaptation* of a group and that their adaptation in turn shapes the rest of their culture. He therefore is sometimes called a *techno-environmental determinist.*

Despite the fact that they are often labeled as determinists, both Steward and White recognized that some parts of a people's culture are more strongly "determined" by technology and environment than are other parts. The way a people organize their productive and other economic activities is likely to be much more affected by their adaptation than the way they arrange marriages, worship deities, recite myths, or construct art. Even so, aspects of culture that are not directly tied to adaptation may be indirectly tied to it, including kinship and worldview.

White and Steward made the investigation of cultural evolution respectable again. Many modern anthropologists specialize in fields such as *behavioral ecology, cul-*tural *ecology,* and *cultural evolution.* Their interests lie in long-term changes in cultures and how people adapt to their environments. Just as importantly, White and Steward felt that anthropology could and should be a *science,* in much the same way that biology or physics are sciences—indeed, White titled one of his books *The Science of Culture* (1949). On this point, a great many contemporary anthropologists disagree, as we shall now see.

Anthropological Thought Today: Divisions

Contemporary cultural anthropologists adopt an enormous variety of theoretical perspectives, far more than we can cover. So we focus on one major division within the field today, that between the **scientific approach** and the **humanistic approach.** (For more detail about the distinction between the sciences and humanities, see A Closer Look.)

Those who hold that anthropology is a science tend to believe that their primary goal is to explain particular cultures and—more broadly—to account for cultural differences and similarities. Scientifically oriented scholars typically emphasize that humanity is part of nature. Therefore, regular patterns develop in cultural systems that can potentially be explained, much as biologists use natural selection and other forces to explain patterns in natural species. Like other animals, *Homo sapiens sapiens* has physical needs and biological predispositions, which makes all humans similar to one another in some fundamental ways. Despite all of our diversity, cultures share some common core elements, so that the differences are underlain by similarities deriving from our evolutionary heritage.

When they do fieldwork, science types tend to quantify and measure. They "gather data." They assume that two trained, objective fieldworkers studying the same community at the same time will come to similar conclusions, so that what one competent fieldworker finds will be replicated by another who studies the same things.

On the other hand, numerous anthropologists reject the whole notion that culture and cultures can or even should be "explained" at all. They think that cultural anthropology should be a more humanistic field, whose main goal is to achieve an empathetic understanding of other cultures. While not denying that humans are animals and primates, they view humanity not primarily as biological life forms but as beings who create their own "realities" by symbolic means. To them, the most important characteristic of people is our capacity for culture, and particularly our tendency to culturally construct our world out of arbitrary symbols. This makes us so unique that our physical/biological needs are really not very im-

Within colleges and universities, anthropology is nearly always classified as a social science, along with fields like economics, psychology, and sociology. Few anthropologists question that two of the main subfields—physical/biological anthropology and prehistoric archaeology—can legitimately be considered sciences. (Indeed, many biological anthropologists hold that their field is more of a "natural" than a "social" science.) But cultural anthropologists are divided on the issue of whether their field is, or even can be, considered a science—even a "social" one.

There are many differences between the sciences and the humanities. Sciences (physics, biology, geology, organic chemistry, and the like) investigate some aspect of the physical/material world with the goal of understanding its structure, how it works, and what makes it the way it is. Ideally, the sciences study the world by means of systematic and replicable observation and experimentation. Here *systematic* means that facts are observed, counted, and recorded using agreed-upon procedures and instruments of measurement. "Facts" thus become "data." *Replicable* means that different observers—trained scientists—will obtain the same findings by using the same procedures. This implies that if two or more observers disagree on the findings, usually someone (or some instrument) has made a mistake.

In contrast, the humanities (literature, philosophy, classics, religion, art, music, drama, and the like) deal with the products of human intellect, emotion, creativity, and imagination. Depending on the discipline, the goals of humanistic fields are enjoyment and appreciation, uplifting the spirit, training the mind, pondering the meaning of life, discovering beauty, broadening horizons, and so on. Because humanities scholars study the products of human minds (poems and other literary texts, ideas, styles, creative expressions, and objects of beauty), their subject is not physical or material—although, of course, the creativity and imagination may be expressed using a material medium (a painting, a written poem, or a musical score). Scholars in the humanities themselves often create, as well as study, their subjects. Once a painting, a sculpture, a poem, a novel, or a play is publicly presented, different people are free to make what they will of it. It is to be enjoyed, interpreted, pondered, experienced, and critiqued. You observe it, listen to it, or read it in any way you choose. And no one expects that his or her discovery of it, experience of it, or opinion of it will be "replicated" by anyone else.

Now: Is cultural anthropology, which studies culture and cultural diversity, more like the sciences or more like the humanities? Are cultures more like "things" (to be explained) or more like "texts" (to be interpreted)? A culture is like a "thing" in that it is the product of (cultural) evolution and has some properties that can be observed and measured, just like a biological life form. But it is like a "text" in that its properties are in part the product of human reason, feeling, and creativity, much like a work of fiction or a play. If culture and cultures are similar to biological life forms, then the basic goals of anthropology can be to "explain" cultural differences and similarities. But if culture and cultures are more like texts, then the anthropologist can only "interpret" other cultures.

Connected to the science or humanity issue are methodological issues of the fieldwork experience. Will two trained fieldworkers studying the same group of people at the same time come up with the same findings? When their findings differ, is one or the other "mistaken"? Given that fieldworkers are human beings studying and interacting with other human beings, can we expect the ethnographies they produce to contain objective and verifiable data?

Such questions seem fundamental to an academic discipline. Students and scholars in other fields are sometimes surprised that cultural anthropologists do not agree on the answer to them. In the conclusion of this chapter, we suggest reasons why agreement on such fundamentals is so difficult to achieve for a field whose focus is describing and understanding human cultural forms in all their diversity.

portant influences on the kinds of cultures we develop to live in. Even our genetic makeup is not very important, because the most important characteristic of the human genome is that it does *not* program our actions, thoughts, and feelings in detail, but allows us to be flexible.

Because humanistically oriented anthropologists emphasize the uniqueness of each culture, they tend to be skeptical of comparisons (because of the old "apples and oranges" problem) and of attempts to generalize about the causes of cultural differences (because cultures are "just too complicated").

In conducting fieldwork, humanistic scholars emphasize participation and interaction over objective measurement of behavior. In their view, ideally fieldworkers become so involved in the life of the community that they come to have a deep understanding of it, almost like an "insider." Because they think that descriptive accounts of a particular culture emerge from interactions between fieldworkers and local people, they believe that the findings of different fieldworkers may be inconsistent. This does not bother them very much, for they tend to think that objectivity is unattainable because

Scientific Approach	Humanistic Approach
Main goal is explaining cultural differences and similarities	Main goal is describing and interpreting particular cultures, ideally achieving an insider's view
Humans are part of the natural world, different only in degree from other animals; emphasizes environment	Humans are unique because they are conscious, cultural beings, different in kind from other animals; emphasizes symbols
Regularities and consistent patterns exist across cultures and are discoverable by empirical observation and systematic comparisons	Individual cultures are so complex that each culture must be understood in its own terms; comparisons distort the cultures compared
All humans are fundamentally similar, sharing a core of motivations, emotions, and behavioral predispositions coming from our evolutionary past	The world's diverse peoples differ in their motives, emotions, and behavioral tendencies according to the particular culture in which they were raised
Field methods emphasize observation and quantification of group patterns of behavior; descriptions are objectively attainable in that two trained fieldworkers can discover the same set of facts, or "data"	Field methods emphasize participation and interaction with individuals; descriptions emerge from interaction of the fieldworker with local people so two fieldworkers will have different accounts depending on their personal characteristics and these interactions

fieldworkers are themselves human beings and not recording devices. (Chapter 5 discusses these points.)

Like most dichotomies, this one is too simple to portray the variety of orientations within contemporary anthropology with complete accuracy. Particular anthropologists do not necessarily view themselves as either "scientists" or "humanists." Indeed, many adopt the assumptions and methods of both approaches, depending on what aspect of culture they are studying. Some even say that the dichotomy is a false one. Nonetheless, the split reflects some of the major divisions and controversies within the field today. Keeping this in mind, the accompanying Concept Review summarizes the differences.

To glimpse how their aims and results differ, we discuss a couple of examples of both perspectives. As an example of the scientific approach, we discuss *sociobiology* and *cultural materialism,* which are quite different. For the humanistic orientation, we use *interpretive anthropology* and *postmodernism.*

Scientific Orientations

Sociobiology and Evolutionary Psychology

As an example—an extreme example, actually—of the scientific approach, in the late 1970s some anthropologists adopted a theory known as **sociobiology.** Social scientists now often call it **evolutionary psychology.** Harvard biologist Edward O. Wilson was instrumental in the development of this theoretical framework in the biological sciences. He was interested in animal social behavior—that is, in why many animals (e.g., lions, ants, many ungulates) live in herds or other kinds of groups whose members help one another in such ways as cooperating in hunting or emitting alarm calls that warn the group of a nearby predator.

Why are such behaviors puzzling? In the animal kingdom, most biologists had long believed that natural selection usually produces organisms that are genetically selfish, meaning that unselfish (*altruistic*) behavior in animals is rare and exists only under very special circumstances. For instance, most cooperative social behaviors and alarm calls appear to be costly to the individual animal, yet the benefits accrue to the entire group—a prairie dog calling to alert its neighbors to a predator might call the predator's attention to itself and thus stand a greater chance of getting eaten. How could natural selection produce animals that act altruistically?

Wilson, along with other biologists such as Richard Dawkins and William Hamilton, noted that the unit of "selfishness" is not individual organisms, but genes. Because genes are the units that are transmitted to offspring through reproduction, only genes that make more copies of themselves in the next generation can survive. Genes, sociobiologists argue, largely program the bodies that temporarily house them into acting in ways that improve their

▲ In the 1970s, the work of Harvard's Edward O. Wilson and other sociobiologists penetrated ethnology. Famous for his work on ants and other social insects, Wilson and other sociobiologists argued that human behaviors and beliefs are shaped by natural selection. Human societies and cultures therefore can be explained by evolutionary processes similar to those operating in other animal species.

biological *fitness*—in ways that increase their frequencies in the next generation. To paraphrase Dawkins, a body and its behavior are a gene's way of making more copies of itself. Some sociobiologists claimed that this statement applied to humans as well as to other animals. Taken seriously, this would mean that *your* body and behavior are your genes' ways of making more copies of themselves.

The main contribution of sociobiology was the insight that related individuals share a greater proportion of their genes with one another than they do with nonrelatives of the same species. For example, a female can potentially increase the fitness of one or more of her genes if she aids her brother, if that brother carries the same genes. By helping her brother, she herself may reproduce less, but this cost can be more than offset if her help significantly improves her brother's fitness. Thus, natural selection will increase the fitness of any gene that programs its body to help a relative if the cost in fitness (to the gene) is lower than the benefit to the same gene housed in the relative's body. So an animal can behave altruistically after all, but only if the benefit of the altruism helps a relative far more than it costs the "altruist" (note that the behavior is not truly altruistic).

Some ethnologists believe that sociobiology contributes to explaining human social behavior. For example, you and I have a genuine interest in the welfare of our relatives. All else equal, the more closely related we are, the more we care for them, and people care most for those bodies that are the main vehicles for transmitting their genes—their own offspring and offspring's offspring. We care little, if at all, for nonrelatives and will assist them only if they somehow return benefits to us or to our relatives, mainly by reciprocating our help immediately or sometime later if we can count on their presence in the future. So evolutionary psychologists claim that selfishness motivates most human actions, although the selfish motive is sometimes disguised when we help family members or friends, in expectations of future returns.

More generally, human sociobiologists note that for much of human history, the most important social groups (bands, discussed in later chapters) were largely composed of relatives who cooperated in foraging, food sharing, child care, and other activities. They also point out that far more human societies allow a man to have several wives than allow a woman to have several husbands, which is consistent with sociobiology for reasons we discuss in Chapter 8. Some anthropologists and psychologists claim that evolutionary psychology explains many widespread behavioral and mental predispositions, including

- xenophobia (hatred or mistrust of strangers, because as nonrelatives they cannot be trusted)
- warfare (braver men who protect the group have more wives and/or sex, and hence more offspring)
- male unfaithfulness to wives or promiscuity (you get more children without the costs of raising them)
- female preference for marrying high status/wealthy males (access to more resources improves the fitness of her offspring)

Critics of such ideas charge that these and other so-called predispositions are more the product of enculturation than of genes, because they vary markedly from people to people. Even if evolutionary psychology "helps" in understanding such widespread patterns, critics say that it tells us little or nothing about the reasons why various peoples exhibit them strongly, only weakly, or not at all. So this kind of "help" is minimal at best, and may even be harmful if it makes us falsely believe we now understand something. And, at any rate, the insights of sociobiology apply mainly if "all else is equal," which it never is in human societies.

There are numerous other arguments both for and against sociobiology/evolutionary psychology, some of which we cover in later chapters. For now, note that it is an excellent example of the scientific side of ethnology: it holds that people are subject to the same principles and pressures as other animals—most importantly, to the forces of natural selection. Potentially, they think, cultural differences and similarities can be explained by these principles and pressures.

Cultural Materialism

Like the evolutionary psychologists, the orientation called **cultural materialism** points out that people face the same kinds of imperatives as all mammals. We must receive adequate intake of food and water, regulate our body temperature (by making shelter and wearing clothing), reproduce, cope with organisms that cause disease, compete successfully with other groups, and so forth. However, most materialists do not agree that human behavior is motivated largely by the selfish desire to transmit one's genes. They note that sometimes people choose not to reproduce at all or voluntarily limit their reproduction. They also think that cooperation is too pervasive in humanity to be simply disguised selfishness. Genuine altruism exists if conditions warrant. Materialists do share with sociobiologists the generalized view that survival in a particular environment is the most important force in human existence.

Like the mid-century evolutionists, cultural materialism holds that the way human populations adapt to their environments, including other organisms and other human groups that might surround them, are the main explanations for most cultural differences. In this context, *adaptation* means that group members must adjust their behavior, and ultimately their ideas and beliefs, to the natural conditions in which they live.

How can adaptation be this important to humanity, with our intelligence, communication skills, technology, and flexibility? To materialists, adaptation requires—or, at the least, makes it advantageous—for groups to organize themselves in certain ways for purposes such as cooperation in producing food, acquiring other material resources, and successfully competing or trading with other groups. In essence, materialists think that how people make a living in their environment is the most important influence on the rest of their cultural existence. Because environments change over time (due in part to the actions of the humans that often modify them), and because technologies can become more efficient, groups change their behaviors and organizations to adjust, producing long-term changes in cultural systems.

If one thinks adapting to environments and acquiring material resources are so important as to be considered "basic," then those aspects of culture that help people adapt and get resources will strongly affect all other aspects. Humans, more than any other animal, depend on *technology* to exploit resources, compete, and cope with other problems of environmental adaptation. Technology includes not just the physical *instruments* (the tools) that people use to produce food, provide shelter, and manipulate the environment. Equally important, technology includes the *knowledge* about the environment, about resources, and about the manufacture and effective use of tools that people socially learn from the long experience of previous generations.

Because humans rely on technology to acquire food and harness other resources, technology is among the most important aspects of culture everywhere, just as

White argued back in the 1940s. By "most important," materialists mean that technology strongly affects other cultural aspects, including family life, political organization, values, and even worldviews. Because the essential purpose of technology is to aid people in making a living in their environment, the environment itself also helps determine culture, just as Steward said. In applying their technology in their environment, over long time periods people discover that certain resources are preferable to others, and that some ways of organizing their groups and activities work better than others. For example, those food resources that are most productive and/or nutritious will become culturally preferred and exploited, and the best ways of scheduling and organizing the work to acquire them will become standardized.

In emphasizing the importance of physical/biological needs, technology, and environment, modern materialists resemble earlier thinkers such as Malinowski, White, and Steward. However, in many ways modern materialists are more sophisticated than their intellectual predecessors. For example, for the most part earlier theories about causation were *linear*, meaning that one thing makes another thing the way it is; thus, A "causes" B, or A "determines" B. White and Steward generally viewed technology and/or environment as causes, and cultures as effects.

But modern materialists are more likely to view technology, environment, and culture as having *feedback* relationships to one another. That is, as people interact with their environment using their technology, they change the environment, and these changes in turn lead people to alter their technology, which then further alters the environment, and so on. For instance, as people exploit a resource, they often deplete its supply for themselves and future generations. They must then work harder to acquire the resource in the future, or develop a new method of acquiring it, or switch to an alternative resource. Other cultural changes accompany these changes in adaptation.

Following this line of argument, the late Marvin Harris proposed that many important changes in human cultures result from a process known as *intensification*. Historically, peoples on all continents invented many ways to reduce the rate at which their population numbers increase, at least in the short term. But over the long term population sizes in many regions increase. As population grows, people tend to overexploit and deplete resources, which leads to degradation or other kinds of changes in their environment. This forces them to develop new ways to use their environment. For example, they turn to resources they previously ignored, which requires them to expend more labor in acquiring energy and materials, which leads them to develop new tech-

nologies to harvest and process resources. They exploit nature more *intensively*. Intensification involves working longer hours to acquire more resources; taking more land out of its natural state and controlling the plants and animals that live on it; developing new technologies like irrigation and fertilization to squeeze more product out of nature; and even warring against neighbors to take over their lands. Both population growth and intensification lead to new social relations and organizations, which develop to facilitate the new ways of exploiting nature. In turn, new social arrangements require new worldviews, values, and norms to reinforce them. If human numbers continue to increase, the process of intensification will necessarily continue until completely new forms of society and culture develop (e.g., civilizations, nation-states, industrial societies, global economies).

We discuss some of these processes in later chapters. For now, note two main arguments of materialists: (1) Many customs and beliefs of a particular culture help the people adapt to their environments, and (2) population growth and intensification are the main factors that drive cultural evolution.

Humanistic Orientations

Of course, no one can argue with some elements of both evolutionary psychology and cultural materialism. Surely, most people do transmit their genes by having children and most of us are more likely to help relatives than strangers. But whether the imperatives identified by sociobiology are all that important is debatable. For example, many scholars find the so-called predispositions identified by evolutionary psychology above quite absurd. Some deny that such universal patterns or tendencies exist at all. Or if they do exist, then trying to explain them has the effect of "justifying" (in the disguise of "explaining") racial hatreds, violence, exploitation, and the like. The notion that human beings are innately selfish is odious to many and probably to most anthropologists. In fact, many believe that any scholar who tries to "explain" culture or cultures dehumanizes people by treating them as objects.

Likewise no one denies that people have material needs. But whether such needs are "basic" and shape all of human existence is debatable. Some think that humans differ from other animals in that these needs can be satisfied in such a multitude of ways that cultural differences cannot possibly be reduced to "material need and want satisfaction." They deny that material factors can explain any specific culture, much less cultural differences and similarities and long-term changes. In fact, they doubt that culture has any *general* explanation, for humans and their diverse ways of living are too complicated to be reduced to a single formula.

We use the phrase *humanistic orientation* to refer to those anthropologists who doubt or deny that any general theory can "explain" culture in the same way that evolutionary theory explains life or that Einstein's relativity theory explains the physical world. People, their cultures, and human minds are too complex and unpredictable to be "explained" in the usual scientific sense of the word *explanation,* humanistic anthropologists feel.

They feel this way for many reasons, but one of the most important is their insistence on *human uniqueness.* Without denying that humans are animals, they think that humans are such a special kind of animal that special methods and analysis are required to understand us.

Human uniqueness, as we already know, lies mainly in our heavy dependence on social learning and our capacity for complex communication—that is, in both culture and language. Our capacity for and reliance on culture and language make us fundamentally different from other forms of life on Earth: Other animals live in the natural world, whereas humans live, in large part, in worlds of their own making and symbolic construction. In part, this means that people manipulate nature (with agriculture, houses, and factories) more than other animals do.

▲ Cultural materialists often hold that how people harness and utilize resources is the main influence on their culture. Humanistic anthropologists counter that whether something found in nature is a resource, and if so, how that resource is used, varies from culture to culture. The sacred cattle of Hinduism, for example, are not the same kind of food resource in India as are cattle in North America or Africa.

But more importantly, it means that the way people perceive the natural and social environment, the way they interpret events in that environment, and their view of the world itself depend on their culture.

To keep our description as clear as possible, we focus on the humanistic critique of only one scientific approach, cultural materialism. Consider the term *resource,* one of the cornerstones of materialist theory. A simple definition is "something that people use to satisfy their needs and wants." By this definition, resources are "out there in the world" available "in nature" for people to use or transform. For materialists, the way people acquire and use resources is one of the main factors that shapes other aspects of their culture. Long-term changes in the way populations acquire resources are one of the main things that leads to cultural change and evolution.

Humanists, though, see resources differently. True, people need resources to live, but to humanists resources are as much cultural concepts as material things. To them, the most important *cultural* fact about resources is that they satisfy *symbolic needs.* Resources are not simply present "in nature" to be "exploited"; rather, they are *culturally constructed.* What one people consider a resource is not defined as a resource for other people. Hindus do not eat cattle; devout Muslims and orthodox Jews refuse pork and abhor the pig; Americans shun dog meat, insects, and horse flesh; and so on. Some perfectly nutritious animals and plants are not culturally constructed as foods, so are not in fact "edible" by a particular people due to their worldview or some other largely ideational factor.

Similar ideas apply to views about the total environment. Materialists emphasize the *objective conditions* under which people live. The natural environment is a reality to which humans must adapt by altering their actions to survive and persist. But is this so-called reality very significant in determining the ways in which any particular people live? Humanists hold that the way a people *subjectively perceive* their environment is as important in shaping their adaptation as is the objective environment itself. Material conditions (e.g., technology, environment, and adaptation) do not "determine" the rest of culture, for cultural constructions, definitions, and conceptions shape people's perceptions of the material conditions.

Materialists and humanists are also likely to disagree on which needs and wants take priority in human life. Materialists assume that material needs and satisfactions like shelter, nutrition, bodily comforts, wealth items, and so forth are generally the main goals and values in life. The desire for nonmaterial satisfactions is less important or is acted upon only after material needs and wants have been satisfied.

© Sylvia Howe/Anthro-Photo File

In contrast, humanists feel that what we put into our stomachs depends largely on what culture has put into our minds. Humans require more than material satisfactions for a sense of well-being and even for survival. People do not live by wheat and meat (or rice and fish) alone: We need rewarding social relationships, intellectually coherent and emotionally gratifying worldviews, a sense of who we are, symbols to become attached to, basic values to cling to, and other nonmaterial rewards. In brief, as *cultural beings* humans seek a meaningful as well as a prosperous existence, and our psychological need for meaning is just as important as our material needs for things. Humanists point out that some people deliberately reject material rewards in the name of cultural preservation or for religious reasons. How could the actions of suicide bombers or the 9/11 terrorists possibly be explained except by understanding Muslim emotional attachments to Islam and to their beliefs about rewards in the afterlife? What "material reward" is earned by such actions?

Lastly, humanists argue that the material conditions people face impose only very broad limits on their behaviors because people can satisfy their needs in a multitude of ways. There are many ways to adapt to a given environment, not just one, and the way a particular people adapts cannot be predicted. The group's history and traditions influence not only how they define *resource* and perceive nature, but also which of the many possible ways of adapting to nature they will adopt.

In summary, humanists believe that the human dependence on culture and capacity for symbolic communication make us such unique animals that attempts to explain cultural diversity in material terms are likely to be futile. In particular, humanists claim that materialist explanations fail for several reasons:

- Resources, which have such an important role in materialist theory, are culturally constructed, not inherent in nature.
- A people's perceptions of the natural world are as important to its adaptation as are the objective conditions of its environment.
- Unlike other animals, material wants are not paramount among humans, who have a variety of social, emotional, intellectual, and symbolic wants as well.
- Material conditions provide great leeway for a people to develop a wide diversity of behaviors and beliefs, based on the group's particular history and unique traditions.

One wonders: *If* all this is true, how is it that materialist scholars have been so wrong about the importance of environment, technology, adaptation, and so forth? How could they be so misguided? Some humanists hold that materialist thinking is a product of Western cultural values and beliefs. Because the West places such a high value on material welfare and consumption, materialists mistakenly impose these values and beliefs on other cultures. Living in a competitive and capitalistic society predisposes cultural materialists to see "economic man" in cultures where he does not exist. The materialist theory is a kind of ethnocentrism, some claim.

Some materialists respond in kind. They point out that most academics are members of the privileged class, in status, in wealth, or in both. Because they so seldom have to worry about filling their stomachs, or sheltering themselves from heat, snow, and rain, or protecting themselves from enemies, some academics too easily conclude that such concerns are not important elsewhere either. The humanists' failure to realize the broad importance of material factors is related to their own wealth and privilege. The humanistic approach is a kind of ethnocentrism, some claim.

There are many particular approaches that we collapse under the term *humanistic.* Here we discuss only two. *Interpretive anthropology* has been around for several decades and reveals especially well how humanistic approaches differ from scientific ones. *Postmodernism* developed in the 1980s.

Interpretive Anthropology

As much as any other one factor, the fascination with cultural diversity distinguishes modern ethnology from other academic disciplines. Many anthropologists say they go into the field in search of "The Other," meaning in quest of peoples and ways of life that contrast with their own. To such scholars, the essence of anthropology is immersing oneself deeply in another culture and, through such immersion, to come to an understanding of it on its own terms. Through the fieldwork experience, they hope to better understand not only the particular culture in which they work, but themselves and the totality of the human condition as well. Through their writings, they hope to communicate their understandings and interpretations of The Other to members of their own culture, to help *them* understand the diverse ways of being human.

This approach is commonly known as **interpretive anthropology.** Like the configurationalists of the early twentieth century, interpretive anthropologists emphasize the uniqueness and particularity of each culture. Every culture has its own ways of doing things, its own worldview, its own values, its own system of symbols, and so forth. Even if two or more cultures look similar, close examination usually shows that the meanings its members attach to behaviors, objects, and concepts are different. This uniqueness makes comparisons between different cultures misleading, at best. And because science relies on comparisons for its generalizations, it follows that anthropology is more of a humanistic discipline than a scientific one. As such, it has more in common with literature and art than with biology or psychology, according to the interpretivists.

For interpretive anthropologists, all social behavior has an inherent symbolic component, in the sense that culture forces people to behave in meaningful ways—ways that others will understand. All social interaction, therefore, is symbolic and meaningful. Meanings exist only by virtue of

▲ Interpretive anthropologists believe that studying culture is more of a humanistic endeavor than a scientific endeavor. Clifford Geertz was influential in formulating the view that culture is essentially a system of symbols, unique to each people, so that our primary goal is interpreting the meanings of symbols in their particular cultural context.

common agreement among the parties to the interaction—whether the interaction is making conversation in China, making change in an American Wal-Mart, making bumpers in a South Korean auto factory, or making time at a party in Spain. Participants cannot tell a foreign observer or fieldworker how they know what other participants "mean" by this or that behavior, for their actions are symbolic (as defined in Chapter 2). Yet participants usually behave in ways that others understand, and they fairly consistently interpret the actions of others correctly.

The job of the anthropologist in studying a culture is not to explain it but to *explicate* it, by interpreting the significance of some elements in light of other elements. Analogously, a dictionary *explicates* the meanings of words in terms of other words. Only if one knows the meaning of many words in the dictionary can one use it to decipher the meaning of unknown words. You must get inside (learn) English, for by understanding the meanings of some of its words, you can potentially learn more and more of them. To explicate a culture, then, the anthropologist shows how one thing in a cultural system makes sense in terms of other things in the same system. This requires "deep immersion" into a particular culture and "thick description" of it, as interpretivists say.

Notice that, for interpretivists, *holism* is a very important principle. In fact, interpretation *is* seeing how things make sense when understood in their context. We seek to understand a people's way of life as the people understand it. In the words of Clifford Geertz, the scholar who more than anyone else founded and shaped the entire approach, we seek to grasp "the native's point of view," for we want "to figure out what the devil they think they are up to" (Geertz 1983, 58). And most interpretivists seem to believe that all "natives" are up to something different and uniquely their own.

According to many interpretive anthropologists, the search for generalized explanations of human ways of life is probably futile. Even if general explanations are desirable as goals (as scientific types assume), too many factors contributed to the formation of a given culture and these factors interacted in too many complex and unpredictable ways. Partial understanding through deep immersion in a particular, unique culture should be our main objective. In this and other respects, interpretive anthropologists exemplify the humanistic perspective in ethnology.

Postmodernism

Postmodernism originated mainly in another field (literary criticism) and is a wider intellectual movement popular in the humanities and some of the social sciences. It attracted many adherents in cultural anthropology in the 1980s. Unfortunately, it cannot be conceptualized as neatly as the other orientations we have covered. Here we discuss only one of its main points (which allows us to avoid using and explaining words like *deconstruction*).

Postmodernists generally believe that the methods and assumptions of all science—including fields such as biology—are suspect. They hold that scientific thinking and methods became prominent during the Enlightenment period (also called the Age of Reason) of late eighteenth- and nineteenth-century western Europe. Enlightenment philosophers emphasized rational thought as the key to advancing knowledge about the world, from the solar system to humanity. Tradition, and especially religion, was viewed as an impediment to discovering Truth. Emotions could also get in the way, especially if they keep otherwise rational thinkers from accepting the reality of a fact or principle just because they don't like it or its implications. For example, if you are a man you might refuse to accept evidence showing that not all societies are patriarchal. You reject or discount the evidence because it is not consistent with what religion has taught you and it makes you feel guilt or other kinds of emotional distress. Your refusal to accept the evidence is not "rational," so it gets in the way of improving your knowledge. This would not matter very much for your society unless, of course, men hold the power in that society and most of them feel and believe as you do.

Postmodernists do not think there is anything very special about this kind of rationality. They say that all of human knowledge (here meaning "ideas and beliefs"— see Chapter 2) originates in a particular social, economic, and political context. *Scientific* knowledge is no exception: because science is a product of a particular cultural tradition—that of the West—it reflects the economy, family organization, political ideology, worldview, and so forth of Western society. Science, in fact, is just one among hundreds of other systems of cultural knowledge. Many postmodernists hold that science has little more claim to absolute Truth than do the ideas and beliefs of other peoples. All are valid on their own terms but none are "privileged," or have any special claim to objectivity. If scientists themselves don't realize this, it is because they are inside the knowledge system and so do not grasp the implicit assumptions of their rationalistic and mechanistic worldview.

Postmodernists also think that the most important thing about the "context" of knowledge is power relationships. Prevalent beliefs and ideas in a community reflect lines of power, largely because those with power have the most influence on which ideas and beliefs become "prevalent." To illustrate with a modern example, most North Americans believe in things like private property, market capitalism, democracy, and various individual rights and freedoms. These beliefs reflect, and support, the interests of some people over other people. Much scholarly knowledge—the kind taught in colleges and universities—is like this, postmodernists claim. For example, sociobiology is often taught more or less as a credible or even correct theory in biology courses, although postmodernists hold its theories support sexism and patriarchy.

As mentioned, postmodernism penetrated anthropology in the 1980s and has attracted more converts in our field than in any other social science. One reason for the popularity of this perspective in anthropology is its apparent consistency with cultural relativism. However, critics of the approach became vocal in the late 1990s. Do postmodernists adopt the tenets of their own ideas in their personal lives? If science is "just another" kind of knowledge, do they refuse to ride in airplanes or use microwaves? How have their own ideas escaped the influence of power relationships? And does the relativity of all knowledge apply to *their* ideas?

So whether postmodernism will remain popular remains to be seen. It does remind us that rationality and science have limits. And it leads us to ask where our ideas come from and who might gain and lose from them.

Either/Or?

As you can see, there are significant differences between ethnologists who believe that cultures can and should be studied scientifically (like a life form) and those who believe that a given culture should be penetrated and interpreted (like a work of literature). The differences in orientation are sometimes presented as conflicting: Humanists often accuse the scientists of dehumanizing people in their effort to explain them, whereas scientists claim that humanists are deceiving themselves if they think they can penetrate the meanings and get inside some other culture.

To some extent, the differences in orientation between materialists and humanists exist because of the differing interests of anthropologists. For example, scholars whose research specializations include subjects such as human adaptation, economic systems, or long-term evolutionary changes in societies are likely to find a materialist approach useful. Those who study dimensions such as mythology, art, oral traditions, or worldviews are more likely to fall into the humanistic camp.

Also, in part, the diversity of modern approaches reflects the fact that human beings and their cultures are complex and multifaceted, so the orientation adopted to understanding one facet (e.g., subsistence) may not prove very useful for understanding another facet (e.g., worldview).

In the interest of balance, in the remainder of this book we try to avoid choosing between the two orientations by taking the following approach. We do think that *it is important* that people are part of nature, like evolutionary psychologists and cultural materialists. But we recognize that different elements of a culture are influenced to different degrees by material conditions. The way an economy is organized is greatly influenced by the local environment, by climate, by technology, and by the size and density of the human population. But the way the members of a culture resolve their disputes, raise their children, perform their rituals, or act toward their fathers-in-law is less influenced by material conditions or is influenced by them only indirectly. The legends they recite, the specific objects they use as religious symbols, or the way they decorate their bodies may have little to do with material forces. Such elements of a cultural system may be only loosely tied to the natural world and to desires for material things. If so, we cannot account for them without considering people's desires for a meaningful existence, for an emotionally gratifying social life, for an intellectually satisfying worldview, for creative self-expression, and so forth.

So we avoid the either/or dilemma by pointing out that different orientations are useful for studying different dimensions of culture. Still, people who are new to anthropology are often puzzled by the diversity of approaches within the field. We therefore conclude this chapter by suggesting answers to the following question:

Why Can't All Those Anthropologists Agree?

Natural scientists such as physicists, chemists, and geologists generally agree on a set of laws or principles that govern the physical world. In geology, for example, processes such as sedimentation, plate tectonics, volcanic eruptions, fossilization, and so forth are fairly well understood and account for the main geological features of our planet. In chemistry, how atoms combine to form molecules and how molecules combine to form more complex molecules is known so well that new chemicals can be created in predictable ways. Biologists, likewise, believe that the process of evolution produced the diversity of all life on Earth, although the relative importance of natural selection and random events in this process remains uncertain.

Yet cultural anthropology lacks a comparable set of general principles (as do the other social sciences except economics). A basic question asked by scientifically oriented ethnologists is: What are the important causes of the differences and similarities between the world's known cultures? If you could ask 100 ethnologists this question, you would get a multitude of answers. Cultural materialists would mention forces such as climate, resources, population sizes, and technology. Interpretivists would say that the question itself is wrongheaded, because anthropologists should be trying to interact with members of particular cultures and achieve an insider's view of them, not to "explain" them. Many would respond that there is no generalized explanation, because cultures are so complex and diverse that the most important causes in culture X are not at all important in culture Y. Still others would hold that the question is ethnocentric, and in some cases racist, because it reduces people in other cultures to the status of "objects" of our explanations.

Why don't anthropologists agree more than they do on the answer to this question and numerous other basic questions about humanity? Several factors contribute to the absence of consensus.

First, we humans are conscious and self-aware beings who state a variety of reasons for why we do and think what we do and think. The zoologist studying an animal observes and records the animal's behavior and quantifies certain aspects of it, then typically tries to identify the elements of the natural and social environment to which the behavior is adapted. But anthropologists must listen to the reasons people themselves give for their behavior. People talk back, and anthropologists must take their talk, as well as their patterns of behavior, into account.

Second, for ethical reasons anthropologists do not set up controlled experiments to study how people respond. Suppose—following Steward's lead—we want to study how the natural environment affects peoples and cultures. We cannot hold everything constant except the food, water, or shelter supply, and then see how people react when the supply of food, water, or shelter is varied. The only way the anthropologist can "control" conditions is by looking around the world for "natural experiments," places where the natural environment is similar and peoples with different histories live. We can choose a sample of peoples who live in environments that appear to be similar, then see whether the peoples who live in these places have similar cultures. For example, we might compare indigenous peoples who live in the world's deserts:

the Sahara of northern Africa, the Kalahari of southern Africa, the American Southwest, the Gobi of northeast Asia, and so forth. To conduct such a comparative study, we will have to rely on the ethnographic reports written by a multitude of earlier ethnographers, whose reports resulted from their observations and discussions with peoples of the various deserts.

Suppose our comparative study finds, as it will, that the cultures are similar in some respects but different in others. Then other problems arise: Natural environments are only similar, never identical. Did we fail to detect a small but critical difference in the environment that might explain the cultural differences? Or are the differences due to some nonenvironmental factor? Likewise, cultures are only similar, never identical. Shall we call customs and beliefs that differ in minor ways between the cultures the "same," or are the subtle differences between them sufficient to call them "different"? Suppose we decide that some behavior, like sharing food within a village, is the "same" behavior in the cultures. But then we discover that people in several of the cultures give different reasons for the behavior—in culture X people say they want to help one another, whereas in culture Y they say they give only because they expect to get something back later. Are both of these behaviors still "sharing food"? Or should we consider them as different because people's stated motivations differ? Or did the various ethnographers falsely believe a certain behavior was "food sharing" when in fact it was something else? Such questions are *inherently* difficult to answer when dealing with human beings, and anthropologists cannot sort them out in laboratories or other experimental settings.

Third, fieldworkers study members of their own species. Being human, fieldworkers enter their research experience with a culture of their own. This culture inevitably affects their objectivity, and, hence, their interactions with the community, their perceptions of what is important, and so forth. Conversely, individuals in the community itself have their own perceptions, opinions, and biases about the fieldworker. Among the many factors that affect how the community reacts are the fieldworker's physical characteristics, sex, personality, the kinds of questions asked, and the historical experience of the community with individuals of the anthropologist's own society. Although most fieldworkers attempt to overcome their own cultural biases and to fit into the community, complete objectivity is impossible. In fact, some contemporary anthropologists—especially postmodernists—write ethnographies that focus far more on their interactions with local people than on the culture of the people themselves. They think that any ethnography is a

"construction"—built out of interactions that another fieldworker would not experience—not a simple report on "facts" about a given group. (We have more to say on such issues in Chapter 5.)

There is another possible reason that anthropology lacks a common theoretical orientation and an agreed-upon set of principles. It is quite likely that people become anthropologists for a wider variety of reasons than people become, say, physicists. Some of us study anthropology because of our curiosity about why the human species is so diverse culturally. Others go into the field to further the cause of social justice—by educating themselves and others about racism, ethnocentrism, colonialism, or sexism, for example. Some want to immerse themselves in travel and interaction with people who are different from themselves, and they become anthropologists because the field provides them with such opportunities. The very broad scope of anthropology (see Chapter 1) helps account for the variety of reasons people choose it as a career: You can study agriculture, family life, political organization, medicine, art, religion, folklore, and almost anything else having to do with humankind. Naturally people who study topics as diverse as these are unlikely to agree on their theoretical orientations to the field as a whole. Indeed, many of them consciously reject any form of theoretical orientation, preferring to concentrate on researching particular cultures.

In sum, there are four major reasons that modern cultural anthropologists have such varied orientations to the study of culture:

- Our subjects—other human beings—are themselves conscious beings who are aware of their own behavior and state their own reasons for why they do what they do. Human subjects talk back.
- Anthropologists cannot set up experiments that allow them to control the conditions under which people live, allowing their behavior to be manipulated. Anthropologists observe people as they live their everyday lives.
- Complete objectivity is impossible to achieve when a researcher is studying humans, both because researchers themselves are culture-bearers and because the subjects of the study react to fieldworkers in varied ways. Ethnographers are different and they encounter different problems as they work in different places.
- The broad scope of the field itself and the enormous diversity of reasons people study anthropology make it unlikely that consensus will emerge. Cultural anthropologists are among the most diverse of scholars.

Summary

1. Anthropology originated as a separate academic discipline in the late nineteenth century, after colonialism intensified contact between peoples of European ancestry and the indigenous peoples of Africa, Asia, the Americas, and the Pacific. Darwin's theory of evolution was one of the main notions that allowed Western intellectuals to make sense of the peoples and cultures of other lands. It seemed to imply that the history of life on Earth was progressive, with simpler organisms evolving into more complex ones.

2. Unilineal evolutionists applied this notion to cultures. Using written accounts as their main source of information about non-Western peoples, they arranged cultures into a sequence of progressive stages, from simple to complex, with Western civilization at the pinnacle. Anthropology thus began as the field that studied how humankind progressed out of rude beginnings into a more "civilized" cultural existence.

3. In the early twentieth century, both American and British anthropologists developed new approaches. The American historical particularists, led by Boas, demolished the speculative schemes of the unilineal evolutionists by arguing that concepts such as "complexity" depend on one's point of view and thus have little objective meaning. Boas popularized the notion of cultural relativism that remains a hallmark of ethnology today. In Great Britain, functionalists such as Malinowski and Radcliffe-Brown tried to show how the various parts of a culture and its social system serve to meet the needs of individuals and society. By emphasizing the interrelatedness of cultural systems, functionalism strengthened the holistic perspective. Both the historical particularists and the functionalists emphasized the importance of firsthand fieldwork as the surest path to objectivity and as essential for the training of anthropologists.

4. In the middle decades of the twentieth century, scholars like White and Steward returned to cultural evolution, avoiding most of the mistakes of the unilineal evolutionists. White emphasized the importance of technology, Steward of adaptation to the local environment, in making cultures the way they are. Both men thought that a group's methods of acquiring resources (energy, food, and so forth) from nature are the main influences on cul-

ture. Both also believed that anthropology is a science, whose main objective is to explain cultural differences and similarities.

5. Contemporary cultural anthropologists are enormously diverse in their theoretical orientations. One very broad modern division is whether ethnology is a scientific enterprise or a humanistic study.

6. Scientifically oriented anthropologists are not all alike, for they differ in their interests and theoretical perspectives. Two examples are sociobiology/evolutionary psychology and cultural materialism. Sociobiology emphasizes that humans are part of nature and that, like other animals, most of our behavior helps us transmit our genes to future generations. Materialists argue that how a given people organizes its groups and activities to acquire energy and materials from their natural environment is the major explanation for other aspects of their cultural system. To materialists, cultural differences and similarities ultimately can be explained by factors such as environment, technology, production, and economic organization.

7. In contrast, humanistically oriented anthropologists mistrust all generalized explanations of cultural phenomena. Interpretive anthropologists emphasize the uniqueness of each culture and favor studying, appreciating, and interpreting each culture individually. This makes them suspicious of the validity of most comparative studies. Postmodernists think that science in general has no particular claim to Truth and that many scientific ideas taught by schools and colleges reflect power relationships in the wider social and cultural context.

8. Contemporary anthropologists, then, do not agree among themselves on many fundamental questions, including even the major objectives of their field. Their lack of consensus, however, is understandable, given that their (human) subjects are self-conscious and willful beings; that anthropologists cannot experiment with people's lives; that total objectivity in fieldwork is impossible; and that the field itself studies such diverse subjects that a single theoretical orientation is unlikely to be able to encompass all of them.

Key Terms

unilineal evolution
historical particularism
diffusionists
configurationalism
functionalism

scientific approach
humanistic approach
sociobiology (evolutionary
  psychology)

cultural materialism
interpretive anthropology
postmodernism

InfoTrac College Edition Terms

cultural evolution
animism
Franz Boas
cultural diffusion

sociobiology and behavior
cultural materialism
Clifford Geertz

postmodern anthropology
  (also postmodernism
  anthropology)

Suggested Readings

Among the volumes that discuss the history of cultural anthropology in detail are:

Barnard, Alan. *History and Theory in Anthropology.* Cambridge University Press, 2000.

  Brief overview of the history of anthropology theory, covering all the approaches mentioned in this chapter.

Salzman, Philip. *Understanding Culture: An Introduction to Anthropological Theory.* Prospect Heights, Ill.: Waveland Press, 2001.

  Very brief overview of anthropological theories, using somewhat different terminology than that used here.

There are two comprehensive readers covering the history of anthropological theory. Both include introductions by the editors as well as key original works by important anthropologists:

Bohannan, Paul, and Mark Glazer, eds. *High Points in Anthropology.* 2nd ed. New York: Knopf, 1988.

McGee, R. Jon, and Richard L. Warms, eds. *Anthropological Theory: An Introductory History.* 2nd ed. Mountain View, Calif.: Mayfield, 2000.

To understand the contemporary divisions between the scientific and humanistic approaches, consult some of the following works:

Geertz, Clifford. *The Interpretation of Cultures.* New York: Basic Books, 1973.

  Collected articles by one of the founders of the American interpretive approach. Three articles are especially well

known: (1) "Thick Description: Towards an Interpretive Theory of Culture," (2) "The Impact of the Concept of Culture on the Concept of Man," and (3) "Deep Play: Notes on the Balinese Cockfight."

Geertz, Clifford. *Local Knowledge: Further Essays on Interpretive Anthropology.* New York: Basic Books, 2000.

  Another compendium of some of Geertz's best known essays.

Harris, Marvin. *Cannibals and Kings.* New York: Random, 1977.

  Intensification hypothesis of cultural evolution is explained and illustrated. Easy reading and an excellent example of materialist thought.

Johnson, Allen W., and Timothy Earle. *The Evolution of Human Societies.* 2nd ed. Stanford, Calif.: Stanford University Press, 2000.

  Theoretical and factual treatment of cultural evolution. Conceptualizes increasing complexity as shifting from family level through local level to regional level, with examples illustrating the cultures of each level.

Marcus, George E., and Michael M. J. Fischer. *Anthropology as Cultural Critique.* Chicago and London: University of Chicago Press, 1986.

  An influential book written from the humanist perspective. Discusses changes in anthropology and ethnography since the 1970s. Argues that anthropologists should take on the task of critiquing their own culture.

Companion Website for This Book

The Wadsworth Anthropology Resource Center
http://anthropology.wadsworth.com

The companion website that accompanies *Humanity: An Introduction to Cultural Anthropology,* Sixth Edition, includes a rich array of material, including online anthropological video clips, to help you in the study of cultural anthropology and the specific topics covered in this chapter. Begin by clicking on Student Resources. Next, click on Cultural Anthropology, and then on the cover image for this book. You have now arrived at the Student Resources home page and have the option of choosing one of several chapter resources.

Applying Anthropology. Begin your study of cultural anthropology by clicking on Applying Anthropology. Here you will find useful information on careers, graduate school programs in applied anthropology, and internships you might wish to pursue. You will also find real-world examples of working anthropologists applying the skills and methods of anthropology to help solve serious world problems.

Research Online. Click here to find a wealth of Web links that will facilitate your study of anthropology. Divided into different fields of study, specific websites are starting points for Internet research. You will be guided to rich anthropology websites that will help you prepare for class, complete course assignments, and actually do research on the Web.

InfoTrac College Edition Exercises. From the pull-down menu, select the chapter you are presently studying. Select InfoTrac College Edition Exercises from the list of resources. These exercises utilize InfoTrac College Edition's vast database of articles and help you explore the numerous uses of the search word, *culture.*

Study Aids for This Chapter. Improve your knowledge of key terms by using flash cards and study the learning objectives. Take the practice quiz, receive your results, and email them to your instructor. Access these resources from the chapter and resource pull-down menus.

Chapter Five

METHODS OF INVESTIGATION

Ethnographic Methods

Ethnographic Fieldwork

Problems and Issues in Field Research

Fieldwork as a Rite of Passage

Ethnohistory

Comparative Methods

Cross-Cultural Comparisons

Controlled Historical Comparisons

© Documentary Educational Resources

Margaret Mead's highly innovative field studies in Samoa and New Guinea made her one of the most widely read anthropologists of the twentieth century.

EVERY SCIENCE HAS A SET of methods used by its practitioners. Cultural anthropologists are primarily interested in human ways of life—particularly the cultural differences and similarities that exist among the world's peoples. Over the decades, anthropologists have developed certain methods of investigating human cultures. These methods are the subject of this chapter.

ANTHROPOLOGICAL METHODS of investigation fall into two broad categories. The first is **ethnographic methods,** which involve the collection and analysis of descriptive data from a single society or several closely related societies. The end product of ethnographic research is either a case study describing the cultural system of some people (e.g., the way of life of the Cheyenne) or a descriptive account of some aspect of a people's cultural system (such as the Cheyenne religion). The second category is **comparative methods,** which involve attempts to test hypotheses about relations between certain aspects of cultural systems by using comparative ethnographic data from a number of societies. The product of comparative research is usually a monograph or article that tries to generalize about causal relations between cultural phenomena.

So ANTHROPOLOGICAL RESEARCH has two purposes: (1) to collect and record new data about specific people (ethnography), and (2) to expand our theoretical understanding of human cultural systems in general through comparative analysis. We first discuss the methods used to describe a single people and then summarize how anthropologists use descriptive accounts to test hypotheses.

Ethnographic Methods

There are two sources of cultural data about a particular people: the living members of the society and written accounts or other records about that group of people. Collecting cultural data by studying and interviewing living members of a society is called **ethnographic fieldwork.** Studying a people's culture using written accounts and other records is termed **ethnohistoric research.**

Ethnographic Fieldwork

Ethnographic fieldwork involves the collection of cultural data from living individuals. The researcher lives with or close to the people being studied and interacts with them on a day-to-day basis for a long period, usually a year or more. Not infrequently, the anthropologist has to learn the group's language and behave according to the group's social norms. By its very nature, fieldwork fosters a close personal relationship between the researcher and members of the society being studied. This social closeness distinguishes anthropologists from other social scientists.

Anthropologists have always used fieldwork as the primary method for collecting cultural information. Over the past century the objective of fieldwork has changed, and with it the data-gathering techniques. Today, a number of techniques are used in the course of any research project.

Interviewing is the most basic method of collecting cultural data. The anthropologist asks questions and elicits answers from members of the society being studied. Interviews may be structured or unstructured. A *structured interview* consists of a limited number of specific questions. It may take the form of a questionnaire that the researcher fills in as the questions are answered. This type of interview is best suited for collecting general quantitative data about the group. For example, most research begins with a census of the community: the number of people in each family, their ages and relationships, and basic economic information about the family. In this manner, the researcher constructs demographic and eco-

nomic profiles of the group. Structured interviews are also used to create genealogies. Most research requires a clear knowledge of how group members are related to one another. Genealogies are important in understanding the social and economic behavior of individuals beyond the immediate family. There are, however, limits to the utility of structured interviews.

In *unstructured interviews* the researcher asks open-ended questions, hoping that the respondent will elaborate on the answers. The questions may be general, about family life, marriage, a particular religious ritual, or economic activity. Most cultural data are collected through unstructured interviews. In these interviews the researcher learns the cultural explanations for information collected in the structured interviews.

Although it is the source of most cultural data, interviewing has severe limitations. The problem usually is not with the answers given by the members of the group, but rather with the questions asked by the researcher. What is relevant or irrelevant to the proper understanding of a particular cultural phenomenon depends on the culture of the individuals involved. Initially, the researcher does not understand the cultural context of the data and thus does not know what questions need to be asked and answered. The early stages of a research project are often characterized by "shotgun" questioning as the anthropologist seeks to learn enough about the culture to ask the right questions. Through interviewing, a researcher can gain a good basic knowledge of a culture's major structural features. However, no matter how knowledgeable and willing the respondents might be, verbal descriptions in themselves are incomplete and do not enable the researcher to gain an in-depth knowledge of the people or an understanding of the true dynamics of their culture.

To understand the limitations of interviewing, ask yourself this question: If an anthropologist from another culture asked you to describe a baseball game, what would you say? How complete would your description be? Chances are, if you are an avid fan, you could relate enough information for the anthropologist to gain a basic understanding of the game. You could tell how many players there are on each side and explain the basic rules about balls, strikes, runs, errors, and innings. From memory alone, it is highly unlikely that you would explain everything that might occur during a game. You would probably give the researcher an idealized model of a baseball game. Certain facts would be left untold, not because you were hiding them but because they are either so commonplace or unusual that they are not part of your consciousness concerning the game. Interviews alone can give the researcher only a simplified overview of a particular cultural phenomenon, an idealized model.

If researchers want to truly understand baseball, they cannot simply talk to someone about it; they need to see a game. In fact, researchers should observe several games and discuss what occurred with a knowledgeable person. It would be even better for researchers to participate, at least in a minor way, in a game. Only by combining interviewing with observing and participating can one begin to understand the rules and dynamics of the game. So it is with the study of any cultural phenomenon.

During the late nineteenth and early twentieth centuries, anthropologists relied primarily on interviews to collect cultural data. This technique was well suited to the anthropological objectives of that time. Early American anthropologists were concerned with collecting general cultural information about Native American groups. These groups had already been placed on reservations, and their economies and cultures had drastically changed. Anthropologists wanted to record earlier Native American lifestyles before all knowledge of the pre-reservation period was lost. The only way the aboriginal culture of these peoples could be studied was by interviewing individuals who had grown to adulthood before the reservations were created. In a relatively short period, anthropologists were able to collect, and thus preserve, a vast body of general descriptive data on Native American cultures.

In the 1920s anthropologists' interest began to shift from just describing the general culture of a society to attempting to understand the basic dynamics of cultural systems. In other words, anthropologists wanted to see how these systems worked and how their parts fit together. A leader in this change was Bronislaw Malinowski, mentioned earlier in the discussion of functionalism in Chapter 4, who popularized a new data-collection technique called **participant observation.** Anthropologists no longer merely recorded and analyzed people's statements. To a greater or lesser extent, they took up residence with the people they were studying and began trying to learn about the culture by observing people in their daily lives and participating in their daily activities.

Participant observation has often been misinterpreted, even by some anthropologists who have taken it too literally. It does not mean becoming a full participant in the activities of the people—in other words, "going native." The emphasis of this technique is more on observation than on participation. Participant observation usually does require that one live in the community, for only by doing so can one observe and record the behavior of individuals as they go about their daily work, visit their friends, interact with their relatives, participate in rituals, and so on. These observations of behavior serve to generate new questions. Why does a man share food with some families but not with others? Why do some men wear a particular type of hat or headdress? Does a particular color of clothing have any meaning? Some behaviors have significance, others do not. For example, variations in types of headdress may be merely the result of personal preferences, or they may reflect status differences. The color may or may not have special significance. In American society, black symbolizes mourning, but in other societies covering one's body with white clay symbolizes the same emotion. Participant observation allows the researcher to collect more detailed data than does interviewing alone, and thus it makes possible a deeper understanding of interrelations between cultural phenomena.

Firsthand observations of the members of a society also allow the researcher to see how people diverge from the culturally defined, idealized model of behavior. An incident that occurred while Malinowski was working in the Trobriand Islands illustrates the divergence between cultural norms—the way people say they ought to behave—and the way they actually behave. One day Malinowski heard a commotion in the village and discovered that a young boy in a neighboring village had committed suicide by climbing a palm tree and flinging himself onto the beach. In his earlier questioning of the islanders, Malinowski had been told that sexual relations between a man and his mother's sister's daughters were prohibited. On inquiring into the suicide of the young boy, he found that the boy had been sexually involved with his mother's sister's daughter, and that in fact such incestuous relationships were not rare. So long as such liaisons were not mentioned in public, they were ignored. In this particular case, the girl's ex-boyfriend had become angry and publicly exposed the transgression. Although everyone in the village already knew of this incestuous relationship, by making it public the ex-boyfriend exposed his rival to ridicule, thus causing him to commit suicide. It is doubtful that such behavior could have been discovered only by interviewing individuals.

Problems and Issues in Field Research

Before we can begin discussing methods of research we need to examine the issue of ethics. In ethnographic fieldwork we are studying the culture of living human beings. What do we tell them about what we are researching and why? What kinds of obligations do we have to them?

Anthropologists have moral obligations not just to their profession, but also to the members of the communities they study. The American Anthropological Association has developed a formal code of ethics for its members. This code applies to all anthropologists, physical anthropologists, archaeologists, and linguists, as well as cultural anthropologists. We will briefly discuss some of the major points that are relevant to cultural research. (For the complete text of the code of ethics see www.aaanet.org/committees/ethics/ethcode.htm). In conducting field research, the primary ethical obligations are to the people being studied. The primary concern must be that the research does not harm the safety, dignity, or privacy of the individuals helping in the research or that of the community as a whole. Researchers should also be open with both individuals and the community as to the nature of the study and what use will be made of the findings. Obligations to the people being studied supersede the goal of gaining new knowledge and thus obligations to the profession as a whole. If it appears that a particular project may be harmful to a community, then it should not be undertaken or it should be discontinued. Although most anthropological studies are read by other academics, it must be assumed that nonacademics will read them as well. Thus collected data that might be misused by others, either within or outside the community, to harm individual members or the community as a whole, should not be reported.

It is easy to say that a researcher should do no harm to the community; in practice it is not always so clear. Thus anthropologists are always confronting moral dilemmas. What should they study and what shouldn't they study? What should they include in their published accounts and what should remain unsaid? The difficulty with the "no harm" doctrine is that the academic world determines what is "harm." Native peoples may not see it in the same way. (See Globalization: Who Owns Culture?)

Every fieldwork experience is, to some extent, unique. Specific problems differ, depending on the individual characteristics of the researcher, the nature of the community, and the particular questions being studied. There are, however, several difficulties that, to varying degrees, affect virtually every field research situation: (1) stereotyping, (2) defining the fieldworker's role in the community and developing rapport, and (3) identifying and interviewing consultants.

Stereotyping. When we think of stereotypes—preconceived generalizations concerning a particular group of people—we usually think only of their effects on the perceptions of one party of a relationship. Anthropologists ask themselves how they can overcome their own stereotypes and cultural biases about the people they study. Stereotyping, however, is a two-way street. Every society has stereotypes concerning members of other societies and of ethnic and racial groups. Thus, although the goal is for anthropologists to put aside their personal stereotypes sufficiently to research the cultural system of another people with some degree of objectivity, those with whom the ethnographer will be living and working will not have shelved their stereotypes. Most anthropologists are of European ancestry, yet most subjects of anthropological research are non-European peoples. Even if a particular anthropologist is of Asian, African, or Native American ancestry, a similar problem exists because anthropologists seldom belong to the local community they study and thus are outsiders. As a result, an anthropologist who enters another community must contend with local stereotypes about the ethnic group with which the anthropologist is identified.

In the case of anthropologists of European ancestry, local stereotyping has most frequently been derived from contact with a limited range of individuals, such as missionaries, soldiers, colonial officials, and government bureaucrats. Regardless of the nature and intensity of this contact, most non-Western peoples have a well-developed idea about the expected behavior of such individuals. The tendency of local people to fit the ethnographer into one of their stereotypical categories can at times prove a burden for fieldworkers. Anthropologists' behavior seldom conforms to the model that the local people have developed. Previous contacts with Europeans and Euro-Americans have often been structured in such a manner as to place the "native" in the position of social inferior. Thus, an anthropologist attempting to gain social acceptance in such a society is typically met with suspicion, if not with hostility. The types of questions anthropologists ask about behavior and beliefs frequently arouse suspicions further and elicit guarded answers. Why does this researcher want to know about our family structure, our political organization, our ritual secrets? What is the person going to do with this information? While the anthropologist is trying to understand the community, the members of the community are attempting to understand the anthropologist's motives. Depending on the nature of previous contacts, some types of questions may provoke more suspicion than others. For example, a minority or tribal group involved

Who Owns Culture?

Since the end of World War II there have been tremendous political changes in the world. The European colonial empires are now gone. Even in countries such as Australia, New Zealand, Canada, and the United States, the native indigenous peoples have increasing political autonomy. No longer do European peoples politically dominate and control most of the other peoples of the world. Although most of the major political issues have been settled, there are many other issues that are yet to be resolved. Disputes over the ownership and use of traditional cultural and intellectual properties are emerging as one of the most emotional and important of these issues. Small indigenous peoples, as well as the national governments of former colonies, are increasingly demanding the repatriation of the human remains, art treasures, sacred objects, and historic items taken from them and now housed in museums and research institutions in Europe and North America. Just as significant to most of these groups is what they see as the continued exploitation by Europeans and Euro-Americans of the intangible expressions of their cultural and intellectual traditions as well as the appropriation and commercialization of their artistic traditions, including art, music, songs, and dances; the publication and production of what they see as degrading, books, photographs, images, and films concerning their cultures and histories; and the exploitation of their traditional knowledge, particularly botanical knowledge, by outside corporations in the development of drugs and other marketable products. Globalization has resulted in the emergence of what might be termed cultural nationalism, as ethnic/religious groups, by various means, attempt to assert proprietary rights over the use of their history, their cultural traditions and knowledge, and even the public use of their images.

The specific issues and demands vary greatly from one ethnic/religious group to another, and even from individual to individual within these groups. Some groups claim absolute control over anything produced about their history or culture—books, photographs, movies, and the like. In other cases the issues involve the misuse of specific cultural elements such as traditional designs, songs, music, or botanical knowledge. Finally in many cases, there are objections to specific books, movies, or advertising images that they feel are insulting or demeaning. Over the last 20 years there have been numerous international, national, regional, and ethnic group meetings and conferences held to address the issues of cultural and intellectual property rights of native peoples. The result has been the creation of numerous organizations and a bewildering array of declarations, position papers, and demands. Here we are just going to limit our discussion to some specific groups and issues illustrative of some of the problems.

Many ethnic organizations today are claiming total control over any portrayals of their people. In 1995, a group calling themselves the All-Apache Culture Committee claimed exclusive control over all things relating to the Apache peoples: culture, history, and all popular and academic materials. They further stated that henceforth anyone wishing to write about the Apaches will have to gain permission of the tribes. Similarly, with the encouragement and support of their local national governments, the San peoples have formed the Working Group of Indigenous Minorities in Southern Africa (WIMSA) to protect their intellectual property rights, art, symbols, folklore, songs, and dances, as well as their medical knowledge of plants. In 1997 WIMSA announced that from now on they would require payments from the media and from researchers wishing to document or study San life and that legal action would be taken against companies for the unauthorized use of San photographs in books, postcards, advertisements, and tourist promotions. There are numerous understandable reasons why the Apaches, the San, and many other indigenous peoples want to exert control over the use of their history and culture and the public use of their image. Many of the books and movies about the Apaches unfairly portray them as ruthless savages, instead of the victims of ethnic cleansing and genocide. The San find that in books and films their traditional culture is frequently ridiculed or portrayed in an extremely degrading manner. Like many indigenous peoples, the Apaches and the San feel that not only are outsiders (usually Europeans or Euro-Americans) profiting by making use of their cultural traditions and history, they are being dehumanized in the process.

It is not just smaller indigenous peoples who find objectionable portrayals of their history and cultural and religious beliefs in Western literature. Hindu civilization is one of the great ancient civilizations of the world. Numbering almost a billion adherents, the Hindus are today one of the world's three largest religious traditions. Like the Apaches and the San, many Hindus have also become incensed about Western writers and their interpretations of Hindu religious beliefs. Recently the works of three American religious scholars have become the center of controversy. Attacks on the works of all three have been posted on web pages. One has been physically threatened, via the Internet, and the Indian edition of his book withdrawn. Another had an egg thrown at her during a public lecture in London. In the most extreme case, not only was the Indian edition of his book recalled, his collaborator in India was physically assaulted, and a mob burned manuscripts in the library in India where he had worked. Some Indian government officials have even threatened to ask for his extradition to India to stand trial for defamation.

While a people do not and can not "own" their history or culture, Western law and even most non-Western legal systems recognize that certain elements within a culture can be "owned" by individuals or groups. Under Western law and international law unique individual creations, inventions, and discoveries may be patented or copyrighted. For example, the Northwest

Coast peoples of Canada and the United States make use of a number of standard designs that are painted or carved on poles, houses, and other items. These designs are the traditionally recognized property of specific groups and even individuals within these societies. Only these groups or individuals have the right to use them. However, today other people frequently make use of these same designs for commercial purposes, printing them on T-shirts, on tourist's posters, on postcards, and in numerous other ways. Are the legal rights of these indigenous groups and individuals, relative to the public use or display of their designs, any different from those of companies who have copyrighted their corporate logos and thus control their use? Similarly among many indigenous peoples, traditional songs, music, and even stories are frequently the property of particular individuals, families, or groups. Although existing only as oral traditions, many indigenous peoples argue that the same copyright protection accorded published songs, music, and stories in other societies should be extended to them as well.

Closely related is the issue of the commercial use of particular elements of traditional cultural knowledge. In the last part of Chapter 18 we are going to discuss the important botanical knowledge of many indigenous people. Some indigenous people are arguing that researchers should not be able to collect traditional plant knowledge and patent and commercialize it without compensation. The San peoples of southern Africa chew slices of the hoodia, a succulent plant, as an appetite suppressant when they are hungry. Based on San cultural knowledge, in 1997 the South African Council for Scientific and Industrial Research (CSIR) was able to isolate the active ingredient in the hoodia cactus and patent it as an appetite suppressant. Eventually the CSIR was sold development rights to Pfizer (U.S.) and to Phytopharm (U.K.). These pharmaceutical companies are planning to market it in the form of a diet pill. This is not a unique case; many of the new drugs being marketed by pharmaceutical companies are based on traditional indigenous plant knowledge. In most cases this traditional knowledge is unique to a single people, such as in the case of the San. Many people argue that the indigenous people should receive royalties for the commercial use of their traditional knowledge. Pharmaceutical companies argue that it

costs them millions of dollars to isolate the active ingredients and develop them into a marketable drug. On the other hand, one may ask, how many generations of trial-and-error research were required before an indigenous people discovered the beneficial use of a particular plant? The difficult research is the initial discovery that a particular plant has certain medicinal properties. The easy part is isolating the active ingredients and making the "new" drug. Are pharmaceutical companies economic profiteers, "biopirates," exploiting the traditional knowledge of indigenous peoples?

The controversy over cultural and intellectual properties is just beginning and little meaningful progress has been made toward resolving the wide range of disputes. As a result, many Native American tribes today require formal permission for anyone to conduct research or even take pictures on their reservations. Similarly, many countries are increasingly regulating the studies of foreign researchers. Other than restricting scholars' access to sources, there is little that most indigenous people and countries can directly do to control the writing of histories or cultural descriptions concerning them. Perhaps it is not surprising that, lacking any legal means, some peoples, such as in the case of some Hindu leaders, have resorted to extralegal means.

In this era of globalization a greater understanding and acceptance of cultural differences is critical. At the same time, the cultural and intellectual rights and interests of all peoples have to be recognized.

Critical Thinking Questions

1. Do indigenous people, or any people, have the inherent right to control their own history and what is written about them? Do indigenous people "own" their own cultural knowledge and creations? What rights, if any, should scholars recognize? Can such rights be made compatible with the basic academic ideas of free inquiry and academic freedom?

2. Is the academic community, particularly the humanities and social sciences, overly dominated by European and Euro-American scholars? Does the academic community, not just cultural anthropology, need to be more inclusive of non-Western scholars?

in some illegal or illicit activity—such as smuggling, poaching, or growing drugs—may wonder if the anthropologist will inform government authorities. Members of groups that have been more exposed to Western culture usually assume that the ethnographer's objective is to make money and that researchers become wealthy by publishing books.

In other cases, members of the community may be aware that Europeans and Euro-Americans do not approve of or believe in certain types of behaviors, and few people will disclose information on topics they think will be met with disapproval or scorn. This reticence is particularly evident for certain types of religious beliefs and practices. As a result of extensive activities of Christian

© National Anthropological Archives/Smithsonian Institution

▲ Among the earliest anthropological researchers and writers was Francis LaFlesche (1857–1932), an Omaha Indian from Nebraska.

missionaries, most non-Western peoples are well aware that Westerners usually deny the validity of witchcraft and the existence of werewolves. Members of societies with these beliefs are usually hesitant about discussing such subjects with Westerners. They are understandably reluctant to talk openly about an uncle who they believe can turn himself into a deer or a snake with someone who will probably view what they say as ridiculous. Likewise, they probably would not say that their father had been killed by a witch if they thought that the outsider did not believe in witchcraft.

Developing a Role and Rapport. Often against a background of suspicion and distrust, an anthropologist has to develop a rapport with the members of the community. *Rapport* in this sense means acceptance to the degree that a working relationship is possible, although ethnographers are rarely, if ever, totally accepted by the people among whom they work. However, over a period of time most anthropologists succeed in gaining some degree of trust and friendship, at least with a few members of the group.

The particular role or roles that anthropologists eventually define for themselves within a society vary greatly with the circumstances of the particular situation. Depending on the amount and nature of research funding, an anthropologist may be an important economic resource, paying wages to interpreters and assistants or distributing

desirable goods as gifts. Anthropologists with a car or truck frequently find themselves providing needed transportation for members of the community. Ethnographers may also provide comic relief by asking "silly questions," behaving in a funny manner, making childlike errors in speaking the language, and generally being amusing to have around. Researchers may also be a source of information about the outside world, disclosing information to which local people would not otherwise have access. Sometimes community members are as curious about the anthropologist's society as the anthropologist is about theirs. Or the anthropologist may be considered just a harmless nuisance. During the course of research, the typical fieldworker adopts all these roles plus many others.

Identifying and Interviewing Consultants. Ethnographers learn a good deal about people simply by living among them and participating in many of their activities. This rather casual, informal participant observation provides a good feel for the general pattern of life. But for most purposes, observation and participation alone are insufficient. We not only want to know what people are doing but also why they are doing it. Because certain realms of culture are not observable (e.g., religious beliefs, myths, stories, and social values), the researcher has to interview members of the group.

An individual who supplies the ethnographer with information is called a **consultant** or **informant.** Field research involves the help of many consultants, who sometimes are paid for their services. Just as no one individual is equally well informed about every aspect of our own cultural system, so no one person in another society is equally knowledgeable about every aspect of that society's way of life. Women are more knowledgeable than men concerning certain things, and vice versa. Shamans and priests know more about religious rituals than other people do. The elderly members of the community are usually most knowledgeable about myths, stories, and histories. Thus, the anthropologist has to attempt to identify and interview those people who are most knowledgeable about particular subjects. Individuals whom the local community considers to be expert in some particular area are known as **key consultants** or **key informants.**

A number of factors affect the quality and accuracy of the data collected through interviewing. The people being studied seldom understand fully what the anthropologist is trying to accomplish. In some instances, especially among minority populations, there may be a deliberate attempt to deceive the researcher. For example, collecting livestock-ownership data on the Navajo reservation can at times prove difficult. The total number of livestock on the reservation is controlled by the tribe, and individual stockowners have a permit that allows them to keep a certain number of animals. Because some people keep more stock than their permits allow, they are reluctant to disclose the actual number in their herds. There is also the problem of humorous deception. Osage men wear a roach made out of deer tail and turkey beard or porcupine hair on their heads at dances. During a dance, an Osage was overheard telling an inquisitive visitor that these roaches were made of horse tails, and that a young Osage male proved his manhood by cutting the hair for his roach from the tail of the meanest horse he could find. In this case, the Osage was simply having fun at the expense of a visitor, but anthropologists also encounter this problem. To get around these and other difficulties, anthropologists try to interview a number of individuals separately about specific points to gain several independent verifications.

Cultural barriers also make it difficult to collect certain types of data. For example, collecting genealogies is not always as easy as it might seem because in many societies it is customary not to speak the names of the dead. Among the Yąnomamö of Venezuela and Brazil, not only is it taboo to speak the names of the dead but it is considered discourteous to speak the names of prominent living men, for whom kinship terms are used whenever possible. When ethnographer Napoleon Chagnon persisted in his attempts to collect genealogies, the Yąnomamö responded by inventing a series of fictitious genealogical relationships. Only after five months of intensive research did he discover the hoax. When he mentioned some of the names he had collected during a visit to a neighboring village, the people responded with "uncontrollable laughter" because his informants had made up names such as "hairy rectum" and "eagle shit" to avoid speaking the real names.

Fieldwork as a Rite of Passage

Fieldwork is important to cultural anthropologists not just because it is the major source of our data on human cultures but because it is a key aspect of the anthropologist's education. It is one thing to read ethnographies about other ways of life, but it is something quite different to live among and interact with individuals from another cultural tradition every day for a year or more. As we have seen, anthropologists usually live in the native community, submerging themselves in the social life of the people, living in native dwellings, eating local foods, learning the language, and participating as fully as an

outsider is allowed in daily activities. Living as social minorities, usually for the first time in their lives, anthropologists depend on the goodwill of people whose norms and values they neither totally understand nor completely accept. Under these conditions, participant observers have to adjust their activities to fit the cultural ideas and behavior patterns of the people. This modification of the fieldworker's own behavior is a necessary part of learning about the community. Because fieldworkers usually work alone, they are socially and physically vulnerable to members of the community. During the course of their research, anthropologists will violate, or at least be perceived as violating, some of the societal norms of behavior. Such incidents may destroy the rapport gained with some key consultants or result in the researcher's being ostracized. In serious cases, the fieldworker may become the target of physical violence.

When in the field, except on rare occasions, the anthropologist is there as the uninvited guest of the community. Regardless of how researchers may rationalize their work as being for the long-term good of the community or humanity, they are basically there to serve their own needs and interests. If a serious problem develops between the anthropologist and members of the community, the fieldworker must bear the primary responsibility and blame.

The fieldwork experience tests and taxes the attitude of cultural relativity that anthropologists teach in their classrooms. It is easy to discuss the concept of relativity in a university setting, but it is more difficult to apply this concept to one's own situation. Regardless of which society it is, certain cultural aspects will offend one's own cultural norms and values. For example, according to the anthropologist's own cultural standards, some local people might "abuse" certain family members or certain powerful leaders might "exploit" lower-ranking members of the society. As the fieldworker develops friendships, this "abuse" or "exploitation" frequently becomes personalized. Under what circumstances, if ever, an anthropologist should attempt to intervene and try to impose her or his cultural standards on the members of another society poses a real and personal dilemma. In theory, such intervention is never permissible, but in real-life situations the answer is not always so clear.

Many people experience a kind of psychological trauma when surrounded by people speaking a language they cannot fully understand and can speak only imperfectly, eating foods that are strange, seeing architecture that is alien, and observing people using gestures and behaving in ways they either do not comprehend or do not approve of. The strange sounds, smells, tastes, sights, and behaviors result in disorientation. Out of their normal cultural context, fieldworkers do not understand what is happening around them, yet realize that their own actions are often being misunderstood. The symptoms of **culture shock** are psychological and sometimes even physiological: paranoia, anxiety, longing for the folks back home, nausea, hypochondria, and, frequently, diarrhea.

The attempts by ethnographers to maintain their relativistic perspective and objectivity in their daily interaction with members of the other society usually compound the normal trauma of culture shock. Socially isolated and unable to release their frustrations and anxieties through conversations with sympathetic others, they often have to cope with their psychological difficulties alone.

For many anthropologists, much of their time in the field is extremely traumatic, and as a result, most anthropologists view fieldwork as a rite of passage. More than any other aspect of their training, fieldwork transforms students of anthropology into professional anthropologists. Although many overemphasize the importance of fieldwork, it is undeniably a significant educational experience. Most individuals return from their fieldwork with a different perspective on themselves and their own culture. Fieldwork often teaches us as much about ourselves as about those we are supposed to be studying.

Ethnohistory

The study of past cultural systems through the use of written records is called **ethnohistory.** Since the late nineteenth century, anthropologists have used written materials in their studies, but the importance of this research has become widely recognized only since the 1970s. The growing interest in ethnohistory has come with the realization that non-Western societies have changed far more dramatically over the past few hundred years than had previously been thought.

Like historians who study their society's past, ethnohistorians make use of such materials as published books and articles, newspapers, archival documents, diaries, journals, maps, drawings, and photographs. Not surprisingly, many scholars treat history and ethnohistory as if they were synonymous. There are, however, critical—yet frequently overlooked—differences that distinguish ethnohistory from history.

- An ethnohistorian is primarily interested in reconstructing the cultural system of the people. The actual historical events themselves are of interest only because they cast light on the cultural system or changes in the system.

- Historical events have little significance outside the cultural context of the peoples involved. Ethnohistorians study nonliterate peoples. Thus, whereas historians can use accounts recorded by members of the society being studied, ethnohistorians have to use accounts recorded by members of other, literate societies. As a result, the problem of interpreting accounts is usually more difficult for the ethnohistorian than for the historian.

The problem of interpretation raises an additional question about the validity of particular reports. Not only do we have to ask about the accuracy of the account but we also have to ask how knowledgeable the recorder was about the cultural context of the events. Ethnohistorians use certain criteria to evaluate the potential validity of an account. How long did the writer live among these people? Did the observer speak the language? What was the observer's role? Soldiers, missionaries, traders, and government officials have different views, biases, and access to information.

The difficulty with ethnohistory is that no hard-and-fast rules can be used in evaluating these data. The longer an individual lived among members of a particular society and the better the person spoke the language, the more reliable the account should be; however, this cannot be automatically assumed. In some cases, the writer may have had little interest in the people, perhaps because the contacts were only related to a job. This attitude is evident in the accounts of many traders and government officials. In other cases, the account may be self-serving, with individuals attempting to enhance their careers. Thus, sometimes soldiers and government officials falsified their official reports. Ethnocentrism is still another factor. Missionary accounts, in particular, often demonstrate overt bias against local customs and beliefs; one has to remember that individuals become missionaries because they are avid believers. However, some of the most objective accounts of other societies were written by missionaries who were scholars themselves.

Thus, in ethnohistoric research, there is no simple way to evaluate a particular document or account. At best, a single event may be recorded in several independent accounts that can each be used to verify the accuracy and interpretation of the others. Unfortunately, multiple observations are the exception, not the rule.

A final limitation on the use of ethnohistoric materials is that seldom are all aspects of a particular society evenly reported. For example, data on economic activities may be the most abundant, whereas information on religious

Marshall Sahlins, Gananath Obeyesekere, and Captain James Cook

In January of 1778 two British ships under the command of Captain James Cook discovered the Hawaiian Islands. They stayed only three days before continuing on to the northern Pacific. In the winter of 1778–1779, they returned and for seven weeks sailed among the islands without making landfall. Finally, on January 17, 1779, they landed on the large island of Hawaii. This second landing was greeted by thousands of Hawaiians, including King Kalani'opu'u. Cook was presented with a great feathered cloak and cap and was greeted with rituals, including a multitude of people prostrating themselves before him and chanting "Lono." On February 4, Cook and his ships departed with a spectacular sendoff. However, the weather quickly turned bad, and one ship sprung its mast, forcing the expedition to return to the island for repairs. The Hawaiians did not welcome this return. Hostilities soon developed and a battle took place in which Cook was killed.

Scholars have long felt that Cook's visit was identified by the Hawaiians as the return of their god Lono. Using ethnohistoric and ethnographic data Marshall Sahlins reexamined this interpretation in his 1981 study, *Historical Metaphors and Mythical Realities,* and reached the same conclusion.

Lono was a mythical god-king whom the Hawaiians believed periodically returned to the islands and ruled in human form, usurping power from the earthly kings who were representatives of the rival god Ku. Several earlier Hawaiian kings had been identified as Lono ruling on Earth. Every year, during a period called *Makahiki,* a series of rituals were performed and

dedicated to Lono. Lono symbolically returned to the islands at the beginning of Makahiki, at which time the priests of Lono took control of the temples from the priests of Ku. During the four lunar months that followed, the priests of Lono were in charge of rituals. Makahiki ended with Lono being symbolically sacrificed and returning to the sky. With Lono gone, control returned to the king and the priests of Ku, the earthly representatives of Ku.

Sahlins found that as Cook sailed among the islands for seven weeks, the timing and direction of his movements coincidentally corresponded with the mythological movements of the god-king Lono. His landing on January 17 took place at the start of Makahiki; his departure on February 4 corresponded with the end of Makahiki. According to Sahlins, the Hawaiians identified Cook as the personification of Lono, an interpretation further strengthened by Cook when he told them during his departure that he would return the next year.

Cook's untimely return to repair one of his ships was ominously interpreted by the king and priests of Ku as Lono returning to claim earthly powers. Not surprisingly the Hawaiian priests had him killed and viewed the killing as the ritual sacrifice of the rival god-king Lono, which they symbolically reenacted every year.

When Gananath Obeyesekere, a Sri Lankan anthropologist, first heard Sahlins present this interpretation of Cook, he was "taken aback." Why would the Hawaiians think that this European was a god? Drawing from his own knowledge of South

ceremonies and beliefs may be absent or limited. As a result, ethnographic studies based on ethnohistoric research lack the depth and balance of those gleaned from research with living individuals. Despite its problems and limitations, however, ethnohistoric research provides us with the only clues we have to the past of many societies, as well as the key to a vast store of cultural data hitherto untapped.

Comparative Methods

So far we have discussed only how anthropologists collect cultural data on peoples, past and present, using fieldwork and historical materials. We have some cultural data available on more than 1,200 societies. As shown in the following chapters, anthropologists have used these data to demonstrate a wide range of cultural variability among human populations. However, we are not merely

interested in describing particular cultural systems and the range of variability they display. We are also interested in attempting to explain why these differences exist. In other words, anthropologists want to make generalizations concerning cultural systems. Generalizations cannot be made based on the study of a single society; we need methods by which many societies can be compared in a systematic way. The objective of comparative studies is to test hypotheses.

Cross-Cultural Comparisons

The most frequently used comparative method is **cross-cultural comparison.** In this method, hypotheses are tested by examining the statistical correlations between particular cultural variables, using synchronic data drawn from a number of societies. Historical changes in the societies examined are ignored; the societies are compared at whatever period they were studied. This research

Asian peoples, he could not think of a single example of Sri Lankans or other southern Asian peoples seeing the newly arrived Europeans as gods. To Obeyesekere this was but an example of European myth building, in which the European explorer/civilizer becomes a "god" to the natives.

In 1992 Obeyesekere published *The Apotheosis of Captain Cook: European Mythmaking in the Pacific,* in which he challenged Sahlins's interpretation. In his criticism of Sahlins and other Western scholars he touches on a broad range of theoretical and substantive issues. We will cover just two of the major points.

Obeyesekere argues that it was the English themselves who first mythologized Captain Cook. He had already made two successful and daring voyages into the unknown waters of the Pacific. Because of published accounts of these trips Cook had become—in the eyes of the British—the very image of the ideal explorer/civilizer. A competent, courageous, generous, decent, and humane individual who understood and was well liked by the native peoples he encountered, Cook embodied all of the qualities and greatness of civilized humanity. His violent death at the hands of a strange and savage people to whom he had brought the prospects of civilization served only to enhance his mythic stature. In his research, however, Obeyesekere found that Cook, particularly on his third and final voyage, was not the Cook of British mythology. Cook could be brutal with both the natives and his crew, as well as arrogant and not always competent. He also found little contemporary evidence that the

members of the crew thought that the Hawaiians viewed Cook as a god. The idea that Hawaiians identified Cook with Lono dates from early nineteenth-century accounts that were compiled well after the events themselves.

Obeyesekere further argues that still prevalent in Western academic thought is the idea that non-Western peoples, such as the Hawaiians, think differently. According to Obeyesekere, "Implicit . . . is a commonplace assumption of the savage mind that is given to prelogical or mystical thought and in turn is fundamentally opposed to the logical and rational ways of thinking of modern man." Thus, the "childlike" natives lacked rational reflection. Even when anthropologists accept the idea that other people can act rationally, rationality is constrained by the boundaries of their own cultural beliefs; "their thought processes are inflexible; [and] they cannot rationally weigh alternative or multiple courses of action." Thus, Obeyesekere further argues that these implicit and sometimes explicit assumptions about the nature of other peoples underlie the interpretation that Hawaiians thought Captain Cook was a god and that that god was Lono.

In his critique of Sahlins, Obeyesekere raises a critical issue. Does anthropology reflect a Western cultural bias? Are anthropological interpretations of other peoples' behavior a reflection of implicit Eurocentric beliefs about others?

Sources: Sahlins (1981), Obeyesekere (1992), and Sahlins (1995) for his response to Obeyesekere.

method involves three steps. First, the researcher must state the idea as a hypothesis—that is, state it in such a way that it can be supported or not supported ("tested") by data drawn from a large number of human populations. Second, the ethnologist chooses a sample of societies (usually randomly) and studies the ethnographies that describe their way of life. Third, the data collected from these ethnographies are classified and grouped in such a manner that the correlations between variables may be shown statistically. What the researcher is attempting to find is the pattern of association: Do two or more cultural variables consistently occur together or not? In most cases, these tasks are far more difficult than they may sound.

To illustrate how the cross-cultural method is used to test a hypothesis, we shall examine the relations between sorcery and legal systems within a group of societies. Sorcery is discussed in some detail in Chapter 13. Here it is sufficient to know that sorcery is the belief that certain

people (sorcerers) have power, either supernatural or magical, to cause harm to others. Some anthropologists believe that sorcery serves as a means of social control in societies that lack a formalized legal apparatus—courts, police, and so forth—to punish wrongdoers. They argue that people will be reluctant to cause trouble if they believe that a victim of their troublemaking has the ability to use supernatural power to retaliate against them. Overall, societies without a formal legal system should have a greater need for a mechanism such as sorcery to control behavior. So, if the hypothesis that sorcery is a mechanism for social control is correct, we ought to find that sorcery is more important in societies without formal means of punishment than in societies with a specialized legal system.

To see if this hypothesis is true across a variety of societies, we use the cross-cultural method. We determine for many societies (1) the relative degree of importance of sorcery, and (2) whether the society has a formal apparatus for punishing wrongdoing. We make a table in which all the possible combinations of the two cultural elements are recorded:

Sorcery	Specialized Legal Apparatus	
	Absent	Present
Important	A	B
Unimportant	C	D

In the cells of the table we record the number of societies in which the four possible combinations are found. If the hypothesis is supported, we should find that cells A and D contain the greatest number of societies. If the hypothesis is not supported, we should find that the distribution of societies in the cells is random, or that cells B and C contain the greatest number of societies, or some other distribution.

In 1950, Beatrice Whiting conducted such a study by surveying the ethnographic literature for 50 societies. Her results were as follows (Whiting 1950, 87):

Sorcery	Specialized Legal Apparatus	
	Absent	Present
Important	30	5
Unimportant	3	12

On the basis of this comparison, we might conclude that the hypothesis is supported because most of the societies fall into the cells predicted by our hypothesis. We would not worry about the eight societies (the "exceptions") that appear in cells B and C. The hypothesis did not claim that social control was the *only* function of sorcery, so the importance of sorcery in the five societies in cell B might be explained by some other factor. Nor did we claim that sorcery was the *only* way that societies lacking a specialized legal apparatus had to control their members, so the three societies in cell C might have developed some alternative means of social control. (Although outside the scope of this text, statistical tests are available that show how confident a researcher can be that such associations did not occur by chance.)

Some confusions are caused by cross-cultural tabulations such as this. One of the most common is to mistake correlation for causation: Simply because two cultural elements (X and Y) are usually found together does not mean that one (X) has caused the other (Y). Y could have caused X, or both X and Y could have been caused by some third element, W. In the preceding example, it was assumed that the absence of formal legal punishments "caused" many societies to need some other social control mechanism, and that sorcery became important to meet this need. On the basis of the data in the table, we might also conclude that societies

in which sorcery is important have little need for a formal legal apparatus, so they fail to develop one.

To acquire the data needed to test her hypothesis, Whiting read through ethnographic information on all 50 societies in her sample. This approach suffers from several disadvantages. It is so time consuming that only a small number of societies can be included in the sample. There is also the problem of bias by the researcher, who must decide, for example, whether sorcery should be considered "important" or "unimportant" among some people. Borderline cases might get lumped into the category that supports the researcher's hypothesis.

Thanks largely to a lifetime of work by George Murdock, another method is available to modern researchers that partially overcomes these two problems (although it has troubles of its own, to be discussed shortly). In the *Ethnographic Atlas,* Murdock and his associates have summarized information on more than 1,200 societies in the form of coded tables. Each cultural system has codes that show its form of kinship, marriage, economy, religion, political organization, division of labor, and so forth. Contemporary cross-cultural researchers no longer need to search through ethnographies for information relevant to their investigations; rather, they use the information already coded and analyze the results by using a computer. This reduces the bias of the researcher, for whoever coded the information on a particular society had no knowledge of the hypothesis under investigation. It also allows a larger number of societies to be included in a sample because the data can be retrieved far more quickly.

Using cross-cultural methods to see if some specific hypothesis applies to a large number of societies is thus easier today than ever before, but some difficulties still exist. One seems to be inherent in the method itself, which dissects whole cultures into parts ("variables," as we called them) and assigns a value (or "state") to each part. In the preceding example, the variables were sorcery, which had two states (important, unimportant), and specialized legal apparatus, which also had two states (present, absent). To test the hypothesis that the states of these two cultural elements are consistently related, we ignored everything else about them. We also ignored everything else about the societies in the sample, such as their family systems and their economies.

A more familiar example makes the point clearly. One element of cultural systems is the number of gods in whom people believe. For purposes of some specific hypothesis, the possible states of this variable might be monotheism (belief in one god), polytheism (belief in many gods), and no gods. Any researcher who included

© Gideon Mendel/Corbis

▲ Christianity, Judaism, and Islam are all monotheistic and have common historical roots. But Christians and Jews do not pray by prostrating themselves toward Mecca, as these Muslims in South Africa are doing. Should cross-cultural researchers consider all of them one kind of religion, or not?

modern North America in the sample would probably consider our primary religion—Christianity—as monotheistic. Most of the Middle East also would be considered monotheistic. The problem is, can North American monotheism be considered equivalent to the Middle Eastern monotheisms? If we consider them the same, we ignore the differences between the worship of the Christian God, the Jewish Yahweh, and the Islamic Allah. When we lump these three varieties of monotheism together into a single kind of religion, we distort them to some degree.

Cross-cultural studies examine data ahistorically, or without reference to time. In other words, the cultural system of a particular society is treated as timeless or unchanging. Thus, in cross-cultural studies and the *Ethnographic Atlas,* there is "a" cultural system coded for the Cheyenne: Cheyenne cultural system circa 1850. However, the cultural system of a society is never stable but constantly changing. For example, today the Cheyenne live in houses, drive cars and trucks, and participate in a wage-money economy. In 1850 the Cheyenne lived in hide-covered tepees, rode horses, and hunted buffalo. In 1650 the Cheyenne lived in permanent earth lodge villages, traveled by foot or canoe, and depended on farming and hunting for their subsistence. Although Cheyenne cultural systems have continuity, all aspects of their culture changed, to some degree, over the period just described. Thus, in reality, there is no stable Cheyenne culture, but an ever-changing system. The ahistorical studies used in cross-cultural research create an artificial picture of the cultural system of a society.

Controlled Historical Comparisons

Only in the past thirty years have anthropologists attempted **controlled historical comparisons.** Unlike cross-cultural studies, controlled historical comparisons use changes in particular groupings of societies over time to define general cultural patterning and test hypotheses.

Controlled historical comparisons, like cross-cultural studies, are usually extremely complex. We illustrate this method by a simple example.

As we discuss in Chapter 9, people organize their family lives in various ways. Two common ways are matrilineal descent and patrilineal descent. In matrilineal societies, family group membership is inherited through your mother; you belong to your mother's family. In patrilineal societies, group membership is inherited through your father; you belong to your father's family. Anthropologists have long attempted to explain why some societies are matrilineal and others patrilineal. Cross-cultural research has shown that a relation exists between matrilineality and patrilineality and the relative economic importance of males and females in the society. However, cross-cultural studies can only show us correlations between descent and other synchronic aspects of the cultural system. For example, these studies can tell us what types of economic systems are most frequently found with matrilineal or patrilineal societies. Cross-cultural studies cannot measure the long-term effects of external changes on matrilineal or patrilineal societies. Is matrilineality or patrilineality more adaptive in some situations than in others? If so, what types of situations favor matrilineal societies, and which favor patrilineal societies? To examine this question, we must turn to controlled historical comparisons.

Michael Allen (1984) has asserted that matrilineal societies in the Pacific appear to be more successful in adapting to European contact than are patrilineal societies. Is there a way to test Allen's assertion? First, we must restructure this statement as a testable hypothesis. What do we mean by success? The term *success* is rather subjective and cannot be directly measured. We have to convert this term into some measurable quantity. One quantifiable measure of the success of a particular system is the relative ability of a society to maintain or expand its population over time. Thus, our hypothesis would be that, given the same degree of disruptive external pressures, matrilineal societies maintain their population levels better over time than patrilineal societies. Now we need to find a group of matrilineal societies and patrilineal societies that experienced a comparable intensity of external contact over a period of time and compare their relative populations at the beginning and end of the period. If Allen is correct, the matrilineal societies should have a relatively higher population at the end of the period than the patrilineal societies.

The farming Native American tribes of the eastern United States present an almost ideal case for testing Allen's assertion. They had similar cultural systems, ex-

cept that some were matrilineal and others were patrilineal. Their collective histories of contact with Europeans were also basically the same. During the historical period, all these societies suffered the effects of epidemic diseases, warfare (with Europeans as well as intertribal), severe territorial dislocation, political domination, and social discrimination.

Now the problem is determining an appropriate time frame to examine and finding comparable population data. One problem with ethnohistoric research is that the researcher is forced to use the data available in the records. It is not until about 1775 that sufficient population data are available in missionary, military, and explorer accounts to estimate the populations of all these tribes with any accuracy. In 1910, the U.S. Bureau of the Census conducted a special Native American census, which was the first truly comprehensive census of Native American societies in the United States. Thus, the time frame we will use is from 1775 to 1910. Using ethnographic data, we can then classify particular societies as either matrilineal or patrilineal and determine their populations for the beginning and end of this period:

	1775	1910	Percent
Matrilineal societies	88,590	82,714	93
Patrilineal societies	36,400	13,463	37
Totals	124,990	96,177	77

From this table we can see that during this 135-year period, the matrilineal societies declined by only about 7 percent of their total population, whereas patrilineal societies lost 63 percent of their population. If maintenance of population is a measure of a society's success, then matrilineal societies in the eastern United States were more successful than patrilineal societies.

As is the case with all comparative studies, findings such as these raise more questions than they answer. Are these population figures and the historical experiences of these societies truly comparable? If they are comparable, is the significant factor differences in descent form, or is it some other cultural factor we have not considered? We need to add at this point that not all matrilineal societies in this study were equally successful in maintaining their population levels, and that a few patrilineal societies studied increased in population during this period. There is room, then, for argument. If, in the final analysis, however, we decide that our findings are valid and that matrilineal societies are, under certain conditions, more adaptive than patrilineal societies, we still cannot directly say why.

Cross-cultural comparisons and controlled historical comparisons give us distinctly different measures of cul-

Ethnographic methods	The collection of cultural data on a particular society or group of societies. The primary purpose is the collection of descriptive data.
Ethnographic fieldwork	The collection of cultural data from living individuals. This usually requires that the researcher live with or close to the people being studied.
Ethnohistoric research	The study of the past cultural system of a people through the use of written records.
Comparative methods	The comparative study of cultural systems of a number of different societies. The objective is to test hypotheses so that we can explain why differences exist.
Cross-cultural	The testing of hypotheses by using synchronic data drawn from a number of different societies.
Controlled historical	The comparative use of historically documented changes in particular groupings of societies over time to define general cultural patterning and test hypotheses.

tural phenomena. They address different questions and test different hypotheses. They are complementary, not competitive, methodologies.

Some anthropologists (especially idealists—see Chapter 4) believe that both kinds of comparative studies distort each cultural system in the sample so much that the whole method is invalid. They think that ripping each element out of the particular context in which it is embedded robs it of its significance be-cause each element acquires its meaning only in its local historical and cultural context.

Despite these and other problems, comparative methods are the only practical means available for determining whether a hypothesis is valid among human cultural systems. Those who use these methods are aware of the difficulties, yet they believe that the advantage of being able to process information on large numbers of societies outweighs the problems.

Summary

1. Anthropological methods fall into two overall categories. Ethnographic methods involve the collection of information on a specific cultural system, whereas comparative methods are used to test hypotheses or to investigate theoretical ideas by comparing information on numerous cultural systems.

2. The basic aims of ethnographic methods are descriptive, whereas comparative investigations aim to determine whether some hypothesis or theoretical idea is supported by the accumulated data on human cultures.

3. The kinds of ethnographic methods used by anthropologists depend on whether they are investigating a contemporary or a past way of life.

4. Research into the past way of life of a people usually involves ethnohistory (perusal of written documents). This method requires considerable interpretation by the researcher. Sometimes those who wrote the documents used in ethnohistoric reconstructions misinterpreted events be-cause of their cultural backgrounds and ethnocentrism. The contents of documents are often affected by the private interests of their authors.

5. Fieldwork is the primary method of acquiring data about the culture of a living people. Fieldworkers usually live among those they study for at least a year, conducting formal interviews and surveys and engaging in participant observation. The difficulties of conducting fieldwork vary with the personality and gender of the fieldworker and with the people and specific topic being studied.

6. In addition there are four problems that all fieldworkers must face. Fieldworkers must not only fight against their own ethnocentrism and tendencies to stereotype those they study, they must also overcome the stereotypes local people have developed about foreigners. It is often difficult to establish a rapport with local people because they may have had no previous experience with the kinds of questions fieldworkers ask.

Identifying reliable informants and finding people willing to participate in intensive surveys may pose a serious problem. Sometimes people deliberately deceive anthropologists because they mistrust their motives, do not want certain facts to become public, or are culturally forbidden to give away secrets of their religion.

7. Fieldwork is viewed as an essential part of the graduate education of anthropologists and almost a prerequisite for professionalism. It is, in some respects, a rite of passage.

8. Comparative methods involve ways of systematically and reliably comparing massive amounts of information collected by previous ethnographers. The use of comparative methods presents many difficulties, including stating the research hypothesis in such a way that it is testable, reliably defining and measuring the variables of interest for many societies, deciding whether similar cultural elements from two or more societies are the "same" or "different," and contending with unintentional researcher bias. The results of comparative studies can be difficult to interpret. Correlation is often confused with causation.

Key Terms

ethnographic methods	participant observation	culture shock
comparative methods	stereotypes	ethnohistory
ethnographic fieldwork	consultant (informant)	cross-cultural comparisons
ethnohistoric research	key consultant	controlled historical
interviewing	(key informant)	comparisons

InfoTrac College Edition Terms

ethnology	anthropological research	cultural anthropology
ethnohistory	methods	fieldwork
culture shock		indigenous property rights

Suggested Readings

Works that deal with research methods and problems include:

Agar, Michael. *The Professional Stranger: An Informal Introduction to Ethnography.* New York: Academic, 1980.

Quite good for the beginning student. Tells how ethnographers do their work, with lots of examples taken from the author's own field experiences.

Brown, Michael F. *Who Owns Native Culture?* Cambridge: Harvard University Press, 2003.

This book is concerned with the issue of native rights and culture, important issues of which every culture researcher should be aware.

Bernard, H. Russell. *Research Methods in Anthropology: Qualitative and Quantitative Approaches.* 3rd ed. Walnut Creek, Calif.: AltaMira Press, 2001.

Now in its third edition, this work has become the standard reference for research methods in anthropology.

Emerson, Robert M., Rachel I. Fretz, and Linda L. Shaw. *Writing Ethnographic Fieldnotes.* Chicago Guides to Writing, Editing, and Publishing. Chicago: University of Chicago Press, 1995.

This is a how-to manual for individuals involved in field research.

Martin, Calvin, ed. *The American Indian and the Problem of History.* New York: Oxford University Press, 1987.

In this edited work, anthropologists, historians, and Native Americans discuss the problems in trying to objectively interpret the cultural history of Indian America. This is a critical book for any ethnohistorian studying Native American culture.

Obeyesekere, Gananath. *The Apotheosis of Captain Cook: European Mythmaking in the Pacific.* Princeton, N.J.: Princeton University Press, 1992.

In part, this study attacks Marshall Sahlins's interpretation of the Cook murder, accusing him of Eurocentric bias. Obeyesekere shows the difficulty in attempting to objectively analyze historical documents.

Spradley, James P. *The Ethnographic Interview.* New York: Holt, Rinehart and Winston, 1979.

Spradley, James P. *Participant Observation.* New York: Holt, Rinehart and Winston, 1980.

Two books that complement each other, one focusing on structured interviewing of informants, the other on detailed observation.

A number of books deal with the actual experiences of ethnographers in the field. They are valuable for conveying the feeling of fieldwork, problems ethnographers encounter, relating to local people, and so forth.

DeVita, Philip R., ed. *The Naked Anthropologist: Tales From Around the World.* Belmont, Calif.: Wadsworth, 1992.

A collection of twenty-seven personal accounts of fieldworkers discussing the situations, issues, and problems they encountered.

Dumont, Jean-Paul. *The Headman and I.* Prospect Heights, Ill.: Waveland Press, 1992.

Account of a fieldworker's relationships with the Panare people of the Venezuelan Amazon.

Freilich, Morris, ed. *Marginal Natives: Anthropologists at Work.* New York: Harper and Row, 1970.

Ten anthropologists discuss the problems of fieldwork.

Golde, Peggy, ed. *Women in the Field: Anthropological Experiences.* Chicago: Aldine, 1970.

Twelve female ethnographers discuss special difficulties they encountered because of their gender.

Hayano, David M. *Road Through the Rain Forest.* Prospect Heights, Ill.: Waveland Press, 1990.

Describes the fieldwork experiences of Hayano and his wife among the Awa, a people of the highlands of Papua New Guinea.

Medicine, Beatrice. *Learning to Be an Anthropologist and Remaining "Native."* Urbana: University of Illinois Press, 2001.

In these selected writings of one of America's foremost Native American scholars and anthropologists, there are a number of excellent discussions of being both a "native" and an anthropologist.

Rabinow, Paul. *Reflections on Fieldwork in Morocco.* Berkeley: University of California Press, 1977.

An interesting discussion of the author's experiences in Morocco.

Ward, Martha C. *Nest in the Wind.* Prospect Heights, Ill.: Waveland Press, 1989.

Wonderfully readable account of Ward's personal experiences and fieldwork difficulties on Pohnpei Island, Micronesia.

Companion Website for This Book

The Wadsworth Anthropology Resource Center
http://anthropology.wadsworth.com

The companion website that accompanies *Humanity: An Introduction to Cultural Anthropology,* Sixth Edition, includes a rich array of material, including online anthropological video clips, to help you in the study of cultural anthropology and the specific topics covered in this chapter. Begin by clicking on Student Resources. Next, click on Cultural Anthropology, and then on the cover image for this book. You have now arrived at the Student Resources home page and have the option of choosing one of several chapter resources.

Applying Anthropology. Begin your study of cultural anthropology by clicking on Applying Anthropology. Here you will find useful information on careers, graduate school programs in applied anthropology, and internships you might wish to pursue. You will also find real-world examples of working anthropologists applying the skills and methods of anthropology to help solve serious world problems.

Research Online. Click here to find a wealth of Web links that will facilitate your study of anthropology. Divided into different fields of study, specific websites are starting points for Internet research. You will be guided to rich anthropology websites that will help you prepare for class, complete course assignments, and actually do research on the Web.

InfoTrac College Edition Exercises. From the pull-down menu, select the chapter you are presently studying. Select InfoTrac College Edition Exercises from the list of resources. These exercises utilize InfoTrac College Edition's vast database of articles and help you explore the numerous uses of the search word, *culture.*

Study Aids for This Chapter. Improve your knowledge of key terms by using flash cards and study the learning objectives. Take the practice quiz, receive your results, and email them to your instructor. Access these resources from the chapter and resource pull-down menus.

Chapter Six

ADAPTATION: ENVIRONMENT AND CULTURES

Understanding Human Adaptation

Foraging

Foraging and Culture

Domestication

Advantages of Domestication

Horticulture

Varieties of Horticulture

Cultural Consequences of Horticulture

Intensive Agriculture

Varieties of Intensive Agriculture

Cultural Consequences of Intensive Agriculture

Pastoralism

Herding Environments

The Karimojong: An Example from East Africa

Adaptation and Culture

How people produce food and handle the problems of adapting to their natural environment is one important influence on the rest of their culture. This Chinese peasant is working in a field of wet rice, one of the most productive agricultural systems in the world.

I**N THIS CHAPTER,** we explore adaptation and its consequences—the ways various human populations relate to their natural environments and how these relationships affect their cultural systems. Adaptation is an appropriate topic to begin our discussion of cultural diversity because many anthropologists (cultural materialists) believe that how people interact with their environment is the primary cause of cultural differences and similarities and the prime mover of cultural change. Future chapters deal with other dimensions of cultural diversity: marriage and family life, kinship systems, relationships between the sexes, political organization, religion and worldview, and artistic expression.

OUR FOCUS is the adaptations of preindustrial peoples—that is, peoples whose traditional economies were based on food production, not on the extraction of resources for factory production. First we provide some concepts that are useful in studying and comparing systems of adaptation. Then we cover the hunting and gathering (foraging) adaptations, which nourished humanity for most of our existence. Adaptations in several parts of the world were dramatically altered between 10,000 and

6,000 years ago, when people first domesticated plants and animals. Agriculture and herding imposed new requirements and opened up new opportunities for human groups, resulting in major changes in cultures, as we shall see.

THE REMARKABLY DIFFERENT WAYS that human groups have adapted to nature is a fascinating study in and of itself. In this chapter, though, we devote most of our attention to how human–environment relationships affect cultural systems.

Understanding Human Adaptation

Adaptation is the process by which organisms develop physiological and behavioral characteristics that allow them to survive and reproduce in their environment. In studying how human adaptation affects cultural systems, it is useful to pay attention to two important features. First, the environment (or *habitat*) includes *natural resources* that people harness to meet their material needs and wants: food, water, wood and leaves for shelters and fires, stones or metals for tools, and so forth. Second, the environment poses certain *problems* that people must solve or overcome: resource scarcity, excessively low or high temperatures, parasites and diseases, rainfall variability, deficient soils, and so forth. If people are to adapt to conditions in their environments, they must harness resources efficiently and cope with environmental problems effectively.

Like other species, humans adapt to their environments physiologically and genetically. For example, bacteria, viruses, and parasites kill susceptible individuals, but those who are genetically resistant survive, reproduce, and pass more of their genes along to the next generation. By this process of natural selection, over many generations human populations will become more resistant to the life-threatening microorganisms to which they are exposed. People are part of nature, and natural selection has helped to adapt us to the environments in which we live, just as it has for other organisms.

However, one way humanity differs from other species is that we adapt to changes in our environments *mainly*—but not exclusively—by cultural rather than by biological/genetic means. If the climate grows colder or if a group migrates into a colder area, they cope mainly by lighting fires, constructing shelters, and making warm clothing, not mainly by evolving physiological adaptations to cold. Humans hunt animals by making weapons and mastering techniques of cooperative stalking and killing, not by biologically evolving the ability to run faster than game. Group cooperation and technology (including both the tools themselves and the knowledge required to make and use them) allow humans to adapt to a wide range of environments without undergoing major alterations in genetic makeup.

Because changes in learned behavior, more than in genetic makeup, allow us to adapt to varying environments, the human species has colonized every type of terrestrial habitat on Earth, from tropical rain forests to Arctic tundra, from the vast grassy plains of central Asia to tiny Pacific islands. The ability to adapt to diverse habitats by means of technology and group living surely is one of the secrets of humanity's success.

People interact with their environments in many ways. One of the most important is the harnessing of energy (e.g., food, fuel) and raw materials (e.g., minerals for tools, wood for shelters) from nature. Acquiring energy and materials from an environment is part of *production*—the patterned, organized activities by which people transform natural resources into things (products) that satisfy their material needs and wants. Indeed, those modern anthropologists who follow the materialist orientation (Chapter 4) think that the process of production is so important that many other aspects of a group's culture are shaped by it.

What does it take to transform a natural resource into a useful product? Production has three components. People apply (1) their own time and energy (*labor, work*) and (2) the tools and knowledge (*technology*) available to them to (3) the *resources* available in their environment. Labor, technology, and resources (called the *factors of production* in economics) are combined in various ways to produce food, shelter, and other material products that people desire.

These concepts are easy to grasp, but there are a few complexities. Many such complications arise from the fact that humans are social animals (see Chapter 2), who live in groups of various sizes and compositions. Because people live in groups, they have to organize themselves to produce what they need and want. Individuals have to know what to do and what to expect others to do, and they have to know when and where to work so they do not come into conflict or violate one another's rights. The *organization of production* solves problems such as who will do which productive tasks, when, where, and how. There are three main factors involved in the organization of production.

First, people usually prefer to spend less rather than more time in work, so they try to use their labor efficiently. Often, people can work most efficiently by dividing tasks among themselves according to factors like sex, age, and skill. The allocation of productive work to different kinds of people is called the *division of labor.* Ideally, but not always in practice, tasks are allocated according to ability.

Second, cooperation helps a group use labor and harness resources efficiently. For example, several hunters may have a better chance of spotting, tracking, and killing large game. Net fishing may be more productive if people work together. Since cooperation usually is more efficient than working alone, a group's *patterns of cooperation* are an important part of how it organizes itself for production.

Third, a group faces the potential problem of conflict over access to natural resources: Which individuals and groups have the right to use a particular resource at a particular time and place? People have to find ways of defining their *rights to resources.* Generally, a given area of land or territory—along with its resources—is allocated to some group. Its members have the right to exploit the area's resources, whereas others are prohibited from doing so, or may do so only with permission.

Industrialized, market societies solve such problems by defining some people as owners of productive property, based in large part on their ability to purchase (or their luck in inheriting) such property. Preindustrial cultures have property rights also, but they often differ greatly from those of industrialized nations. Anthropologists have learned to distinguish *ownership rights* from *use rights* and *group rights* from *individual rights.* A territory and its resources are most frequently owned by some kind of group—most often a family unit of some kind or a residential group—which has collective rights to use the resources. The leader of the group (e.g., the family head, the village chief) allocates the use of the resources among the members. People in the group have the right to use the resources, so long as they do not violate the rights of other group members to use them also. Thus the "property rights" of individuals are always limited by the rights of others.

In sum, productive activities are one important way people interact with their environment. Production involves the application of labor and technology to natural resources. Because humanity is a social species, production is an organized social activity, involving the division of labor, patterns of cooperation, and the allocation of rights to resources.

These concepts are useful in comparing some of the ways various peoples adapt to their environments. Anthropologists generally divide preindustrial adapta-

▶ Production is usually an organized social activity. Everywhere, people cooperate in patterned ways— here illustrated by these African net fishers—to make labor more efficient.

tions into three major categories, based largely on how people produce their food supply:

- **hunting and gathering** (also called **foraging**), in which people exploit the *wild* plants and animals of their territory for food
- **agriculture** (or **cultivation**), in which people intentionally plant, care for, and harvest *crops* (domesticated plants) for food and other uses
- **herding** (or **pastoralism**), in which people tend, breed, and harvest products of *livestock* (domesticated animals) for food, trade, and other uses

It would be very misleading to view these categories as mutually exclusive. People who farm the land may also hunt or keep livestock or both. In fact, since agriculture began several thousand years ago, most peoples have relied on a combination of adaptive strategies, depending on their technologies, local environments, and what their neighbors are doing.

The remainder of this chapter describes these three ways of exploiting the food resources of an environment and discusses some of the main ways that each adaptation affects culture.

Foraging

Foragers, also called hunter-gatherers, get their food from collecting (gathering) the wild plants and hunting (or fishing for) the animals that live in their regions. Foragers do not attempt to increase the resources found in their environments by growing crops or intentionally breeding livestock for meat and other products. But many foragers do make modest efforts to control resource availability in other ways. For example, some Native American peoples periodically burned forests and grasslands to attract game or increase the supply of sun-loving wild berries or other plants.

Most biological anthropologists believe that *Homo sapiens sapiens* has existed for around 200,000 years. But there was no farming of crops or herding of livestock anywhere on Earth until about 10,000 years ago. The foraging adaptation thus supported humanity for the first 95 percent of our existence as a unique species.

However, once plant and animal domestication developed, agricultural and herding peoples increased their numbers and expanded their territories. Over several millennia of expansion, cultivators and herders pushed many foraging peoples into regions that were ill-suited to crops and livestock. As a result, when European contact with people of other continents intensified after about 1500,

hunters and gatherers already lived primarily in regions too cold or arid to support agriculture (see Figure 6.1).

By the beginning of the twentieth century, many foragers had died out altogether or had become assimilated into some other society. European contact was especially hard on Native Americans, who lived on lands highly coveted by Anglo, Spanish, and Portuguese settlers and who were susceptible to a host of diseases brought by Europeans and the Africans they enslaved. Most scholars who have looked seriously at the impact of diseases on Native Americans estimate that 80 to 90 percent of Indians died from epidemics. Europeans did indeed conquer and subdue many Native peoples, but not in the way most people imagine: bacteria and viruses were more important than guns and bullets.

Compared to farmers and herders, hunters and gatherers do not modify their natural environments very much but instead take what nature offers. If edible wild plants are available only at particular places during particular seasons, foraging groups must move to those places at those times to harvest them. If major game animals live in large migratory herds, the hunters must follow them or switch to other animals when the game has left their region. A brief statement that helps to understand both the foraging adaptation and how it affects culture is the following: To acquire resources efficiently, foragers must organize themselves to be in the right place at the right time with the right numbers of people.

Foraging and Culture

Although anthropologists classify hunting and gathering as a single form of adaptation, neither their adaptations nor their cultures are all alike. Foragers living in different habitats differ culturally, partly because environments vary in the kinds and quality of food resources they contain. Peoples of the resource-rich environment of the American Northwest Coast lived a fairly sedentary existence in large permanent settlements, whereas the Shoshone of the arid and resource-sparse American Great Basin roamed in small bands or individual families. In spite of environmental differences, most—but not all—foraging peoples share certain cultural similarities. Our main goal in this section is to describe how the adaptive requirements of hunting and gathering affect the cultures of most foraging peoples.

Division of Labor by Age and Sex. The division of labor among foragers is organized largely along the lines of age and sex, although special knowledge and skill also serve as a basis for assigning tasks. Among the great

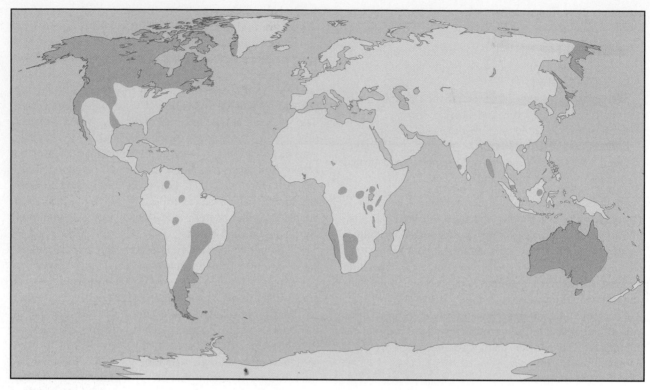

▲ **Figure 6.1** Principal Regions of Foragers at the Time of First Contact with Europeans

majority of foraging peoples, men do the bulk of the hunting and women most of the gathering of plants. However, it is not unusual for either sex to lend a hand with the activities of the other. For example, among the BaMbuti of the tropical forest of Zaire, the women and children help the men with hunting by driving game animals into nets. But in general, hunting is men's work.

Seasonal Mobility. Most foragers are seasonally mobile. None of the Earth's environments offers the same kinds and quantities of resources year round. There may be seasonal differences in precipitation. Outside the tropics there usually are marked seasonal variations in temperature as well. Ordinarily, game animals are available in some places and not others at different seasons, and nuts and fruits tend to be available only at certain times of the year.

Foragers migrate to where food or water is most plentiful or easiest to acquire during a given season. For example, the Hadza people of Tanzania lived in an arid region with a marked distinction between wet and dry seasons. In rainy months the Hadza dispersed around the many temporary water holes that formed, living on the wild plants and animals in the immediate vicinity. At an-

other time of the year, when these ponds evaporated, they lived in large camps clustered around the few relatively permanent water sources.

Seasonal Congregation and Dispersal. To exploit plants and animals efficiently, most hunters and gatherers adjust the sizes of their living groups to match the seasonal availability and abundance of their food supply. At some times of the year, it is most efficient to disperse into small groups, which cooperate in the search for food. During other seasons, these groups come together in larger congregations.

The Western Shoshone live in the arid Great Basin of what is now Nevada and Utah. Until white settlers disrupted their traditional adaptation in the mid-nineteenth century, the Shoshone lived off wild plants and animals. Most of their meat came from deer, antelope, and small mammals such as rabbits and squirrels. Plant foods included roots and seasonally available seeds, berries, pine nuts, and other wild products.

For most of the year the Shoshone roamed the dry valleys and slopes of the Great Basin in tiny bands consisting of a few nuclear families, or even single families. Families occasionally gathered for cooperative hunting of antelopes and rabbits, which they drove into corrals and nets. But a more permanent aggregation of families was difficult because a local area did not have enough resources to support large numbers of people for more than a few days.

One important plant food became available in the fall and in most years was capable of supporting many families throughout the winter. Around October, the cones of the piñon trees on the high mountains ripened and produced large, nourishing pine nuts. During their travels in late summer, Shoshone families noticed which specific mountain areas seemed to have the most promising pine nut harvest. They arranged their movements to arrive at these productive areas in the fall. Ten to twenty families camped in the same region, harvesting and storing pine nuts. During favorable (i.e., rainy) years, the pine nut harvest supported these large camps throughout most of the winter. Spring found the families splitting up again, reliving the pattern of dispersal into tiny groups until the next fall. No family had exclusive access to any particular territory in any season. Rights to resources were essentially on the basis of first come, first served, meaning that whichever group arrived at an area first was free to harvest its plants and animals.

Bands. In most environments efficient foraging requires that people live in small, mobile groups of 50 or fewer, so as not to exhaust the supply of wild foods too quickly. To distinguish these living groups from the settled hamlets, villages, towns, and cities found in other adaptations, anthropologists call these mobile living groups **bands.** Band members cooperate in production and usually share rights to harvest the wild resources of a given territory. The size of bands is usually flexible, allowing the number of people living in the band to be adjusted according to the availability of the food supply. Further, individuals are not attached permanently to any band, but have many options about where to live and whom to live with. This way of organizing bands offers many advantages to foragers.

The !Kung (also known as the Ju/'hoansi) of southern Africa illustrate band organization. Living in what is now southeast Angola, northeast Namibia, and northwest Botswana, the !Kung are the most thoroughly studied of all hunter-gatherers who remained foragers into the twentieth century. The northern part of their environment is an arid tropical savanna, grading into the Kalahari desert toward the south. Until the twentieth century, the !Kung exploited this habitat entirely by foraging. They gathered more than 100 species of plants and hunted more than 50 kinds of animals, including mammals, birds, and reptiles. Plant foods consisted of nuts, fruits, berries, melons, roots, and greenery. A particularly important and nourishing food was the

© Washburn/Arthro-Photo File

▲ Gathering plant foods is mainly women's work among foraging peoples. This !Kung woman is bagging mongongo nuts, a nourishing !Kung staple.

mongongo nut, which ripens around April and provided about half the people's caloric intake.

Because their habitat received so little rainfall and then only seasonally, the availability of water greatly influenced the annual rhythm of !Kung life. From about April to October (winter in the Southern Hemisphere) there was little precipitation, and practically no rain fell between June and September. During this dry season, water for people and animals was available only at a few permanent water holes, around which bands congregated into relatively large settlements of between 20 and 50 individuals. Between November and March—the hot and wet season—temporary water holes formed, and the bands split up to exploit the wild resources around them. But rainfall in this part of the world is not reliable, neither from year to year nor from place to place. In some years, up to 40 inches of rain falls during the wet season; in other years, as little as 6 inches. Drought occurs in about two out of every five years. Precipitation is also spatially unpredictable: One area frequently receives severe thunderstorms, whereas 20 miles away no rain falls.

These characteristics of their physical environment—its aridity, seasonality, and marked temporal and spatial variability in precipitation—influenced !Kung band organization. Because the distribution of wild foods and water was determined by rainfall, the annual cycle of band congregation and dispersal was mainly determined by the seasonal distinction between wet and dry. During the wet months the bands were spread out among the temporary water holes in camps numbering about 10 to 30. When the bands first moved to a "fresh" water hole, wild resources were relatively plentiful; game was abundant and a wide variety of plant foods were easily available. But the longer a band remained around a water hole, the more its members exhausted the surrounding resources. The men had to roam farther afield in their hunting, and the women had to travel longer distances in their plant collecting. After several weeks a camp reached the point at which its members judged that the costs of continuing to forage in the area were not bringing adequate returns in food. They then moved to a new wet-season camp. One ethnographer, Richard Lee, succinctly notes that the !Kung "typically occupy a camp for a period of weeks or months and eat their way out of it" (Lee 1969, 60).

As the dry season approached, !Kung bands made their way back to the area around one of the permanent water holes. These settlements, larger than the wet-season camps, commonly numbered between 20 and 50 and often even more. By the end of the dry season the supply of mongongo nuts and other preferred plant foods was exhausted and the people ate the less tasty bitter melons, roots, and gum. This was considered a relatively hard time of the year, and the !Kung waited in anticipation of the November rains, when they could again disperse into the smaller wet-season groups.

Reciprocal Sharing. It is mutually beneficial for band members to share food and other possessions with one another. The sharing is more or less on the basis of need: Those who have more than they can immediately use share with others. For example, among the !Kung, each day only some members of a band search for food. But foods brought back to camp are widely distributed, so even families who did not work that day receive their share. The fact that most or all members of a single band are relatives further encourages sharing of food.

Reciprocal sharing especially applies to meat: Successful hunters returning to camp share the kill with other families, including those who have not participated in the day's hunt. One reason for the special emphasis on the equitable sharing of meat is the uncertain returns of hunting compared to gathering. Among the !Kung, on most

days women return to camp with their carrying bags full of nuts, roots, fruits, and other wild plants. Men's chances of capturing game, however, are smaller: Richard Lee estimates that only about two out of five hunting trips capture animals large enough to take back to camp. Men who are successful one day may be unsuccessful the next, so one reason they give today is so they can receive tomorrow.

Sharing is usually *normatively expected* behavior, meaning that people who regularly fail to share are subjected to ridicule or other kinds of social pressures. Going along with the expectation of sharing is a positive cultural value placed on equality of personal possessions (property) and even of social status. Families who attempt to hoard food or other products may be ostracized. Men who try to place themselves above others socially by boasting about their hunting skills or other accomplishments are soon put in their place. The result is that there is both economic and social equality between the families of most hunting and gathering bands.

Rights to Resources. Effective adaptation requires that people have familiar, patterned ways of allocating natural resources between individuals and groups. Many hunters and gatherers are similar in how they determine rights to the resources that occur in their territory: who can harvest which resources, where, and when.

One way to organize rights over a territory and its resources is for each group to establish and maintain exclusive claims to particular territories. Cultural ideas about the relationship between people and territory might be, for example, that this area is *mine* or *ours,* whereas that area is *yours* or *theirs.* Among foragers, exclusive access would mean that each band has rights to remain in a specific area during a particular season. One benefit would be that the members of each band would know they alone have rights to harvest the foods found in particular places at definite times. Another advantage is that bands would not interfere in each other's hunting and gathering activities.

Despite these (apparent) benefits, most foragers organize rights to resources in quite a different way. Among the !Kung, for instance, there was a comparatively weak attachment of particular groups of people to specific territories. Particular families tended to return to the same territories year after year, according to season, and over time others came to recognize them as the "owners" of the area. Commonly, the most reliable water holes together with the wild resources around them were "owned" by a set of siblings whose rights grew stronger as they grew older. But by merely asking permission—which was seldom refused—anyone with a kinship relationship to one of the "owners" could come and visit and exploit the area's food and water. Because most !Kung had many relatives who were "owners" of different places, each !Kung family had a multitude of options about where and with whom they would live, work, relax, and socialize. As a consequence of multiple options, the composition of a band fluctuated radically, for each band received visiting relatives several times a year. So instead of establishing exclusive claims to particular places, !Kung were only loosely attached to territories and for the most part came and went as their preferences and circumstances allowed. Similar patterns were found among most other known hunter-gatherers.

To sum up, most hunter-gatherers develop certain ways of organizing their activities and their groups that facilitate their adaptation:

- a division of labor based mainly on sex and age
- a high degree of mobility, especially from season to season
- congregation and dispersal of groups, usually on a seasonal basis
- living in groups of small bands with varying size and flexible composition
- strong values of reciprocal sharing and of equality in personal possessions and social status
- loose attachment of people to territory and flexible rights to resources

Although these characteristics describe most hunter-gatherers reasonably well, we must keep in mind that foragers are diverse. Not all have this set of cultural features.

In fact, in some environments, hunting and gathering peoples lived in quite a different way. Along the Northwest Coast of North America (roughly from Oregon into the Alaskan panhandle), food resources—especially fish—were exceptionally abundant, and the Native Americans who lived there were able to smoke and preserve food for many months. Because of abundance and storage, there was no need to maintain seasonal mobility or small living groups, so people were essentially sedentary. They lived in large permanent villages with elaborately decorated plank houses. In addition, wild resources were also more reliable on the Northwest Coast than in most other environments where foragers lived. Resource abundance and reliability affected property notions along the coast. If a food resource is so abundant that you can usually count on its availability, then it makes sense for you to stay close to it and defend it against other groups that might desire it as well. Northwest Coast people could count on fish being present in their rivers or coastal waters, so they developed

more defined property rights: particular groups were more closely associated with particular locations than were people such as the Shoshone or !Kung.

Another place where cultural systems varied from the patterns predominant among foragers is the North American Great Plains after about 1600. Technically speaking, Native Americans of the Plains were hunters and gatherers since they did not farm and kept no domestic animals except dogs and horses. However, their main food resource was unusually abundant, and during the spring and summer it gathered in huge herds that were most effectively hunted cooperatively by dozens of mounted men. This resource, of course, was bison, tens of millions of which once grazed the tall grass prairies of central North America. In most areas of the Plains, grasses grew luxuriantly in the spring and early summer, leading the bison to congregate in herds of thousands. As the summer progressed, the land became drier and the grass patchier, so the bison broke up into smaller herds for the fall and succeeding winter months.

The Cheyenne are an example of a Plains people. In the early and middle nineteenth century, the Cheyenne lived mainly on the meat of bison, following the seasonal movements of their principal food source. From June until late summer, while the bison gathered in huge herds, the people lived as a single tribe in an enormous camp of several thousand. Men on horseback used bows and arrows and, later, rifles, to hunt the animals for their meat and hides. As the bison herds split up in the fall, so did the tribe, for it was too difficult for the people to remain together as a single enormous camp when their food supply was so widely scattered. By breaking up into smaller bands during the fall and winter, each with its own name and identity, the Cheyenne gained other advantages. Their numerous horses, which were their main source of wealth and pride, were able to graze more easily. And fuel for fires during the freezing winter was easier to acquire, for dried animal dung was a main source of fuel in this place of few trees.

The Plains peoples were unusual foragers in many ways. One way was the size of their summer settlements, which usually numbered in the hundreds, as compared to the maximum band size of 50 to 100 among peoples such as the !Kung and Shoshone. Another was their political leadership form, which included formal leaders ("chiefs"), as covered later in Chapter 12. Like the Northwest Coast cultures, the Plains Indians are a useful reminder of the dangers of overgeneralization.

Perhaps the most surprising fact about the Native Americans of the Great Plains is that the way they were living when Anglos encountered them in the 1700s was

To the Anglo-American public, no Indian people typifies Native American life more than the Plains tribes such as the Blackfoot, Cheyenne, Comanche, Crow, Dakota, and Mandan. Thanks partly to Hollywood, these tipi-dwelling, buffalo-hunting, horse-mounted warriors of the grasslands have come to represent the very essence of "Indianness." When Anglos visualize "traditional" Indian ways of life, they may imagine Red Cloud, Black Kettle, Sitting Bull, or some other Plains leader dressed in beaded buckskin clothing, wearing a feathered "war bonnet," and seated on a horse, most likely in front of a tipi. Most of us do not know that this way of life of the Plains Indians was largely a product of the coming of Europeans.

Indeed, it had to be, because the adaptation of the Plains Indians as most Anglos know them rested upon the horse, and there were no horses in the Americas between about 11,000 years ago and the 1500s. Along with many other large mammals (mammoths, giant sloths, oversized bison, saber-toothed cats, and many others), horses became extinct in the Americas about 11,000 years ago at the end of the last Ice Age. With no way to hunt the bison effectively, the open grasslands of the Great Plains held relatively little attraction for American Indians. Not only were bison difficult to hunt for people on foot, armed with only a bow and arrow or spear, but transporting meat any distance over the vast grasslands was physically arduous. Food and other possessions had to be carried either on their own backs or on those of their dogs, for which they developed harnesses. Before the 1600s, the Plains were inhabited mainly by widely scattered small bands of nomadic foragers who probably depended more on collecting wild plants than on the vast herds of bison.

Ten thousand years after their extinction, horses were reintroduced into the Americas by the Spanish invaders and colonists in the 1500s. Horses were instrumental in defeating and conquering the two great civilizations of the Americas, the Aztecs of central Mexico and the Incas of western South America. They gave the small number of Spanish soldiers big advantages in combat. The mere sight of these huge unknown animals mounted with men wearing armor intimidated the Aztec and Inca foot warriors. Horses reached the Great Plains in sizable numbers only in the late 1600s and early 1700s. It took Native peoples only a few decades to make effective use of their new domesticated animal in hunting and warfare.

Horses revolutionized the cultural existence of some tribes. Not only could a hunter on horseback armed with bow and arrow kill enough bison within a few months to feed his family for a year, but he could pack the meat on horseback for long-distance transport and trade. Families could transport increased numbers of possessions; they could have larger tipis and more (and more finely decorated) clothing and other items. Groups that formerly had to be widely scattered could now gather in large encampments, numbering in the thousands, during favorable seasons.

Horses also altered the relationship between groups that had them and those that did not. Residents of the Plains were now capable of rapidly assembling large parties of horse-mounted young warriors who could raid nearby farming villages with near impunity. Within a few decades, small nomadic bands were transformed into aggressive raiders of their farming neighbors. In response, some farming peoples who lived along the fringes of the Plains took up the mounted nomadic way of life themselves. For example, until the 1600s the Cheyenne lived mainly by farming corn in the region that is now Minnesota, but by the late 1700s they too had turned into "Plains Indians." Some of the Dakota also abandoned the sedentary life and became seminomadic, horseback-mounted, bison-hunting, tipi-dwelling people.

As other peoples moved onto the Plains, eventually they challenged the original Plains tribes for dominance over critical hunting resources, which intensified competition and intergroup conflict. As a result, warfare and the warrior tradition became an integral part of Plains Indian values and social organization. For many Plains peoples, a major way a young man could make a name for himself was by raiding neighboring tribes and taking a few horses. Another is what Anglos know as "counting coup": A man would bravely ride into a throng of enemies and tap one or more of them with his lance.

All of this sounds utterly "traditional." Yet the Plains Indian culture (as Anglos imagine it) emerged well after contact with outsiders in a world that was already being transformed by global forces such as conquests and large-scale migrations. Given the diverse cultural origins of the various Plains tribes, they developed a remarkably homogeneous way of life within a short period: elaborately equipped tipis, beaded (with European trade beads) clothing, the Sun Dance, and the emphasis on the male's role as a warrior. It was not until the latter half of the nineteenth century that Euro-Americans seriously challenged the Plains Indians for control of the Great Plains, three centuries after they had first begun acquiring horses. Because the Plains peoples were the last major tribes to resist Euro-American military dominance, it is not surprising that the wider society mistakenly thinks of them as the "essence of Indianness."

Critical Thinking Question

The discussion argues that the culture of the Plains Indians was not fully indigenous, but was a result of how the horse interacted with preexisting cultural traditions. How often do you suppose we mistakenly believe customs or beliefs are "indigenous" when in fact they are products of interactions between peoples?

Sources: Ewers (1955), Hoebel (1978), Lowie (1954), Oliver (1962)

not their traditional, "time immemorial" way of life. In fact, many or most cultural features of the Plains Indians did not exist until after the introduction of the horse into North America, and this did not happen until the 1600s (the Globalization box discusses this history).

Domestication

Domestication is the intentional planting and cultivation of selected plants and the taming and breeding of certain species of animals. Its main beneficial effect is to increase the supply of the selected species by controlling their location and numbers. This requires new technologies and, in most circumstances, additional labor inputs compared to foraging. With respect to plants, in this book we are concerned with *food crops,* or those species that people intentionally select, plant, care for, harvest, and propagate for purposes of eating. People also grow plants for other purposes, such as for fibers (cotton, flax, hemp) or for drugs (tobacco, coca leaf, opium poppy). With animals we are concerned with *livestock,* or those species that people breed, raise, and control for purposes of providing food (meat, dairy products) or other useful products (hides, wool), or for performing work (pulling plows, carrying people and possessions). People keep animals for other reasons also, such as companionship (pets).

Detailed coverage of the origins of plant and animal domestication is outside the scope of this text. Suffice it to say that in the Old World, domestication occurred by around 10,000 years ago in the Middle East and by about 9,000 years ago in eastern Asia. In the next several thousand years, adaptations based on domesticated plants and animals developed or spread into most African, Asian, and European environments that could support either or both farming and herding. In the New World, a completely different set of plant species was domesticated in Mexico by about 6,000 to 5,000 years ago, and in northern Peru by about the same time. (A Closer Look provides information on the world regions where particular crops and livestock were first domesticated. As you read it think about how much of your diet you owe to the efforts of peoples who lived thousands of years ago and thousands of miles away.)

In the Old World, several animal species were domesticated about the same time as plants. In many parts of the Old World, the availability of livestock meant that men in many regions eventually gave up hunting, putting their labor into farming, crafts, warfare, metallurgy, and other activities instead. But in the New World, except for residents of the Andes, most peoples who relied on the cultivation of crops for their food got all or most of their meat from deer, antelope, small mammals, fish, and other wild animals. Most New World peoples, then, got the bulk of their meat from wild, not domesticated, animals, even though many of them were farmers.

Plant and animal domestication probably had more long-lasting and dramatic effects on cultures than any other single set of changes in adaptation—except, perhaps, industrialization. For example, once certain plants evolved by human selection into crops, people could produce more food in a given area of land. Increased production allowed them to remain in one place for long periods—over time, groups became more *sedentary.* They could also live in much larger settlements than the bands of most foragers—groups settled in *villages* and, later in some places, in *towns* and *cities.*

Advantages of Domestication

For tens of thousands of years, hunting and gathering worked well enough to allow humanity to increase in number to several million. Further, foraging is a flexible adaptation, meaning that it can be applied to any environment with a sufficient quantity of wild, edible plants and animals. Foraging works in rain forests, grasslands, tundras, and mountains—given, of course, adequate shelter, the right kinds of tools and skills, and appropriate ways of organizing production. Because of how quickly people can adapt by means of learning, and how rapidly new ways of doing things can be communicated and spread by social learning if circumstances warrant, hunter-gatherers migrated into all the major continents except Antarctica. By 10,000 years ago, humans were living on all the major land masses of the Earth except Antarctica. The foraging adaptation, then, allowed humanity to be a successful species, if we measure success by population numbers and by geographical distribution.

In fact, most modern anthropologists believe that prehistoric hunter-gatherers actually enjoyed a relatively high quality of life. Richard Lee's quantitative studies of the !Kung in the 1960s show that they worked only about two and a half days per week to acquire their food supply. Even adding in time spent in other kinds of work, such as making tools and housework, the !Kung worked only around 42 hours per week. Most modern-day adults would be happy to have such a short workweek! Further, the !Kung's relatively modest work efforts were sufficient to keep them well fed most of the time: Adults consumed an average of 2,355 calories and 96 grams of protein per day, more than sufficient for their bodily needs.

The domestication of plants and animals occurred independently in the Old World (Europe, Asia, Africa) and the New World (North and South America). Before the age of European colonization the crops grown in the two hemispheres were completely different.

Old World Crops

The first plant domestication occurred in Southwest Asia in the region often called the Fertile Crescent. Wheat, barley, lentils, peas, carrots, figs, almonds, pistachios, dates, and grapes were first grown here. Oats, cabbages, lettuce, and olives were first domesticated in the Mediterranean. In West Africa, sorghum, finger millet, watermelons, and African rice were domesticated; sorghum and finger millet still feed millions of people on the African continent. Eggplants, cucumbers, bananas, taro, and coconuts originated in southern Asia and Southeast Asia. Soybeans, Oriental rice, millet, citrus fruits, and tea were domesticated in ancient China. Sugarcane was probably first cultivated in New Guinea or the islands around it. We get our morning caffeine from coffee, first domesticated in the Ethiopian highlands.

New World Crops

Maize, tomatoes, beans, red peppers, avocados, and cacao (now used in the making of chocolate) originated in Central America and Mexico, in either the highlands or the coastal lowlands, or both. Sunflowers and various members of the squash family (squash, pumpkins, and gourds) probably were first intentionally grown in the same region, although sunflowers perhaps originated in eastern North America. From Peru came numerous crops that are still important to the region and to the world, including potatoes, sweet potatoes, and lima beans. From elsewhere in South America came manioc, peanuts, pineapple, and cashews.

Some plants were domesticated not just once but several times in various parts of the world. Separate species of rice were domesticated in Africa and Asia, apparently independently. Cotton was domesticated independently in three places: South America, Central America, and either India or Africa. Three yam species were grown in West Africa, Southeast Asia, and tropical South America.

Old World Livestock

In the Old World, the earliest animal domestication occurred at about the same times and in the same places as crops were first grown. In the Middle East, the wild ancestors of the most important livestock lived in large herds, including sheep, goats, and cattle. These animals were and are kept for their hides, wool, meat, and milk. Another large mammal, the horse, was first domesticated on the Asian grasslands around 5,000 years ago. When mounted, horses greatly increased the speed of long-distance travel and, of course, increased the mobility of warriors and soldiers. For thousands of years, from Central Asia to North Africa, camels have made it possible for people and products to cross vast stretches of arid land. Along with asses, donkeys, and South Asian yaks, horses and camels allowed heavy loads to be carried long distances, increasing the potential of trade. When harnessed to the plow, cattle, horses, and Asian water buffalos supplemented human labor in farming, and their dung added nutrients to agricultural fields and gardens. Finally, pigs—first brought under human control in Southwest Asia and perhaps East Asia—are an outstanding source of protein and today remain the major source of meat in China and non-Muslim Southeast Asia.

Comparable figures have been reported for other foragers in reasonably productive environments, but quantitative studies are few and of uncertain reliability.

Evidence also indicates that foraging peoples enjoyed a diverse diet and were healthy, compared to farmers. Hunters and gatherers live from plants and animals that naturally occur in their habitats and that are well adapted to periodic droughts and other hazards. In most places their diets were diverse, compared to those of farmers and herders, who focused their attention and efforts on just a few crops and livestock. Foraging bands were small and moved often, which reduced the incidence and spread of infectious diseases. There are, of course, exceptions, but the bulk of the evidence suggests that hunter-gatherers did not have a particularly hard life.

If this is true, then why did the foraging adaptation ever change? Why did so many humans take up farming over the course of centuries? One important reason is that agriculture supports far more people per unit of territory. In trying to account for why agriculture developed at all, most archaeologists point to two factors that led prehistoric foragers to gradually begin cultivating crops. The first is climate change: in the Eastern Mediterranean where agriculture developed earliest—around 10,000 years ago—the climate became warmer about the same time people began domesticating plants and animals.

New World Livestock

Compared to ancient Old World peoples, Native Americans domesticated few livestock. In the Andes, llamas and alpacas (related to camels) were used for meat and transportation. Their thick, long hair was also woven into beautiful clothing by weavers of the ancient Andean civilizations. In South America, guinea pigs were raised for meat. Elsewhere in the Americas, turkeys and Muscovy ducks were the only animals domesticated for food, and these only in a few areas. Dogs, present also in the Old World, were used in hunting and often as food.

Why did American Indians domesticate so few animals compared to Middle Easterners and Asians? The answer is uncertain, but one important reason may be that so many of the large herd animal species in the Americas became extinct shortly after the end of the Pleistocene epoch, about 11,000 years ago. Members of the horse and camel family, in particular, all disappeared (except in the Andes). Horses did not return to the Americas until brought by the Spanish in the 1500s. Still, some large herd animals, such as bison and caribou, survived the extinctions, so the idea that Native Americans had fewer large wild animals suitable for domesticating is debatable.

What's Cooking?

Soon after Spain, Portugal, France, Britain, and the Netherlands began exploring and establishing colonies on other continents, crops and livestock began to spread from continent to continent. Many New World crops were taken to various parts of the Old World, where they became important foods for millions of people. Manioc from Amazonia became a staple in tropical Africa and Asia. Mexican corn spread widely, especially in Africa, Mediterranean Europe, and East Asia. After initial resistance, the Andean potato became a staple food in Russia, northern Europe, and—especially—Ireland. Imagine Italian food without the Mexican tomato! Over the centuries, Native American cultivators had become master farmers, and food crops are one of the greatest gifts they bestowed upon the rest of the world.

Crops and livestock moved across the Atlantic in the other direction also. European colonists took Old World wheat, oats, barley, grapes, and other crops to temperate zones of the Americas. In parts of the Americas with more tropical climates, rice, bananas, and coconuts became important food. But livestock were the most important food introduced from the Old World. Pigs, cattle, sheep, and horses were introduced very soon after the European encounter with the New World. In the next couple of centuries they had multiplied rapidly and spread widely. Old World livestock greatly eased the life of the European colonists—pigs and cattle thrived and multiplied in the Americas and became enormously abundant by the time European settlers began spreading over the landscape. Plentiful, familiar cattle, pigs, and sheep helped attract European colonists to the Americas in the 1700s and 1800s. Plows pulled by horses, mules, and oxen made it possible to turn over heavy soils and break up the matted roots of grasses, allowing settlers to farm the rich earth of the American Midwest and Plains for the first time.

Only a few of us recognize our debt to the prehistoric Middle Easterners, Asians, Africans, Andeans, and Mexicans who domesticated the plants and animals we eat daily. Yet most North American meals include foods brought to the continent from all over the world centuries ago. If you're an all-American, meat-and-potatoes kind of person, only the potatoes are truly American—and they (like another of your favorites, beans) came from south of the border.

Sources: Fagan (1986), Crosby (1972), Diamond (1997), Pope et al. (2001)

The second factor is growing human populations: although prehistoric hunters and gatherers lived well, once their numbers began to increase substantially, wild plants and animals could no longer support the population size in a region. Planting and cultivating crops allow a group greater control over the numbers of *edible* plants that exist in their environment, raising the ability of the land to support people. If a field is planted in wheat, or rice or corn, then nearly all the plants growing there produce foods that humans can digest. If the field is left in its natural state, then only a fraction of the wild plants are digestible and, hence, edible.

How these two factors interacted, and the importance of other factors, is one of the most controversial issues in modern archaeology, but most believe that the single greatest advantage of agriculture over foraging is that agriculture supports far more people. Only in the most favorable environments does the population density of foragers exceed one or two per square mile. In contrast, agricultural peoples typically live at densities of dozens or hundreds per square mile.

Like most benefits, supporting higher population densities entails some costs. Creating and maintaining the artificial community of plants that make up a garden or farm requires labor, time, and energy. First, the plot must be prepared for planting by removing at least some of the vegetation that occurs naturally in the area. In some kinds of agriculture, people modify the landscape itself by constructing furrows, dikes, ditches, terraces, or other artificial landforms. Second, the crops must be planted, requiring more labor. Third, natural processes continually encroach on the artificial plant community and landscape that people have created: Weeds invade and compete for light and soil nutrients, animal pests are attracted to the densely growing crops, and rainfall and flood may wash away physical improvements. Cultivators, therefore, must "beat back nature" by periodically removing weeds, protecting against pests, rebuilding earthworks, and so forth. Fourth, the act of farming itself reduces the suitability of a site for future harvests, by reducing soil fertility if nothing else. In future years the farmers must somehow restore their plots to a usable condition or their yields will fall. All these necessities require labor and other kinds of energy expenditures.

So farming is a lot of work, and much evidence suggests that people who make their living by agriculture work at least as long and hard as most foragers. Cultivation also led to other changes—in settlement size and permanence, in ownership of resources, in political organization, and in many other dimensions of life—that culminated in the evolution of whole new forms of culture, as we shall see.

Commonly, preindustrial farming systems are divided into two overall forms, based partly on the energy source used in farming and on how often a garden or field is cultivated. They are usually called *horticulture* and *intensive agriculture*. Both have many, many varieties—far too many for us to even mention most of them.

Horticulture

In the type of farming called **horticulture,** people use mainly or exclusively the energy (power) of their own muscles to clear land, turn over the soil, plant, weed, and harvest crops. There are no plows pulled by draft animals (like horses or oxen) to help prepare the soil. Instead, hand tools such as digging sticks, shovels, and hoes are used for most tasks. Farmers may clear new fields by burning the natural vegetation. Some horticultural people fertilize their gardens with animal or human wastes or with other kinds of organic matter. If irrigation is necessary, they usually hand-carry water from nearby rivers or streams. Figure 6.2 shows the most important regions where the horticultural adaptation existed at the time of contact by the West.

Varieties of Horticulture

One type of horticulture is *shifting cultivation* (also called *slash and burn*). Once very widespread, in modern times it is limited to pockets of remote tropical rain forests in Central and South America, Southeast Asia, and central Africa. Shifting cultivators farm the forest in a cycle. Using axes, knives, and other hand tools, they first remove a small area of forest. After the wood and leaves dry out, they burn the refuse to recycle valuable plant nutrients. Generally, a given garden plot is cultivated for only two or three years before its fertility declines and it is gradually abandoned. Then another plot is cleared; a new garden is planted, tended, and harvested until its productivity declines. It is abandoned and its natural vegetation regrows until it recovers its ability to produce an adequate harvest, which typically takes 10 or more years.

Shifting cultivation works well so long as population density (the number of people who live in an area of a given size) does not grow too large. For every plot of land under cultivation at any given time, several plots are *fallowed*—they have been left alone for the forest to regrow and the land to recover. For example, if for every acre of land being cultivated, 10 acres are under fallow, then far fewer people could be supported per acre than if only half the land were fallowed at any one time. This is one reason that, in most regions, shifting cultivation has given way to intensive agriculture (discussed later).

Another example of horticulture is *dry land gardening.* It is defined by the main climatic factor with which cultivators have to cope: low, erratic, and unpredictable rainfall. Like other horticulturalists, dry land gardeners use no plow, and simple hand tools—hoes, spades, and so forth—powered by human muscles are the characteristic technology. Dry land gardening occurs in the American Southwest, in arid parts of Mexico, in some of the Middle East, and in much of sub-Saharan Africa. In the more arid regions of Africa it is sometimes supplemented by cattle raising, because rainfall is too light and unpredictable for people to depend entirely on their crops.

Cultivation in arid lands is risky: even if in most years rainfall and harvests are adequate, there is a good chance that in any given year not enough rain will fall. Therefore, people who cultivate in dry regions have developed various gardening techniques to cope with the possibility of drought.

The Western Pueblo peoples—including the Hopi and Zuni—of the North American Southwest illustrate one way to cope with aridity. In this region annual rainfall

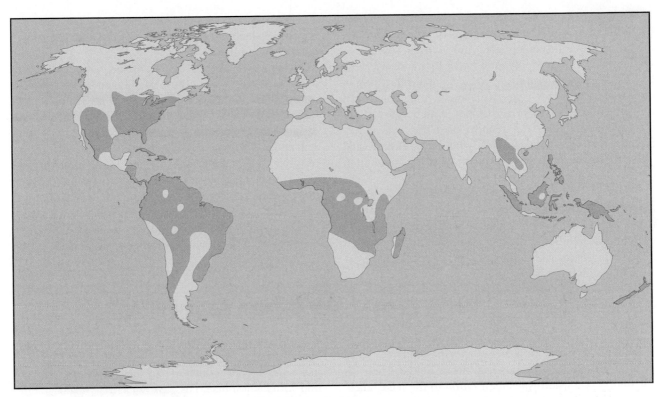

▲ **Figure 6.2** Principal Regions of Horticulture at the Contact Period

averages only around ten inches, concentrated in the spring and late summer. Further, in this high country the growing season for corn—the major food—is only about four months long. The people are faced with extreme uncertainty: If they plant too early, a spring frost may kill their crops; if they wait too long, they will lose some of the critical moisture from the spring rains.

Traditionally, the Western Pueblo coped with risk by planting some crops in those areas most likely to flood, where soil moisture usually lasts until harvest time. Yet in some years the unpredictable rains are so torrential that runoff washes away the crops. To cope with such natural hazards, the people diversify both the place and the time of their planting. They plant the seeds of corn, squash, beans, and other crops in several locations so that, no matter what the weather, some fields produce a harvest. Gardens in low-lying areas may be lost during an unusually wet year, but upland gardens still yield a crop. Staggering the time of planting likewise lowers the risk of cultivation; by planting crops weeks apart, the risk of losing all of a planting because of an untimely frost is reduced. Thus, by mixing up where and when they plant, the Pueblo peoples reduce the risk of cultivation in an arid, highly seasonal environment.

Cultural Consequences of Horticulture

Obviously, shifting cultivation and dry land gardening are quite different types of horticulture, which are adaptations to distinct kinds of environments. But both methods represent successful efforts to increase the amount of food that can be produced in an area if people harvested only wild resources—productivity is well above what would naturally be available to foragers. And even though horticultural methods are sometimes said to represent "simple" agriculture, they require that people remove most of the natural vegetation from the land to plant their crops. Finally, horticulture requires that people invest labor in their gardens or fields (by clearing, planting, and weeding) in expectation of a later return (the harvest). Foragers, as you recall, seldom do such things.

Thus, horticulture improves the productivity of land, modifies the natural environment, and requires people to make labor investments in their lands. These facts alone affect the cultural systems of horticulturalists. How do their cultures differ from those of foragers? Subsequent chapters address this question more thoroughly. For now, we note two of the most important ways in which the horticultural adaptation shapes the cultures of people who live by it.

First, the size and permanence of settlements increase. Rather than living in bands or camps of around 20 to 50, most horticulturalists aggregate into *villages,* sometimes with hundreds of residents. And rather than moving every few weeks, people become more *sedentary,* remaining in the same location for years, decades, or sometimes even longer. Villages are more permanent, both because effective adaptation does not require people to move frequently, and because families who have cleared and planted plots want to stay around at least long enough to recoup their labor investment.

Second, rights to resources differ from those found among most hunter-gatherers. Among horticulturalists, rights to land are better defined, meaning that particular individuals, families, and other groups are more attached to specific places where they or their ancestors have established a claim.

The main reason for more definite claims to resources is as follows. (For now we assume that some kind of family is the group that cooperates in food production.) A horticultural family invests its labor in clearing, planting, and otherwise improving specific and relatively well-defined pieces of land (its plots or fields). Their labor investment establishes their *claim* to the land. Their claim (their *rights* over the plot, including at least the right to deny other families access to it) arises from the fact that they have invested labor to increase the productivity of a plot. Families with claims to specific plots pass their rights along to their children, most of whom marry and transmit the rights to their own children. Over several generations, families and other kinds of kin groups develop recognized ownership over particular plots. (Of course, rights may be under dispute and not every family's rights are regarded as legitimate by everyone else, which leads to "political problems" that make it valuable to develop structured ways of resolving conflicts, as covered in Chapter 12.) In the present generation, any given individual or family thus has ownership rights over specific parcels, which usually include the gardens they are actually cultivating. Rights often extend to abandoned plots that they or their ancestors cultivated in the past and to which they or their children may return in future years.

Among horticultural peoples, then, ownership rights over well-defined parcels of land are usually held by families or some other kind of kinship group. In contrast, foragers most commonly have use rights over large territories with only vaguely defined boundaries. Further, horticultural families usually claim ownership over the land itself, because the soil may be made productive by planting crops on it. For foragers, use rights are typically exercised only over the wild resources of a territory, which is valuable mainly because of the wild plants and animals found there.

In sum, two of the major ways the cultures of horticulturalists differ from those of foragers are: (1) living groups (villages) are larger and more permanently settled, and (2) families have more definite rights of ownership over particular pieces of land. These two consequences, in turn, have other effects on cultures. For example, sedentism means that people can store possessions rather than having to carry them around, raising the potential for wealth accumulation. More definite land rights raises the possibility that some families will inherit or otherwise acquire more productive resources than others. These and other effects are considered in later chapters.

Intensive Agriculture

As we have seen, horticultural peoples use human muscles as the only or main source of power, and mostly they make only modest efforts to improve the soil by fertilization with natural materials. And even though horticulture supports higher population densities than foraging, the number of people it can support is low relative to the farming system known as **intensive agriculture.** (Figure 6.3 shows the major regions where intensive agriculturalists lived at the time of contact with Europeans.)

Intensive farmers keep their fields under cultivation far longer than horticulturalists. Indeed, some intensive agriculturalists have their lands under almost continuous cultivation—the same fields are farmed year after year, with only brief fallow periods. This is what is meant by using land more *intensively:* to produce higher yields, farmers work the land (and usually themselves) harder.

This is possible only if people make efforts to maintain the long-term productivity of their land. In various regions, such steps include substantial fertilization (generally with the dung of livestock), crop rotation, careful weeding, turning the soil prior to planting, composting, and other methods. For some of these tasks, a new tool, the plow, and a new source of energy (power), draft animals, are useful. Using plows pulled by horses, oxen, water buffalo, or other draft animals, a farmer can more quickly prepare the soil. In addition to traction for the plow, livestock provide many other useful products: meat, milk and other dairy products, manure, hides, and transportation. After harvest, livestock may be turned loose to graze on the unharvested stubble, fertilizing fields in the process. In some regions, animal muscle is

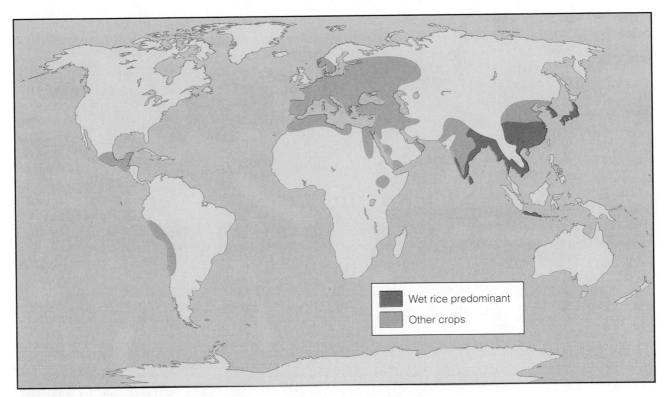

▲ **Figure 6.3** Principal Regions of Intensive Agriculture at the Contact Period

used to power the mechanical pumps that carry irrigation water to the fields. Livestock also were harnessed to the heavy stone wheels used to grind grains into flour.

For all these reasons, intensive agriculture is substantially more productive per unit of land than horticulture. An acre of land produces greater yields and, hence, is capable of supporting far more people—5, 10, and even 20 times the numbers of most horticultural adaptations. Supporting more people is probably the main advantage of intensive agriculture over horticulture.

Varieties of Intensive Agriculture

In the Old World, especially in parts of Asia and Europe, intensive agriculture included the use of the plow. But before the coming of Europeans, New World peoples had no domesticated animals suitable for pulling plows. Indeed, outside the Andes of South America, the only animals domesticated by Native Americans were dogs, turkeys, and muscovy ducks. Andean people also had llamas and alpacas, but these were not harnessed to plows.

Despite this limitation, Native American peoples in places such as the valley of Mexico (land of the Aztecs) and the Andes found ways of increasing yields by inten-

sifying their production efforts. In the valley of Mexico, for example, people transformed swamps and the margins of lakes into productive fields by filling in earth and constructing raised fields in which they planted crops like tomatoes, squash, and corn. By continually adding new organic materials from the lake bottoms, the people could keep their gardens under almost continuous cultivation. In the Andes, stepped terraces were constructed to reduce erosion, and an incredible variety of potatoes and other crops were grown during the summer. Andean peoples also developed a variety of methods for coping with frost in their mountain homelands.

Another method of increasing yields is to augment the water supply by artificial means. Farmers around the world use many ingenious irrigation methods. Sometimes streams are dammed to conserve runoff, and ditches are dug to transport water to the fields. In some Asian river valleys, channels are dug to transport water and fertile silt to fields during the annual monsoons, when rivers overrun their banks. In many mountainous regions of Southeast Asia and China, the level of water in hillside rice fields is controlled with an elaborate system of diked terraces. Rice is produced through a highly coordinated system to supply water in these *wet rice* regions.

© David Austen/Stock Boston

▲ Wet rice is a very productive form of intensive agriculture that has supported large populations in Asia for many generations. If necessary, humans can construct artificial terraces even on steep slopes, as these Indonesian terraces illustrate.

In sum, compared with horticulture, intensive agriculture produces more food per unit of land. Its high productivity is due to factors such as shortened fallow periods, preparing land more thoroughly prior to planting, removing weeds, adding manure and other organic matter to preserve fertility, and manipulating the supply of water. These (and other) inputs give people greater control over conditions in their fields, leading to higher yields per unit of land.

Cultural Consequences of Intensive Agriculture

The development of intensive methods of farming eventually had dramatic cultural consequences in many regions. Some of the most important effects of this form of adaptation result from its relatively high productivity. A single farm family using intensive methods can usually feed many more people than just its own members. Far more than either foragers or horticulturalists, intensive farmers can produce a **surplus** over and above their own subsistence (food) requirements. This surplus can be used to feed other people, families, and other kinds of groups, who no longer need to produce their own food.

What happens to this surplus? Many things, depending on the circumstances. Excess food can be traded for other useful products like pottery, tools, wood, and clothing. If the community uses money (see Chapter 7), families may produce surplus food for sale and use the money to buy other goods. If the village or other settlement has a strong political leader, such as a chief, he can collect the surplus from his subjects and use the food to pay laborers who work on public projects such as trails, temples, and irrigation works. If the community is part of a larger, more encompassing political system, with a ruler and a governmental bureaucracy, then the government will collect part of the surplus as a tax. Political officials then use the tax for public purposes (e.g., support of armies, the judiciary, and the religious hierarchy) or to further its own political interests.

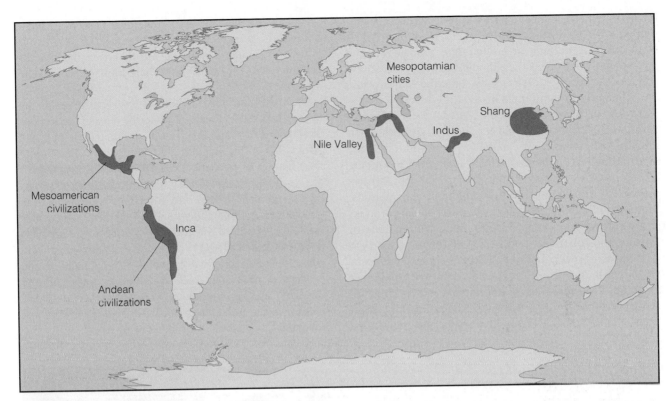

▲ **Figure 6.4** Ancient Civilizations

All these possibilities illustrate a central fact about most peoples who depend on intensive agriculture: Most are not politically independent and economically self-sufficient communities but are instead incorporated into some kind of large organization. The villages in which most of them live are part of a more inclusive political system that dominates or rules them in some way. The surplus production of intensive farmers is traded, sold, or taxed (or all three) and supports people who do not themselves do farm work—people such as rulers, aristocrats, bureaucrats, priests, warriors, merchants, and craft specialists.

Intensive agriculture, then, is strongly associated with large-scale political and economic organization: Local-level farmers in villages produce food and other products for people who live elsewhere, and they, in turn, receive things (products, services) from the larger system. The association of intensive agriculture with large-scale political organization is ancient, going back 5,000 years in parts of the Old World and more than 2,000 years in two regions of the New World.

In a few parts of the world, within a few centuries or a millennium after the development of intensive agriculture, the socially and politically complex organization we call **civilization** (including, among other things, the first cities) emerged. Civilizations have a formal, specialized form of government known as the *state* (discussed further in Chapter 12). States are large-scale political units featuring a ruler, a governing bureaucracy, class distinctions between the elite and common people, and methods of extracting labor and surplus products from those who are responsible for farming the land.

In prehistoric times, intensive farmers were incorporated into the four major civilizations of the ancient Old World: the valley formed by the Tigris and Euphrates rivers of Mesopotamia, the Nile valley of Egypt, the Indus River valley of Pakistan, and the vast empire of China. In the New World, too, agricultural peoples were part of large-scale political units, such as the Mayans, Toltecs, and Aztecs of Mesoamerica, and the Incas of the Andean coast and highlands (Figure 6.4).

All these early civilizations were supported by intensive agriculture based on large-scale irrigation and water control facilities. Intensive farmers produced the food supply and paid tribute or taxes to support the rulers, priests, armies, and officials who staffed the government, protected the city, organized the worship of gods, and performed other roles that had now become necessary. So far as we know, intensive agriculture is virtually a prerequisite for civilization, for no civilization ever developed out of a foraging or horticultural adaptation. (The Mayan civilization was once thought to have been an exception, but recent evidence shows that the Mayans, too, used intensive farming methods.)

In the world we live in today, virtually every human community is politically and economically incorporated into larger organizations, namely, into nations and the international economic system. Rather than producing largely for their own subsistence, many modern farmers produce for sale on local or international markets. Methods of farming the land have also changed dramatically in recent decades. In most industrial nations of Europe, the Americas, and East Asia, farming the land with animal-powered plows has been replaced by mechanized agriculture, with its tractors, combines, and other machinery powered by gasoline and other kinds of energy derived from fossil fuels. Economically, most small, family-owned farms in Canada and the United

States must invest heavily in machinery and other technologies to keep their farms productive, for their livelihood and standard of living are based on their yields and the prices they receive for their crops, livestock, and other products.

Intensive farming methods do survive even in the twenty-first century, especially in the developing regions of southern Asia and Southeast Asia, Latin America, and Africa. Economically, farming communities often fit into their nations as **peasants.** Peasants are rural people who are integrated into a larger society both politically (i.e., they are subject to laws and governments imposed from outside their communities) and economically (i.e., they exchange products of their own labor for products produced elsewhere). In many developing countries, peasants are a numerical majority of the population and produce much of the food consumed by town and city dwellers. Peasants produce goods that are sold for money, traded or bartered, paid to a landlord as rent, and rendered to a central government as taxes.

▲ Even in the modern world, peasants make up the majority population of many Asian nations. These Indonesians of the island of Bali are cooperating in farm work.

© Sergio Dorantes/Corbis

So far as we know, there were no peasants until the emergence of the ancient civilizations just mentioned. The farm work of prehistoric peasants fed the craft workers, the merchants, the state-sponsored priests, the political elite, the warriors, and the builders of palaces and temples. The tribute or tax (paid in food, crafts, labor, or all three) rendered by peasants was extracted from them by armed force or threat of force. This rendering of goods and labor by peasants to members of a more powerful social category continued into historic times. The peasantry of medieval Europe, for example, eked out a meager living, paying a substantial portion of their annual harvest to their lords or working many days a year on their lord's estate.

Given this information, we might well wonder whether the development of intensive agriculture benefited the peasants who actually farmed the land. True, the high productivity of intensive agriculture allowed the specialized division of labor that led to writing, metallurgy, monumental architecture, cities, and the great religious and artistic traditions we associate with civilization. But how about the peasants who produced the food that made such "progress" possible? For them, writing meant that more accurate accounts could be kept of their taxes or the number of days they worked for overlords. Iron and other metals meant that peasants had better farming tools; yet for the most part they were not allowed to use them to ease their own work but instead only to produce more surplus for others to appropriate. Metal also meant that weapons became more deadly and armies more dangerous, allowing one state to make war against other states more effectively. Most peasant families continued to live in hovels, even while engineers designed great palaces, religious structures, and walled cities and towns that were built using peasant tax-labor. Throughout history, most peasants the world over were denied the benefits offered by technological progress, although the food they produced made much of this progress possible.

Pastoralism

Most farming people also keep domesticated animals. Southeast Asian and Pacific horticulturalists raise many pigs and chickens. Intensive agriculturalists raise livestock such as horses, oxen, water buffalo, and cattle that pull their plows, fertilize their fields, and provide dairy products and meat. Livestock do not merely "supplement" the adaptation of farming peoples: Because of the meat, eggs, milk, hides, wool, transportation, fertilizer, and horsepower they provide, they are usually critical to the nutritional and economic welfare of cultivators.

However, cultivators do not depend on their domesticated animals to the same extent or in the same way as do peoples known as *pastoralists,* or herders. Herders acquire much of their food by raising, caring for, and subsisting on the products of domesticated animals. With a few exceptions, the livestock are gregarious (herd) animals. Cattle, camels, sheep, goats, reindeer, horses, llamas, alpacas, and yaks are the common animals kept by herders in various parts of the world.

Agriculture and pastoralism are not necessarily mutually exclusive adaptations, for a great many pastoral peoples also farm the land. When we characterize a people as "pastoral," we mean more than that they keep animals. More importantly, we mean that the needs of their animals for naturally occurring food and water greatly influence the seasonal rhythms of their lives.

The key phrase here is "naturally occurring." Most farmers raise crops that they feed to their livestock or maintain fields in which their animals graze. In general, pastoralists do neither of these. Their herds graze on natural forage and therefore must be moved to where the forage naturally occurs. Some or all of the people must take their livestock to wherever the grasses or other forage is available in a given season. This high degree of mobility, known as **nomadism,** characterizes the pastoral adaptation. Most commonly, pastoralists are seasonally nomadic—they do not wander aimlessly. Their migrations are often "vertical," meaning that animals are taken to highland areas to graze during the hottest season of the year.

Herding Environments

For the most part, herders live in only certain kinds of environments (Figure 6.5 shows where pastoralists lived prior to European expansion). The pastoral adaptation occurs mainly in deserts, grasslands, savannas, mountains, and the Arctic tundra. Obviously, these environments are diverse, but they do share a common feature: Cultivation is impossible, extremely difficult, or highly risky because of inadequate or great yearly fluctuations in rainfall (as in deserts or savannas) or very short growing seasons (as in mountains and tundras). As always, there are exceptions to our generalizations, but most herders live in regions that are not well suited to cultivation.

In such arid or cold environments, the herding of livestock offers several advantages over the planting of crops. First, most of the vegetation of grasslands and arid savannas (grasses and shrubs) and of tundras (lichens, willows, and sedges) is indigestible by humans. Livestock such as cattle, sheep, and reindeer are able to eat this vegetation and transform it into milk, blood, fat, and muscle,

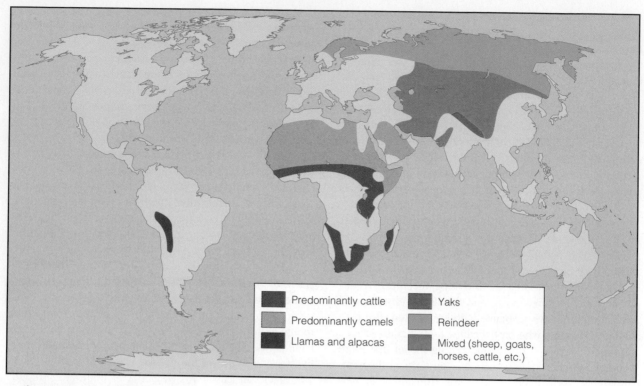

▲ **Figure 6.5** Principal Regions of Pastoralism at the Contact Period

all of which are drunk or eaten by various pastoral peoples. Thus, in some areas livestock allow people to exploit indirectly certain wild plant resources not directly available to them. Livestock convert inedibles into edibles.

Another advantage of herding is to level out fluctuations in the food supply. In areas of low and unreliable rainfall, crops often fail because of drought. Livestock provide an insurance against these periodic, unpredictable droughts and accompanying crop failures. In high altitude mountains, frosts are a threat to crops. Not only do livestock store food "on the hoof," but they can also be traded or sold to neighboring peoples for cultivated foods. Livestock reduce risks.

Finally, a big advantage of livestock is their mobility. Herders can move their animals to areas of freshest or lushest pasture, to sources of water, away from neighbors who have grown too aggressive, or out of easy range of governments that often want the nomads to settle down so they can be taxed, formally educated, or better controlled. Livestock allow people to store their food on the hoof, making it easy to move when necessary.

With advantages like these, you may well wonder why pastoralism was and is not more widespread. Why did the herding adaptation not spread to areas where cultivators lived? Part of the reason is that environmental conditions

are not always conducive. For example, until recently pastoralism was seldom found in tropical forests, largely because of lack of forage. (Today, enormous tracts of tropical forest in Central and South America are cleared and replanted in grasses suitable for cattle grazing.) Livestock diseases also limit the distribution of pastoralists. For example, much of eastern and southern Africa is occupied by cattle herders (most of whom also farm, however). Herders would presumably be even more widespread on the continent were it not for the limitations imposed by the presence of the tsetse fly, which transmits the debilitating disease sleeping sickness to cattle.

But perhaps the main factor limiting the distribution of pastoralism is that herding is not the most productive way of using resources in those areas in which agriculture can be carried out reliably. The best way to understand why is to apply the ecologists' "10 percent rule." The food energy produced by photosynthetic plants lies at the base of all terrestrial ecosystems. In the presence of sufficient water, carbon dioxide, and minerals, plants convert the energy of sunlight into simple sugars. Herbivores (plant-eating animals) consume the vegetation and use it to maintain their own bodies and produce offspring. Carnivores (animal-eating animals) in turn feed on herbivores. At each of these levels of the food chain, most of the energy is lost as it is

▲ Pastoralists use livestock to transport their possessions and to carry products destined for trade or markets. This is part of a camel caravan in the Algerian Sahara.

carried to the next level. Thus, herbivores transform only about 10 percent of the plant energy they consume into their own flesh; and only around 10 percent of the energy carnivores acquire by eating herbivores is available to make more carnivore flesh. At each level, 90 percent of the energy consumed is lost to respiration, waste production, and other processes. The 10 percent rule says that only about 10 percent of the energy locked up in living matter at one level is available to the next level.

Now we can see why herding is not as efficient as agriculture at exploiting an environment: overall, pastoralists eat higher on the food chain. More total food energy can be obtained from an environment by farming because much more energy can be gained from (cultivated) plants than from (herded) animals. People did not necessarily figure out that they could most productively exploit an environment by growing crops rather than raising animals, and then opt for cultivation. More likely, cultivation won out over herding—in areas that are suitable for both—because of its greater labor productivity. Further, the 10 percent rule also translates into higher potential (and actual) population densities for cultivators, who in the past may have outcompeted pastoralists for those territories that both could exploit.

Aridity, temperature, short growing seasons, and other ecological and climatic factors do not totally explain the distribution of the pastoral adaptation, however. Some pastoralists live in areas where crops could be grown, and they certainly know how to cultivate, but they consciously choose not to grow crops. The cattle-herding Maasai of Kenya and Tanzania are an example. In some parts of the Maasai territory cultivation is possible, and in fact most neighboring tribes combine cattle herding with cultivation of sorghum and other crops. The proud Maasai, however, look down on cultivation because their herds represent wealth and are the main symbol of their cultural identity relative to their neighbors. Maasai, therefore, live largely off the products of their cattle—blood, milk, curds—and trade with their neighbors for the cultivated foods they do eat. The reasons they continue their pastoral adaptation are, therefore, as much "cultural" as "ecological."

The Karimojong: An Example from East Africa

The Karimojong of Uganda illustrate many features of the pastoral adaptation. Living on an arid savanna with marked seasonal differences in rainfall, traditionally they subsisted by a combination of horticulture and cattle herding. The Karimojong numbered about 60,000 when they were studied by Rada and Neville Dyson-Hudson in the 1960s.

Karimojong are a fairly representative example of a cultural area anthropologists call the "East African cattle complex." In this complex, found throughout the East African savannahs, cattle are more than a mere food source. East African men love their cattle the way some North Americans love their sports utility vehicles. Cattle represent wealth and manliness. They are the source of prestige, influence in tribal affairs, and wives (an East African man must transfer cattle to his wife's relatives to marry her, a practice we discuss in Chapter 8). Cattle are religious symbols, for their ritual sacrifice is the source of blessings from ancestors and gods. Underlying all these cultural elements of the cattle complex, according to the Dyson-Hudsons, is the important role of cattle in subsistence: "First, last and always the role of cattle in Karimojong life is to transform the energy stored in the grasses, herbs and shrubs of the tribal area into a form easily available to the people" (Dyson-Hudson and Dyson-Hudson 1969, 4).

This transformation is not mainly achieved by eating the animals' flesh, as Westerners might expect. Rather, the Karimojong—and most other East Africans—consume the products of living cattle: milk and blood. Lactating cows are milked twice daily. Every three to five months, several pints of blood are taken from the jugular of some animals and drunk, usually immediately. Cattle meat is consumed mainly on religious occasions; the meat is shared among all participants.

There is a marked sexual division of labor in Karimojong subsistence activities. The central portion of the tribal territory is crossed by several rivers, and hence is relatively well watered during the rainy season. Here the women live in permanent settlements, where they cultivate sorghum (an African grain) and a few other crops. The central area, however, produces good grasses for the herds only during the rainy season, so for most of the year the cattle must be taken to greener pastures, often miles away from the settlements. The Karimojong therefore have another kind of settlement, the mobile "cattle camps" that are run by males, especially by young men. Rainfall is quite unpredictable, especially during the driest half of the year. But localized storms do occur, and for many days afterward grass grows well in restricted areas. The men of the cattle camps—accompanied by the cattle—move frequently in search of pasture. While living in the cattle camps, men live largely from the milk and blood of their animals, supplemented by the beer made from sorghum that the women sometimes bring when they visit.

Both cultivated crops and livestock are necessary foods for the Karimojong. Even a short three-week drought during the sorghum-growing season will seriously reduce the harvest, but the mobility of the livestock allows them to be taken to places where there is sufficient pasture. Cattle thus provide an insurance against climatic and other forces that make cultivation alone too risky to rely on. They also allow the Karimojong to find food in those parts of their territory that are too dry to support cultivation. The cattle convert grasses and shrubs indigestible to humans into milk, blood, and meat, which eventually are eaten by the people.

Adaptation and Culture

In this chapter, we have synthesized an enormous amount of information on the main forms of human adaptation and on how adaptation affects cultural systems. Many complications have not been covered because of space limitations. Many exceptions to our generalizations have been ignored in the interest of understanding broad patterns. Recognizing these complications and exceptions, one major point is the following: *How a group of people harnesses the resources and copes with the problems of living in a particular environment creates important influences on many dimensions of the group's culture.* The accompanying Concept Review summarizes some of these influences.

Just how important these "influences" are, of course, is debatable, as the theoretical approaches known as scientific and humanistic (see Chapter 4) illustrate. Nonetheless, few anthropologists would question certain generalizations about the relation between forms of adaptation and cultural systems:

- In most environments, foraging is most efficient when people live in small, seasonally mobile groups that maintain flexible rights to the natural resources of large territories.
- Horticultural people settle in hamlets or villages in which land and other productive resources are owned by families or other kinship or residential groups.
- Intensive agriculture resulted in the development of towns and cities occupied by elites and specialists and surrounded by rural peasant communities that contribute labor, tribute, and/or tax to support the government and public projects.
- Most pastoral peoples are seasonally nomadic, with grazing rights to pasturelands vested in families or other kin groups or in the tribe as a whole.

In future chapters, as we cover various aspects of culture, we shall sometimes discuss the ways in which adaptation affects family life, gender relations, political organization, and other dimensions of cultural systems.

Major Forms of Adaptation and Their Cultural Consequences

Form of Adaptation	Food Acquired by Means of	Basic Organization of Communities	Rights to Resources	Internal Differentiation
Hunting/ Gathering	Collection/gathering of wild plants; hunting of animals; sometimes fishing	Small, mobile bands of about 10–50, usually varying seasonally	Flexible access to resources over large territories	Division of labor based on sex and age; equality based on sharing
Horticulture	Cultivation of crops using hand tools and mainly human muscle power	Scattered hamlets or villages of 100 or more, largely but variably sedentary	Ownership of land and productive resources by kin groups and/or residential groups	Variable, but little specialization and inequality
Intensive Agriculture	Cultivation of crops with animal-powered plows or other means of using land intensively	Central administrative places with cities and towns surrounded by rural "peasant" communities	Vested in or controlled by multilevel administrative officials responsible to the "state"	Craft and service specialization with social distinctions and major inequalities
Pastoralism	Livestock provide products (meat, milk, hides, wool) to eat, trade, and sell	Seasonally nomadic living units of varying size and composition	Grazing rights based on membership in families, kin groups, or the tribe itself	Variably complex; based on age, sex, and often hereditary distinctions

Summary

1. Adaptation refers to how organisms interact with their environments in ways that lead to their survival and reproduction. One important feature of human adaptation is that it is carried out primarily—but not exclusively—by cultural changes: Humans adapt to new habitats by means of cultural changes in technology and organization, not mainly by alteration in their genes. One of the most important ways in which human populations interact with their environments is by production, which requires labor, technology, and natural resources. To produce a product efficiently, human groups organize themselves by the division of labor, patterns of cooperation, and allocating rights to natural resources.

2. The earliest form of human adaptation was hunting and gathering, or foraging. Foragers live nearly exclusively from the wild plants and animals available in their habitats. All human groups acquired their food from hunting and gathering until around 10,000 years ago, when plants and animals were first domesticated. Over the next several millennia, farmers and herders grew in numbers and expanded into regions previously occupied by foragers. Only a few foraging cultures survived into the twentieth century.

3. The adaptive requirements of living from wild plants and animals greatly affected the cultures of most foraging peoples. People had to organize their activities so that at the proper season, they could be at the places where wild foods were naturally available. Accordingly, the most foraging cultures exhibited the following characteristics: (1) a division of labor based mainly on sex and age, (2) high mobility, (3) congregation and dispersal of groups, usually based on seasonal changes, (4) small living groups called bands, (5) reciprocal sharing, and (6) loose and flexible rights to the resources of a given territory. These features are well illustrated by cultures such as the Hadza, Shoshone, and !Kung. However, in especially resource-rich environments such as the Northwest Coast, the great abundance and high reliability of natural resources allowed people to settle in large, nearly permanent villages, and to develop well-defined rights to territory.

4. Domestication is the attempt to increase the productivity of an environment by planting and cultivating selected plants (crops) and taming and breeding certain animals (livestock). Domestication first arose 10,000 years ago in the Old World and around 5,000 years ago in the New World. Most modern scholars believe that the main advantage of domestication over hunting and gathering is its ability to support far greater numbers of people per unit of land. As plant and animal domestication spread into new regions over several millennia, this new way of adapting to nature modified the way people lived.

5. One of many forms of agriculture is called horticulture. Horticulturalists use only hand tools in planting, cultivating, and harvesting their plots or gardens, as illustrated by shifting cultivation and dry land gardening. Horticulture produces more food per acre than foraging, and it requires that people make a labor investment in particular pieces of land (their plots). Increased productivity and labor investments alone had two important consequences for cultures: (1) people remained in one place for a long time (sedentism), and the size of their settlements increased (villages), and (2) particular families established their own claims to particular pieces of land, producing cultural beliefs that land is the property of specific groups.

6. As populations grew in certain regions, horticultural methods were no longer sufficient to produce enough food, so land had to be worked more intensively. Intensive agriculturalists use various methods to keep yields high, including keeping a single field under production longer, with little or no fallow. In the Old World, livestock were harnessed to plows to till the fields, whereas New World intensive agriculturalists used other methods. Fertilization with animal manure and other organic matter and irrigation are common among intensive agriculturalists. These and other methods eventually raised productivity enough that a single farm family was able to produce a surplus over and above its own food needs. Out of this surplus potential a new form of culture, called civilization, arose in several favorable regions of both the Old World and the New World. Always supported by intensive agriculture, civilization and city life changed human life profoundly, leading to new developments such as writing, specialization, huge architectural structures, roads, and familiar artistic traditions. But whether the class of peasants enjoyed very many of these benefits is questionable.

7. The pastoral adaptation usually occurs in regions unsuitable for agriculture due to aridity, extreme temperature, or inadequate growing seasons for crops. In these kinds of habitats, herding offers several advantages. It allows people to convert, through their livestock, indigestible grasses and other vegetation into edible flesh and dairy products. It reduces the risk of living in an unreliable environment, both because livestock provide a way of storing food on the hoof and because the food supply (herds) can be moved to more favorable places when times are hard. Although herding improves humans' ability to live in cold or arid habitats, agriculture is capable of producing far more total food than herding in favorable regions. This is probably why people usually farm the land where it is possible to do so, with some exceptions such as the Maasai. The Karimojong of Uganda illustrate many of these points about the herding adaptation.

Key Terms

adaptation	bands	surplus
hunting and gathering	domestication	civilization
(foraging)	horticulture	peasants
agriculture (cultivation)	intensive agriculture	nomadism
herding (pastoralism)		

InfoTrac College Edition Terms

Bushmen	slash and burn agriculture	peasants
Plains Indians	(also shifting	herders
origin of agriculture	cultivation)	

Suggested Readings

The following books are good overviews of preindustrial human adaptations:

Campbell, Bernard. *Human Ecology.* 2nd ed. New York: Aldine, 1995.

Describes how humans have adapted to various environments, both prehistorically and today.

Moran, Emilio F. *Human Adaptability: An Introduction to Ecological Anthropology.* 2nd ed. Boulder, Colo.: Westview Press, 2000.

An advanced textbook, with chapters on adaptations to various natural environments.

Sutton, Mark Q., and E. N. Anderson. *Introduction to Cultural Ecology.* Walnut Creek, Calif.: Altamira Press, 2004.

A textbook with discussions of each of the preindustrial adaptations covered in this chapter, along with brief examples of each form of adaptation.

Here are some books on the general relationship between populations and their environments:

Diamond, Jared. *Guns, Germs, and Steel: The Fates of Human Societies.* New York: Norton, 1997.

This Pulitzer Prize–winning book tries to account for why some societies historically were more successful than others. Diamond, a professor of physiology, argues that differences in the natural environments in which prehistoric people lived largely explain why some human societies increased in numbers and expanded geographically at the expense of other peoples. Ultimately, this book argues, all of human prehistory and history was profoundly affected by the natural environment and how diverse peoples adapted to it.

Fagan, Brian. *Floods, Famines and Emperors: El Niño and the Fate of Civilizations.* New York: Basic, 1999.

Argues that periodic shifts in rainfall and climate over large regions help account for the rise and fall of complex societies.

Fagan, Brian. *The Long Summer: How Climate Changed Civilization.* New York: Basic, 2004.

Explains major changes in adaptations and cultures by global climate shifts. Significant focus on Europe.

Krech, Shepard. *The Ecological Indian: Myth and History.* New York: W. W. Norton, 1999.

Many Anglo-Americans hold the view that Native Americans lived in harmony with their environments. By discussion of particular peoples and places, this book argues that the relationship was more complicated.

A few readable case studies of particular hunting and gathering peoples are:

Balikci, Asen. *The Netsilik Eskimo.* Prospect Heights, Ill.: Waveland Press, 1989.

A study of Netsilik adaptation, technology, kinship, marriage, and religion.

Lee, Richard B. *The Dobe Ju/'hoansi.* 3rd ed. Belmont, Calif.: Wadsworth, 2003.

A brief but reasonably comprehensive overview of the Dobe, a local population of !Kung (San) of southern Africa.

Turnbull, Colin. *The Forest People.* New York: Simon and Schuster, 1962.

An ethnography of the BaMbuti (pygmies) of Zaire. Good description of their hunting and organization.

Ethnographies of agricultural and pastoral adaptations include:

Barth, Fredrik. *Nomads of South Persia.* Prospect Heights, Ill.: Waveland Press, 1986.

A study examining the culture of the Basseri, a pastoral, sheep- and goat-herding society of southern Iran.

Lansing, Stephen J. *The Balinese.* Fort Worth, Tex.: Harcourt Brace Jovanovich, 1995.

Describes Balinese culture and the intricate relationship between Hindu temple rituals and the irrigation of wet rice fields.

Netting, Robert McC. *Smallholders, Householders: Farm Families and the Ecology of Intensive, Sustainable Agriculture.* Stanford, Calif.: Stanford University Press, 1993.

Breathtaking in coverage and geographical scope. Discusses relationships between population, land use, work, cultivation methods, productivity, ownership patterns, and household organization.

Companion Website for This Book

The Wadsworth Anthropology Resource Center
http://anthropology.wadsworth.com

The companion website that accompanies *Humanity: An Introduction to Cultural Anthropology,* Sixth Edition, includes a rich array of material, including online anthropological video clips, to help you in the study of cultural anthropology and the specific topics covered in this chapter. Begin by clicking on Student Resources. Next, click on Cultural Anthropology, and then on the cover image for this book. You have now arrived at the Student Resources home page and have the option of choosing one of several chapter resources.

Applying Anthropology. Begin your study of cultural anthropology by clicking on Applying Anthropology. Here you will find useful information on careers, graduate school programs in applied anthropology, and internships you might wish to pursue. You will also find real-world examples of working anthropologists applying the skills and methods of anthropology to help solve serious world problems.

Research Online. Click here to find a wealth of Web links that will facilitate your study of anthropology. Divided into different fields of study, specific websites are starting points for Internet research. You will be guided to rich anthropology websites that will help you prepare for class, complete course assignments, and actually do research on the Web.

InfoTrac College Edition Exercises. From the pull-down menu, select the chapter you are presently studying. Select InfoTrac College Edition Exercises from the list of resources. These exercises utilize InfoTrac College Edition's vast database of articles and help you explore the numerous uses of the search word, *culture.*

Study Aids for This Chapter. Improve your knowledge of key terms by using flash cards and study the learning objectives. Take the practice quiz, receive your results, and email them to your instructor. Access these resources from the chapter and resource pull-down menus.

Chapter Seven

EXCHANGE IN ECONOMIC SYSTEMS

Reciprocity

Generalized Reciprocity

Balanced Reciprocity

Negative Reciprocity

Reciprocity and Social Distance

Redistribution

Market Exchange

Money

On Market Economies

Peasant Marketplaces

© Sean Gallup/Getty Images

In industrialized economies, markets regulate most production and exchange. Many preindustrial economies also have markets, but many products and services are exchanged by other mechanisms.

N THE MID-1970S, when one of your authors (J.P.) conducted fieldwork on a Micronesian island called Kosrae, a man in his sixties told me he had heard that many people in Merike (America) had no land. "Is this true?" he wanted to know. I assured him it was. "But if they have no land, where does their food come from?" "We buy it in stores," I answered. Being familiar with stores, jobs, wages, and money, he nodded. "But where do people live?" He also understood my explanation of rent and the buying and selling of land. "How much does a house cost?" I estimated that he could buy a small house in California (where I then lived) for around $40,000, but that few people had that kind of money on hand and would have to borrow most of it. "Does everyone have to do this in Merike?" "Almost everyone," I replied. He was astonished. "On Kosrae," he said, "everyone gets land from his father [and/or mother, he should have added] and we build our own houses."

THE MICRONESIAN WAS SURPRISED not only because $40,000 was a lot of money for him, but also because almost all Americans have to buy or rent land to live on. The people of Kosrae did occasionally sell land to one another, but those who sold the land they inherited from their father were regarded as unfortunate or short-sighted. In his experience, land was not simply a "commodity," to be bought and sold routinely, like clothing or detergent. A family's land helped define their identity; sometimes people referred to a family by the name of the shared estate it had inherited from its ancestors. Although unmarked, the boundaries that separated one person's land from another's were widely known or, in cases of dispute, debated. How could so many Americans not have any land at all, and how could they pay so much for it?

BY JULY 2004, in California the median price of a small lot with a house was $382,000, up 23 percent from the previous year. In the San Francisco Bay Area, the median price of a lot of about a quarter acre with a house built on it was $550,000 and rising. How, indeed, did it come to cost so much?

THE ANSWER, OF COURSE, is that Americans live in an economy in which land *is* a commodity, whose price (normatively) is determined by supply and demand. Californians (and residents of Texas and Toronto and other places) may complain about the "ridiculous" price of land and housing, but it seems no one can do anything about it. Supply and demand are "impersonal" and land prices are set by the market. In a market economy, prices are not under direct human control, although (paradoxically) human wants and productive and consumptive activities create them.

As people produce the food and other products they need and want, they are engaged in what we call *economic activity*. How they allocate their labor, technology, and resources is part of their *economic system*. But producing a material product is usually only the first step toward the final use (such as consumption or display) of the product. Often, products change hands, or are *exchanged*, between the time they are produced and consumed, displayed, or put to some other use.

In fact, in modern industrial economies organized by the market principle, most products are produced entirely for exchange (sale on the market), and once the value acquired from the market exchange (money) has been gained, the producer has little further interest in the product. Markets, however, are only one way of organizing the exchange of products. In the subsistence-based economies found in traditional Kosrae and much of the preindustrial world, families or other kinds of kinship groups produce mainly for their own needs, not for sale on the market. And rather than exchanges based on supply, demand, and prices, exchanges are organized around other principles. This chapter considers some ways in which these exchanges are structured and how they differ from the buying and selling of market-based exchange.

One research area within cultural anthropology is *economic anthropology,* which is the comparative study of economic systems. Fieldworkers have described and analyzed how economies work in a variety of times and places. Much work has centered on exchange.

Economic anthropologists usually classify various forms of exchange into three major modes or types:

- **reciprocity,** in which individuals or groups pass products back and forth, with the aim of (1) helping someone in need by sharing with him or her; (2) creating, maintaining, or strengthening social relationships; or (3) obtaining products made by others for oneself
- **redistribution,** in which the members of an organized group contribute products or money into a common pool or fund that is divided (reallocated) among the group as a whole by a central authority
- **market,** in which products are sold for money, which in turn is used to purchase other products, with the ultimate goal of acquiring more money or accumulating more products or both

Most products (including land and labor) are transacted through the market mode in modern industrial economies, but reciprocity and redistribution also exist. Examples of reciprocity are various gifts we give and

Reciprocity

Back-and-forth exchange of products, gifts, and objects, symbolic of relationships as well as satisfying material needs and wants

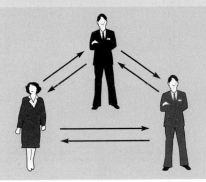

Redistribution

Collection of products and valuables by a central authority, followed by distribution according to some normative or legal principle

Market

Free exchange of products (P_1, P_2) or services (S_1, S_2) for money ($) at prices determined by impersonal forces of supply and demand

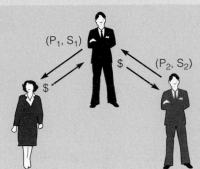

receive on holidays, birthdays, weddings, baby showers, and other culturally special occasions. If you are employed, every pay period you participate in redistribution, for federal, state, and local governments collect a portion of your wage or salary as taxes, which they expend on public purposes or transfer to other members of society.

All these exchange forms thus exist in modern societies, but not all preindustrial peoples have all three. Reciprocity in one form or another occurs in all human populations. But redistribution implies the existence of a central leader(s) whose role(s) carries authority to organize the collection of resources from the group and to make decisions about how they will be reallocated. Redistribution, therefore, is an insignificant exchange mode in societies that lack strong leaders who make decisions on behalf of the group. The market mode of exchange requires money, private property, and certain other features that are absent in nonmarket economies. The accompanying Concept Review illustrates the three forms of exchanges.

Reciprocity

In subsistence economies such as most of those based on foraging, horticulture, and pastoralism, families and households are commonly capable of producing most of the food and other products they consume. That is, most families are *potentially* self-sufficient in the sense that they own or have access to the land, labor, tools, and other resources necessary for survival.

However, in no known society are families, households, or other kinds of social groups self-sufficient *in fact*. Everywhere, such groups exchange products with other groups. Most anthropologists say that this is because families and other groups need or want to maintain relationships with other families and groups, and exchange is necessary to create and sustain these relationships. Examples of why groups need such relationships include ensuring long-term economic security, acquiring spouses, maintaining political ties, and strengthening military alliances.

The form of exchange used for such purposes is *reciprocity,* defined as the mutual transaction of objects without the use of money or other media of exchange. Reciprocity takes several forms: sharing with those in need, providing hospitality, giving gifts, mutual feasting, or bartering. Obviously, each form is motivated by different considerations and values, so anthropologists distinguish three forms of reciprocity to encompass the diversity.

Generalized Reciprocity

The defining feature of **generalized reciprocity** is that those who give goods do not expect the recipient to make a return at any definite time in the future. Generalized reciprocity occurs between individuals who are (or at least are normatively expected to be) emotionally attached to one another and, therefore, have an obligation to help one another on the basis of relative need. In North America, parents who provide their children with

▶ Each member of this Inuit ("Eskimo") whaling crew will receive a share of the whale meat and blubber. Sharing the fruits of cooperative efforts is one form of generalized reciprocity.

© William Bacon/Photo Researchers, Inc.

shelter, food, vehicles, college educations, and interest-free loans are practicing generalized reciprocity. Giving without expectation of return also should occur between parties to certain other kinds of social relations, such as wives and husbands, siblings, and sometimes close friends.

Because it includes various forms of sharing with relatives and other people who are defined as close by cultural norms, generalized reciprocity is found in all societies. However, among some peoples it is the dominant form of exchange, meaning that more resources are distributed using this form than any other form.

For example, most hunter-gatherers expect their band mates to share food and be generous with their possessions, partly because most members of a band are relatives of some kind (see Chapter 6). Among the !Kung (Ju/'hoansi), the band is a social group within which food sharing is culturally expected or even mandatory. Those who are stingy with possessions or who fail to share food with others are ridiculed or socially punished in some other way. Generalized reciprocity between the !Kung and many other foraging peoples ensures an equitable—if not entirely equal—distribution of food among the band's families. It also maintains social and economic equality between the families that make up the band. In fact, the !Kung have a custom they call "insulting the meat" that seems designed to keep even the best hunters from becoming too proud and boastful (see A Closer Look).

Balanced Reciprocity

In **balanced reciprocity,** products are transferred to someone (the recipient) and the donor expects a return in products of roughly equal value (i.e., the exchanges should "balance"). The return may be expected soon, or whenever the donor demands it, or by some specified time in the future. With generalized reciprocity, the giver continues to provide material assistance even though the receiver is unable to return anything for a long time. With balanced reciprocity, the giver tries to apply some kind of sanction against the receiver if the latter does not reciprocate within the appropriate time period. Donors may become angry if the receivers fail to reciprocate, may complain or gossip to others, may try to force reciprocation, or may suspend all relations until goods of appropriate value are returned.

Although the value of the objects transacted is supposed to be equal (at least roughly), balanced reciprocity is characterized by the absence of bargaining between the parties. In some preindustrial economies, the exchange of objects without having to negotiate for each transaction (How much of A will you give me for my B?) frequently is organized by a special relationship between two individuals known as a *trade partnership*. Individuals of one tribe or village pair off with specific individuals (their "partners") from other regions with whom they establish long-lasting trade relationships.

For instance, in the Trobriand Islands off the eastern tip of the island of New Guinea there was a form of bal-

"Insulting the Meat" Among the !Kung

Many gathering and hunting peoples have cultural mechanisms that cut proud and boastful people down to size, reminding them that they are no better than anyone else. A fascinating example of such a mechanism is found among the !Kung, the foragers of southern Africa covered in Chapter 6. !Kung call the custom "insulting the meat," referring to the practice of ridiculing successful hunters' contributions. Their goal is to keep skilled hunters modest, for such modesty is an important value in their culture. In the following extract, Richard Lee describes this custom in his ethnography, *The Dobe Ju/'hoansi* ("Ju/'hoansi" refers to the !Kung):

> When a hunter returns from a successful hunt, or when meat is brought into a camp, one would think that this would be met with open glee and the hunter praised for his skill. Quite the contrary: The people often display indifference or negativity at the news of a successful kill, and I was surprised to see the low-key way in which the hunters would break the news of their success. /Xashe, an excellent hunter for /Xai/xai, put it this way:
>
> When you come home empty-handed, you sleep and you say to yourself, "Oh, what have I done? What's the matter that I haven't killed?" Then the next morning you get up and without a word you go out and hunt again. This time you do kill something, and you come home. My tsu ("older kinsman") sees me and asks: "Well, what did you see today?" "Tsutsu," I reply, "I didn't see anything."
>
> I am sitting there with my head in my hands but my tsu comes back to me because he is a ju/'hoan. "What do you mean you haven't killed anything? Can't you see that I'm dying of hunger?" "Well, there might be something out there. I just might have scratched its elbow."
>
> Then you say, as he smiles, "Why don't we go out in the morning and have a look." And so we two and others will bring home the meat together the next day.

Men are encouraged to hunt as well as they can, and the people are happy when meat is brought in, but the correct demeanor for the successful hunter is modesty and understatement. A /Xai/xai man named /Gaugo said:

> Say that a man has been hunting. He must not come home and announce like a braggart, "I have killed a big one in the bush!" He must first sit down in silence until I or someone else comes up to his fire and asks, "What did you see today?" He replies quietly, "Ah, I'm no good for hunting. I saw nothing at all . . . maybe just a tiny one." Then I smile to myself because I know he has killed something big.

The theme of modesty is continued when the butchering and carrying party goes to fetch the kill the following day. Arriving at the site, the members of the carrying party loudly express their disappointment to the hunter:

> "You mean you have dragged us all the way out here to make us cart home your pile of bones? Oh, if I had known it was this thin I wouldn't have come."
>
> "People, to think I gave up a nice day in the shade for this. At home we may be hungry, but at least we have nice cool water to drink."

To these insults the hunter must not act offended; he should respond with self-demeaning words:

> "You're right, this one is not worth the effort; let's just cook the liver for strength and leave the rest for the hyenas. It's not too late to hunt today, and even a duiker or a steenbok would be better than this mess."

The party, of course, has no intentions of abandoning the kill. The heavy joking and derision are directed toward one goal: the leveling of potentially arrogant behavior in a successful hunter. The !Kung recognize the tendency toward arrogance (/twi) in young men and take definite steps to combat it. As /Tomazho, the famous healer from /Xai/xai, put it:

> When a young man kills much meat, he comes to think of himself as a chief or a big man, and he thinks of the rest of us as his servants or inferiors. We can't accept this. We refuse one who boasts, for someday his pride will make him kill somebody. So we always speak of his meat as worthless. In this way we cool his heart and make him gentle.

Insulting the meat is one of the central practices of the Ju/'hoansi that serve to maintain egalitarianism. Even though some men are much better hunters than others, their behavior is molded by the group to minimize the tendency toward self-praise and to channel their energies into socially beneficial activities. As a result, the existence of differences in hunting prowess does not lead to a system of Big Men in which a few talented individuals tower over the others in terms of prestige.

Source: Excerpt from *The Dobe Ju/'hoansi,* 2nd ed., by Richard B. Lee, pp. 54–55, copyright © 1993 by Holt, Rinehart and Winston, Inc., reprinted by permission of the publisher.

anced reciprocity called *wasi*. Residents of coastal villages traded fish for yams and other garden crops produced in the mountainous interior. The exchange was formalized: A coastal village paired off with an interior village, and within each village individuals formed trade partnerships. The rates at which garden produce was exchanged for fish were established by custom, so there was no haggling at any particular transaction.

In *wasi,* each trade partner received foods not readily available locally, so parties to the transaction gained a material benefit. In other cases, trade partnerships have social as well as material benefits. For example, the

!Kung (see Chapter 6) have a gift exchange custom called *hxaro.* In *hxaro,* the gift exchange is delayed (those who receive a product are not expected to return anything for an indefinite but often long period of time) and nonequivalent (even when a return is made, the value of the object need not be roughly equal to the one received). *Hxaro* partners rely on one another for mutual support in other contexts, such as when one partner asks to forage in the territory of another. The social relationship created and reinforced by *hxaro* matters more to people than the objects given and received.

In *hxaro,* gifts make friends and vice-versa, so gifts have *symbolic value.* More generally, when two people exchange gifts, ideally both gain something more than the sum total of the economic worth of the objects. On your friend's birthday, instead of giving her a CD in exchange for a gift of about equal value on your own birthday, you both could save the cost of wrapping paper and cards by buying the objects yourselves. But then neither of you would gain the symbolic value that is added when the exchange of "goods" becomes an exchange of "gifts." You gain both the emotional satisfactions of expressing and the social value of strengthening your friendship on culturally appropriate occasions. As material symbols of good relations, gifts both create and sustain feelings of solidarity and relations of mutual aid between individuals and groups. This is why, crossculturally, gift-giving ceremonies are frequently part of peacemaking between formerly hostile groups; the gifts symbolize in a tangible form the beginning of a new period of peaceful coexistence.

So the transaction of material symbols (gifts) is one of the ways people express positive social relationships. But gifts are also used to create social bonds that are useful to the giver, and to obligate people from whom the giver wants something. Gift giving makes someone indebted to you, and therefore can be used to create an obligation to return a favor. Lobbyists and sales representatives know that balanced reciprocity can serve one's self-interest.

Among some peoples, balanced reciprocity takes the form of mutual exchanges of gifts or invitations for political purposes. For an example of how balanced reciprocity creates and sustains political alliances, we turn to the Maring, a horticultural people of the mountainous interior of Papua New Guinea. In the 1960s when they were first studied by Roy Rappaport, the Maring lived in settlements composed of clusters of kin groups. Each settlement was engaged in periodic warfare with some of its neighbors. Unless a settlement was unusually large, its members formed a political alliance with one or more

nearby settlements. When warfare occurred, the warriors of each settlement relied on their allies for military support and, in the case of defeat, for refuge.

An important expression of continued goodwill between allied groups was periodic invitations to feasts, accompanied by exchanges of pigs and wealth objects. Every few years, whenever they accumulated sufficient pigs, the members of a settlement invited their allies to an enormous feast, appropriately called a *pig feast.* At the pig feast, which was attended by hundreds of people, allies brought large quantities of wealth objects to exchange and pay off debts; they consumed enormous quantities of pork provided by their hosts; they were on the lookout for potential spouses and sexual partners; and they aided the host settlement in the ceremonial dancing that the Maring believed ritually necessary for success in the fighting that soon occurred. The host group used the occasion of their pig feast to gauge the amount of military support they could expect from their allies: The more people who attended the feast, the more warriors the host settlement could put on the battleground. Later, the guests accumulated enough pigs to reciprocate by hosting a pig feast of their own.

A Maring community sponsored a pig feast to compensate its allies for their previous military aid as well as to reciprocate previous pig feasts. The failure to organize a pig feast large enough or soon enough to compensate allies could result in weakening and even terminating an alliance. Thus mutual invitations to feasts were essential to the military success and continued survival of a Maring settlement. Here, and among many other peoples, the reciprocal flow of products, of invitations and return invitations, and of other forms of give-and-take, are essential for well-being and even survival.

Negative Reciprocity

The distinguishing characteristic of the third kind of reciprocity—known as **negative reciprocity**—is that both parties attempt to gain all they can from the exchange while giving up as little as possible. Negative reciprocity is usually motivated largely by the desire to obtain material goods at minimal cost. Insofar as it is motivated by the desire for material goods, negative reciprocity is like market exchange; it is different mainly because no money changes hands between participants. In economies that use money to purchase goods and services, market exchange partly or largely replaces negative reciprocity.

But in economies with no money, negative reciprocity is an important way for individuals and groups to acquire goods that they do not produce themselves. Few communities are entirely self-sufficient: Some foods they like to eat are not found where they live; some materials they need to make tools are not found locally; or they lack the skill to produce some of the objects they use. To acquire these things, people produce other goods to exchange for "imports."

Negative reciprocity in the preindustrial world often takes the form of barter. In the interior highlands of Papua New Guinea, many indigenous peoples manufactured money or wealth objects by stringing shells together into long chains or belts. Because these shells did not occur naturally in the interior, they were traded from people to people until they reached their final destination. Salt was also a trade object because it occurred in only a few areas. Similarly, in western North America, the obsidian (volcanic glass) used to make stone tools occurred in only a few areas; other peoples acquired it through trade. In some cases these trade routes stretched for hundreds of miles, with the obsidian passing through the hands of numerous middlemen before finally being made into a tool.

Reciprocity and Social Distance

Each type of reciprocity tends to be associated with certain kinds of social relationships. As Marshall Sahlins, who first distinguished the three varieties, noted, the kind of reciprocity that occurs between individuals or groups depends on the **social distance** between them. Social distance is the degree to which cultural norms specify persons should be intimate with or emotionally attached to one another. A given mode of reciprocal exchange is normatively appropriate only with certain kinds of social relationships.

This is illustrated in North American cultural norms. You should practice generalized reciprocity with your children and perhaps with siblings and elderly parents. Others may judge you as uncaring or selfish if you refuse to offer help that is genuinely needed. But if a middle-income person repeatedly lends money to a cousin or puts a niece through college, you are likely to regard the person as either unusually generous or perhaps a bit foolish for having extended generalized reciprocity beyond the range of relatives to whom it seems appropriate.

A normative association between exchange and social distance applies to market transactions, the equivalent of negative reciprocity in modern monetary economies. In buying and selling, people are supposed to be "looking out for themselves" and "trying to get the most for

their money." We regard this as fine—in fact, as smart shopping—with transactions between strangers in a car lot, when everyone is supposed to bargain. But when the seller and buyer are friends or relatives, it is difficult for them to disentangle their economic transaction from their personal feelings for each other. Bonds between relatives and friends cannot easily be combined with market exchange: kinship and friendship are supposed to have an element of selflessness, whereas buying and selling are assumed to have selfish motives. You might buy a used car from your friend, but chances are both of you feel anxious about the transaction: What will you both do if the car is a lemon?

As our social relations with other people change, so does the kind of reciprocity we practice with them. Most adults have experienced one way in which this occurs: As we grow up, our increasing independence from our parents is manifested by a change in the way we exchange goods with them. We go from being the recipients of generalized reciprocity to more of a balanced reciprocity as we become more independent, and finally—at least until the advent of Social Security—to being the provider of generalized reciprocity.

Finally, notice how changing one form of reciprocity into another can be used as a way of changing the nature of a social relationship. Because the form of reciprocity two people practice is related to the degree of social distance between them, the social distance can be decreased or increased by one party beginning to initiate a new form of exchange. Or someone can signal his or her wish to draw another person closer by tentatively initiating a relationship of balanced reciprocity.

So I can let you know that I want to become your friend by giving you an unexpected gift or invitation to dinner. In turn you let me know whether you share my feelings by whether you return my gift on an appropriate occasion, repeatedly find reasons to refuse my dinner invitation, or come to dinner several times at my place without reciprocating. If we both use this "strategy of reciprocity," neither of us needs to be put in a potentially embarrassing position of verbalizing our feelings. I signal my wish by my initial gift or invitation, and you decline or accept my offer of friendship by your response. Reciprocity thus can be a symbolic act, conveying messages about ideal social relationships, hoped-for social relationships, and even rejected social relationships. Because we routinely use reciprocity as a way of conveying feelings and sending social messages, some anthropologists view the exchange of material goods as a form of communication.

Redistribution

The major difference between reciprocity and redistribution—the second major mode of exchange—is how the transfer of products and other resources is organized. With reciprocity, resources pass back and forth between two participants, with no third party to act as intermediary. With redistribution, resources collected from many individuals or groups are taken to a central place or put into a common pool or fund. Some overarching authority (empowered to make decisions on behalf of those who contributed) later draws from this pool or fund in returning public goods and services that allegedly benefit the group as a whole.

In modern nations, the resource (money, in this case) that is redistributed takes the form of taxes on wages, profits, retail sales, property, interest, and other income and assets. Consider how our tax system is supposed to operate. Federal tax revenues, for example, are used for two main purposes. First, they are expended in such a way as to benefit the whole country. The citizens receive police protection, law enforcement, national defense, infrastructure (e.g., dams, roads, airports), regulation of polluting industries, and so forth. Resources collected from the citizenry are expended on public goods and services. Second, taxes are used to provide assistance for individuals in need. These are "transfer payments" in the form of Social Security, Medicaid and Medicare, disaster relief, and so forth. Such public expenditures are based on moral norms and cultural values about social justice, equal opportunity, and helping those in need. Redistribution systems around the world are used for similar purposes: to provide public goods and services and to provide assistance to individuals and groups in need.

But there is another side to redistribution, a side with which we are also familiar. First, there is often conflict over who should provide the public resources, how the resources should be expended, and how much of a share should be given to those who collect and distribute them. One common social and political problem with redistribution is political disagreement: When many individuals have contributed to the public pool or fund, not everyone is likely to agree on how the "public resources" should be spent for the "public good." Much of the conflict between political parties in modern industrial democracies is rooted in disagreements over who should be taxed and how much, and over how government revenues should be spent. Parties and various interest groups are, in many cases, quarreling over redistribution: Who pays? Who gets what? And how much?

Second, elected officials and other officeholders who make important decisions about redistribution sometimes use public resources to further their own interests and ambitions, rather than to benefit the entire country or to help those in greatest need. In the United States, for instance, elected officials make "pork barrel" deals with one another to allocate federal tax dollars to finance highway construction in their districts. Congestion might be reduced for a while, but the real purpose is to provide jobs for their constituencies or to serve special-interest groups who contribute to their reelection. Speaking more generally, political interests—as well as concern for the public welfare—enter into decision making about redistribution.

A common form of redistribution in the preindustrial world is known as **tribute.** The subjects of a chief or other title-holder contribute products (usually including food) into a common pool under the control of the central authority. Often the tribute is culturally viewed as a material symbol showing that the subjects continue to acknowledge the chief's sacred authority. Some of the accumulated products are consumed by the chiefs and their relatives, some are distributed to support the work of crafts specialists (e.g., weavers and potters), and some are redistributed to the whole population at public feasts, celebrations, and ceremonies.

Examples of redistribution systems using tribute payments exist on many of the islands of Polynesia and Micronesia in the Pacific. On many islands, the entire population was divided traditionally into two ranks or classes, noble and commoner (see Chapter 13 for more about rank and class). Members of the nobility did little agricultural or other manual work but instead managed the political system and organized religious ceremonies. Commoners produced the food for themselves and their families and performed most physical labor.

On some islands the king or principal chief was viewed as the ultimate owner of the land and its resources. Nobles generally had ritual functions, which included prayers and sacrifices to deities and ancestors. On most islands, commoners paid periodic tribute to families of noble rank, whether in return for their use of the land or as a sacred obligation, or both. Tribute fed the nobility and their families and supported specialists. The tribute rendered by commoners was used partly for public purposes, such as feeding people who worked on trails and public buildings, providing relief from temporary food shortages, and publicly celebrating special events. On a few of the larger, resource-rich islands such as Hawaii and Tahiti, the nobles were sufficiently powerful to become materially wealthy from tribute: They lived in the best houses, slept on the softest woven mats, wore special clothing, had numerous servants, and ate only the finest foods.

Market Exchange

To say that objects or services are exchanged "on the market" means that they are bought and sold at a price measured in money. Person A possesses goods that person B wants to acquire; B acquires the goods by giving A whatever amount of money that both A and B agree on; A then uses the money to acquire more goods from other people.

Because we are so familiar with market exchange, it sounds obvious. But notice that it requires four things: (1) some object that serves as a medium of exchange, that is, *money;* (2) a rate at which goods and services are exchanged for money, that is, *prices;* (3) parties to exchanges have alternative buyers or sellers and are free to make the best deal they can; that is, prices are determined by *supply and demand;* and (4) most products and resources are privately owned by individuals, families, corporations, or other kinds of groups, that is, *private property* (and legal systems that protect property). On the third point, markets imply the absence of coercion: if prices are set by supply and demand, neither party to a transaction can be forced to buy or sell from the other party, but everyone has alternative ways of spending their money. This is a *free market*—no third party (a government, for example) sets prices or forces anyone to buy or sell from anyone else, and no single supplier of a good (a monopolist) controls enough of the market to force people to buy from him, her, or it (in the case of firms).

In modern market economies, many functions of government protect and enhance the free market. Governments print money and control the money supply; protect private property by means of laws, police, and courts; break up some monopolies; pay for public goods and infrastructure such as highways, ports, and airports; regulate polluting industries; supposedly prevent insider trading in stock markets; and in many other ways allow markets to work smoothly.

▲ The market form of exchange required money, prices determined by supply and demand, and private ownership of most resources and technology. Ownership shares of companies are traded by licensed brokers on the floor of the New York Stock Exchange.

© Spencer Platt/Getty Images

Because markets require the presence of money, we discuss some of the diversity in money objects and money uses.

Money

Money is another of those things we take for granted, so much so that it seems like a simple idea. Actually, the idea of money presupposes a lot of other ideas, so money is actually rather complicated.

Money consists of objects that serve as *media of exchange* in a wide range of transactions of goods, services (including labor), or both. If an economy uses money, individual A can acquire something from individual B without having to return an object desired by B—that is, without having to supply an object or service to trade with or barter. Money is given instead, and B can then use the money to buy a chosen object or service. This facilitation of exchange is the main function of money. Money greases the wheels of commerce.

Other characteristics of money are derived from its function as a medium of exchange. For example, money serves as a *standard of value:* the values of the goods and services that can be exchanged for money can be compared with one another because money serves as a common measure of how much things are worth. This makes it a lot easier for you to decide whether to buy new outfits or a new DVD player, for you can compare their value (i.e., their price) and thus determine how many outfits you would be sacrificing for the new DVD.

Money is also a *store of value:* because you can use it any time to purchase a wide range of goods, it stores your wealth, often in a portable form that can be carried in pouches or pockets. If you are rich and don't want anyone to know it, don't buy anything that displays your wealth; just keep the money, because you can transform it into goods that you can display later if you wish. Or if you want to defer immediate consumption so that you can get something really expensive later, just save your money, since it stores your resources indefinitely (unless, of course, inflation is high; then, without you doing anything at all, your money becomes worth less).

Notice also that money (or more precisely, quantity of money) takes on *symbolic significance.* Because money is both a standard and a store of value and because people and families have access to different quantities of money, we can use money as a means of quickly evaluating people, especially if we don't already know them. We all know that clothing, jewelry, cars, houses, and so forth aren't really indicators of moral character, but they still carry connotations about how much individuals or families are "worth." (If you doubt this, ask what you use to judge people you don't know.) Money can even symbolize national identity or independence: Some English people resist adopting the pan-European currency (the Eurodollar) because they see it as a threat to their sovereignty.

These and other characteristics mean that not just any object is suitable to be used as money. Obviously, money objects must be *durable.* This is why hard objects such as modified stones, shells, and metals often serve as currency.

Money is more useful as an exchange medium if it is *divisible,* so sometimes different kinds of objects will serve as denominations of money—equivalent to nickels, quarters, dollar bills, and thousand-dollar bills. Among the Kapauku, a people of the rugged interior of Papua, small cowrie shells imported from the coast serve as money. As the shells circulate their natural polish wears off, and since the older ones are more scarce they are worth more than the newer ones—thus the "age" of the money serves as a kind of denomination.

The supply of the money object must be *controllable,* because if people can get all they want of it, its value inflates and it becomes worthless as an exchange medium: Who would give you anything in exchange for it? The monetary supply can be controlled by a government, which manufactures the only "legal tender" in the society. Or the supply can be controlled by using only imported or rare objects as money. Shells imported from far away are used as money in many economies because of their scarcity and durability. The money supply can also be controlled by using a currency that requires a lot of labor to make. Minerals or shells can be ground into shapes, drilled with holes, and strung into necklaces. In such cases, money remains scarce because it takes a lot of time to make it.

Most money is *portable,* because of convenience. In different cultures, you can stick it in your pocket, carry it around your neck or waist, wrap it in a bundle, roll it up, or wear it around your arm. But on the island of Yap in Micronesia, huge stone disks weighing hundreds of pounds serve as a kind of money. Yapese stone money is seldom moved; rather, the ownership of it is transacted so that the money stays in one place even when its owner changes.

As the stone money of Yap illustrates, an enormous variety of objects serve as money in one or another region of the world. We are familiar with currencies of modern nations, issued by governments that control the money supply. In preindustrial economies, the kinds of objects that take on the characteristics of money are surprisingly diverse. In Africa, for example, the following objects served as money in one or another part of the continent:

▲ One of the more unusual forms of money is the stone money of Yap island in the Federated States of Micronesia.

iron, salt, beads, cowrie shells, cloth, slaves, gin, gold dust, metal rods, brass bracelets, and livestock.

The range of goods that can be acquired with money varies greatly. In some the range is broad. Many kinds of resources and goods can be bought and sold, including labor, land, tools, and sometimes even people (slaves). In these systems, money serves as a *generalized medium of exchange;* that is, it can be used to acquire many kinds of goods and services, including land and labor. Of course, there are always some things that money just can't buy. Love is the classic example; but if you have enough money, it is not hard for you to *think* everyone loves you.

In many preindustrial economies, the range of money uses is relatively narrow. Only a few categories of products may be purchased with money. For example, it may be possible to buy food, clothing, and a few other goods, but land is not available for sale at any price and labor is almost never sold. Economic anthropologists sometimes call this **limited-purpose money.**

A famous example of limited-purpose money comes from among the Tiv of Nigeria, studied by Paul Bohannan. Tiv money consisted of metal rods, but the rods could not be used as an exchange medium for all other goods. For one thing, land could not be sold, and labor was exchanged among relatives on the principle of generalized reciprocity. For another, among the Tiv goods circulated in different *exchange spheres.* Certain kinds of products could only be transacted for certain other kinds of products. Products were culturally classified into categories, within which they were freely exchangeable, but between which exchange was difficult.

The "subsistence sphere" category included cultivated crops, chickens and goats, and some tools and household goods. Goods within this sphere were exchangeable for one another by means of barter. The "prestige sphere" included slaves, cattle, a special kind of white cloth, and metal rods. Within the prestige sphere, metal rods functioned as an exchange medium: One could sell cattle for metal rods and then use the rods to acquire white cloth or

© Paul Chesley/National Geographic Society

slaves, for example, but the monetary function of metal rods was normally limited to the prestige sphere.

However, it was possible to acquire subsistence goods in exchange for metal rods; but these transactions were rare, for two reasons. First, few people were willing to trade their metal rods for subsistence goods. This is because goods that circulated in the prestige sphere had much greater cultural value to Tiv than subsistence goods. Second, metal rods were worth an enormous amount of subsistence goods. Yet metal rods had no denominations; that is, unlike dollars and cents, they were not divisible into fractions. So for a Tiv to try to exchange one metal rod for subsistence goods would be like an American taking a thousand-dollar bill into a grocery store to buy food, with the clerk unable to make change. As a result of these two factors, Tiv metal rods were largely limited-purpose money.

The Tiv example reminds us that just because we find it convenient to call some object like metal rods "money" does not mean that it has all the characteristics of our own currency. Indeed, some anthropologists believe that money objects are lacking in preindustrial economies and that money is a Western concept that we should not attempt to apply to other cultures. This problem is mainly semantic, however: If we define money simply as a medium of exchange, it is found in many other economies. To avoid confusion and false impressions, we always need to specify its uses and its cultural meaning to local people.

On Market Economies

Just as our readers are familiar with money, so most live in a *market economy*. This means that practically the whole economy is organized on *market principles*. Briefly, the most important of these principles are:

- Practically all privately owned goods and services have a monetary price: They can be bought and sold on the free market.
- Most people make their living by selling something on the market. Some people make their living by selling goods or services to consumers. But most people are workers: They make their living by selling their labor to a group (such as a firm or public agency). Workers have to do this because most of them do not own the natural resources and capital with which to make their own living.
- The factors of production are allocated by the market. Because privately owned resources, capital (including technology and equipment), and labor are bought and

sold, the supply of and demand for these factors of production determine the uses to which they are put. In theory, the market allocates them so that they are used in ways that bring the highest return (profit).
- The economy is self-regulating. The impersonal forces of supply and demand set prices and therefore regulate the kinds of economic activity that occur. The regulation of the economy occurs as if by an "invisible hand," as Adam Smith said back in the late eighteenth century.

Economies organized by market principles have a lot of advantages for individuals—you can shop around until you find the best deal and you are not tied to any particular place or employer. And there is no doubt that an economy organized on free market principles is tremendously productive, as Karl Marx—the nineteenth-century archenemy of capitalism—himself recognized.

Still, it's worth considering some of the ways that living in such an economy affects people and society. For example, compare a market economy in which most people sell their labor to a firm or an agency to an economy in which people themselves own or have access to everything they need to survive and do well (by their standards, of course). Because we have described the hunting and gathering !Kung of southern Africa extensively, we'll use them for comparison and will assume (falsely) that they still live a traditional lifestyle by using the present tense.

Work. It is unlikely that you have what you need to survive on your own. You must get a job. On the job, for the most part your working days and hours are set by your employer. (You have some flexibility, but exercising it too often or too liberally endangers your job.) How much income you earn and how much job security you have vary, but both are highly dependent on your employer. In turn, the employer reacts to impersonal market forces: You may lose wages, benefits, or the job itself if the company that employs you decides to "outsource" your job to "remain competitive."

If you were a !Kung, by virtue of being born into a given family, you have access to a territory that supplies you with almost everything you need. You have to work for your food and other things, of course, but when you have acquired all you and your group need or want you can stop working. If you take a day off, someone else will give you and your family enough food for that day. You have no concept of wage or job security, but you do think about subsistence security: Will there be a drought or other kind of natural calamity? Droughts are as "impersonal" as market forces, and probably even more unpredictable. But everyone knows this from generations of living in the same place, so you have alternatives: You can go live with your husband's brother's band for a while until natural conditions improve.

Family. When you go to work every day, chances are you leave your family. Once you have children, your job will compete with your family for your time and probably for your mental energy. It will be hard for you to balance these demands and preferences. Your boss is sympathetic, and even your boss's boss understands when you have to take personal days, since she also knows you personally. But people higher up the corporate ladder don't know you at all, and all your bosses are ultimately answerable to them. Really, you are interchangeable; someone else can do what you do about as well. So get used to balancing. And get used to someone else wanting the same promotion you do, which is another way of saying get used to not really being able to ease off at work.

If you were a !Kung, you would have no boss, although the elder people in your band will exert some influence over what you do. Everyone knows you, and you know everyone, so within reason everyone can take everyone else's personal situations into account. You don't care too much about getting ahead. Of whom? For what?

Values. You find a lot of things and qualities important and desirable: family, freedom, and fun, just to name a few factors that start with *f*. In fact, so many different kinds of things and qualities are important and desirable that you cannot possibly satisfy them all. When you get one thing, some other desire springs to the forefront to take its place on your wish list. And just in case you should ever come close to satisfying one category of desire—the desire for material goods—advertising will remind you that you want things you never even knew existed. There is never enough. It's a good thing too, because growth in the market economy would cease if too many people decided they have enough, found a way to cut back on their work hours, and stopped spending.

If you are a !Kung, you also care about family, freedom, and fun. You value equality, meaning not that everyone is "equal" (which is a social impossibility), but that it is distasteful when some people have full bellies while others go hungry. You really don't like it when someone you know brags about himself, so you join others in cutting such people down to size. Since you know

that the other people with whom you have spent most of your life feel the same way, you remain outwardly modest too. No one in your camp has very many material possessions—they are too hard to carry around, and if someone has something she doesn't really need someone else will probably ask her for it. When you get enough things, and everyone else around you has about the same things, and no media outlets exist to bombard you with images that make you think you are not sexy enough— well, then enough really is enough.

None of the preceding discussion is meant to disparage market economies, which have done much to improve the lives of millions of people around the world. At any rate, the economies of most of the world's nations are increasingly integrated into a single global market economy (see Globalization: Globalization and Markets), which seems far more likely to expand than to contract for the foreseeable future.

Rather, our main point is this: Some scholars, talk show hosts, elected officials, and the like have completely bought into (pardon the pun) market principles and market economies. They talk and act and support policies as though the costs of markets are so low as to be negligible. But they're not:

• Unlike the !Kung, you probably won't move your family in with your husband's brother if times get tough because it would be humiliating. Relatives care about and care for one another, but not in that way. Markets encourage individual achievement, but with some social costs.

• Since modern technology has made everyone's labor so productive, theoretically we could all be working less. That's probably what the !Kung would do. But the same force (market competition) that fosters technological improvements also means that production has to increase to stay competitive. So productivity gains are used mainly to increase output, not to reduce working hours. Markets encourage people and companies to be competitive, not to take it easy.

• If you are a model citizen, you will try to live what your culture considers the good life. And your culture's definition of the good life is affected by the market economy itself, which requires ever-increasing consumption fueled partly by advertising and the media. Because most people tend to admire others who live out their culture's values, to get their admiration you'll probably need to buy a lot of stuff. Unlike the !Kung, you've got a place to put it. Unlike the !Kung, no one—not even your brother—is likely to ask you for it. And unlike the !Kung, you think it's someone

"**D**eadly Summit Riot," read the July 21, 2001, headline on the front page of the *San Francisco Chronicle*. The story told of the riots that occurred at the G-8 conference in Genoa, Italy. "G-8" stands for the Group of Eight, a gathering of the world's seven richest nations plus Russia, who were discussing issues of mutual concern. Rioters were protesting globalization, which they claimed is increasing the gap between rich and poor, trampling the rights of workers, and spoiling the natural environment. What is market globalization, and why were people protesting it?

In essence, market globalization means that the entire world is increasingly integrated into a single economic system based around market exchange: labor, capital, technology, consumer products, and services move with fewer and fewer restraints across national boundaries. Theoretically, should the entire world become a single integrated market system—a megamarket—then subsistence maize farmers in Uganda would compete with American corn farmers to sell their products in both Kampala and Chicago. Obviously, the implications of such a global market would be profound for Americans, Ugandans, and the rest of the world.

Market globalization has several dimensions, each related to the others. First is the *internationalization of capital and labor*. Corporations from the developed world move their production facilities to other, poorer nations, where they employ people who will work for a fraction of North American, European, and Japanese workers. There are many advantages for companies that relocate factories in regions where the labor force is relatively poor. Wages are far lower. Factory safety regulations are less constraining. Rents are cheap. Environmental laws are relatively lax, or are unevenly enforced. Unions are nonexistent or poorly organized. All in all, these and other advantages lower production costs and, therefore, raise the profits of corporations that locate factories in less developed regions.

Second is the *globalization of consumer products,* along with *marketing efforts.* Products produced in one country are sold in other countries with few or no restrictions. In Europe, the European Union agreement finalized in the 1990s ended all tariffs and quotas on consumer goods for its member nations, and the free flow of products was further streamlined with the advent of the Eurodollar. In the Americas, the North American Free Trade Agreement will eventually make Canada, the United States, and Mexico into a single market. North Americans and Europeans can easily see the impact of consumer globalization. Go to your closet and see if you can find a garment or pair of shoes manufactured in your own country. Check out your DVD, gaming console, TV, CD player, cell phone, and other electronic equipment. Where was it manufactured? What do you suppose you would have paid for it had it been made in Toronto, London, Tokyo, or Chicago?

International markets are not new, but their size and reach expanded dramatically in the late twentieth century. In the 1960s, for example, an agreement between the United States and Mexico allowed U.S. corporations to set up factories in Mexico along the border region with Texas. Components had to be made in the United States, but companies could export the components to Mexico for assembly, then bring them back to the United States for final finishing and sale. There would be no tariffs (import taxes) on the finished products, and Mexico allowed North American companies to retain ownership of assembly plants on its soil in return for the jobs and training received by its citizens.

Since then, these assembly plants (called *maquiladores*) have produced massive quantities of clothing and consumer electronics for American consumers. Cloth is sent to the *maquiladores* to be cut and sewn into garments; electronic components are sent south to be soldered and assembled. Most of the Mexican employees of these multinational firms are young, unmarried women, who come from all over the country to get jobs in the assembly plants. Similar arrangements were made with Asian countries like Taiwan and South Korea.

Since the early 1980s, wage levels in countries like Mexico, Singapore, Taiwan, and South Korea have climbed and their governments have instituted more workplace and environmental regulations. In order to remain competitive by controlling labor and other production costs, corporations have responded by relocating production facilities to other countries with fewer regulations and lower prevailing wages. Countries in Southeast Asia (like Malaysia, Indonesia, and the Philippines), the Caribbean, and Africa have invited foreign companies to establish factories to provide jobs for their people and tax revenues for their governments. The most important country to have expanded opportunities for foreign investment in the past 20 years is the People's Republic of China. Now that the Chinese Communist Party has relaxed some of its restrictions on rural to urban migration, its huge and growing cities soak up the labor of millions of former peasants. The new privately owned factories turn out clothing, toys, machinery, home electronics, housewares, and other products at rock-bottom production costs.

Why has the expansion of global markets occurred? There are a host of reasons, which vary greatly according to who is providing the explanation. High labor costs, environmental regulations, and occupational safety restrictions in the developed countries are part of the reason. Why pay an American garment worker $10 per hour when a Mexican woman will do the same work for $2, and without many of those aggravating labor negotiations and environmental laws?

Technological advances provide part of the reason. Giant freighters hauling hundreds of containers greatly reduce the

◄ The global market ties the regions of the world together into relations based on buying and selling. These Honduran bananas will be sold on the world market.

costs of transporting products from where they are extracted or processed to where they are ultimately sold and consumed. Today electronics can be assembled and clothing can be stitched and sewed in Southeast Asia or Africa, then shipped or flown to North America or Europe, and still produce large profits for factory owners and retailers. Advances in mining and timber extraction make it possible to economically extract minerals and lumber from places where it was too expensive a few decades ago. Modern agricultural technology, with its chemicals and machinery, is applied to land in Mexico and Latin America to supply North American consumers with tomatoes and grapes in January and bananas and mangoes all year round.

Globalization is likely here to stay, barring a worldwide economic collapse. Its causes and consequences are debated by news media, government officials, labor unions, companies, and consumers. The most important questions focus on its costs and benefits, especially the question of who loses and who gains. Nearly everyone agrees that corporations win from globalization, mainly because of reduced labor costs and less restrictive environmental and workplace regulations. Consumers in the rich countries also probably win because prices for many products—from shoes to computers—are lower; indeed, a good case can be made that globalization was largely responsible for the very low inflation rates beginning in the 1990s.

But what about the workers who used to work in the factories in the developed countries, whose formerly high-paying jobs were replaced by people who live half a world away? Many have been "outsourced," becoming the victims of "restructuring" and "increasing efficiency." Those who favor globalization point out that laid-off and fired North American workers have found other jobs and, at any rate, have benefited as consumers from the lower prices made possible by cheap overseas labor. Critics of globalization claim that most of these jobs are lower paid jobs in various service industries and that the alleged decline of the American middle class is due largely to globalization. This dimension of globalization was a major issue in the 2004 American presidential election. Democratic challenger John Kerry charged that President Bush encouraged the outsourcing of American jobs by offering tax breaks to American companies that opened up overseas factories. Kerry promised to put America back to work and save the middle class by keeping good jobs at home. Bush responded (correctly) that the tax incentives had been put in place long before his administration and that the competitiveness of America's businesses would be harmed by more costly regulations, which, in the long run, would hurt American workers.

And what about the workers in the new global production system, whose globally competitive labor provides low-priced products for sale to consumers buying on the global marketplace? Views diverge on their welfare also. Critics of globalization claim that such workers are exploited. Rich companies take advantage of their poverty and lack of alternative economic opportunities by offering low wages and deplorable working conditions in terms of working hours, health, and safety. Those who favor the expansion of global markets respond that these workers are being paid more than they would otherwise be paid, that they receive job experience and training, that their countries receive the taxes paid on their wages, and so forth. Critics fire back that if things are getting so much better in Mexico and Central America, then why are so many Mexicans and Central Americans still illegally entering the United States in search of well-paying jobs?

Finally, what about the effects of globalization on the maintenance of cultural heritages? Is there to be a global cultural melting pot? Will there be a global megaculture if the diverse peoples of the world buy and sell on the global megamarket? People who fear the effects of globalization point out that advertising has infiltrated even remote places such as the interior mountains of New Guinea. Is a culture devoted to megaconsumption the kind of world we want to live in? they ask. Those who favor globalization believe that countries will take what they want and leave the rest. They also hold that companies that sell in particular countries will have to adapt their products and advertising to local cultural preferences. Thus, McDonald's franchises in India accommodate Hindu traditions with burgers made from something besides beef, and you can buy falafel-burgers at Mickey D's in parts of the Middle East. France has fought what it considers cultural imperialism by passing laws against the use of certain English words in the interest of preservation of the French language.

Critical Thinking Question

Obviously, looking into the future is largely speculative, especially if it's the global future. If there is to be only one economic and cultural world, is the one we are currently making the one we want our children and future generations to live in?

else's responsibility to take care of people in need (that's what taxes are for, right?), especially since you don't even know most of those people. Markets encourage consumption, not social responsibility.

If you were raised in a market economy, you may think such things are not "costs" at all, or that they are costs that are worth bearing. But consider the possibility that the *only* reason you think that is because you were enculturated inside a market economy with its norms, values, and worldview.

Peasant Marketplaces

Those of us who live in industrialized market economies purchase most of what we need and want in restaurants, car lots, supermarkets, and shopping malls. We rely on the market to satisfy our needs and wants—we earn money from our jobs and spend the money on goods and services. In the process, we depend on other organizations (companies) to produce and sell the products we wish to buy.

Even in the twenty-first century, millions of rural peasants (see Chapter 6) do not live completely in the global market economy. Rather than selling their labor to others in return for a wage, they work the land and fish the waters to supply food for their families directly. Rather than producing goods that they turn around and sell at a price to others, families consume most of what they produce themselves. There are places in such communities where goods are bought and sold—there are *peasant marketplaces.* But people do not rely on marketplaces for most of what they consume, nor do they spend most of their working hours producing goods to sell at the marketplace.

Peasant marketplaces are ancient and important in West Africa, southern and Southeast Asia, the Caribbean, and Central and South America. Peasant vendors sell food, cloth and clothing, pottery, leather products, livestock, and other goods produced by their families. Traveling merchants (middlemen) bring commodities imported from the developed world or from elsewhere in the region to sell to local people at the local marketplace.

Despite all the buying and selling, peasant marketplaces are not the same as modern shopping malls or department stores. Several notable differences exist. First, the categories of products sold at the marketplace are limited, and in fact, most people produce most of their own subsistence using family labor. Most families rely on the marketplace only for certain kinds of products that they cannot produce for themselves efficiently. Most people are not making the bulk of their living by selling something (objects, labor) on the market.

Second, producing and marketing goods for monetary profit are part-time activities for many vendors (sellers). Many marketplaces are staffed mainly by peasants, who

◄ In peasant marketplaces like this one in Oaxaca City, Mexico, vendors themselves often produce the food and wares they sell.

© Barry D. Kass/Images of Anthropology

sell small quantities of food, pottery, furniture, fibers, crafts, or other objects they have produced with family labor. Indeed, marketplaces often are *periodic,* meaning that they do not open every day, but only for a day or two a week. Traveling merchants typically visit several markets in different regions in a single week, often buying products for sale at one market and reselling them at a distant market a day or two later.

Third, peasant vendors usually sell products that they or their family members, rather than hired laborers, produce. This means that the kinds and quantities of goods offered for sale by any single vendor are usually small. Most marketplaces also feature products sold by people who specialize in buying them wholesale and selling them retail. Such people are dependent on the market—with all its insecurities and risks—for their livelihood. They therefore have developed various strategies to reduce the risks they face.

When we who live in a market economy visit a marketplace—a store or car lot, for instance—we normally buy goods from total strangers. We pay the same price as everyone else. If we need credit, we expect to pay the market rate of interest at some lending institution. We expect sellers to be looking out for themselves, just as sellers expect us to be trying to get the most for our money. This characteristic is referred to as the "impersonality of the marketplace," which is nicely expressed by the old saying that "one person's money is as green as anyone else's."

In contrast, in the small towns and villages of peasant communities, vendors sometimes develop more personal and intimate relationships with some of their customers. For example, in a Philippine marketplace studied by William Davis, vendors establish relationships called *suki* with "special customers," people who regularly buy their wares. The sellers' goal is to reduce their risks by gradually building up a steady, large clientele of customers, rather than by squeezing all the money they can out of each individual transaction. From the *suki,* the customer receives credit, favorable prices, extra quantities of goods at a given price, the best quality of goods the seller has to offer on a particular day, and certain services. The vendor benefits as well: Their *suki* are expected not to buy from any other suppliers of the goods they carry. This is helpful in calculating the quantities of goods they will be able to sell and, hence, helps prevent them from overstocking their stalls.

As *suki* in this Philippine marketplace illustrates, the impersonality of the marketplace can be modified by the formation of personal ties between buyers and sellers. Supply and demand operate to affect prices, yet people may recognize that charging as much as the market will bear on any given day is not necessarily in their long-term interest. This is not surprising in communities in which most people know most other people. Those who have things to sell are often selling them to people whom they know in other, nonmarket and noneconomic contexts.

Summary

1. *Exchange* refers to the patterned ways products are transferred between the time they are produced and the time they are consumed. Economic anthropologists classify the variety of exchanges that exist in human economies into three major modes or types: reciprocity, redistribution, and market.

2. Reciprocity is the giving and receiving of objects or services without the transfer of money. One form, generalized reciprocity, usually occurs between parties who are normatively obliged to assist one another in times of need, as among relatives and sometimes close friends. With balanced reciprocity, a return of an object of equivalent value is expected within a reasonable time. The goal of balanced reciprocity may be the acquisition of goods for their utility, as in Trobriand *wasi*. More often it is motivated by the desire to create or sustain good relations between individuals (as in gift giving) or political alliances between groups (as with the Maring pig feast). Negative reciprocity is characterized by the desire of both parties to acquire as many goods as possible while giving up as few as possible, as in barter.

3. The kind of reciprocity that exists between individuals and groups depends on the normatively appropriate social distance between them. Exchange relations alter as social relationships change. Conversely, one party can attempt to alter a relationship by offering an object (or invitation) and the other party can signal acceptance or rejection by a particular response. Varying the type of reciprocity thus serves as a common means to draw people closer together or to push them further apart. In effect, a reciprocal exchange of goods (and, for that matter, services) can also serve as an exchange of messages about feelings and relationships. Reciprocal exchanges have symbolic as well as material content.

4. In redistribution, the members of a group contribute products, objects, or money into a pool or fund, and a central authority reallocates or uses them for public purposes. Taxes in modern nations and tribute in chiefdoms are examples. Normatively, redistribution is supposed to provide resources to increase public welfare, either to provide public goods or to support those in need. In fact, there is much conflict over collection and allocation, and those officials who do the collecting and allocating frequently use their authority for their private ambition rather than the public interest.

5. Market exchange involves buying and selling commodities. It therefore requires money, prices determined by supply and demand, and private property. Money makes the exchange of goods and services more convenient and also facilitates the making of profit and the accumulation of wealth. Money functions as a medium of exchange, a standard of value, and a store of value. These functions mean that money objects generally (but not always) have certain characteristics: durability, divisibility, limited supply, and portability. The range of goods and services that can be bought with money varies between economies. In market economies, money is a generalized exchange medium, but it has more limited uses in many preindustrial societies, as illustrated by Tiv metal rods.

6. Market economies allow us to be free to choose where to shop and work, and they are also enormously productive and expansive. Some people believe that this advantage is so overwhelming that the costs are negligible. But perhaps these people think this way because they were enculturated into the norms, values, and worldviews that characterize a market economy.

7. Rural peasants of many countries do not completely rely on markets, for they produce most of their food themselves and shop at local marketplaces only for some of their needs and wants. In peasant marketplaces, most vendors are small-scale and part-time. In many regions they develop special relationships with sellers to reduce their risks, as illustrated by *suki* in the Philippines.

Key Terms

reciprocity
redistribution
market

generalized reciprocity
balanced reciprocity
negative reciprocity

social distance
tribute
limited-purpose money

InfoTrac College Edition Terms

reciprocal exchanges
(also social exchanges)

gifts and relationships
child care and job

peasant markets
maquiladora

Suggested Readings

Neale, Walter C. *Monies in Societies.* San Francisco: Chandler and Sharp, 1976.

A brief book about the uses, forms, and functions of money in a variety of economies.

Plattner, Stuart, ed. *Economic Anthropology.* Stanford, Calif.: Stanford University Press, 1989.

A collection of articles on economic systems.

Sahlins, Marshall. *Stone Age Economics.* New York: Aldine, 1972.

Deals with the organization of production and modes of exchange in preindustrial economies.

Weatherford, Jack. *The History of Money: From Sandstone to Cyberspace.* New York: Crown, 1997.

Compares money from a historical perspective.

Wilk, Richard R. *Economies & Cultures: Foundations of Economic Anthropology.* Boulder, Colo.: Westview Press, 1996.

A readable and thoughtful overview of economic anthropology, focusing on major issues and debates.

Companion Website for This Book

The Wadsworth Anthropology Resource Center
http://anthropology.wadsworth.com

The companion website that accompanies *Humanity: An Introduction to Cultural Anthropology,* Sixth Edition, includes a rich array of material, including online anthropological video clips, to help you in the study of cultural anthropology and the specific topics covered in this chapter. Begin by clicking on Student Resources. Next, click on Cultural Anthropology, and then on the cover image for this book. You have now arrived at the Student Resources home page and have the option of choosing one of several chapter resources.

Applying Anthropology. Begin your study of cultural anthropology by clicking on Applying Anthropology. Here you will find useful information on careers, graduate school programs in applied anthropology, and internships you might wish to pursue. You will also find real-world examples of working anthropologists applying the skills and methods of anthropology to help solve serious world problems.

Research Online. Click here to find a wealth of Web links that will facilitate your study of anthropology. Divided into different fields of study, specific websites are starting points for Internet research. You will be guided to rich anthropology websites that will help you prepare for class, complete course assignments, and actually do research on the Web.

InfoTrac College Edition Exercises. From the pull-down menu, select the chapter you are presently studying. Select InfoTrac College Edition Exercises from the list of resources. These exercises utilize InfoTrac College Edition's vast database of articles and help you explore the numerous uses of the search word, *culture.*

Study Aids for This Chapter. Improve your knowledge of key terms by using flash cards and study the learning objectives. Take the practice quiz, receive your results, and email them to your instructor. Access these resources from the chapter and resource pull-down menus.

Chapter Eight

Marriages and Families

Some Definitions

Marriage

Functions of Marriage

Two Unusual Forms

Marriage in Comparative Perspective

Marriage Rules

How Many Spouses?

Marriage Alliances

Marital Exchanges

Kinship Diagrams

Postmarital Residence Patterns

Influences on Residence Patterns

Residence and Households

Family and Household Forms

Two-Generation Households

Extended Households

© Jon Riley/Stone/Getty Images

Extended families of three or more generations are important in many cultures, including China.

WHEN NORTH AMERICAN POLITICIANS proclaim solemnly that "the family is the backbone of our nation," and that their own policies promote "family values," they can hardly go wrong. After all, how many voters see themselves as "antifamily"? Certainly, the bonds of marriage and family are among the central social relationships of most societies. For one thing, a married couple, aided by some kind of extended family, is usually the social group that nourishes and socializes new generations. For another, family ties are the basis of residential groups that not only live together but often own property together, play together, work together, and worship together.

FAMILIES, WE ALL RECOGNIZE, do a lot of things that are quite helpful to their members and to society at large. So when studies show that American divorce rates hover around 50 percent and that around 30 percent of American children live in households with only one parent present, we believe that something is amiss. We fear that broken homes and single-parent families will cause harm to children, communities, and the whole nation. Worrying that marriage between people of the same sex will erode the "sacred institution" of marriage, in 2004 the American president and some members of Congress attempted (unsuccessfully) to include the one man–one woman marital norm in the Constitution.

IN THIS CHAPTER, we look at some of the main ways in which cultures differ in their marriage practices and in the organization of their families and households. Because in most cultures it is the marriage relationship that creates new nuclear families and that begets, nourishes, and teaches children, we begin with it. Before doing so, though, we need to define some terms that will be used in the next couple of chapters.

Some Definitions

Setting aside numerous complexities such as adoption, step-families, and in-law relationships, reproduction is the basis of family relationships. *Biologically* speaking, your relatives are your relatives because they are or were the relatives of your parents: Your grandparents are your parents' parents, your siblings are the other children of your parents, your aunts are your parents' sisters, and so forth.

Anthropologists distinguish between two kinds of relatives. We use the term **consanguines** to refer to "blood" relatives—people related by birth. **Affines** refers to "in-laws"—people related by marriage. So your *consanguineous relatives* are all of your blood relatives—your parents, siblings, grandparents, parents' siblings, and cousins. Your affines are all of your relatives by marriage—such as your sister's husband, wife's mother, and father's sister's husband.

Both consanguineous and affinal relationships can, in theory, serve as the basis for forming all kinds of social groups. For example, you and all your first cousins could form a group if you ever needed to cooperate in some activity like organizing a birthday party for your common grandmother. All societies do, in fact, use kinship relationships as the basis for group formation. But, as societies modernize, the number of specialized groups (e.g., companies, political parties, schools, churches) increases, so the relative importance of kinship groups declines. In contrast, in more traditional societies most of the important groups in the lives of individuals are defined by kinship ties. Among other things, this implies that most of a person's relationships with other people depend on whether, and precisely how, they are related. These kinds of societies are sometimes said to be based on kinship.

When people form an organized, cooperative group based on their kinship relationships, anthropologists call the group a **kin group.** Most of us are intimately familiar with one kind of kin group, the **nuclear family,** which consists of a married couple together with their unmarried children. A nuclear family is a kind—but only one kind—of kin group: The members live together, share the use of family wealth and property, rely on one another for emotional support, pool their labor and resources to support the family, and so on.

Groups with these characteristics (whether nuclear families or not) constitute a **household** (or *domestic group*), whose members live in the same house or compound. Among their many functions, households usually have primary responsibility for nurturing and enculturating children. North Americans usually think of the members of a household as living in a single dwelling such as an apartment, condo, townhouse, or detached single-family dwelling. This conception applies in most other societies as well, but it is fairly common for the families that together make up a single household to live in separate dwellings. In such communities, the entire "household" consists of several couples and their children who live in different "houses" on land owned by the household. So long as the various families use common property (e.g., land, tools), cooperate in work, share income or wealth, and recognize themselves as having distinctive identities, we still consider them to belong to a single *household* although they live in separate *houses*. Households may be very small (e.g., a single person or a parent and her or his children) or quite large (e.g., a set of siblings and all their children).

Households are not always formed exclusively by family or marital ties either, as gay and lesbian couples and heterosexual unmarried couples living together illustrate. In fact, in a great many societies people have the right to incorporate unrelated people into their family and household, acting and feeling toward them in the same way as they do consanguineous relatives. This practice is widespread enough that ethnologists have a phrase for it: **fictive kinship,** which implies that individuals who are not "actually kin" act toward one another as if they were kin.

Term	Meaning
Kin group	Social group formed on the basis of recognized (including fictive) kin relationships between its members
Household	Domestic group, or people who live in the same place and share assets and certain responsibilities
Nuclear family	Married couple and their unmarried children
Extended family	Culturally recognized relatives of varying degrees of distance

People everywhere keep track of, and usually have social relationships with, distant relatives who are part of their **extended family.** Most North Americans of European ancestry recognize extended family ties, if only when cousins of various degrees, aunts and uncles, and other distant relatives get together in large numbers for family reunions, weddings, funerals, and other events. Theoretically, the number of people who make up your extended family could go on "forever" to include third cousins and beyond. Extended families do not have clear social boundaries; rather, recognized relationships are likely to wither and eventually disappear as relatives become more and more distant. You may know and occasionally interact with all of your first and second cousins, but beyond that range whether you even know their names depends mostly on circumstances like whether they live in your town or state. But in societies based on kinship, extended families often are better defined, the rights gained and the duties owed extended family members are more extensive, and their membership "extends" more widely.

By and large, North American middle-class people do not rely on extended family members for access to resources or emotional support. In other societies, however, extended families and even larger groupings of relatives are far more important in the lives of individuals: You may live in the same household with them, you can count on them for economic support, you share access to land and other property with them, you and they have common ritual duties, and so forth. In such societies, nuclear families are important, but they are embedded in larger, more inclusive kinds of kin groups. Some of these groups are enormously large, consisting of hundreds of members, as we see in the next chapter. Here we focus mainly on domestic groups, especially on nuclear and extended families and the ties that create and bind them.

The preceding terms referring to groupings based on family and kinship seem easy enough. But it is easy to use one term when technically you mean another, which will lead to confusion. The Concept Review may help.

Societies everywhere have extended families, households, and kin groups, and all peoples distinguish between consanguineous and affinal relatives. But the nature of these groups and relations between kin is highly variable cross-culturally. This variability is surprising: We can easily understand why adaptations (Chapter 6) and economic systems (Chapter 7) differ from people to people. But family and kinship seem pretty basic, as, for that matter, does marriage. And they are—in the sense that peoples everywhere not only have them, but attach deep importance to them. But exactly what is meant by the word *them* in the preceding sentence varies from people to people.

Marriage

If pressed for a definition of marriage, a North American might say that marriage is a relationship between a woman and a man involving romantic love, sexual activity, cohabitation, reproduction and child rearing, and sharing the joys and burdens of life. People trained in law might also note that marriage has legal aspects, such as joint property rights and child-care obligations. Religious people may want to include their beliefs that marriage is a relationship sanctioned by God, a relationship that should last until the parties are separated by death. Gay, lesbian, and bisexual people may want to add their own provisions.

This definition masks the diversity in the marital relationship that anthropologists have uncovered. For example, we think of choosing one's spouse as a matter to be decided between the couple, although we usually seek the "blessing" of our parents and other relatives. In many cultures, marriage is much more likely to be a *public* matter that concerns a broad range of relatives who must consent to—and often even arrange—the marriage of a couple.

Further, as often as not romantic love between the couple is not considered necessary for marriage, and sometimes it is not even very relevant to the relationship. Couples do not marry because they "fall in love." For example, in traditional China, Korea, and Japan a man and woman seldom had a chance to fall in love before they married because they usually hardly knew each other and often had not even met. Sometimes boys and girls were betrothed at birth or as children. Even when couples married as adults, the marriage was arranged by their parents with the aid of a matchmaker, usually a female relative of the groom's family or a woman hired by them. She tried to find a woman of suitable age, wealth, status, and disposition to become a wife for the young man. The matchmaker would "match" not only the couple to each other, but also the woman to the husband's parents. Once she married, the wife would be incorporated into her husband's family; her labor would be under the control of her husband's parents, especially her mother-in-law; she would worship the ancestors of her husband's family, not those of her own parents; her behavior would be closely watched lest she disgrace her in-laws; and her children would become members of her husband's kin group, not her own.

Even cohabitation in the same house does not universally accompany marriage. In many villages in Melanesia, Southeast Asia, and Africa, the men sleep and spend much of their time in a communal house (called, appropriately, the *men's house*), whereas their wives and young children live and sleep in a separate dwelling.

Similar ideas apply to most other Western cultural notions of and customs about marriage. Many things we consider normal to the marital relation are not practiced among other peoples. Sex is not always confined to the marriage bed (or mat). There may or may not be a formal ceremony (wedding) recognizing or validating a new marriage. The marital tie may be fragile or temporary, with individuals expecting to have several spouses during the course of their lives. Or the tie may be so strong that even death does not end it. In much of traditional India there used to be strict rules against the remarriage of a higher-caste widow, and such a widow often followed her husband to the grave by throwing herself onto his cremation fire (a practice now illegal in India).

And, yes, there are culturally legitimate marital relationships that are not between a man and a woman. Among the Nuer of the southern Sudan, sometimes an older, well-off woman pays the bridewealth needed to marry a girl; the girl takes male lovers and bears children, who are incorporated into the kin group of the older woman. The pastoral and horticultural Nandi of Kenya also allow marriage between females. When a married woman has no sons to inherit the cattle given her by her

husband, she may become the "female husband" of a younger woman. She picks the sexual partner for her young wife, whose male children become the heirs of the "female husband." Regina Smith Oboler, who worked among the Nandi, reported that the relationship was almost identical to that between a married woman and a man. (We have more to say on same-sex relationships in Chapter 10.)

Because of all this diversity, formulating a definition of marriage that encompasses all the cross-cultural variations in the relationship is problematic, for somewhere there will be a society that does not fit the definition. As you can imagine, numerous definitions have been offered, but there is still no agreement on the "best" one. Most anthropologists agree, however, that marriage in most human societies involves

- a culturally defined relationship between a man and woman from different families, which involves and regulates sexual intercourse and legitimizes children
- a set of rights the couple and their families obtain over each other, including rights over children born to the woman
- an assignment of responsibility for nurturing and enculturating children to the spouses and/or to one or both sets of their relatives
- a creation of variably important bonds and relationships between the families of the couple that have social, economic, political, and sometimes ritual dimensions

Defining marriage in this way, do all societies have some form of marriage?

This question is tricky (for example, is the definition above adequate?) but the answer appears to be no. Consider the Na, an ethnic group of Yunnan Province in the south of China. (The Na are ethnically distinct from the Han, China's majority population.) A Na woman remains at her home, with her siblings and other members of her consanguineous family. Men visit her at night for sexual intercourse, but there is no "commitment" or "obligation," for both people have multiple sexual partners, often simultaneously. The man does not spend the night and seems to have no obligation to his children, or even to recognize them as his. Children are raised by their mother and her own family, so the Na have no nuclear families. Either the woman or her male visitor may initiate the communication that leads to their nighttime liaison, but it is always the man who visits, the woman who stays at home. The Na, therefore, lack all four aspects of the definition of marriage given above, so they have no marriage as we define the term, nor do they have marriage as most people understand it. Cai Hua, the Han Chinese ethnographer, says that the Na show that marriage and nuclear families are not universal human institutions.

But Na are very unusual. Nearly all other peoples have some institution that is recognizably "marriage." As we'll soon discuss, marriage varies. But everywhere it does have functions that seem essential.

Functions of Marriage

The near-universality of marriage suggests that marriage does important things for individuals, families, and/or society at large. Three functions are among the most important.

First, marriage forms the social bonds and creates the social relationships that provide for the material needs, social support, and enculturation of children. The creation of a (variably) stable bond between a woman and her husband is recognized in most cultures as one reason

▲ Human children are dependent on adult care for many years, as this photo of a Laotian woman and her children reminds us. Providing for the physical and emotional needs of children is everywhere a major function of families.

for marriage. In the human species, the tie between mothers and fathers is more important than in most other animals because of the lengthy dependence of children on adults. Until they reach 10 or more years of age, human children are totally or largely dependent on adults for food, shelter, protection, and other bodily needs. Equally important, they require the presence of adults for the social learning crucial to complete their psychological and social development. It is theoretically possible that only one adult, the mother, is required; but almost everywhere, marriage helps to create and expand the relationships through which children receive the material support and enculturation necessary for their immediate survival, future maturity, and eventual reproduction.

Second, marriage defines the rights and obligations a couple have toward each other and toward other people. Some rights and obligations, of course, concern sex. The marriage bond reduces (but does not eliminate) potential conflicts over sexual access, by defining and limiting adult sexual access to certain individuals (normatively or legally, at any rate). Extramarital sex is not, of course, prohibited to the same degree in all cultures, but there are always limitations placed on it, and usually it is punished formally or informally. In all known societies, the nurturing and care of young infants are entrusted mainly to females (usually, to mothers), which implies that mothers need to be supported during a variable period after childbirth. Marriage usually facilitates this provision. Other rights and duties concern the allocation of work and other activities. All cultures divide up work by sex and age in some way: Men do some kinds of tasks, women other kinds. Although the work usually overlaps, there is enough differentiation in most communities that the products and services produced by women must somehow be made available to men, and vice versa. Marriage helps to define these rights and duties ("a good husband should . . .") and establishes the household within which family members do things for one another.

Third, marriage creates new relationships between families and other kinds of kin groups. In a few societies, nuclear families are able to produce what they need to survive more or less by themselves. But in no society are the members of the same nuclear family allowed to have sex, marry, and produce children. Sexual relations between parents and children and between sisters and brothers are defined as incestuous and are prohibited normatively or legally. Violators of this prohibition—known as the **incest taboo**—usually are punished, often severely and sometimes by death. Except in a very few cultures in which members of royal families had sexual relations to produce an heir of the highest possible rank, the incest taboo applies to members of one's own nuclear family. It usually is further extended to prohibit sex between some cousins, uncles and nieces, aunts and nephews, and other relatives that a culture defines as close. The near universal prohibition on sexual activity with close family members forces individuals to marry someone other than their immediate relatives. Every such marriage creates a potential new (affinal) relationship between the relatives of the couple. The importance attached to these affinal relationships varies cross-culturally. At the very least, the families of the wife and husband will have an interest in the children. In addition, a great many societies use the relationships created by intermarriage to establish important trade relationships or political alliances, as we see later.

Because marriage—and the new nuclear family each marriage creates—is useful to individuals and to societies in these and other ways, a relationship like marriage and a group like the family are almost universal among the world's cultures. However, no particular *form* of marriage or *type* of family is universal. Cultures evolved various marriage and family systems to perform these functions. To show how diverse these systems can be, we now consider two unusual systems.

Two Unusual Forms

"Marriage" Among the Nayar of South India. Before Great Britain assumed colonial control in 1792, the Nayar were a warrior caste (Chapter 13) of southern India. Because so many Nayar men served as soldiers for several surrounding Indian kingdoms, they were away from their homes and villages much of the time. Frequent male absence affected marriage and family life. The Nayar almost certainly lacked nuclear families, in the sense of a couple and their offspring living together and sharing responsibilities. Depending on how we define marriage, they may have had no marriage either. How did sexuality and provision for children work in such circumstances?

Nayar villages were composed of a number of kin groups. At birth, most children became members of the kin group of their mother. Each group was linked for certain ceremonial purposes to several other groups, either from its own or from neighboring villages. Any Nayar known to engage in sexual relations with anyone in his or her own kin group was put to death because intragroup intercourse was defined as incest. Restrictions on Nayar women were even more severe: Under penalty of death or ostracism, they had to confine their sexual activity to men of their own or a higher subcaste.

Every few years, all the girls of a kin group who were nearing puberty gathered for a large ceremony, the purpose of which was to ceremonially "marry" these girls to selected men from the linked kin groups. At the ceremony, each "groom" tied a gold ornament around the neck of his "bride." Each couple then went to a secluded place for three days, where they may have had sexual relations. Afterward, the "grooms" left the village, and none had any further responsibilities to his "bride"; indeed, he might never even see her again. For her part, the "bride" and the children she would later bear had only to perform a certain ritual for her ceremonial "husband" when he died. The ritual tying of the ornament by a man of a linked kin group did, however, establish a girl as an adult, able to have sexual liaisons with other men when she matured.

After her "marriage," each girl continued to live with her own consanguineous relatives. When she reached menarche, she began to receive nighttime male visitors from other kin groups. She established long-lasting relations with some of her partners, who were expected to give her small luxury gifts periodically, but did not live with her. None of her partners supported her or her children in any way other than these occasional gifts; indeed, they also visited other women and fathered other children. The food and clothing of a woman and her children were supplied by her brothers and other members of her family, who also provided an inheritance for her children. So a woman looked to her own sisters and brothers rather than to her sexual partner(s) for most of the economic support for herself and her children.

A Nayar woman's early "marriage," then, did not establish a nuclear family, nor did her later sexual partners live with her or support her children. There was only one other thing a woman required from her partners: When she got pregnant, one of them had to admit that he could have been the father of her child by paying the fees for the midwife who helped deliver the baby. If none of her partners did so, it was assumed that she had had sexual intercourse with someone of a lower caste. She, and sometimes her child, would be expelled from her kin group or killed.

Cross-Generational Marriage Among the Tiwi of Northern Australia. In most societies, people who marry are comparable in age. Often males are older, and sometimes significantly older. The Tiwi, who traditionally lived on the Bathurst Islands just off the coast of northern Australia, were unusual because both sexes frequently married people of markedly different ages—in fact, most spouses belonged to different generations. Ethnographer C. W. M. Hart worked among the Tiwi in the late 1920s, and Arnold Pilling worked there in the early 1950s. Jane Goodale's later work focused on Tiwi women.

Like other aboriginal peoples of Australia, the Tiwi were exclusively hunters and gatherers. Male elders made most of the important decisions in a band, including those about foraging activities and the distribution of food. Many elderly men were polygynous—that is, they had more than one wife. Polygynous men had access to lots of food from their wives' gathering and fishing, and they could acquire prestige by distributing the food widely to other families. Other male elders were desired as allies, and allies could be acquired by food distribution and by another means to be discussed in a moment. Tiwi prized meat, but as men reached their 50s and 60s they were unable to hunt effectively. To hunt meat, they needed sons, which they generally had, and sons-in-law, which they could get by marrying off their daughters.

Tiwi marriage is unusual because of two rare customs. First, when a girl was born she was almost immediately promised as a wife to some other man. This is "infant betrothal," with the husband selected by the infant's father. Second, there was a cultural requirement that all females be married virtually all their lives. So an infant girl was not simply betrothed. Tiwi seemed to have thought of her as already married. And when a woman's husband died, she remarried almost immediately, which we may call "widow remarriage."

An astute Tiwi father did not marry his infant daughter to just anyone. He used her marriage to win friends and gain allies. The allies who were most valuable were men of about his own age, so naturally he tended to marry his daughters to these men. But the relationship created by one such marriage was often reciprocated—if you married your daughter to a friend, you would likely receive his daughter, sooner or later. So a man might gain a wife in return for a daughter.

If a man's wives had daughters when he was in his 40s and 50s (which was common, since wives were so young), then he married some of them to men his own age. Not all of them, though, because a man also wanted sons-in-law to come live in his band and help supply meat. So an elder would look around for a young man in his 20s who seemed like a diligent and skillful hunter and a promising ally. He married some of his daughters to these younger men. When his daughters grew up, his sons-in-law would supply him and his household with meat.

From the perspective of a girl growing into womanhood, she would already have a husband, most likely one who was perhaps 20 or 30 years older than herself, and often even 40 or 50 years older. That is, most women were married to men one or two generations removed from themselves. Most women spent their younger years working with their cowives gathering plants for themselves, their children, and their joint husband.

Of course, most wives outlived their husbands but did have children by them. By Tiwi custom, widows had to remarry. But to whom? Some young men in their 20s had failed to attract the notice of the elders and therefore had no wives of their own. But they still could be friends and useful allies of the sons of these widowed women. So at the death of her husband, her sons (usually with her consent and approval) married their mother to a man 20 or 30 years her junior. That way, she would have the support of a strong hunter as she aged, and her sons would strengthen a friendship and gain an ally. (Incidentally, Tiwi wives might seem like "pawns," but in fact they were active participants in marital machinations, as Jane Goodale documented in her book *Tiwi Wives*.)

Should you have visited the Tiwi during their traditional life, what would you have observed about marriage? Many elderly men had several wives, many of whom were between 20 and 40 years younger than themselves. Young men had either no wife at all or only one wife, and that one wife was probably at least 20 years older than her husband. Elderly men were married to women in the prime of their lives, whereas many younger men in their "prime" had wives who were old enough to be their mother. Looked at from the point of view of a typical female's life cycle, she is first a cowife of a much older man; then after he dies she and her male children arrange for her to marry a man who is young enough to be her son.

We emphasize again that both the Nayar and the Tiwi had unusual marriage systems. (Both systems are no longer operating.) Of course, we can assume that neither people viewed their marriage practices as "unusual." It was just what they did. Perhaps they even thought it was only natural.

Marriage in Comparative Perspective

The relationship we call marriage varies enormously cross-culturally. For one thing, most cultures allow multiple spouses. For another, the nature of the marital relationship—living arrangements, what wives and husbands expect from each other, who decides who marries whom, authority patterns, how the relatives of the couple relate to one another, and so forth—differs from people to people. Some of this diversity is described in this section.

Marriage Rules

Everywhere, the choice of a spouse is governed by norms that identify members of some social groups or categories as potential spouses and specify members of other groups or categories as not eligible for marriage. One set of rules is called **exogamous rules.** Exogamy ("outmarriage") means that an individual is prohibited from marrying within her or his own family or other kin group or, less often, village or settlement. Because the incest taboo applies to those people whom the local culture defines as close relatives, members of one's own nuclear family and other close kin are almost everywhere prohibited as spouses. (Note, incidentally, that the incest taboo prohibits *sex,* whereas rules of exogamy forbid *intermarriage.*)

Other kinds of marriage rules are known as **endogamous rules.** Endogamy ("inmarriage") means that an individual must marry someone in his or her own social group. The classic example of an endogamous group is the caste in traditional Hindu India (see Chapter 13). Other kinds of endogamous categories are found in orthodox Jews, races in the American South during slavery, and noble classes in many ancient civilizations and states.

Endogamous rules have the effect of maintaining social barriers between groups of people of different social rank. Rules of endogamy maintain the exclusiveness of the endogamous group in two ways. First, they reduce the social contacts and interactions between individuals of different ranks. Intermarriage creates new relationships between the families of the wife and husband and potentially is a means of raising the rank of oneself or one's offspring. Endogamy has the effect of keeping affinal relationships within the caste, class, ethnic group, race, or whatever; this reinforces ties *within* the endogamous groups and decreases interactions *between* the groups. Second, endogamy symbolically expresses and strengthens the exclusiveness of the endogamous group by preventing its "contamination" by outsiders. This is most apparent with Indian castes because the cultural rationale for caste endogamy is to avoid ritual pollution: The Hindu religion holds that physical contact with members of lower castes places high-caste individuals in a state of spiritual danger, precluding the possibility of marriage between them.

Technically, the term *endogamy* applies only to cultural rules (or even laws) about confining marriage to those within one's own group. But it is important to note the existence of *de facto endogamy,* meaning that although no formal rules or laws require inmarriage, most people marry people who are like themselves. De facto racial and social class endogamy exists in most modern nations, including North America. This is partly because opportunities for members of different classes to get to know one another are often limited. For instance, members of different classes often go to different kinds of schools and often hang out with different sets of friends. Such practices decrease social interactions between classes and thus reduce the possibilities for people of different classes to meet and fall in love. De facto endogamy also exists because of powerful norms against marrying outside one's own "kind." Members of elite classes (and parents and other relatives of young people) may worry that would-be spouses of lower-class standing would not fit in with their social circle (to phrase their objection politely). Likewise, interracial couples are warned about the social stigma attached to their relationship and about the "problems" they and their children will encounter. Of course, these problems exist largely because so many people continue to think that interracial marriages are problematic!

How Many Spouses?

One way cultures vary in marriage practices is in the number of spouses an individual is allowed to have at a time. There are four logical possibilities:

- **Monogamy,** in which every individual is allowed only one spouse
- **Polygyny,** in which one man is allowed multiple wives
- **Polyandry,** in which one woman is allowed multiple husbands
- **Group marriage,** in which several women and men are allowed to be married simultaneously to one another

The last three possibilities are all varieties of **polygamy**— meaning "plural spouses." Notice that the three types of polygamy refer to the number of spouses *allowed* to a person, not necessarily to how many spouses most people have. For example, in polygynous cultures, men are permitted more than one wife, but only a minority of men actually have more than one.

It may surprise members of monogamous societies to learn that most of the world's cultures historically allowed polygamy. The most common form of plural marriage is polygyny. In the past, before colonialism had affected most of the world's peoples, about three-fourths of all societies allowed a man to have two or more wives. Today polygyny is allowed in many modern nations such as the Middle East, and it remains common among indigenous tribal peoples of Africa, Southeast Asia, and Amazonia.

Polyandry, on the other hand, is rare. There are fewer than a dozen societies in which it is documented—less than 1 percent of the world's cultures. Group marriage, so far as we know, has never been a characteristic form of marriage of a whole human society. Indeed, most anthropologists believe that group marriage, where it has occurred, has been a short-lived phenomenon brought about by highly unusual circumstances.

Many Westerners misunderstand the nature of polygamous marriages, seeing them mainly as attempts, usually by men, to get access to more sexual partners. We fail to recognize the social and economic conditions that make these forms of marriage advantageous. We now look at these conditions for polygynous and polyandrous societies.

Polygyny. Even in societies that allow polygyny, only a minority of men actually have more than one wife. Thus polygyny exists as an alternative form of marriage, rather than as the predominant (most common) form. But in those societies that allow it, polygyny ordinarily is the preferred form of marriage, at least for men. Speaking generally, men of high rank/status or wealthy men are the ones who have plural wives, although there are many exceptions.

Even with only a minority of men married polygynously, an obvious problem exists for some other men: If some men have two or more wives, this reduces the number of marriageable women so that some men cannot marry. This is in fact often the case. But in other cases this problem is not as serious as one might think, because in many populations there are more marriageable women than men at any one time. In some societies more males than females die prematurely because they engage in hazardous activities, such as warfare and hunting. Higher male death rates increase the number of men who are able to find wives, even though some men are polygynous.

Looked at from the female perspective, polygyny may have the beneficial effect of ensuring that virtually all women find husbands. In a great many societies, becoming married is important for a woman's welfare because marriage legitimizes her children, and in many cultures children are her main or only source of social security—they are the people she depends on to support her in old age. There is another reason why a woman wants to marry: to ensure that her children are well provided for. In the majority of polygynous societies, inheritance of land, livestock, and other wealth and productive property passes from fathers to sons. A woman need not marry to bear children, but she does want a husband to ensure that her sons have an adequate inheritance (her married daughters usually acquire their resources from their own husbands). Thus, in societies in which for some reason there are more adult women than men, polygyny provides a means for almost all women to gain the benefits of husbands for both themselves and their children.

For their part, most men prefer to have two or more wives. Men usually have both social and economic in-

▶ Polygyny is allowed as a form of marriage in many of the world's cultures. This is a Maasai man with his wives and children. Maasai are a cattle-herding people of Kenya and Tanzania.

© Emil Muench/Photo Researchers, Inc.

centives for marrying several women. Socially, a man's status commonly is directly related to the size of his family and, hence, to the number of his wives and children. Also, when a man marries more than one woman, he acquires a new set of affines—fathers- and brothers-in-law whom he can call on for support, trade, or political alliances. Economically, there are also short- and long-term benefits, especially in horticultural and pastoral adaptations where a woman's labor is important in providing food and wealth to her family. The more wives and children a man has, the larger the workforce available to his household. In pastoral societies in Africa and elsewhere, polygyny enables a man to increase the size of his herds, since he has more herders (wives and children) to tend livestock. Similarly, in those farming societies in which female labor is important, a polygynous man has more family members to tend fields and harvest crops. As he grows older he will have more children and grandchildren to look after his herds or work his fields and care for him. Thus, as long as he has the resources to support them, a man usually tries to acquire additional wives.

What determines whether a particular man is *able* to acquire more than one wife? The answer is usually wealth: only well-to-do men are able to afford more than one wife. "Afford," however, does not mean what North Americans might think; it is often more a matter of being able to *acquire* additional wives than of being able to *support* them. Most polygynous peoples have the custom of bridewealth (discussed later), which requires a prospective groom and his relatives to give livestock, money, or other wealth objects to the kin of the bride. Although fathers and other relatives are typically obliged to help a young man raise bridewealth for one wife, only a minority of men can get together sufficient resources to provide bridewealth for additional wives.

There may be social and economic advantages for the cowives of a polygynous man. Many North Americans think that no woman would want to be part of a "harem." But the most prestigious marriage for a woman is to a husband of wealth and status—the type of man who is most likely to have married other women. Not only will the woman herself be better provided for, but her children may also receive larger inheritances of land, livestock, wealth, or other property. In addition, cowives may lighten a woman's workload. Cowives usually work together and cooperate on chores such as producing, processing, and preparing food, tending livestock, and caring for children. Thus, in many societies it is not unusual for a wife to encourage her husband to take additional wives to assist her in her chores.

Despite their advantages for both men and women, polygynous marriages also have inherent problems. A common problem is rivalry between cowives and favoritism by husbands. Several strategies are used in polygynous societies to minimize friction within these families. One way is for a man to marry women who are sisters, a widespread practice known as *sororal polygyny.* The rationale for sororal polygyny most often is that sisters are raised together, are used to working together, have preexisting emotional bonds, and are likely to be less jealous of one another. Sisters are, therefore, likely to be more compatible than unrelated wives. In most cultures in which a man marries a number of women who are unrelated, each wife usually has her own separate dwelling, which helps to minimize conflict with her cowives. Also, cowives are usually allocated different livestock to care for, and/or they will have separate gardens to tend and harvest. The effect of such practices is that each wife, together with her children, is semi-independent from the other wives. Despite such practices, rivalry and jealousy among cowives are problems in many polygynous marriages.

Polyandry. Polyandry, the marriage of one woman simultaneously to two or more men, is a documented practice in only about a dozen societies. Much has been written about this unusual form of marriage, but ethnologists have not yet satisfactorily explained it. Some believe that female infanticide is partly responsible, arguing that the death of large numbers of girls would produce a shortage of adult women, which would lead several men to be willing to share a wife. All else being equal, female infanticide does indeed have the effect of decreasing the number of marriageable women, but far more human groups allow many of their female infants to die than practice polyandry. Female infanticide is not a *general* explanation for polyandry.

Rather than discussing general explanations, we note that wherever polyandry exists, it does so as an alternative form of marriage. Like polygyny, polyandry is *allowed,* but it is not the *predominant* form of marriage; most couples are monogamous even where polyandry is allowed. Therefore, to understand the reasons for polyandry, we indicate some of the special conditions that lead some people (namely, husbands and their joint wife) to choose to join in a polyandrous marriage.

The insufficiency of a family's land to support all its heirs is one such condition. Many families in farming communities have faced the following dilemma: Our land is barely adequate, and all available farmland is already owned by another family or by a landlord, so we cannot provide all our children with enough land to support them and their families. Many European peasants faced this problem during the Middle Ages and even into the nineteenth century. In Ireland and some other parts of Europe, one solution was *primogeniture,* or inheritance by the eldest: The oldest son inherited the farm and most of its property, and the younger sons had to find other ways of supporting themselves. Younger sons served in the army or became priests or found some other occupation. Daughters who did not marry usually either remained at home or joined a nunnery. After the Industrial Revolution in the late 1700s, many migrated to cities and went to work in factories.

Some peoples of the Himalayas developed another solution—polyandry. The rugged topography and high altitude of Tibet and Nepal sharply limit the supply of farmland. A farm may be adequate to support only a single family, but many couples have three or more sons. If the sons divide their inheritance by each taking his own wife, the land would become so fragmented that the brothers' families would be impoverished. To solve this problem, sometimes all the sons marry one woman. This form of polyandry, called *fraternal polyandry,* helps to keep the farm and family intact and limits the number of children in the family. Although the oldest son usually assumes primary responsibility for the wife and children, the joint wife is not supposed to favor him or his brothers sexually. When children are born, ideally each brother treats them as if they were his own, even if he knows that a particular child was fathered by one of his brothers.

What are the benefits of fraternal polyandry? For the brothers, sharing a wife preserves the family property, keeping the land, the livestock, the house, and other wealth together. Also, one brother can stay in the village and work the family land during the summer, while another brother takes the livestock to high mountain pastures and a third brother (if present) visits towns in the lowlands to sell the family's products. This system also has advantages for the wife, who has multiple husbands to work for her and help support her and her children. Her life is usually less physically strenuous and she usually has a higher standard of living than a woman married to only one man.

Although Himalayan polyandry has economic advantages, sometimes problems arise. A younger brother can decide at any time to end the arrangement, claim his portion of the family property, marry another woman, and establish his own family. The oldest brother does not have this option because as head of the family he bears primary responsibility for supporting their wife and children.

Marriage Alliances

Cultures vary in the importance they attach to the tie between wives and husbands. In some cultures, there is no formal wedding ceremony. Instead, a couple is socially recognized as "married" when they regularly live together and as "divorced" when one of them moves out. Each partner retains her or his own separate property, so the separation or divorce is not very "messy." In the contemporary United States, the wedding ceremony is often a big and expensive affair, marriages are supposed to endure, and couples usually own houses, furniture, and other property jointly. Yet about half of all new American marriages will end in divorce, many quite messy because of conflicts over property and custody of the children. For many Americans, monogamy turns out to be *serial monogamy,* meaning only one legal spouse at a time.

Many cultures consider the marital relationship to be far more serious. In many, marriage establishes lasting social relationships and bonds not just between the couple but also between their families and other relatives. The affinal ties between kin groups created by intermarriage are frequently important not just socially but also economically, politically, and often, ritually. Marriage establishes an *alliance* between the members of two kin groups, and in many cultures **marriage alliances** are critical for the well-being and even survival of the intermarried groups. This appears to have been the case among the ancient Israelites because Moses says in Genesis (34:16): "Then we will give our daughters unto you, and we will take your daughters to us, and we will dwell with you, and we will become one people."

A good example of how intermarriage creates and maintains ties between kin groups comes from among the Yąnomamö, a horticultural and hunting tribe of the Amazon rain forest of South America. Many Yąnomamö villages were under periodic threat of attack, so each had to be prepared to defend itself; likewise, the men of each village periodically went on raids intended to capture the women and resources of their enemies. It was, therefore, advantageous for villages to establish and maintain military alliances for mutual defense and offense, because the more men a village could mobilize as warriors, the more likely it was to be successful in conflicts. Smaller villages in fact almost had to form alliances or they would be victimized by their more numerous enemies. Having allies was also helpful in case of military defeat: a defeated group could take refuge with an allied village, whose members would feed and protect the refugees until they could establish productive gardens in a new location.

Marriage was a key strategy in creating and maintaining these alliances. When the men of a Yąnomamö village wanted to make an alliance with another village, they began by trading. For instance, one village might tell the other it needed clay pots and would be willing to trade its bows for them; or it might say that it needed hallucinogenic drugs used in shamanistic curing and would trade its hammocks for them. The people of each village were capable of making all these products for themselves, but trade provided the excuse for visiting one another to begin alliance formation. If no trouble broke out during the trading—for a Yąnomamö village did not even trust its longtime allies, much less its prospective allies—the relation might extend to mutual invitations to feasts. If the feasts did not turn violent, the men of the two villages would agree to give some of their "sisters" (female relatives) to one another. This was considered the final stage of alliance formation; once the villages had exchanged women, the alliance was—by Yąnomamö standards—secure.

The Yąnomamö illustrate how intermarriage creates bonds and establishes important political relations between villages. Among many peoples, these bonds and relations are important to families or entire communities. If marriages are a means of establishing ties that are critical to a group's material well-being or survival, then the choice of which group to marry into may be too important to be left entirely up to the woman and man whose marriage creates the relationship. Older, wiser, and more responsible people should be making such critical decisions.

The fact that who marries whom is often so important to families and even larger groups helps to explain one widespread custom—*arranged marriages*—that many Westerners view as an infringement on a person's freedom to choose. To offer an alternative view, a couple's freedom to choose their own spouse is an infringement on the freedom of their parents and other relatives to form advantageous relationships with other kin groups. How serious this infringement is, and whether the "freedom" of one party or another takes precedence, is not absolute but depends on circumstances. Perhaps some of our readers will find arranged marriages less offensive when they realize that a poor marital choice often puts more people at risk than just the couple themselves—though the couple may put themselves at risk by their own choices.

The importance of the ties between kin groups created by intermarriage is also revealed by two other widespread customs. In one, called the **levirate,** if a woman's husband dies, she marries one of his close kinsmen (usually a brother). The relations between the intermarried kin groups are too valuable for a woman to be returned to her own family, because then she might marry into an-

▲ In most highly urbanized, industrialized countries, marriage emphasizes the relationship between the woman and her new husband rather than bonds between the families of the newlyweds. This is a wedding procession in Hungary.

other kin group. Therefore, a male relative of her deceased husband takes his place. Because both her dead and her new husband belong to the same kin group, the relationship between the two groups remains intact. The converse custom, the **sororate,** also preserves the affinal ties between kin groups. With the sororate, if a woman dies, her kin group is obliged to replace her with another woman, for which no additional bridewealth need be transferred. The Zulu of southern Africa, as well as many other African peoples, practiced both the levirate and the sororate. In societies with these customs, marriages—and the affinal ties they create—endure even beyond death.

Marital Exchanges

In most cultures, the marriage of a man and a woman is accompanied by some kind of transfer of goods or services. These *marital exchanges* take numerous forms, including the North American custom of wedding showers and wedding gifts. In these, the presents given by relatives and friends supposedly help the newlyweds establish an independent household. We give things that are useful to the couple jointly, with food-preparation and other household utensils easily the most common type of gift. Many couples even register at stores so that their relatives and friends will provide the items they want.

Comparatively speaking, the most unusual feature of North American marital exchange is that nothing is transferred between the relatives of the groom and bride: the couple treats the gifts as their private property. Like most of our other customs, this seems natural to us. Of course the gifts go to the couple—what else could happen to them?

Plenty else, as we shall see in a moment. For now, notice that the fact that the couple receives the gifts fits with several other features of Euro-American marriage. First, in addition to creating new nuclear families, marriage is the bond through which new independent households are started. So the husband and wife "need their own stuff." If, in contrast, the newlyweds moved in with one of their relatives, they would not have as great a need for their own pots and pans, wine glasses, silver candlesticks, dishes, and other household items. Second, our marriage-gift customs fit with the value our culture places on the privacy of the marital relationship: It is largely a personal matter between the husband and wife, and their relatives should keep their noses out. If the in-laws get along and socialize, that's great, but our marriages generally do not create strong bonds between families of the bride and groom. (In fact, the two families often compete for the visits and attention of the couple and their offspring.) As we saw in Chapter 7, gifts make friends and vice versa; the fact that the in-laws do not exchange gifts with each other is a manifestation of the absence of a necessary relation between them after the wedding. If, in contrast, the marriage created an alliance between the two sets of relatives, some kind of an exchange would probably occur between them to symbolize and cement their new relations. Third, the gifts are presented to the couple, not to the husband or wife as individuals, and are considered to belong equally and jointly to both partners. But there are marriage systems in which the property of the wife is separate from that of her husband; if divorce should occur, there is no squabbling over who gets what and no need for prenuptial legal contracts.

With this background in mind, what kinds of marital exchanges occur in other cultures?

Bridewealth. **Bridewealth** is the widespread custom that requires a man and/or his relatives to transfer wealth to the relatives of his bride. It is easily the most common of all marital exchanges, found in more than half the world's cultures. The term *bridewealth* is well chosen because the goods transferred are usually among the most valuable symbols of wealth in the local culture. In sub-Saharan Africa, cattle and sometimes other livestock are the most common goods used for bridewealth. Peoples of the Pacific islands and Southeast Asia usually give their bridewealth in pigs or shell money and ornaments.

One of the most common rights a man and his relatives acquire when they transfer bridewealth to his wife's family is rights over the woman's children. Reciprocally, one of a wife's most important obligations is to bear children for her husband. This is well exemplified by the Swazi, a traditional kingdom of southern Africa. A Swazi marriage is a union between two families as well as between the bride and groom. The payment of bridewealth—in cattle and other valuables—to a woman's relatives establishes the husband's rights over his wife. A woman's main duty to her husband is to provide him with children. If she is unable to do so, her relatives must either return the bridewealth they received for her or provide a second wife to the husband, for which he need pay no extra bridewealth. Reciprocally, a man must pay bridewealth to gain rights of fatherhood over the child of a woman, even though everyone knows he is the child's biological father. If he does not do so, the woman's relatives will keep the child; if the woman herself later marries another man, her new husband will not receive rights over the child unless he pays bridewealth.

Brideservice. **Brideservice** is the custom whereby a husband is required to spend a period of time working for the family of his bride. A Yąnomamö son-in-law is expected to live with his wife's parents, hunting and gardening for them until they finally release control over their daughter. Among some !Kung bands (Chapters 6 and 7), a man proves his ability as a provider by living with and hunting for his wife's parents for 3 to 10 years, after which the couple is free to camp elsewhere.

Brideservice is the second most common form of marital exchange; it is the usual compensation given to the family of a bride in roughly one-eighth of the world's cultures. However, sometimes it occurs alongside other forms of marital exchange and occasionally can be used to reduce the amount of bridewealth owed.

Dowry. A marital exchange is called **dowry** when the family of a woman transfers a portion of its own wealth or property to the woman (their daughter) and/or to her husband and his family. The main thing to understand about dowry is that it is *not* simply the opposite of bridewealth; that is, it is not "groomwealth." The woman and her family do not acquire marital rights over her husband when they provide a dowry, as they would if dowry were the opposite of bridewealth; rather, the bride and her husband receive property when they marry, rather than when the bride's parents die. By doing so, parents give their female children extra years of use of the property and also publicly demonstrate their wealth.

Sometimes dowry is the share of a woman's inheritance that she takes into her marriage for the use of her new family. Dowry may represent an occasion for a family to display their wealth publicly by ostentatiously moving furniture and clothing from their house to that of their daughter's husband. Among other peoples, the family of a man will not allow him to marry a woman unless she and her family are able to make a dowry payment. Typically, the cultural rationale is that women do not contribute as much to a family as do men, so a family must be compensated for admitting a new female member. (Interestingly, this rationale is usually found among societies in which the domestic labor of the female is both difficult and valuable.)

Historically, dowry transfers were common in Eurasian (Europe, southern Asia, and the Middle East) cultures. Most peoples that practiced it were intensive agriculturalists and had significant inequalities in wealth. It has always been a relatively rare form of marital exchange, occurring in only about 5 percent of the societies recorded by anthropology.

Although a minority of societies practice dowry, some of these societies are quite populous. Dowry is common today in parts of India, where it includes jewelry, household utensils, women's clothing, and money. Much of the dowry is presented to the bride on her wedding day, but her parents and maternal uncle often provide gifts periodically throughout the marriage.

In recent decades, the demands of Indian families for dowry have led to thousands of tragic deaths. Rather than a one-time marital exchange, some Indian families demand additional, continual payments from the parents of a woman who has married one of their sons. They ask for large sums of cash, for household appliances like refrigerators and televisions, motorbikes, and other kinds of consumer goods. If the wife's family refuses, their daughter may be severely injured or even killed by burning (in "accidental kitchen fires"), beatings, withholding food, falls, or other retaliations. Around 7,000 Indian women suffered "dowry deaths" in 2003, according to official figures, but the actual number is likely much higher. If these numbers sound large, be aware that India has over a billion people, so dowry deaths are not common statistically.

There are other forms of exchanges that occur at marriages, including some in which both sets of relatives exchange gifts as a material symbol of the new basis of their relationship. And the three forms discussed above are not mutually exclusive. For example, in most of traditional China, both bridewealth and dowry occurred at most marriages. The groom's family would make a payment to the bride's, and the bride's family would purchase some furniture and other household goods for their daughter to take with her when she moved into her husband's household. For wealthier families, dowry was usually displayed by being transported ostentatiously over the streets between the households of the bride and groom. Dowry thus became a Chinese status symbol. Sometimes, if the bride's family was substantially poorer than the groom's, part of the bridewealth payment would be spent on purchasing goods for the woman's dowry. This was legal and common until after the Communist Revolution in 1949, when Communist Party leaders outlawed both bridewealth and dowry, with only partial success.

Although the preceding information about marriage rules, forms, alliances, and exchanges has barely introduced these complicated topics, enough has been presented for you to glimpse both the cross-cultural diversity of marriage customs and the societal importance of marriage. Marriage is tied up with adaptation, with economics, and, quite obviously, with politics and religion. Similar interrelationships between marriage, politics, and religion are seen in the contemporary United States, as the recent political wars over gay marriage illustrate (see A Closer Look).

Kinship Diagrams

At this point we need to introduce a set of notational symbols used in the remainder of this chapter and the next. This notation allows us to express diagrammatically how any two persons are (or believe themselves to be) related by bonds of kinship. The symbols appear in Figure 8.1, along with an example of how they would be used to show a married couple with five children. By stringing a number of symbols together, it is possible to make a complete chart—called a *genealogy*—that shows all the relatives of a given individual and how they are related to that individual. In these charts, or kinship diagrams, it is useful to have a reference individual, or a person to whom everyone on the chart is related. It is customary to call this reference individual "ego." In Figure 8.1, ego is symbolized by a square to show that his or her gender is irrelevant for the purposes of the genealogy. (If ego's gender mattered, we would symbolize him or her with either a triangle or a circle.)

In early 2004, the newly elected mayor of San Francisco began issuing marriage licenses to gay couples. In May, the state of Massachusetts legalized same-sex marriages. Alarmed over the prospect of other states passing similar legislation, by summer President George W. Bush and conservatives in the U.S. Congress pressed for an amendment to the U.S. Constitution. After several rewrites, when brought to a vote on July 14, 2004, the amendment read:

> Marriage in the United States shall consist only of the union of a man and a woman. Neither this Constitution, nor the constitution of any state, shall be construed to require that marriage or the legal incidents thereof be conferred upon any union other than the union of a man and a woman.

In the July vote, the proposed amendment failed to gain even a majority in the Senate, where a two-thirds vote is required for passage of an amendment. Leftists, liberals, and most moderates opposed it. Liberals saw it as either the latest attempt at gay-bashing or just another symbol of cultural intolerance. Some viewed it as a shameless effort by neoconservatives, Fundamentalists, and other Republicans to gain political support for the November 2004 elections by forcing their opponents (mainly Democrats) to vote yes or no, which would then allow them to claim that the "no" voters were antifamily and didn't share mainstream values. But even some conservatives opposed it because they believed it infringed on states' rights.

Why did gay marriage become so politicized? The short answer is that the issue is part of the American "culture wars." Among the battles are whether there are absolute standards of right and wrong; the role that Christian teachings should have in schools, courtrooms, and other public institutions; whether individuals are morally responsible for all their actions; and how much multicultural diversity "one nation under God" can absorb without tearing itself apart from within. Same-sex marriage provides spring-loaded ammunition for the culture warriors: Is it morally wrong or an alternative lifestyle? Given that many Protestant denominations welcome gays and lesbians and some even allow their ordination, is it against biblical teachings? Are homosexual desires rooted in genes and hereditary, or is being openly gay merely a "lifestyle choice"? What would happen to the nation as a whole if diverse forms of marriage were legalized? If same-sex marriage is legalized, will polygamy be next?

Some of the strongest opponents of same-sex marriage hold that marriage between one woman and one man is the bedrock of human society, so changing it is likely to endanger social order in lots of unpredictable ways. In July 2004, in a Saturday radio address supporting the amendment, President Bush said, "The union of a man and a woman in marriage is the most enduring and important human institution. . . ." Obviously, the president meant that *one form of marriage*—monogamy ("a man and a woman")—is the most enduring and important institution. On this point, at least, he was mistaken, for polygyny is widespread and even polyandry exists.

And no matter how fiercely culture wars are fought to preserve the marriage practices that are at the present normative and positively valued, these practices are sure to change, and change again. Whether people can marry outside their race or ethnicity, what goes on during courtship, how people choose their spouse, what they expect from marriage, what obligations wives have toward husbands, how enduring specific marriages will be, how the children resulting from the "union" of a man and a woman are raised—all these and most other features of marriage as we know it today would be viewed with consternation and even horror by North Americans of a century ago. No doubt at least some of them would have foretold the horrific effects on society if blacks and whites were ever able to marry, if premarital sex were the norm, if many women were the main family breadwinners, if half of all marriages ended with divorce, and if large numbers of couples entrusted their preschool-aged children to something called "day care centers" for 40 hours a week.

Sources: San Francisco Chronicle, Monday, July 12, 2004, pp. A1, A8; Thursday, July 15, 2004, pp. A1, A14.

Postmarital Residence Patterns

In modern Euro-American societies, most newly married couples establish a new domestic group (household) in their own apartment, condo, or house. Elsewhere, couples do not set up a new household, but more often move into an existing household, either that of the husband or that of the wife. Where most newly married couples in a society establish their residence is known as the **postmarital residence pattern.** Cross-cultural research shows that our own pattern, in which couples form new households separate from their parents, is uncommon.

What are the other common patterns? By splitting enough hairs, it is possible to identify a dozen patterns, but here we present only six. In order of most frequent to least frequent, they are as follows:

- **Patrilocal** Couples live with or near the parents of the husband.
- **Matrilocal** Couples live with or near the wife's parents.

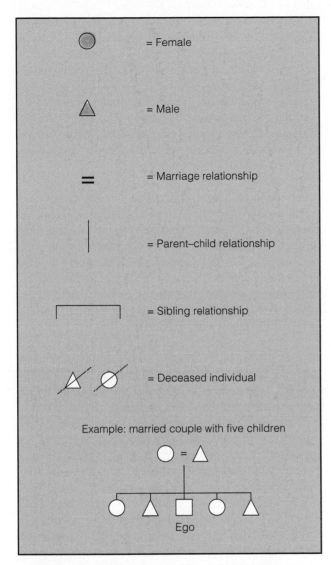

▲ **Figure 8.1** Symbols Used on Kinship Diagrams

- **Ambilocal** Postmarital residence is optional between either the wife's or the husband's kin; roughly one-half of all couples choose each.
- **Bilocal** Couples move back and forth between the households of both sets of parents, according to preferences and circumstances.
- **Neolocal** Couples live apart from both parents, establishing a separate dwelling and independent household.
- **Avunculocal** Couples live with the maternal uncle of the husband.

About 70 percent of all societies have patrilocal residence as the predominant pattern. Thirteen percent have matrilocal residence. These two patterns are easily the most widespread, accounting for about 83 percent of all societies. Bilocality, ambilocality, neolocality, and avunculocality together account for the remaining 17 percent.

Influences on Residence Patterns

What sorts of factors affect postmarital residence patterns? What determines whether newly married couples live separately or move in with some kind of relative? And if most couples co-reside with some relatives, as they do in most societies, what affects which set of relatives?

There is no simple answer, but property rights and inheritance forms are important influences on postmarital residence. In societies in which the most important productive property is held by men, and in which inheritance passes from fathers to sons, brothers have good reasons to join their fathers (and each other) in a common household to cooperate and protect their interest in land, livestock, or other wealth. When the sons of most families in a society bring their wives and children into their father's existing household, this pattern of behavior leads to the residence anthropologists call patrilocal. Where important resources are controlled or owned by women, and especially if female labor is important in supplying food for their families, then sisters tend to live and work together, and matrilocal residence is most likely to develop as sisters bring their husbands to live with them.

Ambilocal and bilocal patterns are most common in societies in which inheritance of important resources passes through both sexes and the labor of both women and men is important to household subsistence. Most hunter-gatherers have one of these two patterns. As explained in Chapter 6, most families in a foraging band need or want to maintain access to several territories, so rights to gather and hunt in a particular area are flexible. Nuclear families may live off and on with the husband's and wife's bands, depending on sentimental ties or short- or long-term availability of resources. If all or most couples do this, the result is bilocal residence. Or the couple may settle with whichever parental family has the most resources or with whichever they have good relations, leading to ambilocality.

Modern industrialized nations are usually neolocal, for two major reasons. First, job availability forces many couples to move away from their home town. This is especially true for "upwardly mobile" couples seeking increased income, better opportunities, and the more materially rewarding lifestyle valued by many. Second, in industrialized countries most workers do not rely on their family connections for access to their livelihood but sell their labor on an impersonal market to an employer they have never met. In other words, most ordinary citizens do not inherit productive property from their parents and do not rely on their parents for their livelihood, so they establish independent domiciles free from parental control and interference. The result is neolocal residence and an emphasis on nuclear family ties.

Although control over resources and form of inheritance are important overall influences, no single factor "determines" postmarital residence. For instance, if most couples rely on the wife's family for access to the resources they need to survive and raise children, then most couples will live with the wife's family and matrilocal residence will be the pattern. But a multitude of other factors also affect residence choices. In fact, in some societies even though women have much control over land, residence is not matrilocal because these other factors are locally more important than keeping sisters together in a common household. Similar complexities apply to the other residence patterns, so there is no single explanation.

We conclude this section by pointing out a few more complications that make generalizations difficult. For one thing, there are many exceptions to almost all generalizations about humanity: for example, the Tiwi of Australia (discussed earlier) are patrilocal, although they are foragers. For another, a great many peoples do not have a single residence pattern. Rather, where people live varies over time. Among some Inuit ("Eskimo") peoples, often couples lived neolocally in the summer, patrilocally in the winter. Among western Shoshone, most families lived neolocally during the dry summers but came together with a mixture of other relatives during the fall and winter. Lastly, even within a single society, different families make different choices. For example, China's industrial economy is growing at a staggering rate, and its residence is transforming from the pre-twentieth-century patrilocal pattern to a neolocal pattern. Yet many rural couples live with the husband's family, and even many young urban couples live with relatives due to housing shortages and the (ever-weakening) obligation to support one's elderly parents.

The subject of postmarital residence might seem trivial. What difference does it make whether newly married couples live alone or with one set of parents?

Residence and Households

In fact, there are good reasons for our interest in residence patterns: they greatly affect the kinds of family relationships that are most important in a human community.

A moment's reflection shows that both matrilocal and patrilocal residence places a new nuclear family (usually, created by a new marriage) with one set of relatives rather than the other set. In turn, whom a newly married couple lives with influences whom they will cooperate with, share property with, feel close to, and so forth. If postmarital residence is patrilocal, for instance, then the husband lives with and works with his own consanguineous relatives (his father and brothers, paternal uncles and cousins *through his father*). The wife is likely to cooperate in household chores, gathering, gardening, and other tasks with members of her husband's family, more than with her own.

Postmarital residence also affects the relatives with whom children are most likely to develop strong emotional bonds. If residence is matrilocal, for example, then the children of sisters (who are cousins *through their mothers*) live together in a single household (much like biological sisters and brothers) and are likely to view their relationship as being like real siblings. The children of brothers, on the other hand, will live in different households and are less likely to play together and develop strong emotional attachments.

Most importantly, the prevailing form of residence affects the kinds of household and family units that exist among a people. Consider neolocal residence, for example. If all or most newlyweds set up their own households, distinct from and independent of that of either of their parents, then a new household and family unit is established with each new marriage. This emphasizes the social and economic importance and independence of nuclear families because mothers and fathers—and not more distant relatives—are most likely to be the main teachers of children and breadwinners for the household. The couple maintains relations with their parents, siblings, and other relatives, of course, but neolocal residence tends to lead to an emphasis on nuclear families as the most culturally important and stable family unit.

Comparing neolocal to the other forms of postmarital residence might lead you to think differently about some statements of North American political leaders. For the most part, when politicians worry about the decline or breakup of "the" American or Canadian family, they are usually talking about the nuclear family. "The" family is threatened by high divorce rates, unmarried couples living together, absent or deadbeat fathers, high illegitimacy rates, the gay lifestyle, and so forth. In recent years so many families have split up that family stability has become a major social problem. But the disintegration of *extended family* relationships is treated differently: No one worries much about the separation of adult married children and their parents, or about how many married siblings have not seen one another for years. We consider it normal—not a social problem—when married children move out from their parents' homes and away from their siblings. Indeed, most view it as unfortunate if newlyweds live with either set of parents; surely only economic necessity could force them to do so. (It helps the market economy that we feel this way, since the housing industry would collapse if very many of us abandoned neolocal in favor of matrilocal residence.) Perhaps you join many of your peers in thinking young marrieds who visit or seek advice from their parents too often are a little strange. Why can't they make their own choices and break away from their mom and dad?

Family and Household Forms

One of the most important differences in households is the number of generations they include. Nuclear families include only two generations (parents and children), whereas extended families include three or more generations.

Two-Generation Households

Some people believe that the nuclear family is the basic unit of kinship. (Notice that "individuals" cannot be the basic unit of kinship, since kinship is inherently about *relations* between individuals.) Other kinds of kin groupings arise when nuclear families associate together in patterned ways. For example, patrilocal residence associates the nuclear families of brothers with one another in the same household. Neolocality does not associate nuclear families with one another *residentially*, although of course related nuclear families have other kinds of socially and emotionally important ties.

Possibly, though, those who think the nuclear family is somehow "basic" only believe this because they live in a society in which a couple and their offspring are the most visible family form. Perhaps they view other forms as morally perverse, or as unfortunate compromises a particular nuclear family has to make due to special circumstances such as lacking the income to get a place of their own.

There is another view: that the "basic unit" of kinship is a woman and her offspring. People who think this point out that fathers are more frequently separated from their children than are mothers, implying that the mother–child bond is more "basic." Fathers may separate temporarily or permanently for many reasons. In subsistence economies, men may be absent for long periods hunting, herding, trading, raiding, or carrying out other duties. In communities—and in modern countries—where most families depend on wage labor, husbands/fathers may take jobs in distant cities or countries for many months or even years. The money they send back to their families at home (called *remittances*) is surprisingly large: in 2004, around 10 million migrants (predominantly men) from Mexico and other Latin American countries remitted $30 billion to their home countries.

Historically, male absence for extended periods was especially common in regions that were colonies of a major world power. In sub-Saharan Africa, especially, European colonial powers imposed taxes on men or introduced new commodities that soon became virtual necessities. In order to earn money to meet expenses, married men went to work for foreign companies on distant diamond or gold mines or would leave their families to work on plantations owned by Europeans. This pattern continues in much of Africa and other regions even today. For the families left behind, the result is the **matrifocal family,** where a mother (with or without a husband) bears most of the burden of supporting her children economically and nurturing them emotionally and intellectually.

Matrifocal families occur in modern industrial societies as well, whenever households are "female-headed," as the United States Census Bureau calls them. Around half of all African American children live in households with a female head. Some say that matrifocal families are an important cause of poverty, crime, and other social problems today. Adult men would act more responsibly if they had jobs that supported their nuclear families. Sons need male role models and supposedly find them elsewhere if their fathers are not around. Mothers would be much better mothers if they didn't have to struggle so hard to pay the bills.

In modern nations, it is true that poor families are more likely to be female-headed than affluent families. But this does not mean that matrifocal households are a significant cause of poverty and other social ills. Matrifocal families can also be viewed as a consequence of poverty: lack of job skills or other factors lead to high unemployment among men, leading many women to decide that having a permanent male presence is too costly. Female-headed households in the United States and elsewhere are not necessarily the result of men's refusal to act responsibly, nor of women's moral choices: they also are adaptations that people make to their economic and social environment.

Extended Households

Extended families are made up of related nuclear families. Because the related nuclear families usually live in a single household, here we use *extended family* and *extended household* as synonyms. Extended households typically include three and often four generations of family members.

Many anthropologists think that the form of family (household) that is prevalent in a society depends on its postmarital residence pattern. For example, with patrilocal residence the married sons of an older couple remain in the household of their parents. Alternatively, each son builds his own house on his parents' land, near their dwelling, but they cooperate with one another and pool or share resources. As they grow up and marry, the daughters depart to live with their husbands' parents. If all the sons and daughters of a couple do this, the resulting household is of a type called *patrilocally extended*—brothers live in a single household with their own nuclear families and parents (see Figure 8.2a). If all families in the village, town, or other settlement follow this pattern, then the settlement consists of patrilocally extended households. Notice that the residents of each household are related to one another through males. The married women of the community live scattered in the households of their husbands. Perhaps many of them have married out of the community altogether.

The converse occurs with matrilocal residence. The mature sons leave as they marry, and the daughters bring their husbands to live with them in or near their parents' households. The household type formed by the co-residence of daughters and sisters with their parents is called the *matrilocally extended household* (see Figure 8.2b). The sons of an elderly couple are scattered in the households of the women they have married, either in their own home community or in another community. If most people follow this residence pattern, then the community consists of numerous households, each of which is lived in by women related through females, plus their husbands and children.

The same relationship between residence and prevalent household form applies to the other residence patterns. With bilocal and ambilocal residence there is no consistency in whether households are made up of people related through males or females: Some couples live with the husband's family, others with that of the wife. The household type is *bilocally* (or *bilaterally*) *extended* (see Figure 8.2c). The community's households are a mixture of people related through both sexes, in roughly equal frequency. With neolocal residence the settlement—be it village or modern suburb—consists of relatively small domestic units made up of nuclear families.

The avunculocal residence pattern associates nuclear families with the husband's mother's brother. If everyone resided this way (which they usually do not), then the settlement would consist of households composed of older men (the household heads) and the families of their sister's sons. This is called the *avunculocally extended household* (see Figure 8.2d). It includes men (and their wives and children) who are related to one another through women (their mothers). (Confused by this one? We shall see in Chapter 9 that avunculocal residence

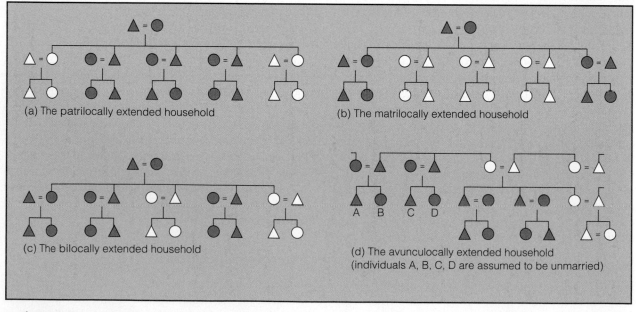

(a) The patrilocally extended household

(b) The matrilocally extended household

(c) The bilocally extended household

(d) The avunculocally extended household
(individuals A, B, C, D are assumed to be unmarried)

▲ **Figure 8.2** Household Forms

makes good sense in many societies that trace their main kinship relationships through women.)

We can now see the main reason postmarital residence patterns are important: They give rise to various household and family forms. The kinds of family and domestic groups found among a people result from where newly formed families go to live. Stated differently, the prevalent household type in a human community represents the crystallization of the pattern of postmarital residence. And who lives with whom—the household type—is important, since households so often hold property in common, cooperate in production and other economic activities, enculturate children together, and sometimes even worship the same ancestral spirits.

In this chapter we have given an overview of some variations in domestic life. If we were writing a book about industrial, market economy societies, we might stop our discussion of groupings formed on the basis of kinship relations at this point. This is because, among the industrialized, urbanized portion of humanity, other kinds of relations and groupings—economic, educational, political, religious, and so on—are organized by relationships other than kinship—by specialized firms, schools, parties, governments, churches, and so on. But, as we discuss in Chapter 9, in preindustrial cultures kinship principles are used to form much larger kin groups that organize and perform a wide range of other activities.

Summary

1. All societies have some kind of family groupings to organize and facilitate child-rearing and other essential domestic activities. Marriage serves many functions, including reducing conflict over sexuality, forming social bonds that provide for children, organizing the exchange of goods and services between husbands and wives, and establishing new relations between intermarrying families. Some form of marriage is nearly universal in human societies, although the form of marriage, the kinds of rights and duties it establishes, and many other aspects of the marital relationship vary. The Nayar and Tiwi illustrate unusual forms of marriage, and the Na of southern China seem to have no marriage at all.

2. Marriage is everywhere governed by rules, many of which pertain to exogamy and endogamy. Marriage systems are commonly classified by the number of spouses an individual is allowed: polygyny, monogamy, polyandry, and group marriage, in order of relative frequency in human societies. In preindustrial societies, marriage is often the cornerstone of alliance relations between families or larger kin groups. The Yąnomamö illustrate the use of strategic marriages to create and sustain military alliances, a practice quite common in the preindustrial world. The levirate and sororate are customs that preserve affinal relationships even after the death of a spouse.

3. New marriages are usually accompanied by the exchange of goods or services between the spouses and the families of the bride and groom. The most common forms of marital exchange are bridewealth, brideservice, and dowry. These exchanges are used to create affinal relationships, compensate a family or larger kin group for the loss of one of its members, provide for the new couple's support, or provide a daughter with an inheritance that helps attract a desirable husband.

4. *Postmarital residence patterns* refers to where newly married couples establish their residence. From most common to least common, the patterns are patrilocal, matrilocal, ambilocal, bilocal, neolocal, and avunculocal. There are many influences on which of these forms will be most prevalent in a given community, including economic forces and inheritance patterns. But no single factor is adequate to explain the cross-cultural variation in residence patterns.

5. Anthropologists are interested in postmarital residence patterns mainly because where a newly married couple goes to live influences which kinship relationships will be most emphasized in a society. In particular, the prevalent forms of family and domestic groups in a community arise out of many couples living with one or another set of relatives. Patrilocally, matrilocally, bilocally, and avunculocally extended families are often interpreted as the crystallization of postmarital residence patterns.

Key Terms

consanguines
affines
kin group
nuclear family
household
fictive kinship
extended family (extended household)
incest taboo
exogamous rules
endogamous rules

monogamy
polygyny
polyandry
group marriage
polygamy
marriage alliances
levirate
sororate
bridewealth
brideservice

dowry
postmarital residence pattern
patrilocal residence
matrilocal residence
ambilocal residence
bilocal residence
neolocal residence
avunculocal residence
matrifocal family

InfoTrac College Edition Terms

family and culture
marriage definition (yields articles on legal issues)

polygamy
marriage in China
bridewealth

dowry in India
gay marriage

Suggested Readings

Collier, Jane F. *Marriage and Inequality in Classless Societies.* Stanford, Calif.: Stanford University Press, 1988.

Compares marriage systems and marriage exchanges in small-scale societies from a theoretical perspective, discussing their impact on male–female relationships.

Stockard, Janice E. *Marriage in Culture: Practice and Meaning Across Diverse Societies.* Fort Worth, Tex.: Harcourt College Publishers, 2002.

Describes and compares postmarital residence and marriage in four cultures: !Kung, traditional China, Iroquois of around 1800, and the polyandrous Nyinba of Nepal. Probably the best brief (129 pages) recent comparative treatment of marriage for introductory students.

Suggs, David N., and Andrew W. Miracle, eds. *Culture and Human Sexuality: A Reader.* Pacific Grove, Calif.: Brooks/Cole, 1993.

A collection of articles dealing with sexuality and related topics from a cross-cultural perspective. Includes both case studies and theoretical articles.

Most ethnographies contain a description of the domestic life of the people studied. Here are a few ethnographies that focus narrowly on domestic life.

Levine, Nancy. *The Dynamics of Polyandry: Kinship, Domesticity, and Population in the Tibetan Border.* Chicago: University of Chicago Press, 1988.

Case study of fraternal polyandry in the Himalayas.

Malinowski, Bronislaw. *The Sexual Life of Savages.* New York: Harcourt, Brace, Jovanovich, 1929.

Not what you may think from its title. An ethnography that describes courtship, sexual norms, marriage, domestic relations, and love magic in the Trobriand Islands. A "classic."

Shostak, Marjorie. *Nisa: The Life and Words of a !Kung Woman.* New York: Vintage Books, 1983.

A wonderfully readable biography of a !Kung woman, much of which focuses on her relationships with family, husbands, and children.

Wolf, Margery. *The House of Lim.* Englewood Cliffs, N.J.: Prentice-Hall, 1968.

An ethnographic study of family life in a Taiwanese Chinese farm family.

Companion Website for This Book

The Wadsworth Anthropology Resource Center
http://anthropology.wadsworth.com

The companion website that accompanies *Humanity: An Introduction to Cultural Anthropology,* Sixth Edition, includes a rich array of material, including online anthropological video clips, to help you in the study of cultural anthropology and the specific topics covered in this chapter. Begin by clicking on Student Resources. Next, click on Cultural Anthropology, and then on the cover image for this book. You have now arrived at the Student Resources home page and have the option of choosing one of several chapter resources.

Applying Anthropology. Begin your study of cultural anthropology by clicking on Applying Anthropology. Here you will find useful information on careers, graduate school programs in applied anthropology, and internships you might wish to pursue. You will also find real-world examples of working anthropologists applying the skills and methods of anthropology to help solve serious world problems.

Research Online. Click here to find a wealth of Web links that will facilitate your study of anthropology. Divided into different fields of study, specific websites are starting points for Internet research. You will be guided to rich anthropology websites that will help you prepare for class, complete course assignments, and actually do research on the Web.

InfoTrac College Edition Exercises. From the pull-down menu, select the chapter you are presently studying. Select InfoTrac College Edition Exercises from the list of resources. These exercises utilize InfoTrac College Edition's vast database of articles and help you explore the numerous uses of the search word, *culture.*

Study Aids for This Chapter. Improve your knowledge of key terms by using flash cards and study the learning objectives. Take the practice quiz, receive your results, and email them to your instructor. Access these resources from the chapter and resource pull-down menus.

Why Study Kinship?

Cultural Variations in Kinship

Unilineal Descent

Unilineal Descent Groups

Descent Groups in Action

Avunculocality Revisited

Cognatic Descent

Cognatic Descent in Polynesia

Bilateral Kinship

Influences on Kinship Systems

Classifying Relatives: Kinship Terminologies

Cultural Construction of Kinship

Varieties of Kinship Terminology

Why Do Terminologies Differ?

© Mark Segal/Stone/Getty Images

Among all peoples, kinship relations are important both in the lives of individuals and for the well-being of society as a whole. Among some families in the United States, large numbers of kinfolk gather for weddings, funerals, and family reunions like this one in Maine.

H UMANS ARE AMONG THE MOST SOCIAL of all mammals. We are born into, live with, and die among other people. Young children rely totally on parents and other adults for the food, shelter, protection, and learning needed to raise them to social maturity. Even as adults, we rely on cooperation with others for survival, economic well-being, and emotional gratification. When we die, many members of the groups to which we belonged mourn our passing.

OF THE MANY KINDS OF ORGANIZED groups in society, those based on kinship, or culturally recognized biological ties, are among the most important. In many cultures, the specific persons with whom one cooperates in everyday life are relatives of some kind. The groups that organize large-scale cooperative activities are established on the basis of kinship ties. Within those groups, the nature of individuals' relationships with one another depends largely on what specific kinds of relatives they are.

IN THIS CHAPTER we cover how kinship relationships are used in a variety of ways by different peoples to organize relationships and create cooperative groupings. We also describe some of the main ways that members of different cultures define and classify their relatives into labeled categories.

Why Study Kinship?

Why do anthropologists pay so much attention to kinship? In Western cultures, kinship relations are important—to varying degrees—in individuals' lives. But, compared to many other peoples that anthropologists work among, kinship is not an important organizing principle of modern Western society as a whole. Instead, different kinds of activities are organized by different kinds of institutions and groups. When we distinguish between economic, political, religious, and educational institutions, for example, we mean that different kinds of institutions specialize in different kinds of organized activities that perform different kinds of functions.

Further, in industrialized nations, each person is a member of and participates in the activities of a number of formal and informal groups and associations. For example, you might belong to formal groups such as a university, conservation organization, church, political party, and company that pays your wages. (Here *formal* means that the group is organized *as a group,* with officers, membership criteria, and so forth.) At the same time, you are active in many informal associations made up of your coworkers, fellow students, neighbors, and friends, with whom you socialize or share common interests.

Notice two important characteristics of these groups and associations. First, they are *voluntary:* if your interests change, or if you find another group in which membership is more satisfactory, you are free to change jobs, churches, neighborhoods, and friends. Second, for the most part, they have *nonoverlapping membership:* each group typically consists of a different collection of people. We cooperate and interact with different individuals in the various groups to which we belong. Members of each group have varying and sometimes contradictory expectations about how we should behave; after all, we perform different roles in each of the groups. In many ways our behavior differs according to the identity of the particular group of people (the *social context*) we are associating with at the moment—we act one way at home, another at church, and yet another at work. (Our fellow church members might be surprised if they could see how we act on the job, but— probably fortunately—ordinarily they do not.)

In contrast, among many indigenous peoples, one lives with, works with, socializes with, and often worships with the same people, most of whom are relatives. Kin groups and kin relationships are *multifunctional,* meaning that they organize many kinds of activities. Most of the activities organized by the firms, schools, governments, churches, and other specialized groups in an industrial society are organized by one or another kind of kin group. We can no more understand such societies without studying their kinship systems than we could understand the modern world without knowing about nations.

Cultural Variations in Kinship

In more than a century of studying kinship systems and analyzing their role in cultures, anthropologists have discovered surprising variations. Among the most important variations are the following.

Ways of Tracing Kinship Ties. In North America and most of Europe, most people believe they are related equally and in the same way to the extended families of both their mother and their father. Particular individuals may develop closer ties with one or another side of their family according to circumstances and personal preferences, such as whether only one set of grandparents lives in one's town. But there is no systematic *cultural pattern* of feeling closer to or socializing with relatives according to whether they are paternal or maternal kin.

In contrast, most other peoples place primary importance on one side of the family—either the paternal or the maternal side—in preference to the other. For example, in many cultures most individuals become members of their father's kin group. They might live with their father's relatives, inherit property from their father but not their mother, and worship their paternal but not their maternal ancestors. In such systems, relatives through one's mother usually are considered to be kin, but kin of a fundamentally different and less important kind than paternal relatives. There are also systems in which kin groups are organized around maternal relationships, and paternal kin are culturally deemphasized.

Normative Expectations of Kin Relationships. The kinds of social relations a people believe they should have with individuals related to them in a certain way are part of the norms of kinship. Cross-culturally, kinship norms are surprisingly variable. There are kin systems in which brothers must strictly avoid their sisters after puberty; in which sons-in-law are not supposed to speak directly to their mother-in-law; in which a boy is allowed to joke freely with and appropriate the property of his maternal uncle but must show utmost restraint and respect toward his paternal uncle; and in which people are expected to marry one kind of cousin but are absolutely forbidden to marry another kind of cousin. In sum, many of the patterns of social behavior toward relatives that members of one culture regard as normal are absent in other cultures.

Cultural Classifications of Relatives. Except for fictive kinship (Chapter 8), kinship relationships are created through biological reproduction. When a woman gives birth, her relatives and those of her mate become the biological relatives of the child. Thus the kinship relationship between any two people depends on how these individuals are related biologically.

Yet anthropologists claim that kinship is a cultural— as opposed to a biologically determined—phenomenon. We make this claim mainly because societies differ in the way they use the biological facts of kinship to create groups, allocate roles, and classify relatives into various kinds. In our own kinship system, for example, whether a woman is our maternal or paternal aunt makes no difference: We still call her *aunt* and think of both our maternal and paternal aunt as the same kind of relative. But the side of the family makes a difference in some other kinship systems: the father's sisters and mother's sisters are completely different kinds of relatives and are called by different terms.

Keeping this overview of kinship diversity in mind, let's look at kinship in more detail.

Unilineal Descent

Consider what it means to be consanguineous relatives. If "kin" are defined in strictly biological terms, then someone is your relative because you and they share a common ancestor in a previous generation. Thus your sister is the female child of your parents; your aunts and uncles are the children of your grandparents; your first cousins are the grandchildren of your grandparents; and your second cousins have the same great-grandparents as you.

Stated differently, a man is your biological relative if you and he are *descended* from a common ancestor who lived some number of generations ago. The greater the number of generations back this common ancestor lived, the more distantly you and the man are related.

Notice that you are descended from 4 grandparents, 8 great-grandparents, 16 great-great-grandparents, and 32 great-great-great-grandparents. Everyone alive today who is descended from these 32 people is related to you. Going back in time, the number of your ancestors doubles every generation. So you have an enormous number of living *biological* relatives—all people descended from any of your ancestors are related to you, however distantly— even if you count back only four or five generations.

Obviously, we do not keep track of all our biological kin. Nor does any other society. From the total range of potential relatives, all cultures consider some kinds of relatives as more important than others. The reduction in the number of relatives is accomplished in two main ways: (1) forgetting or ignoring the remoter kinship relationships and (2) emphasizing some kinds of kinship relationships and deemphasizing others. North America and western Europeans use mainly the first method: Most people forget who their kin are beyond the range of second cousin because they have little reason to keep track of more distant relatives.

Many peoples also use the second method: they consider that some kinds of relatives are more important than others. The most common way of making some relatives more important than others is to use the sex of connecting relatives as the basis for defining which kin are close or most socially important. For example, if people consider that relatives traced through males are most important, then individuals will think that their father's relatives are more important than their mother's relatives— for some purposes at least. Relationships through females will be deemphasized and perhaps forgotten in two or three generations. If you lived in such a culture, some of your second cousins on your father's side would be quite important relatives, but your second cousins through your mother might be barely known to you, if at all.

Kinship relationships, then, are defined by how people trace their descent from previous generations. How people in a given culture trace their descent is called their **form of descent.** Descent can be traced through males, females, or both sexes. The Concept Review may help in distinguishing the three descent systems.

In many cultures, relationships traced through only one sex are considered most important. Such cultures have **unilineal descent,** a phrase that refers to the fact that people place importance on either their mother's an-

Forms	Characteristics	Associated Kin Groups
Unilineal		
(a) Patrilineal	through male line	(patri)lineages and (patri)clans
(b) Matrilineal	through female line	(matri)lineages and (matri)clans
Cognatic	through either male or female line	cognatic descent groups

cestral line or their father's ancestral line, but not both. There are two categories of unilineal descent:

- **Patrilineal descent** People trace their primary kinship connections to the ancestors and living relatives of their father (see Figure 9.1). In cultures with patrilineal descent, a person's father's relatives are likely to be most important in his or her life. Individuals are likely to live among their father's kin, and most property is inherited by sons from fathers.
- **Matrilineal descent** People trace their most important kinship relationships to the ancestors and living relatives of their mother (see Figure 9.2). In matrilineal descent, it is the mother's relatives who are most important in a person's life. People are most likely to live with or near their mothers' relatives and usually inherit property from their mother or mother's brothers.

Of these two forms of unilineal descent, patrilineal is the most common. There are about three times as many patrilineal as matrilineal cultures.

Let's look at each of these forms of unilineal descent more closely to see which relatives are considered most important for an individual. In Figure 9.1, the patrilineal relatives of the person labeled *Ego* are shaded in. The kinship diagram shows that Ego's patrilineal kin include only those relatives related to Ego through males. For instance, Ego's father's brother's children are related to Ego through males, whereas Ego's other first cousins (through Ego's mother or father's sister) are not.

Looking at patrilineal descent another way, Ego's patrilineal kin include all the people descended *through males* from the man labeled *Founder* in Figure 9.1. In fact, any two individuals shaded in the diagram are related to one another through males. This includes women as well as men, but the children of these women are not related through males and, therefore, are not patrilineal kin. Why aren't the children of the women counted? Because they have their own set of patrilineal relatives, which they take from their fathers.

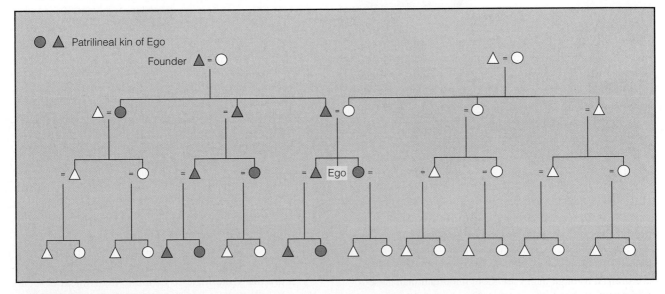

▲ **Figure 9.1** Patrilineal Descent

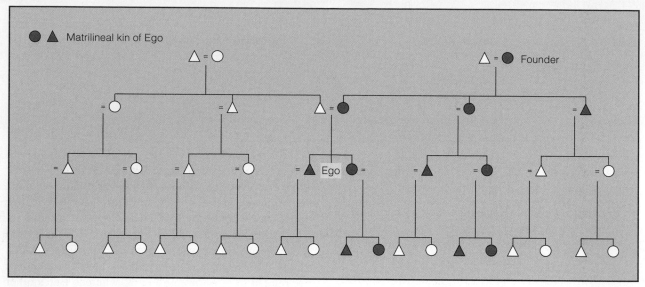

▲ **Figure 9.2** Matrilineal Descent

▲ Some cultures place primary emphasis on only one side of an individual's family, either the mother's side or the father's side. In these two men's Middle Eastern homeland, relationships traced through males are more important than those traced through females.

How does patrilineal descent affect behavior between different relatives? In all sorts of ways, but probably the most widespread and noticeable effect is in the inheritance of property. In patrilineal societies, property is passed down through the male line or, in other words, from fathers to sons. We can see the significance of this effect on inheritance by contrasting it with inheritance in North American society, where the dominant ethnic group makes no distinction between males and females in tracing kinship relationships. You probably do not distinguish between your two grandfathers but think of yourself as related in the same way to both. But if your culture were patrilineal, your father's father would play a far more significant role in your life, and it would be from him that you would expect to inherit wealth or receive land rights. Your mother's father would pass his property on to his sons and sons' sons—not to you because you are related to him through his daughter, not his son. A similar distinction would exist between paternal and maternal uncles: Paternal uncles would be far more important. Finally, some of your four sets of cousins would be more important than others—those related to you through males, or your father's brothers' children. It is these people who would be primarily responsible for your economic and social welfare, and it would be with them and your own siblings that you would probably cooperate and associate.

Apply the same logic to examine matrilineal descent. Your matrilineal kin are related to you through female links. They include your mother, mother's mother, mother's mother's mother, plus the daughters of all these women and their children. The sons and brothers of these women are your matrilineal kin, but their children are not. In Figure 9.2, we have shaded the people who are Ego's matrilineal relatives. Note that only one set of cousins—Ego's mother's sisters' children—is shaded in the diagram. They are all related to ego through female links, and therefore, Ego is likely to have closer relationships with them than with other cousins. Property is most likely to be inherited from one's mother and maternal grandmother and from the brothers of these women. In matrilineal societies, men usually leave most of their property not to their own children but to their sister's children. As a result, maternal uncles (mother's brothers) are important figures in one's life, and in some respects they assume the role we usually associate with fathers.

In unilineal descent systems, relations such as aunt, uncle, and cousin differ from those to which most of our readers are accustomed. Some cousins, in particular, will be more important relatives than other cousins: father's brothers' children in patrilineal systems, mother's sisters' children in matrilineal systems. Not all cousins are culturally perceived as the same kinds of relatives in unilineal societies. This fact has led anthropologists to distinguish between *parallel cousins* and *cross cousins*. Two sets of cousins are parallel cousins if their parents are of the same sex, so your parallel cousins are your mother's sisters' children and your father's brothers' children. People are cross cousins if their parents are siblings of the opposite sex, so your cross cousins are your father's sisters' children and your mother's brothers' children. The significance of this distinction is that in unilineal descent systems, one set of parallel cousins always belongs to the same kin group as Ego, as you can see by contrasting the cousins shaded in Figures 9.1 and 9.2. On the other hand, no cross cousin is ever in Ego's kin group in a society with a unilineal descent form.

Unilineal Descent Groups

In Chapter 8, we saw how various peoples form household groups by associating nuclear families together in patterned ways. Much larger kin groups of people—also known as **descent groups**—can be established on the basis of kinship ties.

Take matrilineal descent, for example. A matrilineal descent group exists when people descended from the same woman through females recognize their group identity and cooperate for some purposes. When a matrilineal rule of descent establishes a group of people all re-

lated to one another through females, we say that the group is created using the *matrilineal principle.* We can state the matrilineal principle as "everyone joins the descent group of his or her mother." Alternatively, we can say "only children of the female members of a group become members." Looking back to Figure 9.2, all the individuals in the diagram are members of a single descent group. Check for yourself that only the female members pass their membership in the group along to their offspring. (What happens to the children of the group's men? They join the descent groups of their mothers, which usually are a different group because incest taboos and exogamy rules usually prohibit sex and marriage between any of the group's members.)

Conversely, groups can develop by repeated application of the *patrilineal principle:* In any given generation, only males transmit their membership in the group to their offspring. The result of applying this principle for several generations is a group of people related to one another through males. Check this in Figure 9.1: all the shaded individuals are in the same descent group, and everyone joined the group of their father. Assuming the patrilineal kin group is exogamous, the children of the group's women become members of their father's patrilineal group.

A **unilineal descent group** is a group of relatives all of whom are related through only one sex. A *matrilineal descent group* is a group whose members are (or believe themselves to be) related through females, or who trace their descent through female links from a common female ancestor. A *patrilineal descent group* comprises people who trace their descent through males from a common male ancestor.

Unilineal descent groups can be small or enormous, depending mainly on the genealogical depth of the group—that is, on how far back in time any two members of the group must go to trace their relationships to each other. A small matrilineal group with a few dozen members might consist of people descended matrilineally from a woman who lived 4 or 5 generations ago. A large matrilineal group with many hundreds of members might consist of people who trace their ancestry back to a woman who lived 9 or 10 generations ago. Anthropologists often use genealogical depth as a way to define different kinds of unilineal groups. From "shallowest" to "deepest," these groups are called unilineally extended families, lineages, and clans. (There are other types, but they are not discussed here.)

Unilineally extended families consist of people who cooperate and have mutual obligations based on their descent from an ancestor who lived only three or four generations ago. Extended families may be defined either patrilineally or matrilineally. Such families may or may not live in the same household (see Chapter 8), but they recognize their close ties, may hold common property, may cooperate in work, and may have shared ritual responsibilities.

Lineages are unilineal groups composed of several unilineally extended families whose members are able to trace their descent through males or females from a common ancestor who typically lived four or five or more generations in the past. By the conventional definition, the extended families that make up the group must be able to state how they are related to one another for anthropologists to call the group a lineage. Lineages may be either patrilineal (patrilineages) or matrilineal (matrilineages), depending on the form of descent prevalent among a given people.

Clans are unilineal descent groups whose members believe they are descended from either a common ancestor through the male line (patriclans) or a common ancestor through the female line (matriclans). The major difference between a clan and a lineage is generational depth. With clans, the common ancestor lived so far in the past that not all the members of the clan are able to state precisely how they are related to one another. Like lineages, clans are usually exogamous. Members of the clan think of themselves as relatives and frequently refer to one another as "clan brother" or "clan sister." In many societies, clans own or control land and other forms of property. Generally, each clan is further subdivided into two or more lineages.

Among many peoples, clans are *totemic,* meaning that their members are symbolically identified with certain supernatural powers associated with particular animals, plants, and natural forces such as lightning, the sun, and the moon. Clans commonly take the name of their primary totemic symbol, and thus have names such as the bear clan, the sun clan, the reed clan, and the eagle clan. The association with particular supernatural powers often gives specific clans control over particular religious rituals. Although the function of clans varies from one society to another, they are usually among the most significant economic, social, and political units in the society.

Often people need to call upon different numbers of relatives for different purposes. A woman may need help with her gardening chores and will ask her extended family members for help. Or a group may need to defend itself against enemies, for which purpose they need to mobilize dozens or even hundreds of men to serve as warriors, so they call upon their lineagemates or clanmates for aid. Unilineal descent is a useful organization

for these and many other purposes because it allows people to mobilize varying numbers of their relatives when they need assistance. Using one of the unilineal descent principles, smaller kin groups can be nested inside larger ones.

For example, in a patrilineal society, a nuclear family is a part—a "segment"—of a patrilineally extended family. In turn, the extended family is a segment of a larger group (a small patrilineage), whereas the small patrilineage is a segment of a larger patrilineage, which in turn is a segment of a patriclan. Using this *segmentary organization,* dozens, hundreds, or even thousands of relatives can be mobilized, depending on the circumstances. The flexibility of segmentary unilineal descent systems makes them useful for many economic, political, and ritual purposes (see Chapter 12).

Descent Groups in Action

The preceding description of descent forms and groupings is abstract. But, like families, descent groups are made up of living people who work in gardens, quarrel, conduct rituals, go to war, teach their children, construct their dwellings, and carry out innumerable other activities together. If people are to work together for common purposes, they must have ways of creating groups and ensuring their continuity over time; they must have ways of assigning group members to roles and allocating tasks to them; they must have ways of making decisions that affect the members. In a word, they must be *organized.* More often than not, descent groups and kinship relations provide the organizational basis on which various cooperative activities are carried out.

Two examples illustrate how unilineal descent principles organize cooperative activities. One is a patrilineal people of a Pacific island who call themselves the Tikopia. The second is the Hopi, a matrilineal Native American people of the Southwest.

Tikopia: A Patrilineal Society. Tikopia is a western Pacific island with only 6 square miles of land area. In the late 1920s, when it was studied by Raymond Firth, Tikopia had a population of about 1,200. Tikopians trace their descent patrilineally and use this principle to establish groups of people related through males. They view the people of their island as members of one of four patriclans, each with a name that passes from fathers to sons. Each patriclan is subdivided into several patrilineages, averaging about thirty to forty members. The members of each patrilineage trace their descent in the male line back to a common ancestor—the founder of the patrilineage—

who lived four to six generations ago. Each patrilineage ordinarily considers the oldest male descendant of this founder to be its head. The women of a lineage marry men of other lineages, so the children of the lineage's women do not become members of it.

What sorts of activities do Tikopian lineages and clans organize? The lineage controls rights to land and certain other kinds of property. Each lineage owns house sites and several parcels of land planted in crops, including yams, taro, coconut, and breadfruit. The families that make up the lineage have the right to plant and harvest crops on lineage land; once they plant a parcel, they have the right to continue to use it. They cannot, however, sell, trade, or give it away to members of other lineages. The patrilineage, then, owns land and allocates use rights to parcels among its members, and each family acquires most of its food through farming the land of their lineage.

Ordinarily, each nuclear family cultivates mainly the lineage land of its husband-father. In Tikopia, the female members of a patrilineage retain their use rights to lineage land even after they marry. When a woman marries, a parcel of the land of her lineage is divided off for her own and her husband's and children's use. A woman may not, however, pass any of her rights to this land along to her children, for when she dies the use of the parcel reverts back to the patrilineage into which she was born. Thus each patrilineage allows its female members who marry out of it to use plots of land for subsistence during their lifetimes but not to transmit rights to the land to their offspring.

The social rank of individuals is also determined largely by their kin group membership and their status within it. One lineage of each clan is considered the senior lineage. Because its living members are believed to be descended (through males) from the founder of the clan, it is the highest ranking lineage of that clan, so its members receive certain kinds of respect from their clanmates. The senior lineage of each clan also has the right to select one of its male members to serve as the clan chief. Just as the lineages are ranked relative to one another by genealogical closeness to the senior lineage, so families within a single lineage are ranked by their closeness to the head of the lineage. Tikopian kinship thus has a political dimension, since authority over others is granted or denied to an individual or group largely through their descent group membership and rank.

Tikopians do not live by breadfruit alone. Their worldview includes belief in supernatural powers. These beliefs are also tied into the descent system because each descent group has specific ritual duties to perform. Each of the four clan chiefs serves as the religious leader and organizer of certain religious ceremonies. Each clan has its own ancestral spirits, which were the deceased former chiefs of the clan. Each clan also has its own gods, with whom its chief acts as intermediary.

One religious function of a clan is to carry out rituals that ensure the availability of food. Each of the four major subsistence crops is mystically associated with one of the clans. The gods of this clan control the crop. The chief of the clan performs the rituals that ensure the continued supply and fertility of whichever crop "listened to" (as the Tikopia phrase it) the gods of his clan. Thus each clan—in the person of its chief—has ritual responsibilities toward the other three clans. A patrilineage, too, has an ancestral home with sacred shrines where its members gather to honor their ancestors.

Tikopians exemplify the diverse functions that are often assigned to kin groups. Patrilineages control use rights to land and some other kinds of property, influence an individual's social rank, and perform joint rituals. Patriclans have political functions and their chiefs carry out rituals that Tikopians believe essential for the well-being of all islanders.

Hopi: A Matrilineal Society. In northeastern Arizona lives a matrilineal people known as the Hopi. The Hopi divide themselves into about 50 exogamous matriclans (some of which are now extinct). Clans are not residential groups; most have members who live in more than one of the Hopi's nine *pueblos*. A Hopi pueblo, or village, often is a single large apartment-like building divided into many rooms in which families reside. Each clan is subdivided into several matrilineages. The female members of a Hopi matrilineage usually live in adjoining rooms within a single pueblo.

The Hopi postmarital residence pattern is matrilocal, so after marriage a man usually joins his wife, her sisters, and her other matrilineal relatives to form a matrilocally extended household. Most Hopi extended families consist of one or more older women, their daughters together with their husbands, and sometimes even their granddaughters and their husbands. Because of lineage and clan exogamy and matrilocal residence, husbands are outsiders, and—as the Hopi say—their real home is with their mother's extended family. The residential core of a matrilineage thus consists of its women, who live close to one another throughout most of their lives. The married men of the lineage are scattered among the households of their wives, although they frequently return to their matrilineal home for rituals and other responsibilities or in case of divorce.

Most property, both secular and ceremonial, is inherited matrilineally. Living space, for instance, is passed from mother to daughter. Farmland, on which the Hopi formerly depended for more of their subsistence, is owned by a clan, with each lineage having use rights over particular parcels at any one time. The husbands of the lineage's women do most of the farming to support their families, although they themselves do not own the land.

Membership in a matriclan not only defines one's primary social relationships but also establishes one's relationships with the supernatural world. Each clan is mystically associated with a number of supernatural powers called *wuya.* Clans usually take their name after their principal *wuya,* such as bear, rabbit, corn, snake, cloud, sun, and reed. The members of a matriclan pray to their *wuya,* asking for protection and for bountiful harvests.

Hopi religion features a ritual calendar that includes a large number of annually required ceremonies. In most cases, each ceremony is "owned" by the members of a certain clan, meaning in Hopi culture that this clan has primary responsibility to see that the ceremony is performed on time and in the proper manner. Every clan represented in a village has a clanhouse in which the masks, fetishes, and other sacred items used in the ceremonies it owns are kept when not in use. The clanhouse usually consists of a room adjoining the dwelling of the senior female member of the clan. This woman, the *clan mother,* is in charge of storing ritual objects and of seeing to it that they are treated with the proper respect. The position of clan mother is passed down from a woman to either

her younger sister or her daughter, depending on age and personal qualities. There is also a male head of each clan whose duties likewise are partly religious because he is in charge of the performance of ceremonies owned by his clan. A male clan head passes his position, together with the ritual knowledge required to hold it, down to either his younger brother or his sister's son. In this way, culturally important ritual knowledge is kept within the clan.

Among the Hopi, as with most other matrilineal systems, the roles of father and husband differ from those in patrilineal systems. As we have seen, a husband moves in with his wife and her relatives after marriage. Traditionally, a man brings little property into the marriage other than his clothing and a few personal items. Nor does he accumulate much property as a result of his marriage because the house, its furnishings, the food stored there, and other goods remain the property of his wife's family. Although a man provides food for himself and his family by working in the fields of his wife, the products of his garden labor belong to his wife. The children similarly are viewed primarily as members of their mother's lineage and clan, and indeed they have no rights to use land or any claim to ritual knowledge or property of their father's kin group.

The combination of matrilineal descent and matrilocal residence profoundly affects relationships between fathers and children. Children's relationship with their father is usually close and tolerant. A man seldom punishes his own children. Culturally, this is not considered his ap-

▶ The unmarried status of these young Hopi women is shown by their hairstyle. In Hopi villages, traditionally the husbands of women worked the land of their wife's family and moved into their wives' households. Hopi matrilineages and matriclans also organize many other economic and ceremonial activities.

propriate role, for—after all—children and fathers belong to different descent groups. The father's sisters and brothers likewise exhibit warm feelings for their nieces and nephews, often providing them with gifts and affection. The main disciplinarians of children are their mother's brother and other members of their mother's kin group. This is partly because a child's behavior reflects well or poorly on the kin group of the mother, so members of this group have the primary duty of monitoring and correcting children.

The Hopi illustrate how the matrilineal principle recruits individuals into kin groups in which they perform various economic, religious, and social roles. They also show how the form of descent found among a people influences interpersonal relationships between relatives, including between fathers and children and maternal uncles and their nieces and nephews.

Neither the Tikopia nor the Hopi system "typifies" patrilineal and matrilineal kinship. A wide range of diversity occurs in patrilineal and matrilineal systems. The two peoples do illustrate some of the main differences between patrilineal and matrilineal peoples with respect to recruitment into groups, allocation of roles, nature of emotional attachments, and organization of common activities. They also exemplify a fundamental organizational feature of many preindustrial societies: Multifunctional kin groups carry out most of the cooperative activities that more specialized groups perform in industrialized nations.

Avunculocality Revisited

Comparatively speaking, Hopi women have a great deal of influence on domestic life and control over property—land in particular. (As we discuss in Chapter 11, Hopi women owe their relatively high status partly to their control over land and partly to matrilineality and matrilocality.) Because they are a matrilocal people, sisters live together and their husbands live apart from their matrilineal relatives for as long as the marriage lasts.

But not all matrilineal people are matrilocal. A common pattern of postmarital residence among matrilineal peoples is avunculocality, in which married couples live with or near the husband's mother's brother (Chapter 8). More than one-third of all matrilineal societies have avunculocal residence as the predominant pattern. Most of the others are matrilocal or patrilocal. Now that we are aware of matrilineal descent groups and know that they often control property, we can understand this unfamiliar residence pattern.

First, the fact that a people are matrilineal does not necessarily mean that women control property and politics. That is, *matrilineality*—descent through females—should not be confused with *matriarchy*—rule by women or dominance by women over men. Even in most matrilineal societies, men control and make decisions about the use and allocation of land and other forms of wealth and have more of a say than women do in public affairs. The oldest competent man of a lineage usually has the greatest control over life-sustaining or culturally valuable property in a matrilineal society. Of course, in contrast to patrilineal peoples, in a matrilineal society a lineage elder has authority over his sister's children rather than his own children. This is because a man's children are not members of his own descent group and supposedly have their property and loyalties with the group of their mother.

How can a male lineage elder have his sisters' sons living with or near him, where he can keep an eye on them, and where they can look after their own interest in land and common property? The answer is avunculocal residence (see Figure 8.2d in the previous chapter). If a man's sisters' sons bring their wives to live with them in a common residence, then the elder and young male members of a single matrilineage are localized in a single place. The married women of the matrilineage are scattered among the households of their own husbands' mothers' brothers. The children of the matrilineage's women are likewise scattered among the households of their fathers, so long as they are unmarried. But as they marry they return to their own mother's brothers' households—the place of their own lineage.

In short, avunculocal residence has the effect of localizing male matrilineal relatives who have a common interest in land, wealth, or other material property and/or who share ritual responsibilities. It therefore makes perfect sense once we see how the matrilineal principle forms kin groups that hold common property, and once we realize that men have control over wealth and public affairs among most matrilineal peoples.

Cognatic Descent

In patrilineal cultures, most people become members of the kin group of their father. If enough people do this over several generations, patrilineages and perhaps patriclans develop, the members of which are related through males. Conversely, in matrilineal cultures most people join the group of their mother; over time matrilineal descent groups develop whose members are related through females.

Social life usually is not so clear-cut. In real societies where either of these unilineal principles is the norm and the pattern, the membership of lineages and clans is not as well defined as the principles make them appear. For instance, in matrilineal systems circumstances vary and change: adoptions, childless women, inability to get along with one's matrikin, insufficiency of land owned by the matrigroup, and other factors make it likely that some individuals will join a group other than that of their mother. As a result, many matrilineages include some members who are not matrilineally related in terms of biological relatedness. Thus, even in unilineal systems there is often some degree of choice about which group to join, depending on personal preferences and circumstances. Still, there is a norm or rule about what "should" happen.

Cultures with **cognatic descent** have no formal principle or rule about whether individuals join the group of their mother or father. Some people join with their father, others with their mother, entirely or largely according to preferences and circumstances. A **cognatic descent group** consists of all the individuals who can trace their descent back to the common ancestor (founder) of the group through both female and male links.

More than in unilineal systems, in cognatic descent people make choices about the groups they want to join. The choice is commonly based on factors such as one's chances of inheriting rights to land use or other forms of property or wealth, the desire to associate with a relative of high status or rank, childhood residence, and emotional ties. For example, in a cognatic system you might decide to reside and cooperate with your mother's relatives if her kin group has a lot more land available for you to cultivate than does your father's group. Or if a coveted political office or honorific title is about to become vacant in your father's group, you might decide to try to acquire it by moving in and working with his relatives.

Cognatic Descent in Polynesia

Cognatic descent is found in all world regions, but it is especially prevalent among Polynesians, including Samoans, Hawaiians, Tahitians, and New Zealand Maori. Details vary from island to island, but generally speaking, people can join any cognatic group or groups to which they can trace ancestry. Membership in the group bestows rights to agricultural land, house sites, and some other kinds of property.

In cultures with patrilineal and matrilineal descent, individuals ordinarily become a member of only one group—their father's or their mother's, respectively. With cognatic descent, everyone potentially belongs to several groups because everyone has the opportunity to join all the groups to which their parents belong, and each parent is probably a member of at least two groups.

Unlike unilineal groups, cognatic descent groups have *overlapping membership*. This potentially poses a problem for access to land and other culturally valued things. For example, if all members of a group have rights to the land collectively owned by this group, and if one-half or more of the entire population potentially has such rights, then the "right" does not mean much.

In the cognatic societies of Polynesia, most people keep up their membership in several groups simultaneously by contributing labor and foods to feasts sponsored by the groups and generally showing their interest in and commitment to the groups. The islands of Samoa provide an example. Each Samoan village has a council that plans public activities, levies fines, and performs other functions for the whole community. Each village is composed of several cognatic kin groups known as *'aiga*. Although each *'aiga* has branches represented in several villages, every *'aiga* has an ancestral homeland village. In its homeland village, each *'aiga* has the right to select one or more of its men to hold titles, or *matai*. These titleholders serve as the *'aiga*'s representatives to the village council. Acquisition of a *matai* carries great honor, as well as authority to regulate use of the *'aiga*'s land, resolve disputes among the *'aiga*'s members, organize feasts and ceremonial gifts, and assess the members for contributions to marriages, funerals, and other events.

When a title becomes vacant because of death or some other reason, all members of the entire *'aiga* have a voice in choosing a new *matai,* whether they live in the homeland village or not. Because people belong to several *'aiga* at the same time, they have a voice in choosing the new *matai* for several groups, although they may not exercise their rights in every *'aiga* to which they belong. Because men belong to several groups, they have the right to compete for and gain a title in these groups. A young man might anticipate a future title vacancy in one of his *'aiga* and decide to move to the village where that *'aiga* is represented on the council to concentrate his energies on acquiring that particular *matai*. This general kinship and village-level political organization persists in rural Samoa to this day.

The Samoan *'aiga* illustrates some of the common functions of cognatic kin groups: They can hold property and regulate access to land, organize cooperative activities, and serve as the structural basis for acquiring honored and authoritative political roles. In these respects they are similar to the lineages and clans of unilineal systems. But in cognatic systems the range of individual choice about group membership is much wider than in unilineal descent.

Bilateral Kinship

Bilateral (two-sided) kinship systems differ from unilineal descent in that kinship relationships are traced through both genders. Individuals regard their relatives through both parents as equal in importance; cousins are seen as the same kind of relative, for instance, regardless of whether they are related to Ego through the mother or the father.

Bilateral kinship, as you may recognize, exists in most contemporary Western countries, but it is also common in other parts of the world. Bilateral kinship differs from both unilineal and cognatic descent in that no large, well-defined, property-holding groups exist. Rather than lineages and clans, the tracing of kinship relationships bilaterally produces associations of relatives known as the **kindred.** A kindred consists of all the people that a specific person recognizes as relatives through both sides of the family.

To understand bilateral kinship and the kindred, imagine a Canadian named Liz. Liz recognizes her relatives through her father and mother as equivalent and interacts with them in much the same way (unless she has established strong bonds with someone because he or she lives close by, or for some other reason). The more distant the relationship, the less likely Liz is to interact with or even know who her relatives are. The only times she is likely to see many of her kindred in the same place are at events such as weddings, funerals, and family reunions. Many of Liz's relatives do not know one another (her cousins on her mother's side are unlikely to know her cousins through her father, for example). All the members of her kindred do not consider themselves relatives, and they certainly do not own any common property. The only thing that ever brings them together is the fact that they are related to Liz.

As this hypothetical example shows, a kindred is *ego-focused,* meaning that each individual is the center of his or her own set of relatives. Only you and your siblings share the same kindred; your mother has a different kindred, as do your father and all your cousins. Unilineal and cognatic descent groups, in contrast, are *ancestor-focused,* meaning that people are members of a descent group by virtue of the fact that they recognize descent from a common ancestor.

The Iban, a people of the tropical island of Borneo in Malaysia, provide a non-Western example of bilateral kinship. The Iban are shifting cultivators who traditionally lived in longhouses that are subdivided into numerous apartments. Each apartment is occupied by a single bilocally extended family called a *bilek.* Most *bilek* include three generations: an elderly couple, one of their married sons or daughters and spouse, and their children. The *bilek* owns the section of the longhouse where its members live. Each *bilek* owns separate land, farmed largely in rice by its members.

The *bilek* is the main residential and property-owning group among the Iban. Compared with the unilineal and cognatic descent groups, the *bilek* is relatively small, averaging only six or seven members. When an individual Iban needs more people for some purpose, he can ask for help from his kindred, people who are related to him through bilateral ties. In organizing hunting or periodic long-distance trading or warfare expeditions, for example, a man would call out dozens of his first and second cousins to get enough people together to help him for this specific purpose. In other words, a man *mobilized* his kindred to help him accomplish some particular task or achieve some goal. The bilateral relatives he mobilized, however, came together and cooperated only occasionally. They did not constitute a permanent kin group and did not hold any common property because the *bilek* was the property-holding unit.

Influences on Kinship Systems

Why does a given culture develop one form of kinship rather than another? Are there any general explanations? Ethnologists have worked on this question for decades, but so far no one has identified a single factor or even a small number of factors that account for why different cultures develop different kinship systems. There are, however, a number of factors that seem to *influence* (as opposed to *cause*) which form of kinship a people will have.

One influence is how a people adapts to its environment (Chapter 6). For example, about 60 percent of all foraging cultures are bilateral or cognatic. These two kinship systems allow individuals and nuclear families a great deal of choice about which of their many kinship relationships they should activate at any given time. Generally, they can move to and harvest the resources of any band to which they can trace a kinship tie. Given that most foragers must adapt to seasonal, annual, and spatial fluctuations in wild food availability, keeping one's options open is advantageous.

Adaptation affects other descent forms also. About three-fourths of pastoral societies have patrilineal descent. According to one hypothesis, the association between nomadic herding and patrilineal descent exists because livestock are most often owned and managed by men. To conserve labor devoted to protecting and moving animals to seasonally available pastures, brothers often combine their animals into a single herd. Also, inheritance of animals typically passes from fathers to sons. Brothers tend to stay together to cooperate in herd management and look after their common inheritance; therefore, they will reside patrilocally. Patrilocal residence associates male relatives together in a single location, whereas it disperses females. Over many generations, descent through males develops as a consequence.

Patrilineal descent has also been interpreted as a way to improve success in intergroup warfare. It keeps a group of related males together and thereby increases their willingness to cooperate in battles, as well as decreases the chances of male relatives becoming antagonists. Several cross-cultural studies have found an association between patrilineal descent and warfare frequency. But exactly why this correlation exists is a subject of much dispute, especially since war is important in many matrilineal societies.

What are some hypotheses about the causes of matrilineal descent? Some anthropologists think that it is connected to the way matrilineal peoples acquire their food. Matrilineal descent is more likely to be found among horticultural peoples (Chapter 6) than it is with any other adaptation; nearly 60 percent of matrilineal cultures are horticultural. This association is probably related to the fact that women perform so much of the daily subsistence work in most horticultural populations, as we discuss in Chapter 11.

A study by Melvin Ember and Carol Ember suggests that horticulture plus long-distance warfare or trade is likely to lead to the development of matrilineal descent. The reasoning is that if the men are far away fighting or trading much of the time, they cannot at the same time be doing garden work, so women will have to take over most of the subsistence labor. Women are unlikely to do this effectively if postmarital residence is patrilocal because then they would be working for their husbands' relatives rather than for their own. At any rate, a middle-aged or elderly couple will want to keep their daughters around after they marry, to work their land and help support them in their old age. So postmarital residence is typically matrilocal in horticultural cultures in which men are often absent. Matrilocality has the effect of localizing a group of sisters and other female matrikin in a single household or village. Their brothers move away after their marriage, and the children of these brothers develop closer relationships with their mother's family than with their father's relatives. This ultimately leads to the tracing of descent through females (i.e., to matrilineal descent).

This hypothesis is not accepted by all anthropologists, many of whom believe that there is no universal explanation. It does seem to work reasonably well for some matrilineal cultures, such as the Iroquois and the Huron of North America and the Nayar of south India (Chapter 8). Almost certainly, no single determinant can explain all cases of matrilineality, or for that matter the other forms of kinship. It may be that cross-cultural variations in kinship are influenced by so many kinds of complex factors that no generalized explanation is possible. Or perhaps anthropologists have not yet looked in the right places for causes.

Classifying Relatives: Kinship Terminologies

In Chapter 2 we noted that one of the major components of cultural knowledge is the way a people classifies (or constructs) natural and social reality. As is by now apparent, kinship relationships and kinship groups are a major part of social reality in all human cultures. Just as cultures differ in the ways they trace their descent and form social groupings of relatives, so do they differ in how they place relatives into types, or labeled categories. The labeled categories are called **kin terms,** and the ways in which people classify their relatives into these categories are called their **kinship terminology.**

Most people think that the kin terms they use to refer to different relatives reflect the way those relatives are related to them biologically (genetically). In fact, this is true for *some* English kin terms: *mother, father, sister, brother, son,* and *daughter* all define individuals related to you in distinct (unique) biological ways. The female persons you call *sister,* for example, have the same two parents as yourself, and no other female relative shares your parentage (setting aside considerations of fictive kinship, such as adoption, foster parenting, and step relatives).

However, there are other English kin terms that do not faithfully reflect genetic relatedness. Consider the terms *uncle* and *aunt.* They refer to siblings of your parents, and they differ only by their gender. But the individuals you call *aunt* and *uncle* are related to you in four different ways: your father's siblings, your mother's siblings, your father's siblings' spouses, and your mother's siblings' spouses. Note that both consanguineous and affinal relatives are included in the English terms *uncle* and *aunt.* The same idea applies to some other terms: A particular term groups together several individuals related to you in different ways. Thus *grandfather* includes both mother's father and father's father; *grandmother* is used for both mother's mother and father's mother; and *first cousin* refers to a wide range of people who are connected to you biologically in different ways.

Thus a people's kinship terminology reflects the biological relationships between individuals only imperfectly. More fundamentally, kin terms reflect the various norms, rights and duties, and behavioral patterns that characterize social relationships between kinfolk. Speaking broadly, collapsing relatives of different kinds into a single term reflects the cultural fact that people think of them as the same kind of relative. In turn, people conceive of them as the same kind of relative because they have similar kinds of relations with them. Thus the men we call *uncle* have the same general kinds of social relationships with us regardless of whether they are our mother's or our father's brothers or are the husbands of the many women we call *aunt.*

Cultural Construction of Kinship

Because the way various relatives are lumped together into labeled categories does not perfectly reflect the degree of genetic relatedness between them, anthropologists commonly say that kinship terminologies are *culturally constructed.* The **cultural construction of kinship** implies two things: (1) as children grow up in a certain community, they socially learn the logic by which their culture classifies "relatives" into categories, and (2) those categories do not simply reflect biological/genetic relationships. (If they did, we might be justified in saying that kinship is *biologically determined.*) In fact, as we'll see in a moment, the labeled categories of kinship sometimes hardly match up at all with biological relationships.

Before we can discuss particular kinship terminologies, we need to understand the logic by which they are culturally constructed. By "logic" we mean the principles that people use to distinguish one kind of relative from others. There are many principles, but only four are relevant for our purposes.

First, every kin term has a reciprocal term. For example, the reciprocal of *grandfather* is either *granddaughter* or *grandson.* If you call a woman *mother,* she will call you *son* or *daughter.*

Second, for at least some terms, the gender of the individuals to whom the term applies makes a difference. In English, gender matters for terms like *brother* and *sister, uncle* and *aunt,* and *grandfather* and *grandmother.* Indeed, gender is the only criterion that distinguishes the relatives just mentioned from one another. Gender is irrelevant, however, for another of our kin terms, *cousin.*

Third, kinship terms usually reflect whether the individual referred to is of the same or a different generation than Ego's. In English, specific terms are used for relatives in Ego's own generation (like *cousin*), in Ego's parents' generation (*aunt*), and in Ego's children's generation (*niece*). In describing kinship terminologies we call Ego's parents' generation the *first ascending generation* and Ego's children's generation the *first descending generation.* Although the terms used in most kinship terminologies reflect generational differences, several systems of terminology use terms that transcend generations.

Side of the family is a fourth criterion by which kin terminologies are constructed. In English, side of the family is actually irrelevant: Your relatives through your mother receive the same terms as relatives through your father. As we know, many other cultures place special emphasis on relationships through females (mothers—matrilineal) or males (fathers—patrilineal). As you suspect, this emphasis is reflected in terminological systems.

Varieties of Kinship Terminology

By using these four principles in different ways, the world's diverse peoples have developed many ways of classifying relatives into labeled categories. The classification systems have names like Eskimo, Hawaiian, Sudanese, Iroquois, Omaha, and Crow. (Don't be misled by the names of these systems. The American anthropologist Lewis Henry Morgan developed the classification system for kinship terminology in 1871. He named each system after the first people among whom he encountered it. In fact, all the systems are found on many continents, though four of them were named after the Native American peoples that Morgan learned about.)

Here we cover only four systems: Eskimo, Hawaiian, Iroquois, and Omaha. We further simplify things by considering only terms used for consanguineous relatives in Ego's generation and in Ego's first ascending (parental) generation. To make these systems easier to understand, we translate the terms into their closest English equivalents. Keep in mind that these translations are only rough approximations, and that some terms have no exact English equivalents.

Eskimo. Eskimo terminology is the easiest for English speakers to understand because this is the system most of us are familiar with (see Figure 9.3). In this system, Ego's biological mother is called *mother* and Ego's biological father is called *father.* These are the only two persons to whom these terms apply. The term *aunt* is used for both Ego's father's sister and Ego's mother's

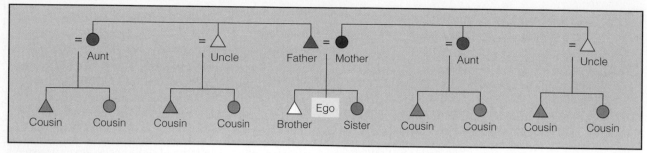

▲ **Figure 9.3** Eskimo Kinship Terminology

sister, and the term *uncle* is used for father's brother and mother's brother. The terms *brother* and *sister* are used only for the children of Ego's mother and father. The term *cousin* is used for all children of Ego's uncles and aunts.

Hawaiian. The **Hawaiian** system of kinship terminology is the simplest because it uses the fewest terms (see Figure 9.4). All of Ego's relatives in the first ascending generation are called either *mother* or *father:* the term *mother* is extended to include Ego's mother's sister and Ego's father's sister, and *father* is extended to include father's brother and mother's brother. In Ego's own generation, everyone is called either *brother* or *sister.* Thus Hawaiian terminology includes no terms equivalent to the English terms *uncle, aunt,* or *cousin.* Although the Hawaiian system extends the terms *mother* and *father,* this does not mean that individuals are unable to distinguish their biological parents from their other relatives of the parental generation.

Iroquois. **Iroquois terminology** categorizes relatives very differently than the Hawaiian and Eskimo systems (Figure 9.5). The term *father* includes father's brother but not mother's brother. *Mother* includes mother's sister but

not father's sister. The term *uncle* is used only for mother's brother; *aunt* is used only for father's sister. If we look at Ego's generation, we also see a difference. The children of father's brother and mother's sister are called *brother* and *sister.* The term *cousin* is used only for the children of mother's brother and father's sister. Thus, in the Iroquois system, Ego distinguishes between kinds of cousins (of course, they are not "cousins" to *them*).

Although this distinction may seem unusual to us, it also exists in the Omaha (and in many other) systems, so we need to understand the logic behind it. Peoples who use the Iroquois system distinguish between parallel and cross cousins. They give their parallel cousins the same terms they use for their own brothers and sisters. They distinguish cross cousins from parallel cousins, calling cross cousins by a unique term (here we translate the term as *cousin,* although obviously it has no English equivalent).

To understand the logic behind calling parallel cousins *brother* and *sister* and cross cousins by a different term, go back to the terms used for ego's parents' siblings. Ego's father's brother and mother's sister are called *father* and *mother,* respectively. Thus, it is logical to call their children *brother* and *sister.* (After all, what do you call the children of the people you call *mother* and *father*?) Ego calls his father's sister *aunt* and his mother's brother *uncle,*

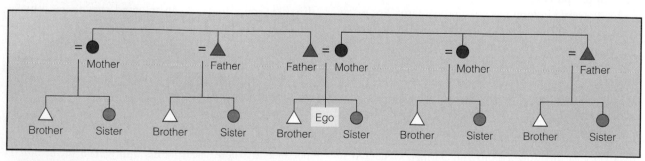

▲ **Figure 9.4** Hawaiian Kinship Terminology

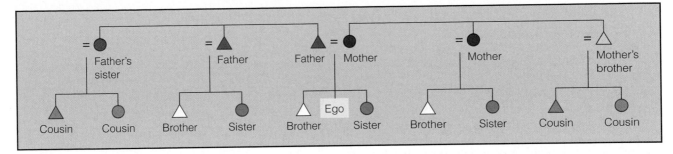

▲ **Figure 9.5** Iroquois Kinship Terminology

so it is logical to call their children (who are Ego's cross cousins) by another term we might translate as *cousin.*

Omaha. **Omaha** is a difficult kinship terminology for English speakers to understand (see Figure 9.6). The terms used in the first ascending generation are identical to the Iroquois system and parallel cousins are called *brother* and *sister.* The only difference between Iroquois and Omaha is how cross cousins are treated. Omaha terminology has no equivalent to the English term *cousin.* In addition, in Omaha terminology a distinction is made between cross cousins on the mother's side (the children of mother's brother) and cross cousins on the father's side (the children of father's sister). Mother's brothers' daughters are called *mother,* and mother's brothers' sons are called *mother's brother* (or *uncle*). Thus, Ego's maternal cross cousins are grouped with individuals in Ego's parents' generation. For Ego's paternal cross cousins, the term depends on Ego's sex. If Ego is a male, he calls his father's sisters' children *niece* and *nephew.* If Ego is a female, she calls her father's sisters' children *son* and *daughter.*

Why are there two separate terms for father's sisters' children, depending on the sex of Ego? This distinction is perfectly logical. Remember that kinship terms are reciprocal and that Figure 9.6 only shows the terms used by Ego. To understand why the sex of Ego is important in this relationship, ask: What would father's sisters' children call Ego? In Figure 9.6, you see that Ego is their mother's brother's child. Thus, if Ego is female, they would call her *mother,* and she would reciprocate by calling them *son* or *daughter.* If Ego is male, they would call him *uncle,* and therefore he would call them *niece* or *nephew.*

There are other systems, but these four are the most common and widespread. This diversity is surprising, and some of the ways of classifying relatives are puzzling. Can we account for them?

Why Do Terminologies Differ?

In previous chapters we emphasized that cultures are integrated: One aspect "fits" with others and sometimes makes sense only when understood in context.

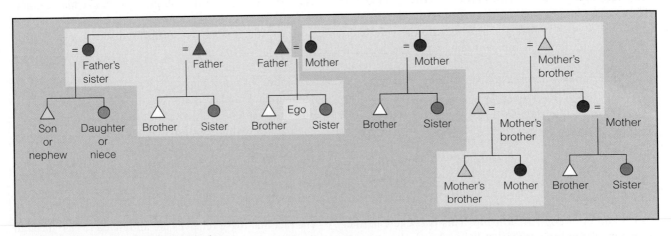

▲ **Figure 9.6** Omaha Kinship Terminology

In kinship terminology systems we have a great example of cultural integration.

A good way to begin is by noting that the four terminologies described can be separated into two types. In the Eskimo and Hawaiian, the side of the family does not matter in classifying relatives; in the Iroquois and Omaha it does. Stated another way, among the diverse peoples who use the Eskimo or Hawaiian system, the principle of distinguishing relatives according to the side of Ego's family is irrelevant; they *could* recognize the distinction between mother's and father's kin, but they do not. Among the many cultures who use the Iroquois or Omaha system, the principle of distinguishing relatives according to family side is relevant. Why should the side of the family matter in some terminological systems but not in others?

As you've already guessed, the side of the family matters in some terminologies because some people trace their descent through only one of their parents. The side of the family makes no difference in other systems because these populations trace their kin connections equally through both parents. *In general*—for there are exceptions—the way a people trace their descent affects the relationships between kin, which affects the terms used to refer to various kin.

Consider the Eskimo classification. Comparing it with the other terminologies, it differs in two main ways: (1) it makes no distinctions between ego's father's and mother's relatives, and (2) no other relatives of any kind are lumped together with nuclear family relatives. Assume that these two features reflect people's ideas about how various kin are related. We might conclude that people think (1) that both sides of the family are of equal importance to an individual (or, rather, there is no systematic *social pattern* of importance through one side over the other), and (2) that nuclear family relatives are somehow special and thought of differently than are other kinds of relatives. In the case of North America, our surnames are inherited mainly through males, but other than this, we are no more likely to have special relationships with our kin through our fathers than through our mothers. And, generally, the members of our nuclear families *are* special: We do not expect to inherit much, if anything, from other relatives; we usually do not live in extended households; kin groups larger than the nuclear family do not usually own property in common; and so on.

More generally, we expect the Eskimo classification of relatives to be associated with cognatic or bilateral kinship. And usually it is: about 80 percent of all societies that use the Eskimo terminological system have either bilateral or cognatic kinship. This is because neither side of the family is consistently emphasized, so people do not think of their mother's or father's relatives as being any different. The absence of a special relation with kin through either parent is reflected in the terminological system.

What about the Hawaiian system? As in the Eskimo system, family side is irrelevant. Logically, then, it ought to be associated consistently with cognatic or bilateral kinship. The fact that it lumps other relatives with nuclear family members seems to indicate that the nuclear family is submerged or embedded in larger extended households. Ego should have important relations with the siblings of his or her parents and with their children. Despite this logic, the Hawaiian terminology is not as consistently associated with cognatic or bilateral kinship as is the Eskimo terminology; in fact, about 40 percent of societies that use the Hawaiian classification are unilineal. The Hawaiian system is apparently also compatible with unilineal descent.

And the Iroquois? Ego's father and father's brother are assigned a single term, which is different from mother's brother. Mother and mother's sister are given the same term, which is not the same term that Ego uses for father's sister. Thus Ego distinguishes between maternal and paternal aunts and uncles in the first ascending generation. The fact that the side of the family matters in this generation seems to imply unilineal descent. And in fact the Iroquois system is usually found among peoples who trace their descent unilineally: around 80 percent of all Iroquois terminologies occur in unilineal descent forms. If you look back to Figure 9.5, you will see that Ego classes with his own brother and sister the children of relatives he classes with his mother and father. This certainly makes logical sense—if you call someone *mother,* it follows that you will call her son *brother.* The cross cousins have a separate term because their parents are not classed with Ego's own biological parents, which again is logically consistent.

The Omaha system also distinguishes between sides of the family. In fact, it carries the distinctions between the mother's and father's side "down" into Ego's own generation. If you compare Figures 9.5 and 9.6, you will see that the Omaha differs from the Iroquois by its splitting of cross cousins according to whether they are related to Ego through Ego's mother or father. Mother, mother's sister, and mother's brother's daughter are lumped together, although they are members of different generations. Mother's brother and mother's brother's son likewise are lumped together under a single term.

What can explain this way of classifying relatives? The fact that these relatives are all related to Ego through Ego's mother must mean something; and the fact that they are classified together and distinguished only by their gender must be significant. Indeed, both these features are clues to the logic behind the Omaha terminology. It is found among peoples who use the patrilineal principle to form kin groups.

How does patrilineal descent make sense of the Omaha system? In Figure 9.6, we have shaded all those relatives in the diagram who belong to Ego's own patrilineal group. Notice that the cousins in Ego's group are called *brother* and *sister,* to reflect the fact that they are in Ego's own lineage. We have also shaded those relatives who are members of Ego's mother's patrilineal group. Notice that all the members of this latter group are assigned only two terms—one for the male members of the group and one for the female members of the group. The two terms have no English translation, but they mean roughly "female member of my mother's group" and "male member of my mother's group." Their common *social identity* as members of Ego's mother's kin group overrides the *biological fact* that they are members of three generations. If you have followed the argument, you will agree that the Omaha system makes perfect sense, provided it is associated with patrilineal descent forms. And, indeed, more than 90 percent of all cultures that use the Omaha terminological system are patrilineal.

Another system, the Crow, is essentially the mirror image of the Omaha. You will not be surprised to learn that the Crow system is strongly associated with societies that have the matrilineal form of descent.

Thus, terminological systems make sense once we understand that they reflect the prevalent relationships and groupings produced by various ways of tracing kinship connections. The ways in which various people classify and label their relatives reflect the social realities of their kinship system, though not perfectly. These ways look mysterious until we understand these classifications and labels in the context of the kinship systems that give rise to them. The Eskimo terminology used by Americans would probably look strange to people who use, say, the Omaha terminology. Our failure to distinguish between relatives through one's mother and father would be strange because to them these relatives would be clearly differentiated, given the way their kinship systems place people in different kin groups.

Along these same lines, the various peoples who use one or another of these kinship classification systems cannot state the logic of their classifications in the same way we just did. For instance, people who use the Omaha terminology cannot tell you why they label their relatives as they do, because they lack a comparative perspective of their own kinship system. To them, their mother, mother's sister, and mother's brother's daughter are called by the same term because all these women are the same kind of relative, just as *aunts* are all the same kind of relative to us. They do not realize that in Eskimo systems these females all have separate terms; nor are they aware that their terminology reflects the groupings and relationships of their kinship system.

But then again, people like us who use the Eskimo system cannot account for our own classification system either, until of course we become aware of the diversity in human kinship systems discovered in the past century by anthropologists. The way people—including you and me—classify their kinfolk seems quite natural to them until they learn that other people do it differently.

Summary

1. Relationships and groups based on kinship are especially important in the social organization of preindustrial peoples. Kinship is based on biological relatedness, but societies vary in their kinship systems. There is diversity in the kinds and sizes of groups formed using kinship principles, in the norms attached to kin roles, and in the way people culturally categorize their relatives.

2. One variation is in how people trace their relationships back to previous generations—in how they trace their *descent.* One form is unilineal descent, meaning that relationships traced only through one sex are emphasized. Unilineal descent groups may be formed using the matrilineal or patrilineal principle, yielding kin groups composed of people related through females and males, respectively. In order of increasing inclusiveness and genealogical depth, the main kinds of descent groups are extended families, lineages, and clans. All these descent groups may be based on either the matrilineal or the patrilineal principle. The multifunctional nature of descent groups and the diverse kinds of activities organized by such groups are illustrated by the patrilineal Tikopia and the matrilineal Hopi. The avunculocal residence pattern is understandable once we realize that it consistently occurs in matrilineal cultures.

3. In cognatic descent, people trace their ancestry through both males and females. Cognatic descent groups exist that own common property and cooperate in various contexts, but individuals are able to join all the groups to which they can trace ancestry and can choose those groups with which they want to associate closely. The Samoan *'aiga* illustrates the functions of cognatic descent groups.

4. People who trace their kinship relationships bilaterally have no true kin groups larger than extended families because the kindreds of different people overlap so much. In most industrialized nations, kinship is bilateral, and individuals trace their bilateral relatives outward from themselves. Unlike unilineal descent, kindreds are ego-focused, and large numbers of "Ego's" relatives are likely to congregate only on certain occasions such as weddings, funerals, and family reunions. Individuals in preindustrial bilateral societies, such as the Iban, mobilize their kindreds to help them in various tasks, such as hunting, trading, and construction.

5. One of many influences on kinship is adaptation. Cognatic descent and bilateral kinship are common among foragers, most of whom find it beneficial to maximize social contacts and access to diverse territories. Nomadic pastoralists are usually patrilineal, which is probably related to the tendency for males to own and manage herds. Patrilineal descent is also likely to be found among peoples who are heavily engaged in warfare with close neighbors. Matrilineality is most likely to occur among populations that are horticultural and whose men are absent for prolonged periods when engaged in long-distance trade, warfare, or both. These very general associations are supported by cross-cultural studies, but so many forces influence descent forms that no single explanation suffices to account for their occurrence.

6. Kinship is culturally constructed, meaning that people culturally classify their relatives into labeled categories by recognizing some differences between relatives and ignoring others. This classification gives rise to various systems of kin terminology, of which we discuss four: Eskimo, Hawaiian, Iroquois, and Omaha. Very generally speaking, the ideas people have about how they are related to one another are strongly influenced by how the descent form of their society sorts people into groups and establishes relations of one or another kind between kinfolk.

Key Terms

form of descent	lineage	kinship terminology
unilineal descent	clans	cultural construction of
patrilineal descent	cognatic descent	kinship
matrilineal descent	cognatic descent group	Eskimo terminology
descent groups	bilateral	Hawaiian terminology
unilineal descent group	kindred	Iroquois terminology
unilineally extended	kin terms	Omaha terminology
families		

InfoTrac College Edition Terms

Hopi	totemism	pastoralism and family
Samoan family		

Suggested Readings

There are a number of texts and collections of readings on kinship, descent groups, and the classification of relatives:

Collier, Jane F., and J. Yanagisako, eds. *Gender and Kinship: Essays Toward a Unified Analysis.* Stanford, Calif.: Stanford University Press, 1987.

Collection of articles focusing on relationships between the sexes and kinship.

Fox, Robin. *Kinship and Marriage: An Anthropological Perspective.* New York: Cambridge University Press, 1984.

Comparative introduction to marriage forms, kinship systems, and their causes and consequences. Was for years the standard text in this technical subject.

Schneider, David M., and Kathleen Gough, eds. *Matrilineal Kinship.* Berkeley: University of California Press, 1961.

Contains a description of nine matrilineal systems and an analysis of some dimensions of variation in matrilineal societies. Introductory essay by Schneider is a good overview.

Stone, Linda. *Kinship and Gender: An Introduction.* 2nd ed. Boulder, Colo.: Westview, 2000.

As the title suggests, looks at the interrelationships between kinship systems and gender. Many case studies illustrate the author's general points. Includes discussion of new reproductive technologies.

The following ethnographies include descriptions of specific kinship systems:

Chagnon, Napoleon A. *Yąnomamö.* 5th ed. Fort Worth, Tex.: Harcourt Brace Jovanovich, 1997.

Description and interpretation of a patrilineal horticultural and hunting people of the Brazilian and Venezuelan rain forest. Shows how conflict and cooperation are based on kinship ties between individuals and lineages. Findings are controversial.

Eggan, Fred. *Social Organization of the Western Pueblos.* Chicago: University of Chicago Press, 1950.

A study describing and comparing the social organization of the Hopi, Hano, Zuni, Acoma, and Laguna pueblos.

Evans-Pritchard, E. E. *The Nuer.* Oxford: Clarendon, 1940.

An ethnography of an African society, long considered one of the classic studies in social organization.

Companion Website for This Book

The Wadsworth Anthropology Resource Center
http://anthropology.wadsworth.com

The companion website that accompanies *Humanity: An Introduction to Cultural Anthropology,* Sixth Edition, includes a rich array of material, including online anthropological video clips, to help you in the study of cultural anthropology and the specific topics covered in this chapter. Begin by clicking on Student Resources. Next, click on Cultural Anthropology, and then on the cover image for this book. You have now arrived at the Student Resources home page and have the option of choosing one of several chapter resources.

Applying Anthropology. Begin your study of cultural anthropology by clicking on Applying Anthropology. Here you will find useful information on careers, graduate school programs in applied anthropology, and internships you might wish to pursue. You will also find real-world examples of working anthropologists applying the skills and methods of anthropology to help solve serious world problems.

Research Online. Click here to find a wealth of Web links that will facilitate your study of anthropology. Divided into different fields of study, specific websites are starting points for Internet research. You will be guided to rich anthropology websites that will help you prepare for class, complete course assignments, and actually do research on the Web.

InfoTrac College Edition Exercises. From the pull-down menu, select the chapter you are presently studying. Select InfoTrac College Edition Exercises from the list of resources. These exercises utilize InfoTrac College Edition's vast database of articles and help you explore the numerous uses of the search word, *culture.*

Study Aids for This Chapter. Improve your knowledge of key terms by using flash cards and study the learning objectives. Take the practice quiz, receive your results, and email them to your instructor. Access these resources from the chapter and resource pull-down menus.

Chapter Ten

ENCULTURATION AND THE LIFE CYCLE

Growing Up

Diversity in Child Care

Two African Examples

Aka

Gusii

Implications for Modern Parents

Life Cycle

Infancy

Childhood and Adolescence

Initiation Rites

*Male Initiation Rituals:
A New Guinea Example*

*Female Initiation Rituals:
Mescalero Apache*

Adulthood

Old Age

© Jeff Greenberg/Photo Edit

As children grow up, they are enculturated in the proper ways to think, feel, and act. These Chinese children seem to be enjoying the experience.

As WE KNOW FROM CHAPTER 2, the development of a human being requires the social learning of culture. Because the acquisition of some form of culture is necessary to make a complete, functioning individual, anthropologists are interested in *enculturation* (or *socialization*), the process by which newborns learn the cultural knowledge needed for physical survival, getting along with others, and interpreting the world around them. Human groups vary in how they nourish, support, teach, and value children, as we shall see in this chapter.

As CHILDREN MATURE, they pass through various stages of life: They reach puberty, get married, become parents, and grow old. Progress through these temporal phases brings new roles, privileges, and responsibilities, which vary from people to people. In all cultures, formal ceremonies called rites of passage mark and celebrate at least some of these changes in the life course. We also cover life cycle changes and their associated rites of passage in this chapter.

Growing Up

Children learn how to think, feel, speak, and behave in the context of a social environment made up of other people and the cultural traditions they live by. Theoretically, children socialized in similar social environments should think, feel, and act in similar ways.

This is sometimes the case but, as most parents know, not always. Even within the same society or other cultural group—indeed, even within the same family—individuals can be remarkably different. They react differently to people, situations, occurrences, and circumstances. Sometimes we say that individuals feel and act differently because they have different *personalities,* but in everyday speech this is just another way of saying that there is something inside their heads that makes them the way they are. It seems obvious that what makes an individual is the interaction between that individual's unique biological makeup and total life experiences. But this interaction must be incredibly complex, since even identical twins raised in the same household are different, sometimes surprisingly so.

Cultural anthropologists have paid a lot of attention to how diverse peoples enculturate children. Enculturation practices include things such as how children are nursed, held, weaned, and toilet trained; how parents and other adults interact with children; the kinds of behaviors that are punished and rewarded and how they are punished and rewarded; how kids are taught the basic skills needed for success in their society; how much attention and love children receive from their parents and other caretakers; how they relate to their peers; what kinds of work expectations are placed on them; and so forth.

Although it is convenient to speak of "the" way people who live in the same group and share culture raise their children, it is important to note that there is always variability in how families interact with their young, even within a single cultural tradition. Nonetheless, adults share many ideas and beliefs (such as norms and values relevant to raising children) by virtue of the fact that they were raised in the same culture, which impacts how they rear their children. They may broadly agree on how to interact with toddlers, on the proper age and methods for nursing and weaning infants, on appropriate awards and punishments, and on other practices. For example, most North Americans agree that it is possible to "spoil" young children by indulging their every whim, whereas most Japanese mothers are less likely to worry about this.

Although norms, ideals, values, and other cultural knowledge about raising children affect parental *behavior,* child rearing is affected by factors other than parental *beliefs.* In some societies, families are subject to economic or social pressures that do not let them raise their children the way their ideals say they ought to be raised. For example, if men are frequently away on hunts, in wars, or on jobs, then fathers and other male relatives may not take as active a role in child care as women, and this will affect child rearing.

Thus, many North American fathers today want to be more involved in the care of their children, feeling that both they and their children will benefit from a close relationship. Most mothers, too, have to balance job and career against home and family. It used to be different in the old days, with breadwinning fathers and stay-at-home mothers, right? No—the circumstances of their lives constrain the actual child-rearing behavior of mothers, fathers, and other caretakers everywhere, not just in industrialized nations, as we shall see.

Diversity in Child Care

Significant cross-cultural differences exist in ideas and behaviors related to child rearing. A brief discussion of weaning and discipline methods illustrates the diversity.

Cultures differ in their ideas about whether infants should be allowed to nurse whenever they desire or only at certain times. Mothers in many sub-Saharan African ethnic groups practice on-demand nursing, meaning that infants feed whenever they wish. There are culturally variable norms about the proper age of weaning and how it should be accomplished. The !Kung (Ju/'hoansi) are a southern African people who used to get their food supply by gathering wild plants and hunting wild animals (Chapter 6). It is normal for a !Kung mother to breastfeed her children for about 4 years, or even longer. How children are weaned from breast milk likewise varies: some people believe that infants should be allowed to wean themselves, whereas other mothers coat their nipples with bitter substances to discourage nursing after a certain age. In some African societies, it is believed that one or both children will be harmed if a mother becomes pregnant again before her previous baby has been weaned.

Norms about disciplining children likewise vary from people to people. In some societies, people believe that physical punishment is an integral and necessary part of childhood discipline (as in the saying "spare the rod and spoil the child"). In other societies, correcting children's behavior by slapping or beating them is rare. Parents and siblings may ridicule a child for misbehaving, or children may be indulged until they reach a certain age, after which they are punished severely for their misdeeds. On many Micronesian and Polynesian islands, an infant of either gender is caressed, fondled, and played with, and is generally the center of interest of the whole family. Such indulgence and attention continue until a younger sibling is born, then attention shifts to the newborn. In some cultures, adults threaten children with animals, ghosts, spirit beings, and the like (as in "the boogey man will get you if you act like that"). Among the Hopi of Arizona, children are threatened by *kachinas,* or masked dancers impersonating spiritual beings whom Hopi believe live in the mountains to the west of their villages. When a Hopi child seriously misbehaves, parents often get someone to put on a costume (including a frightening mask) of a kachina believed to eat children. When the kachina tries to steal the child for misbehaving, the parents come to the child's rescue. Kachinas also reward "deserving" children by passing out gifts of toys or food during their dances.

Numerous other differences in child-rearing norms and practices exist. Everywhere, the care of infants is entrusted almost entirely to mothers, but by the time children are walking caretaking roles vary from people to

people. In some places, parents do almost all the care of their toddlers, but elsewhere children aged 6 to 8 competently look after their 2- and 3-year-old siblings. Fathers in many cultures are hardly involved with their children and in fact are absent much of the time, but in other cultures men are more equal partners in child care. The kinds of social interactions with adults vary widely—children are constantly fussed over among one people, left alone more to amuse themselves among others. On some islands of the Pacific, sisters and brothers associate freely until both reach puberty, but after that they are supposed to avoid being alone together.

Two African Examples

As an illustration of differences in socialization, we consider two African peoples in some detail: the Aka of the rain forest of west Africa and the Gusii of Kenya.

Aka

The Aka are one of several short-statured (Pygmy) groups who have lived in the west African rain forest for centuries. Like other Pygmies of Africa, Aka are mainly foragers who exploit the natural products of the forest by a combination of hunting, fishing, collecting honey, and gathering fruits, roots, and leaves of plants. Although they do not plant gardens for themselves, for 3 or 4 months of each year the Aka trade with and work in the fields of their agricultural neighbors in exchange for manioc (cassava) and other cultivated foods. Most of the year, though, they live largely on the animals and plants of the forest.

Barry Hewlett, who studied the Aka in the 1970s and 1980s, reports that Aka parents are indulgent toward infants and children. Infants have physical contact with a parent or other caregiver most of the time. Mothers and fathers deal with their crying almost immediately. Whenever they wish, their mothers nurse them, and continue to do so until the child is 3 or 4 years old or until the mother becomes pregnant again. Infants sleep with their parents, as do other dependent children. Parents do not worry about spoiling their children or creating too much dependency. Children crawl and walk whenever they are ready, for Aka do not believe that they have to be systematically taught how to do such things.

After infants learn to walk and talk, they are capable of taking on some tasks and responsibilities. Parents may ask them to gather firewood or fetch water, for example. But the Aka place great value on individual autonomy, even of children, so parents usually do not enforce their

▲ Enculturation practices are affected by parents' circumstances as well as by their ideas about child care. Is this dad spending as much time with his son as he would like?

commands. Like parents in most groups, they may yell at their kids, but corporal punishment is rare—indeed, should one parent strike an infant, the other parent has a reason to ask for a divorce. By accompanying adults on their gathering and hunting trips, 7- or 8-year-old children learn the tasks needed to assume adult roles. Generally speaking, boys learn from their father, girls from their mother, but there is considerable overlap between the two.

Aka infants typically have many caregivers. As foragers, the people travel in small groups that average about 25 or 30 members. Most adults in the camp are relatives of the children. Aunts, uncles, grandparents, and older siblings care for infants much of the time, actually holding them more often than their own mothers while they are resting in camp. Despite this pattern, caregiving is not "communal," for the mother and father are considered to have the main responsibility for nurturing and teaching children.

Aka fathers are heavily involved in the care of their infants and young children. On the basis of his detailed field study, Hewlett reports that the Aka have the highest degree of father participation and involvement in infant care of any known human group. Fathers of infants younger than 4 months old hold or carry their babies one-fifth of the time when they are in camp, in spite of the fact that infants are so dependent on their mothers for nourishment. Fathers also make it a point to be generally available to their infants and children. Far from the role of remote but respected disciplinarian found in many other cultures, Aka fathers talk to their babies and are intimate with them. As a result, older children become attached to their father and report having as warm feelings toward him as toward their mother, Hewlett says.

The reasons why a particular people bring up and enculturate their children in a particular way are complex. Is the main factor their worldview? Their values? How they make their living? Their family organization? Obviously, all these and many other forces matter to different degrees among different peoples.

In the case of the Aka, how their bands are organized is one of the important factors. Married couples have their own sleeping huts, but the entire band of about a

▲ Compared to most other peoples, Pygmy fathers are heavily involved in the care of infants and young children.

dozen families live in close proximity, with little domestic privacy. Both men and women are needed to get food for the family, and in fact mothers and fathers contribute about equal amounts to the daily food supply. Cooperation beyond the range of the nuclear family is essential. Often the entire band, including women and men, cooperate in hunting with nets. From the child's perspective, both the mother's and the father's side of the family are about equally important. There is almost no difference in access to valued resources within an Aka band. Sharing is so ingrained as a norm that Hewlett calls it "demand sharing," meaning that an individual will give up an object if someone else asks for it. Finally, like many other people who make their living by hunting and gathering (Chapter 6), the Aka practice "prestige avoidance." No one brags about his or her accomplishments or skills, and in fact a man who shows a tendency to flaunt his talents may find other men and women putting him in his place by joking about the shape and size of his genitals.

Gusii

The Gusii's child-care beliefs and behaviors contrast with those of the Aka. The million or so Gusii live in the highlands of southwest Kenya. Unlike the hunting and gathering Aka, the Gusii traditionally made their living by growing crops and herding livestock (cattle, sheep, and goats). In modern times, though, many Gusii men have taken up working for a wage, and women improve their own economic welfare by selling grain at local markets. Robert A. LeVine, Suzanne Dixon, Sara LeVine, and their collaborators studied infant and child care among the Gusii for a period of 17 months in the 1970s. Their 1994 book, *Child Care and Culture: Lessons from Africa,* focuses especially on children from birth until about 30 months of age.

Gusii care of infants and small children differs both from the habits of the Aka and from those practices familiar to most Westerners. Most North Americans observing Gusii mothers interacting with infants would find the mothers very attentive to their children in some respects, but lacking in other maternal qualities considered essential or desirable for childhood development in Europe, Canada, or the United States.

In providing for the physical needs of their infants, Gusii mothers are quite diligent. Infants are rarely allowed to cry for more than a moment before the mother begins to nurse or soothe them. This is easy for a mother, for she and her baby are in nearly constant contact—mothers carry infants with them almost everywhere, either in their arms or tied into a sling on their back. Even when a

woman is working in her garden, her baby is on her back or on a mat beside her. Infants sleep with their mother every night, for on-demand nursing is customary and no decent mother would deny her milk to her demanding child during the night. A mother continues to nurse her child for the first 16 to 20 months, with no fear of creating "dependence" on herself. She is constantly available. Aside from nursing and comforting, mothers are careful that their children avoid physical danger, such as fires and animals. Although a mother continues her agricultural work even when she has an infant, the needs of the baby are paramount, so she takes the baby with her.

On the other hand, a Westerner might feel that the Gusii mother–infant relationship is deficient in stimulation and emotional attachment. Gusii think that a mother can take good care of her baby without engaging in much "baby talk," many adoring looks, a lot of play, and frequent affectionate touching and loving caresses. Crying babies are always calmed, but intellectual stimulation, smiles, and excitement are not important goals of the mother during infancy. Language development, too, does not seem high on a Gusii mother's priorities: When babies "babble," mothers do not encourage it with baby talk of their own, but tend to avert their gaze to avoid exciting the infant. Why talk to an infant who cannot understand you?

After an infant has grown into a toddler, mothers ease off in their attention. A Gusii woman, after all, has a lot of work to do. There are fields to plant and weed, grain to harvest, meals to cook, and firewood to gather. There are likely to be other children to attend to, for most women bear several children during their lifetime. So after the phase of high physical dependency has passed in the life of her child, a mother resumes her full workload in the house and garden. When she is away, the 1- to 2-year-old child is left behind in the care of older siblings, some of whom are only 5 or 6 years old themselves.

Westerners might consider such "infant day care" under the supervision of children a kind of parental neglect, but it is normal in Gusii families and in most other parts of Africa. Older sisters are responsible for much socialization. They assist their younger siblings in language, work skills, and social development.

A Gusii woman in her 30s or 40s typically has several children. A mother continues with garden work and other physical labor, but as her children grow up more of her time is spent managing their activities and supervising their work. For the most part, she issues commands and assigns tasks, which children are expected to complete—although actual task completion varies a lot. Mothers seldom give detailed instructions or show their youngsters how to do something, although their older siblings do. Nor do mothers provide much encouragement or praise for a task well done. Mothers who praise their kids are felt to be encouraging selfishness, disobedience, and overly large egos. Apparently, the development of their children's self-esteem is not a high maternal value among the Gusii.

Gusii mothers also differ from Western mothers in how their relationship to children changes over time. During infancy, they are always available and protective, though most Westerners would say the relationship is emotionally distant. As infants begin to walk and talk, mothers tend to pull away and spend much less time with the child, entrusting child care to her other children. She becomes a more authoritarian presence to all her children, although she remains diligent in supplying them with food.

By the time they are in their early teens, most daughters will marry and move in with their new husband. When they become strong and responsible enough by the teen years, sons will join young men at the cattle camps—small roaming groups of young males that tend and protect cattle. When they first marry in their 20s, most sons will bring their wives to live with them near their mother, for sons are a woman's primary support in old age.

So far we have said nothing about Gusii fathers. This is because most Gusii fathers are barely involved in caring for their children, and most are seldom around even when their wife is caring for an infant. The Gusii and Aka live only about 1,200 miles away from each other on the African continent. But in the degree of paternal care, the two peoples are worlds apart. To understand the difference between their child-care practices, we must consider additional facts about the Gusii way of life. We must put them in the total context of the way the people live.

The most relevant facts are these: The Gusii are a patrilineal, polygynous, patrilocal, decentralized tribal people with high fertility and child mortality rates. How does this context affect Gusii child rearing?

Because of *patrilineal* descent, important kinship relationships are traced primarily through males, rather than through both sexes, as for the Aka and in North America. Patrilineality has many implications, one of which is the inheritance pattern: a male inherits most of his land and livestock from his father and father's father. Another is that men are clearly the heads of Gusii extended family units, or homesteads. Normatively speaking, a wife obeys her husband, but she often responds to his demands by assigning tasks and responsibilities to her children. Family life, then, is fairly hierarchical and authoritarian, compared to that of the Aka (and to that of most Western nations, at least in modern times).

As a *polygynous* people, many Gusii women do not have a husband all to themselves, but are cowives of the same man. In the 1950s about 40 percent of men had more than one wife, and nearly 60 percent of Gusii wives were cowives of some man (polygyny is much less common today). Which men have more than one wife? Basically, those who can come up with the resources (in livestock, mainly cattle) to pay the bridewealth for several wives. Accumulating so many livestock takes time, so it is mainly older men who can afford to be polygynous. Most men's first marriage is in their early 20s, but most women marry much younger, in their midteens.

Because Gusii are *patrilocal,* a wife leaves her own mother and father and goes to live on the family lands of her husband, using his land for gardening and his livestock to feed herself and her children. When a man has several wives, one of his obligations is to provide each of them with a separate dwelling, where she lives with her children. He also must provide each wife with garden land and a few livestock for support. Within the larger extended household (the husband–father together with his wives and all their children), each wife–mother thus has her own mini household (the woman plus her dependent children). The place where the mother–children family unit lives is called by a term that translates as "house," indicating that it is culturally regarded as semi-independent from the larger, extended household. Generally, wives provide for their own offspring, though cowives may mutually help one another and share some tasks.

The phrase *decentralized tribal people* means that the Gusii have no formal chiefs or other kind of political authority that issues commands, settles disputes, or prevents warfare among Gusii themselves or between Gusii and neighboring tribes. There is no standing professional army; rather, each settlement must defend itself and its livestock. Therefore, men—especially young men—must be available and willing to fight with spears to defend themselves, their families, and their local community against attack. Being a willing warrior was a valued male role. At the very least, men had to be ready to retaliate if their group was attacked. Any group whose men did not fight back would be considered weak and would be repeatedly attacked and have its livestock stolen.

High fertility means that a woman has many children during her childbearing years. An average woman has eight or nine children between her marriage in her teens and menopause. For most of her reproductive life, she is pregnant, nursing, or looking after young children. Indeed, she expects to become pregnant again soon after she has weaned her last infant. If her husband doesn't visit her often enough, she may even demand one of her rights as a wife—that her husband impregnate her.

High child mortality means that many children die during their first 2 years of life. About 1 in 10 babies dies before the age of 2. If a baby survives the first year or two, the mother considers it to be relatively safe. Most who survive the first couple of years grow into adulthood, although in olden times young male lives were at risk from violent clashes.

These factors interact in complex ways, but here the key point is to realize how Gusii care of infants and children makes sense in light of the overall context of Gusii life.

Why are Gusii families so large? The short answer is that children are "valued." This is true, but there are good reasons why Gusii value having lots of children. A man prefers to have several wives (though most cannot afford to do so) for many reasons. He wants the labor of his wives and their future children, to work the land and tend the livestock that are his main forms of material wealth and the main source of economic security for his relatives. His sons will tend his animals when they grow up and protect them from theft, whereas his daughters will bring in additional livestock from the bridewealth he receives when they marry. He wants his patrilineal family line to continue and to prosper in future generations, for which large numbers of sons are useful. When a man dies, he wants his sons to bury him—an important custom in the Gusii worldview—and his later descendants to pay homage to his memory. A man also enhances his status and reputation by having several wives and many children.

As for a woman, she also wants many children, to assist her with her work and to help her meet her husband's demands. Further, since a woman lives on her husband's land, she finds that having many sons is economically beneficial in her old age: Her daughters will marry and move out, but her sons will remain near where she lives to help her with her work and provide her with food. Also, since child mortality rates previously were so high (though they have declined in recent decades), a woman needs to have several children to make sure she has enough surviving sons. If a woman is a cowife, it is useful to have many sons to help protect her interests against her husband's other wives, who are in some ways rivals.

In sum, Gusii parents do value large families, but the value they place on children is sensible and rational to both mothers and fathers, given the way Gusii live.

Why are Gusii mothers so attentive to their infant's physical needs, yet leave their older toddlers in control of

their other children? Because so many children die before the age of 2, the main goal of a mother for her infant is simple survival, not providing a warm and nurturing social environment to improve the child's intellectual and emotional development. For those women who have been married long enough to have several children, spaced 2 to 4 years apart, older siblings are available to look after toddlers. It is good training for their own parenting skills, and LeVine and his colleagues believe that the toddler has few problems. Assuredly, in a culture such as Gusii, it is not a form of child neglect, as it would be considered in North America.

Why are Gusii fathers hardly involved in child care, in sharp contrast to Aka fathers? There are several reasons:

- Aka mothers and fathers regularly work together in acquiring food by cooperative net hunting. Gusii couples rarely work together. This allows Aka fathers to be more continuously available to their infants.
- Aka couples live in the same hut along with their children. If married to a polygynous man, a Gusii wife has her own house and semi-independent household and the husband–father does not live with her on a permanent basis.
- Aka are like most hunters and gatherers in that resources are widely shared, so the families of an Aka band have about the same amount of resources (Chapters 6 and 13). Some Gusii men and families have more land and livestock than other men and families. Their land can be worked and their herds increased by having a lot of dependents, that is, wives and children. So the most successful Gusii men have several wives and too many children to be as attentive as Aka fathers.
- Aka share objects and food widely and almost daily within the band on the principle of generalized reciprocity (Chapter 7). Gusii men gain social advantages by engaging in balanced reciprocity with other men to make alliances. Exchanging and feasting take a lot of organizing. Children benefit from their father's success, but it reduces his contact with them.
- Aka do occasionally have physical fights with one another. But living in the rain forest, they have no true enemies against whom they must mobilize for defense. Gusii have land and livestock that are sometimes coveted by other Gusii as well as by other tribes, so they have to be ready and able to defend themselves from attack and theft. This takes time and energy away from fathering.

Some readers may conclude that Aka men are "better fathers" than Gusii men. But this view ignores the different ways of life of the two peoples. Good Gusii fathers look after the welfare of their children in their own customary and culturally appropriate way. They provide their wives with land, livestock, a house site, and other resources to support herself and their children. When their sons are ready to marry, fathers give them an adequate inheritance and assistance with bridewealth. They provide all their family dependents with protection from enemies. They try to increase the size of their herds so that their sons will inherit more animals and thus have better chances to succeed in life. All this is facilitated by having a large family and political connections and alliances, and maintaining such connections and alliances consumes much of a Gusii man's time.

Implications for Modern Parents

In brief, Aka and Gusii children are brought up in different cultural worlds. Different kinds of knowledge and personal qualities are needed for success, so naturally child-care and enculturation practices are not the same. Notice also that the different degrees of paternal caregiving among the two peoples is not *simply* determined by their ideas and beliefs about the proper way to care for and teach children.

Consider Gusii fathers, for example. Surely at least a few fathers wish they could remain physically and emotionally close to their children. But protecting their property, providing an adequate inheritance for their sons, and achieving success in the wider society do not allow them to achieve their ideal parenting goals. A Gusii father's circumstances—the conditions in which he lives and to which he must adapt his parenting—do not allow him to act as he wishes.

Likewise, many factors affect how a Gusii mother relates to her children. She has ideas and beliefs about the proper way to treat and enculturate her children. She acquired these ideas in her own childhood and from a lifetime of talk, observation, and other kinds of social learning. But she also encounters circumstances and conditions as she lives her own life and tries to be a good mother. These are external factors or constraints that affect a mother's actual child-care behavior (see Chapter 2 on the relation between cultural knowledge and behavior).

A mother's beliefs and circumstances together affect how she raises her children. Because of her *beliefs,* she thinks certain ways are better than others. Because of her *circumstances,* she finds certain behaviors to be necessary or more feasible than others. The mother may prefer to remain as attentive to her 2-year-old child as

▲ In Africa and on other continents, young children frequently assist with the child care of their younger siblings, as this Baggara girl of Sudan is doing with her baby sister.

she is to her newborn, but her circumstances do not allow this: She has obligations to her husband, to other relatives, and to her older children, so she cannot always do what she prefers.

The wider message is that economic, social, and political factors outside the control of parents and other caretakers are *universally* important influences on how parents rear their children. Many employed parents in twenty-first-century industrial nations bemoan their inability to spend as much time with their children as they would like, or as much as they believe is necessary for their children's emotional well-being or intellectual development. To make up for the hours spent on the job instead of at home with the kids, modern parents have adopted the idea of devoting "quality time" to their children. The implication is that in the past no one had to worry about such things.

But parents everywhere have to cope with conditions that affect how they rear children. Societies have adjusted

◄ These newlyweds in Seoul, South Korea, pose with their families. A wedding ceremony is a rite of passage that recognizes and legitimizes a major transition in status and role.

© Noboro Komine/Photo Researchers, Inc.

to these conditions, and they have readjusted as these conditions have changed. Thus far in the United States, working parents themselves have had to make most of the familial rearrangements needed to find child care. Only a small percentage of companies offer on-site day care or help parents through flexible work scheduling. Given the alleged concern for family values in the United States, perhaps it is time for more employers to find ways of accommodating the child-care needs of their employees.

Life Cycle

In all societies, chronological age makes a difference in the kinds of roles people perform and in their relationships with others. Everywhere, individuals are culturally classified on the basis of their age into categories such as infant, child, adult, elderly person, and so forth. People also make subdivisions of age categories as needed by the context (e.g., the age category "child" may be divided into infant, toddler, preschooler, first-grader, and so on).

The labeled age categories of other cultures may not exactly parallel those derived from one's own cultural classifications. A Gusii female, for example, passes through the following culturally defined age categories during her life: infant, uncircumcised girl, circumcised girl, married woman, female elder. At each age level, certain events should happen in a female's life, and she is concerned if the events do not happen within the appropriate time frame. Thus, to become a "female elder," a woman must have married children, and so women worry about the number of their children and whether their sons and daughters will marry early enough.

So all peoples have age categories, but societies vary in the number of recognized categories, the sharpness with which they are defined, their importance relative to other distinctions such as sex, and the roles members of the category are expected to adopt.

A person's **life cycle** consists of the culturally defined age categories through which he or she passes between birth and death. It includes stages such as infancy, childhood, sexual maturation (puberty), adulthood, and old age. At specific ages, a particular person will be a member of one of these age categories, whereas at other times she or he is in between the various categories and stages of life.

Transitions between stages may take place gradually and not receive any special notice. In all cultures, though, transitions between at least some stages of life are sharply and formally defined by a rite of passage. A **rite of passage** is a public ceremony that marks, rec-

Stage	Cross-Cultural Variations
Infancy	Begins at or after birth. Timing and significance of naming.
Childhood	Domestic and subsistence work responsibilities. Care of younger siblings. Degree of separation of boys and girls.
Adolescence	Degree of recognition and elaboration as an age category. Responsibilities and privileges relative to adults. Presence, elaboration, and significance of initiation rituals.
Adulthood	Defined roughly by age or by life events and experiences.
Old Age	Degree of respect received from younger people. Age of "retirement." Degree of control over family resources.

ognizes, celebrates, or is believed to actually cause a change in a person and her or his status, usually brought about or related to increasing age. Examples of rites of passage that most North Americans experience include birth ceremonies, birthday celebrations, graduation ceremonies, weddings, and funerals. Other familiar rites of passage are baptisms, bar and bat mitzvahs, baby and wedding showers, and installations of officials (inaugurations). All of us enjoy (endure?) such rituals that mark new stages of our lives but, as we shall see, some human groups "ritualize" certain kinds of transitions to extraordinary degrees.

Physical changes are visible evidence of some life cycle transitions, such as puberty and, in a few cultures, menopause. Here again, physical and biological markers of maturation and aging are interpreted differently and made culturally meaningful in a host of ways. Stages in the life cycle are intertwined with physical maturity, but in many cultures an individual does not pass through a certain stage until something has happened to him or her. A person may not become an "adult" with all the rights and responsibilities the culture associates with "adulthood" until the person has married, for example. In many cultures, an initiation ritual is necessary to make a boy into a man or a girl into a woman, as we shall soon see with some examples from New Guinea. So people do not grow up on the basis of physical changes alone. Maturation is a cultural as well as a biological process, so the details of the life cycle vary from people to people. A brief overview of a few of these variations is provided in the accompanying Concept Review.

Each stage in the life cycle carries certain expectations. As individuals move through these stages, their overall role in society changes. All societies recognize at least four major distinctions in the life cycle: infancy, childhood (including puberty), adulthood, and old age.

These stages serve as a convenient way to organize our discussion of the life cycle, but it is important to recognize that cultures vary in how they conceive of these stages and in how transitions from one to the other are recognized and marked.

Infancy

It seems obvious that infancy begins at birth. But actually the life cycle stage of infancy is more complex, for peoples differ in their beliefs about when life begins. Like other phases of the life cycle, "infant" is a culturally defined category of person in addition to being a physiological stage of physical and mental development. For example, does one become a human person at the time of conception, at some later phase in the mother's pregnancy, at birth, or at some time after birth?

Anthropologists often use the phrases *social birth* and *social person* in recognition of the fact that not all newborns are viewed as completely human in some cultures. Obviously, there are important consequences of beliefs about when human status is attained. Parents and families may not mourn the death of a newborn who they do not believe is yet fully human. In the wider society, an individual may not be granted legal protection until he or she is culturally considered a living human being. The American legal system has struggled with this issue for years, for people of different religious beliefs, ethnic affiliations, and political persuasions do not agree on when human life begins, whether at the time of conception, late in pregnancy, or at birth itself. Among the Cheyenne of the American Great Plains, children in the womb were thought to be completely human and were accorded legal protection. A woman who aborted her child was considered a murderer. She might be banished for a while, because taking a life polluted the whole group.

In other cultures, though, even birth itself does not automatically confer the rights that come with human status. Where infant mortality rates are high, sometimes it is too painful for mothers and fathers to become emotionally attached to newborns. Northeast Brazil is one of the poorest regions of the Americas. Here many children are born into matrifocal families, and many mothers are unable to care adequately for some of their babies. To become social persons, babies must exhibit signs that they are likely to survive. Infants who are small and weak, who do not nurse vigorously, and who are frequently ill are believed to "want to die" and to become angels who fly up to heaven. There is little ceremony at their burial, their graves are unmarked, and the mother does not show much grief. (If a mother weeps, her tears dampen the wings of the little angel, so he or she cannot fly to heaven.) Nancy Sheper-Hughes, who worked among these women, sees the mothers' reaction as a response to their desperate circumstances: women cannot afford to invest financially and emotionally in babies who probably will not live.

In most cultures, an infant receives a name at birth. The act of assigning a name to a child is one symbol that she or he is recognized as a social person. The formal naming of a child is often the first rite of passage.

For the Osage, a matrilineal Native American people now living in Oklahoma, the naming rite bestowed human status on the individual. Osage parents often waited several months—in the case of a sickly child, possibly more than a year—before naming a child. A child who died before acquiring a name was quietly buried and the family did not have to observe a year of mourning. After they were convinced the infant was going to survive, parents began to prepare for a naming ritual. A ritual specialist called a "little-old-man" from the child's father's clan organized and directed the ceremony. Little-old-men representing all 24 Osage matriclans gathered in a ritual lodge to hold the ceremony. Each little-old-man recited a long prayer asking God's blessing for the child. After all clan prayers were recited, the child was handed to each of the little-old-men, who in turn blessed the child with water, cedar, corn, and other symbolic substances. Then the baby was seated on a specially prepared robe in the center of the lodge and given a name belonging to the child's clan by the leader of the ceremony. Giving this name symbolized the acceptance of the child as a member of a particular clan. The ritual participation of members of the other 23 clans indicated the acceptance of the child as an Osage. The ritual ended with the father of the child giving horses and blankets to the main little-old-men and

lesser gifts to the other little-old-men. Only after the naming ritual occurred did Osage infancy truly begin.

Childhood and Adolescence

At some point, infants begin to toddle around, stop nursing, and learn the proper places and techniques for eliminating their bodily wastes. Such events usually mark the passage into childhood. Childhood is the period when people begin to acquire technical and mechanical skills. In most societies, learning technical skills begins early by Western standards, by about age 5 or 6. Simple tasks not demanding great strength are done even earlier—3-year-olds may sweep the house, feed the animals, wash the baby, pick up the yard, run errands, deliver messages, and so forth.

In industrial societies, much technical learning takes place in schools, where trained specialists provide instruction in the skills needed to succeed in life. Elsewhere, children learn most skills informally by watching and imitating adults and following their instructions. For example, among the Navajo of New Mexico and Arizona, 6- and 7-year-old boys and girls begin helping with the herds of sheep and goats. While Navajo boys learn the technical skills needed by men, girls learn the skills of women helping their mothers prepare wool for weaving, grinding corn, making clothing, and caring for their younger brothers and sisters.

Most people experience physiological puberty between ages 12 and 16. In most societies, sexual maturation alone does not convey full adult status, with all its rights and responsibilities. Biologically determined sexual maturation usually precedes culturally defined social maturation, especially for males.

This intermediate stage of transition from childhood to adulthood is what we call *adolescence*. An earlier generation of anthropologists debated whether all peoples recognized a stage of life comparable to adolescence: did some peoples go directly from childhood to adulthood, with no transition period for training in fully adult roles and for achieving emotional maturity? Certainly, not all peoples have a word for adolescence in their language. Certainly, too, in many societies girls are married before or very shortly after their first menstruation and so early on assume the role of wife. But neither of these facts means that adolescence is absent as a cultural concept, though its length may be short and its importance slight.

For males in many cultures, adolescence is a period when they prove their worth and establish their reputa-

◄ Some of these Micronesian boys are nearing adolescence. Will their teen years be filled with the same emotional responses as those of American adolescents?

© James Peoples

tion. Among the Cheyenne and some other Plains Indians, older adolescent boys were expected to join war parties and to be daring and aggressive warriors and raiders. Along with adult males, they were expected to take part in hunts and help supply food for their family. In societies in which warfare is a serious concern, adolescence is frequently a period in which young male associations are responsible for defending a group's land and livestock against aggressors. By being vigorous and fierce in warfare, a young man could establish a reputation that might endure for the rest of his life.

On the Micronesian island of Chuuk (formerly Truk), most young men in their late teens and early 20s get intoxicated on alcoholic beverages. There is almost no "social drinking"; men drink mainly to get drunk. While drunk, Chuukese say that a man loses control of himself and goes out of his head "like a sardine" (which come headless in cans). While out of his senses, a man usually acts fierce and often picks fights with other young men. More seriously, he may physically attack a close relative, which ordinarily is normatively forbidden. Mac Marshall, who worked among the people of Chuuk, believes that drunkenness is a role that young men adopt. While in the role of a drunk, they get away with actions that ordinarily are not allowed. This phase of their life cycle proves their manhood—they are fierce, they won't back down, they are someone to be respected. But the role

of drunk is a temporary phase for almost all males: once they have children, almost all men soon become responsible adults, joining the church and giving up the role of drunk. Those who continue to drink are stigmatized.

In American society, adolescence is often a troubled stage, filled with conflict, experimentation, rebellion against parental authority, mood swings, and the like. Some researchers attribute the problems that arise during this period primarily to physiological changes, but others consider cultural factors to be the major causes. In the 1920s Margaret Mead examined adolescence in a Pacific culture in her classic study, *Coming of Age in Samoa.* Mead found that adolescence was not a particularly traumatic time in the life of Samoan girls. She argued that the problems Americans associated with adolescence were the result of cultural factors, not physiological changes. In 1983 Derek Freeman challenged Mead's findings in his book *Margaret Mead in Samoa,* arguing that Samoan adolescents have about as much trouble and conflict as do American teenagers. He went on to suggest that the physiological changes occurring during adolescence have similar effects among all peoples, so this stage of the life cycle is always stressful despite the cultural context. Most anthropologists of today agree that even if physiological changes create problems for adolescents everywhere, these problems are manifested in various ways, depending on the cultural context.

Initiation Rites

How individuals become adults and gain adult rights and responsibilities varies. In the United States, the transition to the adult stage of life is marked by rites of passage, such as graduation ceremonies (from high school or college): one leaves the status of "student" and (the parents hope) becomes an independent, wage-earning adult.

In many societies, the transition from childhood to adulthood is marked by an elaborate set of ceremonies known as **initiation rites.** Initiation rites often occur around puberty, so sometimes they are called *puberty rites,* although they do far more than simply mark a person's sexual maturation. During many rituals, the initiates are educated in the intricate responsibilities of adulthood. Elders tell them about the changes that will soon be expected in their behavior and often share ritual secrets.

Some societies have initiation rituals for males only, others for females only, and still others for both sexes. But even those societies that hold initiation rites for both males and females almost always have separate ceremonies for each sex. This generalization suggests that an important function of initiation rituals is to incorporate children not just into adulthood but also into the adult responsibilities culturally appropriate for their sex (see Chapter 11). In fact, the most common theme of initiation rituals is to make girls into women and boys into men.

Victor Turner pioneered the modern study of rites of passage. In his study of male initiation rites among the Ndembu of Zambia, Turner noted that most rites have three phases: separation, liminality (transition), and incorporation. The phases are revealed by common cultural themes and behaviors involved in male initiation rituals among numerous peoples. The boys are often forcibly removed from their home, a frequent practice being to separate them from the company of women (especially their mother, who sometimes is expected to mourn as if her son has died), so they can become real men.

Turner noted that, once separated from their former home and roles, boys go through a liminal phase. Typically, they are secluded and subjected to tests of their ability to endure pain without crying out. They may have to fast or go without water for days. Nearly always, painful operations are performed on their genitals; they may be circumcised or have their penises mutilated in other ways. Scarification of face and body is common because it is a visible symbol that a male has gone through the proceedings and is entitled to the privileges of manhood. Although sometimes the proceedings last for years, the initiates may have to refrain from eating certain foods or from coming into contact with females or female

things because the period of transition into manhood is regarded as a dangerous time. A simple social structure usually characterizes the liminal period: to symbolize their equal status, the boys are typically stripped of all possessions, their faces or bodies are painted in an identical way, they are dressed alike, and their heads are shaved. All these actions make them look alike and emphasize their common identity and subordination to the elders in charge of the proceedings. (Incidentally, notice that some of these practices are similar to those that new recruits in modern militaries experience during the early weeks of their training, when they too are in the liminal phase of "no longer civilians, not yet full soldiers.")

After their common experience, the youths are reincorporated into the group, but often with new rights and responsibilities. Sometimes, they are now eligible to be married or betrothed. They may receive a small inheritance. They may dress differently or wear new jewelry. Often, the initiation ritual marks their independence from their mother, symbolized by a change in residence. Details vary, but the youths are brought back into normal social life as new persons.

Male Initiation Rituals: A New Guinea Example

Some of the most unusual initiation rituals for males occur in the highlands of New Guinea. Before describing an example, we must point out that in many of these societies (and there are many hundreds of them) people believe that females can pollute males. In their worldview, a woman's body contains substances that endanger a man's health or that can even kill a man unless preventive measures are taken. Above all else, men fear contact with women's menstrual discharges, which they believe can cause them to sicken and die. Because of such beliefs, among many New Guinea peoples women must remain in seclusion during their periods, either in a menstrual hut away from the main settlement or in a special place in their house, which men never enter.

These beliefs about feminine contamination have many implications for women's lives. Women must take precautions to avoid accidentally causing injury to their husbands by polluting the food they serve. In some New Guinea societies, women must travel on separate paths from men, lest a man unknowingly step on a female secretion and become polluted. Women have to suffer through having their young sons taken away from them by force because, according to beliefs, continued association with their sons endangers the boys once they reach a certain age.

Finally, it is common for husbands and wives to live in separate dwellings. A man's wife or wives have their own house, where they live with their children. The husband lives in a separate men's house, together with all the older boys and men of the hamlet or village. By the time they are around 10, boys are usually taken away from their mother—because even contact with one's own mother is dangerous for a boy—and brought to live in the men's house. Male initiation rituals usually begin when a boy is taken from the company of his mother and other women and inducted into the men's house.

The details of male initiation vary from people to people in highland New Guinea. One common cultural rationale for the rituals is to transform a boy into a man: Boys do not grow up naturally but must go through a lengthy series of rituals to give them masculine qualities. Masculine courage, strength, aggressiveness, and independence are desirable not only for the boys themselves but for the group as a whole, because most New Guinea peoples traditionally were heavily involved in warfare with their neighbors and so needed warriors to survive. Another goal of the rituals is to protect boys from feminine contamination: initiates learn ritual procedures that will allow them to have sexual relations in relative safety.

The Awa, a New Guinea people numbering about 1,500 who were studied in the 1970s by Philip Newman and David Boyd, illustrate both themes: "maturation" and "protection." Like many of their neighbors, Awa men believe that if female substances penetrate male bodies, the men will become sick or old before their time. Beginning in their early teens, boys go through a series of rituals that have five stages and last well into their 20s. When several boys in a region have reached the appropriate age of 12 to 14, they are taken from their mothers' houses. In Turner's terminology, this is a rite of separation. They are inducted as a group into the men's house during an intimidating ritual involving food and water restrictions, beating with stinging nettles to toughen them, and rubbing the inside of their thighs with a coarse vine. This is the first stage of their initiation.

In the second stage, about 1 year later, the boys experience the first cleansing of their bodies from female pollution. At a secluded site in the forest they are forcibly bled and made to vomit. Small bundles of sharp-edged swordgrass are jabbed into their nostrils and two small cuts are made in the glans of their penis to bleed out contamination. A vine is looped and thrust down their throat, inducing the vomiting that also cleanses and helps dry out their body—for the Awa believe that desiccation is necessary for boys to achieve maturity. The purpose of

© David Boyd

▲ Beginning in their early teens, Awa boys participate in a prolonged series of rituals intended to strengthen, protect, and instruct them. This second-stage initiate is having his nose bled to remove harmful substances from his body.

these acts is to protect the boys' health and promote their physiological maturity by removing female substances from their bodies.

The third ritual stage occurs when the males are between 18 and 20. They again are purged of female contamination by nose bleeding, penis cutting, and induced vomiting. They are also told certain ritual knowledge, known to all adult men but kept secret from women and boys. After they have been through the third stage, the young men are taught why too much contact with women is so dangerous. They learn how menstrual pollution can overstimulate their growth and age them prematurely. Because they have not yet learned to protect themselves from female substances, they are warned to avoid sexual intercourse altogether until they are married.

About 5 years later, when in their mid-20s, men go through the "sweat ceremony," which is the fourth stage of initiation. They sit together next to the fire in the men's house and sweat profusely for a week or more. The older men lecture them about their upcoming responsibilities as husbands and fathers. They are told about how to protect themselves from the dangers of sexual intercourse and are emphatically warned about the evils of adultery. When the men emerge from the men's house after the sweat ceremony they receive new clothes and body ornaments, including a pair of boar's tusks that they wear in their pierced nose as a symbol of their adult status. In Turner's terminology, stages one through four are the liminal period in Awa male initiation: the youths have been ritually separated from their former lives as boys, but have not yet achieved the full maturation of adulthood, which in the Awa view implies marriage.

The fifth stage—appropriately called the "severe penis cutting"—occurs only a few days later. The young men are again subjected to food and water taboos, to nosebleeding and vomiting, and to penis cutting. This time, however, canes are driven deep into their nose to cause severe bleeding. Small wedges of flesh are cut from either side of their penis, producing deep gashes in the glans. In fact, at the final stage of initiation, all the adult men who are present line up and expose their penis to puncture wounds made by tiny stone-tipped arrows. This treatment is necessary to remove harmful female substances that have entered the body through the penis during sexual intercourse.

The fifth stage is an Awa man's rite of incorporation. Once a man has been through the fifth stage, Awa believe that he has been sufficiently strengthened by the hardships of initiation to be capable of withstanding feminine pollution, although he must continue to undergo ritual bloodletting to maintain his strength. After this stage, the men are in their early 20s. To celebrate their manhood, they are fitted with a boar's tusk that shows they are ready for sexual relations and marriage. They are usually married soon afterward.

The Awa illustrate several themes common in male initiation rituals: inducing physical maturation, strengthening and protecting, imparting secret knowledge, learning the importance of masculine responsibilities, symbolically marking the transition to adulthood. Awa initiation also exemplifies another practice, common not just in New Guinea but around the world: the rituals are usually painful and traumatic to the boys. They frequently involve scarification, beatings, genital mutilation, intimidation by threats and frightful stories, social seclusion, fasting, going without water, and so forth. These pains and traumas are usually considered necessary to strengthen the boys and prepare them for the rigors of adulthood. Certainly such ordeals indelibly mark the transition from boy to man in the minds and usually the bodies of the males.

In discussing the example of the Awa, we must note that their initiation rites are not "typical" of rites in other cultures, which are not usually so severe. But, again, it is interesting to know that male physical maturation—growing into a man—is a cultural as well as a biological process. Indeed, to the Awa, the series of rituals do not just "mark" or "symbolize" the maturation, but are believed to actually cause the physical changes that make men out of boys.

Female Initiation Rituals: Mescalero Apache

Fewer societies make the attainment of adulthood for girls into an initiation ritual. Some say that this is because the physical signs of maturity are more obvious in the female body, so it is less essential for them to be socially recognized and proclaimed. Whatever the reason, where they occur, initiation rites for females most often emphasize attainment of physical maturity, instruction in sexual matters and childbearing, and reminders of adult duties as wives and mothers.

Mescalero Apache are one people who have puberty ceremonies for girls. Each year, around the Fourth of July, the people celebrate the attainment of womanhood in a ceremony that lasts 4 days and 4 nights. Apache girls in the region who have had their first menses in the last year go to a place where a large tipi is erected. During the ceremony, the girls are regarded as reincarnations of White Painted Woman, a spiritual being who gave many good things to the people. During the ceremony, the girls are blessed by singers (specialists who have gone through lengthy training to learn the stories and chants) and by their relatives and friends. Those attending participate in traditional songs and dances dedicated to the four directions and to spirits associated with them. The Apache ceremony places a lot of emphasis on the girls becoming the "Mothers of the Tribe," perhaps because the Apache are a matrilineal people. On the fourth day, singers recount the history of the Apache and the girls are reminded of their ancestry and obligations. The ceremony honors the girls as individuals, reaffirms their commitment to the community and vice versa, urges them to act responsibly, and upholds and re-creates Apache traditions annually. According to ethnographer Claire Farrer (1996, 89), "almost invariably, the girls report having been changed, not only into social women but also at a very basic level. They are ready to put aside their childhoods and become full members of their tribe and community." The ceremony thus helps the girls make the social transition to adulthood, with all its rights and responsibilities.

Adulthood

When is a person considered an adult? Partly because there are no obvious physiological transformations or psychological indicators of adulthood, some peoples

▲ Apache girls have a four-day puberty ceremony to publicly acknowledge and celebrate their attainment of adulthood. The initiate is coated in clay to symbolize her identification with a benevolent female spirit.

have no clear idea of when the stage begins (as is also true with old age). But almost all peoples hold that adults have both more rights and more duties than adolescents, thus recognizing adulthood (at least implicitly) as a stage of life.

In many societies, marriage is the rite of passage that most clearly denotes the transition to adult status. When people marry, usually they are assumed to be sufficiently mature socially and physically to assume the workload and social responsibilities required of spouses and parents. Thus marriage in most societies is marked ceremonially with a rite of passage—a wedding.

The importance of marrying and having a family has lessened in Western industrialized societies. In most preindustrial societies, however, the eventual marriage of nearly every individual is expected, and there are relatively few unmarried people. Why should marriage be so important for the attainment of adulthood in so many preindustrial societies?

There are several reasons. Sociobiologists/evolutionary psychologists hold that reproduction is a primary human motive, for it is the means by which genes are transmitted. In nearly all societies, marriage is the bond by which legitimate reproduction occurs. Marriage legitimizes children in the eyes of others and makes children more likely to receive favorable treatment in inheritance and in social life generally. Both women and men can and do have children outside of marriage, of course, but marriage helps stabilize the female–male bond for purposes of child care and gives children greater standing and rewards in the community.

The sociobiological view is plausible, but it is not very helpful in accounting for why there is a greater expectation of marriage in preindustrial than in Western industrial societies. For that, we need to bring in the economic and social benefits of marriage while recalling that marriage concerns a wide range of people (Chapter 8).

In preindustrial cultures, marriage is important to an individual because children often provide the only form of economic security available for elderly people, so one needs children for support in later life. Relationships created by marriage are also important for various kin groups. Socially, a person's family members usually urge or command him or her to marry in order to establish useful economic relationships with other families or useful political alliances with other villages. Access to resources is usually enhanced by marriage, or, rather, by strategic choice of spouses. The desire to establish some degree of economic and social independence is another reason for high marriage rates among preindustrial peoples. Some kind of family unit is usually responsible for producing and processing the food and other products required. Because the domestic tasks done by wives and husbands are often complementary, each sex requires the goods and services provided by the other (see Chapter 11). Most people who do not marry remain dependent (and typically low-status) members of someone else's household.

More than among industrialized people, then, marriage established a person's prestige, security, and social and economic independence. That modern industrial nations have relatively high percentages of never-married people, as well as high rates of separation and divorce, is partly explained by the fact that marriage has lost many other economic and security-providing functions it so often performs in preindustrial cultures, as explored in Chapter 8.

Old Age

Gerontology, the study of elderly people, has only recently become an important interest of anthropologists. Part of our interest stems from conditions in our own society, in which elderly people are too often seen as a burden, both to their children and to those of us who pay Social Security taxes.

One popular notion is that the neglect of and contempt for elderly people in modern American society are something recent. Sometimes we hear or read statements like "The elderly were respected and admired for their wisdom in primitive societies." As we have emphasized, however, "primitive" people are enormously diverse in all respects, including the way they regard and treat elderly people.

Among some preindustrial peoples, adults who can no longer economically contribute to the family because of age, physical injury, or severe illness become burdens to their families. As they become dependent on the goodwill of others, their prestige declines. Among the Comanche,

old men were often the victims of pranks by young boys, who sometimes slashed the prized painted buffalo robes of the old men. As elderly people became increasingly helpless, they frequently were "thrown away" or abandoned by their relatives and friends. Little time was spent mourning the death of an old or "useless" person. Intense mourning was reserved for people who died while still physically in their prime because only their death constituted a true loss to their community.

Among some Inuit peoples of Canada, conditions for survival were even more tenuous, and parricide (the killing of close relatives) sometimes occurred. The old or infirm who could no longer keep up with the migratory movements of the group were abandoned by their families. In some Inuit groups, an elderly person who was no longer able to travel would be abandoned in a sealed igloo with a little food and a seal-oil lamp for warmth. Further south, in the subarctic forests, the Athabaskan tribes sometimes abandoned elderly people. Animals, particularly wolves, were likely to find these helpless individuals before death and kill them. To avoid leaving relatives to such a fate, a family member frequently killed them.

Such ethnographic cases are not "typical"—there is no generalization that can be made about *the* treatment of elderly people among preindustrial cultures. They do suffice to show that modern attitudes toward the elderly are not unique.

Other preindustrial peoples come closer to the romantic ideals some of us have about all such peoples: Authority over family and community, control of resources, and the respect one receives increase with advancing age. Senior members of the family and community are elevated to positions of leadership. Knowledge and wisdom gained from experience replace physical strength and stamina as the elderly person's contribution to the well-being of the family and community.

In East Asia (China, Korea, and Japan), respect for and care of one's aged parents was a much more important cultural value in Confucian philosophy than in the Judeo-Christian commandment to honor one's father and mother. In old China and Korea, the Confucian ethical philosophy held that *filial piety* (extreme respect and almost blind obedience to one's parents) was a primary human virtue. Parents made most of the important decisions for their children about matters such as when and whom to marry, education, and daily work activities. In China, many brief stories were told to teach and reinforce these filial values. In one story, the parents of an 8-year-old boy are bitten by swarms of mosquitoes during the summer months. To spare his parents, the boy allows them to bite his stomach and doesn't even swat at them for fear they will fly away and bite his parents. In another, a 70-year-old man amuses his very elderly parents by acting like an infant in front of them, stumbling around and crying like a baby to make them laugh. During the Qing dynasty (1644–1911), many violations of filial piety were considered serious enough to warrant harsh legal punishments. For example, a magistrate (acting as judge) could order the execution of a son who struck one of his parents.

In industrialized societies, most retired individuals are supported partly or entirely through investments, retirement funds, and/or government programs. In many instances, the elderly physically withdraw from daily contact with their families, moving to retirement communities or to areas of the country with warm climates, such as California, Arizona, and Florida. Thus many individuals culturally classified as elderly are segregated and isolated (sometimes by their own wishes) from younger adults and children, living in their own relatively closed communities.

Why do cultures vary in their regard for and treatment of elderly people? A cultural materialist argument is that the elderly receive greatest respect and authority in those societies in which they control the land, livestock, and other resources of their family group. Younger family members rely on elders for rights to land and other resources needed for survival and success, so children have economic as well as emotional reasons for acceding to the wishes of their parents and deferring to their judgments. Obedience and deference, though, are not permanent, for almost everyone who lives long enough will attain the status of elder and the esteem and authority it brings. Rather than fearing old age, many people look forward to it in such settings.

Some anthropologists argue that the explanation lies not in economics per se but in the contrast between literate and nonliterate people. In societies without writing, elderly people become the major repositories of historical, religious, and technical knowledge, functioning as the de facto libraries of these societies. Their control of knowledge makes them indispensable to the community

▲ In many societies, advanced age brings increasing prestige and authority, as in these elders' homeland in Xinjiang, China.

and gives them power over its members, enhancing their social value and the respect they receive. This might be termed the "knowledge is power" explanation.

Another contributing factor is the rate of change a people is experiencing. In slowly changing societies with relatively stable technologies, knowledge is seen as cumulative and wisdom as the product of age and experience. The older people within the group are viewed as the repositories of community wisdom and knowledge, so they are the individuals most capable of making important political and economic decisions.

In contrast, industrialization unleashes rapid and profound changes in the technologies of modern societies, and existing technologies quickly become obsolete. Therefore, we tend to view knowledge not as fixed but as evolving. Experience alone does not generate the wisdom necessary for effective decision making. Like yesterday's technology, elderly people are often viewed as obsolete and out of step with today's realities. Their ideas and knowledge are thought by many to be antiquated ("dinosaurs") and of limited value in decision making. From this perspective, it is not surprising that older individuals are sometimes forced out of positions of authority and replaced by younger individuals thought more capable of making the critical decisions.

Summary

1. Cultures differ in their child-rearing practices—in nursing and weaning norms, the degree and methods of discipline, toilet-training practices, nurturing, sexual permissiveness, caretaking roles, and so forth. The Aka and Gusii, both African peoples, illustrate some of the diversity in child-care and enculturation beliefs and behaviors. They also show that child care everywhere is affected by people's circumstances as well as by their beliefs.

2. The changes that occur in people's lives as they mature and age are referred to as life cycle changes. Age is everywhere a relevant social characteristic used to allocate roles. This is shown by the fact that transitions from one age category to another are so often marked by formal public ceremonies called rites of passage.

3. Exactly when infancy begins and ends is affected by culture as well as by actual biological birth and physi-cal maturation. Often, as among the Osage, a naming ritual confers human status to an infant.

4. Among preindustrial peoples it is typical for children to begin contributing to the support of their families at a much younger age than among ourselves. The passage from childhood to adolescence is often accomplished and marked by an initiation ritual, which sometimes involves severe physical and psychological trauma, as illustrated by the Awa.

5. Human societies vary enormously in their regard for and treatment of the elderly. The chronological age at which an individual is considered elderly likewise varies. The degree to which elderly people exercise control over important property and its inheritance is one influence on how they are regarded. Other influences include the degree of literacy and the rate of technological change a people are experiencing.

Key Terms

life cycle	rite of passage	initiation rite

InfoTrac College Edition Terms

socialization variations	adolescence in Samoa	Apache women
Gusii	liminal (liminality)	filial piety

Suggested Readings

Farrer, Claire R. *Thunder Rides a Black Horse: Mescalero Apaches and the Mythic Present.* 2nd ed. Prospect Heights, Ill.: Waveland, 1996.

A brief and readable description of the author's experiences with the Apache girl's initiation ceremony. Focuses on the ceremony itself, the roles surrounding it, the symbolism, and the place of the ceremony in the people's culture.

Hewlett, Barry S. *Intimate Fathers: The Nature and Context of Aka Pygmy Paternal Infant Care.* Ann Arbor: University of Michigan Press, 1991.

Fathers among the Aka Pygmies of Central Africa are more involved in the care and nurturing of infants than in any other known culture. An excellent study of Aka paternal care and how the case relates to wider issues of adaptation and gender egalitarianism.

Leiderman, P. Herbert, Steven R. Tulkin, and Anne Rosenfeld, eds. *Culture and Infancy: Variations in the Human Experience.* New York: Academic, 1977.

A volume of 23 articles, mostly dealing with infancy in various cultural settings.

LeVine, Robert A., Suzanne Dixon, Sarah Levine, and Amy Richman. *Child Care and Culture: Lessons from Africa.* Cambridge: Cambridge University Press, 1996.

Examines parenthood, infancy, and childhood among the Gusii of Kenya and compares it to child care and parent–child relations in the American middle class.

Mead, Margaret. *Coming of Age in Samoa.* New York: Morrow, 1928.

Account of adolescent girls in Samoa and one of anthropology's great classics. Few anthropological studies have been more widely read by the general public.

Turnbull, Colin. *The Human Cycle.* New York: Simon & Schuster, 1983.

A readable summary of life cycle changes in various cultures.

Companion Website for This Book

The Wadsworth Anthropology Resource Center
http://anthropology.wadsworth.com

The companion website that accompanies *Humanity: An Introduction to Cultural Anthropology,* Sixth Edition, includes a rich array of material, including online anthropological video clips, to help you in the study of cultural anthropology and the specific topics covered in this chapter. Begin by clicking on Student Resources. Next, click on Cultural Anthropology, and then on the cover image for this book. You have now arrived at the Student Resources home page and have the option of choosing one of several chapter resources.

Applying Anthropology. Begin your study of cultural anthropology by clicking on Applying Anthropology. Here you will find useful information on careers, graduate school programs in applied anthropology, and internships you might wish to pursue. You will also find real-world examples of working anthropologists applying the skills and methods of anthropology to help solve serious world problems.

Research Online. Click here to find a wealth of Web links that will facilitate your study of anthropology. Divided into different fields of study, specific websites are starting points for Internet research. You will be guided to rich anthropology websites that will help you prepare for class, complete course assignments, and actually do research on the Web.

InfoTrac College Edition Exercises. From the pull-down menu, select the chapter you are presently studying. Select InfoTrac College Edition Exercises from the list of resources. These exercises utilize InfoTrac College Edition's vast database of articles and help you explore the numerous uses of the search word, *culture.*

Study Aids for This Chapter. Improve your knowledge of key terms by using flash cards and study the learning objectives. Take the practice quiz, receive your results, and email them to your instructor. Access these resources from the chapter and resource pull-down menus.

Chapter Eleven

GENDER IN COMPARATIVE PERSPECTIVE

Cultural Construction of Gender

Sex and Gender

The Hua of Papua New Guinea

Gender Crossing and Multiple Gender Identities

Cross-Gender Occupation or Work Roles

Transvestism

Associations with Spiritual Powers

Same-Sex Relations

The Sexual Division of Labor

Understanding Major Patterns

Understanding Variability

Gender Stratification

Universal Subordination?

Influences on Gender Stratification

Gender Stratification in Industrial Societies

© Malcolm S. Kark/Peter Arnold, Inc.

Anthropologists study gender from a comparative perspective. This perspective can challenge many stereotypes about sex roles, including the one that men are normally the "breadwinners" for their families. These women from Papua New Guinea are fishing to feed their families, as do women in a great many other societies.

ALL HUMAN BEINGS THINK and act within the framework of a cultural system that affects their interests, concerns, worldviews, social behavior, and so forth. Since anthropologists are humans too, our own research and teaching interests are affected by the changes that have occurred in our own culture in the past several decades. So it is hardly surprising that the feminist movement—one of the most powerful social and political forces of the late twentieth century—has led to increased anthropological concern with the role of gender in human relationships and in society generally. In the early twenty-first century, the investigation of issues connected to gender is one of the most popular specializations within ethnology. Even those of us who do not "specialize" in gender now take gender into account in our research on other subjects, due to the recognition that most human relationships are permeated by beliefs about gender.

ALONG WITH KINSHIP AND AGE, gender is a universal basis for organizing group activities and allocating roles to individuals. Everywhere, your identity as a male or female or as a member of another gender matters: it makes a difference in who you are, what you have, how you interact, and what you can become. But anthropologists have found that in different cultures, gender matters to different degrees and in different ways. These cultural variations and the factors that affect them are the subjects of this chapter.

THIS FIELD IS SO VAST that we must focus our coverage on only four of the main issues to which anthropologists have made important contributions: (1) the cultural construction of gender, (2) multiple (as opposed to "dual") genders, (3) the sexual division of labor, and (4) gender stratification. Where relevant, we suggest specific ways in which anthropological findings and perspectives help in understanding gender roles and beliefs about gender in contemporary societies.

In any society, gender is a key dimension of a person's *social identity:* how other people perceive you, feel about you, and relate to you is influenced by the gender to which they assign you and by how your culture defines gender differences. Less obviously, an individual's *self-identity* is affected by cultural beliefs and ideas: your conception of yourself depends partly on how your culture distinguishes masculinity and femininity, allocates roles to one or the other sex, and uses symbols (such as dress, behavior, speech style, and sexual preferences and practices) to help define differences between females and males.

The importance of a person's self-identity as a member of a particular sex is apparent in social relationships. Certainly, you are aware of how important your sexual identity is when you interact with someone of the opposite sex. But even in same-sex interactions, your social behavior is affected by your culture's norms, categories, worldviews, symbols, and other ideas and beliefs that influence your group's conceptions about gender. Cultural conceptions of "masculinity" and "femininity" matter just as much in same-sex as in opposite-sex interactions.

Finally, just as sexual identity affects interactions between individuals, so do beliefs about gender affect behavior in a variety of social settings and contexts: in the workplace, home, school, church, and political arenas, to name a few. Our culture's ideas about males and females—and about masculinity and femininity—permeate most of our personal relationships and our society's institutions, whether or not we are consciously aware of it.

Cultural Construction of Gender

Ideas about gender itself and differences between the sexes vary from people to people. The world's peoples differ in how much importance they attach to whether a person is female or male and in what specific behaviors they expect from females and males.

Sex and Gender

To emphasize such cultural variations, anthropologists make a conceptual distinction between *sex* and *gender*. A person's *sex* is determined by biological inheritance, namely, by the X and Y sex chromosomes, as well as by other aspects of genetic makeup. A person's genetic makeup—which interacts with the environment to affect physical and social maturity—forms physical characteristics like genitals, hormonal frequencies, and secondary sexual characteristics (breasts, body size and musculature, and the like). Of course, not all individuals can be identified as a member of a *dichotomous* (female/male) category on the basis of their genetic makeup. Various peoples treat this ambiguity in different ways, as we shall see.

In contrast, *gender* is culturally defined, not strictly biologically determined. How males and females perceive and define themselves and each other, what it means to be a woman or a man, what roles are seen as appropriate for men and women—these and many other dimensions of femaleness and maleness are learned during socialization rather than fixed at birth. They are culturally variable, not universal to the human species or constant across all cultures. Anthropologists use the phrase **cultural construction of gender** to emphasize that different cultures have distinctive ideas about males and females and use these ideas to define manhood/masculinity and womanhood/femininity.

The notion that gender is culturally constructed is too easily and often misunderstood. Some scholars (especially those in the biological sciences) mistakenly believe that anthropologists claim that genetic (physical) differences between the sexes do not matter. They think we claim that differences in male and female behaviors are determined by culture, not genes.

Some anthropologists do claim this, of course, especially those whose theoretical orientation is more humanistic than scientific (Chapter 4). But most accept that biological differences between females and males "matter"—are relevant for both ideas and behaviors—in all cultures. However, our discipline's focus on cultural diversity has made us aware that human groups define and make use of these differences in a multitude of ways. In *symbols,* various peoples attach cultural meanings to female–male differences that go well beyond biological/anatomical distinctions. In cultural *classifications of social reality,* male–female differences are minimized in some cultures, maximized in others. In *values,* "patriarchy" crudely describes some groups, "sexual equality" others. In *behavior patterns,* some groups fairly rigidly differentiate between female and male activities and roles, whereas others allow both sexes to participate in similar kinds of activities according to individual preferences and circumstances. Anthropologists are fascinated by such variations between human communities. But this fascination does not imply that we are not aware of cross-cultural similarities or that we deny biological realities.

One implication of the cultural construction of gender is that no single culture's constructions are entirely based on the biological differences between the sexes. In other words, there are no cultures that are "natural" with respect to their conceptions of gender. We cannot find a people whose women or men act "exactly as their genes dictate," or whose conceptions of femininity or masculinity are based "entirely on biological factors." This fact makes it very difficult to determine the impact of biological (sexual) differences on the behaviors of females or males, for everywhere cultural (gender) constructions obscure and complicate the impacts of genes. (Notice, though, that this does not mean that genetic differences are not important. It only means that their effects are hard to determine.)

The Hua of Papua New Guinea

The Hua are one people whose cultural construction of gender differs markedly from that familiar to most of our readers. Hua are one of several hundred tribal peoples who live in the interior mountains of Papua New Guinea. Studied by Anna Meigs in the 1970s, the Hua are a patrilineal, horticultural people who live in villages of around 100 to 300 people. As we shall see, Hua culture constructs gender on the basis of female–male differences that most people outside of Papua New Guinea do not recognize. Because of this cultural construction, Hua believe that later in life a woman can become like a man and a man can become like a woman.

Each Hua village contains one or more large men's houses, occupied by initiated people (see Chapter 10 on the Awa) who belong to one of the village's patrilineages. Initiated people include mainly adult men, but also some older women who have become "like men" (as discussed later). Uninitiated people—including young women, girls, and boys who have not yet been through the male initiation ceremonies—live in separate houses.

How do Hua culturally construct gender? They believe that bodies contain a life-giving substance (like a vital essence) that they call *nu. Nu* is thought of as a real, physical substance—not a mystical or magical power—that can be transferred from one person to another and gained and lost in various ways. Female bodies contain an excess of *nu,* which in Hua thought makes women grow faster and age more slowly than men but also makes them unattractively moist. On the other hand, men naturally contain a smaller amount of *nu.* This means that men have difficulty with growth and maintenance of vitality later in life, but they are attractively dry and hard. Hua explain many of the differences between men and women by the amount of *nu:* men are stronger and fiercer because they are dry, for example.

Nu takes several forms. It is both gaseous (breath) and liquid (blood, sweat, semen, female sexual secretions). A transfer of *nu* between individuals may be either harmful or helpful, depending on the nature of the relationship between the giver and the recipient. Transfer of *nu* may occur during eating, sexual intercourse, and other kinds of direct and indirect contact. For example, a woman transfers her *nu* to people when she serves food to them. *Nu* from her bodily secretions and under her fingernails adheres to the food and gets ingested by her children or her husband.

A woman also transfers *nu* to a man (including her husband) when she has intercourse with him. The giving of feminine *nu* to a man in the act of intercourse is harmful to the man because it pollutes and debilitates him. Intercourse is also damaging to a man because he contributes his scarce *nu* (in the form of breath and semen) to a woman during sex, so she gains strength and vitality at his expense.

The amount of *nu* one has can be regulated by one's activities and by the kinds of food one eats. Various events in people's lives require regulation of the amount of *nu* they should have. Women need extra *nu* during pregnancy, so they eat lots of foods that are considered rich in *nu*. (Broadly speaking, these are fast-growing foods with high moisture content.) During menstruation, though, women have too much *nu*, so they avoid the same kinds of food.

For their part, males do not have enough *nu* for full growth and maturation, so during certain periods of boyhood they are encouraged to eat foods with lots of *nu*. At other times, when they are undergoing the initiation ceremonies that make them into strong men able to fight to defend the village, they are supposed to strictly avoid *nu*-rich foods because such foods will weaken and pollute them. In fact, during initiation ceremonies there are strict taboos not only on the eating of these foods but also on eating foods from gardens tended by women or foods prepared by women. These taboos keep the boys free of the pollution caused by contact with women.

Nu is the substance that makes women polluting to males. The greater the difference in *nu* between a woman and a man, the more dangerous that woman is to that man. But both men and women can and do lose or gain *nu*, depending on their activities, their diet, and their age. After decades of engaging in sexual intercourse with women and eating foods touched by their wives and other women, middle-aged and elderly men have picked up lots of *nu*. They become invulnerable to further contamination by contact with females and therefore may eat *nu*-rich foods and participate in sexual intercourse with less anxiety than younger men. Gaining *nu* over the years makes them become "like women," Hua believe.

Women lose *nu* whenever they menstruate, handle and prepare food, and have babies. Their *nu* is transferred to others by these activities and events. Over their life course women thus are drained of *nu*. This draining of *nu* from female bodies means that they become less and less dangerous to males as they grow older. Women who have given birth to more than two children are considered to have lost enough *nu* so that they are no longer polluting. They therefore have become "like men," Hua say.

In these ways Hua culture constructs gender categories on the basis of beliefs about quantity of *nu* as influenced by a person's stage in the life cycle. Women normally possess more *nu*. In fact, women at the height of their procreative years—when they are menstruating, sexually active, giving birth, and nursing infants—generally need and have the most *nu* of all. Men most of the time have much less *nu*. Most women lose *nu* as they age, so they become more "like men," whereas older men have accumulated *nu* from a lifetime of relations with women, so become more "like women."

Constructing gender classifications on the basis of the quantity of *nu* allows for more than two gender categories. Indeed, Hua culture recognizes gender distinctions on two bases. One is a person's genitals, which makes one either male or female. The other is the quantity of *nu* in a body. The latter criterion gives rise to two additional nondiscrete (more/less) gender categories that the Hua call *figapa* and *kakora*. Although the *figapa/kakora* distinction is relevant only in certain ritual contexts, it is significant that people who are genitally male or female can be classified with the opposite gender for certain purposes.

Figapa, or "uninitiated person," are persons whose bodies contain lots of substances associated with femininity (e.g., menstrual blood, vaginal secretions, fluids associated with childbirth). *Figapa* include the following kinds of people:

- Children of both sexes because they have recently been in intimate contact with a woman (their mother)
- Women in their childbearing years because they are the essence of femininity and their bodies contain maximum amounts of feminine substances
- Postmenopausal women who have not had at least three children because their bodies are not sufficiently drained of feminine substances
- Elderly men because female *nu* has been transmitted to them by their lifetime of activities (sexual intercourse, eating food prepared by women) that exposed them to contact with women.

These people—whether or not their genitals are female genitals—are all "like women" because their bodies contain lots of substances the Hua symbolically consider feminine.

Kakora, or "initiated person," includes the following kinds of persons:

- Males in their early teens through the prime years who have been initiated (not including elderly men) because during the initiation procedures they have rigorously avoided female foods and contact with women and so have minimal quantities of nu

- Postmenopausal women with more than two children because giving birth to three or more children has drained them of most feminine substances, so they are no longer a source of danger to males.

People who are *kakora* are eligible to live in the men's house and to obtain the secret "male" knowledge gained during initiation ceremonies. As Meigs (1990, 109) puts it, the feminine substances in *kakora* bodies have been "massively cleaned out three or more times," and without these substances culturally associated with femininity they are "like men." Therefore, they may live in the men's house.

Anna Meigs's work is presented in such detail because the Hua so clearly illustrate the cultural construction of gender. The objective physical distinctions between the sexes—genitals, beards, breasts, and so on—are differences that are recognized and relevant for behavior in all known cultures. But, as the Hua show, cultures use the raw material (to speak metaphorically) of these differ-

▲ Many North Americans believe that women are emotionally better suited to caretaker roles than are men. This belief helps to account for why women predominate in occupations dealing with the care and education of young children.

ences to construct varying beliefs about the ways in which females and males differ. (Thus Hua believe that men and women differ not only in the usual physical ways but also in the quantity of *nu* each has.) These beliefs in turn affect the attitudes each sex holds about the other and the behavior each sex adopts toward the other. (Thus Hua men in some contexts fear the possibility of feminine pollution and therefore try to minimize their contact with women, their intake of food prepared by women, and their sexual relations with women.)

The more different some culture's beliefs are from your own, the more obvious it is that those beliefs are a cultural construction rather than biologically determined. Because Hua beliefs pertaining to male–female relationships seem exotic to most Westerners, the fact that gender is culturally constructed among these people is readily apparent. However, all people's ideas about gender are culturally constructed, including yours and mine. To stimulate thought, we briefly present some ideas on the construction of gender in Euro-American culture.

Speaking generally, many North Americans see females as caring toward others, emotional, socially skilled, physically fragile, and family oriented. Males are taken to be more selfish, rational, tolerant of physical discomfort ("tough"), coordinated, and individualistic.

Consider the possible effects of these cultural conceptions on the uneven distribution of occupational roles between women and men in the modern American economy. The predominant pattern is for members of each sex to move into jobs for which they are believed to be best suited, given American cultural conceptions of gender. This happens for at least two reasons. First, individual men and women more often seek those jobs that they find appropriate for their sex or believe they have the best chance of getting or succeeding in; people apply for certain kinds of jobs according to their preferences, based in part on their beliefs about "sex roles." Second, employers tend to hire people according to their own cultural conceptions of which sex is likely to do well in a particular job; the employment market (the market for labor) itself allocates men and women into certain kinds of jobs.

Cultural constructions of gender are changing rapidly, but many jobs remain disproportionately female or male. Thus women predominate in jobs that involve nurturing (e.g., nursing, day care, teaching elementary students, pediatric medicine), routine interactions with the public (e.g., receptionists, store clerks, restaurant waiters), repetitive use of fine motor skills (word processing, sewing and stitching), and cleaning and housekeeping. A few of the jobs in which men predominate are those involving outdoor activity (equipment operation, driving,

© Lawrence Migdale/Photo Researchers, Inc.

carpentry and construction), high-level decision making (management, administration), and knowledge of mathematical principles (science, engineering, computer programming). How much of the occupational difference between the sexes results from the American cultural construction of gender, which defines females as having certain inherent characteristics and males as having a contrasting set?

Of course, to say that gender is culturally constructed is not the same as saying that physical differences between males and females are irrelevant. But, as we now discuss, some peoples allow for the existence of gender identities other than female and male.

Gender Crossing and Multiple Gender Identities

Many peoples tolerate and even institutionalize diversity in gender roles and sexual orientation. Biologically male or female individuals who, for one reason or another, wish to adopt aspects of the role or behavior of the other sex are allowed to do so, with little or no social stigma or formal punishment. A boy who cannot or does not wish to conform to male roles is not forced to follow norms nor is he socially ostracized, but he is allowed to act like a woman in certain respects or contexts. Conversely, a girl who shows an affinity for activities culturally defined as male is allowed to participate in manly roles when she becomes an adult. In short, people can adopt the behaviors and roles typical of the other sex in features such as clothing, work, and sexual preference without experiencing social or legal punishment from other members of their communities.

These practices or customs are often called **gender crossing,** for obvious reasons. It is important to know that, in many cultures, gender crossing is *institutionalized.* It is expected that a certain number of people are born who will, when they mature into adulthood, become like the other sex in some ways. Rather than stigmatizing such persons or trying to force them to uphold the group's standards of femininity or masculinity, they are accommodated and integrated into social life; that is, their alternative sexual identity is institutionalized.

Most North Americans will interpret "institutionalized gender crossing" as a way to accommodate lesbians, gays, and bisexuals. This interpretation is generally correct, but in fact there is much more to gender crossing than sexual orientation, as we shall see. First, let's consider briefly how anthropological thinking about gender crossing has changed recently.

Until the 1970s or 1980s most ethnologists viewed gender crossing in the following way. In any society, some individuals are born who do not fit into the existing sexual identities of "male" or "female." There will always be some boys who do not want to go to war, hunt, or compete in politics, but prefer to play with girls, do domestic work, tan skins, or otherwise act in ways culturally considered feminine. Likewise, some girls display an affinity for actions culturally associated with masculinity, preferring to play boy games, use weapons, dress like males, or whatever. In many human societies, such persons eventually learn to outwardly conform to the normal sex roles. If they do not conform, they are considered deviant and punished or stigmatized throughout their lives. In some societies, though, a legitimate role exists that allows them to satisfy their inclinations while serving the group in various ways. In this view, institutionalized gender crossing is interpreted as a cultural mechanism that provides a legitimate outlet for people who otherwise might be unhappy or cause problems in the social life of the community.

Certainly, this view presents a favorable image of cultures that allow gender crossing. Anthropologists have often seen this as a lesson "we" can learn from "them." Some human groups do not insist on rigid conformity to their sexual stereotypes, but allow diversity, in contrast to chauvinistic cultures like the anthropologists' own. Unlike "us," "they" normalize individual variation in aspects such as dress style, sexual orientation, work activities, mannerisms, and the like, rather than rigidly insisting on uniformity. And unlike many of "us"—who view men who act like women and women who act like men as morally degenerate, dangerous to society, or genetically abnormal—"they" do not despise or ostracize such individuals, but provide them with legitimate roles in the community's social life. The usual lessons were two: (1) "We" ought to be more like "them" by tolerating variation and accepting people as individuals whom we value and who can contribute in various ways. (2) Not all peoples in the world require conformity to their society's normal sex roles, so there is no reason to think that our intolerance is universal and, therefore, inevitable. These two lessons are well worth learning or, at least, pondering.

Still, some anthropologists today feel that this view disparages gender-crossed individuals, because, it assumes that they cannot live up to the expectations of their "real sex," so they are allowed to "alter their sex." Further, it assumes that, in all cultures, people classify individuals as belonging to one of only two genders (female and male), so that a woman who doesn't want to be completely a woman must become partly like a man, and vice versa. In fact, the term *gender crossing* itself implies that there are only two alternative genders.

In contrast, some contemporary anthropologists argue that many societies have more than two gender identities. Rather than dual genders, they say, such societies culturally construct **multiple gender identities.** Such peoples define a third or even a fourth gender of "man–woman" or "woman–man" (or "not woman–not man," or "half man–half woman," as some indigenous terms often translate). These third or fourth gender identities go beyond Euro-American definitions of homoeroticism, transvestism, transsexualism, or other concepts familiar in the Western cultural tradition.

Multiple gender identities are well documented for many Native American peoples. In his 1998 book *Changing Ones,* Will Roscoe reports that more than 150 Native American cultures had institutionalized multiple gender identities for males, or females, or both sexes. Males adopted the dress, tasks, family roles, or other aspects of womanhood. Females took on activities usually associated with manhood, such as warfare or hunting. When they did so, they did not become the opposite sex, but took on alternative third or fourth gender identities. Far from being ridiculed, ostracized, despised, or otherwise socially stigmatized, such individuals in most cases were treated with respect and valued for their contributions to their families or group.

Among the Navajo of the Southwest, for example, families and local communities generally welcomed third-gender persons. An anthropologist in the 1930s quoted a Navajo elder:

> If there were no *nadle* [men–women], the country would change. They are responsible for all the wealth in the country. If there were no more left, the horses, sheep, and Navaho would all go. They are leaders just like President Roosevelt. (Quoted in Roscoe 1998, 43)

The elder surely exaggerated, but his statement does indicate the Navajo's recognition of the contributions of men–women. They often managed their family's property, supervised work, and became medicine men or took on other ritual responsibilities. On the other hand, we should assume that Navajo (like other people) vary in their opinions, so there was unlikely to have been unanimous approval or tolerance of *nadle.*

People with female genitals could adopt alternative roles as well, which also were valued in many Native communities. A girl who came to be known as Woman Chief was adopted by a Crow family during the nineteenth century. Like boys, she hunted deer and bighorn

sheep while growing up. When the man who raised her was killed, she took responsibility for the family, acting as both father and mother. Later in life, she helped save her camp from an attack by the Blackfoot and went on horse raiding parties. Eventually Woman Chief took four wives and participated in council deliberations in her band, a role usually reserved for men.

Most Native tribes had a special word for such roles in their language, but gender identities varied so much from people to people that applying a single English word is problematic. To refer to males assuming an alternative gender, most anthropologists use the term *berdache,* taken from a term used by early French explorers of the Southeast. Some Natives and scholars today find this term inaccurate and offensive because the original Arabic term meant "male prostitute." But the Arabic meaning of *berdache* is not popularly known, so we continue to use it here, along with *man–woman, woman–man,* or *third or fourth gender identity,* depending on context.

As you might expect, most early Anglo observers of Native American men–women or women–men misunderstood these individuals and their roles in society. They overemphasized the sexual orientation of the person, whereas in fact their sexual behavior varied from tribe to tribe and from individual to individual within the same tribe. In most cases, even when *berdache* were homosexual, sexual behavior was not the aspect of the role that was considered the most important element by the people themselves. Further, male *berdache* rarely engaged in homosexual activity with *one another.* Where homosexuality was an aspect of the role, the men with whom relations occurred were not considered homosexuals at all.

Another common feature wrongly believed to define the role is transvestism, which, although common, was not found in all cultures. Sometimes men–women dressed like men, sometimes like women, and sometimes their choice of clothing depended on the situation. Among the Navajo, some *nadleehi* (men–women) wore women's clothing; others did not or only sometimes did so. Woman Chief, the adopted Crow woman, did not wear men's clothes, although she adopted many other aspects of the male role.

A complete portrayal of third and fourth genders defines the roles as multidimensional, thus recognizing that practices varied not only from tribe to tribe, but from individual to individual within the same tribe. Nonetheless, certain patterns are apparent. Serena Nanda identifies several features of gender variants that were widespread (but not universal) among Native American peoples. Four of the main characteristics are:

1. Cross-gender occupation or work activities—a preference for the work of the opposite sex and/or for work set aside for their third- or fourth-gender identity.
2. Transvestism—in most cultures third- and fourth-gender individuals were distinguished from men and women in their dress style. Most commonly they cross-dressed, but sometimes they wore a combination of female and male garments.
3. Associations with spiritual power or a spiritual sanction—possession of special powers derived from spiritual forces, usually combined with a personal experience interpreted by the group as a calling.
4. Same-sex relations—the formation of sexual and emotional bonds with members of the same sex, who were not themselves men–women or women–men.

These four widespread characteristics of third- and fourth-gender identities provide a convenient way to organize our discussion, but the variability of the role must always be kept in mind. No single dimension is "typical."

Cross-Gender Occupation or Work Roles

Adopting the work roles of the opposite sex was a widespread feature of men–women or women–men. This aspect often received special attention in various Native communities. Probably more than any other single dimension, occupation/work best defines the role. A famous Navajo *nadleehi* who died in the 1930s was unusually skilled in weaving blankets, a typically female task. In many tribes, individuals who performed the tasks of the opposite sex often excelled at the work, in the opinions of their communities. Sioux *berdache* (called *winkte*) dressed like women and lived in their own tipis at the edges of camps. The quill- and beadworks of a *winkte* were often highly valued because of their fine quality. Among the matrilineal, matrilocal Zuni of the American Southwest, a *lhamana* (man–woman) was looked upon favorably by the women of his family, for it meant he would stay with the household of his birth rather than leave upon marriage. Matilda Cox Stevenson, a nineteenth-century ethnographer, wrote that Zuni *lhamana* would do almost double the work of a woman, for they were not burdened by childbirth or the heaviest duties of child care. In spite of such examples, to say that all gender variants exhibited "sex role reversal" in work performance is simplistic, for the most famous Zuni man–woman was We'wha, who participated in both female and male tasks.

▲ An old photo of the Zuni *berdache* whose name was We'wha. We'wha was a valued member of his family and community. Here he is dressed as a woman.

Courtesy National Anthropological Archive, Smithsonian Institution

Commonly, a child who showed an inclination for the work of the opposite sex was considered by others to be suited for an alternative gender role. For example, girls who acted as though they wanted to go hunting or use weapons were seen as potential women–men. A Mohave adult told a 1930s ethnographer that "[adults] may insist on giving the child the toys and garments of its true sex, but the child will throw them away" (Roscoe 1998, 139). A child could not control such behavior, in the Mohave view, for the kinds of dreams a child had affected whether the child would become a man, a woman, a man–woman, or a woman–man. Among the Zuni, as children grow up they experience several rites of passage that initiate them into ceremonial groups and also instruct them in the ceremonial and work duties appropriate for their sex. While a child, one Zuni man–woman underwent the first male initiation ceremony but not the second, making him an "unfinished male" (Roscoe 1991, 144), who could participate in some male activities but not others, such as warfare and hunting.

Transvestism

Transvestism was one of the most common ways in which alternative genders expressed their identity. Wearing the clothing of the opposite sex was especially common and culturally significant among the tribes of the Great Plains, including the Arapaho, Arikara, Blackfoot, Cheyenne, Crow, Gros Ventre, Hidatsa, Iowa, Kansa, Mandan, Omaha, Osage, Oto, Pawnee, Ponca, and speakers of the Siouxan language. After whites began settling the West, most regarded men–women (which many simplistically categorized as "sodomites") as disgusting or sinful. Because it was a visible manifestation of the *berdache* role, transvestism was especially abhorrent to Anglo government officials, missionaries, educators, and settlers. Due to formal punishments and white ridicule, this symbol of alternative gender identity had largely disappeared by the early twentieth century.

Associations with Spiritual Powers

Usually, communities perceived men–women and women–men as having some sort of unusual powers or abilities derived from spiritual sources. The Cheyenne of the Great Plains used a term that translates "half man–half woman." They served as masters of ceremony for the important Scalp Dance that followed a successful raid by a war party. They also possessed powerful love medicines, so their services were sought by young men and women who wanted to attract heterosexual partners. Lakota believed that *winkte* could predict future events and could bestow lucky names on children. Osh-Tisch (whose name translated as "Finds Them and Kills Them"), of the Crow tribe, had a vision as a youth and became a powerful medicine person. One Navajo man–woman memorized numerous curing chants and learned to construct dozens of the intricate sandpaintings used in curing rituals (see Chapter 15). He was widely credited with near-miraculous healing powers.

Same-Sex Relations

The sexual orientation of Native American *berdache* varied from people to people (and from person to person within a single tribe). Understandably, reliable information on the sexual orientation of third- and fourth-gendered persons is rare. Some seem to have refrained

from sex altogether. But the most common pattern was for men–women to be sexually active with men and sometimes women, but not with other men–women. These relations (most Anglo-Americans or Canadians would culturally categorize them as "homosexual relations") in most cases were an expected aspect of the third- or fourth-gender role. Thus a (genitally) male *berdache* would engage in sex with men of his group, without stigma or punishment for either party. The man would not be considered homosexual, for he had not had relations with *another man,* but with a *man–woman.* In some tribes, a man would take a man–woman as a second "wife"—again apparently without stigma.

Even less is known about the sexual practices of women–men, and often early observers just stated that they were women who avoided marriage, or refused to marry. It appears, though, that they most commonly had relations with females. The complications of characterizing a person's sexual orientation are shown by a Mohave woman–man who had three wives (sequentially). All three eventually left her, and later in life the woman–man became very active sexually with men.

After contact with Euro-Americans, multiple gender identities were suppressed in most regions where Native Americans still lived, especially after the confinement of so many Natives to reservations in the 1800s. The majority of whites—settlers, traders, government agents, missionaries, and others—found the existence of a *legitimate* role such as man–woman or woman–man abhorrent. Because most viewed the custom as sinful, as harmful to Indian character, or as an obstacle to Native assimilation into Anglo society, they often imposed legal or social punishments for third and fourth genders. For example, in the 1920s, large numbers of Indian children were taken away from their families and communities—by force when necessary—and placed in on- or off-reservation government-run boarding schools. In these Indian Schools (as they are known today), the explicit goal was to socialize and educate Indian children into Anglo culture. By separating Native children from their families and traditions, the theory was, they could be more quickly and thoroughly assimilated into white society. Of course, young people who showed signs of assuming alternative gender identities were punished.

Through such educational and legal mechanisms, multiple gender identities were suppressed. Even some tribes that had once accepted third and fourth genders came to reject such persons. For instance, in the 1940s, some Winnebago told an ethnographer that "the *berdache* was at one time a highly honored and respected person, but that the Winnebago had become ashamed of the custom because the white people thought it was amusing or evil" (quoted in Roscoe 1991, 201).

In North American society generally, popular ideas about gender crossing and homosexuality changed dramatically in the late twentieth century. Polls show that most U.S. citizens favor giving spousal benefits such as medical care and life insurance to same-sex domestic partners. But the majority of people oppose same-sex marriage. Thus, in the November 2004 national elections in the United States, 11 states had ballot initiatives that defined marriage as a relation between a man and a woman. The initiatives passed in all states, and by very wide margins. Many large corporations now provide spousal benefits such as health insurance for domestic partners of either sex, partly reflecting the modern realities of the labor market and partly reflecting changes in society's attitudes about sexual preference. Despite such changes in attitudes, most North Americans still regard cross-dressing, transsexuality, and homoeroticism as deviant or perverted. Most conservative religious people view them as sinful, and even some Protestant denominations generally considered fairly liberal do not allow ordination of gays and lesbians.

Cultures such as the Native American examples mentioned here show that attitudes of fear, hatred, and intolerance of transsexuals and homosexuals are not universal. Indeed, acceptance and even appreciation of alternative genders is fairly common among Native peoples. Perhaps the knowledge that there are lots of cultures in which alternative genders are accepted is relevant for our attitudes about diversity in sexual orientation and other gender-related issues in twenty-first-century societies. Knowledge of such cultures must, however, be balanced by noting that there are a great many other peoples whose attitudes toward homoeroticism and gender crossing are highly negative.

The Sexual Division of Labor

The **sexual** (or **gendered**) **division of labor** refers to the patterned ways productive and other economic tasks are allocated to men and women. Each sex has access to the products and/or services produced by the other, making the tasks of males and females, to some extent, complementary. The sexual division of labor is one aspect of a human group's **gender** (or **sex**) **roles**—the rights, duties, expectations one acquires by virtue of one's sex. Of course, the specific tasks performed by the two sexes vary.

It is interesting to compare humans with other primate species, particularly with African apes (gorillas and chimpanzees). One type of work that most human groups divide up according to sex is subsistence work—productive activities that provide domestic groups with food. Whether African apes can be said to "work" in the same sense as humans is debatable, but we can think of their foraging for food as equivalent to human work. It then would be accurate to say that African apes do not divide up work to the same degree as most human groups. Male and female gorillas forage separately for leaves and fruits, and for the most part each sex eats what they "gather." Among chimpanzees, a species that does engage in some hunting and meat eating, it is the males who hunt. Sometimes they share the meat with females, sometimes not. Chimpanzees do share food, however, and even have behavior that looks like "begging." And of course mothers regularly provide food to their offspring. Still, on a day-to-day basis, only humanity systematically divides labor by sex and allows or requires each sex to make the products of work available to domestic partners.

It may be an exaggeration to say that the sexual division of labor is one of our species' unique attributes, but clearly no ape divides work to the same degree as do human groups. It is also true that various populations of gorillas and chimpanzees hardly vary in the degree to which male apes dominate female apes. In contrast, human groups not only divide labor by sex, but also do so in diverse ways, and human groups do vary in the degree to which one sex "dominates" (controls, makes decisions for) the other. This raises an interesting possibility: Could variations in the sexual division of labor be related to variations in the degree of sexual dominance? We pursue this topic in the next section.

In more developed nations, the sexual division of labor, and indeed the roles of males and females in general, is rapidly changing: males are performing tasks and holding occupational roles that 20 or 30 years ago were associated with females, and vice versa. In many other societies, however, the social roles of females and males are more sharply divided and the sexual division of labor is more clearly defined.

One misconception about this topic should be corrected immediately: that it is only natural for men to be the breadwinners for their family. Hundreds of field studies provide all the data needed to falsify this idea. Breadwinning—that is, producing the supply of food and other material needs and wants of domestic groups—is definitely not an activity of men exclusively, or even largely. As we shall see, in many societies men produce most of the food, but in others women's contribution to daily subsistence equals or exceeds that of men.

This finding contradicts the opinion of those who think that the widespread domination of men over women is rooted in the "fact" that men's work is more important to physical survival and material well-being than women's work. Those who hold this view argue that women are everywhere economically dependent on men, which in turn makes women everywhere socially subordinate to men. But where females are subordinate to males, it is not because the things men do are somehow more important to family and group survival than the things women do. (What could be more important to group survival than bearing children?) This ethnocentric idea probably comes from the way most modern industrial economies worked in the mid-twentieth century: by and large, men earned the money that allowed their families to purchase the goods they needed to survive. It is falsely concluded that the same economic dependence of wives on husbands characterized other peoples.

This is the anthropologist's usual warning about confusing the beliefs and practices of one's own experience with those of all humans. Most people's ideas about what is and is not "natural" for humans to think and do are products of a specific culture at a particular time. Unless we become educated about the cultural diversity of humanity, we consistently—and usually mistakenly—conclude that the ideas and practices of our own society are universal or even inherent in human nature.

So Man the Breadwinner and Woman the Homemaker do not accurately describe the sexual division of labor in other cultures. Humankind is too diverse for that. But despite cultural variation, there are some cross-cultural regularities and patterns in the sexual division of labor. What are these patterns, and can they be explained?

Understanding Major Patterns

Table 11.1 summarizes a vast amount of comparative work on the sexual division of labor. It lists some specific tasks and whether they are more likely to be performed

Table 11.1 Patterns in the Sexual Division of Labor

General Category of Activity	Tasks That Are Performed By				
	Exclusively Males	**Predominantly Males**	**Either or Both Sexes**	**Predominantly Females**	
Extracting Food and Other Products	Hunting Trapping	Fishing	Gathering small land animals	Gathering shellfish, mollusks	Gathering wild plant foods
		Clearing land Preparing soil	Planting crops Tending crops Harvesting crops		
		Tending large animals	Milking animals	Care of small animals	
	Woodworking Mining Lumbering			Gathering fuel	Fetching water
Manufacturing, Processing, and Preparing Goods for Consumption	Butchering				Processing, preparing plant foods
	Boat building Working with stone, horn, bone, shell	House building Making rope, cordage, nets	Preparing skins Making leather products	Cooking Making clothing Matmaking Loom weaving	
	Smelting ore Metalworking			Making pottery	

Source: Adapted from Murdock and Provost (1973).

by females or males. Those tasks toward the left of the table are more likely to be performed by males; those to the right are more likely to be done by females. The nearer a task is to the left, the more likely it is to be performed by males, and vice versa for females.

A few comments are needed to clarify Table 11.1. First, the table does not portray the sexual division of labor in any specific society. Rather, it represents a kind of composite or aggregate of information drawn from hundreds of societies in various parts of the world. For example, the tasks listed as "Predominantly Females" should be interpreted as those that are done by women in most societies, although in some specific societies one or another of the tasks are performed mainly by men. Tasks listed as "Exclusively Males" should be understood as those that are carried out by men in all or almost all societies, with very few exceptions.

Also, Table 11.1 includes only those activities that produce some kind of material product. Left out of the table are other activities that are predominantly or exclusively male, such as holding political office and fighting in wars. Also omitted are some activities, such as caring for infants, that are predominantly or exclusively women's work in all cultures. Of course, there is a sense in which all activities are "productive" (of social order, group defense, or children, for example), but here our discussion is limited to activities usually considered to be "economic tasks."

Two patterns are revealed by Table 11.1. First, all human groups divide *some* kinds of labor by sex in similar ways. That is, some tasks are done mainly or nearly exclusively by one sex in most societies. For instance, hunting, land clearing, soil preparation, working with hard materials, and cutting wood are exclusively or predominantly men's work in the great majority of societies. Gathering wild plants, processing plant foods, and cooking are mainly the work of females in almost all cultures. In short, although the table shows that groups vary in the kinds of tasks allocated to women and men, there are *widespread* (although not *universal*) patterns; consistently, some tasks are more likely to be done by men, others by women. The first thing to explain is: Why are some tasks done mostly by women, whereas others are done mainly or entirely by men?

Second, notice the tasks listed under the column labeled "Either or Both Sexes." These tasks are not sex-specific—that is, they are about equally likely to be performed by men or women, depending on the particular society. Members of either sex may do them, or both may work cooperatively on them. For example, whether men or women plant, tend and harvest crops, milk animals, or

work with skins or leather varies from people to people, with no clear pattern apparent. In sum, which sex performs these kinds of tasks is so culturally variable that we cannot generalize about who will do them; whether they are done by women, men, or both depends largely on local circumstances. The second thing to explain is: What determines the cultural variability in the sexual division of labor? Why are women more heavily involved in agriculture (planting, tending, and harvesting crops) in some societies than in others, for example?

This section focuses on hypotheses that deal with the first question. We put off discussion of the second question until the next section.

What explains why some tasks are nearly always done by men, whereas others are performed by women in most cultures? Biological/physical differences between the sexes provide one possible explanation. Perhaps tasks are assigned in such a way that the members of each sex do what they are physically able to do best.

This notion seems like biological determinism. If stated properly, though, it is not. Physical differences between men and women are only *relevant* in explaining the sexual division, not *determinative*. To claim that biological differences alone account for (determine) similarities

▲ Certain tasks are carried out largely or exclusively by men in all premodern cultures. Cutting wood is one such task, perhaps because it requires significant strength.

▲ Processing and preparing food is largely a female task in most cultures. This Central African Republic woman is grinding cassava.

would be outrageously wrong. The sexual division of labor *varies* cross-culturally, whereas the biological differences between females and males are *similar* everywhere. You cannot explain something that *varies* from people to people by something that is the *same* among all people.

Rather, to say that physical differences between the sexes are relevant is to say something like the following: Because of biological differences, men can perform certain kinds of tasks more effectively than women, and vice versa, and these differences are reflected in the widespread cross-cultural similarities in the sexual division of labor.

Consider an example. Anthropologists used to say that there was one task that was everywhere done by men: hunting. Hunting seems to require certain biological capabilities—such as speed, strength, and endurance—that gives men an advantage over women. Hunting also was thought to be incompatible with certain responsibilities universally borne by women for biological reasons: pregnancy, lactation (breastfeeding), and child care.

Pregnant women would have a hard time chasing game; lactating mothers would have to quit the hunt several times a day to nurse their infants; and the risk of injury to both mother and young child would be high. Because men could hunt more effectively than women, in foraging populations men hunted. In contrast, gathering required less strength and endurance. Since men had to spend so much of their time hunting, which women couldn't do as effectively, gathering became largely women's work.

These arguments are partly valid, but female and male biological differences do not make it physically mandatory that males are the hunters and females are the gatherers in foraging populations. For one thing, not all kinds of hunting, and not all tasks connected to hunting, require superior strength, speed, and endurance. For another, there are questions about whether males typically have more "endurance" than females. Finally, there is no necessary biological reason why a woman could not give up hunting only during her pregnancy and lactation and leave her older children in camp under the care of someone else.

In fact, it is just not true that hunting is *universally* a male activity. When BaMbuti Pygmies of the Zaire rain forest hunt animals with nets, the women help by driving game into the nets held by men. In another part of the world, Agnes Estioko-Griffin describes hunting by women among the Agta, a mountain tribe of the Philippines who live on the island of Luzon. Agta men do most of the hunting, but women often accompany them in teamwork efforts, and women frequently hunt together without the company of men. Interestingly, sometimes women take their infants with them on the hunt, carrying the children on their backs. There are some differences between the methods used and types of game hunted by women versus men. Still, people like the Agta and BaMbuti show that the "man the hunter" image is oversimplified.

But such cases do not make it entirely wrong. The great majority of peoples in which hunting is a significant means of acquiring food are foragers or horticulturalists. In most foraging cultures women do most of the gathering of wild plants, although men may contribute among the !Kung, Aka, and BaMbuti Pygmies, and other peoples. Among horticultural peoples, the *pattern* is for women to do most planting, weeding, and harvesting of cultivated plants, whereas men hunt to provide meat. These patterns are not *universal* (no pattern is among humanity), but they are *widespread* enough that many anthropologists believe that there must be some physical differences between men and women that are relevant in explaining it.

© Barry D. Kass/Images of Anthropology

Factors Affecting the Major Patterns in the Sexual Division of Labor

Fertility Maintenance	Heavy, prolonged physical exercise by women results in lowered body fat and hormonal changes that reduce female fertility, so most strenuous tasks are done by males.
Reproductive Roles	Only a few males are needed to sustain and increase population size, so societies protect their females by assigning hazardous tasks to males.
Physical Strength	Most men are stronger than most women, so tasks requiring greater strength generally are performed by males.
Child-Care Compatibility	Women are everywhere the bearers and primary caregivers for infants and young children, so they tend to perform those tasks that can be combined efficiently with child care.

What specific female/male biological differences are likely to be most relevant in explaining cross-cultural similarities in the sexual division of labor? Four main arguments have been proposed, briefly summarized in the Concept Review: (1) the possibility that regular heavy exercise depresses female fertility, (2) the fact that women and men have different roles in reproducing the population, (3) the relative overall strength of the two sexes, and (4) the biological fact that only women give birth to and nurse infants and young children. We discuss each factor, although the first two do not seem very plausible in the view of the authors.

Fertility Maintenance. One potentially relevant physical characteristic is that heavy exercise can reduce a woman's fertility. Modern female athletes—especially long-distance runners—often do not menstruate and ovulate monthly. Apparently, this is because of a low ratio of body fat and complex hormonal changes in women who engage in prolonged physical exercise. Some anthropologists suggest that work activities requiring heavy exertion would reduce the fertility of women. For example, with preindustrial technologies, hunting often requires weapons such as bows and spears that are powered by muscles alone, locating and tracking prey, and running down animals once they are shot. Lumbering and clearing land for planting also involve physical exertion such as swinging heavy axes for hours at a time. Conceivably, female fertility would be so decreased by such strenuous activities that the population would not be sustained over the course of many generations.

However, hunting among most foragers and horticulturalists is not as strenuous as portrayed, nor are many other activities that are exclusively or largely done by males. In fact, women commonly do work that is as physically demanding as that done by men: hauling water, gathering firewood for fuel, and planting and harvesting crops are among many work tasks that women perform in a great many societies. Although fertility maintenance could be relevant among a few peoples, it is unlikely to be a widespread factor and certainly does not account for any widespread patterns in the sexual division of labor.

Reproductive Roles of Women versus Men. Another possibility arises from the fact that fewer men than women are biologically necessary to maintain or increase a population size. As sociobiologists point out, a man produces enough sperm to father many thousands of children (theoretically). A woman can only bear a child every year or so. Because only a few sexually active men can impregnate a large number of women, the size of the population seemingly depends more on the number of women than the number of men. Also, in all known societies, women are far more involved in the care of infants and young children than men. For these reasons, speaking only of reproduction, fewer males than females are needed to sustain a population. For the sexual division of labor, this biological difference might imply that males are more expendable, which helps explain why so many hazardous roles (most importantly, hunting and fighting battles) are male roles: the group can afford to sacrifice some of its males but must protect its females as much as possible. If men "have" to perform such dangerous roles, then many other tasks are left to women by default.

However, males are only expendable "theoretically," and if "all else is equal." In those societies—and there are a great many of them—in which warfare is a serious threat, large numbers of males are needed to protect the entire group. In fact, among many peoples, group survival itself depends on the ability to mobilize many warriors and to make political/military alliances with friendly neighbors. Only in their reproductive role are males "expendable"; in other respects, large numbers of males are essential for group survival. *If* there is a biological explanation for males performing more hazardous activities, it is because they are better equipped physically to do so, not because a group finds many of its males to be expendable.

Relative Strength. Another biological factor is the average difference in physical strength between men and women, which allows men to perform tasks requiring great strength more efficiently. In Table 11.1, superior average male strength is *relevant*—once again, no anthropologist claims it is "determinative"—in many tasks under the heading "Exclusively Males" and in some of the tasks labeled "Predominantly Males," such as clearing land and preparing soil. On the other hand, male strength has no obvious relation to other exclusively or predominantly male tasks, such as trapping, butchering, and working with fibers. Also, note that women often do tasks

▲ The relative average strength of the sexes is one factor in the sexual division of labor, but this Pygmy woman carrying a heavy load of firewood illustrates that strength is not a "determinant."

that require significant strength, such as gathering fuel and fetching water. Relative strength does influence patterns in the sexual division of labor, but other factors also matter.

Compatibility with Child Care. A fourth biologically based difference is that women are the bearers, nursers, and primary caregivers of infants and young children. This reproductive fact means that women are most likely to perform those tasks that can be combined with pregnancy and child care. Back in 1970, Judith Brown argued that such tasks have several characteristics:

• They are fairly routine and repetitive, so they do not require much concentration.
• They can be interrupted and resumed without significantly lowering their efficient performance.
• They do not place the children who accompany their mothers to the site of the task in potential danger.
• They do not require women and children to travel very far away from home.

The gathering of various products and the domestic work listed in Table 11.1 are highly compatible with child care. In addition, among horticultural peoples, garden tasks such as planting, weeding and tending crops, and harvesting usually are done by women; these activities, too, generally seem to be highly compatible with caring for children. Notice that child-care compatibility is likely to be a more important factor among peoples with high fertility. Where most couples have few children, this factor becomes less relevant as a basis for allocating productive work.

In sum, biological factors do help explain cross-cultural patterns in the sexual division of labor. Female–male differences in strength and child-care roles have the most widespread relevance, although the other two factors might matter among specific peoples. Notice, though, that even if all four factors in combination "explain" the widespread patterns in the sexual division of labor shown in Table 11.1 (which they do not), none of them can explain the *differences*. In fact, no biological difference between males and females alone can explain the cross-cultural diversity in the sexual division of labor. The biological differences between the sexes in strength, reproductive physiology, and ability to care for infants are roughly constant in all human populations. But a condition that is constant in all groups cannot, by itself, account for things that vary between the groups. Constants cannot explain variability and diversity. We need other hypotheses to account for the cross-cultural variability in the sexual division of labor.

Understanding Variability

Here we focus on only one of the most important variations. Comparative studies reveal a fairly consistent pattern in the degree of women's versus men's involvement in certain agricultural tasks, specifically in those tasks labeled "Either or Both Sexes" in the middle column of Table 11.1. Recall the distinction between horticulture and intensive agriculture (Chapter 6). In most horticultural groups, much—and in some societies nearly all—of the everyday garden work is done by women. For example, in traditional cultures in parts of the Pacific, the Amazon basin, tropical Africa, and North America, women do most of the planting, weeding, tending, and harvesting of crops, whereas men participate in farming by clearing new land and preparing the plots or fields for planting. In contrast, among peoples who rely more heavily on intensive agriculture, women's actual work in the fields and direct contribution to the food supply are less important. To phrase the relationship in a few words: Women are more likely to be involved in direct food production in horticultural than in intensive agricultural communities.

There seem to be several reasons for this general pattern. First, in the New World horticultural Native Americans had few or no domesticated animals, so men's contribution to the food supply focused on hunting. Most routine garden work fell to women, for such work is generally compatible with pregnancy and child care. In contrast, most intensive agriculturalists relied on livestock for meat, dairy products, hides, wool, and other products derived from animals, so men spent relatively little time in hunting. They had more time for farming.

Also, prior to the twentieth century, in Europe and Asia nearly all intensive agriculturalists used the animal-powered plow to turn the earth prior to planting. Some researchers have suggested that most women are not strong enough to perform the heavy work of plowing efficiently. (You might remember, though, that draft animals provide most of the muscle power for plow agriculture, which makes this suggestion difficult to evaluate. Also note that men are stronger than women only "on average.")

There is another reason women are less involved in direct cultivation in intensive agricultural societies. In Europe and Asia ("Eurasia") the horticultural and intensive agricultural adaptations tend to involve the farming of different kinds of crops. Roughly half of horticultural societies grow *root crops* like yams, sweet potatoes, manioc (cassava), or taro. In contrast, about 90 percent of intensive agriculturalists rely on *cereal crops* like rice, wheat, corn, barley, and millet.

This difference in crop type affects the sexual division of labor. Root crops can be stored in the ground for long periods after they first become ready to eat, so they typically are harvested continuously during the growing season (think of familiar root crops like carrots or potatoes, which you pull or dig up as needed). Either daily or a few times weekly, a woman goes to the garden and returns with root crops for herself, her children, and her husband. In contrast, cereals (because they are the seeds of plants) tend to ripen at about the same time each year, usually near the end of the growing season. They have to be harvested in a short period of time, dried and processed, and stored for the rest of the year.

How does crop type affect the work of men and women? Cereal crops generally require a lot of labor to process (e.g., winnowing, drying, grinding) before cooking. Plant processing labor is women's work in most cultures (Table 11.1). Further, people who rely on wheat, rice, barley, or other cereal grains usually face periods of intense labor requirements: At the beginning of the growing season and at harvest time, there is a need for laborers who can do a lot of hot, heavy work in a short period that is best not interrupted by other tasks. Such work is generally done by men (see the previous section). In contrast, root-growing horticultural peoples tend to spread cultivation tasks out more evenly over the entire year, making gardening a day-in, day-out, repetitive task that requires less strength and that is more compatible with child care.

A third influence is warfare. Men in most horticultural communities were responsible for defending the local village, neighborhood, or kin group from their enemies. In regions such as highland New Guinea and parts of the Amazon, group survival depended on the ability to defend land and resources from attack. Community welfare often was improved by taking over the land of enemy neighbors, so offensive as well as defensive warfare was common. Men were not actually fighting their enemies most of the time, of course, but maintaining community defenses and guarding against surprise raids did require significant amounts of (predominantly male) time.

For most peoples, the odds of success in warfare were improved by making alliances with other groups, which required a lot of politicking, mutual visiting, and exchanges, further consuming male time and energy. Also, male solidarity ("male bonding") was advantageous, so in many groups where warfare was prevalent there were elaborate male-only rituals or social events that strengthened ties between men and helped socialize boys into manhood and the warrior role (see the discussion of the Awa in Chapter 10 for an example). All these pressures connected to defensive and offensive warfare led men to concentrate much of their time and resources in fighting, preparing to fight, or maintaining political relations needed for success in organized fights. Routine garden tasks were left to women, partly by default.

To summarize, comparative research indicates that women are less involved in direct food production in intensive agricultural systems than in horticultural systems. Three of the most important factors that influence female involvement in cultivation tasks are:

- In horticultural adaptations, more of men's time is spent in hunting than in intensive agricultural adaptations, so men have less time for producing plant foods.
- Compared to horticultural communities, intensive agriculturalists are more likely to grow cereal crops, which makes it more likely that men will concentrate more on farm work, women more on domestic work, including processing foods.
- Horticultural peoples tend to be subjected to pressure from hostile neighbors, so men are busier fighting, guarding, politicking, exchanging, and creating bonds and relationships among themselves.

In brief, as agricultural systems become more intensive, other factors change that usually lead to reduced women's involvement in direct food production.

It is important to emphasize that these relationships are *generalized,* meaning that they may not hold for any particular people. Horticultural peoples "tend to" be more affected by warfare pressures, intensive agriculturalists are "more likely to" grow cereals than roots, and so forth. Obviously, there are many exceptions to the general patterns.

Consider the Kofyar of Nigeria, for example. They construct terraces, spread goat manure over their fields, use compost, and practice other methods of increasing yields that lead anthropologists who observe them to call their farming "intensive." Yet quantitative studies in the 1990s reveal that Kofyar women work about as much as men in agriculture. The Kofyar and many other peoples do not have the relationship between cultivation intensity and male labor that comparative research says they "ought to have" or "predicts they will have."

The Kofyar and other exceptions to the general pattern illustrate two other points. First, the existence of a general relationship established by comparative research does not tell us what any particular group of people are doing or thinking. The culture of any people is a product of a complex interaction among their history, adaptation, beliefs, and other factors. In any particular group, factors *unique* to that group may be more important than factors that are *generally* important. So the fact that Kofyar women work the land about as much as men, even though the Kofyar farm the land intensively, does not "disprove"

the general point that women's labor becomes less important as land use becomes more intensive.

Second, just because there are exceptions does not invalidate a generalization provided, of course, that the general pattern is well established. If we are interested in the factors that influence the cultural variations in the sexual division of labor, then we must do comparative work to look for general patterns. The fact that particular cultures do not fit the pattern does not invalidate the generalization—at least not until the number of exceptions becomes large enough to make us suspicious of the existence of the general pattern.

At any rate, the preceding discussion represents an excellent example of cultural materialism, discussed in Chapter 4. The way a population exploits its habitat (by horticulture or more intensive methods) greatly affects the kinds of tasks women and men do (given the physical differences between the sexes and given the biological fact that women give birth to and nurse children). So the material conditions of life in a certain kind of adaptation interact with biological differences between women and men to produce the overall pattern of the division of labor along gender lines. That, at least, is the argument.

Gender Stratification

A fourth main issue in the anthropological study of gender is **gender stratification,** or the degree to which human groups allocate material and social rewards to women and men *based on their gender.* Other sources of unequal rewards include class, caste, family origins, and race (as discussed in other chapters). Here we discuss only rewards based on whether one is a male or a female. We ignore such complications as third- or fourth-gender identities.

Gender stratification is also often referred to as "the status of women," with the implied phrase "relative to men." Whatever we call it, gender stratification is difficult to define, for it includes many components that interact in complex ways. Here are some of these components, including for each component questions whose answer would indicate high, moderate, low, or nonexistent gender stratification for some culture:

- The kinds of social roles men and women perform: Are some roles limited to males only or to females only? If so, which roles and how are they valued?
- The cultural value attached to women's and men's contributions to their families and other groups: Are men's contributions viewed as more important and more rewarded than women's?

- Female deference to males: Do women defer socially to their husbands or male relatives? How much and in what contexts?
- Access to positions of power and influence: Do women hold offices in the political arena? Can and do women control family or household members and domestic tasks?
- Control over personal decision making: Do women control their own lives by making marital, sexual, childbearing, work, leisure, and other important decisions for themselves?
- General beliefs and ideas about the sexes: Are men considered to be superior to women intellectually, psychologically, and/or physically?

These are some of the main dimensions that should be considered in evaluating the degree of gender stratification in particular cultures. Think of the list as some of the main features that constitute the overall pattern of gender stratification in particular cultures. Obviously, gender stratification is *multidimensional,* which makes it difficult to categorize it as "high" or "low" even within a single culture. Why is it so difficult?

For one thing, some of the components are not consistent with other components. For example, studies of family life often report that women have a great deal of control in making decisions about child rearing and about the allocation of domestic resources, even though they have little independence outside the domestic context. For instance, in two Andalusian towns of south Spain, David Gilmore's fieldwork showed that wives have great autonomy in managing household affairs. He believes this is because many women are able to live near their own mothers, so that wives and their mothers frequently "gang up" on a husband. Even in male-dominated societies like traditional Korea, Japan, and China, the eldest female in a household usually had the right to manage household affairs with a fair degree of autonomy. Yet in these countries, and in many other societies, women were not allowed to participate in public affairs, had hardly any property of their own, had little say over whom they married, and were clearly subordinate to their fathers, husbands, and husband's fathers socially and even legally.

Added to the fact that specific aspects of women's status vary according to social context and situation is the fact that distinctions of rank or class (considered in Chapter 13) or of ethnic affiliation (Chapter 17) often override male–female distinctions. In modern North America, most professional white women enjoy higher living standards and achieve more of what their culture values than do working-class black men—what shall we say about overall stratification when "gender stratification," "ethnic stratification," and "class stratification" do not coincide?

A final factor complicating gender stratification is that, in most cultures, a woman's status changes over the course of her life. For example, most scholars agree that "the status of women" was comparatively low in most of traditional East Asia and South Asia. In all three regions, most families were patrilocally extended (Chapter 8), so when women married they left their own family and moved into or near the house of their husband's parents. A young wife was subjected to the authority of her husband's mother and was duty-bound to work extremely hard. But as a woman settled into the household, had a son, and aged, her status improved and she gradually took over control from her mother-in-law. When the latter died, she became the everyday manager of the household and became an authority figure over her own daughters-in-law after her sons married. The same pattern of women's status improving with age appears in numerous other cultures.

So we must avoid thinking of gender stratification as a unitary phenomenon. Like other social relations, male–female relations are complex. This is not surprising. Concepts like "the status of women" or "gender stratification" are concepts used by contemporary social scientists, not universal concepts. The people whose lives anthropologists study may not have such cultural concepts at all. Nor are women's and men's lives in any community so simple that anthropologists (or for that matter, anyone else) can categorize them unambiguously by statements like "women have low status in culture X." (This point— that simple categorizations are misleading—is one you might remember when a friend bemoans how some region, or country, or religion "suppresses women.")

Universal Subordination?

In spite of the complications, there are significant cross-cultural variations in gender stratification. Even those humanistic anthropologists who mistrust comparisons and objective measurements recognize that there is much less gender stratification among the Native American Hopi and Iroquois than among the Yąnomamö of the Amazon basin. Gender stratification is a meaningful concept to use for answering certain questions such as: Are there societies in which women and men are equal? Are there societies in which women dominate men?

The answer to the second question is no. Despite the stories we sometimes read or the occasional old adventure movie in which the hero finds himself captured by "amazons," not a single instance of clear female domination over men has ever been found by ethnographers. *Matriarchy*—rule by women over men—does not exist, nor has it ever existed, to the best of our knowledge. Clearly there have been and are individual women who hold great power, control great wealth, and are held in high esteem. Certainly there are queens, female chiefs, and individual matriarchs of families and kin groups. But no clear instance of matriarchy—women as a social category holding power over men as a social category—has been documented.

The first question, of whether cultures exist in which men and women are equal, has a more uncertain and complex answer. Even anthropologists who have devoted their careers to studying gender cannot agree. On the one hand, some scholars believe that women are never considered to be fully equal to men. They interpret the ethnographic record as showing that an asymmetry always exists between the sexes in one or more areas of life.

Those who believe that male dominance/female subordination is a cultural universal point to two fairly well-established generalizations. One applies to political institutions. In political life, sexual asymmetry always exists. In no known society are the primary political authority roles restricted to females. But in many societies all women are denied the right to succeed to political offices. In the majority of cases even kin-group leadership roles are dominated by men. Male elders of the lineage or clan decide how the group's land and other resources are to be used and allocated, how the group's wealth objects are to be disposed of, whether the group is to engage in a battle to avenge a wrong, and so on. (But as we shall soon see, women often do have significant influence over these matters, especially in matrilineal societies.)

The other realm of life in which sexual asymmetry is found is religion. In many societies women are excluded from performing major religious leadership roles. To be sure, there are societies—lots of them, in fact—in which women have their own *particular rituals* from which men are excluded. But there are no known societies in which males are excluded from participation in all important rituals. In contrast, there are many societies in which females are forbidden to participate in the most important rituals. Finally, in some cultures men believe that women are dangerous to their health and well-being. In many New Guinea societies—the Hua and Awa, for instance—men believe that their health or masculinity is jeopardized if they come into contact with women's menstrual discharges, so women must seclude themselves during their periods to avoid harming the men. Women may be punished—sometimes severely—for suspected violations.

According to some scholars, then, the activities of males are everywhere regarded as more important than those of females. Women as a social category are everywhere culturally devalued relative to men as a social category. Women are universally subordinate to men.

But the ethnographic record can be interpreted differently. Many scholars note that most fieldworkers—and hence most of the ethnographic data available to shed light on the issue of universal female subordination—have been biased in two ways. The first is the *androcentric* (male) bias. Most of the fieldwork until the 1970s was done by males, who usually were uninterested in the females of the cultures they studied. At any rate, simply because they were themselves males, fieldworkers had little access to women's points of view, so they often unwittingly took the men's values, attitudes, and opinions as representative of the entire group. Female points of view were largely unreported.

The second source of fieldwork bias in the study of gender is *Eurocentric* bias. Because of the inequalities in wealth, power, and status in Western (European-derived) societies, Western anthropologists might perceive relations of inequality, hierarchy, and domination/subordination even among cultures where they are less developed. For instance, when a wife greets her husband by bowing her head or stays behind him while walking, Western fieldworkers may interpret such behaviors as indications of female subordination, when in fact they are merely public demonstrations of politeness.

In short, some scholars think that many fieldworkers have been sexually and culturally biased. Because of this bias, the ethnographic record is not objective; it "records" a universal female subordination not justified by the real world. It is worth mentioning, though, that those who accuse others of bias may be biased themselves, and especially if a subject is as politically charged as that of gender.

Some ethnologists who have looked at the "ethnographic facts" have found examples of what they consider sexual equality. Anthropologists who believe that female–male equality does exist in some cultures can point to particular peoples whom they think document their belief. The Iroquois, a matrilineal and matrilocal people of northeastern North America, are the most famous ethnographic example of women achieving equality (or is it only relative equality?) with men. Iroquois women produced the corn and other cultivated foods, put them in storage, and largely controlled how they were distributed from the storehouses. Iroquois men were away from their apartments in the longhouse much of the time, engaged in warfare or cooperative hunting expeditions. After the introduction of the fur trade into northeastern North America in the seventeenth century, men often were away searching for beaver pelts or raiding their neighbors for pelts. The matrilineally related women of a longhouse influenced their inmarried husbands' behavior by withholding provisions from their hunting trips and war parties. Only men had the right to hold the most powerful political leadership offices because only males could be elected to the great council of chiefs. But it was the older women of the various matrilineages who selected their groups' representatives to the council. These women also had the right to remove and replace men who did not adequately represent the group's interests. Also, women had a voice in the deliberations of the council itself. They could veto declarations of war and introduce peace-making resolutions.

So are women subordinate to men in all societies or not? Certainly, some male ethnographers have been biased—but does this bias account for their reports of female subordination? Certainly, the Iroquois, the Hopi (Chapter 10), and many other peoples demonstrate that women in some cultures have achieved considerable control over their own lives and over public decision making—but do such cases represent *full equality* of males and females? Indeed, would we know "total equality" if we saw it in a society? What would it look like? Would men and women have to carry out the same kinds of economic tasks before we could say they are completely equal? Is monogamy necessary, or can a society be polygynous and still qualify? Shall we require that women occupy 50 percent of all leadership roles before we say they have equal rights? How should family life be organized before we can say that husbands in culture X do not dominate their wives?

As you can see, many questions must be answered before we can say whether women are everywhere subordinate—the most important of which is how we would know complete gender equality if we were to encounter it!

Perhaps too much weight is given to the issue of universal male dominance. Many anthropologists think their discipline must ferret out human cultures in which women and men are equal for ethnographic data to lend support for the feminist cause. Feminist psychologists, sociologists, historians, biologists, and other scholars likewise have examined ethnographic descriptions of various Other Cultures, looking for "matriarchy" or "equality." Their reasoning is that, if numerous cultures can be found in which women have achieved equality, then women will be more likely to achieve equality in the future. Their hope is that there are many such cultures. Their fear is that there are few or none.

But the ethnographic record on the issue of sexual equality—though not silent—is filled with ambiguity and uncertainty. At any rate, how much does it matter for the cause of sexual equality *today* if women are "universally" or "nearly universally" subordinate? Perhaps what matters most is that women and men are a good deal more equal in some societies than in others, which allows us to study the conditions under which future equality is likely to be possible. To argue that, because women have always or usually been subordinate they will forever be subordinate, is analogous to pre-twentieth-century arguments that humans will never be able to fly. Just because no human group has achieved some state in the past does

◄ Iroquois women's control over cultivated foods and their distribution gave them relatively high status.

© Stock Montage

not mean that none will achieve it in the future. It does not mean that we should give up trying to achieve it today and for the future. And it certainly does not mean that women alive in the twenty-first century have achieved about all the equality they are likely to achieve.

So anthropologists really can't say whether women are universally subordinate, because it is too difficult to decide what would constitute "complete" gender equality. A more answerable question, though, is: What influences the degree of gender stratification in a society?

Influences on Gender Stratification

Gender stratification is affected by a multitude of factors. So far no one has shown that any small number of forces are the primary determinants of women's status in all times and places. Here we discuss only a few generalizations that point to the kinds of influences that are most widespread and important.

Women's Contributions to Material Welfare. Many people argue that women's role in production strongly influences their property rights, their role in public affairs, their degree of personal freedom, and other dimensions of their overall status. One idea is that, where women produce a high proportion of the food, shelter, clothing, and other necessities of existence, men will recognize their contributions and reward women with influence, property, prestige, dignity, and other benefits. In other words, the sexual division of labor and the proportion of valued goods women produce are strong influences on women's overall status.

Such ideas might apply to some foraging and horticultural peoples, among whom women's gathering or gardening contributes much of the food consumed by their domestic groups. Women's productive labor might give them a status that is closer to equality with men than they have in other forms of adaptation in which their subsistence contributions are not as great. For example, among the BaMbuti and Aka, two foraging Pygmy groups of the central African rain forest, women's labor is critical for success in net hunting, and ethnographic reports on both these Pygmy peoples report male–female equality or near equality. Among the !Kung, too, considerable equality exists between women and men.

But everyone's status is "closer to equality" in most hunter-gatherer and many horticultural populations (see Chapters 7 and 13). So perhaps the relative lack of gender stratification in these adaptations results not from women's importance as food providers but from some other factor or influence "leveling out" social inequalities of all kinds.

Women's Control over Key Resources. A more complex proposal is that women's contribution to production, by itself, is not enough to "earn" them relative equality. It is *necessary* for women to contribute heavily to material welfare to gain resources, rights, and respect, but this alone is not *sufficient*. (To see why, consider enslaved persons.) One specific hypothesis is that women must also own productive resources (land, tools), or have considerable control over the distribution of the products of their labor, or both. If women own productive resources and have a great deal of say over what happens to the goods they produce, then they can have some influence on the activities of men. Overall, this gives them more equality. Peggy Sanday found some support for this hypothesis in a cross-cultural study done in the 1970s.

This hypothesis seems to account reasonably well for some specific cases. For instance, Iroquois women controlled the production and distribution of important resources. They used this control to nominate their kinsmen to chiefly positions and to influence the public decision making from which they were formally excluded. Likewise, Hopi (see Chapter 10) women owned land and had considerable control over the distribution of its products. Women had relatively high status in both these societies, as they did among many other Native American peoples.

Along the same lines, in many West African and Caribbean societies, women are more active than men in market trade in foodstuffs, handicrafts, textiles, and other goods produced by themselves. Sometimes market-trading women are able to transform their independent control over exchangeable resources into more equitable relations with men. Wives commonly maintain a separate income from that of their husbands, which they are free to spend on themselves and their children. Among the Yoruba of Nigeria, women are active in market trade and in craft production, which gives them access to income and economic security independent of their husbands and other men. Many women purchase houses in urban areas and use the rent to improve their own and their children's economic well-being and social autonomy. According to Sandra Barnes (1990, 275):

> Property frees the owner from subordinating herself to the authority of another person in domestic matters. It places her in a position of authority over others and in a position to form social relationships in the wider community that are politically significant. Property owning legitimates her entry into the public domain.

The economic independence that some Yoruba women are able to acquire translates into increased participation in neighborhood associations and other public affairs and

▲ Where women commonly earn income for themselves by marketing products, as in Jamaica, their overall status tends to be relatively high.

allows them much freedom from male authority. A wider generalization would be that control over resources increases women's independence from men and allows women to form associations with other women that act like mutual support networks.

Thus, many ethnographic and comparative studies suggest that controlling resources is one way for women to get respect and independence from their husbands, brothers, and other men. This ability to acquire some measure of control over family resources helps to account for why many late-twentieth-century North American wives demanded and received more help from their husbands in housework and child care. In recent decades, married women in increasing numbers have acquired wage- and salary-earning jobs by selling their labor and skills to the private or public sector. Between 1960 and 1990, in the United States, the percentage of all married women who were employed doubled, from around 30 percent to 60 percent. Even the presence of young children does not keep most American women from entering the workforce: Between 1960 and 1990, the percentage of women with preschool-aged children who were working for a wage tripled, from about 20 percent to about 60 percent. Among the reasons why so many married women have

entered the workforce since the 1960s are the insufficiency of one person's (formerly, the husband's) income to support the family at an acceptable living standard; structural changes to a more service-oriented (less goods-producing) economy; the increasing value women place on personal fulfillment through career advancement (partly because of the feminist movement); and high divorce rates.

As a result of entering the workforce as wage and salary earners, many American women have gained considerable economic independence from their husbands and other men. The legal system has also helped by increasingly considering family violence more than just a private family matter, as well as by prosecuting or garnishing the wages of "deadbeat dads." Husbands have, therefore, lost considerable economic leverage in the household relative to their wives. In the twenty-first century, working wives have psychological ammunition against their husbands' domestic incompetence or laziness—they've put in 8- or 10-hour days on the job just like their husbands. Increasingly, women have the resources to back up their demands—they don't really need the loser, anyway.

In the early twenty-first century, increasing numbers of North American couples are "role reversed," to use the phrase of sociologists Theodore Cohen and John Durst. Husbands/fathers stay at home with young children while wives/mothers are the breadwinners. Some believe this pattern reverses the natural order of male/female family roles and thus is both immoral and harmful to children, who look up to their parents as role models. However, others believe the feminist movement has helped liberate men as well as women from old cultural attitudes: as economic or familial circumstances warrant, or as couples prefer, parents can reverse, switch, or alternate caretaking and breadwinning roles. They believe that feminism has given both sexes the freedom to choose.

With most women now out in the world of work, and with the families of so many married women now virtually dependent on their income to pay the bills, more women are demanding equal pay for equal work, equal treatment and opportunity in the workplace, equal legal rights, and equal respect. As in other societies, in North America women's success in obtaining control over important resources empowers them relative to men.

Descent and Postmarital Residence. The form of descent and postmarital residence also influences the degree of gender stratification. Women in matrilineal and matrilocal societies have greater equality in many areas of life. What is it, specifically, about matrilineality and matrilocality that gives relatively high status to females? It is not that "women rule" in these societies. Generally speaking, men hold positions of both political and domestic authority in matrilineal societies (see Chapters 9 and 10). The main difference is whom among their relatives men have authority *over:* their sisters and sisters' children in matrilineal systems, versus their sons, unmarried daughters, and sons' children in patrilineal systems.

But other elements of matrilineality and matrilocality benefit women. In a cross-cultural study Martin Whyte found that women enjoy more authority in domestic matters, have more sexual freedom, and have more worth placed on their lives in these societies. Two factors contribute to their equality. First, because husbands live with the families of their wives, sisters remain with or close to

▶ One generalization is that equality between the sexes is greatest in societies in which women control resources, their own labor, and how the products of their labor are distributed. This woman from Bangalore, India, is a jet pilot. Do such women also control how their salary is expended?

© David Wells/The Image Works

one another throughout their lives. A typical wife thus has her mother, sisters, and other female relatives around to support her in domestic quarrels. Second, in many matrilineal and matrilocal societies, domestic authority over a married woman is divided between her husband and her brother. Alice Schlegel suggests that this arrangement increases her freedom because each man acts as a check on the other's attempts to dominate her.

Contrast this situation to patrilineal and patrilocal China before the mid-twentieth century (our remarks apply to the Han, the majority ethnic group in China). When a Chinese woman married she was incorporated as a member of her husband's household. This was symbolized by the fact that she began to pay homage to his deceased patrilineal ancestors rather than to her own. A woman's relationships with her own parents and siblings were sharply curtailed when she married. Her main duties were to work for her husband and his parents, to obey them in all things, and to bear them male heirs. In many respects a new wife was treated as a domestic servant to her father- and mother-in-law: she was given arduous household tasks to perform for most of her waking hours, and she could be berated and even beaten with impunity. Only when she herself bore sons and heirs to her husband's family did her status improve, and only when she herself became a mother-in-law to her sons' wives could she relax a bit. The Confucian social and moral philosophy, which held that women must be submissive to men, affected the way wives and daughters-in-law were treated. But also important were the social facts that wives were fully incorporated into the households of their husbands' parents, and the lines of authority over them were clearly and legally redrawn on their marriage. A Chinese wife had few viable alternatives to submission to her husband's family and few sources of social support when she was treated poorly. In contrast, in most matrilocal and matrilineal cultures women do have alternatives to suffering the dominance of their husbands, and they likewise receive support from their own relatives.

Gender Stratification in Industrial Societies

We conclude by bringing together some of the information and ideas covered in this chapter and briefly suggesting how they might be relevant to women living in industrialized, modernized nations.

Anthropological research on gender stratification provides women with a hope and a warning. Part of the hope derives from the fact that women's roles and rights, and the restrictions placed upon them, vary from place to place and from time to time. Although it may be very difficult or impossible to say whether women and men have "totally equal status" in any culture, we certainly know that sexual equality varies—and varies significantly. So there is reason to think that modern societies can move further toward eliminating barriers to female opportunity and achievement. Patriarchy does not seem to be in the human genome.

Anthropological work on gender offers another hope. Some of our discussion of gender stratification suggests that any change that improves women's independent access to material resources and to social support will have positive impacts on their status in other realms of life. If married women have their own source of income independent of their husbands, then they are better able to become empowered within their families and to escape relationships with men who are physically or psychologically abusive. If, as in matrilineal and matrilocal societies, women are able to maintain relationships of "sisterhood" (i.e., support from other women) and/or of extended family ties (i.e., aid from their own relatives), then they can mobilize these supportive relationships in times of hardship. If women have legal recourse to sue discriminating employers and would-be employers, then their opportunities and compensation on the job will be improved by the threat of monetary damages.

And going back to the very first point in this chapter: The knowledge that ideas and beliefs about gender are culturally constructed rather than biologically given should—if taken seriously and understood properly—lead women and men alike to realize that at least some of the sexual differences they believe exist are differences of our own culture's making. It is a biological reality (with minor qualifications) that women have the tools to bear and nurse children, but is the belief that this makes women generally more nurturing than men also a reality? or is it a "construct"?

The warning? Cross-cultural studies have not yet discovered the key that unlocks the door leading to "total equality" (whatever that might look like) between the sexes. Comparative anthropological work—like most work dealing with human behavior and beliefs—is highly suggestive, but it is not conclusive. Thus far we cannot identify the one or two or three things that women can do that will lead to equal treatment in the workplace, in the household, in the bedroom, and in the political arena. No one or two or three male-dominated institutions could be changed to radically improve the position of women in various realms of their lives. For example, outlawing sexual discrimination in the workplace and making comparable pay for comparable work legally mandatory might not be translated into greater female–male equality in other contexts such as family life or politics. Even a female CEO can be abused by her husband. Therefore, feminists—of both sexes—need to continue to work on a broad front to achieve their objectives.

Summary

1. Physical differences between females and males are recognized and relevant to social behavior in all known cultures. Whether one is a male or female matters to all peoples, but it matters in different ways and to different degrees.

2. A person's sex is determined biologically by genes, but gender is a cultural construct. The cultural construction of gender means that cultures vary in how they perceive the physical differences between the sexes, in the significance they attribute to those differences, and in the way those differences are made relevant for self-identity, task and role allocation, access to property and power, and so forth. The Hua illustrate the cultural construction of gender.

3. Human groups differ in their tolerance of individual variations in gender identities. Many peoples allow gender crossing, in which males are allowed to enact female roles and vice versa. Others recognize multiple sexual identities, in which there are not only two, but three or four genders, roughly corresponding to man–woman or woman–man. Native American peoples seem especially tolerant of gender crossing and to allow for multiple gender identities.

4. The sexual division of labor varies cross-culturally. Sexual stereotypes holding that men are breadwinners and women are caretakers are not supported by comparative research. For example, male domination is not rooted in men's supplying the "material necessities of existence" because it is women's work that produces much or most of the food supply in a great many societies. Despite variation, there are certain widespread patterns in the sexual division of labor. Four biological factors that have been proposed to influence the broad cross-cultural similarities are (1) the depression of fertility that seems to occur when a woman engages in heavy exercise; (2) the possibility that women are more necessary than men to maintain population size, so women need to be protected from hazardous tasks; (3) superior male strength; and (4) the degree of compatibility of a task with the care of infants and young children. The first two factors might be important in a few times and places, but the last two biological differences between women and men are most significant cross-culturally.

5. No biological difference between the sexes can account for the cross-cultural variations in the sexual division of labor. One important and well-supported variation is that of women's subsistence contributions in various societies. It is well established that female labor is more important in subsistence tasks in horticultural populations compared with intensive agriculturalists. Reasons for these differences are related to the types of crops grown (root crops versus cereal grains), the amount of time spent in food processing, and the greater prevalence of warfare in horticultural groups.

6. A fourth issue in gender studies is the causes of cultural diversity in sexual stratification. Even specialists in this subject cannot agree whether ethnographic studies reveal that females are universally subordinate to males. This is mainly because no explicit criteria can be used to judge whether there are populations in which males and females are fully equal. It does seem to be true that females as a social category are never dominant over males as a social category. Many forces influence women's overall "status" in a culture, including their relative contributions to subsistence, their control over key resources, and the prevalent pattern of descent and postmarital residence. These conclusions have relevance for women in twenty-first-century societies.

Key Terms

cultural construction of
   gender
gender crossing

multiple gender identities
sexual (gendered)
   division of labor

gender (sex) roles
gender stratification

InfoTrac College Edition Terms

social construction of
   gender
berdache
genetic differences sex

women's work (occupa-
   tion) United States
status of women compar-
   ative (cross cultural)

Iroquois Native American
matriarchy
patriarchy

Suggested Readings

Books that are excellent brief introductions to the anthropological study of gender include:

Gilmore, David D. *Manhood in the Making: Cultural Concepts of Masculinity.* New Haven, Conn.: Yale University Press, 1990.

Nanda, Serena. *Gender Diversity: Crosscultural Variations.* Prospect Heights, Ill.: Waveland Press, 2000.

Roscoe, Will. *Changing Ones.* New York: St. Martin's Press, 1998.

The following books investigate gender from a comparative perspective:

Buckley, Thomas, and Alma Gottlieb, eds. *Blood Magic: The Anthropology of Menstruation.* Berkeley: University of California Press, 1988.

Dahlberg, F., ed. *Woman the Gatherer.* New Haven, Conn.: Yale University Press, 1981.

Martin, M. K., and B. Voorhies. *Female of the Species.* New York: Columbia University Press, 1975.

Sanday, Peggy R. *Female Power and Male Dominance.* Cambridge: Cambridge University Press, 1981.

Some useful edited volumes for introductory students are:

Cohen, Theodore, ed. *Men and Masculinity: A Text Reader.* Belmont, Calif.: Wadsworth/Thomson Learning, 2001.

di Leonardo, Micaela, ed. *Gender at the Crossroads of Knowledge: Feminist Anthropology in the Postmodern Era.* Berkeley: University of California Press, 1991.

Morgen, Sandra, ed. *Gender and Anthropology: Critical Reviews for Research and Teaching.* Washington, DC: American Anthropological Association, 1989.

Sanday, Peggy Reeves, and Ruth Gallagher Goodenough, eds. *Beyond the Second Sex: New Directions in the Anthropology of Gender.* Philadelphia: University of Pennsylvania Press, 1990.

Companion Website for This Book

The Wadsworth Anthropology Resource Center
http://anthropology.wadsworth.com

The companion website that accompanies *Humanity: An Introduction to Cultural Anthropology,* Seventh Edition, includes a rich array of material, including online anthropological video clips, to help you in the study of cultural anthropology and the specific topics covered in this chapter. Begin by clicking on Student Resources. Next, click on Cultural Anthropology, and then on the cover image for this book. You have now arrived at the Student Re-

sources home page and have the option of choosing one of several chapter resources.

Applying Anthropology. Begin your study of cultural anthropology by clicking on Applying Anthropology. Here you will find useful information on careers, graduate school programs in applied anthropology, and internships you might wish to pursue. You will also find real-world examples of working anthropologists applying the skills and methods of anthropology to help solve serious world problems.

Research Online. Click here to find a wealth of Web links that will facilitate your study of anthropology. Divided into different fields of study, specific websites are starting points for Internet research. You will be guided to rich anthropology websites that will help you prepare for class, complete course assignments, and actually do research on the Web.

 InfoTrac College Edition Exercises. From the pull-down menu, select the chapter you are presently studying. Select InfoTrac College Edition Exercises from the list of resources. These exercises utilize InfoTrac College Edition's vast database of articles and help you explore the numerous uses of the search word, *culture.*

Study Aids for This Chapter. Improve your knowledge of key terms by using flash cards and study the learning objectives. Take the practice quiz, receive your results, and e-mail them to your instructor. Access these resources from the chapter and resource pull-down menus.

Chapter Twelve

THE ORGANIZATION OF POLITICAL LIFE

Forms of Political Organization

Bands

Tribes

Chiefdoms

States

Social Control and Law

Social Control

Law

Legal Systems

Self-Help Systems

Court Systems

© Jarrick Bailey

In modern urban societies such as England, uniformed police are an important part of the legal system.

EVERY SOCIETY HAS SOME FORM of political system, meaning those institutions that organize and direct the collective actions of the population. In small societies, political leadership and organization may be informal and even ad hoc. Only when a specific need for leadership arises does some individual assume an overt leadership role. In general, the larger the population, the more formalized the leadership and the more complex the political organization.

LIKEWISE, AS MENTIONED in Chapter 2, all societies demand some minimal degree of conformity from their members. All, therefore, develop mechanisms of social control by which the behaviors of individuals are constrained and directed into acceptable channels. There are always behavioral patterns that are approved or acceptable and patterns that are disapproved or unacceptable. By means of social control, a society encourages normatively proper behavior and discourages unacceptable actions, the objective being the maintenance of harmony and cooperation. The most serious deviations from acceptable behavior, which threaten the cohesiveness of the group, fall under that aspect of social control known as law, also discussed in this chapter. In the least organized societies, law and political organizations exist independently of each other. As political organization becomes increasingly formalized and structured, governmental institutions take over legal institutions, until legal institutions become part of the formal political structure.

Forms of Political Organization

When we speak of the political organization of a particular cultural system, we frequently are left with the impression that political boundaries and cultural boundaries are the same. But the boundaries of a *polity,* or politically organized unit, may or may not correspond with the boundaries of a particular way of life. For example, the Comanche of the Great Plains shared a common language, customs, and ethnic identity, yet politically, they were never organized above the local group. Thus, the term *Comanche* refers to a people with a common language and culture who never united to carry out common political activities.

At the other extreme we find highly centralized polities that incorporate several culturally and socially distinct peoples. The United States is unusual in this regard only in the degree of cultural heterogeneity in the population. France, although predominantly "French," also includes Bretons and Basques. India has several hundred different ethnic groups. Russia, China, Indonesia, and the Philippines also integrate highly diversified populations into a single polity. In fact, every large and most small countries in the world today politically integrate several ethnic groups (see Chapter 17).

Political organization falls into four basic forms. From the least to the most complex, these forms are bands (simple and composite), tribes, chiefdoms, and states. Today, few societies exist that are not integrated into state-level political systems. Thus, to understand societies organized at less complex levels, we have to reconstruct the structure of such societies at an earlier period.

Bands

As the least complex form, bands were probably the earliest form of human political structure (see Chapter 6). As more complex political systems developed, band-level societies were unable to compete for resources. Thus, bands survived until the modern period only in regions of the world with limited natural resources. Most known band-level societies were found in the deserts and grasslands of Australia, Africa, and the Americas. A few others lived in the tropical forests of Africa, Asia, and South America and in the boreal forest and tundra regions of North America and Asia.

Bands consist of a number of families living together and cooperating in economic activities throughout the year. Band-level organization most frequently was found among peoples with foraging economies, which usually dictated low population densities and high seasonal mobility. As a result, only a relatively small number of people could stay together throughout the year. Bands ranged in size from only a dozen to several hundred individuals. The adaptive significance of the band's size and seasonal mobility is described in Chapter 6. In this chapter we are concerned with leadership statuses and political organization of bands.

The smallest bands, called **simple bands,** usually were no larger than an extended family and were structured as such. Leadership was informal, with the oldest or one of the older male members of the family serving as leader. Decision making was reached through consensus and involved both adult males and adult females; simple bands operated as families. Because all members of the band were related either through descent or by marriage, they were exogamous units, and members of the band had to seek spouses from other bands. Thus, although an autonomous economic and political unit, every band was, by social necessity, allied through intermarriage with other bands, usually territorially adjacent ones. Simple bands usually had names, although names may have been informal and may have simply referred to some prominent geographical feature associated with the band's usual territory.

Resource availability influenced the formation of such small groups. Simple bands often were associated with the hunting of nonmigratory game animals, such as deer, guanaco, moose, or small mammals, which occupy a limited territory on a year-round basis and are found either singly or in small herds. The foraging activities of simple bands usually did not generate any significant surpluses of food, which necessitated the year-round hunting of game animals. Effective hunting required only a few male hunters who had intimate knowledge of the seasonal shifts in range of these animals within their territory. The game resources of such areas could be exploited

Form	Characteristics	Associated Equalities and Inequalities
Bands	Local, economically self-sufficient residence group.	Egalitarian
(a) Simple	Single extended family, usually numbering 25 to 50 people.	
	Family head with leadership based on influence.	
(b) Composite	Local, economically self-sufficient residence group.	Egalitarian
	Several extended families, usually numbering from 50 to several hundred individuals.	
	Big-man leadership based on influence.	
Tribes	Several economically self-sufficient residence groups.	Primarily egalitarian with some societies showing the traits of ranking
	Usually numbering between 1,000 and 20,000 people.	
	A few formal leadership positions with limited authority, with access based on inheritance and/or achievements.	
	Group cohesion maintained by sodalities.	
Chiefdoms	Several economically interdependent residence groups.	Ranked societies
	Usually numbering from a few thousand up to about 30,000.	
	Centralized leadership, with a hereditary chief, with full formal authority.	
States	Usually numbering from the tens of thousands up to several million.	Stratified societies
	Centralized leadership, with formal full authority, supported by a bureaucracy.	

most effectively by a small and highly mobile population. In addition, such bands depended on the seasonal collection of wild roots, berries, nuts, and other edible plants, as well as on limited fishing and shellfish collection.

Composite bands consisted of a larger aggregation of families, sometimes numbering in the hundreds. In contrast to simple bands, composite bands encompassed unrelated extended families. Although leadership in composite bands was informal, it was more defined. Such leaders frequently have been called **big men.** Big men did not hold formal offices, and leadership was based on influence rather than authority over band members. **Influence** is merely the ability to convince people that they should act as you suggest. **Authority** is the recognized right of an individual to command another person to act in a particular way. Thus, a big-man leader could not, by virtue of his position, make demands or impose rules on the members of the band, and his decisions were not binding on others. Because big-man status did not involve a formal office, no prescribed process for attaining leadership status existed. A man might emerge as the leader through a variety of personal accomplishments or qualities, such as his proven ability in hunting or warfare, the supernatural powers he possessed, or merely his charisma. There was no set tenure

in the position, which was filled by a man until he was informally replaced by some other leader.

Like simple bands, many composite bands were nomadic groups that moved within a relatively well-defined range. Because of their greater size, composite bands were not as cohesive as simple bands and were politically more volatile. Disputes between families could result in some members joining another band or even the band splitting into two or more bands.

The formation of composite bands resulted from economic pressures that facilitated or necessitated the cooperation of a larger number of individuals than found in a single extended family. As in the case of simple bands, the behavior of the principal game animals was an important influence. Composite bands were associated with the seasonal hunting of migratory animals that form large herds, such as bison and caribou. Migratory herd animals usually appeared only seasonally in the range of a particular composite band as the herd moved between its summer and winter ranges. Because bison and caribou migrated in herds that sometimes numbered in the tens of thousands, there was no difficulty in locating the herds on the open grasslands and tundra. Unlike the nonmigratory-animal hunters, who secured game steadily throughout the year, hunters of migratory animals took

241

most of their game only twice a year, as the herds passed through their territories during migrations.

Successful hunting of large herds of animals effectively requires maneuvering the herd into situations where large numbers could be slaughtered. Herds might be run over a cliff, into a holding pen, or into a lake, where hunters in boats could kill them. Regardless of the method used, all these strategies required the presence of a larger group of hunters than was available in a simple band. Thus, composite bands were formed to bring together a sufficiently large number of hunters to control the movements of large herds of animals.

The Comanche of the southern Great Plains of the United States illustrate the nature of composite bands. These horse-raising, bison-hunting people were politically autonomous until the Red River War of 1875. During the early and middle years of the nineteenth century, the Comanche numbered about 6,000 to 7,000, divided between 5 and 13 main bands. Comanche bands had only vaguely defined territories, and 2 or more bands frequently occupied the same general area or had overlapping ranges. Membership in Comanche bands was fluid: Both individuals and families could and did shift from one band to another, or a number of families might join together to establish a new band. Some anthropologists have theorized that there were only 5 major bands, with a varying number of secondary bands appearing and disappearing from time to time.

A band consisted of a number of families, each headed by an older male member who was "peace chief" or "headman." One of these family heads also served as the peace chief for the entire band. There was no formalized method of selecting either the family heads or the head of the band. As the Comanche say, "No one made him such; he just got that way." A Comanche peace chief usually was a man known for his kindness, wisdom, and ability to lead by influencing other men. Although a war record was important, peace chiefs were not chosen from among the most aggressive or ambitious men. Such men usually remained war chiefs—great warriors who periodically recruited men to raid neighbors—but frequently had little influence outside war and raiding.

A band peace chief was responsible for the well-being of the band. Through a consensus of the family heads, he directed the seasonal movement of the band and the bison hunts. He did have men who voluntarily assisted him. In the morning the peace chief usually sent out two men to scout the area around the camp for the presence of enemy raiding parties. He also sent a crier through the camp periodically to announce plans for the movement of the camp, an upcoming hunt, or some other cooperative activities. During the bison hunts, the peace chief called on a number of men from the camp to police the hunt and restrain overly eager hunters from scattering the herd and thus spoiling the hunt for others.

In an extraordinarily individualistic and egalitarian society, Comanche band leaders had to strive for and maintain consensus. If a dispute arose and a consensus could not be reached, individuals and families were free either to shift residence to another band or even to form a new band under another leader.

Comanche bands were economically and politically autonomous units. Only seldom did two or more bands come together for any unified action, and never did leaders of the bands come together to discuss issues. At the same time, there was a strong consciousness of common identity, of being Comanche. Comanches freely traveled between bands to visit, marry, and even shift residence. There was an informally reached general consensus on whether relations with a particular neighboring group were friendly or hostile. Comanche bands also usually refrained from attacking other Comanche bands, although on occasion some did ally themselves with foreign groups.

Thus, on the band level of political organization, populations are fragmented into numerous independent political units that operate only at the local-group level. These various communities share a common cultural identity and usually attempt to maintain harmonious relations with one another, but they lack any political structure capable of organizing all the various communities into a single unit for collective actions.

Tribes

Tribes differ from bands in that they have formally organized institutions that unite the scattered residential communities, give the society greater cohesiveness, and make possible a more united response to external threats. These institutions are called **sodalities.** Sodalities take various forms: they may be based on large kin groups, such as clans and lineages; on nonkinship units, such as age sets (see Chapter 9); or on voluntary associations, such as warrior societies. Regardless of their exact nature, sodalities unify geographically dispersed communities into political units. Although tribal-level societies usually are egalitarian, with leadership dependent in part on the persuasive abilities of individuals, formalized political offices with institutionalized authority exist. Although tribes vary greatly in structure, here we can examine only one tribal-level society.

The Cheyenne of the Great Plains numbered between 3,000 and 3,500 during the early 1800s. The Cheyenne, like the neighboring Comanche, were horse-mounted bison hunters. They were divided into 10 main nomadic villages, which averaged between 300 and 350 persons. Village membership was not based on kinship, although the members of a particular village usually were related either by blood or by marriage. Village membership was relatively stable, and marriages between villagers were common. Despite this stability, myths concerning village origins were not well developed, and band names were only nicknames (e.g., Grayhairs, Hair-Rope Men, Ridge Men, or some other trivial characteristic). Although a particular village usually frequented a certain range, there was no sense of village territoriality. Periodically and seasonally, family camps and subvillage camps broke off from the main village.

The only time the entire tribe came together was in early summer, when all the widely scattered villages gathered into a single camp at a predetermined location. This crescent-shaped encampment stretched for several miles from end to end, with the open portion facing east. Within the tribal encampment every village had a designated location, and while camped together, they performed the great tribal ceremonies (e.g., the Arrow Renewal, the Sun Dance, or the Animal Dance). At least one and possibly two of these rituals were performed, depending on the particular ritual needs of the tribe at that time. After the performance of the ritual, the tribe as a unit staged the great summer bison hunt. After the hunt, the tribe again scattered into smaller village camps.

Politically, the tribe was controlled by the Council of Forty-Four and the warrior societies. The Council of Forty-Four, which had both political and religious duties, was headed by the Sweet Medicine chief, who was responsible for keeping the Sweet Medicine bundle, a sacred package of sweet grass. Second to him in importance were four other sacred chiefs, each representative of specific supernatural beings. Under these five sacred chiefs were 39 ordinary chiefs.

Chiefs served in their positions for 10 years and could not be removed for any reason. Serving as a chief placed a burden on the individuals. Chiefs usually were selected from among the older men, all of whom had war records. When an individual was chosen as a chief, he was to act like a chief, not an aggressive warrior. If the man was an officer in one of the warrior societies, he had to resign his position, although he remained a member of the society. A chief was to be generous, kindly, even tempered, and aloof from everyday disputes. In short, he was expected to display ideal human behavior at all times. He was to take care of the poor, settle disputes between individuals, and be responsible for the ritual performances that protected the tribe.

The major sodalities were the warrior societies, of which there were five. These were formal voluntary associations of men, each with its own style of dress, dances, songs, and set of four leaders. As young warriors, men were recruited by the different societies until all had joined one or another. The term *warrior societies* is slightly misleading. The heads of the various societies constituted what some call the *tribal war chiefs*. Although this group planned and led attacks on their enemies, the different societies did not fight or operate as military units in battles. In battles men fought as individuals, and members of several societies may have been present in a particular raiding party.

Subordinate to the council of chiefs, the warrior societies cooperated as a group only in the policing of the camps. During the summer tribal encampment, the Council of Forty-Four appointed one of the societies as camp police. Later, when the village scattered into separate camps, the members of the council resident in the village appointed one of the warrior societies to police the camp. After being appointed, the warrior society usually carried out its function with little direction from the chiefs. Its members scouted the area around the camp to check for the presence of any enemy raiding parties and intervened in any serious disputes between village members.

There are two points to be emphasized about the political organization of tribal societies. First, although there were some formalized political and religious offices that bequeathed some limited authority and prerogatives, on the whole, tribal societies were basically egalitarian (see Chapter 13). Few positions were hereditary, and most leaders were selected on the basis of personal qualities and individual merit.

Second, there was little economic specialization, either individual or regional, among tribes. Except for cooperation in communal hunts, families produced their own food and manufactured their own clothes and other material goods. From an economic perspective, each band or village was capable of sustaining itself without support from other communities; therefore, it was not economic necessity, convenience, or efficiency that led to the supracommunity political organization of tribes. Although sodalities unite tribes at a higher level of cohesiveness than bands, the mere existence of sodalities is not sufficient to generate or maintain the cohesiveness of a tribe. It is likely that external threats, either real or perceived, necessitated the cooperation in warfare of a large group of people and was the major factor that united geographically dispersed communities. Thus, warfare—the existence and activities of hostile human neighbors—was an important force in creating the political integration of separate communities.

Chiefdoms

Like tribes, **chiefdoms** were multicommunity political units. Unlike tribes, chiefdoms had a formalized and centralized political system. A chiefdom (see Chapter 7) was governed by a single chief, who usually served as both political and religious head of the polity. The chief had authority over members of the chiefdom, and the position often was hereditary within a single kin group, which based its rights chiefly on supernatural powers. Thus, a chiefdom was not an egalitarian society but a ranked or stratified society (see Chapter 13) with access to resources based on inherited status. With authority and power conferred by supernatural beings, governing was not by consensus but by decree.

Most chiefdoms were associated with horticultural societies in which craft or regional specialization in production had emerged. There was a need for regularized exchanges of goods either between geographically dispersed communities or, at times, within a single community. This economic exchange was managed through redistribution, with the chief occupying the central position in the flow of goods (see Chapter 7).

In earlier historic periods, chiefdoms probably were found throughout much of the Old World. During more recent periods, such political systems were primarily concentrated in Oceania (Polynesia, Micronesia, and Melanesia) and in the Americas (the circum-Caribbean and coastal portions of South America and the northwestern coast of North America).

The Polynesian-speaking people of Tahiti, an island in the southeastern Pacific, illustrate many characteristics typical of a chiefdom. This relatively large, mountainous, volcanic island had a population of about 100,000 at the time of European discovery. Tahiti was divided among about 20 rival chiefs. Although most of these chiefdoms were about the size of the average tribe and significantly smaller than the largest tribes, their political organization differed significantly.

The economy of Tahiti was based largely on farming. Taro, breadfruit, coconuts, and yams were the main crops; pigs and chickens were also raised, and fish and other seafoods supplemented the food supply. Food production was sufficient not only to meet the needs of the population but also to produce surpluses for export to other islands. Although sufficient food was produced in all regions, there were significant regional differences in types of food produced because Tahiti varied ecologically.

Tahitian society had at least three and possibly four distinct classes, depending on how finely one wants to divide the units. *Arii,* or chiefs, and their close relatives formed the ruling elite. The arii were divided into two groups: the *arii rahi,* or sacred chiefs, and the *arii rii,* or small chiefs.

Under these chiefs were the *raatira,* or subchiefs, and the *manahune,* or commoners. The sacred chiefs were viewed as descended from the gods, whereas the commoners were merely created by the gods for their use. The subchiefs were the offspring of intermarriage between the sacred chiefs and commoners, whereas the small chiefs were the products of still later intermarriages between sacred chiefs and subchiefs. Once these four classes were established, class endogamy became the rule.

The sacred chiefs, viewed as gods on Earth, evoked both reverence and fear. Whatever the highest-ranking sacred chiefs touched became *tabu,* or sacred, and could not be used for fear of supernatural punishment. Such a chief had to be carried on the back of a servant, lest the ground touched by his feet became tabu. He could not enter the house of another individual for the same reason. The lifestyle of the chief's family differed from that of others: they had larger and more elaborate houses, the largest canoes, insignia of their rank, and particular clothing.

Unlike band and tribal societies, resources in chiefdoms were individually owned. Land was owned mainly by the chiefs and subchiefs, but ultimate authority rested with the sacred chiefs within the polity. Although sacred chiefs could not withhold the title to lands from the families of subchiefs, they could banish an individual subchief. Crafts were specialized, and craftspeople were attached to particular sacred chiefs and produced goods for them. Thus, the sacred chiefs directly controlled craft production and communal fishing. The chiefs could make demands on the property of the subchiefs and commoners. If someone refused, the chief could have the recalcitrant banished or make him or her a sacrificial victim. Theoretically, the sacred chief was the head judicial figure in the polity, but some believe that the chief seldom intervened in disputes between individuals; the chief usually used these powers only against people who challenged his authority.

The sacred chief in each polity was the focal point for redistributive exchanges. The chief periodically demanded surplus production from all his subjects for a public redistribution. Such events were associated with a number of occasions: a rite of passage for a member of the chief's family, the organizing of a military attack, religious ceremonies, or the start of the breadfruit harvest. During such ceremonies, the chief distributed the goods collected to all his subjects.

States

Although they had a centralized political system, chiefdoms were still kinship-based structures. Even in Tahiti, the sacred chief's authority rested in large part on his control over families of subchiefs, each of whom had his own inalienable rights to lands—and thus families—of commoners. As a result, the number of people who could be effectively integrated into a chiefdom was limited. In Polynesia, most chiefdoms ranged from only a few thousand to 30,000 persons. Polities with larger populations require a political structure based on institutions other than kinship.

States, like chiefdoms, have a centralized political structure. States are distinguished from chiefdoms by the presence of a bureaucracy. A chiefdom is basically a two-level system: (1) the chiefs (which in Tahiti included the subchiefs), who have varying levels of authority and power, and (2) the commoners, or the great mass of the populace. A state has three levels: (1) the ruling elite, (2) a bureaucracy, and (3) the populace.

In states, as in chiefdoms, highest authority and power reside in the ruling elite, the formal political head or heads of the polity. States vary greatly in the types of political leaders present and in the basis for the leaders' authority and power. Leaders in the earliest states frequently were considered to be the descendants of gods, and thus themselves gods on Earth. The Inca of Peru and the pharaohs of Egypt were leaders who ruled as gods. Other political leaders, although not claiming to be gods, have legitimated their positions with claims of having been chosen by God. Early European kings legitimated their claims to leadership on such a basis; and as English coins still proclaim, the queen rules *Dei gratia*—by the "grace of God." Other states have evolved political leadership that uses strictly secular ideas to justify its power. In countries where leaders are elected by a vote of the populace, rule is legitimated by the internalized acceptance of such ascendence to office. Even strictly secular kingdoms, dictatorships, and oligarchies can, if in power for a sufficient time, have their rule accepted by the populace as "legitimate." We have more to say about legitimation in Chapter 13.

Although they differ greatly in political leadership, states all share one characteristic: the presence of a bureaucracy that carries out the day-to-day governing of the polity. In simple terms, a bureaucrat is a person to whom a political leader delegates certain authority and powers. The bureaucrat thus acts on behalf of the political leader. Lacking any inherent authority or powers personally, bureaucrats depend on the continued support of political leaders. Using bureaucrats as intermediaries, political leaders could expand the size of their polities both geographically and demographically, while strengthening their political control over the population. Bureaucrats could engineer such expansion without threat of revolution and political fragmentation because they lacked any personal claims to independent political legitimacy.

Inca Empire. The Inca empire of ancient Peru was typical of a state-level organization. From the capital of Cuzco, the ruler, or *Sapa Inca,* controlled a multiethnic empire of between 6 and 12 million subjects speaking dozens of different languages and extending over 2,500 miles from modern-day Ecuador to central Chile. Dissected by some of the highest mountain ranges and most inhospitable deserts in the world, the Inca empire also existed without a writing system for communication, a monetary system for exchange, or wheeled vehicles for transporting goods. In spite of this limited technology and hostile terrain, the central government was able to organize human labor for massive public works projects, ranging from the construction of buildings and terraced fields to a 9,500-mile highway network that stretched the length and breadth of the country.

The *Sapa Inca* was also able to mobilize and supply armies numbering in the tens of thousands for extended periods of time. The Inca empire was a conquest state created through the military conquest and incorporation of smaller neighboring states. However, it was the administrative abilities of its leaders, more than their military might, that gave the empire its political cohesiveness.

The *Sapa Inca* was believed to be the direct descendant of the Sun God. Thus, the *Sapa Inca* was a divine being, with absolute authority over and control of all the people and resources of the empire. Succession was not clearly defined. Any son of the *Sapa Inca* had a legitimate claim to his father's position. To avoid conflict, the *Sapa Inca* usually chose one of his sons as his successor before his death, but the death of the *Sapa Inca* usually resulted in conflicts between potential heirs.

The empire was administratively divided into four geographical regions, each with its own head. The regions were divided into provinces, with governors and regional capitals. The provinces were in turn organized on the basis of what some have called a "decimal administration" of hierarchically nested administrative units based on population size. The largest, with a population of 10,000 households, was called a *huno*. A *huno* was divided into units of 5,000, 1,000, 500, 100, 50, and finally 10 households. Each unit had an official head responsible to the person above him. Periodically, a census was conducted and adjustments made. This was the ideal administrative model; the actual structure varied somewhat from province to province due to local demographic and ethnic factors.

Regional heads were members of the Incan royal family. In some provinces, relatives of the *Sapa Inca* also filled the position of governor. However, in most cases provincial governors and other provincial officials were drawn from local elite families, and these families even

© Mirelle Vautier/Woodfin Camp & Associates

▲ Manco Capac, as portrayed in this eighteenth-century painting, was the mythic founder of the Inca. The son of the Sun, he and his descendants were considered to be gods.

held hereditary rights to these offices. Beneath these officials and their families was the great mass of people, the commoners.

Land was divided into plots used by individual families and households, and land used for the support of public functions. Every household in the empire was given sufficient land to meet its economic needs. Households and local communities were basically self-sufficient. Food and other goods produced on their land and within the family belonged to the family.

The government of the empire was supported by a labor tax, not a tax on production. Every household was required to supply labor for state purposes. Some assignments were for a number of days per year, others were yearlong, and still others lifelong. The major function of provincial officials was to assign tasks, organize work parties, and oversee the work.

The majority of commoners paid their labor tax by working part of the year farming public fields, tending herds of state-owned animals, weaving cloth, making pottery, repairing public buildings, working on public roads, or performing some other local task. In every province, food, clothes, and other utilitarian goods produced by state tax labor were stored in public buildings. State-owned food, clothes, and other goods were used to support the army, visiting government officials, and commoners who had been assigned long-term labor tasks that made it impossible for them to be self-supporting. In return for their services, all provincial officials in charge of 100 households or more were allowed to use tax laborers to farm their fields, tend their herds, build their houses, and make their clothes and other goods.

In the 1530s, the Spanish conquered the Inca Empire and murdered the last *Sapa Inca.* However, the provincial governmental structure and the "decimal administrative" system were incorporated into the government of colonial Peru.

The emergence of states increased the complexity of political units. Bureaucracies not only allowed for specialization in governmental functions but also made possible the effective integration of large land areas and populations into political units. For example, chiefdoms seldom exceeded 30,000 persons, whereas modern states such as China and India have populations of 1 billion people or more.

Social Control and Law

All societies have clearly defined rules that govern the relationships between members. Not all individuals in any society will conform to these rules. There will always be some who behave in a socially unacceptable manner. Thus, among all peoples there exist formal and informal ways to correct the behavior of individuals. In general, we call these mechanisms social control. One form of social control is called law.

Social Control

Social control refers to the diverse ways in which the behaviors of the members of a society are constrained into socially approved channels. All cultures have certain behavioral norms that most people learn and begin to conform to during enculturation. But all societies have individuals who, to one degree or another, deviate from those norms. Violations of norms usually result in sanctions or punishments for the offender, which serve both to correct

The Global Economy and the Future of the Nation-State

One of the creations of the global economy has been the transnational corporation. The global economy has allowed corporations to grow in size and economic power far beyond the wildest dreams of their founders. In 1999 the combined sales of the 200 largest global corporations were equal to 27.5 percent of combined gross domestic products (GDPs) of all of the countries of the world. If one compares corporate sales and GDPs of the 100 largest economies, 51 would be corporations and 49 would be countries. In the corporate world, globalization has been the avenue by which the big have gotten bigger. In the global economy, economic power is rapidly passing from the control of governments to corporations. The CEOs and boards of directors of the world's largest corporations now have more economic power than the political leaders and governments of all but a handful of the world's countries.

To understand the significance of this shift in economic power, one has to understand that corporations and governments have very different interests and interest groups. The basic function of a government is to promote the collective well-being and economic interests of its citizens. The interest of a corporation, on the other hand, is far more limited. In most cases today, corporations exist only to produce profits for their owners, an ever-changing and anonymous group of stockholders. As a result, there has always been friction between governments and corporations. Ideally, governments attempt to regulate corporate activities so as to increase the economic and social benefits to their citizens. Corporations, on the other hand, attempt to minimize governmental constraints on their activities so as to maximize profits for their owners. As long as corporations were basically domestic corporations, companies whose operations were confined to a single country, there was no question as to the power of the government to regulate corporate behavior. If a corporation or group of corporations acted in a manner that the citizenry opposed, then the government, particularly in democracies, would respond to public pressure and pass laws regulating corporate behavior. In the United States and most other countries there is a large body of corporate regulatory laws, minimum wage laws, worker safety laws, environmental laws, and product safety laws, to name only some. In almost all cases these laws are vigorously opposed by corporate groups. The reason is simple: Regulations cost companies, and thus stockholders, money.

With globalization, the relationship between corporations and government is changing. In 1948, the General Agreement on Tariffs and Trade (GATT) talks were established. These talks, initially involving the United States and a few other industrial countries, were concerned with negotiating reductions in tariffs with the eventual objective of achieving "free trade" throughout the world. Free trade is a central element in global economy. Free trade means that goods, raw materials, commodities, and services may be moved and marketed across international borders without regulations or restraints.

Free trade sounds good. But what does it really mean? For a transnational corporation it means that not only can it market its products in any country it wishes, it can produce those products wherever it wishes. If wages are relatively high in one country, it can simply move its production facilities to other countries where wages are lower. If environmental laws are too stringent in one country, it can move its production facilities to a country with less demanding environmental protection laws. Thus free trade allows transnational corporations to play countries, particularly underdeveloped countries, against one another, suppressing wages and lowering worker safety and environmental protection standards. It also means that domestic companies cannot develop. Being forced to compete directly with economically powerful transnational corporations, they are either forced out of business or absorbed.

Although GATT agreements have changed, lowered, or eliminated many tariffs and quotas, every country still has some import and export duties as well as trade quotas. World trade is far "freer" than it was 50 years ago, but numerous tariffs and quotas still exist. In 1995 the World Trade Organization (WTO) became the successor to GATT. Headquartered in Geneva, Switzerland, the WTO monitors and enforces existing binding agreements between the 142 member countries, and is working to develop still other agreements. However, unlike GATT, which was limited to the elimination of import tariffs and quotas, WTO has much broader powers. WTO has the same legal status as the United Nations, and serves as a global commerce agency. The stated objective of the WTO is to ultimately create a fully integrated global economic system in which not only goods, services, and capital flow without any interference or control of local national governments, but the property rights of corporations, both physical and intellectual, are fully protected.

Many individuals object to the fact that once the government of a country adopts one of these agreements, the WTO has the power to enforce the agreement. Under these agreements any existing law in any of the member countries may potentially be considered an obstacle to free trade, and thus illegal. The power for determining if the law of a particular country is "protectionist" and thus a barrier to free trade and illegal, rests solely with panels of appointed bureaucrats of the WTO. Any member country can challenge any law of any other member country if that law presents a barrier to trade or investment. The proceedings of the WTO tribunals are conducted in secret and only governments, not the public, have direct voice in these proceedings. If the WTO tribunal finds against a country, that country has one of only three options: (1) change the law, (2) pay compensation, or (3) have trade sanctions imposed. There is no appeal of a WTO decision.

Almost any law has potential economic consequences, thus most of the existing laws of the 142 member countries of the WTO are subject to WTO review. So far the WTO's tribunals have made only a handful of binding rulings, while over a hundred additional challenges await action. The few rulings made by the WTO demonstrate the authority it has assumed.

Among other provisions, the U.S. Clean Air Act set cleanliness standards for oil refiners. These requirements were applied to both domestic refiners and foreign refiners who sold their production in the United States. The WTO ruled against the United States, forcing the law to be amended.

The European Union (E.U.) countries, for public health concerns, ban the sale of beef containing artificial hormones. The United States challenged this ban, and the WTO ruled against the E.U., saying that a country cannot ban the import of a food as a precautionary health measure. The E.U. has to present scientific proof that artificial hormones are unsafe. The E.U. also has a similar ban on the importation of genetically altered crops, and the United States is challenging this law as well.

Even the threat of bringing a challenge before the WTO has resulted in smaller countries changing their laws. Following guidelines developed by the World Health Organization, Guatemala adopted a set of measures regulating the marketing of infant formula to reduce its infant mortality rate. Citing this law, the Guatemalan government made Gerber's stop running an ad stating that Gerber's infant formula was better than mother's milk. Gerber's prevailed on the U.S. government to bring this issue before the WTO. The mere threat resulted in Guatemala dropping the regulation.

Supporters of the WTO argue that for the global economy to reach its full potential there has to be a uniform set of rules and regulations that everyone follows, and sanctions have to be imposed on those who do not. In this regard they are correct. The question is, Who will set these rules and regulations, who will

determine if they have been violated, and who will impose sanctions? Opponents argue that the WTO consists of 500 publicly faceless and nameless hired trade specialists in Geneva who are exercising governmental and judicial prerogatives. The decisions they reach are based solely on economic considerations, not the cultural, social, health, and environmental concerns and interests of the public whose lives they affect. No one elected these individuals to these positions of power, and they are not directly responsible to the citizenry of the member countries. In fact, individuals and nongovernmental organizations cannot directly bring complaints before the WTO. The WTO responds only to member governments and these governments usually react only to the requests of transnational corporations.

Critical Thinking Questions

1. Does globalization make some form of world government inevitable? The World Trade Organization is not the only global organization assuming more and more governmental prerogatives; the World Bank and the International Monetary Fund are moving in similar directions.

2. Is the authority of the nation-state and its citizens being eroded?

3. Will the governments of nation-states of the world become increasingly subordinate to the bureaucratic oligarchies of the World Trade Organization, the World Bank, and the International Monetary Fund, or will some new, more representative and democratic form of global governance evolve?

Sources: Noam Chomsky (2000); Public Citizen (n.d.); World Trade Organization (n.d.), "The WTO in Brief"; Globalisation Guide (n.d.); "Is Globalisation Shifting Power from Nation States to Undemocratic Organizations?" (see Globalisation Guide Web page, www.globalisationguide.org).

the behavior of particular people and to show others the penalties for such deviance. The severity of sanctions and the process by which sanctions are imposed differ greatly, depending on the seriousness culturally attached to the violated norm, the perceived severity of the violation, and the overall political and legal system of the people.

Children who get into mischief usually are corrected by their parents. In our own society, parents may impose sanctions ranging from scolding to spanking to withdrawing privileges. Correcting children trains individuals in proper behavior at an early age.

The community also applies informal sanctions against children and adults who are not behaving properly. Gos-

sip, or fear of gossip, serves as an important method of social control in most societies. Most people fear the contempt or ridicule of their peers, so they try to conform to acceptable behavioral norms. People attempt to hide behavior that would be the subject of gossip, scandal, and ridicule. Individuals whose known behavior consistently violates social norms may even find themselves ostracized by friends and relatives (the severest of informal punishments). Informal economic penalties also may be imposed. A family may withdraw economic support in attempts to modify the errant behavior of a member.

A wide variety of supernatural sanctions may assist in controlling individual behavior, and in some cases these supernatural sanctions are automatically imposed on particular types of behavior. Whether the commission of these acts becomes public knowledge or not, and thus regardless of whether other punishments are inflicted on the individual, the commission still endangers one's immortal soul. Supernatural sanctions can be more specifically directed. In many societies, including some Christian ones, an individual may place a curse on another person by calling on a supernatural being. Fear of sorcery or witchcraft (see Chapter 14) frequently serves as another important form of social control. Most victims are people who offended a witch or sorcerer in some way, often through a breach of social norms.

Law

Law is the highest level of social control, and legal punishments usually are reserved for the most serious breaches of norms. The question of how law can be distinguished from other forms of social control is not easy to answer. In societies with court systems the distinction is formalized, but in societies without such formalized legal systems the division is not as clear. E. Adamson Hoebel (1954, 28) defined law in the following way: "A social norm is legal if its neglect or infraction is regularly met, in threat or in fact, by the application of physical force by an individual or group possessing the socially recognized privilege of so acting." Law so defined was and is present in virtually every society.

In a legal action, some individual or group must have publicly recognized authority to settle a case or punish a violation. In societies with courts the authority is obvious, but in societies that lack courts the authority becomes less clear. What emerges frequently is an ad hoc authority; that is, because of the peculiarities of the case, a particular individual or group becomes recognized by the community as the authority responsible for its resolution. In some cases, the victim may be the recognized authority. In the victim's absence (as in the case of murder), the victim's family, clan, or kin group may be placed in the role of authority. Such ad hoc authority is discussed later in some of the examples.

Implicit in all legal actions is the intention of universal application, which means that in identical cases the sanction imposed is the same. Although one might argue that no two legal cases have been or will ever be identical, the notion of universal application requires that the law be consistent and thus predictable; the arbitrary imposition of sanctions is not law.

Hoebel limited legal sanctions to physical sanctions. However, other scholars have argued that this definition

▲ Gossip is one of the primary means of social control.

is too narrow. A legal sanction does not have to be some form of corporal punishment, nor does it have to involve the loss of property. Based on his work with the Kapauku of New Guinea, Leopold Pospisil contended that the impact of psychological sanctions can be more severe than that of actual physical punishment. For this reason he stated, "We can define a legal sanction as either the negative behavior of withdrawing some rewards or favors that otherwise (if the law had not been violated) would have been granted, or the positive behavior of inflicting some painful experience, be it physical or psychological" (Pospisil 1958, 268).

Legal Systems

On the basis of procedural characteristics, two main levels of complexity and formality can be defined: self-help legal systems and court legal systems.

Self-Help Systems

Self-help legal systems, also called *ad hoc systems,* are informal and exist in the absence of any centralized or formalized legal institutions capable of settling disputes. Such systems are associated with band-level societies and most tribal-level societies. In such systems there is only civil law. All legal actions concern only the principal parties and/or their families. The reason for terming the legal procedure in these societies *self-help* will become clear.

Self-help legal systems fall into two main forms: (1) familial and (2) mediator. In *familial* systems, all actions and decisions are initiated and executed by the families or larger kin groups involved. *Mediator* systems add the formal presence of a neutral third party—the mediator—who attempts to negotiate and resolve the dispute peacefully.

In familial systems, legal actions are handled by the families involved. A legal offense only indirectly concerns the community as a whole. When an individual and/or family determines that its rights have been violated, the imposition of the proper sanction falls to the plaintiffs; in other words, the offended party assumes the role of authority. Such a system has some problems in implementation, but not as many as one might anticipate. This is not a system of "might makes right." Certainly cases arise in such societies in which the physically (or militarily) weak are victimized by the strong. However, in cases of legal redress there is a community consensus in support of the victim and usually a recognized means by which even the weakest members of the community can gather support adequate to impose appropriate sanctions on the strongest.

The Comanche exemplify how a familial legal system operated and how victims weaker than their opponents could nonetheless obtain redress. One of the most frequent Comanche offenses was "wife stealing." Most older Comanche men were polygynous, and some of their wives were significantly younger than their husbands. Among young Comanche men it was considered prestigious, although illegal, to steal the wife of another man. Under Comanche law the injured husband could demand either his wife back or some property, usually horses, in compensation. The husband had the responsibility of imposing these sanctions. In such actions the community played no direct role, but a husband could not ignore the loss of a wife. If he did ignore it, the community would ridicule him, and his prestige would decline. Thus, not only did the community support the husband in pressing his claim, but they informally pressured him to act.

In imposing these sanctions the husband was allowed to use whatever physical force was needed, short of killing the offender. In cases in which the men involved were physically about equal, the two met to negotiate and discuss the husband's demands. Behind these negotiations was the potential threat that the husband might physically assault the defendant.

In cases where the husband presented little or no physical threat to the defendant, institutionalized means existed whereby the husband could gain physical backing. Although it lowered his prestige in the community, he could call on his relatives for support; with his male relatives present and prepared to support his demands phys-

ically, the husband could then negotiate with the defendant. The defendant always had to stand alone. Even if he had asked his kinsmen for support, they would not have responded for fear of community ridicule.

In cases where the husband was an orphan or lacked kinsmen, he could call on any other man he wanted to prosecute his case. He usually asked for the assistance of one of the powerful war leaders in the band. Such a request was so prestigious that a war leader could not refuse. At the same time, such a request was demeaning to the man asking for help and greatly lowered his prestige. As a result, it usually required a great deal of social pressure to force a man to ask for assistance. Once the request was made, the issue was between the defendant and the war leader alone. On approaching the defendant the war leader would call out, "You have stolen my wife," and then proceed to exact whatever demands the husband had requested. For his action the war leader received nothing in payment other than the admiration of the community; the husband received the settlement. Although this process most commonly was used in wife-stealing cases, it could be used for other issues as well. Thus, Comanche legal institutions gave any individual the means to marshal overwhelming physical force in the protection of his rights.

A more formalized type of legal procedure is found in the mediator system. Under this system, disputes are still between individuals and families. The offended party and/or the person's family fills the position of authority. However, a third party is called on, usually by the offending individual or his or her family, to attempt to negotiate a mutually agreeable solution. The mediator has no authority to impose a settlement. The aggrieved party and/or family must agree to accept the compensation negotiated.

The Nuer, a pastoral tribal society of Sudan, provide an example of how mediator systems operate. The Nuer live in small villages of related families. Although villages are tied together through lineages and clans, there is no effective leadership above the village level. The only formalized leaders who transcend the local units are *leopard-skin chiefs,* whose position is indicated by the wearing of a leopard-skin cloak. These men have no secular authority to enforce their judgments but only limited ritual powers to bless and curse.

The most important function of leopard-skin chiefs is mediating feuds between local groups. The Nuer are an egalitarian, warrior-oriented people. Disputes between individuals frequently result in physical violence, and men occasionally are killed. The killing requires that the kinsmen exact retribution. Any close patrilineal kinsman of the murderer may be killed in retaliation, but at least initially the kinsmen of the victim attempt to kill the murderer himself. Immediately after committing a murder the killer flees to the house of a leopard-skin chief. This dwelling is a sanctuary, and as long as the man stays in the chief's house he is safe. The victim's kinsmen usually keep the house under surveillance to try to kill the murderer if he ventures out.

The leopard-skin chief keeps the murderer in his house until a settlement is arranged. The chief will wait until tempers have cooled, which usually requires several weeks, before he begins to negotiate the case. First, he goes to the family of the murderer to see if they are willing to pay cattle to the victim's family in compensation. Seldom do they refuse, because one of them might be killed in retaliation. After the murderer's family has agreed to pay, the chief proceeds to the family of the victim, offering so many cattle in compensation. Initially the victim's family invariably refuses, saying that they want blood, that cattle cannot compensate them for the death of their beloved kinsman. The leopard-skin chief persists, usually gaining the support of more distant relatives of the victim who also pressure the family to settle. The leopard-skin chief may even threaten to place a curse on the family if they continue to refuse to settle for a payment rather than blood. The family finally agrees and accepts cattle, usually about 40 head, as compensation. Even though the matter is formally settled, the killer and his close patrilineal kinsmen will avoid the family of the victim for some years so as not to provoke spontaneous retaliation.

Up to this point we have examined legal systems that operate without a formalized or centralized political structure capable of resolving disputes. In many of these societies law, not subordination to a common set of formal political institutions, defines boundaries. To see what we mean, consider the Nuer. The Nuer distinguish among a *ter*, or a feud within a tribe that is a legal action subject to arbitration; a *kur*, or a fight between members of two tribes that cannot be arbitrated; and a *pec*, or a war with non-Nuer people. Nuer believe that disputes within a tribe should be resolved by legal means (that is, peacefully), whereas disputes between individuals who are not members of the same tribe should be resolved by extralegal means, including organized warfare. Legal processes serve to repair and maintain social relations between families; thus, law serves both to maintain the cohesiveness and to define the boundaries of the society.

The Jívaro, a horticultural and foraging people of eastern Ecuador, illustrate how law defines social boundaries. By the 1950s, the Jívaro had been reduced to slightly more than 2,000 persons settled in more than 200 scattered family households. Such households usually consist of a husband, his wife or wives, their children, and possibly a son-in-law or other relatives. Households are grouped into "neighborhoods," which consist of a number of households living within a few miles of one another; the membership of a neighborhood is fluid. Poor hunting, a dispute with other households, or other factors might result in a family's moving away. Neither corporate kin groups nor formalized leadership positions exist. Except for household heads, only a few men are called *unta*, or "big," but their informal leadership role is limited and transitory.

Politically, the Jívaro are organized at a band level. Although they have only limited political institutions, the Jívaro have a strong sense of common cultural identity and territorial boundaries. Living in adjacent or nearby territories are four other "Jívaroan" groups, who speak mutually intelligible dialects, share the same basic customs, and at times trade with Jívaro households. Despite their minimal political integration, there is little question about which households are Jívaro and which belong to the other four groups.

With this political organization, the methods used to settle disputes define the effective boundaries of the society. Disputes between Jívaros are resolved by legal means, whereas disputes with members of other societies are resolved through extralegal means. Like the Nuer, the Jívaro make a sharp distinction between a feud and a war. A **feud** is the legal means by which a sanction is imposed on another family for the murder of a kinsman. As a legal procedure, a feud proceeds in a manner quite different from a war.

As in most societies, murder is the most serious offense. According to Jívaro beliefs, few deaths are attributable to natural causes; most are the result of physical violence, sorcery, or avenging spirits. Deaths caused by physical violence and witchcraft are considered murders, which have to be avenged by the kinsmen of the deceased. In most cases of physical violence, the murderer is readily identifiable. In cases of poisoning and witchcraft, divination is used to determine the guilty party.

Determination of the guilty party and whether they are Jívaro or non-Jívaro affect how the victim's kinfolk avenge the death. If the guilty party is Jívaro, the kinsmen of the victim attack the household of the murderer with the goal of killing the man himself. If they are not successful in finding him, they may kill a male relative of his, even a young boy. They normally will not harm women or little children, except when the victim was a woman or a child. Even if they have the opportunity to kill more, only one individual will be killed. This is a legal action, and Jívaro law allows only a life for a life.

If the guilty party is determined to be a non-Jívaro, the relatives of the murdered person attack the household of the guilty party, trying to kill as many people as possible. They attempt to massacre the entire family, with no regard for either sex or age. In some cases they attack nearby households as well, attempting to kill even more members of the group. This is a war, not a legal action.

The Jívaro, the Nuer, and other peoples who lack a centralized and formal political structure nonetheless have definite means of maintaining social control. To those of us who have formal governmental institutions that are supposed to handle our grievances and right the wrongs done to us, self-help systems look rather anarchic. However, rules govern such systems. Some anthropologists believe, in fact, that the best definition of *society* in self-help systems is those individuals whose vengeance-taking activities are constrained by procedural rules.

Court Systems

A number of factors distinguish a **court legal system** from a self-help legal system. First, authority resides not with the victim and his or her family but with a formalized institution, the court. The court has the authority and the power to hear disputes and to unilaterally decide cases and impose sanctions. Authority in legal matters is a component of political authority; thus, fully developed court systems can exist only in societies that have centralized formal political leadership, that is, chiefdoms or states. Second, most court systems operate with formal public hearings, presided over by a judge or judges, with formally defined defendants and plaintiffs. Grievances are stated, evidence is collected and analyzed, and, in cases of conflicting evidence, oaths or ordeals may be used to determine truthfulness. Finally, only in court systems does one find substantive law clearly divided into criminal law and civil law.

Court systems in turn may be divided into three categories: (1) **incipient courts,** (2) **courts of mediation,** and (3) **courts of regulation.** All court systems mediate disputes as well as regulate behavior; however, as societies become increasingly complex, the primary focus of the court shifts from mediating disputes to regulating behavior. This shift results in a qualitative difference not only in courts but in the nature of the law itself. Associated with this shift is an increasing codification of the laws. Laws and their associated sanctions become standardized and rigid, and civil laws are steadily transformed into criminal laws. Court systems begin to emerge with the concept of "crime against society"—the need to control individual acts that might endanger the society as a whole, as opposed to acts that threaten only individuals. Herein lies the distinction between criminal law and civil law.

Incipient Court Systems. True court systems can only be found in societies with centralized political systems—chiefdoms or states. However, some tribal societies have what might best be termed *incipient courts.* Although a tribal-level society, the Cheyenne, as described earlier in this chapter, demonstrate the development of an incipient court system. At times, both the Council of Forty-Four and the warrior societies assumed the role of de facto judges and courts. The Cheyenne recognized that certain individual actions threatened the well-being of the group and thus had to be controlled. Some of these actions were purely secular, whereas others were religious. Designated warrior societies were formally empowered by the council to enforce secular laws and regulations. For example, in preparation for a communal bison hunt, camp members would be told to refrain from independent hunting for some days. If the policing warrior society discovered someone hunting illegally, the men present became the de facto judges and court and immediately imposed sanctions on the offender, often beating him with whips, shooting his horses, and slashing his tipi with knives.

Other secular criminal violations were handled just as swiftly. The Council of Forty-Four was responsible for the religious, or sacred, well-being of the tribe; thus, any action that endangered the supernatural well-being of the Cheyenne was their concern. The murder of a Cheyenne by another Cheyenne was the most heinous of crimes. Such a crime was said to bloody the sacred arrows, the most sacred of Cheyenne tribal medicine bundles. The arrows were symbolic of Cheyenne success in hunting (their main economic activity) and warfare. Murder within the tribe polluted the arrows and thus made the Cheyenne vulnerable to their enemies and less successful in their hunting. When a Cheyenne died at the hands of another Cheyenne, the Council of Forty-Four became a de facto court. Although there was no formal hearing, the council met and discussed the case: Was it murder? If so, then the sacred arrows had to be "renewed," or ritually purified. They also decided on the sanction to be imposed—usually exile for a period of years. With the Cheyenne there could be no capital punishment without again polluting the sacred arrows. In A Closer Look we have a further discussion of the Cheyenne.

Courts of Mediation. The key difference between court systems is not how the legal hearings are conducted, but the manner in which breaches of the law are determined and suitable sanctions imposed. In courts of mediation few laws are codified, and the judges follow few formalized guidelines as to what constitutes a legal violation or the sanction that should be imposed. This is not to say that

Murder Among the Cheyenne

The killing of one Cheyenne by another was not only a "sin" that "polluted" the murderer and endangered the well-being of the tribe but also a crime against the society. This pollution of the sacred arrows caused the game animals that Cheyenne depended on for their subsistence to shun their hunting territory. A killing required the ritual purification of the sacred arrows. However, not every killing was considered a criminal act. On hearing of a killing within the band, the members of the Council of Forty-Four assembled. Exactly how and what they discussed in such cases we shall never know; but the council members had to decide when a killing was to be treated as a murder. Was suicide murder? Was abortion murder? Was a killing ever justifiable? Was drunkenness a mitigating circumstance? If the council determined that a murder had taken place, the chiefs ordered the immediate banishment of the murderer. Such banishment usually included not only the murderer but also the murderer's family and sometimes friends who went along voluntarily. This banishment usually lasted between 5 and 10 years. During the period of exile, the banished individual usually lived with a friendly group of Arapahos or Dakotas.

The act of suicide was not typically considered murder. Several cases are known of Cheyenne women committing suicide for what were considered trivial reasons. Such cases were not considered murder, and as far as can be determined, the sacred arrows were not renewed. In other instances, however, suicide was treated as murder. For example, one mother became infuriated when her daughter eloped with a young man of whom she did not approve. The mother found the girl and beat her with a whip while dragging her home. Inside the tipi the girl seized a gun and shot herself. In another case, a young girl divorced her husband and returned to her parents' home. At some later time, her mother found the girl participating in a young persons' dance and beat her; the girl subsequently hung herself. In both cases, the chiefs ruled that the girls were driven to suicide by their mothers, who were thus considered the murderers. In both cases the sacred arrows were renewed, and the mothers were banished.

Was a killing ever justifiable? In one case, a man attempted to rape his daughter, who resisted and used a knife to kill her father. The sacred arrows were renewed, but the chiefs did not order the girl banished, nor did the people treat her as a murderer. In another case, a man named Winnebago took the wife of another man, who retaliated by taking one of Winnebago's wives. Winnebago was enraged and killed the second man; he was then banished. After his return from banishment Winnebago argued with and killed a second man, so he was banished again. While living among the Arapaho, Winnebago became involved in a dispute with a Cheyenne named Rising Fire, who knew of Winnebago's murders and therefore shot Winnebago out of fear.

Although the facts are unclear, it appears that Rising Fire was not exiled for this killing. Thus, under some circumstances, such as incestuous rape and the fear of a known murderer, the chiefs thought that killing was justifiable. In such instances the sacred arrows had to be renewed, but the killer was not exiled.

Was drunkenness a mitigating circumstance? During a drunken brawl, Cries-Yia-Eya killed Chief Eagle. In another case, during a drunken party, Porcupine Bear stabbed Little Creek and then called on his relatives to stab Little Creek as well. They did so, killing Little Creek. Cries-Yia-Eya and Porcupine Bear and his guilty relatives were banished by the chiefs; drunkenness was not a defense for murder.

The chiefs were faced with a second issue regarding Little Creek's killers. After their banishment, Porcupine Bear and his relatives continued to stay close to the band camp. When the tribe organized a revenge attack on the Kiowas, Porcupine Bear and his relatives kept their distance but followed along with the other Cheyenne. In the attack on the Kiowas, Porcupine Bear and his six relatives distinguished themselves by bravely attacking first and killing about 30 Kiowas. What about war honors for acts of bravery accomplished during banishment? The council ruled that exiles could not receive recognition for their military acts, no matter how courageous they might be. In a sense, during their period of banishment they were not Cheyenne.

Was abortion murder? In one case, a fetus was found near a Cheyenne camp. An investigation by a warrior society discovered that a young girl had concealed her pregnancy. The young girl was banished, but only until after the sacred arrows had been renewed. Thus, the chiefs considered abortion a less serious type of murder that required a shorter period of banishment.

The chiefs had to answer many other questions concerning murder and banishment. About 1855 one of the chiefs, a member of the Council of Forty-Four, killed another Cheyenne. The sacred arrows were renewed and the chief was banished; but what was to be done about his position on the council? The council ruled that the man could not be removed from office and that he remained a chief even though he could not participate in the council.

From the discussion of these cases emerges some of the reasoning behind Cheyenne legal decisions. The chiefs considered a range of factors in reaching their final determinations. Murder included not merely the cold-blooded killing of one Cheyenne by another, it also included abortion and acts that compelled another to commit suicide. At the same time, the chiefs thought that in particular instances killing was justifiable, but that intoxication was not a mitigating factor.

Source: Llewellyn and Hoebel (1941).

judges act arbitrarily in these matters, but that they have tremendous latitude in their actions. What they apply is a **reasonable-person model.** Using prevalent norms and values, they ask the question, How should a reasonable individual have acted under these circumstances? To determine this, an individual's actions have to be examined within the social context in which the dispute occurred: What was the past and present relationship between the parties involved? What were the circumstances leading up to the event? Thus judges attempt to examine each case as a unique occurrence. Although some sanctions are imposed as punishments, other sanctions are designed to restore as fully as possible a working, if not harmonious, relationship between the parties involved.

One difficulty in attempting to describe courts of mediation is our limited knowledge of such systems. Polities having courts of this nature were some time ago brought under European colonial rule. Their courts were soon modified by and subordinated to European colonial courts, which were more regulatory in nature. The example we use is that of the Barotse judicial system, as described by Max Gluckman. The Barotse made up a multiethnic state in southern Africa that at the time of Gluckman's study in the 1940s had been under British rule for 40 years. More serious offenses had been removed by the British from the jurisdiction of this court. Despite these factors, the basic Barotse legal concepts aptly illustrate a mediation type of court system.

The Barotse state had two capitals—a northern capital, where the king resided, and a subordinate southern capital, ruled by a princess. All villages in the state were attached to one or the other of these capitals. The capitals were identical in structure; each had a palace and a council house. Courts of law were held in the council house.

The titular head of the court was the ruler; in practice, the ruler seldom was present at trials. In the center at the back of the house was the dais, or raised platform, where the ruler was seated if present. There were three ranked groupings of judges. The highest-ranking group of judges was the *indunas,* or councilors, who sat to the right of the dais. The second-highest-ranking group was the *likombwa,* or stewards, who sat to the left. These two groups were divided into senior members, who sat in the front, and junior members, who sat behind. The third group consisted of princes and the husbands of the princesses, who represented their wives. This group sat at a right angle to the *likombwa.*

A case was introduced by a plaintiff, who was allowed to state his or her grievance at length with no interruption; the defendant was then allowed the same privilege. The statements of witnesses for both sides followed.

There were no attorneys for either side; the judges questioned and cross-examined the witnesses. After all the testimony had been heard, the judges began to give their opinions, starting with the most junior *indunas,* followed by the others in order of increasing seniority. The last judge to speak was the senior *induna,* who passed judgment on the case, subject to the ruler's approval.

In judging a case, the Barotse judges used a reasonable-person model. The reasonableness of behavior was related to the social and kinship relationships of the individuals involved. Also, a breach of the law usually did not happen in isolation, and many individuals could be at fault; so one case frequently led to a number of related cases. In passing judgment and imposing sanctions, the judges considered numerous factors. One of the most important was the kinship relationship between the parties. The judges attempted to restore the relationship and reconcile the parties—but not without blaming those who had committed wrongs and not without imposing sanctions. The judges' opinions frequently took the form of sermons on proper behavior. As Gluckman (1973, 22) notes:

> Implicit in the reasonable man is the upright man, and moral issues in these relationships are barely differentiated from legal issues. This is so even though . . . [they] distinguish "legal" rules, which the . . . [court] has power to enforce or protect, from "moral" rules which it has not power to enforce or protect. But the judges are reluctant to support the person who is right in law, but wrong in justice, and may seek to achieve justice by indirect . . . action.

Courts of mediation have great potential for meeting the basic social purpose of the law, which is the maintenance of group cohesiveness. There is one serious drawback: such a system is workable only in a culturally homogeneous political unit; that is, it works only if the judges and the parties involved share the same basic norms and values.

Courts of Regulation. In the second millennium B.C. the Code of Hammurabi, the earliest known set of written laws, was created in Babylon. The code covered a variety of laws. One section dealt with physicians. It set the prices to be charged for various types of operations, based on the ability of individuals to pay. It also decreed, among other things, that if a surgeon operated on an individual using a bronze knife and the patient died or lost his eyesight, the surgeon's hand was to be cut off. The laws defined in the Code of Hammurabi reflect the emergence of regulatory laws. The role of the court was no longer to merely arbitrate disputes and strive for reconciliation but to define the rights and duties of members of an increasingly heterogeneous community.

Form	Characteristics	Associated Political System(s)
Self-Help (a) Familial	Legal concepts based on accepted social norms and behaviors of the society. Ad hoc sanctioning authority limited to victim and/or victim's family, with implicit support of other community members.	Band
(b) Mediator	Legal concepts based on accepted social norms and behaviors of the society. Ad hoc sanctioning authority limited to victim and/or victim's family, with implicit support of other community members. Use of a third-party mediator, with limited if any authority, to negotiate a settlement.	Found among composite bands and most tribal peoples.
Courts (a) Mediation	Legal concepts based on the reasonable-person model. Formal judges who have the authority to hear cases and impose sanctions.	Some tribal peoples have rudimentary court systems. However, true court systems appear with chiefdoms and smaller states.
(b) Regulation	Laws and sanctions are formally codified. Formal judges who have the authority to hear cases and impose sanctions.	States

Courts of regulation were a natural outgrowth of state-level polities, which evolved socially and economically distinct classes and encompassed numerous culturally distinct peoples. As relationships between individuals in the population became depersonalized, the law, too, became increasingly depersonalized. This change in the nature of law was compounded by the political incorporation of diverse peoples who frequently had conflicting cultural norms and values. The use of a reasonable-person model is workable only as long as there is a general consensus on what is "reasonable." In increasingly complex and stratified societies, the possibility of such consensus declined. Mediation of disputes works well in small, kinship-based societies, where all parties recognize the need for reconciliation through compromise. In sharply divided societies, the need for mediation is not as great because reconciliation in itself is not seen as a gain. Compromise is viewed only in terms of what is lost. Laws were thus created to bring order and stability to the interactions between individuals who were not social equals. With law divorced from social norms and values, justice was no longer simply a moral or ethical issue, but came to be viewed in terms of consistency, or precedent.

The separation of law from social norms and values also allowed for the "politicization" of the laws. Laws were created to serve political ends, as various groups vied with one another for the creation of laws that would protect, express, or further their own goals, interests, and values. This situation is particularly evident in multiethnic and religious and economically diverse state-level systems such as that of the United States. Given the cultural pluralism, religious diversity, and economic inequality of the United States, it would be impossible to create a code of laws that could equally protect the interests of all classes and that would be consistent with the norms and values of all groups. As a result, many people find themselves subject to laws and sanctions, many of which they judge either immoral or unethical; at times, people find that laws violate their own cultural values. We see this with groups who think that abortion is murder and thus should be made illegal, and with groups who oppose capital punishment on the grounds that the state does not have the right to kill individuals. During the Vietnam War, we saw it with draft resisters who argued that the state did not have the right to order men to fight in a war they considered immoral. Less obvious is the manner in which numerous ethnic minorities, notably Native Americans, subordinate their cultural norms and values to comply with the legal system. With the emergence of states and courts of regulation, law ceased to be an expression of social norms and values and became their molder.

Summary

1. Political organization and social control are distinct but overlapping cultural institutions. Group action—in both economic and social activities—is a prerequisite for the survival of the population. To be effective, group activities must have leadership and organization, which are the basis for political structure. At the same time, individual differences, conflict, and competition within the group must be controlled and channeled in such a manner that the internal cohesiveness and cooperation of the individual members of the group are maintained—thus the need for social control.

2. Four major categories of political organization are bands, tribes, chiefdoms, and states. Found among foraging societies, the band is the simplest and least formal level of political organization. The two forms of band organization are simple bands and composite bands.

3. In simple bands, the highest level of political organization is the extended family, with the highest level of political leadership being the heads of the various families. These simple bands are economically self-sufficient and politically autonomous. Because a simple band has as its core a group of related individuals, band members are forced to seek spouses from outside the band; they are exogamous units. Thus, kinship ties through marriage serve as the primary link between bands. Simple bands most commonly are found among foragers who hunt game animals that are present in small numbers year-round.

4. Composite bands are larger than simple bands and include a number of distinct families. Leadership in composite bands is vested in "big men," or informal leaders, who have influence but not authority. Composite bands most often are found among foragers who hunt migratory herd animals.

5. At the tribal level, institutions transcend local residence groups and bind the geographically scattered members of the society into a cohesive unit. The key element in tribal societies is the sodality, which may be either kinship-based, as in the case of clans, or nonkinship-based, as in the case of warrior societies or age grades. Leadership in such groups is more structured, with formal political offices.

6. Chiefdoms have formal, hereditary leadership with centralized political control and authority. The associated redistributive economic exchange system focused on the chief economically integrates the various communities within the political unit.

7. The state is the most complex level of political organization. States have centralized power and control, but the key characteristic of a state is the presence of a bureaucracy—individuals acting on behalf of the political elite, thus enabling the centralized power figures to maintain control of a greater number of individuals.

8. Social control consists of the various methods used to control and channel the behavior of individual members of a society into approved behavior. Law and legal systems are merely the highest level of social control. Law is defined as having three attributes: (1) authority, (2) intention of universal application, and (3) sanction. By this definition, all societies have law.

9. In societies without centralized political systems, legal systems are self-help. In self-help systems, the responsibility and authority for determining a breach of the law and imposition of the proper sanction fall to the victim or victim's family (or both). As discussed, this system is not as arbitrary as we might think. In the case of murder or killing, the result may be a feud between families, but a feud—sharply distinguished from a war—is part of the legal process.

10. Law in societies with centralized political systems is handled by courts. Court systems usually can be categorized as either courts of mediation or courts of regulation. In relatively homogeneous societies, most court systems take as their primary objective the mediation of disputes between individuals and the restoration of harmonious social relationships. In more heterogeneous groups, courts usually become more regulatory in nature, with formally defined laws and sanctions.

Key Terms

simple bands
composite bands
big men
influence

authority
tribes
sodalities
chiefdoms

states
social control
law
self-help legal systems

feud
court legal systems

incipient courts
courts of mediation

courts of regulation
reasonable-person model

 InfoTrac College Edition Terms

big men leader
chiefdom

reasonable-man

tribal law

Suggested Readings

Cohen, R., and Elman Service, eds. *Origins of the State: The Anthropology of Political Evolution.* Philadelphia: Institute for the Study of Human Issues, 1978.

A collection of essays from various perspectives examining the development of state-level political systems.

Fried, Morton. *The Evolution of Political Society.* New York: Random House, 1967.

A theoretical study that traces the development of political systems from egalitarian societies, through ranked, to stratified and state-level societies.

Haas, Jonathan (ed.). *From Leaders to Rulers.* New York: Kluwer Academic/Plenum Publishers, 2001.

Making use primarily of archaeological data, the 10 scholars whose papers appear in this volume discuss one of the most critical issues in the evolution of political leadership. How and why did centralized systems develop and leadership shift from informal leaders with only influence, to formal rulers with the authority to command their followers?

Hoebel, E. Adamson. *The Law of Primitive Man.* Cambridge, Mass.: Harvard University Press, 1964.

The first major comparative study of non-Western legal systems. Although somewhat dated, it remains a classic study.

Newman, Katherine S. *Law and Economic Organization: A Comparative Study of Pre-Industrial Societies.* Cambridge: Cambridge University Press, 1983.

A cross-cultural analysis of 60 societies to show that legal institutions systematically vary with economic organization.

The following ethnographies are excellent descriptions of political and/or legal systems within particular societies.

Gluckman, Max. *The Ideas in Barotse Jurisprudence.* Manchester: Manchester University Press, 1965.

————. *The Judicial Process Among the Barotse.* Manchester: Manchester University Press, 1973.

These two studies of the Barotse of Zambia not only describe a system in a non-Western state but also—and more important—illustrate the legal reasoning used in their court systems. Good description of the political structure and legal system of a band-level society.

Kuper, Hilda. *The Swazi: A South African Kingdom.* 2nd ed. New York: Holt, Rinehart and Winston, 1986.

An excellent short ethnography of Swaziland, now an independent nation. Has a good discussion of recent changes.

Llewellyn, Karl, and E. Adamson Hoebel. *The Cheyenne Way.* Norman: University of Oklahoma Press, 1941.

A classic study of the legal system of a tribal society.

Companion Website for This Book

**The Wadsworth Anthropology Resource Center
http://anthropology.wadsworth.com**

The companion website that accompanies *Humanity: An Introduction to Cultural Anthropology,* Seventh Edition, includes a rich array of material, including online anthropological video clips, to help you in the study of cultural anthropology and the specific topics covered in this chapter. Begin by clicking on Student Resources. Next, click on Cultural Anthropology, and then on the cover image

for this book. You have now arrived at the Student Resources home page and have the option of choosing one of several chapter resources.

Applying Anthropology. Begin your study of cultural anthropology by clicking on Applying Anthropology. Here you will find useful information on careers, graduate school programs in applied anthropology, and internships you might wish to pursue. You will also find real-world examples of working anthropologists applying the skills and methods of anthropology to help solve serious world problems.

Research Online. Click here to find a wealth of Web links that will facilitate your study of anthropology. Divided into different fields of study, specific websites are starting points for Internet research. You will be guided to rich anthropology websites that will help you prepare for class, complete course assignments, and actually do research on the Web.

InfoTrac College Edition Exercises. From the pull-down menu, select the chapter you are presently studying. Select InfoTrac College Edition Exercises from the list of resources. These exercises utilize InfoTrac College Edition's vast database of articles and help you explore the numerous uses of the search word, *culture*.

Study Aids for This Chapter. Improve your knowledge of key terms by using flash cards and study the learning objectives. Take the practice quiz, receive your results, and e-mail them to your instructor. Access these resources from the chapter and resource pull-down menus.

Chapter Thirteen

SOCIAL INEQUALITY AND STRATIFICATION

Systems of Equality and Inequality

Egalitarian Societies

Ranked Societies

Stratified Societies

Castes in Traditional India

Classes in Industrial Societies: The United States

Maintaining Inequality

Ideologies

American Secular Ideologies

Theories of Inequality

Functionalist Theory

Conflict Theory

Who Benefits?

© Darkside Productions/Corbis

In stratified societies, large differences in wealth exist and are tolerated and even encouraged. These people in Cape Town, South Africa, seem to be doing well in life.

"WE HOLD THESE TRUTHS TO BE SELF-EVIDENT, that all men are created equal, that they are endowed by their Creator with certain unalienable Rights . . ." As you can guess by now, whether in fact all "men" are believed to have been created equal depends on which society you happened to have been born into. Whether you have certain "unalienable rights," and the nature of these rights, also varies from people to people. In this chapter we consider another dimension of cultural diversity—the differential allocation of rewards.

Systems of Equality and Inequality

All human groups assign individuals to roles (Chapter 2). Your role in some group to which you belong, or in society at large, affects your tasks or jobs, your relationships with other group members, and, in some cases, your access to rewards. **Inequality** refers to the degree to which culturally valued material and social rewards are given disproportionately to individuals, families, and other kinds of groups. To the extent that inequality exists in a group or whole society, the members receive varying levels of benefits.

Before discussing cross-cultural variations, we must consider the nature of rewards. They are commonly divided into three categories. The most tangible reward is *wealth*—ownership of or access to valued material goods and/or to the natural and human resources needed to produce them. A second reward is *power*—the ability to make others do what you want based on coercion or legitimate authority. A final type of reward is *prestige*—the respect, esteem, and overt approval other group members grant to individuals they consider meritorious. Prestige (or *honor*, or *status*) is a social reward, based on judgments about an individual's personal worthiness or the contributions the individual makes to others in the group.

The distribution of each kind of reward varies between societies. Some allow ambitious individuals to acquire wealth, power, and prestige, whereas others make it difficult for anyone to accumulate possessions, gain control over others, or put themselves above their peers socially. For instance, many North Americans admire "self-made" men and women who have supposedly earned higher income (wealth) than other people by their own talents and efforts. But such individuals would be looked down on as self-centered and ungenerous in many other cultures.

The best way to introduce the ways societies differ in inequality is with an influential classification used by Morton Fried back in 1967. Fried identified three basic types of societies based on their degrees of inequality. He labeled these societies **egalitarian, ranked,** and **stratified.** A description and examples of each type appear later in this section. The differences among the three forms are summarized in the Concept Review. We need to clarify three points about Fried's classification.

First, the categories do not refer to access to rewards based on sex or age. When we call a society *egalitarian,* for example, we do not mean that females and males receive equal or nearly equal rewards, or that elderly people and young people are socially equal. Even in egalitarian societies there are social distinctions based on sex and age. Essentially, *egalitarian* means that there are few differences in the rewards received by families or other kinds of kin groups within a society. At the other end of the continuum, in societies we call *stratified,* there are major differences in access to rewards between families and/or kin groups, in addition to any distinctions based on sex or age.

Second, Fried's three categories are merely points along a continuous spectrum of inequality. It is impossible to pigeonhole all human societies into one of these types because most fit somewhere in between the three categories. The terms *egalitarian, ranked,* and *stratified* are useful mainly as short descriptions of the kinds and range of variation in inequality found cross-culturally.

Third, egalitarian–ranked–stratified is the temporal order in which the three forms developed. Until about 10,000 years ago, most people lived in egalitarian societies. Ranked societies developed in a few areas about then, and a few thousand years later stratification developed in some early chiefdoms and in the great civilizations. Archaeologists have devised some clever means to find out about inequality in prehistoric societies, and there is wide (but not universal) agreement that most of the world's people were quite egalitarian until the development of agriculture. Afterwards, over the next 4,000 to 5,000 years, stratified societies spread throughout most of the world, as some peoples and nations conquered and ruled over others.

Egalitarian Societies

In egalitarian societies, aside from distinctions based on sex and age, there are minor differences between individuals and families in rewards. People who work hard, or who have attractive personalities or valuable skills, may be rewarded with respect and prestige from other members of their group. But egalitarian groups have various cultural mechanisms to prevent any individual from becoming too "big." And even people who are respected have few, if any, more possessions or power than others.

Mobile hunting and gathering peoples such as the Inuit, !Kung, Hadza, BaMbuti, and Aka are egalitarian. Back in 1982, James Woodburn identified several reasons why rewards are rather evenly distributed among such foragers. First, and most obviously, frequent seasonal movements of the band or camp are necessary for effective adaptation (Chapter 6). Mobility makes it difficult to transport possessions, and hence to accumulate wealth.

Second, the cultural value foragers place on reciprocal sharing (see Chapter 7) helps prevent individuals or family groups from becoming wealthier than their band mates. Because sharing of food and most durable possessions is normatively expected, hoarding and accumulation are negatively evaluated. So even if someone should try

Form	Main Characteristics
Egalitarian	Rough equality across families in access to possessions and wealth objects
	Wide availability and sharing of productive resources
	Influence and prestige based on age and personal qualities and achievements
Ranked	Limited number of formal positions (offices, titles) that grant authority
	Access to prestigious titles and offices determined largely by kinship and heredity
	Rights to resources allocated by those of higher rank
Stratified	Highly unequal distribution of resources and wealth, with large differences in access to power and social rewards (prestige)
Caste	Named, endogamous, hierarchically ranked groups with membership normatively determined by birth
	Occupation and economic activities limited by caste category
	Social rules constraining interaction between members of different castes (e.g., segregation, pollution)
Class	Hierarchically ranked groups, often with ambiguous membership determined by a combination of birth and achievement
	Productive resources privately owned by a minority, with lower-class persons working for higher-class persons

to, he or she would find it difficult to accumulate because other people demand their share, and failure to adhere to norms of sharing and to live up to egalitarian values is socially punished by public ridicule or worse.

Third, among mobile foragers, families are not tied to specific territories but have the right to visit and exploit the resources of many areas, often due to bilateral kinship relations (Chapter 9). If anyone tries to give orders or exercise control over others, people have enough options that they are free to leave and live elsewhere.

In sum, if people move around in their environments a lot, are required to share food and other possessions, and have a range of options about where to live and whom to live with, then inequality in wealth and power does not have much chance of developing. If it should develop, it does not have much chance of persisting for very long.

Not all foragers are or were egalitarian, however. The Native Americans of the Northwest Coast, for instance, lived in ranked societies because in their rich environment the three conditions just listed did not exist. Northwest Coast people were more sedentary, accumulated wealth in order to distribute it to validate and acquire rank, and formed kin groups that were mostly associated with particular territories (see Chapter 6).

Most hunting and gathering bands do have informal leaders whose decisions are respected because others defer to their age or skill at particular activities or because they seem to have some kind of spiritual powers. By and large, such leaders are *headmen,* who have only influence, not authority (Chapter 12). Only rarely is decision-making authority vested in a formal office or title to

which certain individuals automatically succeed. This is the most important difference between egalitarian and ranked societies.

Ranked Societies

In ranked societies there are a limited number of high-ranking social positions, usually named titles or some kind of formal offices that grant authority: people who hold the title can issue commands and expect to have them obeyed. The titles also confer high honor on people who hold them. In most cases, the privilege of holding a title or occupying an office is largely or entirely hereditary within certain families, lineages, clans, or other kin groups. If you are born into a group that does not have the hereditary right to the title or office, normatively (but not always in fact) you cannot succeed to the office regardless of your talents or ambitions.

In one of the most common types of ranked societies, all kin groups are ranked relative to one another, with each group having its own unique rank relative to every other group. Further, within each kin group, each member is ranked relative to all others, usually on the principle of genealogical seniority (elders being superior in rank to younger people). The highest-ranking individuals of the highest-ranking kin group hold the most valued positions that bring the highest rewards in prestige, power, and in some societies, wealth. This way of ranking individuals and kin groups existed among many peoples of the Northwest Coast and also is well documented for several ancient Polynesian chiefdoms.

▲ Like most mobile hunter-gatherers, the !Kung (ju/'hoansi) are an egalitarian people.

An excellent example of such a ranked society is Tikopia, a tiny Pacific island whose kinship system is described in Chapter 9. When studied by Raymond Firth in the 1920s, Tikopia's 1,200 persons were divided into four patriclans, each with its own chief who exercised authority over his clanmates. Each clan in turn was divided into several patrilineages. Every patrilineage had a head, believed to be the oldest living male descendant of the man who founded the lineage about four to six generations ago. Alongside this ranking of individuals within a single lineage, the various lineages of a single clan were ranked relative to one another. One lineage of each clan, supposedly the original, "senior" lineage from which the "junior" lineages had budded off, was considered the noble lineage. Members of other lineages of the clan had to defer socially to members of the noble lineage, according to Tikopian standards of etiquette. In addition, the noble lineage of each clan selected one of its members to be the chief of the whole clan. Clan chiefs had authority to punish troublemakers and the duty to perform rituals connected to agriculture and other common concerns.

But chiefs and other members of the noble Tikopia lineages had little more wealth than anyone else. The nobility did receive tribute from other lineages of their clan, but they gave away most of it in the many public activities that they organized and financed through redistribution (see Chapter 7). The chief and nobility of each clan had no way to deny access to land and ocean resources to members of other lineages, for each lineage was considered to have inalienable rights to certain pieces of land. The Tikopia nobility, then, received much prestige and token tribute from other islanders, but they did not use this tribute to make themselves notably more wealthy than lower-ranking people. They were honored, but their wealth and power were not great. It is mainly in this respect that ranked societies contrast with stratified societies.

Stratified Societies

Within a society or nation, a *social stratum* consists of families who have about the same degree of access to rewards. Stratified societies have two distinguishing characteristics. First, there are marked and enduring inequalities between strata in access to all three kinds of rewards: wealth, power, and prestige. The inequality may endure because the positions that bring rewards are themselves hereditary or because being born into a certain stratum gives individuals better or worse opportunities in life. Second, inequality is based primarily on unequal access to productive resources such as the land and tools people need to make their living or the education and training needed to succeed. In some stratified societies a minority of people control access to the resources other people need to survive at culturally acceptable levels.

Stratified societies vary in their cultural beliefs about the possibilities of social mobility—that is, about movement up and down the social ladder. In some, such as North American and other contemporary democracies, upward or downward mobility is possible, although numerous studies have shown that most people die in the stratum of their birth. In others, especially in preindustrial societies, one's position is considered fixed, often because of beliefs that existing inequalities are hereditary and/or ordained by supernatural beings.

Cross-culturally, we distinguish two major kinds of strata: **classes** and **castes.** Two general differences between class and caste systems stand out. First, by definition, castes are *endogamous* groups: they have cultural norms or laws that require individuals to marry within their caste. As discussed in Chapter 8, rules that mandate marriage within one's own group have the effect of maintaining the distinctiveness of the group relative to other groups. This is because there is no possibility of upward mobility through intercaste marriage, and because there are no children who have potentially anomalous group membership. In contrast, class societies allow people to marry someone of a different class; in fact, intermarriage between classes is a common avenue of social mobility. It follows from the endogamous nature of caste that one's caste membership is theoretically hereditary: one is born into the caste of one's parents, one marries someone in the same caste, and one's children are likewise born into and remain members of one's own caste. (We say theoretically because social reality often differs from cultural norms, in caste societies as in all others.)

Second, caste systems have powerful norms or laws regulating social relations between members of different castes. For example, norms or laws prohibit direct physical contact between castes or may forbid members of different castes from eating from the same bowl or drinking from the same wells. In some societies, high-caste members believe they will be spiritually polluted if they

should touch members of other castes. In[c] must perform rituals to cleanse themselv[e] tal contacts.

Both of these general differences mea[n] more permanent membership and more r aries than classes. This does not mean t[h] whether some particular stratified soci[e] classes. Some societies have elemen[t] stance, some scholars have suggested lations in the American South were classlike until the mid-twentieth ce possibility of upward mobility into blacks because no one could overco of black skin color. Interracial ma[r] hibited or culturally taboo, so that tually endogamous. Explicit laws "intercaste" contacts and interacti[o] *tion laws*—forced blacks to live a[t] them to enter certain white bus public restrooms, prohibited drir fountains, made them send t[h] schools, and so forth. Most w blacks were "polluting" in the but many whites did believe t[h] another sense and tried hard t

Castes in Traditi[onal]

The best-known caste sy caste system is complex a[nd] so we can present only a ally, the people of India egories, four of which a[re] caste.) Each category i[s] honor and degree of rit sociated with certain k

The highest *varna* scholars; next is the Kshatriyas; third are sans; and ranked l[ow] craftspeople, and c *varna* are associate[d] one in a given *va[rna]* category—outside the untouchables, ing to the *varna.*

The *varnas* (w when the Aryar northern India) specific castes

▲ The income a

Where do you work?" is one of the first questions American adults ask of new acquaintances, the answer to which gives a lot of information about a person very quickly.) Occupation is generally a good indication of income, and one's income influences so much else: overall lifestyle, access of one's children to education, the kinds of people with whom one associates socially, the kind of church or club to which one belongs, and so on.

Unfortunately for our desire to make societies neat and orderly, there are problems with defining a class on the basis of occupation or any other single criterion. For one thing, different criteria used to define class membership do not always agree. For instance, people do not agree on the prestige of many occupations—attorneys, physicians, and academicians are despised by some but granted high prestige by others, for example. For some occupations, there is disjunction between income and prestige—nurses and teachers are held in higher regard than plumbers and assembly-line workers, but often do not earn as much.

It may be difficult to decide to which class some individual belongs. One way around this ambiguity, favored by some sociologists, is to separate the three kinds of rewards from one another and define a separate class ranking for each reward. We can distinguish classes defined on the basis of prestige (*status groups,* as some call them) and on the basis of income or wealth (*economic classes*), for instance. The definitions and methods used for ranking the classes depend partly on the interests of the social scientist.

In the United States, the most widely accepted approach to stratification uses the concept of economic class. The class membership of individuals and families depends largely on their wealth. Using wealth as the primary basis for assigning class ranking has four major advantages. First, it is more measurable than other indications of class membership (although cash income alone does not measure it adequately).

Second, wealth is the best single indication of the overall benefits individuals and families are receiving from their citizenship in the nation. Money cannot buy you love, happiness, brains, or many other things, but it can buy you much of what Americans value (including, nowadays, better looks and tighter bodies).

© Vivane Moos/Corbis

The income and wealth gap between the very rich and the poor is enormous in the United States. This is a homeless family.

Third, extremely high wealth is generally correlated with ownership of productive resources such as factories, financial institutions, and income-producing real estate. Many of the very wealthy people own the nation's large businesses. Either they built their companies themselves, or their ancestors made fortunes through business activity and passed their ownership along to the current generation.

Fourth, wealth levels broadly determine people's access to political power. Through political contributions, the wealthy have a greater say in who gets nominated and elected to important offices, which is why many Americans push for campaign finance reform. Through lobbying efforts, the rich enjoy greater influence on the laws and policies of the nation than their numbers warrant. By providing much of the funding for think tanks and other public advisory groups, the wealthy subsidize the expertise of many economists, political scientists, sociologists, and other social scientists who advise government. Many appointed officials in the executive branch of the federal government are members of the elite. People who serve in the government as an elected or appointed official may later work in the private sector, which covets both their expertise and their political connections.

For these and other reasons, we can learn most about class inequalities in the United States by focusing on the distribution of wealth. We begin with the distribution of annual income. Table 13.1 summarizes the distribution of income for 2003, the latest year for which the U.S. Census Bureau provides information (data in the "Amount Earned" column are for 2002, because 2003 figures have not been released as we write this). In the table, American households are divided into fifths based on their 2003 cash income. For example, the poorest one-fifth (20%) of households earned only 3.4 percent of all income, whereas the richest one-fifth (the wealthiest 20 percent) of American households earned almost 50 percent of the total income earned by all households. The table also shows

that the richest 5 percent of American households earned about 22 percent of the total family income in 2002.

Census Bureau data over the past two or three decades also show that inequality in the distribution of yearly income has increased in the United States since the 1970s. In 1973, the bottom three-fifths (the "poorest" 60 percent) of American households earned 31.8 percent of all cash income, but by 2003 their share had fallen to 26.9 percent—a *loss* of 5.4 percent. In 1970, the richest one-fifth earned 43.3 percent of all cash income, but by 2003 their share had increased to 49.8 percent—a *gain* of 12.5 percent for the most affluent 20 percent of American households. Thus the most well-off families in 2003 had an even greater share of the total income than the most well-off families in 1970.

To make the same point in another way, in 1973 the ratio of the incomes of the richest fifth to the poorest fifth was 10.4, whereas in 2003 the ratio was 14.6. It is true that the real cash incomes of all quintiles increased in the past 30 years. But the relative benefits of economic growth over the last three decades have been distributed unequally, going far more to the affluent than to the poor, and even to people who view themselves as middle class.

So inequality in the distribution of yearly income has increased in the past 30 years. But the distribution of income does not accurately reflect the extent of economic inequality in the United States, because figures on annual *income* do not show how much *wealth* is owned by families of different classes. Yearly income figures such as those given in Table 13.1 greatly underestimate the degree of economic inequality in the United States. People's material standards of living (consumption levels) are not determined directly by their income, nor is their voice in local, state, and national political decision making (influence on government policies). If we consider the distribution of wealth, we see that middle income families, and even families who are generally considered affluent, own little in comparison with the truly wealthy.

Table 13.1 Distribution of Household Income in the United States, 2000

Percentage of Income Earned By		Amount Earned, 2002 (nearest thousand)
Poorest fifth	3.4	Less than $18,000
Second fifth	8.7	Between $18,000 and $34,000
Third fifth	14.8	Between $34,000 and $53,000
Fourth fifth	23.4	Between $53,000 and $84,000
Richest fifth	49.8	Over $84,000
Top 5% (for 2002)	21.9	Over $150,000 (2002)

Source: U.S. Bureau of the Census (2004, Table A-3).

Surveys funded by the federal government allow estimates of the net worth (wealth) of American families. *Net worth* includes all the family assets (property) owned minus debts. Assets include material property such as residential homes and other real estate, motor vehicles, boats, household possessions, and the like. Material assets directly affect standards of living. Assets also include money saved and invested in institutions like banks, bonds, and stocks. Saving and investment assets vastly increase a family's economic security and, of course, can be withdrawn from banks or sold on the stock market to acquire material assets. Savings and, especially, investments also earn additional future income and wealth, although not without risk.

The Federal Reserve Board (the "Fed") is the semigovernmental institution that tries to regulate the economy by its policy on interest rates. Every 3 years the Fed publishes a *Survey of Consumer Finances* that estimates the distribution of the wealth of American families. The most recently available *Survey of Consumer Finances* is based on information gathered in 2001.

In a 2004 publication, the Economic Policy Institute, a private nonprofit institution, used the 2001 Federal Reserve survey to estimate the concentration of net worth in the United States. In the *State of Working America 2004/5,* the Economic Policy Institute concluded that the richest fifth of families held 84 percent of the wealth, the middle fifth held 4 percent, and the poorest fifth had negative net worth (they owed more than they owned). The net worth of the vast majority of the population was actually less than the amount owned by the top 1 percent: the richest percent of families owned 33 percent of the wealth, whereas the bottom 90 percent owned 29 percent of the wealth. Considering only the ownership of stocks, the top 1 percent of stock owners held 45 percent of all the dollar value of stocks, whereas the bottom 80 percent of stock owners held just 6 percent of the value of stocks. And nearly half of American families owned no stock at all.

High levels of economic inequality also exist within other modernized nations, though the United States leads all industrialized nations in the gap between the rich and everyone else. At the international level, too, there are huge gaps between nations and continents. The Globalization box for this chapter discusses some issues related to global inequality.

Maintaining Inequality

There are many theoretical issues in studying stratification. One problem is figuring out such large differences between people developed long ago, in prehistory. This problem cannot be addressed in this book, other than to note that large differences between groups of people usually arise from a complex combination of intensive agriculture, control over scarce resources, large-scale cooperation, and conquest warfare. Most archaeologists and other scholars who study stratification in prehistory agree that significant inequalities (deserving of the term *class*) did not exist until after the evolution of civilization (Chapter 6).

▶ The difference between the net worth of the very rich and everyone else is much larger than the gap in annual income.

© Wartenberg/Picture Press/Corbis

Globalization affects the standards of living of most of the world's nations and peoples. Scholars, officers and boards of directors of corporations, leaders of the rich and poor nations, and members of the working class disagree on whether globalization will raise or lower the income and wealth of the poorer nations.

On the positive side, expansion of international trade provides overseas markets for the products of rich and poor alike, presumably allowing many people in poor countries to produce and sell more than they otherwise would. On the negative side, the richer countries and their companies have advantages due to their greater access to productive technology, shipping and marketing facilities, skills and information, and other resources that allow them greater control over prices and other terms of trade.

It is fairly clear that economic inequality between the world's regions and nations increased in the past century, largely because the growth of economies in the richer regions of North America, Europe, and East Asia outpaced growth in Africa, Latin America, and South Asia. Some people think that the inequality caused by globalization began in the twentieth century. In fact, the origins of global inequality are much older. As early as the 1500s and 1700s, the products of the two American continents were shipped to Europe. Mesoamerica and the Andes were the homelands of the two great New World civilizations, the Aztec and the Inca, respectively. Like the upper classes in Europe, the Aztec and Inca elite surrounded themselves with treasures, many in gold and silver. The trade of these precious metals produced huge fortunes for some Europeans, helped to finance the industrial revolution of the late eighteenth century, and changed balances of military power and political influence.

By the 1700s and 1800s products were pouring out of the conquered regions of the Americas and Asia. In the Caribbean, northern Brazil, and the American South, enslaved Africans produced the cotton, tobacco, sugar, and cacao that were worn, eaten, and otherwise consumed by western Europeans. In Asia, spices, tea, porcelain ("china"), and other products produced by peasants and craftsmen were shipped over land or, later, over sea to satisfy European appetites and tastes. Britain's colony in India, for example, provided early English textile factories with cotton and other fibers. In the process, India's own highly skilled textile weavers suffered. Although the costs of transporting goods from Asian, African, and American colonies was high, Europe's climate did not allow the production of tropical crops, and the labor of both African American slaves and Asian peasants was a fraction of the cost of production. So the effects of globablization on world inequality are several centuries old, at least.

In the world today, globalization has intensified as the economic interdependence between the world's nations has increased. Whether future globalization will increase or decrease the economic gap between poor and rich nations is hotly disputed. But within the poorer regions themselves, there is much evidence that inequality increases in the early phases of globalization. This is largely because companies from the richer nations open factories or other enterprises in the poorer countries mainly in order to lower their production costs. To do so, they hire local managers or make contracts with local business people. They hire workers at low wages, which is possible because of the high unemployment in the host country and because labor laws are usually lax. Local managers and subcontractors generally benefit disproportionately.

China, which has experienced the world's fastest growth since the 1980s, is a recent example. China's economic growth rate has hovered between 8 and 10 percent for over two decades because of its plentiful labor supply, its authoritarian central government, the work ethic of its citizens, and the loosening of restrictions on worker mobility and foreign investment. Tens of millions of Chinese have enjoyed a dramatic increase in their living standards by working in factories. Hundreds of thousands of Chinese factory owners, real estate investors, and market entrepreneurs have become fabulously wealthy. But there are 1.3 billion Chinese, and hundreds of millions in rural areas have yet to participate significantly in the economic boom. Will the bonanza ever reach them? How much longer will it take?

Critical Thinking Questions

1. Some think that recent advances in information technology such as e-mail, the World Wide Web, and cell phones will lessen inequality both within and between nations. How might this occur? What other changes will be required if it is to happen?

2. Students from the poorer nations often receive higher education in North America or Europe. Will they take their skills back home or seek jobs where wages are highest, increasing the problem known as the *brain drain* in the countries of their birth?

© Matthias Clamer/Stone/Getty Images

▲ Economic globalization has affected inequality within countries that used to be called Third World. In this man's homeland of China, some people who can take advantage of China's privatization and opening of markets have grown fabulously wealthy through production and sale of exports to the rich countries.

Further, we know enough about the preindustrial world to know that in most stratified societies a conquering militaristic group imposed their rule over the indigenous population of a region. This was true in African states such as Bunyoro and Zulu and in the ancient civilizations of the Americas such as the Aztec and Inca. Conquest of the weaker by the militarily stronger was also important in forming the most ancient Old World civilizations of East Asia, Mesopotamia, and India. Historically speaking, the lower classes did not consent to their low standing but had it forced on them.

A question that applies to stratification in contemporary societies is: How do such high degrees of inequality in stratified societies *persist*? As the United States illustrates, a small percentage of the population typically controls most of the wealth and wields a great deal of influence over public affairs. Why does the relatively un-

derprivileged majority allow them this power and privilege? Why doesn't inequality produce more conflict? Why don't the "have nots" revolt?

In fact, there is conflict between strata in a wide range of stratified societies. Resentment, rebellion, and occasional attempts at revolution occur in stratified societies in all parts of the world (which is not to say that they are universally present). A great many powerless and poor people do not simply accept their place in the social hierarchy. Inequality is a major source of social unrest. Arguably, global economic inequality and concerns about cultural imperialism are as much responsible for international terrorism as ethnic conflicts and religious ideologies.

One possible explanation of how stratification persists is that members of the highest stratum (hereafter called the *elite*) use their wealth and power to organize an armed force stronger than that of their opposition. If the elite somehow monopolize control over weapons or organize a loyal army, then they can use coercion and threat to maintain their access to rewards and resources. Elites do sometimes use armed force to put down rebellions, and certainly the ever-present threat of coercion and fear of punishment deters resistance to the elite's wealth, prestige, and power.

Yet in most stratified societies, the elite only occasionally find it necessary to actually use force. Use of military might is costly to the elite. Suppose the elite wait for rebellions to occur and then use police or armies to put them down. Even if no rebellion succeeds, every time armies suppress one, more hatred and resentment and more awareness of the relative wealth and power of the elite are produced. Increased hatred and awareness caused by suppression can backfire and lead to a greater probability of future rebellion. Notice also that the elite's reliance on brute force and oppression to maintain their wealth and power potentially reduces or eliminates their honor and esteem, one of the three major rewards offered by stratification, and one that they presumably covet. Further, those who supply the military might—the army, guards, thugs, or police—must be paid or otherwise provided for by the elite. Payment requires resources. Either the elite can take these resources from their own wealth, thus reducing it, or they can increase their exploitation of the majority population, thus breeding more hatred and resentment toward themselves. Finally, relying entirely on the loyalty of an army is risky because this allegiance may change. In sum, reliance on threat and armed force alone is both costly and risky.

None of these points denies that armed force is an important reason why high degrees of inequality are maintained for many generations. Probably few elites have maintained themselves for many generations without using force and periodically suppressing rebellions and dissent. Nonetheless, stratification systems that rely entirely or largely on force seem to be short-lived and unstable and have been replaced by those that use other mechanisms. What other mechanisms are available?

Ideologies

We can begin to address this question by noting yet another reason why coercive force alone seldom is solely responsible for maintaining inequality. A single rebellion can have many causes, but a persistent *pattern* of rebellion is caused mainly by the lower strata's perception that they are exploited or not receiving their fair share of rewards. Seeking out and eliminating rebels (or, one might suggest, terrorists) does little to change the reasons why people rebel. The instigators may be sanctioned or eliminated, but the underlying discontent that causes persistent conflict remains. Sooner or later there will be new instigators who organize new rebellions and attacks. Also, innocents are usually killed, injured, or harmed economically by the use of military might, which can alienate those who otherwise would be passive about their place in the world. For these and other reasons, armed force alone is unlikely to eliminate the perceptions of unfairness, injustice, cultural domination, or other attitudes that cause rebellions.

One mechanism available to maintain elite privileges is to change the perceptions of the underprivileged about why they are underprivileged. For example, if poor people think it is God's will that they are poor, they are less likely to rebel than if they believe they are poor because of exploitation. Or if they think the elite use their property and power to benefit everyone in the society, then they are less likely to challenge the elite. Or if they think that a concentration of property and power is inevitable because that's just the way human life is, they will be less likely to resist. Or if they think that they, too, can acquire property, power, and prestige through their own achievements, they are more likely to put their effort into improving their own position rather than into causing trouble.

If, to state the general point, members of the lower strata adopt a set of beliefs that justifies and legitimizes the rewards received by the higher strata, then they are more likely to try to join the system rather than to beat it. In such beliefs the elite have a powerful and relatively cheap tool with which to reduce the amount of opposition to their power and privileges. Further, these ideas increase the prestige of the elite. If people believe that inequality is God's will, or that the activities of the elite benefit all, or that the elite became elite through intelligence and hard work, then the elite deserve the honor and respect of everyone else. (Not surprisingly, elites themselves find it easy to believe such things about themselves.)

We shall call those ideas and beliefs that explain inequality as desirable or legitimate **ideologies.** The term *ideology* also has a broader meaning, referring to any set of ideas held by a group—as in the phrases *leftist political ideology* and *feminist ideology*. Here we use it in the narrow sense, to refer only to ideas that justify the status quo of inequality.

In many stratified societies, ideologies are based on religion. We are familiar with the notion of the "divine right of kings" from feudal Europe—certainly a handy supernatural mandate for kings and aristocracies! Similar notions are common in non-Western stratified societies. For instance, in Bunyoro, a kingdom in East Africa, the health and welfare of the ruler were mystically associated with the fertility and prosperity of the whole kingdom. Anything that threatened his life was believed to be a threat to everyone. In many ancient civilizations, such as the Aztec, the Inca, the Japanese, and the Egyptian, the ruler himself was believed to be a divine or semidivine being. In pre-twentieth-century China, the emperor had the "Mandate of Heaven," meaning that Heaven itself had granted him secular authority over the vast Chinese empire for so long as he ruled it wisely and humanely. In traditional India, as we have seen, Hindu beliefs about reincarnation and pollution were so intertwined with the caste system that they rendered its inequities both explicable and legitimate.

In the ancient complex chiefdoms of Hawaii there was a marked social distinction between the noble and the commoner class. The nobility was viewed as endowed with a supernatural power called *mana*. *Mana* was partly hereditary, and within a single family the eldest child inherited the most *mana* from his or her parents. The highest-ranking noble, the paramount chief, was believed to be descended from one of the gods of the islands through a line of eldest sons. This descent gave him the right to rule because he had more *mana* than anyone in the chiefdom. Other nobles (lesser chiefs and their families) were relatives of the paramount chief and thus also were endowed with *mana*. *Mana* gave chiefs the power to curse those who were disloyal or disobedient or who violated some taboo, which further reinforced their authority. Hawaiians believed that the prosperity of a chiefdom and everyone in it depended on the performance of certain religious rituals held in grand temples. Because commoners did not have enough *mana* to enter a temple, only priests and nobles could perform the rituals needed to ensure prosperity. Everyone in the chiefdom thus relied on the social (and religious) elite for their well-being.

The preceding examples illustrate a few ways religion serves ideological functions in some societies. In stratified societies, religion commonly gives the elite a supernatural mandate, provides them with the supernatural means to punish people, and gives them ritual functions to perform that are believed to benefit the whole population.

American Secular Ideologies

Do similar kinds of religious ideologies exist in modern industrial societies, some of which are as highly stratified as any preindustrial society? In the United States, for instance, some people claim that the most prevalent religion (Christianity) helps preserve the status quo. But in fact, Christian teachings historically have been and still are used to support social and political movements of all kinds. Many such movements are far from supportive of the status quo. The nineteenth-century antislavery movement is one example. More recent examples include the civil rights and liberation theology movements. And a variety of Christian churches and denominations are resolutely against the Establishment in their beliefs.

Further, most American citizens do not believe that the richest Americans have a supernatural mandate for their wealth. The wealthiest families generally do not justify their income and claim their ownership of stocks by invoking religious authority. At most, they claim to be "blessed," but the majority take credit for their own success.

As for power, although many officeholders attend church and find ways to work their religious faith into their speeches to certain audiences, few get very far by claiming they are God's chosen official. (There are reasons to think this reality may be changing in the United States.) Religion does perhaps reinforce some of America's "basic values," but it is not generally used to justify the wealth and power of particular individuals and families.

In brief, with regard to the issue of who has what and why, most Americans are *secularists:* They understand the unequal distribution of rewards by events here on earth, not in heaven.

In industrial societies such as the United States, then, ideologies are not based mainly on religion. But they do not have to be, for there are only two essential features of ideologies:

- They reinforce inequality by affecting people's consciousness, not by threatening physical coercion.
- They are believable to large numbers of people, based on existing cultural knowledge.

On the first requirement, *consciousness* refers to cultural attitudes, values, worldviews, and so forth. On the second requirement, *believable* means that effective ideologies match up with people's general ideas about how their society works. They must make sense in terms of existing cultural knowledge, or they will be ineffective. **Secular ideologies** can meet these requirements as well as religious ideologies.

Many social scientists argue that two major secular ideologies exist in the modern United States. One is that the whole nation benefits from inequality. Because a few people are very wealthy, many citizens believe that "the masses" are better off than they would be if wealth were distributed more equally. After all, the chance to get rich motivates people to do their best, and we all win when our fellow citizens perform up to their potential. Besides, the accumulation and investment of wealth are necessary to create jobs, from which poor and middle-class people benefit. "Workers don't want a handout. They want a hand," politicians claim as they debate legislation that they say will generate jobs by cutting business taxes. Tax cuts that benefit mainly the very wealthy are justified by the claim (ideology?) that they lead to more consumer spending, thus stimulating investment and creating jobs that eventually trickles down to everyone.

A second feature of secular ideology is the belief that elite earn their rewards through their own merit and efforts. They are more intelligent, ambitious, hard working, and willing to take risks, and generally possess more admirable personal qualities than other people. In short, elite are given credit for their success. This is, of course, accurate for some members of the elite. But those who inherited their wealth, or were lucky enough to buy the right stock at the right time, or to get into the right housing market early enough, receive the same rewards as those who "really" earned their rewards.

To the extent that they are widely believed, these two ideas fit with Americans' other beliefs about the way people are and how their society works. They are compatible with widespread beliefs about human motivation—people need strong incentives before they will make the effort to get a good education and have a responsible career. They also fit in with many American values, such as individual freedom, progress, the work ethic, and private property.

Of course, many Americans do not believe these two ideas. (If you do not believe them, then they are not effective ideologies for you.) Others believe that these ideas are an accurate portrayal of how the whole nation benefits from economic inequality. (If you fall into this camp, you will think that these ideas are objectively true, rather than merely ideologies.) Your personal opinion depends on your class, upbringing, ideas about human nature, political views, and so forth. Can the comparative perspective of anthropology shed any light on the issue of whether stratification benefits society at large, or mainly members of the elite class themselves? To answer this question, we must first look at the major theories of inequality.

Theories of Inequality

Many sociologists and anthropologists apply two kinds of theories to analyze stratification. One holds that a high degree of inequality in the distribution of rewards is necessary, morally justified, and beneficial to all members of society. Unless society offers unequal rewards for unequal talents and efforts, the most talented people will have no incentive to put their talents to work for the welfare of all. This view is called the **functional theory of inequality.**

A contrary view holds that a high degree of inequality is not only immoral but robs the whole society of the benefits of much of its potential talent, which lies undeveloped in many of those at the bottom of the socioeconomic ladder. Stratification is not beneficial to society as a whole, but only to elites, who use their wealth to influence the passing of laws and regulations that benefit mainly or only themselves. This view is known as the **conflict theory of inequality.** It holds that a high level of inequality offers few benefits to anyone except the elite and, indeed, is harmful to the whole society because of the conflicts it creates.

Functionalist Theory

The functionalist theory holds that inequality is necessary for society to motivate its most talented and hard-working members to perform its most important

roles. Some roles (including jobs) require more skill and training than do others. Ordinarily, the more skill and training required to perform a job, the fewer the number of people qualified to do the job and the more valuable their abilities are to the whole group. Functionalists argue that unequal rewards are effective ways to recruit the most able individuals into the most socially valuable roles. Unless there are rewards for those with the talents most of us lack, they will have no incentive to put those talents to work in activities that benefit all of us.

Further, in the functionalist view, inequality is not only socially useful, it is also morally justified. If society as a whole is to enjoy the fruits of the labor of its small number of well-trained, talented, and hard-working individuals, it is only fair and right that it reward these individuals with material goods, respect, and control over public decision making.

The functionalist analysis of inequality does make sense. Functionalists claim that people who do the most valuable things get the greatest rewards. It is perfectly reasonable that rewards be proportionate to qualities like effort and skill. But two objections to such an analysis are possible within the framework of the functionalist theory itself.

First, there is no reason to believe that the high degree of inequality that actually exists in stratified societies is necessary to ensure that those with scarce talents will fill the most valuable roles. In industrialized nations, for example, how many dollars does it take to motivate a qualified individual to manage a major company? In the United States, chief executive officers (CEOs) of large corporations enjoy relatively large compensation packages. In 2002, on average, American CEOs earned 185 times the amount of compensation paid to workers. This is part of a 40-year upward trend from the 1965 earnings ratio (24), the 1977 ratio (35), the 1989 ratio (71), and the 1995 ratio (101). (It is interesting that the ratio peaked at 300 in the year 2000, but has declined since then. The decline is due to several factors, two of which are stockholder concerns about the effects of CEO compensation on dividend earnings and share prices and the corporate scandals of the early twenty-first century.)

Comparing the 1977 ratio of 35 to the 2002 ratio of 185, CEOs in 2002 earned about five times what CEOs earned in 1977. Were the top managers of American companies responsible for a fivefold increase in productivity between 1977 and 2002? American CEOs also earn about three times the average of CEOs in those 13 other advanced countries for which the compensation packages can be compared. Do American CEOs contribute three times as much to the profitability of their companies as the CEOs in Europe and East Asia? If the compensation of American CEOs were more in line with the America of 1977 and with other advanced nations today, would American firms sell fewer or more products domestically or internationally? Do the contributions of CEOs to their companies match the compensation paid to CEOs?

Phrasing the question more generally, is there an actual relation between compensation (rewards) of the elite and their contributions to their groups or to the nation as a whole? Obviously, there is no way to measure this relation. So one objection to the functionalist theory is that no one knows how much inequality is needed to motivate people nor does anyone know how to calculate the benefits that the elite actually offer to their group or to society at large. There is no reason to think that the *high degree* of inequality that actually exists in some stratified society is necessary to enjoy the societywide benefits of *some degree* of inequality. There is no reason to think that America as a whole would be worse off if the wealthiest 20 percent owned only 40 percent of the wealth rather than 84 percent.

Second, functionalists assume that the system of stratification *effectively* places qualified individuals in important roles. But it is a large assumption that those who are best able to perform the most important roles are those who are usually recruited into them. In all systems of stratification there is a powerful element of inheritance of wealth, prestige, and power. Even assuming that most of the elite of the present day actually earned their rewards, many will pass their resources along to their heirs, who may or may not be talented, hard working, and meritorious. And even if elite families do not transmit wealth to their children, the latter still have a head start in life by the extra help they get in education, job prospects, and other privileges. Certainly, children born to poor families can and do succeed, but they must overcome more obstacles than those born to privilege. If every generation were born with nearly equal access to the means to succeed in life, we could be more confident that those who occupy the most important roles are those who are best qualified to fill them. The functionalist theory that those who receive the highest rewards are most deserving would be more plausible if the (metaphorical) playing field in which people compete were leveled.

Suppose there were some way to calculate the amount of inequality that is optimal for a given society. Suppose further that a society could devise some way of beginning each generation on an equal footing, with truly equal opportunities to compete. (This could be partly accomplished by steep inheritance taxes.) Then the functionalist theory of inequality might apply. But no stratified society has ever achieved this condition, partly because these questions are unanswerable and partly because the wealthy and powerful would have to consent to such a change, and they have no incentive to do so.

Conflict Theory

The conflict theory takes off from objections to functionalism, such as the two just given. But it goes much further. Conflict theorists claim that stratification is based ultimately on control over productive resources such as land, technology, information, and labor. Once the elite gain control over these resources—by whatever means—they get other people to do work that benefits themselves. How this is organized varies between different kinds of economic systems. In ancient preindustrial states and some chiefdoms, the noble class controlled the land and the commoners had to provide tribute and labor to the nobility in return for the privilege of using it. In parts of feudal Europe, the serfs were tied to their estate and ordinarily had strong rights over the land they worked, but they still had to contribute a certain number of days of work or a certain proportion of their harvest to their lord per year.

As for the capitalist economic system, Karl Marx—the nineteenth-century "father" of conflict theory—argued that capitalist societies include only two fundamental classes. Members of the capitalist class (or *bourgeoisie*) own the factories and tools. Members of the working class (or *proletariat*) have only one thing to sell on the market: their labor. To earn their living, workers must sell their labor to some capitalist. This seems like an equitable arrangement: the capitalists buy the labor they need to operate their capital to sell goods and make profit; the workers get the jobs they need to support their families by selling their time and skills for a wage.

But, Marx noted, the goods the workers produce must be worth more on the market than the workers themselves receive in wages or there would be no profit for the capitalists. The difference between the amount the capitalists receive for the goods they sell and their costs (including the amount they pay their workers) is *profit*. In Marx's controversial view, profit is based on the exploitation of workers. The belief that workers receive a fair day's wage for a fair day's work is merely an ideology.

Conflict theorists have been criticized for being ideologues themselves, although of a different political per-

◄ Conflict theorists hold that stratification exists because some groups are able to exploit others. For example, in a capitalist economy, workers like this woman, who is boxing up clothing for shipment, do not receive a fair wage for their contributions to their employers. Does this mean they are "exploited," as Karl Marx claimed?

© William Taufic/Corbis

suasion than functionalists. If one wants to find exploitation in an unequal relationship, one can usually do so. Critics of conflict theory claim that the value-laden term *exploitation* does not adequately characterize relations between chiefs or kings and commoners, between lords and serfs, or between capitalists and workers. Conflict theorists play down the valuable services that elite classes perform, such as maintaining social control, organizing the society for the provision of public goods, and accumulating productive resources (capital) put aside to increase future production.

Many conflict theorists assume that it is possible to organize a complex society without unequal rewards. This is a rather unrealistic view of human nature, according to some critics of the approach, which may be one reason "communism" has collapsed almost everywhere. Complex societies are always hierarchically organized, with centralized leadership. Many critics believe that the functions of leaders, controllers, and organizers are so valuable to society at large that they deserve the rewards they receive.

Who Benefits?

Contrasting the two theories, we see that functionalism emphasizes the positive aspects of stratification, whereas conflict theory emphasizes the negative side. Conflict theory points to the costs of stratification not just to those on the bottom of the social ladder but also to society at large. A country or other form of society loses the undeveloped potential of its underprivileged members. Societies also suffer the periodic violent conflicts (rebellions, revolutions) and/or ongoing disorder (crimes, labor strikes, political dissent) related to a high degree of unjust inequality and inherited privilege.

Conflict theorists argue that many of the problems that have afflicted modern North America in the last couple of decades are caused (or at least made worse) by increasing inequality. Much resentment toward "the system" comes out of people's sense that their lives will not get better or are getting worse. Unable to identify the causes of their frustrations, some white conservative groups find scapegoats in African Americans and Jews, immigrants, the United Nations, and overseas laborers who work for

Comparisons between stratified societies in the preindustrial world and those of modernized, industrialized nations help in viewing class inequalities from new perspectives. In general, comparison shows that many services performed by elites are useful, but only *given the way an existing stratified society works and the kinds of cultural knowledge (beliefs) common among its members*. Some roles performed by members of the elite are valuable only because of the way a society's institutions are organized and because of its members' beliefs about what is necessary or useful and their acceptance of their cultural system as a whole.

To illustrate, consider two provocative examples. First, if there were no such occupation as "attorney" (an important role in the existing legal system), how often would you need to hire one? You might hire one if sued or accused of a crime for many reasons: because laws are complex, courtroom procedures are intricate, you don't know all your "rights," and the opposing side has an attorney, which places you at a disadvantage. For these and other reasons, you would be stupid to go into court "unrepresented," as any lawyer will tell you. But how did all this complexity in the legal system develop in the first place, and how much of it benefits society and how much of it benefits only attorneys?

Second, medical costs are so high (in 2000, 14 percent of gross domestic product in the United States) that many Americans who lack medical insurance are unable to obtain adequate medical care. Two of the most important institutions involved in health care are private medical insurers and the professional association of physicians, the American Medical Association (AMA). Health Maintenance Organizations (HMOs) and other kinds of private insurers claim to help provide Americans with excellent medical care by spreading the risks of catastrophic illness and disease among many clients. The AMA also claims to improve health care by licensing physicians and controlling the curriculum of medical schools. But medical insurers themselves help to make medical costs high by their bloated bureaucracies and, for some patients, insurers actually reduce the quality of care by refusing to pay for diagnostic tests and other services. And the AMA, which probably does improve the quality of health care by its regulatory functions, nonetheless raises the cost of health care by its lobbying efforts on behalf its members and its control of medical school admissions numbers. Both HMOs and the AMA do provide beneficial services, just as they claim. But these services exist partly because of how medical care institutions work.

We make these points not to disparage lawyers or the medical industry, but to state a more general implication: occupants of some roles or managers of institutions justify their high wealth by claiming they have "earned it." But the earning power of the roles they perform or the institutions they manage is due at least as much to the social and economic structure of the legal and medical professions as to the actual usefulness of their services to clients and patients.

Along these same lines, note that many of the institutions we regard as beneficial to the public do not, in fact, benefit everyone to the same degree. A good example of this is laws regarding the protection of private property. Most Americans are enculturated to believe that private property is a basic human right and that the general welfare requires laws to protect everyone's property. But, as shown previously, the bulk of the private property is owned by a small percentage of citizens. It may be true that we all benefit somewhat from the legal safeguarding of our private property, but we do not all benefit equally, if only because we differ so vastly in the amount of property that needs to be protected.

"peanuts." Unable to make a personally acceptable living in a socially acceptable manner, inner-city youths turn to dealing drugs. Economic hardship contributes to family breakups. Poorer people need more social programs, funded by taxpayers, who watch stories in the media about people cheating the government and so elect representatives who provide *fewer* services—for the poor, at least. More generally, the sense of national unity and social responsibility is undermined by worsening inequality, according to conflict theorists.

Does the comparative perspective of anthropology have anything to say about who benefits from inequality? In preindustrial stratified societies, elites did indeed perform some vital roles for the whole population, just as functionalists claim. For example, elites often organized labor for the construction and maintenance of public works projects, provided relief to regions struck by famine, and raised a military force to provide for the defense of the political unit (see Chapter 12). Some kind of central authority is useful and may even be necessary for such tasks to be coordinated effectively. Cooperative activities require organization; organization (at least on a large scale) requires leadership; such decision makers deserve to be rewarded.

On the other hand, elites performed some roles that probably were created to maintain their positions at the top of society. Thus their religious functions were often viewed as indispensable to the general welfare, but in fact the rituals they sponsored did not bring rain, sustain the fertility of women, or assuage the anger of the gods. Elite's regulation of access to land and other resources might have seemed necessary, but it was partly because they themselves controlled so many resources that other people's access to them had to be "regulated." The law and order they helped maintain benefited everyone, but the elite's power, wealth, and internal political rivalries produced violent conflicts that otherwise would not have existed.

With the insight gained from this comparative perspective, we can question whether some of the "functions" carried out by the elite in industrialized nations are imaginary. We also wonder whether some of the "benefits" other people receive from the roles performed by the elite exist only because society's institutions are organized in such a way that the roles of elites are widely perceived as beneficial. (Some provocative ideas about this point are presented in A Closer Look.)

Who does benefit from the inequality found in stratified societies? Functionalists are probably correct in their assumption that some degree of inequality is needed for motivation. Many people also agree that unequal rewards for unequal efforts and talents is a fair and just standard. But we do not know how much inequality is necessary to provide incentives, much less whether some particular stratified society—including our own—has just the right amount. We do know that power and privilege are partly inherited and, therefore, the current members of the upper class are not automatically more talented and diligent than everyone else. In looking at other stratified societies, we see that elites do provide some useful services for the population at large. But we also see that many popular ideas about their functions are "just ideologies," and that many of their "essential roles" are useful only under circumstances that previous elite classes had a hand in creating and that present elites help perpetuate by their privilege and power.

Perhaps most citizens in stratified societies would benefit from inequality, if only there were some way to find out what the optimum amount of inequality is for a particular society, if only there were some way to achieve this optimum initially, and if only there were some way to ensure that opportunities to succeed and achieve are equal for all children. But no known human society has ever achieved this utopia.

Summary

1. *Inequality* refers to the degree to which individuals and groups experience differential access to socially valuable rewards of wealth, power, and prestige. Fried's typology of egalitarian, ranked, and stratified societies provides a useful description of the range of cross-cultural diversity in inequality.

2. Most foragers are egalitarian. This is largely because their adaptation makes it difficult for anyone to exercise control over productive resources and the behavior of others. Such adaptive features include high rates of mobility, ability of individuals to choose their band affiliation, a cultural value placed on sharing and the social pressure against making oneself stand out, and the difficulties of maintaining exclusive access to a territory.

3. In ranked societies there are a set number of honored positions (chiefs, titles, offices) to which only a small number of people are eligible to succeed. Succession may be determined by genealogical ascription, or membership in a particular kin group may establish a pool of candidates from which one will emerge or be selected. Tikopia illustrates one form of ranking.

4. Stratified societies have marked inequalities in access to all three kinds of rewards, and this inequality is based largely on unequal access to productive resources. One system of stratification is the caste system. Castes are best known from India, where they were intimately associated with the Hindu doctrines of reincarnation and pollution.

5. Class systems are characteristic of all modern nations. In the United States the best criterion of class membership is wealth. Studies conducted by scholars and by the federal government reveal an enormous disparity in the distribution of wealth, especially if net worth rather than annual cash income is used to measure a family's wealth.

6. How such highly unequal distribution of rewards persists in stratified societies is puzzling. The mobilization of armed force by the elite is an insufficient explanation. Cultural beliefs that inequality is inevitable, divinely ordained, legitimate, and/or beneficial to society as a whole provide ideologies that justify and reinforce the power and privilege of elite classes. Among

preindustrial peoples, religious beliefs were the main form of ideology, as exemplified by ancient Hawaii.

7. In modern countries, ideologies are more secular in orientation, because effective ideologies must be compatible with people's overall cultural ideas about how their society works. In the United States, Americans' ideas about the social and economic usefulness of inequality, about the fairness of unequal rewards for unequal talents and efforts, and about how the well-to-do achieved their wealth are often interpreted as secular ideologies.

8. The two major theories about inequality are the functional and the conflict theories. Functionalists hold that societies offer unequal rewards to those individuals who have the scarcest talents and who use them to perform the most socially valuable roles. Conflict theorists claim that inequality is based ultimately on control over productive resources. Anthropology's comparative perspective suggests that although elites often do perform valuable services for society at large, many of their "functions" are illusory. Others exist only because past elites have set up the structure of society so that their "services" are necessary. Although functionalists are correct that some degree of inequality is necessary for incentive, we have no way of knowing whether any society has the amount it "needs," nor has any society ever succeeded in establishing the equal opportunity required for the functionalist theory to be correct.

Key Terms

inequality	class	functional theory of
egalitarian	caste	inequality
ranked	ideology	conflict theory of
stratified	secular ideology	inequality

InfoTrac College Edition Terms

egalitarian United States	India caste	wealth (income)
social strata	social class	distribution
Hinduism	inequality	

Suggested Readings

Domhoff, G. William. *Who Rules America: Power and Politics.* 4th ed. Mountain View, Calif.: Mayfield, 2001.

Ehrenreich, Barbara. *Nickel and Dimed: On (Not) Getting By in America.* 2002. New York: Henry Holt.

A popular columnist describes her personal experiences in temporarily living like the poor in the United States.

Lenski, Gerhard. *Power and Privilege.* New York: McGraw-Hill, 1966.

A treatment of stratification comparing the range of inequality in preindustrial and industrial societies. Best known as an attempt to reconcile the functionalist and the conflict perspectives.

Newman, Katherine. *Declining Fortunes: The Withering of the American Dream.* New York: Basic, 1993.

Newman, Katherine. *Falling from Grace: The Experience of Downward Mobility in the American Middle Class.* New York: Vintage, 1988.

Written by an anthropologist, the interview and observational data in these two books show the impacts of job loss or declining income on former members of the American middle class and how they cope with downward mobility.

Scheper-Hughes, Nancy. *Death Without Weeping.* Berkeley: University of California Press, 1992.

How poor northeast Brazilian families cope psychologically with high rates of infant and child mortality.

Companion Website for This Book

The Wadsworth Anthropology Resource Center
http://anthropology.wadsworth.com

The companion website that accompanies *Humanity: An Introduction to Cultural Anthropology,* Seventh Edition, includes a rich array of material, including online anthropological video clips, to help you in the study of cultural anthropology and the specific topics covered in this chapter. Begin by clicking on Student Resources. Next, click on Cultural Anthropology, and then on the cover image for this book. You have now arrived at the Student Resources home page and have the option of choosing one of several chapter resources.

Applying Anthropology. Begin your study of cultural anthropology by clicking on Applying Anthropology. Here you will find useful information on careers, graduate school programs in applied anthropology, and internships you might wish to pursue. You will also find real-world examples of working anthropologists applying the skills and methods of anthropology to help solve serious world problems.

Research Online. Click here to find a wealth of Web links that will facilitate your study of anthropology. Divided into different fields of study, specific websites are starting points for Internet research. You will be guided to rich anthropology websites that will help you prepare for class, complete course assignments, and actually do research on the Web.

InfoTrac College Edition Exercises. From the pull-down menu, select the chapter you are presently studying. Select InfoTrac College Edition Exercises from the list of resources. These exercises utilize InfoTrac College Edition's vast database of articles and help you explore the numerous uses of the search word, *culture.*

Study Aids for This Chapter. Improve your knowledge of key terms by using flash cards and study the learning objectives. Take the practice quiz, receive your results, and e-mail them to your instructor. Access these resources from the chapter and resource pull-down menus.

Chapter Fourteen

RELIGION AND WORLDVIEW

Defining Religion

   Beliefs About Supernatural Powers

   Myths and Worldviews

   Rituals and Symbols

Theories of Religion

   Intellectual/Cognitive Approaches

   Psychological Approaches

   Sociological Approaches

Supernatural Explanations of Misfortune

   Sorcery

   Witchcraft

   Interpretations of Sorcery and Witchcraft

Varieties of Religious Organization

   Individualistic Cults

   Shamanism

   Communal Cults

   Ecclesiastical Cults

Revitalization Movements

   Melanesian Cargo Cults

   Native American Movements

© Giampero Sposito/Reuters/Landov

The religious rituals practiced by a people involve customary methods of communicating with and sometimes worshipping gods, ancestors, and other supernatural powers. At this ordination of new deacons, the candidates ritually symbolize their submission.

ALL CULTURES HAVE SOME FORM of religion. A people's religion is related to their worldview—the conceptions of reality that affect their interpretation and perceptions of things and events and, therefore, their patterns of behavior. Like other dimensions of culture, religion and worldview vary greatly among the world's diverse peoples. In this chapter, we introduce this diversity. We begin with an extended definition and overview of religion. Then we cover some of the main theories social scientists use to understand it. Next we look at some of the major forms of religion that have most interested anthropologists. We conclude by discussing religious movements, which often occur when a society is undergoing rapid change and foreign domination.

Defining Religion

How can we best define religion so as to encompass all the diverse religions of humanity? A nineteenth-century definition that many scholars still use is E. B. Tylor's **animism,** or "belief in spiritual beings." Most modern conceptions follow Tylor's lead: they specify that, at the least, all religions include beliefs that some kind of spiritual or supernatural powers exist. As we expand on Tylor's definition we present an overview of religion in cross-cultural perspective.

Beliefs About Supernatural Powers

Religion does include belief in supernatural beings such as gods, but "beings" are not the only kind of spiritual powers. The worldview of various peoples includes belief in other supernatural powers that are more like forces and substances than beings. For example, before becoming predominantly Christian the peoples of Polynesia believed in *mana,* a diffuse, incorporeal power that permeated certain people and things. *Mana* lent supernatural potency to objects, which explained unusual qualities. The gods gave *mana* to certain people, which explained unusual success or why chiefs had the right to receive privileges and issue commands. People and objects could be infused with greater or lesser amounts of *mana.* Having a lot of *mana* explained why some chiefs always won battles, why some fishing equipment seemed to work so well, why certain gardens produced such fine crops, and so forth.

Other peoples—and sometimes the same peoples—hold that there are mystical substances that can be transmitted by direct or indirect contact with people or things. An example is pollution, which can be passed between people of different statuses based on differences such as gender or caste (see Chapters 10, 11, and 13). Unlike *mana,* pollution is harmful to individuals who receive it, and cleansing or other forms of purification are required to remove it.

Spiritual *beings* usually have qualities such as the ability to assume a bodily form, a personality with emotions, and a consciousness and will. Usually gods and other kinds of beings respond to human actions in some way: if you communicate with them (by prayer) they will listen and if your actions displease them they will react. Some beings have human origins or are associated with living or deceased persons, such as souls, ancestral ghosts, and important people who did such notable things that they became gods. There are numerous other kinds of beings: spirit helpers, nature spirits, demons, zoomorphic spirits, forest spirits, disease spirits, and so on. The characteristics people attribute to supernatural beings vary enormously: they can be capricious or consistent, stubborn or reasonable, vengeful or forgiving, amoral or just.

In the religious traditions of Western civilization, the supreme being is all-knowing and all-powerful, expects sacrifices or worship, and is mindful of human behavior and morality. But the gods that many peoples believe in have none of these characteristics. They can be tricked or otherwise manipulated. They are commanded more than worshipped. And quite often people do not believe gods are concerned about the morality of human actions: they do not punish wrongdoing, in either this life or the next. There is no belief that *sin* (violation of a commandment or moral precept) exists.

In contrast to beings such as gods, supernatural *forces* or *substances* generally cannot take on a physical appearance and have no will of their own. Rather, they are known mainly by their effects: *mana* makes a chief successful, pollution sickens a man. In many cultures, the beliefs about how powers are effective are indefinite: One performs a ritual and utters an incantation (spell), and the effect that the rite and spell are intended to cause simply happens. This is generally known as *magic* and is discussed later in this chapter.

Myths and Worldviews

Belief in supernatural powers is only part of religion. Religion also includes **myths**—oral or written stories (narratives) about the actions and deeds of supernatural powers and cultural heroes. Sometimes myths explain how the entire universe was created. They may recount how and why people, animals, plants, and natural features originated. Myths may explain how a people acquired their tools and customs and how they came to live where they do. They often tell why people should or should not act in certain ways and what happened to someone in the past who did something people are forbidden to do.

North Americans mostly learn their mythology in formal settings: myths are taught at church and, to a lesser extent, at home. (Here we need to emphasize that calling the Bible, Quran, Torah, and other religious texts *myths* does not mean that we regard them as false.) In many societies, there is no formal church service. Elders recount myths more informally, including in moments of leisure. Myths are repeated regularly on days set aside for religious performances. They are sung or chanted while one is doing daily tasks. The fact that myths sometimes are recounted rather casually does not mean that their importance in a people's way of life is negligible. A people's worldview is greatly affected by their mythology.

It has been argued, for example, that the Judeo-Christian mythology makes it easy for North Americans to view nature as something to be conquered and used for their own profit and gratification. God gave humans "dominion" over nature and told us to "subdue" the earth and its living creatures (see Genesis 1:26–30). Because of the biblical account of creation, when it suits our purposes and interests we have no divine prohibitions against polluting the air and water, ruining the habitats of other creatures, destroying the landscape with strip mines and highways, and so forth. According to this argument, because of the religious heritage of Western civilization—which influences the worldview of Europeans and peoples culturally derived from Europe—Westerners are more likely to believe that God gave the earth to humans to conquer and exploit than to preserve and protect. In contrast, Westerners might show more respect for other living things if (as in some cultures) the sacred myths of our religious heritage recounted how some of us came from bears, some from coyotes, some from whales, and so forth. We might hesitate to destroy a forest if the scriptures told us explicitly that trees are just as precious to God as are humans. In short, if Western mythology emphasized the importance of living in harmony with nature rather than subduing nature, perhaps the modern ecological crisis would be less of a crisis.

However, Judeo-Christian scriptures can be interpreted in many ways and used for many purposes, not all of which involve the uncontrolled exploitation of resources for profit or material self-gratification. The Old Order Amish of North America, for example, are thoroughly Christian, but they reject much of the materialism of modern society, which they fear threatens their values and the integrity of their communities. Several New Testament passages warn against the accumulation of wealth, an injunction that some Christians take seriously.

A people's myths—and this is our general point—are more than stories they tell after dark or recite on appropriate occasions. They do more than satisfy curiosity and help pass the time. Myths help to form a people's worldview: their conceptions of reality and the interpretations of events that happen in society and the natural world. Worldview and myths affect people's beliefs about how they ought to relate to the world and to one another (Chapter 2), and therefore affect how people behave in their everyday lives.

Rituals and Symbols

People everywhere believe that gods, ghosts, demons, devils, and other supernatural beings take an active interest in worldly affairs, particularly in the lives of human beings. Such beings can be asked for blessings or aid through prayer, or sometimes they can be commanded to do things for or to people. Because people believe that supernatural powers can make natural events occur and can intervene in human affairs, all cultures prescribe certain behaviors used to control or influence powers. In the context of religion, the organized performance of behaviors intended to influence spiritual powers is known as **ritual.**

Rituals are always *stereotyped:* There are definite patterns of speech or movement, or definite sequences of events, that occur in much the same way in performance after performance. In general, people performing rituals want supernatural powers to do things on their behalf. For example, some central Canadian Inuit believe that failure to locate game animals may be caused by an undersea goddess who is angry over the misconduct of members of the camp. They persuade her to release the game by performing a ritual in which camp members publicly confess their violations.

Rituals the world over have *symbolic* aspects. They often occur in *places* that have symbolic significance to the performers. For example, they may be held where some mythological event occurred, or where the women who founded a matrilineage were born. Rituals often involve the display, touching, and manipulation of *objects* that symbolize an event (e.g., the cross), a holy person (statues of Jesus and Mary), a relationship (wedding rings, the symbol of holy matrimony), and a variety of other things. Symbolic significance is usually attached to the *language* and *behavior* of ritual, as in the Christian rituals of worship, hymn singing, prayer, baptism, communion, and confession. The symbolic aspects of rituals are so important that some anthropologists define ritual itself as symbolic behavior.

Cross-culturally, people perform rituals for a bewildering variety of purposes. Diverse peoples use rituals to make someone (or everyone) healthy or fertile, to bring rain, to make the crops grow, to save souls, to provide blessings, and so forth. People may pray, worship, make sacrifices, and follow ritual procedures scrupulously to ensure that their gods, their personal spirits, or the ghosts of their dead ancestors intervene favorably in their lives.

Anthropologists often classify rituals on two bases. The first basis is their conscious purposes—the reasons people themselves give for performing them. For example, there are divination rituals that people believe allow them to acquire information from a supernatural power about the future or about some past event. Divination is commonly employed to determine the source of sickness or misfortune or to help people make decisions in uncertain situations. There are curing, sorcery, sacrificial, and exorcism rituals. There are rituals to renew the world, to make a man out of a boy and a woman out of a girl, and to free the soul from a dead person's body. There are rituals held for single individuals, for kin groups, for people of similar age, for whole societies, and so forth.

In many cultures, there are rituals for weather control. The Hopi of the American Southwest believe that rainfall that fills springs and streams and nourishes crops is brought by supernatural beings. These beings, called *kachinas,* live in the peaks of mountains to the west of Hopi villages. They bring life-giving rain to Hopi cornfields when they come in the form of clouds. In the spring and summer, Hopi believe, kachinas dwell in the villages. During this period men wearing masks of the kachinas perform ritual dances, impersonating and honoring the spirits. The spirit enters the body of the dancer, who thus becomes the kachina. The dances bring rain to the Hopi cornfields.

The second basis of classification is when rituals occur—whether they are held on a regular schedule (like weekly church services) or simply whenever some individual or group wants or needs them (like funerals or prayers for a sick person). If rituals are held regularly (seasonally, annually, daily, monthly), they are called *calendrical rituals.* Hopi, for example, follow a ritual calendar in which certain rituals are performed by certain groups at the same time every year. One ritual begins the sequence, then other rituals follow in regular sequence. The same cycle is repeated the following year.

In contrast, *crisis rituals* are organized and performed whenever some individual or group needs, wants, or asks for them—for purposes of curing, ensuring good hunting or fishing, or other events that happen sporadically or unpredictably. The supernatural curing practiced by shamans, considered later, is the most widespread type of crisis ritual.

With this brief and broad overview of religion in mind, we consider some of the major theoretical orientations offered to understand or explain religion.

Theories of Religion

Why do all cultures have religious beliefs, myths, and rituals? With regard to beliefs, people cannot prove the existence of supernatural powers such as ghosts, gods, demons, angels, souls, *mana,* and so forth. And although people who follow a particular form of religion may believe that traditional accounts of their past

▲ In this depiction of a biblical myth, Eve offers forbidden fruit to Adam. Their original sin explains the origin of evil in the Judeo-Christian worldview.

reflect historical events, outsiders to the religion are more likely to consider at least parts of them mythical. Indeed, some people who do not share the beliefs of a given culture think such beliefs result from ignorance or superstition.

As for rituals, people who are outsiders to a religion and worldview may not share the opinion that they help achieve the goals the performers have in mind. To them, most rituals may seem like a waste of time and resources. For example, when a Trobriand Islander plants a yam garden, he does some things that "work" in the way he thinks they do: he clears the land, removes the weeds, and so forth, just as anyone should for success. But a Trobriander believes certain acts that many outsiders consider superfluous are also necessary for success in gardening. He hires a magician to perform rites and spells to improve his yam harvest. Outsiders

▶ In many religions, certain places are considered sacred, as the wailing wall of Jerusalem is for Jews.

© Barry D. Kass/Images of Anthropology

(nonbelievers) to Trobriand beliefs understand what the gardener gets out of the first kind of activity: a yam harvest, if nature cooperates. But what does he get out of the performance of magic? How did Trobrianders come to believe that magical rites are needed?

We can state this problem another way to see a main problem in understanding rituals in other cultures. From an outsider's perspective, when the Trobriander plants a crop and weeds his garden, his actions are effective in attaining the goal he has in mind—they work in more or less the way he thinks they do. But when the garden magician performs rites and spells, his actions do not achieve the result he has in mind. The magic does not really work. How, then, did the Trobrianders get the idea that they do?

Speaking broadly, rituals do not have the effects performers intend. The crazy woman is not made sane by exorcizing the demon; no spirits enter the body of the medicine man; there were no genuine witches in Salem, Massachusetts, in 1692. Why, then, do so many people believe in the power of ritual?

Some people who consider themselves sophisticated say that religious beliefs and rituals rest on ignorance and superstition. This nonanswer to the question "Why religion?" is (or should be) rejected by all anthropologists. Its ethnocentrism is apparent: superstition is

something that someone else believes in but you do not. Yet many of your own beliefs seem superstitious to others, and undoubtedly many of the accepted truths of the twenty-first century will be considered superstitious by the twenty-second. Besides, even if we feel that such beliefs and practices are superstitious, we have not explained them. Why does one form of superstition develop in one place and another form in another place?

You may already have thought of possible answers. If rituals do not work in the way performers believe they do, perhaps they work in some other way. If they do not have the effects people intend, they may have other effects that people find useful or satisfying. If the conscious reasons people state for performing rituals seem inadequate explanations, perhaps their meaning is entirely symbolic: They convey and reinforce deep meanings and values that help people cope with life or that tie people together. As for myths, if they are not accurate historical accounts, perhaps they are symbolic statements that help people make sense of reality and give meaning to real-world things and events.

Social scientists have proposed many theories for why religion exists. Some theories hold that beliefs, myths, and rituals provide benefits that people want or need but cannot acquire without religion. Broadly, social scientists have proposed three types of theories: the intellectual (or cognitive), the psychological, and the sociological.

Intellectual/Cognitive Approaches

Those who follow the **intellectual** (or **cognitive**) **approach** assume that humans want explanations for the world around them. Religious beliefs help satisfy the uniquely human desire to understand and explain things and events. Without religion, much of the world would be incomprehensible and inexplicable, which (these scholars argue) would be intolerable to the mind of a conscious, reasoning, problem-solving species like *Homo sapiens.* For example, religion satisfies the human demand for understanding by providing explanations for the movements of the sun, moon, and stars. *Origin myths* explain things like the creation of the sky, land, and water; where animals and plants come from; and where people got their language, tools, rituals, and other customs and beliefs. The essential purpose of religion, in the intellectual view, is to provide people with explanations.

Sir James Frazer was an influential scholar who championed the intellectual approach. His most famous work was the *The Golden Bough,* published in 12 volumes around the turn of the twentieth century. Among other things, Frazer was interested in the development of rational thought. He argued that thought had progressed through three stages that he called magic, religion, and science. The earliest cultures practiced what he called *magic,* which attempted to control the world by performing rites and spells. Later cultures came to believe in the existence of supernatural beings, who demanded that people worship them or make sacrifices to them, giving birth to *religion.* Finally, people realized that neither magical techniques nor worship of imaginary beings allowed them to explain or control events. This realization came about with the advent of *science,* which replaced the errors of magic and religion with knowledge of true cause-and-effect relationships. In Frazer's view magic, religion, and science are alternative worldviews: each provides people with an intellectual model of the way the world works and a means to manipulate events and people. Because science is a superior system of knowledge, Frazer thought it to be in the process of replacing magical and religious beliefs.

The idea of Frazer and others that religious beliefs provide people with explanations for things and events is correct, as far as it goes, but it is an incomplete explanation for religion. Religion does satisfy curiosity about the world, but this is not its only function. The people whom Frazer called "savages" possess and use practical knowledge just as "civilized" peoples do—a Trobriander knows that he must care for his yams as well as perform garden magic. Conversely, many "scientific" folk believe in and practice religion—including many of those who make their living practicing the science for which religion supposedly substitutes. Those scientists who go to church apparently find little or no contradiction between their religious beliefs and worship and their scientific knowledge and practice. Religious beliefs do not substitute for objective knowledge; in some way that we do not fully understand, they supplement and complement it.

Although few scholars today hold that religion exists solely or even mainly to provide "prescientific" people with explanations their culture would otherwise lack, the intellectual approach is by no means passé. Clifford Geertz, a leading modern humanistic theorist (Chapter 4), holds that religion provides its believers with the assurance that the world is *meaningful*—that events have a place in the grand scheme of things, natural phenomena have causes, suffering and evil happen to specific individuals for a good reason, and injustices are corrected. Cultural beings (i.e., humans) cannot tolerate events that contradict the basic premises, categories, and worldview of their cultural tradition. Yet such events do occur periodically. Because of religion, people are able to maintain their worldview in spite of events that seem to contradict it. Religion, Geertz believes, reassures believers that the world is orderly rather than chaotic, all within the framework of their existing cultural knowledge.

Stewart Guthrie is another contemporary scholar who views religion in cognitive terms. Guthrie thinks the essence of religion is the belief that natural phenomena have humanlike properties. He points out that people tend to see the world *anthropomorphically*—we tend to attribute human motives, purposes, feelings, senses, and other characteristics to living and nonliving things that are not human. For example: thunder is the voice of the gods, clouds are the spirits of our ancestors, the sun is our life-giving father, Mother Earth is alive, the wind is the breath of a god. Anthropomorphism is natural to human thought, and most of us regularly think this way, as when you think your car or computer hates you or when you interact with your pet as if it is a person.

When people see the world as "peopled" with spirits (as in animism), or think that different gods control various aspects of nature (as in polytheism), or believe that one god created and controls everything (as in monotheism), they are attributing human characteristics to the natural world. In Guthrie's view, this actually is a smart thing to do. If you think there are no human-like beings making things happen, and you are wrong, then the consequences are costly: If the earth is in fact our mother, but we treat her as nonliving, then she might punish us. But if we think anthropomorphically about the earth and take steps to worship and protect her, then no harm is done. If there is a war god, and our enemy sacrifices to him but we do not, we may all be killed, so why take the chance? As Guthrie phrases it, religion is then a "good bet."

However, not all the rituals that result from beliefs that humanlike beings control natural processes are "harmless." In fact, many rituals are quite costly: They require sacrifices to deities or ancestors, and they consume time and energy that could be used in other ways. In some societies, religious beliefs are costly indeed: among some ancient Mesoamerican civilizations, priests pierced their bodies with thorns to make themselves bleed because they believed that the gods demanded blood sacrifices. Human sacrifice occurred as well. Attributing human properties to nonhuman entities is not always harmless: religion often helps motivate individuals and groups of individuals to do horrific things to others—and sometimes to themselves.

Psychological Approaches

The notion that religion helps people cope psychologically with times of trouble, stress, and anxiety is a common one. Sicknesses, accidents, misfortunes, injustices, deaths, and other trials and tribulations of life can be better handled emotionally if one believes that there is a reason and meaning to them or that one's troubles can be controlled or alleviated by means of ritual. Scholars who make such arguments follow the **psychological approach.**

In anthropology a well-known psychological theory of religion is that of Bronislaw Malinowski, whom we introduced in Chapter 4. Malinowski thought that religion (including magic) serves the valuable function of giving people confidence when they are likely to be unsuccessful despite their best efforts. There are always natural phenomena that people cannot control and that constantly threaten to ruin their plans and efforts. Belief in the power of ritual to control these (otherwise uncontrollable) elements instills confidence and removes some of the anxiety that results from the uncertainties of life. Not only do rituals relieve our worries, they may also help us be more successful in activities by making us more confident of success.

Another specific psychological theory of religion holds that, as self-conscious beings, we humans are aware of our own mortality. Knowing that we will eventually die causes us great anxiety and leads us to worry about our own death. Experiencing the serious illness or death of one's parent or other relative likewise produces grief and psychological stress for most people. We must have some way of coping emotionally with the grief over the death of our loved ones, and with the anxiety caused by the knowledge of our own mortality. Religion helps us cope by denying the finality of death—that is, by inculcating beliefs about the existence of a pleasant afterlife, in which our immortal souls live forever.

The notion that belief in life after death helps to calm our fears and alleviate our anxieties seems reasonable. However, this theory is tainted by an ethnocentric assumption: although most religions do include beliefs about some kind of afterlife, in a great many cultures the afterlife is far from pleasant. The Dobu people of Melanesia believe that human bodies also have a ghostly form, seen as a shadow or a reflection. During life, the ghostly self goes out at night and appears in the dreams of other people. Once the corpse rots after death, the ghosts of people go to a place called the Hill of the Dead, where they have a "thin and shadowy" existence and mourn for their homeland. How are such beliefs about the afterlife "comforting"?

Certainly, religion is psychologically useful. For some people some of the time, it relieves anxieties, calms fears, and helps one cope emotionally with life's uncertainties and hardships. That religion often serves such functions is indisputable. On the other hand, sometimes religious beliefs actually increase our anxieties, fears, and stress levels. Consider the Kwaio, a people of the Solomon Islands. Kwaio believe that women are polluting to men, so Kwaio wives are expected to take elaborate precautions to avoid polluting their husbands when preparing food for them. If a man dies of an illness, his wife may be blamed, and perhaps killed, for her "offense." Just whose anxieties and fears are relieved by this belief?

The general point of the Dobu and Kwaio examples is that, from a psychological perspective, religion has two faces. On the one hand, it does—for some people, some of the time, in some respects—help us to cope emotionally with times of trouble and hardships. On the other hand, beliefs about the supernatural often create fears and anxieties that would not otherwise exist. Pleasant afterlives ("Heaven") offer us comfort and hope. But what *psychological* benefit does the threat of eternal damnation ("Hell") offer?

▲ Psychological approaches hold that religion helps individuals and groups cope with crisis, uncertainty, grief, stress, trauma, and other times of emotional distress. This Iraqi woman cries at a funeral.

Sociological Approaches

"Societies need religion to keep people in line," you may have heard people say. The idea of the **sociological approach** is that religion instills and maintains common values, leads to increased conformity to cultural norms, promotes cohesion and cooperation, promises eternal rewards for good deeds and eternal damnation for evil acts, and so forth. Those who champion the sociological approach hold that religion exists because of the useful effects it has on human societies—because of its *social functions*. Religion helps societies maintain harmonious social relationships between individuals and groups. It encourages people to respect the rights of others and to perform their proper duties. It is part of the socialization process that instills deeply held values in children.

Consider the Ten Commandments, for example, which serve as a moral code for Christians and Jews. Two prescribe how people ought to feel and act toward God and other people, and eight give rules for actions, including the five "thou shalt nots" (see Exodus 20:3–17). Note that five of the divinely ordered prohibitions are against the commission of acts that could result in harm to others, such as killing and stealing. God gave us commandments that will, if obeyed, lead to good relations with others and therefore promote earthly social order. More general Judeo-Christian moral guidelines are the Golden Rule ("do unto others as you would have them do unto you") and love of one's neighbor (Matthew 19:19), both of which are useful prescriptions for harmonious social life.

Another social function of religion is to enhance the cohesion of society by making people sense their interdependence on one another and on their traditions. Émile Durkheim, a French sociologist of the early twentieth century, was influential in formulating this perspective. Durkheim's view was that the main function of religion in human society is to promote *social solidarity,*

▲ These people are gathered for a ritual in Irian Jaya, Indonesia. French sociologist Émile Durkheim proposed that rituals involve gatherings and common activities that enhance social solidarity.

meaning that religion has the effect of bringing people together and enhancing their sense of unity, cohesion, and reliance on their society's customs. Groups of people who share the same beliefs and who gather periodically to perform common rituals experience a feeling of oneness and harmony.

The most important social function of religion, Durkheim believed, is to strengthen social solidarity. There also are other versions of the sociological approach. One is that religion help maintain social order (that is, religion serves as a social control mechanism—see Chapter 12) by increasing conformity to norms, inculcating shared values in children, reminding people to act responsibly, teaching moral lessons through myths and doctrines, and so forth.

One mechanism by which religion serves social control functions is by offering rewards for good behavior and punishments for antisocial behavior. In this life, when people have an accident or get sick, they may think they are being punished for some crime or deviant action, for example. This deters the individual from future deviance and also serves as an example to others, leading them to act properly in the future. In the next life (the afterlife, which some peoples believe lasts for eternity), gods may reward virtue and punish sinful behavior. Such socially useful effects of religion are widespread.

But not all peoples have such beliefs. In some worldviews, gods and other kinds of spiritual beings have little or no interest in the morality or immorality of human actions. There is no concept of "sin"—in the sense of behavior that violates a doctrine or divine will—and the fate of a person in this life or in the afterlife is not related to her or his moral character or conduct.

There is a relation between whether spiritual beings punish and reward people according to their character or conduct and the general nature of the cultural system. In a cross-cultural study done back in the 1960s, Guy Swanson found a striking relationship between the degree of social inequality in a society and the likelihood that its religion will include beliefs that spiritual beings punish wrongdoing. Generally, societies in which there is greater inequality (class societies, discussed in Chapter 12) are much more likely than egalitarian societies to believe that gods or other spirits will reward and punish individuals according to how well they behave.

Supernatural Explanations of Misfortune

One occurrence that many peoples attribute to the action of spiritual powers is personal misfortune, including death, illness, and events that many Westerners consider accidents. Many beliefs and rituals of various societies are concerned with explaining, preventing, and curing illness and disease.

Cross-culturally, two major complexes of beliefs about misfortune are common. First, as already discussed, many people believe that sickness or some other unfortunate occurrence is caused by the action of spiritual powers. The violation of a taboo can lead some supernatural power to cause sickness. The ancestral spirits of kin groups cause their members to become ill because of conflict or bad feelings within the group. Similar beliefs may apply to accidents that many Westerners attribute to bad luck or carelessness. Drownings, falls, snakebites, prolonged failure to succeed at some activity—such events are likely to be seen as evidence of unfavorable supernatural intervention. The victim has offended a god or spirit, who brings an "accident" as punishment.

Second, many people think that illnesses or other misfortunes are caused by the action of some evil human who is using special supernatural powers against the afflicted person. Belief that certain people, called *sorcerers* and *witches,* have powers to harm others by mystical means is enormously widespread among humanity. Sometimes witches and sorcerers are thought to strike randomly and maliciously against people who are innocent of any wrongdoing. More commonly they direct their evil magic or thoughts toward those against whom they have a grudge. Sorcery and witchcraft are worth considering in more detail.

Sorcery

Sorcery is the performance of rites and spells intended to cause supernatural harm to others; that is, it is a form of evil magic. In some cultures, almost everyone learns to harm their enemies by sorcery techniques, for such techniques are a form of everyday magical self-defense. Among other peoples, sorcery is a more specialized practice: only certain people inherit or acquire the knowledge of how to recite spells and perform the rites correctly.

In 1890, Sir James Frazer proposed that magic (including sorcery) is based on two kinds of logical principles or assumptions. Both involve a symbolic identification of something (e.g., an object or action) with something else (e.g., an event or a person).

One kind of logical principle on which magic is based is the *imitative principle,* often stated as the premise that "like produces like." That is, if an object resembles a person and the sorcerer mutilates the object, then the same effect will happen to the person. The so-called voodoo doll is a familiar example of the imitative principle: An image or effigy is made that symbolizes the enemy; some act is performed on the effigy; and the enemy supposedly experiences the same fate. In another kind of imitative magic, the magician or sorcerer mimics the effects she or he wants to produce. For example, sorcerers among the Dobu of Melanesia cast spells by imitating the symptoms of the disease they want to afflict on their victims.

The second kind of logical premise underlying magic and sorcery is called the *contagious principle,* which is the assumption that "power comes from contact." That is, things that were once in contact with someone can be used in rites and spells to make things happen to that person. By performing sorcery rites and spells on such objects as hair clippings, bodily excretions, nail parings, infant umbilical cords, or jewelry and clothing, harm can be done to one's enemies. In societies in which sorcery rests on the contagious principle, people must be careful to dispose of objects they have been in contact with, lest one of their enemies use them for sorcery. As with the imitative principle, a symbolic identification is made between the objects and the victim. But in the case of the contagious principle, the symbolic equation comes from previous contact rather than from resemblance: by acquiring possession of something once belonging to a person, supernatural power is acquired over that person.

Whether based on the imitative or contagious principle, beliefs about sorcery are affected by the patterned relationships between individuals and groups. In all societies, certain kinds of social relationships are especially likely to be beset by conflicts. Co-wives of a polygynous man may be jealous over their husband's favors or be in competition over an inheritance for their children. People who have married into a kin group or village may be viewed as outsiders who retain loyalty to their own natal families. Two men who want the same woman, or two women who want the same man, have reasons to dislike one another. Men who are rivals for a political office have conflicts of interest.

These and other kinds of relationships are sources of strain and conflict within a human group. Which relationships are likely to cause strain and conflict depend on the way the society is organized: Brothers-in-law are allies in one society, but their interests regularly conflict in another society, for instance. The relationships most likely to be troublesome are *patterned,* meaning that individuals who have these relationships with one another are likely to experience difficulty.

Suppose you were brought up in a culture that explained illness or accident by sorcery. If you or a relative became ill or suffered misfortune, you would not suspect just anyone of harming you. You would ask: Who has a motive to perform evil magic against me? Who envies me? Who would profit from my sickness or death? With whom have I recently quarreled? These people are your prime suspects, and they are the ones you or your family are most likely to accuse.

Members of most cultures reason in much the same way. They believe that sorcerers do not strike randomly but harm only their enemies or people toward whom they feel anger, envy, or ill will. But bad feelings are more likely to exist in certain kinds of relationships than in others, within a single society. Accusations of sorcery, therefore, usually follow the prevalent lines of conflict: because people who stand in the same kinds of relationships are likely to accuse one another again and again, sorcery accusations are patterned.

Witchcraft

Witchcraft is another explanation that people in many societies give for misfortune. There is no universally applicable distinction between sorcery and witchcraft. Whereas sorcery usually involves the use of rites and spells to commit a foul deed, here we define **witchcraft** as the use of psychic power alone to cause harm to others. Sorcerers manipulate objects; witches need only think malevolent thoughts to turn their anger, envy, or hatred into evil deeds. (The English language's main distinction between the two—witches are female, sorcerers usually male—is not useful cross-culturally.) Many cultures believe in the existence of both kinds of malevolent power, so sorcery and witchcraft are often found among the same people. Like sorcery accusations, accusations of witchcraft are likely to be patterned, for people most often believe that both witches and sorcerers harm only people they dislike, hate, envy, or have a conflict with.

Cultures vary in the characteristics they attribute to witches and in how witches cause harm. A few examples illustrate some of the diversity.

- The Navajo of the American Southwest associate witches with the worst imaginable sins—witches commit incest, bestiality (sex with animals), and necrophilia (sex with corpses); they change themselves into animals; they cannibalize infants; and so on.
- The Nyakyusa of Tanzania hold that witches are motivated mainly by their lust for food; accordingly, they suck dry the udders of people's cattle and devour the internal organs of their human neighbors while they sleep.
- The Azande of the southern Sudan believe that witches possess an inherited substance that leaves their bodies at night and gradually eats away at the flesh and internal organs of their victims. Witches, as well as their victims, are considered to be unfortunate, because the Azande believe that a person can be a witch without even knowing it. Witches can do nothing to rid themselves permanently of their power, although they can be forced to stop bewitching some particular individual by ridding themselves of bad feelings against their victim.
- The Ibibio of Nigeria believe that witches operate by removing the spiritual essence (soul) of their enemies and placing it in an animal; this makes the victim sick, and he dies when the witches slaughter and consume the animal. Sometimes Ibibio witches decide to torture, rather than kill, a person. In that case they remove the victim's soul and put it in water or hang it over a fireplace or flog it in the evenings; the afflicted person will remain sick until the witches get what they want out of him or her.
- The Lugbara, a people of Uganda, claim that witches—who are always men—walk around at night disguised as rats or other nocturnal animals. Sometimes they defecate blood around the household of their victims, who wake up sick the next morning.

Such beliefs, it might appear to someone who does not share them, are logically outrageous; no one's soul leaves his or her body at night to cavort with other witches, for example. It might seem that these beliefs are socially harmful as well. Beliefs about witchcraft, fear of witchcraft, and accusations of witchcraft engender conflict and aggression among a people. Finally, the treatment many suspected and "proven" witches receive offends our notions of social justice. As we know from the witch hunts of European and American history, the truly innocent victims of witchcraft are often the accused witches, who sometimes are cruelly executed for crimes they could not have committed.

Interpretations of Sorcery and Witchcraft

Given their seemingly harmful effects and the injustices that frequently result from them, why are beliefs about and accusations of sorcery and witchcraft so widespread? Why should most of the world's peoples think that some or all of their misfortunes are caused by the supernatural powers of their enemies?

Many answers have been offered to such questions. In line with the overall theoretical approaches discussed earlier, the answers fall into two categories: cognitive and sociological. (In the following discussion, for simplicity, we use the term *witchcraft* to refer to both witchcraft and sorcery because the ideas presented have been applied to both kinds of beliefs.)

Cognitive Interpretations. The most influential cognitive approach is that witchcraft explains unfortunate events. The argument is that most people find the idea of coincidence or accident intellectually unsatisfying when some misfortune happens to them or their loved ones, so they search for other causes. Their logic is something like this: I have enemies who wish me harm, and harm just came to me, so my enemies are responsible.

The classic example of how people account for misfortune by reference to the actions of witches comes from among the Azande, an African people. The Azande attribute prolonged serious illnesses and many other personal misfortunes to witchcraft. Ethnographer E. E. Evans-Pritchard describes their beliefs:

> Witchcraft is ubiquitous. . . . There is no niche or corner of Zande culture into which it does not twist itself. If blight seizes the groundnut crop it is witchcraft; if the bush is vainly scoured for game it is witchcraft; if women laboriously bail water out of a pool and are rewarded by but a few small fish it is witchcraft; . . . if a wife is sulky and unresponsive to her husband it is witchcraft; if a prince is cold and distant with his subject it is witchcraft; if a magical rite fails to achieve its purpose it is witchcraft; if, in fact, any failure or misfortune falls upon any one at any time and in relation to any of the manifold activities of his life it may be due to witchcraft. (1976, 18)

This does not mean that the Azande are ignorant of cause and effect and therefore attribute every misfortune to some witch who is out to get them. When a man seeks shelter in a granary and its roof falls and injures him, he blames witchcraft. But the Azande know very well that granary roofs collapse because termites eat the wood that supports them. They do not attribute the collapse of granaries in general to witchcraft; it is the collapse of this particular granary at this particular time with this particular person inside that is caused by witchcraft. Do not granaries sometimes fall with no one sitting inside them? And do not people often relax in granaries without the roof falling? It is the coincidence between the collapse and the presence of a particular person—a coincidence that many other peoples consider bad luck—that Azande witchcraft explains.

Another cognitive benefit is that witches serve as scapegoats. When things are going poorly, people do not always know why. Witchcraft provides an explanation. It also provides people with a means to do something about the situation: identify, accuse, and punish the witch responsible. If, as is often the case, things still do not improve, there are always other yet-to-be-identified witches. People can blame many of their troubles on witches—evil enemies conspiring against them—rather than on their personal inadequacies or on bad luck.

Sociological Interpretations. One sociological interpretation is that witchcraft reinforces the norms and values that help individuals live harmoniously with one another. Every culture has notions of how individuals ideally ought to act toward others. Witches typically are the antithesis of these cultural ideals. They act like animals, or actually change themselves into animals. They mate with relatives. They often put on a false front, pretending to be your friend by day while they eat your liver by night. They have no respect for age or authority. They are in league with the forces of evil (in the Judeo-Christian tradition, witches made compacts with the Devil, agreeing to be his servant in return for worldly pleasures). All the most despicable personal characteristics of people are wrapped up in the personality of witches, whom everyone is supposed to hate. So witches symbolize all that is undesirable, wicked, and hateful. Just as one should despise witches, so should one hate all that they stand for. In short, by providing a hated symbol of the abnormal and the antisocial, the witch strengthens cultural conceptions of normatively approved social behavior.

Another argument is that witches provide an outlet for repressed aggression, and thus beliefs about witches lower the overall amount of conflict in a society. Writing about the Navajo in 1944, Clyde Kluckhohn argued that Navajo culture emphasizes cooperation and maintenance of good relationships between members of the same extended household. When bad feelings do develop within the household, Navajo culture leads people to suppress them. But pent-up hostilities have an outlet in the form of witches, whom people are allowed to hate and gossip about. Because most of the persons the Navajo believe to be witches are members of distant groups, usually little action is taken against them. Solidarity between relatives of the in-group is preserved by displacing hostility to people of the out-group.

Another sociological interpretation is that witchcraft beliefs serve as a mechanism of social control. This might work in two ways. First, many people believe in the existence of witchcraft but do not know which specific members of their community are witches. This leads individuals to be careful not to make anyone angry, since the offended party may be a witch. Second, individuals who fail to conform to local norms of behavior are most likely to be suspected and accused of being witches. People who are always mad at somebody; who carry grudges for prolonged periods; who always seem envious and resentful of the success of others; who have achieved wealth but selfishly refuse to share it in the culturally accepted manner—such violators of these and other normative standards frequently are believed to be the likely perpetrators of witchcraft. Fear of being accused and punished presumably increases adherence to norms and ideals of behavior.

Varieties of Religious Organization

To describe various dimensions of culture, ethnologists develop classifications based, hopefully, on major differences and similarities. Any classification distorts the "real world" of actual cultural diversity: to be useful, classifications must be broad, but their very broadness inevitably masks many details. In classifying diverse religions into a relatively few forms or types, we oversimplify and, to some degree, distort, as humanistic anthropologists remind us. Just as we oversimplify a given culture when we classify it as (for example) horticultural, polygynous, patrilineal, tribal, and egalitarian, so do we simplify when we pigeonhole its religion as (for example) shamanistic or monotheistic. Nonetheless, a classification of religion is useful because it gives a general picture of religious diversity among humanity.

In the 1960s, Anthony Wallace proposed a classification of religions that is influential. His typology is based on the concept of *cult*. As Wallace used the term, *cult* does not refer to some exotic, offbeat, and (usually) short-lived set of beliefs that grow up around a "cult leader." Rather, he used the term in a neutral way to refer to an organized system of beliefs and practices pertaining to the control or worship of specific supernatural powers. Thus rituals intended to help sick people get well might be called *curing cults;* rituals believed to bring precipitation might be called *rain cults;* and so forth.

Defined in this way, cults have diverse and sometimes specific purposes. It is important to understand that the members of a given society can participate in many different kinds of cults, each with a specific orientation such as hunting, rain, war, agriculture, salvation, protection, initiation, divination, and so forth. Therefore, a "cult" is not the same as "the religion" of a people. Rather, religion is a more inclusive concept: A society's total religion may include many different cults devoted to different purposes like curing illness, controlling weather, worshipping gods, foretelling the future, renewing nature, protecting people from enemies, saving souls, and keeping ancestral spirits happy.

Wallace originally distinguishes four kinds of cults.

- **Individualistic cults** Each individual has a personal relationship with one or more supernatural powers, who serve as the person's guardians and protectors. The aid of the powers is solicited when needed for personal goals.
- **Shamanistic cults** Some individuals—shamans—are believed to have relationships with the supernatural that ordinary people lack. They use these powers primarily for socially valuable purposes, to help (especially cure) others in need. They may also act on behalf of their band or village to cause supernatural harm to the group's enemies.
- **Communal cults** The members of a particular group gather periodically for the performance of rituals that they believe benefit the group as a whole, or some individual in it. There are no full-time religious specialists, as is also true of individualistic and shamanistic cults.
- **Ecclesiastical cults** The hallmark of ecclesiastical cults is the presence of full-time religious practitioners who form a religious bureaucracy. The actual practice of religion is managed or carried out by formal, specialized officials—priests—who perform calendrical rituals. The priesthood is usually materially supported by institutionalized gov-

© Catherine Karnow/Corbis

▲ Religious healing aids people in societies at all levels of complexity and development. This South Korean woman is leading a *kut,* a ritual that helps her clients with physical, psychological, and family problems.

ernmental authorities through taxation or redistributive tribute (see Chapters 7 and 12).

The Concept Review summarizes these four forms of religious organization.

Although any given culture has more than one of these kinds of cults, the varieties are not randomly distributed among the peoples of the world. Rather, there is a rough evolutionary sequence to their occurrence. For example, in many foraging bands and horticultural tribes—such as the Inuit, !Kung, and Yąnomamö—shamanistic cults are common, whereas ecclesiastical cults occur mainly in stratified chiefdoms and states. If we consider the religion of a people to be composed of some number of cults, more kinds of cults are found in states than in tribes.

But the evolutionary matching of kinds of cults with kinds of economic and political organizations is very rough and general. For instance, the aboriginal peoples of Australia had communal cults, although they were foragers and lived in bands. Many tribes of the North American Great Plains had individualistic, shamanistic, and communal cults, although they were primarily foragers.

Further frustrating our desire to "pigeonhole" religious diversity is the fact that in many societies there are several religions, sometimes at odds with one another. In the Caribbean nation of Haiti, voudon (voodoo) persists even though the official hierarchy of the Catholic Church has tried to eliminate it for over a century. Multiethnic nations, of course, have a variety of religions within their borders (see Chapter 17). Even nations that are linguistically and culturally homogeneous are religiously diverse. South Korea, for example, is a heavily industrialized, urbanized nation most of whose 43 million people are Buddhists or Christians or express no religious affiliation. But many Buddhist or Christian Koreans today seek the services of shamans (who are usually women) to help with illness or difficulties in their personal lives. Many Japanese people have Christian-style weddings and Buddhist funerals, and they may honor their ancestors at Shinto shrines. Some North Americans pay spirit mediums

Varieties of Religious Organization

Form	Major Characteristics
Individualistic cults	Individuals have a relationship with one or more supernatural powers who serve as personal guardians and protectors.
Shamanistic cults	Shamans have power to contact supernatural beings to help (especially cure) individuals. Shamans may also act on behalf of their band or village to cause harm to enemies.
Communal cults	Members of a well-defined group gather periodically for collective rituals that benefit the group as a whole or some individual member. "Elders" often have special roles in rituals.
Ecclesiastical cults	Include full-time religious officials (priests) organized into a religious bureaucracy supported by tribute and/or redistribution. Priests officiate at mainly calendrical rituals believed to benefit the society or political unit as a whole.

("channelers") large sums of money to put them in contact with deceased relatives, a practice that is comparable in many ways to shamanism.

But these and other complications should not obscure the general pattern. The religions of hunter-gatherer bands do differ generally and significantly from those of complex chiefdoms and states. We now discuss these varieties of religious organization. Because our major point is that religious beliefs, myths, and rituals can only be understood in the contexts of a people's entire cultural system, we discuss how they relate to economic and political organization.

Individualistic Cults

The defining characteristic of individualistic cults is that individuals intentionally seek out particular spirits or other supernatural powers to protect and help them. The most well-known example of individualistic cults is the **vision quest.** It is widespread among Native American peoples but is especially important for the Great Plains tribes. To the Plains peoples, the world is charged with spiritual energy and supernatural power. Power exists in inanimate objects such as rocks or mountains and in living animals and plants. Human beings require the aid of the supernatural in many activities—in hunting, warfare, and times of sickness or other troubles.

Spiritual power most often comes to individuals in visions. These visions play an important role in religious life because it is through them that people achieve the personal contact with the supernatural that is essential in various endeavors. Spiritual powers occasionally make contact with individuals for no ap-

parent reason, coming to them as they sleep or even as they are walking or riding alone.

More often humans—especially young men—have to seek out these powers through an active search, or quest, whose purpose is to acquire a vision. There are places that supernatural powers are believed to frequent: certain hills, mountains, or bluffs. A young man goes to such a location alone. There he smokes and fasts, appealing to a power to take pity on him. Among one tribe, the Crow, sometimes a man will even amputate part of a finger or cut his body to arouse pity. The vision commonly appears on the fourth day, since four is a sacred number to the Crow.

The way in which the power manifests itself varies. Sometimes the man hears the spirit speak to him. Sometimes it comes in the form of a dreamlike story. In other instances it simply materializes before his eyes, taking the form of a bear, a bison, an eagle, or some other large animal. Sometimes small animals like rabbits, field mice, and dogs also appear. The power tells the man how it will help him. It might give him the ability to predict the future, locate enemies, find game, become a powerful warrior, or cure illness. It tells him the things he will have to do to keep his power—what songs to sing, how to paint his war shield, how to wear his hair, and so forth. It also tells the man some things he cannot do; for example, if the power comes from the eagle, the man might be prohibited from killing "his brother," the eagle. As long as he continues to behave in the prescribed manner, the power will be his supernatural protector, or *guardian spirit.* Through the spirit, the man acquires special powers other men do not have.

There is no known culture in which individualistic cults constitute the entire religion. Even among Plains

Indians, among whom the vision quest is unusually well developed, shamanistic and communal cults also exist.

Shamanism

A **shaman** is a person who people believe has a special relationship to supernatural powers, which he frequently uses to cure sickness. In many societies (especially among many foraging peoples), the shaman is the only kind of religious practitioner; that is, he possesses the only kinds of abilities not available to ordinary people. Usually, shamans are not full-time specialists in curing. Rather, they carry out their tasks whenever their services are needed, usually in return for a gift or fee; but otherwise they live much like everyone else.

Shamans are believed to possess several qualities. They have access to the power of spiritual beings, usually called *spirit helpers.* The effectiveness of a shaman in curing (or causing harm) is believed to derive from the potency of his spirit helpers and from his ability to contact them and get them to do his bidding. Contact with one's spirit helpers commonly is made by achieving an altered state of consciousness. This altered state (referred to as a *trance*) is reached in various ways: through intake of drugs, ritual chanting, or participation in percussive or rhythmic music. The Tungus, the northeast Asian people from whom we borrowed the word *shaman,* use tambourines and drums to achieve the trance in which they journey to the spirit world to discover the cause of illness.

Among peoples who practice shamanism, trance is interpreted as a sign some spirit, often one of a shaman's spirit helpers, has physically entered (possessed) the shaman's body. The spirit takes over his body and speaks to the assembled audience through his mouth. When possessed, the shaman becomes a *medium,* or mouthpiece for the spirits—he may lose control over his actions and his voice changes its quality because a spirit is speaking through him. The unusual behavior and strange voice are seen as evidence of genuine possession, which is a sign of a shaman's power.

The way a person becomes a shaman varies from people to people, for the details of the role are defined by local cultures. Many scholars argue that shamans are individuals who are unusual in some way: they hear voices, parts of their bodies tremble uncontrollably, they dress or act in strange ways, and so forth. Other members of their community interpret their "difference" as a sign they have been chosen by a spirit to become a healer. Other observers report that shamans are quite normal

people who act like everyone else when not enacting the role of shaman. Obviously, whether shamans are "different" varies from people to people.

Shamans are usually considered to have knowledge and powers lacked by others. They acquire these in three major ways. In some societies they undergo a period of special training as an apprentice to a practicing shaman, who teaches the novice chants and songs and how to achieve the trance state. Among other peoples, shamans must have endured difficult deprivations, such as prolonged fasting, the consumption of foods culturally considered disgusting, or years of sexual abstinence. Finally, in many societies shamans are individuals who have experienced some unusual event. For example, they have miraculously recovered from a serious illness or injury, or they claim to have had an unusual dream or vision in which some spirit called them to be its mouthpiece.

In most cultures, the shaman's major role is curing. Again, how the shaman performs this role varies. By considering an ethnographic example of sickness and curing, we can see shamans in action. We can also use the case to suggest an answer to one of the questions frequently asked about shamanism: How does the belief that shamans have the power to make people well persist, even though many of their clients die?

The Jívaro are a rain forest people of Ecuador. Jívaro believe that most sickness is caused by the actions of their human enemies (rather than by natural causes). Jívaro shamans acquire their power from their control over their personal spirit helpers, which live in their bellies in the form of tiny magical darts. A man becomes a shaman by presenting a gift to an existing shaman, who regurgitates some of his spirit helpers, which the novice swallows. If the novice drinks a hallucinogenic drug nightly for 10 days and abstains from sexual intercourse for at least 3 months—the longer the better—he will acquire the power to transform any small objects (insects, worms, plants, etc.) he ingests into magical darts.

The Jívaro recognize two kinds of shamans: bewitching shamans, who have the ability to make people sick, and curing shamans, who try to make people well by counteracting the evil deeds of bewitching shamans. By ingesting and storing many magical darts in his body, a bewitching shaman can later harm his enemies. He causes illness by propelling one or more magical darts into the body of his victim; unless the darts are removed by a curing shaman, the victim will die. To effect the cure, a curing shaman first drinks tobacco juice and other drugs, which give him the power to see into the body of

▲ Shamans call on the power of their spirit helpers to cure their patients. Here two Mentawai healers treat a woman in Siberut Island in Indonesia.

the victim. Once he locates them, the curer sucks out and captures the magical darts; if the cure is successful, the darts return to their owner and the patient recovers.

Many patients die, which means that the curing shamans are often ineffective. How, then, does the belief in curing abilitics of shamans persist? The answer is that the Jívaro believe that a supernatural battle is waged between the bewitching and the curing shamans. Bewitching shamans have two special spirit helpers. One, called a *pasuk,* looks like an ordinary tarantula to people who are not shamans; the other takes the form of a bird. A bewitching shaman can order his *pasuk* or spirit bird to remain near the house of the victim, shooting additional magic darts into him as the curing shaman sucks them out. If the victim dies, Jívaro believe it may be because the darts shot by the *pasuk* and spirit bird were too many for the curing shaman to remove. Or it may be because the bewitching shaman has more power than the curing shaman.

Aside from serving as an example of shamanism, the Jívaro show how beliefs about supernatural causes and

shamanistic cures for illness form a logically coherent system. If the patient recovers, as usually happens, the ability of the shaman to cure is confirmed. If the victim dies, Jívaro believe this event, too, is explained in terms that are consistent with the existing worldview. Events in the real world—getting better or getting worse, living or dying—do not invalidate the shamanistic worldview because the belief system itself covers such events and contingencies.

As the Jívaro illustrate, in some cultures shamans, as the experts of healings, work alone during the actual cures, although many other people may be physically present. Sometimes, though, shamans have human helpers who perform tasks. Navajo shamans (also called "singers") have assistants who fetch objects, help construct the elaborate drawings in sand used in curing, supply food and drink for all-night cures, and perform other duties.

Shamanistic cults can be more complexly organized also. Among the Zuni, who now live on a reservation in western New Mexico, there were 12 special groups of people (sometimes translated into English as "medicine societies") who were recognized as knowledgeable about curing. Different medicine societies knew the secret techniques for curing various illnesses. If a Zuni became ill with specific symptoms, he or she would go to the appropriate society to be healed. Once healed, the person had learned the secrets of the society, so was usually then initiated into it. Among Zuni, both sexes could join the medicine societies.

Communal Cults

Like shamanism, communal cults have no full-time religious specialists who make their living as practitioners. Communally organized rituals do have leaders—often an elderly person or someone with a special interest in the results of a ritual—who manipulate the symbolic objects or who address the supernatural.

Communal rituals are held to intercede with the supernatural on behalf of some group of people, such as a kin group, an age group, a village, or a caste. To illustrate, we consider two widespread kinds of communal rituals organized by descent groups: ancestral cults and totemism.

Ancestral Cults. Practically all worldviews hold that people have a spiritual dimension—a *soul*—that lives on after the physical body has perished. Beliefs about the fate of the soul after death vary widely. Some peoples—such as Hindus—believe that it is reincarnated into another person or animal. Others hold that the soul passes into a spiritual plane, where it exists eternally with a community of other souls and has no further effects on the living. Still others believe that souls become malevolent after death, turning into ghosts that cause accidents or sickness or that terrify the living.

Another common belief about the fate of souls after death is that they interact with and affect the living, especially their descendants. The many peoples who hold such beliefs use rituals to induce the spirits of their deceased ancestors to do favors for them or simply to leave them alone. Beliefs and rituals surrounding the interactions between the living and their departed relatives are called **ancestral cults,** or *ancestor worship.*

The Lugbara, a people of Uganda, illustrate ancestral cults. The patrilineage is an important social group to the Lugbara. As the most important members of the lineage, lineage elders oversee the interests and harmony of the entire group. They serve as the guardians of the lineage's morality, although they have no power to punish violations physically. The Lugbara believe that the spirit of a deceased person may become an ancestral ghost of her or his lineage. The ghost punishes living descendants who violate Lugbara ideals of behavior toward lineage mates. People who fight with their kinsmen (especially their older relatives), who deceive or steal from their lineage mates, or who fail to carry out their duties toward others are liable to be punished by an ancestral ghost. Sometimes this happens because a ghost sees an offense committed and causes illness to the offender. More commonly, the ghosts do not act on their own initiative to make someone sick. Rather, the ghosts act on the thoughts of an elder who is indignant because of the actions of some member of the lineage. John Middleton describes Lugbara beliefs about the power of lineage elders to cause illness by invoking ghosts:

> [The elder] sits near his shrines in his compound and thinks about the sinner's behavior. His thoughts are known by the ghosts and they then send sickness to the offender. He "thinks these words in his heart"; he does not threaten or curse the offender. For a senior man to do this is part of his expected role. It is part of his "work," to "cleanse the lineage home." Indeed, an elder who does not do so when justified would be lacking in sense of duty toward his lineage. (Middleton 1965, 76)

In the Lugbara example we see how elders maintain harmony and cooperation in the lineage by invoking the power of deceased members. This is a common feature of ancestral cults.

Matrilineal peoples often have ancestral cults as well. The Ndembu of Zambia provide an example. When a woman experiences fertility problems, people often say that she is forgetting her ancestress or doing something disapproved by an ancestress. The cure consists of a lengthy ritual involving the participation of many members of the matrilineage that makes the victim "remember" her relative.

Why do some societies have ancestral cults, in which the spirits of deceased ancestors are concerned with the affairs and behaviors of their descendants? Like other "why" questions, this one is controversial. But many anthropologists agree that such beliefs are related to the degree of importance of large kin groups in a society. The greater the importance of kin groups such as lineages and clans in making public decisions, regulating access to resources, allocating roles, controlling behavior, and so on, the more likely a society is to develop an ancestral cult. Someone who follows the sociological interpretation might argue that ancestral cults provide a religious mechanism by which behavior can be channeled and controlled.

Totemism. Another widespread form of communal cult is **totemism,** the cultural belief that human groups have a special mystical relationship with natural objects such as animals, plants, and, sometimes, nonliving things. The object (or objects) with which a group is associated is known as its *totem.* The group most often is a unilineal kin group, such as a clan. The totem frequently serves as a name of the group; for example, the Bear clan, the Eagle clan, the sun clan.

The nature of the relationship between the members of the group and its totem varies widely. Sometimes the totem is used simply for identification of the group and its members, much like our surnames. Often there is a mystical association between the group and its totem object. People believe they are like their totem in some respects. Or the totem object may be used as a symbol of differences between clans. In many populations—most notably among some of the aboriginal peoples of Australia—the members of a clan treat their totem like a clanmate, believing that the totem gave birth to their ancestors in a mythical period. The welfare of the clan is mystically associated with the welfare of the totem, so periodically the clan gathers for rituals that ensure the reproduction of its totem.

Ecclesiastical Cults

In Chapters 6 and 12, we discussed how a high degree of specialization accompanied the development of civilization. Among New World peoples such as the ancient Incas, Aztecs, and Mayans, and in the Old World cities of ancient Mesopotamia, Egypt, East Asia, and India, this specialization extended into the religious dimension of cultural systems. Rather than organizing rituals on a communal basis—in which a wide range of people controlled and participated in the performance—a formal bureaucracy of religious specialists controlled many public rituals. The religious bureaucracy probably also had a large voice in formulation of the religious laws, which prescribed certain kinds of punishments for those who violated them.

These religious specialists are known as **priests.** It is instructive to compare priests with shamans. In addition to their more specialized status, priests differ from shamans in several respects. First, most shamans perform their ritual functions without aid from other shamans; indeed, as the Jívaro illustrate, many peoples believe that enemy shamans engage in supernatural battles with one another. In contrast, priests are hierarchically organized and usually subsidized and supported by a formal government, either by the high-ranking chiefs of a large

chiefdom or by the state (Chapter 12). Second, priests undergo a lengthy period of special formal training because they must master the complex rituals needed to perform their role. Third, the priesthood was at or near the top of the social ladder in ancient civilizations, so individual priests lived much better than the population at large. Fourth, shamans typically perform mainly crisis rituals, whenever some person requires their services. The rituals at which priests officiate tend to be calendrical—they occur at regular intervals because the gods that the rituals are intended to appease demand regular praise or sacrifice. Fifth, shamans usually derive their powers from their personal characteristics that they have from birth or that they acquired from experiencing some ordeal. In contrast, priests are effective because they have learned the specific skills needed to perform rituals correctly.

A final difference is especially revealing. With the development of a *priesthood* comes a strong distinction between priest and layperson. The layperson has little control over the timing of religious performances or the content of myths. The population at large relies on the priesthood to keep it in proper relation to supernatural powers. This creates a sense of spiritual dependence on the priesthood and on the state apparatus that so often sponsors it, a dependence that reinforces the high degree of stratification found in states.

These state-sponsored cults are called *ecclesiastical* (meaning "of or pertaining to the church") because their priesthood was highly organized and their rituals usually were held in grand buildings that served as temples. The entire ecclesiastical cult was under the control of the government. Officials exacted tribute or taxes to finance the construction of temples, the livelihood of the priesthood, the sacrifices that often accompanied state rituals, and other expenses needed to support and organize religious activities on a fantastically large scale.

There is little question that ecclesiastical cults provided a body of myth and belief that supported the domination of the ruling family or dynasty. (This is not to say that this function totally explains these cults or that it constitutes their entire significance.) This is seen by the content of the cults' beliefs, myths, and rituals, which almost invariably express the dependence of the entire population on the ruler's well-being and on the periodic performance of rituals. A common belief of official state religions is that the ruler is a god-king: He not only rules by divine mandate but is himself a god or somehow partakes of divine qualities. This was true of most of the ancient civilizations and of the states that developed in sub-Saharan Africa. Many complex chiefdoms of Polynesia and the Americas had comparable ideas.

▲ Ecclesiastical cults feature grandiose temples, awe-inspiring physical symbols, and specialized priests needed to mediate between laypersons and gods. This Catholic mass is performed at the Vatican.

Many official rituals of ecclesiastical cults are held to keep the entire polity in beneficial relationship with supernatural beings. For example, the state religion of the ancient Aztecs held that the gods had to be periodically appeased or they would cause the world to end in a cataclysm. To keep the gods' goodwill, the priesthood periodically performed human sacrifice at temples, offering the heart of the victim (usually a war captive) to the deities. The ancient Egyptians believed that their pharaoh would rule in the afterlife—just as in the present world—so when he died, he took much of his wealth, his wives, and his servants into the next world with him. The emperors of Japan were believed to be descended through males from a sun goddess; in later Japanese history the emperors were so set apart from the mundane world that political affairs were handled by the shogun, who ruled in the name of the emperor. The emperor of old China—who was at various times in the more than two millenia history of Chinese civilization the most powerful man on the planet—ruled so long as he had the mandate of heaven.

Ecclesiastical cults everywhere consumed enormous resources, but they did not necessarily wipe out other kinds of cults. Common people usually continued to rely on local shamans for curing, to practice magic, to believe in witches and sorcerers, and to worship their ancestors. In ancient China, Korea, and Japan, for example, each household and lineage continued to revere its own ancestors and to make offerings to them at family shrines.

In medieval Europe, Catholicism was ecclesiastical: the authority of the Church was tightly interwoven with the exercise of secular power, although there often was conflict between popes and various kings. Only in the past few centuries has the formal alliance between the power of government and the will of the gods been broken for any length of time. We should not assume that even this official separation between church and state will necessarily be permanent. As the recent history of Iran and Afghanistan suggests, the intermingling of political and ecclesiastical authorities can be reborn in the modern world—perhaps even in democratic nations.

Revitalization Movements

So far in this chapter we have discussed religion in cultures that are changing only slowly. Under conditions of rapid change, many peoples have turned to supernatural beings for aid and protection when their way of life or their very survival is threatened by contact with powerful outsiders. To preserve their way of life or to cope with changing conditions, large numbers of people join organized movements, usually called **revitalization movements.**

Revitalization movements are most likely to occur in a society when three conditions coalesce: (1) rapid change, often caused by exposure to unfamiliar people, customs, and objects; (2) foreign domination, which leads to a sense of cultural inferiority; and (3) the perception of relative deprivation, meaning that people see themselves as lacking wealth, power, and esteem relative to those who dominate them. Historically, the movements were especially common during colonialism, in which a foreign power subjugated an indigenous people. Colonialism did not always lead to revitalization movements, however.

Revitalization movements usually originate with an individual—a *prophet*—who claims to have had a dream or vision. Sometimes the prophet claims to be a *messiah*, or savior, sent by a spiritual being to save the world from destruction. In the dream or vision the prophet received a message—a *revelation*—from a god, an ancestor, or another spiritual power.

Revelations typically include two kinds of information given by the spirit. The first is a statement about what is wrong with the present-day world, about why people's lives have changed for the worse. Prophets and their followers commonly blame the introduction of corrupting foreign objects and habits—such as tobacco, alcohol, money, new religions, formal schooling, the relaxation of old moral standards—for the troubles of today.

Second, prophets' revelations usually include a vision of a new world and a prescription for how to bring it about. In some cases the message is vague and secular, the prophet claiming that earthly lives will improve if people do (or stop doing) certain things. However, the message is often *apocalyptic:* the prophet says that the present world will end at a certain time, and only those who heed his message will be saved. The expulsion or death of foreigners is a frequent theme of apocalyptic visions: foreigners will be drowned in a flood, burned in a fire, swallowed up by an earthquake, or killed by deities or ancestors. Another common theme is the reversal of existing political and economic dominance relations: foreigners will work for us, we will have the wealth instead of them, we will tax them and make laws that they must

obey, or some other inversion of the existing structure. Nearly always, the prophets' revelations are *syncretic;* that is, they combine elements of traditional myths, beliefs, and rituals with introduced elements.

Examples from two regions illustrate revitalization movements.

Melanesian Cargo Cults

The area called Melanesia in the southwest Pacific experienced numerous revitalization movements in the twentieth century. Melanesians placed great cultural emphasis on wealth and its distribution as the means to become a big man or powerful leader. It is therefore not surprising that they were most interested in the material possessions of German, English, French, and Australian colonial powers. Because European wealth was brought to the islands by ship or plane, it became known as *cargo,* and the various movements that sprang up with the aim of acquiring it through ritual means became known as **cargo cults.**

To Melanesians, all Europeans were fantastically wealthy; yet the Melanesians seldom saw them do any work to earn their possessions. The whites who lived in the islands certainly did not know how to make cars, canned foods, radios, kerosene lanterns, stoves, and so forth. In many traditional Melanesian religions, technology was believed to have been made by deities or spirits, so it followed that European objects were made by their God. Further, when the whites living in Melanesia wanted some new object, they simply made marks on papers and placed them in an envelope or asked for the object by speaking into metal things. Some weeks later, the object was delivered in ships or airplanes. Surely the goods were made by spirits, and the acts the whites did to get their spirits to send cargo were rituals. Melanesians therefore believed that they, too, could acquire this wealth through the correct ritual procedure, which they frequently believed the whites were selfishly withholding from them.

Numerous prophets sprang up among diverse Melanesian peoples, each with his own vision or dream, each with his own story to explain why the Europeans had cargo and the Melanesians had none, and each claiming to know the secret ritual that would deliver the goods. The prophet often claimed to have received a visit from one of his ancestors or a native deity, who told him that the whites had been lying to people about how to get cargo.

The Garia, of the north coast of Papua New Guinea, illustrate some common themes of cargo cults. Like most other indigenous peoples, the Garia were visited by mis-

◄ Members of the John Frum cargo cult in Tanna, Vanuatu, perform a ritual march. They await the return of their messiah, John Frum, who will bring wealth and a new life. This movement, which has also become a political party, has existed on the island of Tanna since the 1940s.

© Lamont Lindstrom

sionaries. Also, like many other peoples, the Garia initially adopted Christianity for reasons other than those the missionaries had in mind. They assumed that the whites knew the ritual that was the "road to cargo." The missionaries would give it to the Garia if only they practiced what the missionaries preached: church attendance, monogamy, worship of the true God, cessation of pagan practices such as sorcery and dancing, and so forth. Based on their belief that the missionary lifestyle and Christian rituals held the secret of cargo, many Garia converted to Christianity early in the twentieth century.

But the cargo did not arrive. The Garia grew angry with the missions because they concluded that the missionaries and other Europeans were withholding the true ritual secret of how to get cargo to keep all the wealth for themselves. In the 1930s and 1940s, two Garia prophets arose. They told the people that the missionaries had been telling them to worship the wrong gods. God and Jesus were both really deities of the Garia, not of whites. The Europeans knew the secret names of God and Jesus and asked them for the cargo with secret prayers. All along, Jesus had been trying to deliver the goods to the Garia, but the Jews were holding him captive in heaven. To free him, the Garia had to perform sacrificial rituals. To show him how poor they were and to make him feel sorry for them, they had to destroy all their native wealth objects. If they did these things, Jesus would give the cargo to the ancestral spirits of the Garia, who would in turn deliver it to the living.

Native American Movements

Revitalization movements also occurred among American Indians, whose tragic sufferings at the hands of white traders, settlers, armies, and administrators are known to all Americans. Two movements were especially important, both of which were precipitated by a deterioration of tribal economic, social, and religious life.

Handsome Lake. In the 1600s and 1700s the Seneca of New York were one of the members of the League of the Iroquois, a loose confederation of different tribes who agreed to maintain peaceful relations between themselves and to come to one another's aid in case of attack by surrounding tribes. Like other members, the Seneca traditionally were horticultural and matrilineal. Men hunted, traded for furs, and went on raids against neighboring tribes, whereas the women owned most of the farmland and did most of the planting and harvesting of corn and other crops.

By 1800 the Seneca had lost most of their land to the new state of New York, Anglo settlers, and land speculators. Whites committed many atrocities against the Seneca in the 1780s and 1790s, partly because most Seneca supported the British during the American Revolutionary War. There were also devastating diseases—such as smallpox and measles, which wiped out millions of Native Americans all over the continent—that reduced the tribe to a fraction of its former numbers. Seneca men had been proud warriors, hunters, and fur traders, but all these activities became more difficult because of the loss of land and the presence of whites. The American government waged psychological warfare against them, intentionally corrupting their leaders with bribes and liquor and generally attempting to dehumanize and demoralize them.

Seneca men became victims of alcoholism and drank up most of what little money they could still earn from the fur trade. Neighboring peoples, who once feared the Seneca and other members of the League of the Iroquois, ridiculed them. A growth in witchcraft accusations increased the internal conflict and divisions of their communities. Many women lost their desire for children and took medicines that caused them to abort or become sterile altogether. A way of life—and perhaps an entire people—was dying.

In 1799 a Seneca man named Handsome Lake lay sick. He was cured by three angels, who gave him a message from the Creator. Handsome Lake reported that the Creator was saddened by the life of the people and angry because of their drunkenness, witchcraft, and use of abortion medicines. The Seneca must repent such deeds. Handsome Lake had two more visions within the next year. There would be an apocalypse in which the world would be destroyed by great drops of fire, consuming those who did not heed Handsome Lake's teachings. People could save themselves and delay the apocalypse by publicly confessing their wrongs, giving up sins such as witchcraft and drinking, and returning to the performance of certain traditional rituals.

The apocalypse did not occur, but Handsome Lake was able to give his teachings a new, more secular twist between 1803 and his death in 1815. He continued to preach temperance because, he said, the Creator had never intended whiskey to be used by Indians. He taught peace with both whites and other Indians. He urged that the scattered reservations of the Seneca be consolidated, so that the people could live together as one community. Family morality must be impeccable: sons were to obey their fathers; divorce (commonplace among the Seneca in aboriginal times) was no longer to be allowed; adultery and domestic quarreling were to cease. Most important, Handsome Lake succeeded in changing the traditional division of labor, in which cultivation of crops was done by women and garden work by men was considered effeminate. Seneca men took up farming and animal husbandry and even fenced their fields and added new crops to their inventory.

Peyote Religion. Peyote is a small cactus that grows in the Rio Grande valley of Texas and northern Mexico. It produces a mild narcotic effect when eaten. The ritual use of peyote among northwestern Mexican Indians predated European conquest. However, its consumption as the central element in a revitalization movement dates only from the last two decades of the nineteenth century.

In 1875 the Southern Plains tribes, the Kiowa and Comanche, lost their land after they were defeated militarily. During their confinement to reservations in southwestern Oklahoma, the Lipan-Apache introduced them to peyote. By the 1880s the two tribes had made consumption of the cactus at religious services the central ritual of a revitalization movement. Peyotism was syncretic, adopting many elements of Christian theology and worship alongside the consumption of peyote as a sacrament. Like many movements, peyotism subsequently spread, reaching about 19 Indian groups in Oklahoma by 1899. During the early twentieth century, the church spread rapidly to other Indian communities throughout the western United States and Canada.

The peyote movement had no single prophet or leader. Local churches developed their own versions of services and rituals. One early leader was John Wilson, a Caddo/Delaware from western Oklahoma who had learned to use peyote from the Comanche. While eating dinner in the early 1890s, Wilson collapsed. Thinking him dead, his family began preparations for the burial. But Enoch Parker, a Caddo, told the family that he had learned in a vision that Wilson was not dead. Indeed, Wilson revived 3 days later. He reported that a great Water Bird had sucked the breath and sin out of his body, causing his collapse. Jesus brought him back to life 3 days later, telling him that his sins had been removed and that he was to teach the Indian people to believe in God and to use peyote to communicate with him.

Until his death in 1901, Wilson proselytized the peyote religion among the Osage, Delaware, Quapaw, and other groups. He preached that they needed to believe in God and Jesus, work hard, act morally, and abstain from alcohol consumption. They were to abandon their traditional religious practices because the spirits that formerly had aided them could be used for evil as well as good purposes. Wilson attracted a great number of adherents among the Osage, who combined the use of peyote in worship services with the Christian teachings they had learned in mission schools.

Peyote provided meaning and moral direction to tribal life during a period of rapid and harmful change. The peyote religion exists today on many reservations, especially in the central and western United States. It was legally incorporated as an official church—now known as the Native American Church—in 1918. Those who follow the Peyote Road eat pieces of the cactus during services, treating it as a deeply meaningful sacrament. Many members of the Native American Church say that the Creator intended peyote to be used by Indians. Periodically, the governments of some states have tried to outlaw the use of peyote, for it is a legally banned substance defined by the wider society as a "dangerous drug." So far, the courts have upheld the right of Church members to consume peyote as a part of their religious sacraments.

What is the fate of revitalization movements? Many with apocalyptic messages simply disappear when the end of the world does not occur. Other movements have been remarkably tenacious. In Melanesia, certain areas saw the rise and fall of numerous prophets, each claiming to have the cargo secret. People followed again and again because they had no other acceptable explanation for the existence of cargo, for why whites had it and they lacked it, or for how they could acquire it. Certainly their own worldly efforts—working for Europeans in mines and plantations, growing and selling coffee, copra, cocoa, and so forth—showed no signs of rewarding them with the fantastic wealth that whites enjoyed with virtually no effort. Cargo cults did not exactly disappear in some regions; instead, they transformed into a political movement or party. This was the fate of cargo cults among the Garia, Manus, Tannese, and some Malaitans.

Other movements do not wither away or transform into a more secular, political movement. They retain their religious character, frequently teaching that contentment is to be found within oneself rather than in worldly material things. After his death in 1815, Handsome Lake's exhortations on how to live became codified and still persist as a church—the Old Way of Handsome Lake, also known as the Longhouse religion. Peyotism also became formally organized. Like many other revitalization movements that give birth to new religions, the adherents of peyotism are thus far largely confined to a single ethnic category: Native Americans.

Still other movements grow in scale over the centuries. From humble beginnings they eventually attract millions of believers. They develop a formal organization, with priests rather than prophets. Revelations become religious texts held to be sacred by believers. Beliefs become formal written doctrines. Followers and disciples become organized into a church. The teachings and rituals cross national and ethnic boundaries. Beliefs and rituals go from being "local" to being "international." Most of the major religions of the modern world began as revitalization movements, including Judaism, Christianity, Islam, and Buddhism. These religions are sometimes called *world religions*, for they have spread outside their original homelands.

Summary

1. In the anthropological conception, religion includes three components: beliefs about the nature of supernatural powers, myths about the historical actions of such powers and culture heroes, and rituals intended to influence them. The stereotyped behaviors of rituals have many symbolic dimensions.

2. Religion is a cultural universal despite the facts that beliefs and myths can never be shown to be true or false and that most rituals do not achieve the results people have in mind when they perform them. Most theories of religion fall into three basic categories: intellectual/cognitive, psychological, and sociological. Among one or another people, religion is probably helpful in all these ways, but no single theory seems able to explain religion itself or the great diversity of human religions.

3. Most religions include a belief that supernatural beings or forces cause or influence group or personal misfortune, such as deaths, illnesses, and "accidents." The malevolent powers of sorcerers and witches are blamed for misfortune in a great many societies. Accusations of sorcery and witchcraft tend to be patterned and to reflect prevalent conflicts and tensions in the organization of society. Although beliefs in sorcery and witchcraft might seem to be harmful, anthropologists have argued that they have intellectual, psychological, and social functions.

4. Religions may be classified according to the types of "cults" they include, although any such classification is inadequate to depict the diversity of the world's religions. Cults may be characterized as individualistic, shamanistic, communal, and ecclesiastical. In a generalized way, there is an evolutionary sequence to cults, in that they tend to be associated with different degrees of cultural complexity. Ecclesiastical forms are regularly found in complex chiefdoms and states, where they legitimize and rationalize the powers and privileges of ruling families and elite classes.

5. Revitalization refers to religious movements that aim to create a new way of life to replace current conditions that are intolerable. Most revitalization movements originate with prophets who claim to have received a revelation, which usually is syncretic and often apocalyptic. Twentieth-century Melanesian cargo cults are among the best-studied movements. The Handsome Lake religion among the Seneca of New York and the peyote religion are two of the many North American revitalization movements. Most revitalization movements disappear, but some are transformed and develop into formal churches that evolve into world religions if they eventually attract tens of millions of members.

Key Terms

animism

myths

ritual

intellectual/cognitive
  approach

psychological approach

sociological approach

sorcery

witchcraft

individualistic cults

shamanistic cults

communal cults

ecclesiastical cults

vision quest

shaman (medicine man)

ancestral cults

totemism

priests

revitalization movement

cargo cults

InfoTrac College Edition Terms

creation myths (origin
  myths)

theory of religion

anthropomorphism

religious healing

witch

sorcerer

spirit medium

ancestor worship

peyote

Suggested Readings

Four recent textbooks provide basic introductions to the anthropological study of religion:

Bowen, John R. *Religions in Practice.* 2nd ed. Boston: Allyn & Bacon, 2002.

Bowie, Fiona. *The Anthropology of Religion: An Introduction.* Oxford: Blackwell Publishers, 2000.

Crapo, Richley. *Anthropology of Religion: The Unity and Diversity of Religions.* Boston: McGraw-Hill, 2003.

Stein, Rebecca L., and Philip L. Stein. *The Anthropology of Religion, Magic, and Witchcraft.* Boston: Pearson, 2005.

Three recent readers prepared for undergraduates are:

Hicks, David, ed. *Religion and Belief: Readings in the Anthropology of Religion.* 2nd ed. New York: McGraw-Hill, 2002.

Lehman, Arthur C., James E. Myers, and Pamela A. Moro, eds. *Magic, Witchcraft, and Religion.* 6th ed. Boston: McGraw-Hill, 2005.

Scupin, Raymond, ed. *Religion and Culture: An Anthropological Focus.* Upper Saddle River, N.J.: Prentice-Hall, 2000.

A few of the accessible "classic studies" (ethnographies) of particular religions include:

Boyer, Dave, and Stephen Nissenbaum. *Salem Possessed.* Cambridge: Harvard University Press, 1974.

Evans-Pritchard, E. E. *Witchcraft, Oracles, and Magic Among the Azande.* Oxford: Oxford University Press, 1937.

Keesing, Roger. *Kwaio Religion.* New York: Columbia University Press, 1982.

Kluckhohn, Clyde. *Navaho Witchcraft.* Boston: Beacon, 1967.

Kraybill, Donald B. *The Riddle of Amish Culture.* Rev. ed. Baltimore: Johns Hopkins University Press, 2001.

Stoller, Paul, and Cheryl Olkes. *In Sorcery's Shadow: A Memoir of Apprenticeship Among the Songhay of Niger.* Chicago: University of Chicago Press, 1987.

Some of the better-known books dealing with movements include:

Anderson, Edward F. *Peyote: The Divine Cactus.* 2nd ed. Tucson: University of Arizona, 1996.

An excellent description of peyote and its religious uses among Native Americans.

Kehoe, Alice Beck. *The Ghost Dance: Ethnohistory and Revitalization.* Fort Worth, Tex.: Holt, Rinehart and Winston, 1989.

Descriptive account of the 1890 Ghost Dance that began among the Nevada Paiute and spread to the Lakota and other peoples of the plains. Shows the impact of the religious movement on Native American cultures today.

Stewart, Omer. *Peyote Religion.* Norman: University of Oklahoma Press, 1987.

Detailed study of the peyote religion, with a historical focus.

Wallace, Anthony F. C. *The Death and Rebirth of the Seneca.* New York: Vintage, 1969.

An account of Handsome Lake, the revitalization movement that first appeared among the Seneca of New York State in the early 1800s.

Companion Website for This Book

**The Wadsworth Anthropology Resource Center
http://anthropology.wadsworth.com**

The companion website that accompanies *Humanity: An Introduction to Cultural Anthropology,* Seventh Edition, includes a rich array of material, including online anthropological video clips, to help you in the study of cultural anthropology and the specific topics covered in this chapter. Begin by clicking on Student Resources. Next, click on Cultural Anthropology, and then on the cover image for this book. You have now arrived at the Student Resources home page and have the option of choosing one of several chapter resources.

Applying Anthropology. Begin your study of cultural anthropology by clicking on Applying Anthropology. Here you will find useful information on careers, graduate school programs in applied anthropology, and internships you might wish to pursue. You will also find real-world examples of working anthropologists applying the skills and methods of anthropology to help solve serious world problems.

Research Online. Click here to find a wealth of Web links that will facilitate your study of anthropology. Divided into different fields of study, specific websites are starting points for Internet research. You will be guided to rich anthropology websites that will help you prepare for class, complete course assignments, and actually do research on the Web.

InfoTrac College Edition Exercises. From the pull-down menu, select the chapter you are presently studying. Select InfoTrac College Edition Exercises from the list of resources. These exercises utilize InfoTrac College Edition's vast database of articles and help you explore the numerous uses of the search word, *culture.*

Study Aids for This Chapter. Improve your knowledge of key terms by using flash cards and study the learning objectives. Take the practice quiz, receive your results, and e-mail them to your instructor. Access these resources from the chapter and resource pull-down menus.

Chapter Fifteen
Art and the Aesthetic

The Pervasiveness of Art

Forms of Artistic Expression

Body Arts

Visual Arts

Performance Arts

Art and Culture

Secular and Religious Art

Art and Gender

Social Functions of Art

© Kevin R. Morris/Corbis

The Shakers of the nineteenth century emphasized simplicity and utility, not ornamentation and aesthetics, in the objects they manufactured. Yet today many of their products are considered works of art. Shaker chairs such as those hanging from the walls of this house are highly prized by collectors.

THERE IS MUCH MORE TO HUMAN LIFE than the acquisition of necessities like food, clothing, and shelter. There is also more to living than the production and use of things for their utilitarian value. All peoples have both a sense of and a desire for the aesthetic: those things that appeal to the eye, the ear, the taste, the touch, the emotions, and the imagination. Such sensory experiences are important not only for their functional value but because their color, form, design, sound, taste, or feel are pleasurable in their own right. Commonly, these experiences are sought after to stimulate our imaginations and emotions through the creation of feelings of happiness, fear, and even anger. These expressions of the aesthetic are what we generally call art—the subject of this chapter.

Art is one of those elusive terms we all know and use, and think we understand, but it is difficult to define. Some scholars have defined *art* by saying what it is not: It is not utilitarian. The difficulty is, when does something stop being utilitarian and become art? Richard Anderson uses a Tikopean wooden headrest as an example. Any block of wood, even a log of proper size, might serve as a headrest. A person might go further by cutting away portions of the block or log to form legs, which Anderson argues still serve the utilitarian purpose of lessening the weight of the block. If, however, the person carves designs on the headrest, this carving becomes its artistic component, and the object becomes art. According to Anderson, it is this artistic component, the design, that transforms the object from the realm of the utilitarian to the realm of art. Thus it is ornamentation placed on the object—not its functional design—that defines it as art.

If this way of defining art seems simple enough, consider the Shakers, a religious communal group that reached its height in the early nineteenth century in the United States. As "plain folk" they emphasized the utilitarian. The qualities of simplicity and function were incorporated into everything they made and used in their communities. Their wooden furniture was simple, delicate, and superbly crafted, but unpretentious with stark straight lines or gentle curves. There were no accessories, carvings, extravagant turning, or inlays. In keeping with their idea of natural purity, wood was usually finished with light stains and varnishes. Their furnishings were very different from those of their neighbors, and some Shakers said that their designs came from heaven, communicated to them by angels.

Extremely functional and utilitarian, the beauty of Shaker furniture is in its masterful simplicity of form. Collected today as art, Shaker furniture is among the most highly prized and pricey American furniture. Form and superb craftsmanship, not ornamentation, make Shaker furniture art.

So at what point is a piece of wood, stone, or ivory transformed into a work of art? When does noise become music? When do body movements become dance, and words become poetry, literature, or song lyrics? When does a shelter become architecture? Are there any limitations on what can be considered art? Can the preparation and serving of food be considered art? Is the painting or alteration of the human body art?

Something becomes **art** when its purely utilitarian or functional nature is modified for the purpose of enhancing its aesthetic qualities and thus making it more pleasurable to our senses. Artists can produce art objects that only they themselves will see or hear, but most of the time art is displayed publicly or used in social events such as gatherings or ceremonies. In such contexts, art objects sometimes take on an additional function: they become material means of communication. Thus Western artists often claim that they are trying to "make a statement" through their artwork, although we all recognize that the artistic message is in the eye of the beholder. In other cultures, too, artistic creations communicate messages that can have both religious and secular meanings.

Obviously, art is inseparable from the **aesthetic,** and the aesthetic is an elusive quality since it is subjective. Anthropologists since Franz Boas have argued that there are no universal standards for art. Something that one society might find beautiful or pleasing, others might consider ugly, disgusting, or even repulsive. As we frequently hear, "There is no accounting for taste."

Aesthetics cannot be separated from culture. Just as we learn other aspects of our culture, so we also learn what is beautiful. Beauty is culturally determined. Aesthetics is unrelated to complexity, difficulty, or skill in creation or performance. Although we might appreciate the craftsmanship that went into making a piece of pottery, or the difficulty in performing a particular piece of music, we may or may not find them aesthetically pleasing. During a visit to Scotland, the English writer Samuel Johnson complained about bagpipe music. On being informed that bagpipes were an extremely difficult instrument to play, Johnson replied, "I wish it was impossible."

Not only does every culture, as well as every individual, have its own ideas as to what is aesthetically pleasing, but aesthetics change within a culture over time. For example, examining European or Chinese art over the past 2,000 years, one finds dramatic changes in both the nature and the complexity of designs. Thus, not only is the idea of what is beautiful subjective, it is also volatile and ever changing.

The Pervasiveness of Art

In the urban, industrial world, we usually think of artistic creation as a separate and distinct kind of activity, and artistic objects as a special set of things. We also commonly think of art only in terms of "fine art": painting, sculpture, music, and dance. If pressed, we might add great architecture, literature, and even poetry. We tend to categorize as art only those things whose sole or basic value is aesthetic. Artists, in turn, are those painters, sculptors, composers, writers, architects, performers, and others who produce these things of aesthetic value. Individuals who are not directly involved in the production of "art" are commonly seen as merely the audience or consumers—people who buy, see, and hear art.

The notion that art is a conceptually separate realm of social and cultural existence is not found among all peoples. As anthropologists have long noted, Native American peoples had no word for art in their languages. Similarly, other traditional peoples in other parts of the world also frequently lack words for art. The basic reason for this is that art is integrated into virtually every aspect of their lives and is so pervasive that they do not think of it as something separate and distinct. The idea of "art for art's sake" is a recent Western cultural phenomenon that in some ways both distracts and diminishes the reality of human creative expressions. If we define art broadly, then it permeates virtually every aspect of our lives. All of us search for and attempt to create that which is aesthetically pleasing and, thus, we are all "artists." Creative artistic expressions are found in even the most mundane and commonplace acts of the daily lives of all peoples. Consider, for example, three behaviors that most of us think of as "mundane" rather than "artistic": dressing for the day, residing in a particular place, and eating.

We begin the day by ornamenting our bodies. From among our clothes we make choices as to what to wear based on colors and styles appropriate for the day's events. We make choices on how to wear our hair and even the color of our hair. We may paint our faces and further adorn our bodies with jewelry of varying kinds, worn on our fingers and arms, around our necks, in our ears, noses, and—in recent years—other parts of our bodies. Some of us have our bodies permanently decorated with tattoos. By these everyday acts we are artists, attempting to enhance the aesthetic qualities of our persons by making ourselves a work of art. In these acts we are also adept communicators of messages about ourselves, for through hair, makeup, dress, jewelry, and other ways of adorning our bodies we present to the public certain kinds of images of ourselves.

Consider your living space. In finding or building a place to live, we don't just look for something that will meet our physical needs; aesthetic appeal also plays an important role. We alter our homes by changing walls, adding rooms, remodeling the bathroom or the kitchen, and repainting everything in different colors inside and outside. We decorate the inside with furniture, rugs, paintings, posters, mirrors, and a host of knickknacks and smaller things. If we have a yard, we may remove or add trees, shrubs, flower beds, and fences. Even temporary apartment and college dormitory dwellers try to make a place their own. Although some of these additions and changes may be of utilitarian value or need, most serve to enhance the aesthetic appeal of the place where we live.

Finally, think about mealtimes. Whether we eat food raw or cooked, boiled, baked, fried, hot, or cold, and whether we season it with salt, pepper, garlic, or other herbs and spices, we are attempting to create something that is pleasing to our sense of taste. Our quest for new and

► Notice the ways the clothing and jewelry of these Masai women serve to enhance their appearance.

© Barry D. Kass/Images of Anthropology

exciting ways of preparing food seems endless, giving rise to the steady flow of new cookbooks from publishers. Nor is eating food a purely utilitarian act. We set the table and arrange the repast in bowls and on plates, which have usually been purchased for their aesthetic appeal. In our food preparation and serving we attempt to create something that is appealing to both the palate and the eye. (Chinese, incidentally, are far more conscious of this artistic quality of food than are most North Americans.)

Even in our daily lives, then, we attempt to immerse ourselves in the aesthetic. The search for the aesthetic is reflected in the appearance of our persons, our homes, and our meals, as well as in our places of worship, recreation, and work. Much of our day is filled with music, song, dance, drama, comedy, literature, and sports, which we listen to, participate in, and sometimes create. Art, anthropologists recognize, is a cultural universal. But beyond this the artistic impulse is seen in the everyday lives of individual human beings, for we are all both producers and consumers of art.

Forms of Artistic Expression

Although art permeates most aspects of human activity, from clothing and furniture to music and theater, space constraints do not permit us to discuss all these diverse forms of artistic expression. For this reason we limit our discussion to certain categories: body arts, visual arts, and performance arts.

Body Arts

People around the world are highly creative in altering their physical appearance. Almost anything that can be done to the body is probably being done or has been done in the past. In Euro-American societies, for example, parts of the body are now being pierced that few people even thought of as pierceable a decade or two ago. For convenience, we focus on the **body arts** of physical alterations, body painting, and tattooing and scarification.

Physical Alterations. In most societies people attempt to physically alter their bodies. Head and body hair is treated in many different ways. In Western societies hair is styled and often artificially colored. Some people shave their head, their beard, and even their legs and armpits. Others let their beard and mustache grow and style them in various ways. Still others, particularly middle-aged males, attempt vainly to have replacement hair grown on the top of their head. In most Western societies these actions are mainly a matter of fashion or personal taste; in other societies such actions may have deeper cultural meanings.

In parts of Africa a woman's status—for example, whether she is unmarried or married, or is a mother or a widow—is indicated by hairstyle. Among the Hopis, adolescent girls of marriageable age wear their hair in a large whorl on each side of the head, creating the so-called butterfly hairstyle. After marriage they will wear their hair long and parted in the middle. Children among the Omahas had their hair cut in patterns indicating their clan membership.

Wearing beards is not always a matter of personal taste and fashion. In many societies, such as Hasidic Jews, Mennonites, Amish, some Muslim sects, and Sikhs, wearing a beard is an act of religious belief. In the ancient world social status was frequently associated with beards. In Egypt only the nobility were allowed to wear beards. Not only did noblemen wear beards, but women of the nobility frequently wore artificial beards as well to indicate their social rank. In contrast, in ancient Greece only the nobility were allowed to be clean shaven; men of commoner status had to let their beards grow.

Hair alterations are usually reversible, for hair will grow back. Other parts of the body are altered on a permanent basis. Cranial deformation or head shaping has been and is still widely practiced among the peoples of the world. The skull of a baby is soft and if the baby's head is bound the shape of the skull can be permanently changed, flattening the back and the forehead or lengthening the head. In parts of France cranial deformation was virtually universal until the eighteenth century. A baby's face was tightly wrapped in linen, resulting in a flattened skull and ears. In the Netherlands, babies once wore tight-fitting caps that depressed the front portion of the skull. The elite classes of the ancient Andean civilizations elongated the skull, as did the ancient Egyptians. For the first year of its life a Chinook baby was wrapped on a hard board, with another board bound against the top and front of the head. This technique resulted in a head with additional breadth. Some peoples of central Africa bound the heads of female babies to create elongated skulls that came to a point on the back.

Some peoples permanently altered other parts of the body as well. In China the feet of female children of high-status families were bound at the age of 5 or 6 to deform the feet and keep them small. This was not only considered attractive, it was practiced as a visible indication of the fact that the family was sufficiently wealthy that its women did not have to do much physical labor. In parts of Africa and among some Native American peoples holes were cut in earlobes or the lower and upper lips were expanded so that ear plugs and large lip plugs could be inserted. Some of these plugs were up to three inches in diameter. Some central African Pygmy peoples file their front teeth into points, which in their culture enhances their attractiveness. In parts of Africa, a series of rings was placed around a girl's neck over a period of time, so that when she reached womanhood her shoulders were pressed down, her neck appeared longer, and she could wear multiple neck rings.

Such alterations continue in modern nations. Much of the lucrative work of plastic surgeons in contemporary Western nations is concerned with altering physical appearance by changing the shapes of the eyes, nose, mouth, and jowls, or increasing or decreasing the size of breasts, lips, thighs, hips, or waistlines.

Body Painting. Painting is a less drastic and temporary manner of changing an individual's appearance. Some peoples paint only their faces, while others paint almost their entire bodies. Face painting is more common than body painting. Native American peoples commonly painted their faces for war. Among the Osage, before attacking their enemy, the men would blacken their faces with charcoal, symbolic of the merciless fire and their ferocity. In other Native American groups face painting was individualized, each man using different colors and designs to create a ferocious appearance. Sometimes the manner in which a man painted his face depended on a vision and his spiritual helpers (see Chapter 14). However, not all face painting was associated with war. Faces were commonly painted for religious rituals as well. In ritual face painting the painted symbols usually had religious significance. In addition, many Native American peoples simply painted their faces to enhance their social appearance. Thus, Native Americans painted their faces for a variety of reasons—warfare, religious rituals, and social appearance—just like other peoples in the world.

Body painting refers to painting the entire body, or most of it. Like face painting, body painting is found all over the world. In some cases, body painting has religious significance and meaning; in other cases, it is purely secular, designed to enhance the person's physical appearance. Many peoples in Papua New Guinea cover their faces and limbs with white clay when a relative or important person dies as a sign of mourning and respect for the deceased. Among the aboriginal peoples of Australia, bodies were painted with red and yellow ocher, white clay, charcoal, and other pigments. During rituals individuals were painted with elaborate designs covering most of the body. The colors and designs were standardized and had symbolic meaning. Ritual specialists who knew these designs did the painting for religious ceremonies. Outside of ritual contexts, for many Australian peoples, body painting was a secular and daily activity, performed by family members on one another. Individuals were free to use whatever colors and designs pleased them, so long as they were not ritual designs.

Tattooing and Scarification. Tattooing and the related practice of scarification are widespread practices. Tattoo designs, achieved by etching and placing a colored pigment under the skin, have been practiced by diverse peoples. When the skin is too dark for tattooing designs to be seen, people may use scarification, the deliberate scarring of the skin to produce designs on the body.

Tattooing has a long history as an art form. Tattooing was practiced in ancient Egypt, as well as by the ancient Scythians, Thracians, and Romans in Europe. The ancient Bretons, at the time of the Roman conquest, were reported to have had their bodies elaborately tattooed

▲ This Kikuyu man has painted his face for participation in a dance. Face and body painting is commonly used in many cultures for ceremonial and ritual occasions.

© Barry D. Kass/Images of Anthropology

with the images of animals. In the fourth century A.D., when Christianity became the official religion of the Roman Empire, tattooing was forbidden on religious grounds. Tattooing virtually disappeared among European peoples until the eighteenth century, when it was discovered in the Pacific and Asia by sailors and reintroduced to Europe as purely secular art.

Robert Brain noted an important difference between body painting and tattooing and scarification: paint is removable; tattooing and scarification are indelible and permanent. As a result, tattooing and scarification are usually associated with societies in which there are permanent differences in social status. In complexity of designs and parts of the body tattooed, peoples differed. Among some people, tattooing was limited to a few lines on the face, chest, or arms. Among others, complex designs covered most of the body from the face to the legs. In some cases, every adult had some tattoos; in other societies, only certain individuals had tattoos. The significance and meaning of tattoos varied, but most had socioreligious significance. The more fully tattooed an individual was, the greater the social status.

The adornment of the body by tattoos is most elaborate in the scattered islands of Polynesia. In fact, the word *tattoo* itself is Polynesian. The word, like the practice of tattooing sailors, came into use as a result of the voyages of Western explorers and whalers in the seventeenth and later centuries. Tongans, Samoans, Marquesans, Tahitians, the Maori of New Zealand, and most other Polynesian peoples practiced tattooing, which everywhere was connected to social distinctions such as class or rank, sex, religious roles, and specialization. Polynesian peoples are all historically related, so it is not surprising that marking the body with tattoos is found on almost all islands, albeit to different degrees and with somewhat different styles.

Many Maori had large areas of their bodies covered with tattoos, which could be placed on the torso, thighs, buttocks, calves, and, most notably, the face. Several instruments were used by skilled tattoo artists to incise the curvilinear patterns characteristic of most Maori tattoos. One was a small chisel made of bone and etched into the skin with a hammer. Apparently, no anesthetic was used to relieve the pain and, in fact, tolerating the pain of the procedure may have been part of its cultural significance. To make pigment, several kinds of wood were burned for their ashes. After the artist made the cuts, pigment was rubbed into the wounds to leave permanent markings. The most skilled tattoo artists were rewarded with high prestige and chiefly patronage, and their craft was in such high demand that they traveled widely over New Zealand's two huge islands.

Both Maori men and women wore tattoos, although men's bodies were more thoroughly covered. For both sexes, tattoos were seen not merely as body ornamentation or expression of one's personal identity. Having tattoos brought certain privileges. Men who did not undergo tattooing could not build canoe houses, carve wood, make weapons, or weave nets. Untattooed women could not help in the gardens with sweet potatoes, the Maori staple vegetable crop.

Maori facial tattoos, called *moko,* have special importance. Women were tattooed on the lips and chin, often near the time of their marriage. Male facial tattoos were designed by splitting the face into four fields—left versus right of the nose and upper versus lower at roughly eye level. *Moko* were basically symmetrical on the vertical axis, with curvilinear designs on the forehead and eyebrows, cheeks, and mouth regions. In many cases, virtually the whole male face was tattooed. Not just any *moko* design could be worn by just any male, for designs were related to factors such as hereditary status, place of birth, and achievement in battle. Social restrictions thus were placed on the wearing of facial tattoos, suggesting that they were important symbols of group identity and personal achievement. North Americans might see echoes of their own styles of clothing, jewelry, hairstyle, and other personal ornamentations in Maori and other Polynesian tattoos.

In other Polynesian islands tattooing was similar to the Maori in broad pattern but varied in detail. In Samoa, for instance, a group of boys was tattooed together on the hips and thighs in their early teens, accompanied by much ceremony. The primary recipient of the tattoo was the son of a high-ranking chief, and other boys participated to share his pain and, therefore, publicly show their respect and loyalty. Supposedly, Samoan women disdained men as sexual partners if they did not have tattoos. Traditionally, Samoan girls received tattoos only on the backs of their knees, which they were not supposed to reveal to others. It is interesting that in Samoa greater and more elaborate male tattoos were connected to different sexually based biological functions. There was a saying:

The man grows up and is tattooed.
The woman grows up and she gives birth. (Milner 1969, 20)

According to one interpretation, voluntary tattooing gives pain to men just as childbirth causes pain to women. Perhaps the male experience of pain by tattooing is connected to Samoan women's contempt for tattooless men.

In all of Polynesia, it was the people of the Marquesas whose bodies were most covered by tattoos. The highest

▶ The Maori of New Zealand are well known for their elaborate tattoos. The designs of Maori facial tattoos are important symbols of identity and achievement.

© Paula Bronstein/Getty Images

ranking chiefs even had tattoos on the soles of their feet. Alfred Gell argues that this relatively thorough covering of the body in the Marquesas was necessary to wrap the body in images in order to protect it from spiritual dangers. Gods and spirits were not tattooed; tattoo images protected the human body from spiritual harm.

Decorating the body by cutting and creating scars, or scarification, is more limited among the world's peoples than tattooing. As in tattooing, scarification is practiced for numerous reasons. Depending on the culture, both men and women may be scarred. Sometimes the scarred design is on the face; in other cases, the chest, breast, back, and even the legs and arms may be elaborately covered with such designs. Sometimes scarification forms part of the puberty rite or some other initiation rite. Among the Nuer of the southern Sudan, a series of horizontal cuts is made on the foreheads of men who have completed male initiation rituals. On young men, these cuts symbolically mark and communicate their maturity and courage. After they scarify, these cuts become permanent symbols of Nuer manhood.

Visual Arts

Visual arts are produced from material, tangible objects, so they are part of the material culture of a people. They may be religious or secular in meaning and use. Usually

they are permanent in that they are meant for long-term use, but sometimes they are created for one-time use only and then destroyed. Visual arts encompass a wide range of basketry, ceramics, textiles, clothing, jewelry, tools, paintings, masks, and sculpture, to name only a few examples. Metal, wood, stone, leather, feather, shell, paper made of fibers, pigments, and other materials are used in their creation. The two main factors that transform a material item into a visual art are form and ornamentation.

Form. The physical form or shape of an object is a reflection of its utilitarian function, the materials available, the technical knowledge and skill of the person producing it, and the general lifestyle of the society. Nomadic or seminomadic foraging and pastoral people often produce items that are light in weight and easily transportable. One might think that the visual arts of nomadic or seminomadic people are "less refined" than those of more settled peoples. But Inuit peoples of northern latitudes precisely carved small art objects out of soft soapstone, and decorated many of their portable tools with figures of animals. Shields and hides were elaborately painted among many nomadic peoples of the American plains. Plains Indians heavily decorated their clothing and moccasins with shells and beadwork, thus allowing people to carry their art along with them. Native Americans of the western United States, especially the Southwest, used

The artistic tradition of the Osage of the central United States was, and still is, distinctly different from art in Western societies. Not only was Osage art fully integrated into the everyday material culture of the community, it was also an expression of their religious beliefs. Even by Native American standards the Osage were extremely religious. Religion governed virtually every aspect of their lives and their behavior. The Osage believed that everything in the universe was a creation as well as a manifestation of a great invisible force that they called Wah-kon-tah. Collectively the visible universe was the tangible expression of Wah-kon-tah. Thus the more one understood the visible universe, and the meanings and purposes of every type of animal, bird, plant, and other nature phenomenon, the more one understood this great mysterious and controlling force. Of course the Osage realized that no one could ever fully understand the universe in all of its complexity. Thus no humans could ever fully understand Wah-kon-tah. From their observation of the world about them the Osage did come to understand certain things. Everything created by Wah-kon-tah was born and would eventually die. Everything created by Wah-kon-tah passed through the stages of birth, maturity, old age, and death. This was true for all animals, plants, birds, humans, and even natural phenomena. It was seen in the passing of the year, in spring, summer, fall, and winter. This was true individually as well as collectively. Someday even the Osage, like all other peoples, would disappear.

Many of the things created by Wah-kon-tah were blessings that had been bestowed on humans for their use. The sun and the associated fire gave warmth and comfort to humans. Certain animals and plants could be used for food and nourishment. The skins of certain animals and the bark, wood, and/or fibers of certain trees or plants could be used for clothing, shelter, and other material wants. Still other plants could be used to heal the sick. Everything created by Wah-kon-tah was for a purpose. Wah-kon-tah did not reveal the purposes of these creations to humans. Humans were unique among Wah-kon-tah's creations in that only they possessed *wa-thi'-gethon,* the power to search with the mind. Thus humans were responsible for studying the universe about them, in a never-ending search to gain ever-greater knowledge of the meanings and purposes of all of Wah-kon-tah's creations. Wah-kon-tah also bestowed on humans the ability to take their knowledge and use it to create new things.

So, endowed with the power to reason and to create, humans were responsible for securing for themselves the continued blessings of Wah-kon-tah. The greatest of these blessings were children, indicative of Wah-kon-tah's will that they as a people would continue to live. To this end the Osage consciously structured every aspect of their lives and behavior in such a manner as to show respect for Wah-kon-tah. Just as all things created by Wah-

kon-tah had purpose and meaning, so it had to be with them. Everything they did had to have purpose and meaning, with the ultimate goal of receiving Wah-kon-tah's continued blessings.

Based on their observation of the universe, they noted that there were two main divisions, the sky and the earth. The sky was the source of life, the father, and the earth was the nourisher of life, the mother. All living things existed in a narrow lens between earth and sky, which they called the *hoe-ga,* or snare. The countless other creations, animals, birds, plants, and other natural phenomena of Wah-kon-tah were associated with either the earth or the sky. Based on this cosmic model, the Osage organized their life as a symbolic mirror image of the cosmos. The basic unit was the clan, which symbolically represented a portion of Wah-kon-tah's creations. Collectively, 9 of these clans, acting together symbolically, represented the forces of the sky, while the other 15 of these clans collectively symbolized the earth. All marriages had to be between a member of a sky clan and an earth clan with the children belonging to the clan of their father.

The village structure was modeled after the cosmos, with each village having two chiefs, a sky chief and an earth chief. The houses of the sky clan families were placed in a specific clan order along the north side of an east–west street. The houses of the earth clan people were placed in a specific clan order along the south side. The street itself symbolized the path of life, the passage of the sun from east to west, and the *hoe-ga* or snare. Rituals were organized following the same model; priests of the sky clans sat in a precise order on the north, while earth clan priests sat on the south.

Every morning before sunrise the people of the village would arise and greet the sun with prayers. This ritual was repeated at noon and at dusk. Their lives were organized as one continuous prayer for Wah-kon-tah's blessings. Warfare, hunting, planting, harvests, marriage, death, and the naming of children were all structured as religious rituals.

Everything created by Wah-kon-tah had meaning and purpose, and thus it had to be with all of the material items used in their daily lives and rituals. Every animal, bird, shellfish, and plant had its own behavioral characteristics; bears, mountain lions, and eagles were powerful in different ways; otters could swim; wolves were tenacious; hawks were courageous; pelicans and shellfish lived for a long time; cedar trees did not "die" in the winter like other plants. The hides, feathers, shells, bones, wood, or bark of these and other animals, birds, and plants symbolically represented specific qualities of Wah-kon-tah. Colors also had meanings; red and white as in the sun and fire were colors of birth and life; black as in the night, charcoal, and the fur of the black bear was the color of death and destruction; blue as in the sky on a cloudless day was the color of peace and tranquility; and green as in the cedar tree in winter was the color of everlasting life. Form and designs also had meanings. A disk shape or design was the form of the sun and thus life. A design divided with each side the mirror image of the other represented the sky and earth balanced as in the universe. A line with four lines descending from it was the *hoe-ga.*

Every object created by the Osage consisted of a number of different elements, raw materials, color, and form and/or designs. Each of these elements had a specific symbolic meaning. All objects consisted of several elements, each with its own symbolic meaning, which collectively gave meaning and purpose to the object. Ritual items were the most symbolically complex. A good example of symbolism in Osage art is found with the staff used in the Osage peyote church meetings.

Osage peyotism is an Osage form of Christianity. Established at the turn of the twentieth century, it replaced the traditional religion while retaining much of the traditional symbolism. Unlike other forms of peyotism, each Osage meetinghouse has a permanent concrete altar in the middle of the floor, and a set of ritual interments that have been consecrated for use in that specific church. The most important of these interments was the staff or *mon,* a word that means "arrow." This staff consists of a straight wooden pole about 4 feet in length. At the base end it is carved into a four-sided arrow point. On the top is a crown of eagle and hawk feathers. Attached to the staff are "drop feathers," a narrow strip of otter skin, a narrow strip of opossum hide, and a string of bells. When not in use during the meeting the staff stands upright in a hole at the head of the altar. During the singing, the staff is passed in a clockwise direction from singer to singer. Each singer holds the staff in one hand while he sings.

Every aspect of the staff has multiple symbolic meanings. Each part has a distinct meaning; however, in association with other parts, new composite meanings are created. The staff in its entirety is symbolic of the ideal man. The upright feather crown, like a war bonnet, and the downward dropping scalp feathers, such as men wear in dancing, mean that this man is "Indian." Some say that the staff represents Jesus Christ, the ideal man, clothed as an "Indian." The arrow point at the end not only gives the staff its name, *mon* or arrow, but also introduced another dimension to this symbolic man. Arrows had traditionally been used in both war and hunting. The arrow in the context of the staff introduces the symbolic meanings of spiritual protection

and nourishment. The symbolic meaning of nourishment is further enhanced by the carving of the staff out of the wood of a tree that bears fruit, and is thus a source of food. The fact that the wood is from a deciduous tree adds the symbolism of death (loss of leaves in the fall) and rebirth (new leaves in the spring). The feathers add still another dimension to the *mon.* Among all creatures birds fly in the air and thus come closest to the life-giving powers of the sun. As a result, feathers are spiritually pure and serve to guard one or cleanse one of evil. The fact that there were both eagle and hawk feathers is also of symbolic importance. The eagle was symbolic of power; however, the hawk was considered the most courageous of birds. Even a small hawk will attack a large bird in defense of its nest. Together they symbolized the ideal man as both powerful and courageous. The otter is an animal much admired. At home on the land as well as in the water, it moves swiftly and is protective of its young. The otter in its swiftness symbolized the ability to avoid evil and protection. The opossum is a clean animal, pure in its habits. It can also feign death. Thus the strip of opossum hide conveys the meaning of purity as well as death and rebirth. When the staff is moved the bell will tinkle, like the sound of raindrops, symbolic of the life-giving rain. Just as the universe consists of land, water, and sky, so symbolic elements of land, the wood and the hides; water, the otter and the bells; and the sky, the bird feathers, are brought together in the construction of the staff. The staff was thus a symbolically constructed Christ-centered universe, emphasizing the qualities of purity, safety, courage, power, and death and rebirth. Finally the ordered movement of the staff during the ceremony was symbolic of an ever-moving, changing universe. A traditional Osage ritual involved first the symbolic creation of the universe, and then putting it in motion through the use of ritual objects, song, movements, and other acts. Their peyote church ceremonies were structured in the same manner.

To the Osage everything had to have meaning and purpose. Everything in the universe was a creation of Wah-kon-tah. Thus everything was sacred. The Osage, like all humans, had the abilities to alter and change material objects to meet the special needs of humans. However, these changes, to work properly, had to be in accordance with the meanings and purposes that Wah-kon-tah had given to the objects they made use of.

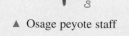

Courtesy Thomas Gilcrease Museum, Tulsa

▲ Osage peyote staff

Source: Bailey, Swan, Nunley, and StandingBear (2004).

pigment to paint or hard stones to etch images of animals, celestial objects, people, mythological beings, and other things on rocks. The prehistoric people who created these images might have moved according to season, but their art was stationary and long lasting. Today we know these images as pictographs and petroglyphs, also called rock art.

Rock seems like a difficult object to use as a canvas, but the world's peoples have used other unusual materials, including sand (as we shall see later). Of course, the availability of wood, stone, clay, hides, and other natural materials does influence what people can create and how. The kinds of tools the artist uses to paint, etch, or sculpt are also important influences on the final artwork. Metal tools have advantages over stone tools in giving artistic form to a raw material. Peoples also differ in their technical knowledge of how to work stone or wood, and how to model clay or metals.

Within these natural and technical limitations, the form of an object is the result of the interplay of utilitarian function and aesthetic style. The function/style debate has long interested archaeologists. Prehistoric stone tools display a bewildering variety of forms. In North American archaeology, extensive typologies have been created to classify projectile point types, which differ in size, relative length and width, and shape (straight, concave, convex, or even serrated). Some are unnotched; others are notched on the bases or sides. Many of these differences are undoubtedly related to function, but others seem to be purely stylistic. Great variability is also present in the vessel shapes and decorations of another archaeological favorite, pottery. Pottery vessels vary tremendously from one group to another, as well as within the same group of people over time.

One does not have to look at peoples remote in time or space to see that the form of an object that has utilitarian purposes is part of the artistic expression of a people. Look at something as mundane and "functional" as the legs of tables and chairs in our own culture. The legs can be straight or tapered, or round, square, or rectangular. The table may have a pedestal base. All are equally functional; they keep the seat or the top off the floor. The differences are a question of aesthetics, not of function. Thus the physical form of an object may be part of its aesthetic appeal; however, it is sometimes difficult to determine where function ends and the aesthetic begins.

Ornamentation. Ornamentation is design added to the physical form of an object. Humans are highly creative in developing ways of adding ornamentation to material items. Ornamental designs may be woven or carved into

an object. They may be painted, incised, molded, or sewn onto an object. Or a combination of these techniques may be used to decorate.

In basketry and textiles, designs are commonly woven onto the item during its construction. For baskets, different colors of plant fibers, either natural or artificially dyed, are used for the designs. The same is true in the weaving of textiles, for which different colored yarns are used. However, not all textile designs are created using fibers of contrasting colors. By using different types of weaving techniques, designs may be created in a single color.

Carving refers to creating a design by removing parts of the original form. Wood, stone, clay, ivory, shell, and bone may have carved designs. An object may be carved in three dimensions so that the form itself becomes the design, as in a piece of sculpture. Or the form of the object will remain the same, with only shallow relief carving of a design on the surface.

Painting is certainly one of the easiest and most versatile methods of ornamenting an object. It is possibly the oldest method of ornamentation; European cave paintings are at least 20,000 years old. All one needs to paint is a range of colors. To make colored pigments, a variety of different materials may be mixed with water, oil, or fat, such as charcoal, plant materials, and natural mineral pigments. Paintings can be applied to wood, stone, clay, textiles, paper, or leather. Paintings can be applied to flat surfaces, such as cave walls, exposed rocks or cliff walls, wooden furniture, or canvas. They may be made on round or irregular surfaces, such as pottery, masks, and sculpture.

Incising consists of decorating an object by scratching lines into the surface. Like painting, incising appears to be one of the earliest ways of adding designs to an item. Incising is most commonly used on ivory, bone, and shell. In these cases, the scratched lines are frequently accentuated by adding some type of colored pigment, usually black or dark in color, so one can more readily see the design itself. Incised designs are also occasionally used for decorating clay pots and leather.

Designs on ceramics and metal are commonly modeled by raising certain areas above the surface. There are two ways in which this form of ornamentation can be accomplished. One is by making additions to the object after the surface area is finished. In pottery, for example, designs may be formed by placing little balls or coils of clay on the surface after the body of the pot has been formed. A similar technique is sometimes used in adding designs to metal items, as when metal wires shaped into designs are welded to the surface. More commonly, though, molds are created with designs carved into the surface area. Clay can be forced into these molds, or metal poured into them.

▲ These women in Chaing Mai, Thailand, are producing traditional pottery.

After the object is removed from the mold the design areas stand out as raised areas on the object surface.

Sewing is often used to add ornamentation to cloth or leather. Glass, bone, or shell beads may be sewn on an item forming designs, as on moccasins or clothing. Designs may be created by sewing with various colored threads of hair, plant fiber, quills, or metal, or by sewing different colors of fabrics together, as in a patchwork quilt.

This discussion has only touched upon some of the ways in which peoples add ornamentation to and create design on objects. When it comes to ornamenting objects, humans are highly creative. When most people think of artistic creativity, they think of the artist as creating a novel object (e.g., a unique drawing or sculpture) using some medium (e.g., paper or wood). Looking in broad cross-cultural perspective, we see that humanity as a whole has also been enormously creative not only in its styles but also in its techniques of ornamentation and in some of the surprising materials used.

Art of the Northwest Coast: An Example of Style. In visual arts, some two-dimensional image (e.g., a painting or drawing) or three-dimensional form (e.g., a sculpture or mask) is created. Cultures vary in many ways in their visual arts: the themes or subjects portrayed, the purposes of the artwork, the relation between the artist and the public, and so forth.

Stylistic conventions are an important variation. In visual arts, stylistic symbolism may be especially important, for artists in many cultures are not especially concerned with realistic portrayals of people or nature, but use conventional representations that are understood by themselves and the public. But even when the intention is a realistic portrayal, symbolic representation may be necessary. In a painting or drawing, for example, three-dimensional reality is portrayed on a two-dimensional surface, and the stylistic conventions of different cultures may handle this problem of representation in various ways.

The art of some of the Native Americans of the Northwest Coast, from southern Alaska to Oregon, is one example of stylistic variation in imagery and two-dimensional representation. Although they were hunters, gatherers, and fishers—rather than cultivators—Northwest Coast peoples were largely sedentary villagers, which was made possible by the abundance and reliability of coastal and riverine food resources, especially fish (see Chapter 7). Their social and political organization included large descent groups, chiefly roles, and hierarchical ranking. Sponsoring the creation of art objects, displaying them, and/or using them in ceremonies was one way groups and high-ranking people proclaimed their wealth and social position.

Northwest Coast art is famous for its sheer quantity, quality, and style. Most major Canadian and American museums west of the Rockies contain substantial collections of masks, wooden sculptures, incised silver jewelry, carved boxes, finely woven blankets, and sometimes larger objects such as "totem poles" and painted housefronts. Animals, humans, and spirits are the most common subjects of the art of these peoples, although many creations represent animal–human–spirit at the same time. Because of the unique style used to represent these subjects, most Northwest Coast art is easily recognizable.

Animals such as beavers, ravens, hawks, frogs, bears, and killer whales were common subjects of the art, but their depiction was not intended to be realistic. Artists created animals by combining design elements representing what was culturally considered their most distinctive body parts. For example, beavers have two large incisors, a scaly (often hatched) tail, a rounded nose, and forepaws (often holding a stick). Hawks are portrayed by emphasizing their distinctive beak, which is turned backward and often touches the face. Frogs are suggested by wide and toothless mouths. Bears usually are identified by paws with claws and a large and heavily toothed mouth. Images of killer whales have a large toothed mouth, a blowhole, and an exaggerated dorsal fin. Using such conventional design elements, Northwest Coast artists carved animals onto boxes, masks used in a multitude of ceremonies, huge cedar tree trunks representing a group's or individual's ancestry (commonly mislabeled "totem poles"), and other three-dimensional objects.

Painters are familiar with the problem of representing the world on flat surfaces. In the Western and many other artistic traditions, three dimensions are represented on two-dimensional surfaces (canvas or paper) by such techniques as relative sizes of images, perspective, and coloration, all intended to create the visual illusion of depth. Northwest Coast artists painted on many two-dimensional surfaces, including the flat sides of boxes and communal housefronts. They also wove representations of animals into blankets and incised lines into bracelets and other metal jewelry. Most often, their work on flat surfaces tried to retain as many as possible of the design elements characteristic of each animal, so that each animal representation would be identifiable. A common technique was to split the animal down the middle and paint profiles on each half of the surface. The result was a representation that distorted the actual shapes of the body and its characteristic parts, but retained the elements that conventionally identified the animal.

Yet another stylistic characteristic of Northwest Coast art is the artists' apparent intolerance of empty spaces. The subject's body, limbs, and even hands and feet were generally filled in by design elements. Most commonly, curvilinear patterns, stylized eyes, or faces were painted or carved inside body parts. Thus, one frequently observes a face on an animal's torso or an eye pattern on a leg joint.

Although meaningful cross-cultural studies of visual arts are difficult, comparative studies have been made of stylistic elements found in ornamental designs. Working with the idea that art reflects the creator's view of society, John Fischer studied the use of stylistic elements in 28 different societies around the world. He divided the societies on the basis of their degrees of social equality and inequality (see Chapter 13), feeling that the artistic expressions of egalitarian (primarily foraging) societies would differ from those of socially stratified (primarily intensive agricultural) societies. Stylistic elements were examined in terms of relative complexity, use of space, symmetry, and boundedness. Fischer found that in egalitarian societies designs tended toward repetition of similar, symmetrical design elements, with

▲ Along the Northwest Coast, houses were elaborately decorated with designs that were symbolic of the family and its heritage. This Tlingit house is in Ketchikan, Alaska.

large areas of empty space without enclosures. In more stratified societies, ornamentation was characterized by asymmetrical designs that integrated unlike elements and more fully filled enclosed areas. Fischer interpreted these differences as symbolically reflecting the differing social realities of egalitarian and stratified peoples. Egalitarian peoples tend to live in small, scattered isolated groups, while in stratified societies people live in crowded communities.

Performance Arts

Performance arts encompass music, song, and dance, which use voice, instruments, and movement to delight the senses and communicate. (Theater/drama is also a performance art, but we do not cover it here.) Music, song, and dance are closely interrelated. Dancing is usually to the accompaniment of music, especially rhythms created partly by drumming, clapping, or other kinds of percussion. Singing is often accompanied by instrumental music. Traditional religious ceremonies and pageants commonly integrate music, song, and dance.

An interesting aspect of performance arts is that not only do we watch or listen to such formal performances but we also frequently perform them ourselves, in many cases for pure pleasure. We play our own pianos or guitars, we sing in the shower or as we drive, and we take part in social dances. The dual dimension of these art forms has been questioned by some anthropologists. Speaking only of dance, Adrienne Kaeppler has asked, "Is participation in rock and roll in any way comparable to watching ballet? Indeed, should 'dances of participation' and 'dances of presentation' be classified as the same phenomenon either in our own or other cultures, let alone cross-culturally?" She further questions if dance performances for the gods should be categorized with social dancing, since their purposes are so different. Similar questions may be asked of music and song, which so often are part of religious rituals. For example, Osage rituals integrated music, song, physical movements (including dance), and theatrical performances to communicate ideas that could not be expressed by words alone. In his studies of Osage religious rituals, Francis LaFlesche argued that these rituals were not merely prayers for supernatural assistance but were educational as well. They were a manner of recording and transmitting the collective knowledge of the society, communicating social messages to the assembled participants. Thus, even within a society the purposes of performance arts may differ significantly, depending on whether they are religious or secular in nature.

People raised in the Judeo-Christian religious tradition are quite familiar with the many functions of music in religious services. The lyrics of familiar hymns sung to praise God are an integral part of worship rituals. Music also helps to create the mood and sense of reverence for the service and is capable of altering the emotional state of the participants. The shared experience of singing in unison may help draw the congregation together, enhancing what many Christian denominations call their fellowship. In these and other ways, music is important in making the congregation receptive to the messages delivered by the sermon and prayers.

Music and other forms of performance arts are essential to the religious experience for diverse peoples in all parts of the world. The *voudon* (voodoo) religion of the Caribbean heavily incorporates performance arts into religious ceremonies. Followers of *voudon* consider themselves to be people who "serve the spirits" (*loa*). Many *loa* originated and now live in West Africa, where the ancestors of modern Afro-Caribbean peoples were enslaved during the era of slave trade beginning about 1500. *Voudon* temples are elaborately decorated with sacred objects, paintings, and symbolic representations of various *loa*, which show the devotion of the worshippers and make the temple attractive to the spirits. Through drumming, music, and energetic dancing, *voudon* wor-

shippers induce the *loa* to leave their spiritual homes and take over the bodies of those who worship them. When the *loa* possess their human servants, the latter speak with the voices of the *loa*, wear the *loa*'s favorite clothing, eat their foods, drink their beverages, and generally assume their identity. Visiting petitioners with problems can ask questions of the worshipper/*loa*, who may answer with directions about what course of action to take. *Voudon* drumming, music, and dancing are so totally integrated into temple rituals that the religion is unimaginable without it.

Among many peoples, music, dance, and other forms of performance arts are essential elements of curing ceremonials. !Kung shamans (see Chapters 6 and 14) use percussion, song, and dance to induce the trance state they believe is necessary for curing sick people. The power to heal, !Kung believe, comes from a substance called *n!um*, which when heated up by dancing and trance allows shamans to draw sickness out of people. While women produce a definite rhythm by clapping and singing, the curers circle the fire in short, synchronous dance steps. The experience of music and dance causes the *n!um* inside their bodies to boil up into their heads, inducing trance. In this spiritually powerful state, shamans heal by placing hands on the sick, shrieking at the same time to drive out the affliction.

Music is essential to the healing process among many other African peoples. The Tumbuka-speaking peoples of northern Malawi combine singing, drumming, and dancing in all-night curing sessions. Some kinds of illness are caused by a category of spirits called *vimbuza*. *Vimbuza* are the powerful spiritual energy of foreign peoples and wild animals (especially lions). *Vimbuza* cause various kinds of illness and even death when they possess someone. Tumbuka believe that health requires a balance between bodily cold and hot forces (similar to the bodily "humours" of old Europe). When *vimbuza* enter the body, they create an imbalance between hot and cold forces, leading to the buildup of heat that is culturally interpreted as sickness.

Tumbuka diviner-healers (curers) both diagnose illnesses and direct elaborate healing ceremonies that include drumming, music, and dance. The most essential part of the curing ritual is a shared musical experience in the context of a group gathering, with every individual present expected to contribute to the music making. Even patients themselves participate in the total experience by singing, clapping, and dancing. As the sick person dances to the accompanying rhythm of drums and music, the heat inside the person's body increases. This leads the possessing spirit to expend excess energy and cool off.

Body Arts	Alterations to the physical appearance of the body, including, but not limited to, physical alterations, painting, tattooing, and scarification
Visual Arts	Material, tangible objects that are part of the material culture of a people, including, but not limited to, basketry, pottery, textiles, clothing, jewelry, tools, furniture, painting, masks, and sculpture
Performance Arts	Arts meant to be heard, seen, or personally performed, including music, song, dance, and theater

By thus restoring the balance between hot and cold, the individual is cured, at least temporarily.

Steven Friedson, who worked among the Tumbuka, briefly summarizes the importance of music and performance to healing among just a few African cultures:

> Africans approach healing through music and dance. Azande "witch doctors" eat special divinatory medicines, activated by drumming, singing, and dancing. In northern Nigeria among the Hausa, the sounds of the *garaya* (two-stringed plucked lute) and *buta* (gourd rattle) call the divine horsemen of the sacred city of Jangare to descend into the heads of *boorii* adepts, thus healing the people they have made sick. Similarly, the various *orisha* and *voudon* spirits of the Guinea Coast, called by their drum motto, mount their horses (possess their devotees). The resultant spirit-possession dance, though religious in nature, is in the first instance often a therapy for those afflicted by the same spirits. Spirit affliction is healed through music and dance in Ethiopia and Sudan, wherever *zar* cults occur. . . . Central, southern, and parts of Equatorial Africa have examples of the *ng'oma* type of healing complex, whose name . . . points to the centrality of music in curative rites. (Friedson 1998, 273–274, references in the original deleted)

In the early 1980s, the authors of this book first heard about a medical practice that involves integrating music into the treatment of both biomedical and psychological disorders. At the time, we thought the field now called music therapy was a new mode of treatment and a new occupation. As the previous examples illustrate, many other cultures have long recognized the connection between music and healing and have integrated the performance arts into their treatments.

As with other forms of aesthetic expression, comparative studies of performance arts are difficult and few. Alan Lomax's comparative studies of dance and song rank with the most ambitious. Lomax and his collaborators analyzed film footage of peoples from around the world, comparing body movements in everyday activities with their dance movements. What they found was that dance movements were formalized repetitions of the movements found in daily life. Lomax further argued that the form of dance was correlated with the relative complexity of the society.

In his comparative study of songs, Lomax found that differences in song styles were also correlated with societal complexity. The songs of less complex peoples, such as egalitarian foragers, included more vocables (sounds, not words). Words were not enunciated as clearly in their songs and there was greater repetition of vocables and words. The songs of the most complex peoples included fewer vocables, less repetition, and more words, which were more clearly enunciated. Although Lomax's conclusions concerning the correlation between dance and song and relative cultural complexity have been questioned, there are some interesting parallels between his findings and those of Fischer on stylistic elements in ornamental designs.

Art and Culture

Anthropologists are not interested in art simply for art's sake. As we have already seen with the examples of body, visual, and performance arts, art is embedded in a cultural context. Three of many features of this context are religion, gender, and identity.

Secular and Religious Art

In our discussions of the various forms of art, we mentioned that certain artistic products are sacred and others are not. There are both sacred and secular designs, forms, dances, songs, music, and literature. This division between secular and sacred cuts across many forms of art and across most cultures.

In contemporary industrial society, the greatest artistic energies are expended in the creation of secular art, although such art may at times include religious themes. If, for example, you examine the works of the greatest Western painters, architects, and composers of the last century, you will find that most of their work is secular. This was not always true. The great art of earlier periods was for the most part concerned with religion, partly because religious and political authorities so often sponsored artists and their creations. The pyramids and great temples of ancient Egypt were related to conceptions of the afterlife and other dimensions of the supernatural world. While visiting pyramids and great statues of the pharaohs, one must remember that the pharaohs were gods on Earth.

In classical Greece, the cradle of western European artistic traditions, religion was a central focus for most of the greatest artistic accomplishments. The Parthenon in Athens was the temple of Athena. Most of the greatest Greek public statuary depicted gods such as Poseidon, Zeus, Apollo, and Venus. Much Greek drama had strong religious overtones and was associated with the god Dionysus. In Rome, secular art became more prominent. The great buildings were usually palaces and theaters, while public monuments honoring the triumphs of living or recently dead heroes filled Roman cities. In the Middle Ages religion regained preeminence. The great buildings of the medieval and Renaissance periods were cathedrals, while the greatest artists of the time labored to fill these buildings with frescoes, mosaics, paintings, statuary, and other artistic works, as well as music, song, and pageantry dedicated to the worship of God.

The 1700s saw an emphasis on reason and science, the Industrial Revolution, the rise of capitalism, and the beginnings of modern political democracy. Ever since, Western art has become increasingly secular. The largest buildings in our cities are no longer dedicated to religion, but to government, commerce, or athletics. Contemporary painters choose secular subjects, from realistic landscapes and buildings to abstract designs and cans of Campbell's soup. The most illustrious composers and performers today seldom produce or perform religious music, but focus on secular and, at times, even irreligious themes. For those of us who learned our culture in a society dominated by secular art, it is important to remember that for most peoples and for most of human history, religion and religious art have been preeminent. The most elaborate artistic achievements of a great many peoples are associated with religious ceremonies: visual arts, music, dances, ornamentations, architecture, and their associated mythologies.

We have already discussed examples of the integration of performance arts like music and dance into African healing practices. Another people for whom art—both visual and verbal arts in this case—is part of curing rituals is the Navajo of the American Southwest. In Navajo belief, the most common cause of illness is the loss of harmony with the environment, often caused by the person's violation of a taboo or other transgression. When illness strikes and a diagnosis is made, a Navajo "singer" (curer or medicine man) is called on to organize a complex curing ceremony.

In curing ceremonies (and there were traditionally hundreds of such ceremonies), the singer addresses and calls on the Holy People, who are spiritual beings believed by Navajo to have the power to restore sick people to harmony and beauty. Ceremonies usually occur in a hogan (house) at night, and in theory the procedures must be executed perfectly for the cure to work.

For the ceremony, the singer creates images of the Holy People out of sand, called sandpaintings. Navajo sandpaintings are visual and sacred representations that are created, used in a single ceremony, and then destroyed. Most sandpaintings are stylized scenes of events involving various Holy People that occurred in the mythological past. Each sandpainting is part of a ceremony that also includes other sacred objects (such as rattles and prayer sticks) and lengthy songs or chants recited by the singer. The songs/chants that are recited over the sandpainting and the patient may last for hours. Most songs/chants tell of the myths depicted in the specific sandpainting. Thus, each curing ceremony calls to mind the Navajo worldview to the patient and the audience present.

In their years of learning to become singers, Navajo singers must memorize the lengthy songs and chants that they recite over sick people to restore their harmony with the world. Singers also learn to make precise sandpaintings that represent specific mythical scenes and events. To make the images, a singer, usually with the help of his family members and/or apprentices, collects and mixes sand and other materials of various colors, including white, red, yellow, black, and blue, with charcoal, corn pollen, and various plant materials. Pictures are created by carefully dribbling fine grains of sand through the fingers onto the prepared floor of the hogan.

There are literally hundreds of sandpaintings. Most ceremonies involve a combination of many sandpaintings used in association with particular chants. Because some are quite large and enormously detailed, they often take hours to create. But all must be exact representations of the ideal model of the mythical scene or event depicted. The images are stylized drawings of the Holy People, many of whom are depicted with weapons and armor. Most scenes represented in the sandpaintings are from particular myths familiar to the patient and audience.

Sandpaintings are made for the express purpose of inducing the Holy People to come to the hogan where the ceremony is held. The Holy People are attracted by the beauty of the sandpainting, the compelling chants recited by the singer, and the manipulation of powerful ritual objects. During the ceremony, the patient is usually sitting on the sandpainting itself, which contains drawings of the Holy People whose presence in the hogan imbues the images with power. The singer completes the transfer of power to the patient when he rubs the patient's body with the sand of the images of the Holy People. After each phase of the ceremony is finished, the sandpainting is destroyed, for the Holy People commanded the Navajo not to make permanent images of them.

Navajo sandpaintings certainly are works of art. Some Anglos who have seen them think it is a shame to destroy such beautiful images that singers and their helpers have worked so hard to create. But in the context of Navajo beliefs, sandpaintings are made for specific curing ceremonials held for particular patients. That purpose—not expressing the singer's creativity, making an artistic statement, celebrating Navajo culture, or publicly displaying the singer's talents—is their objective. For Navajo, fulfilling that purpose requires that the paintings not be permanent.

Navajo sandpaintings and the singing of curers clearly have strong religious overtones, but the division between their secular and religious purposes is not always clear. The kachina dolls of the Hopis are small figures carved out of cottonwood root and painted to look like one of the kachinas or supernatural beings that are a central focus of their religious life (see Chapters 10 and 14). Traditionally, these dolls were given to girls at ceremonial dances by people wearing kachina costumes and masks. The dolls themselves were not ritual items, but rather a way to help the children learn about and recognize the 500 or so different kachina spirits. Similarly, the Hispanic peoples of New Mexico have a tradition of producing *bultos,* which are carved wooden crucifixes and figures of saints, and *retablos,* which are flat wooden boards, painted with images of Christ or saints. Today in New Mexico there are dozens of artists who produce and sell *bultos* and *retablos.* Some of these paintings and figures of saints find their way into churches or family chapels and altars, but the majority are used in a more secular context as decorative art for the home. Religious symbolism is often used to decorate clothing and other items of everyday use, blurring the distinction between secular and sacred art.

Religious considerations have other effects on secular art as well, frequently placing limits on secular artistic expressions. The use of certain types of motifs or themes may be religiously forbidden. The Koran prohibits the use of human images, which are viewed as idolatry. Thus many Islamic peoples extended this ban to include any pictorial representation of humans or animals. As a result, much of the art of Islamic peoples is devoid of naturalistic representations, focusing instead on elaborate geometric or curvilinear designs. The Shakers emphasized singing and dancing as important parts of their religious services but prohibited the use of musical instruments.

Art and Gender

Gender differences are often reflected in body, visual, performance, and verbal arts. Colors and designs are sometimes considered male or female, most familiarly reflected in clothing and body decoration. Gender also influences who creates and/or performs certain types of visual, performance, or verbal arts. The BaMbuti Pygmies of the African rain forest have a ritual performance involving dance and music they call *molimo.* They view the forest as like their parent and, like any parent, the forest looks after its children—themselves. Therefore, when misfortune strikes, it must be because the forest is asleep. To wake up the forest, at night the women and children retire to their huts while the men make *molimo* music. Women are not supposed to know that the *molimo* is just a long, flutelike instrument stored in a local stream, but instead believe it to be some kind of forest animal. (In fact, women seem to know all about the *molimo.*)

As discussed in Chapter 11, men and women are usually involved in the production of different types of durable items, and usually the individuals involved in production decorate the items as well. In many cases, the aesthetic qualities of the items are an integral part of the production process itself, as with the shape of a pottery vessel or metal tool, or the design in a blanket or a basket. However, in other instances, decorative arts are separate and distinct from the production of the basic item, and decorative artists may be defined by gender.

Among the Plains Indians, beadwork and quillwork were produced by women. The only men who produced beadwork and quillwork were *berdaches,* men who dressed and acted as women (see Chapter 11). Although both women and men painted hides, there were distinct differences in subject matter. Women painted only geometric designs. The hide containers called *parafleches* used for the storage of food and clothing were made by women and were painted only in geometric designs. Representational designs of people, horses, and other animals and supernatural beings were painted only by men. Tipis and buffalo robes, though made by women, were painted by either men or women depending on whether the design was to be geometric (by women) or representational (by men).

Some visual art objects are made for specific rituals or ceremonies. Initiation rites are usually held for only one sex (see Chapter 14). The art produced for them, therefore, is sometimes "sex-specific." In many cultures of the highlands of Papua New Guinea, long bamboo flutes are played at male initiation ceremonies. Women are not supposed to know about the existence of the flutes. Many initiation ceremonies also include carved and painted masks, supposedly kept secret from women and uninitiated boys.

Performance arts are often carried out during religious ceremonies. Men have historically played the dominant role in most religions. Not surprisingly, in most societies men dominate the performance arts associated with religion. For example, even though many of the Hopi kachinas are female, in traditional kachina dances all dancers, even those impersonating female spirits, are men. In ancient Greek drama, the roles of women were played by men. In the West, women were not allowed to participate in certain performance arts long after they had become secularized. The role of Juliet, in the original production of Shakespeare's play, was performed by a young boy, for women could not be actors in Shakespeare's time. It was not until the late seventeenth century that women could perform in the English theater.

Social Functions of Art

Does art exist solely to satisfy the human desire for the aesthetic? Perhaps, but if so, why have humans expended such incredible energy in its creation? Perhaps art also has a critical role in human social life and cultural existence. Through the use of art people can simultaneously express their identities as members of particular groups, while at the same time demonstrating their individuality. Through the production, consumption, and use of art we can express our personal individuality, our group identities (including ethnic affiliation), and even our social status.

Individuality. Many of us attempt to express our individuality by creating art or displaying art, as shown by the widespread appeal of handmade goods produced by skilled craftspeople. Since the advent of the Industrial Revolution in the nineteenth century, the attraction of handmade over machinemade goods has been their individuality. This individuality is not solely the result of the differing technical skill of the makers, but rather that the makers have consciously tried to make every item unique by varying colors and designs. Thus, if one looks at Oriental rugs, Native American jewelry, pottery and baskets, Maya textiles from Guatemala, or wood carvings from New Guinea, rarely does one find two identical items. If they are, it is probably because they were produced for the commercial market.

Similarly, our clothing and houses express our individuality. Even though we usually conform to the norms of our society in clothing styles, most of us abhor uniforms, and thus we enhance our clothes in some manner to make them uniquely ours. In their dwellings people also attempt to express their individuality. While all Maori dwellings were carved and painted, different designs and images were used. Today in suburban North America builders of subdivisions usually vary the houses by using a range of floor plans, building materials, and colors. Many residents of older neighborhoods, though, still consider the new subdivisions as lacking in character, style, and individuality.

Social Identity. As well as displaying our individuality, art is a means of expressing social identity, publicly displaying what kind of person you are or which group of people you identify with. In the 1960s and early 1970s, many young people wore long hair, beads, and baggy clothes decorated with peace signs and upside-down flags. Some traveled the country in old Volkswagen minibuses or school buses that were hand painted in strange colors and designs. The minute you saw them you knew they were "hippies." Clothing styles, hairstyles, and other art forms are commonly used to indicate social group identity, from the black leather jackets painted with club emblems of motorcycle gangs to the shepherd crook spears and red sashes of the Cheyenne Dog Soldier society.

A widespread use of art to express social membership has to do with ethnic affiliation. In Chapter 17 we discuss ethnic boundary markers in more detail, but here it is important to note that art is one of the common expressions of ethnic identity. Clothing styles and decoration are important visual markers of ethnic identity. Plaid kilts are markers of Scots, as much as beaded clothing and feather headdresses are of Native Americans. A woman in Guatemala wearing a *huipuli* is a Maya. If you see a man wearing a cowboy hat and boots in Europe, you can guess that he is an American tourist, even though he has probably never ridden a horse or seen many cows.

Ethnicity is expressed in more than clothing. The full range of artistic forms—body, visual, performance, and verbal arts—is employed to display one's ethnic identity. Thus we speak of ethnic art, ethnic dance, ethnic music, ethnic songs, ethnic literature, and ethnic foods. Despite our use of the word *ethnic* in such contexts, ultimately, of course, all art is ethnic art, since it is associated with a specific ethnic group and everyone is a part of some ethnic group. For various reasons, people value and pay premium prices for the art produced by ethnic groups other than their own.

From an anthropological perspective, much of the multicultural movement in contemporary North America—and particularly in colleges and universities—is really

The visual arts of traditional rural peoples of the world are integrated into virtually every aspect of their lives, with some of the most important forms found in the everyday material items they make and use. Depending on the society, these artistic traditions find expression in clothing, pottery, basketry, and other furnishings of their homes. Although these material items may be elaborately decorated, for the most part these items are utilitarian, valued not just for their beauty but for their usefulness as well.

In the capitalist global economy all goods and services have to compete for market share. Thus, as traditional peoples become economically integrated into larger capitalist markets, local traditional handmade goods must compete with mass-produced imported goods. Aluminum, tin, ceramic, and plastic pots, pans, kettles, jugs, jars, plates, bowls, and cups compete with locally made pottery, basketry, hide, horn, and wooden items. Machinemade cloth, blankets, canvas, plastic sheets, and mass-produced clothing compete with traditional woven textiles, bark cloth, felt, and handmade clothing. Both cost and quality are factors in this competition. For the most part, these imported items are more durable and more useful than locally made goods. Because traditional goods are labor intensive to produce, once a group becomes even marginally involved in a cash economy, they are no longer competitive in terms of costs. As a result the global economy is resulting in rapid and dramatic changes in the material culture. Throughout the world local traditional handmade goods are being replaced by mass-produced, machinemade items. As people stop making their own material goods, the artistic traditions associated with making them are disappearing as well.

There are exceptions to this trend. For a variety of reasons, some groups have been able to commoditize and market their traditional goods, not as utilitarian items but as "ethnic art." A handmade basket that takes a hundred hours or so of labor to make cannot compete with a plastic bowl that costs 50 cents or less, even in the most impoverished regions of the world. However, if that basket can be sold as "art" and not as a utilitarian bowl, then it might be economically feasible for people to continue to make them. The price for art is based on totally different standards of supply and demand, and that same basket might sell for $10, $100, or even several thousand dollars.

The traditional craft arts of many societies throughout the world have been successfully commoditized and marketed as ethnic art. The Kuna of Panama now have a good market for their *molas,* patchwork blouses worn by women. Pottery made by the Shipibo of Peru is sold in the United States and Europe. Traditional wood carvings from New Guinea and the Northwest Coast peoples of Canada and the United States are widely collected. Paintings on bark and canvas of the native peoples of Australia have a small but well-established market even outside Australia. However, no groups have been more successful in commoditizing and marketing their art than the Native Americans of the United States. The Indian art market in the United States is estimated to be worth about $1 billion a year.

The ethnic art market is unique in that buyers and sellers belong to different ethnic groups. The producers are members of small indigenous societies. The items are not being produced for use within the native community but for sale to outsiders. The buyers or consumers of this art are for the most part middle- and upper-class members of Western societies. The reasons why wealthier Western peoples collect art produced by indigenous non-Western peoples are varied. However, the primary appeal of these items is that they reflect the artistic tradition of a particular indigenous people, and that they are made by individuals from these societies. Thus the market value of a particular item depends not only on its aesthetic appeal but also on the ethnic identity of the artist. It is the ethnic authenticity of an object that gives it higher value. Since such objects command higher market value than comparable items made by others, there is a problem with misrepresentation. Recognizing this factor, in 1990 Congress passed the Indian Arts & Crafts Act, which states that only an object made by a legally enrolled member of a tribe can be sold as "Indian art." In the ethnic art market, "Indian" is a de facto brand name and, like all brand names, serves to enhance value. In the Indian art market tribal affiliation is a secondary brand name, and the relative value of a particular object is also dependent on tribal identity. Thus, whether a basket is Western Apache, Hopi, Pima, or Navajo affects its market value.

An important question is how "authentic" ethnic arts are once they have been commoditized and marketed. The traditional arts of the American Indian peoples of the Southwest are a good case study. The commercialization of these arts began over a century ago in the last decades of the nineteenth century. At that time mass-produced Euro-American trade goods were rapidly replacing traditional native-made craft items. Many local traders realized that the developing tourist industry in the region and the growing demand for authentic regional souvenirs could be a profitable market for Indian-made items. However, traditional Indian-made craft items had limited appeal. Traditional Navajo blankets were too thin to be used as rugs, and their designs were not appealing to most tourists. Navajo jewelry was too heavy to appeal to female tourists. Pottery was usually large and frequently had a round bottom. It was not easily transported by a tourist on a train and was frequently difficult to display on a table or shelf. Basketry, while lightweight, usually consisted of shallow, round-bottomed bowls. Like much of the pottery it was difficult to display.

Local traders and craftspeople worked together to develop new items to appeal to the tourists. Navajo weavers were encouraged to weave thicker, larger textiles, which could be sold as rugs. Designs were changed to make them appear more "Indian." Certain colors such as orange and pink were discouraged. The use of stereotypical Indian design elements such as arrows, feathers, and swastikas was encouraged. Some traders had new designs drawn and placed on the walls of their trading posts to show the weavers the types of designs they should weave. Navajo silversmiths were encouraged to make lightweight silver bracelets and necklaces, and to decorate them with arrow and swastika designs. Potters were encouraged to make smaller items. A wide range of new forms also appeared: animal figures, human figures, pitchers, creamers, teapots, flower vases, salt and pepper shakers, cups, and miniatures of all shapes and forms. Basketry underwent similar changes. To be marketable, baskets had to have flat bottoms and high sides so that the designs could be easily seen. Wastepaper baskets, lidded trinket or jewelry baskets, smaller high-sided baskets, cup-shaped baskets, and baskets woven in the shape of humans, animals, and birds were produced. By the middle of the twentieth century the sizes, forms, and designs of southwestern American Indian textiles, jewelry, pots, and baskets were quite different from what they had been in the late nineteenth century.

During the early twentieth century, Indian arts were marketed by the tribe or pueblo of origin. Individual weavers, jewelers, potters, and basketmakers were rarely recognized and craftspeople were encouraged to conform to certain recognized standards identified with their tribe or community. This changed during the last decades of the twentieth century as the market began to recognize and value the work of individual artists. Today most American Indian art is marketed as the work of a specific named artist. As a result most artists at-

▲ An American tourist buys a textile from a Maya in Antigua, Guatemala.

tempt to be highly original in what they produce, and it is becoming increasingly difficult to identify the tribe or community of the artist who produced a particular work.

Critical Thinking Questions

Contemporary ethnic art in the American Southwest is the result of more than a hundred years of adaptation to market forces.

1. What is "authentic"? Is contemporary American Indian art still an "authentic" expression of an indigenous artistic tradition?

2. How much, and in what ways, does it reflect Native American aesthetics? How much, and in what ways, does it reflect Euro-American stereotypes and aesthetics? Does it make any difference?

about understanding and appreciating "ethnic" forms of artistic expression. When Anglo-Americans talk about "other cultures," as often as not they are referring to African, Hispanic, Asian, and other "non-Anglo" Americans. When they "celebrate diversity," as often as not they are celebrating differences in literature and other forms of verbal art, interpreting graffiti as a legitimate art form, listening to African or Mexican music, eating South Asian or Vietnamese foods, and so forth. Overall the multicultural movement has had a positive influence on intercultural tolerance and understanding. In fact, multiculturalism is part of what anthropologists have been trying to get across to their students for nearly a century. But perhaps more people ought to realize that appreciating

multicultural diversity should mean far more than celebrating diversity in forms of artistic expression.

Social Status. Finally, relative social status within societies is reflected in the use of art. As discussed earlier, body arts are frequently an indicator of social status. Other art forms also indicate status. In many ranked and stratified societies the rights to use certain art forms may be the property of families or status groups. Only certain individuals will have the right to wear or use particular colors or designs, sing particular songs, dance particular dances, and even tell particular stories. This control over the use or performance of particular artistic expression is a symbolic indicator of individual social status.

Similarly, in contemporary Western society we use art to demonstrate our relative status. We display our status in our homes, automobiles, furnishings, and clothing, communicating to the world, "Look what we can afford to buy." We also demonstrate our status in what we hang on our walls, read, listen to, and watch. In our consumption of visual, performance, and verbal arts the evaluation, of course, is more subjective and difficult to measure. But for many people opera, ballet, and classical music have higher status than comedy, square dancing, and country-western or rap music. Classical literature has higher status than romance novels, science fiction, and comic books.

Summary

1. All cultures have artistic objects, designs, songs, dances, and other ways of expressing their appreciation of the aesthetic. The aesthetic impulse is universal, although cultures vary in their ways of expressing it and the social functions and cultural meanings they attach to it.

2. People raised in the Western tradition are inclined to think of art as something set apart from everyday life—as when we use the phrase "fine arts"—yet we all express ourselves aesthetically in many ways, including how we dress, decorate our houses, and eat our meals.

3. In addition to allowing people to express themselves aesthetically, art serves communicative functions by encoding meanings and messages in symbolic forms.

4. Art takes a multitude of forms, including, at minimum, body, visual, and performance arts. People around the world change their bodily appearance by such means as physical alterations, application of body paints, tattoos, and scarification. These decorations of the body are used for a variety of purposes, including beautification, expression of individual or group identity, display of privilege or social position, and symbolic indication of social maturity. The tattooing practices of the Maori of New Zealand and other Polynesians exemplify some of these functions.

5. In the visual arts, humankind as a whole has shown enormous creativity in form, style, design, techniques, materials, and many other features. Ornamentation of tools, clothing, basketry, houses, and practically all other material objects is a universal practice. The Northwest Coast peoples illustrate one way in which art varies in style and two-dimensional representation.

6. Performance arts include the use of sound and movement for both aesthetic and communicative purposes. In preindustrial cultures, performances of music (including song and percussion), dance, and theater often involve heavy audience participation, as they often do in the everyday lives of people everywhere. Often, performance art is tightly integrated into a people's spiritual and religious life, from Judeo-Christian worship services to possession trances in the *voudon* religion of the Caribbean. The integration of music and dance into the healing practices of the Tumbuka of Malawi and many other African peoples shows that using music to help cure both physical and psychological ills is not a recent, Western innovation.

7. Perhaps many forms of art began as "sacred" in that they were connected to the appeal to or worship of spiritual beings. Certainly, the religious elements of artistic expression are important not only in the history of Western art but also in the artistic traditions of people the world over. In their complex curing ceremonies, Navajo singers used both visual arts (sandpaintings) and performance arts (chants/songs) in appealing to the Holy People. Distinguishing "sacred" and "secular" art seems like a simple thing, but objects with religious significance are often used for practical purposes.

8. Art is connected to other social and cultural elements such as gender, identity, and status. In many societies certain arts and art forms are associated with women and others with men. Ethnic identity is commonly expressed in art and serves as ethnic boundary markers. Finally, within societies, relative social status is frequently expressed in the consumption of art.

Key Terms

art	body arts	performance arts
aesthetic	visual arts	

InfoTrac College Edition Terms

primitive art
ethnic art

Maori art
American Indian art

African art
Shaker art

Suggested Readings

Bailey, Garrick, Daniel C. Swan, John W. Nunley, and E. Sean StandingBear. *Art of the Osage*. Seattle: St. Louis Art Museum and Washington University Press, 2004.

In this study by two anthropologists, an art historian and an Osage artist/craftsman, Osage art is examined within its cultural historical context. Symbolism in Osage art is shown to be both an appeal to Wah-kon-da (god) for continued blessings, as well as an important mnemonic device for communicating and perpetuating traditional cultural knowledge and beliefs.

Boas, Franz. *Primitive Art*. New York: Dover Publications, Inc., 1955 (original 1927).

The first systematic treatment of the subject by an anthropologist. Despite its original publication date over 75 years ago, this book remains insightful today.

Brain, Robert. *The Decorated Body*. New York: Harper & Row, 1979.

Although written in popular style, this is a well-researched introduction to the broad range of techniques used by humans to decorate their bodies.

Faris, James C. *Nuba Personal Art*. London: Duckworth, 1972.

The Nuba people of Sudan are famous for their body painting. This book presents the classic study of Nuba painting and is a good general introduction to body painting as well.

Kirk, John T. *The Shaker World: Art, Life, Belief*. New York: Harry N. Abrams, 1997.

The Shakers, a communal religious sect, were a small but influential group in nineteenth-century America. This book discusses the evolution of their religious beliefs and practices and how they influenced their distinctive art styles.

Levenson, Jay A., ed. *Circa 1492: Art in the Age of Exploration*. Washington, D.C.: National Gallery of Art and New Haven, Conn.: Yale University Press, 1991.

The catalog for a museum exhibition at the National Gallery of Art, this is an excellent visual introduction to the range of major artistic traditions present at the dawn of globalization.

Mead, Sidney Moko. *Te Maori: Maori Art from New Zealand Collections*. New York: Harry N. Abrams, 1984.

A museum exhibition catalog, the edited text provides an excellent discussion of Maori art within the broader context of Maori culture.

Nunley, John, and Judith Bettelheim. *Caribbean Festival Arts*. Seattle: University of Washington Press, 1988.

This edited work focuses on the history and development of festivals in the Caribbean with particular attention to their elaborate costuming. Although African American peoples form the vast core of the participants, on some islands east Indians and other groups contribute and actively participate.

Phillips, Ruth. *Trading Identities: The Souvenir in Native North American Art from the Northeast, 1700–1900*. Seattle: University of Washington Press and Montreal: McGill-Queen's University Press, 1998.

In this study the author discusses early European influences on Native American art in eastern Canada and the northeastern United States, as well as the manner in which some of these arts were commoditized and marketed to Euro-Americans.

Price, Sally, and Richard Price. *Afro-American Arts of the Suriname Rain Forest*. Berkeley and Los Angeles: University of California Press, 1980.

During the late seventeenth century, escaped African slaves were able to establish their own free communities in the jungles of northern South America. This study examines the distinctive art tradition these communities developed.

Schevill, Margot Blum. *Maya Textiles of Guatemala*. Austin: University of Texas Press, 1993.

The text of this book serves as an excellent introduction to Maya textiles, while the accompanying catalog of the Eisen Collection of the Hearst Museum presents a good visual picture of the diversity of Maya textiles at the end of the nineteenth century.

Companion Website for This Book

The Wadsworth Anthropology Resource Center
http://anthropology.wadsworth.com

The companion website that accompanies *Humanity: An Introduction to Cultural Anthropology,* Seventh Edition, includes a rich array of material, including online anthropological video clips, to help you in the study of cultural anthropology and the specific topics covered in this chapter. Begin by clicking on Student Resources. Next, click on Cultural Anthropology, and then on the cover image for this book. You have now arrived at the Student Resources home page and have the option of choosing one of several chapter resources.

Applying Anthropology. Begin your study of cultural anthropology by clicking on Applying Anthropology. Here you will find useful information on careers, graduate school programs in applied anthropology, and internships you might wish to pursue. You will also find real-world examples of working anthropologists applying the skills and methods of anthropology to help solve serious world problems.

Research Online. Click here to find a wealth of Web links that will facilitate your study of anthropology. Divided into different fields of study, specific websites are starting points for Internet research. You will be guided to rich anthropology websites that will help you prepare for class, complete course assignments, and actually do research on the Web.

InfoTrac College Edition Exercises. From the pull-down menu, select the chapter you are presently studying. Select InfoTrac College Edition Exercises from the list of resources. These exercises utilize InfoTrac College Edition's vast database of articles and help you explore the numerous uses of the search word, *culture.*

Study Aids for This Chapter. Improve your knowledge of key terms by using flash cards and study the learning objectives. Take the practice quiz, receive your results, and e-mail them to your instructor. Access these resources from the chapter and resource pull-down menus.

Chapter Sixteen

GLOBALIZATION

Globalization

The Development of Global Trade

European Expansion

The World and the Industrial Revolution

The Emergence of the Global Economy

Globalization: The Continuing Process

Population Growth and Inequalities in the Global Economy

Consequences of Globalization and the Global Economy

© Paul Chesley/Network Aspen

Globalization has resulted in the increasing homogenization of urban architecture. Only the writing on some of the signs indicates that this is a street in Tokyo and not some other major city in the world.

UNTIL THE VIOLENT STREET PROTESTS at the meeting of the World Trade Organization in Seattle in late 1999, few Americans had given more than passing attention to issues of globalization and free trade. To most, globalization seemed to be part of the natural evolution of the world economic system, which during the decade of the 1990s had resulted in economic prosperity for the United States. We assumed that globalization was bringing or eventually would bring prosperity to the rest of the peoples of the world as well. Since Seattle, virtually every major international economic meeting or summit has brought increasing numbers of protesters into the streets. At the G-8 meetings in Genoa, Italy, in the summer of 2001, between 100,000 and 150,000 demonstrators filled the streets. What was the problem? The protesters have been variously labeled "anticapitalists," "anarchists," "environmentalists," and even "Luddites." But no single label can be readily applied to these protesters since they range widely in their concerns about the effects of globalization and in their ideologies.

GLOBALIZATION IS NOT SIMPLY AN ECONOMIC ISSUE. Globalization has far-reaching political, social, and cultural implications for the world's peoples. In boxes in the preceding chapters we have discussed some of the more specific questions concerning globalization. In this chapter we will discuss the history of globalization together with some of its consequences.

Globalization

It was not until the 1980s that the term *globalization* first came into common usage. Today, although we hear and use the term almost daily, we might find it difficult to define. Globalization is not a thing or a product, but rather a process. **Globalization** refers to the worldwide changes that are increasingly integrating and remolding the lives of the people of the world. Most commonly we speak of the global economy and think of globalization primarily in economic terms. Although economic changes are certainly the driving force behind globalization, it is having far more profound effects on our way of life than merely what we eat, what we wear, and how we make our living. It is having an impact on our political, social, and cultural institutions as well.

Globalization began 500 years ago, with the voyage of Columbus, and has had two stages of development. The earliest stage, the period from about 1500 to the mid-twentieth century, saw the development of a global trade network, which eventually connected, directly or indirectly, every group of people in the world. The second stage, which began to develop at the end of World War II, saw the development of global marketing of products and the emergence of a global economy.

The Development of Global Trade

Before A.D. 1500 the major world regions were relatively isolated from one another. Most contact was limited to societies that occupied adjacent territories. Trade was minimal, and the long-distance trade that existed between Europe and China or Africa seldom involved direct exchange between members of those societies. Trade was managed by intervening groups whose members acted as middlemen. Thus, although Europeans were aware of the existence of places like China, India, and Ethiopia, their knowledge was extremely limited and seldom based on firsthand accounts. Although innovations in technology and cultural institutions spread from one population center to another, diffusion was slow because direct contact was lacking.

Although the terms *Old World* and *New World* are ethnocentric, this distinction is useful from a cultural–historical perspective. The Old World—Europe, Africa, and Asia—did form a unit within which trade and contact, however tenuous and limited, allowed for the spread of technology and institutions. *New World* is a term usually applied only to the Americas, but it could just as well be applied to Australia and most of Oceania because both of these regions were outside this exchange network before 1500. Thus, before European expansion the world consisted of two broad geographical regions with peoples who for much of their history had developed technologies and lifeways in isolation from one another.

European Expansion

With the "discovery" of the Americas by Christopher Columbus in 1492, the age of European expansion began. In population and technological achievement, Europe was not the most developed region of the world during the fifteenth century. Asia had a total population four to five times that of Europe, and in overall technology Asia was ahead of Europe. Compared with the states of Asia, European countries were small. The populations of such soon-to-be-imperial powers as England, Portugal, Spain, and the Netherlands were insignificant in comparison with those of China or the Mogul (Islamic) states of India. Even the Aztec Empire in the Americas may have had a population equal to the total of these four European countries.

The major advantage that European societies possessed was their military technology. Guns, crossbows, iron weapons, armor, and horses gave them significant advantages over the stone-tool military technologies of the peoples of the Americas and Oceania. To a lesser degree, Europeans also enjoyed a military advantage over most peoples of Africa. The same was not true in Asia: on land, European armies enjoyed no technological advantage. Only in naval warfare were the Europeans technologically superior to the Asian states.

These factors influenced European expansionist policies during the early period and caused the histories of contact with Asia, Africa, the Americas, and Oceania to differ significantly. With some exceptions, principally in the Americas, the expansion of Europe during the sixteenth, seventeenth, and eighteenth centuries consisted of the development of maritime mercantile empires, as opposed to actual overseas colonies and territorial empires.

Because European contact took such different forms from one region to the next, it is necessary to examine the history of contact region by region (see Figure 16.1).

Conquest of the Americas. In 1492, Columbus found a new world inhabited by numerous peoples, who still had only an advanced stone-tool technology. Initially, the Spaniards were disappointed in their new discoveries because they failed to find the immense treasures of the Indies they were expecting. On the island of Hispaniola, where they first settled, there were some gold deposits, but most Spanish settlers quickly turned their attention to the development of sugarcane plantations and cattle ranches.

During the first quarter-century after its discovery, the New World attracted only a few thousand Spaniards. In 1519, the Spanish landed on the coast of Mexico and by 1521 had completed the conquest of the Aztec Empire. Aztec gold and silver sent back to Spain encouraged the migration of others to search for still more wealth and plunder. Between 1532 and 1534, a Spanish military expedition conquered the Inca Empire and took the wealth of Peru for Spain. By the late 1500s, Spanish expeditions had explored much of the Americas and had located and conquered every major Native American state. In little more than half a century, the Spaniards had conquered the richest and most populous portions of the Americas: the West Indies, Mesoamerica, and Peru.

The Treaty of Tordesillas, signed in 1494, divided the non-Christian world between Spain and Portugal. The easternmost part of South America, Brazil, fell into the

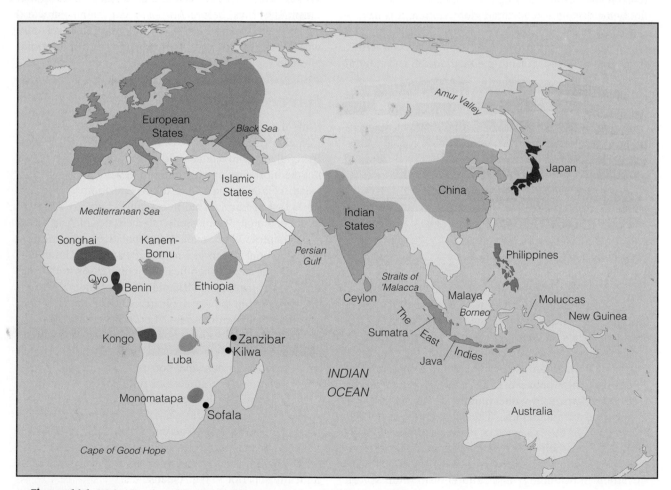

▲ **Figure 16.1** Major States and Regions of Europe, Asia, and Africa (ca. 1500)

Portuguese portion. The coastal regions of Brazil were well suited for sugarcane plantations. Starting in 1500, Portuguese settlers began colonizing Brazil, and by 1550 small settlements were scattered along most of the coast.

The Spanish and Portuguese were able to conquer large portions of the Americas in a surprisingly short time. As the Spanish demonstrated in their conquests of the Aztecs and Incas, their military superiority was so pronounced that their small armies numbering in the hundreds were able to vanquish well-organized native armies whose troops numbered in the thousands. Small groups of European troops could move with near impunity throughout the length of the Americas. Only lack of manpower limited Spanish and Portuguese expansion and kept them from subjugating all of the Americas.

The main period of conquest and territorial expansion had ended by 1600, and Spanish settlers turned their attention to exploitation of the West Indies, Mesoamerica, and Peru, where they developed silver and gold mines, ranches, and plantations. The Portuguese contented themselves with coastal sugarcane plantations in Brazil.

The cultural impact of the Spanish and Portuguese was most pronounced in those regions directly under their control. Existing native political organizations were either replaced or modified and integrated into a colonial government. European technology and livestock were introduced—iron tools, plows, cattle, horses, sheep, and so forth—as existing economic systems were altered to meet European needs. Indian labor was used in the mines and on the plantations and ranches that were developed. Missionaries flooded the Americas seeking converts. Temples were replaced by Christian churches. In some regions, such as Mexico and Peru, native peoples managed to maintain their languages and Indian social and ethnic identity, but even these societies were given a veneer of Christian customs and beliefs. Even Native American peoples beyond direct European control were affected. Old World crops, domesticated animals, and metal tools in limited numbers were diffused to these autonomous peoples. In some regions the introduction of European items and animals, such as the horse, revolutionized native societies.

As important as these material elements were in altering Native American culture, they were not the only causes of change. Old World diseases such as smallpox, measles, influenza, bubonic plague, diphtheria, typhus, cholera, malaria, and scarlet fever were also introduced by early Europeans. Isolated as they had been, the peoples of the Americas had no natural immunities to these diseases. Because these illnesses spread well in advance of European contact, it is impossible to estimate with any exactness the size of native populations before that contact. The massive population decline caused by European diseases is best documented in regions under direct Spanish and Portuguese control. Father Bartolome de las Casas reported that there were 1,100,000 Indians 14 years of age or older on Hispaniola in 1496; even the most conservative estimate of the Indian population of the island at that time is 100,000. Regardless of the original figure, we do know that the native population underwent rapid decline and that by 1535 there were only 500 Indians left on Hispaniola.

In Mexico the decline was also severe, but not as devastating. One study places the contact population at 25,200,000 in 1519, with a decline to 16,800,000 by 1532, 2,650,000 by 1568, and 1,075,000 by 1605. Although these estimates are open to question, there is no doubt that Native American societies suffered severe population declines after European contact.

From the very beginning the Spanish and Portuguese were heavily dependent on Indian slave labor to work their mines and plantations and to perform other menial tasks. As the native populations under their control decreased, they faced a labor shortage. One answer to this problem was to "recruit" new labor by raiding other Native American groups for slaves. Thus peoples who were not under direct Spanish or Portuguese control suffered heavy losses from slave raiders during the sixteenth and seventeenth centuries. This, however, proved only a stopgap measure since these new recruits also died rapidly from European diseases. New sources of human labor had to be found to fill the expanding vacuum.

Awareness of the rapid and dramatic decline in Native American population is critical to understanding not only the history of the Americas during the past 500 years but the histories of Africa and Europe as well. The population decline of the Native Americans created a vacuum that was filled by the massive migration of Old World peoples. However, since neither Spain nor Portugal sent sufficient emigrants to offset the declining Native American population, another source of labor had to be found. This was the genesis of the African slave trade. Starting in the 1490s, ever-increasing numbers of African slaves were sent to the Spanish and Portuguese colonies. By the eighteenth century, these colonies had more individuals of African ancestry than of European ancestry.

During the late sixteenth and early seventeenth centuries other European powers—England, France, and the Netherlands—began contesting Spanish and Portuguese dominance of the Americas. For the most part, these countries occupied portions of the Americas outside the limits of Spanish and Portuguese control: some of the small islands in the West Indies and the Atlantic coast of North

▶ Conversion of native peoples to Christianity was one of the primary interests of the Spanish in the Americas.

© Garrick Bailey

America. The Native American populations in this region had already suffered the devastating effects of Old World disease and were of little interest to northern Europeans as a source of labor. Unlike the Spanish and Portuguese to the south, these settlers were primarily interested in the land the Indians occupied, and they considered Native Americans to be a hindrance and a danger to their settlements, not an economic resource. As these northern European settlers pushed their frontiers into the interior, Native American populations were evicted and forced west.

As early as 1619, English colonists in Virginia were purchasing African slaves. The number of African slaves in the French, English, and Dutch West Indies and in English North America steadily increased during the 1600s and 1700s, paralleling the pattern in the Spanish and Portuguese colonies.

Although Native Americans were seldom enslaved in the northern European colonies, their labor was used indirectly. Unlike the Spanish and Portuguese, the French, English, and Dutch quickly established trading networks in the interior regions, exchanging cloth, metal tools, guns, and other items of European manufacture for hides and furs. By the late 1700s most of the Native American societies in North America were in regular trade contact with these Europeans and dependent on this fur trade. By the end of the eighteenth century, virtually every Native American society had been affected by European expansion. Many had already become extinct. Others were under the direct

political and economic control of European colonial governments. Even those societies that had been able to retain their autonomy had seen their populations sharply reduced through disease or warfare and their lifestyles changed by the introduction of European material goods and technology. No "pristine" societies were left in the New World.

Sub-Saharan Africa. Portuguese explorers first made contact with sub-Saharan Africans in 1444 and 1445. Trade quickly followed, and Portuguese explorer-traders steadily expanded farther south down the west coast of Africa. In the 1470s they reached the Gold Coast and found the area so rich in gold that in 1482 they erected a fort to protect their trading interests. This fortification was the first of a series of coastal forts that the Portuguese established to exclude other European powers from the region. By 1488, Portuguese explorers had reached the Cape of Good Hope, the southern extremity of the African continent. Between 1497 and 1499, Vasco da Gama successfully sailed to India and back by way of the Cape. By the end of the fifteenth century, the Portuguese had established the basis for a trading empire that stretched along the coast of Africa and all the way to Asia. The problem confronting the Portuguese was strengthening and maintaining their hold against European rivals. Trading ports were created along the African coast not only to acquire gold and ivory but also to serve as way stations for ships bound to and from Asia.

In 1482 the Portuguese discovered one of the largest states in Africa, the Kongo kingdom, near the mouth of the Congo. The Portuguese developed friendly relations with the Kongo, and in 1490 missionaries and various artisans were sent there. The missionaries soon converted the king and many of the people, and the capital of the kingdom was rebuilt on a European model and renamed Sao Salvador. Many younger Kongo went voluntarily to Portugal for formal education.

Although gold and ivory were the primary trade items, early Portuguese traders dealt in other commodities as well: slaves, sea lion oil, hides, cotton cloth, and beeswax. Slaves eventually emerged as the most valuable trade item of the African coast, and this factor led other European countries to challenge Portuguese control.

Slavery and the slave trade existed in portions of Europe before European expansion. On the Iberian Peninsula in Spain and Portugal, slavery knew no racial or religious boundaries: slaves could be black or white, Christian, Jewish, or Muslim. However, the number of slaves in Europe was limited. During the early 1500s, the market for African slaves in the New World grew rapidly.

The magnitude of the African slave trade cannot be determined with any exactness. We know that the slave trade grew steadily during the sixteenth and seventeenth centuries, reached its zenith during the last decades of the eighteenth century, and ended about 1870. Estimates of the number of African slaves sent to the Americas range from about 10 million to about 50 million, but the actual number was probably closer to 10 million. Likewise, estimates of the number of slaves taken to the Americas during particular centuries vary. Estimates for the sixteenth century range from 250,000 to 900,000; for the seventeenth century from 1,341,000 to 2,750,000; and for the eighteenth and nineteenth centuries from 6 million to 11 million.

The Portuguese became the first major traders of African slaves in the Americas. In the earliest period of the trade, slaves brought to America had already been slaves in Africa. However, as the demand for slaves increased, the Portuguese turned to raiding to acquire them. As early as 1575, Portuguese mercenaries and African "allies" began systematically to stage slave raids throughout much of central Africa.

In the late 1500s, the English and French began competing for a share of the African slave trade and marketing slaves in the Spanish colonies. During the early 1600s, with the establishment of French, English, and Dutch colonies in the West Indies, even more traders attempted to tap this lucrative trade. French, English, Dutch, Swedes, and Danes obtained slaves along the west coast of Africa. For the most part, these new traders concentrated on West Africa, where they established their own fortified trading stations and drove the Portuguese out of many posts. The French, English, and Dutch were not just challenging the Portuguese in Africa; they were also competing for the Asian trade. To reach Asia, they also had to circumnavigate Africa, and they needed ports. In 1652, the Dutch East India Company established a colony of Dutch farmers at the Cape of Good Hope to supply their ships.

By the late 1700s, the French, English, Dutch, Portuguese, and Spanish controlled ports scattered along the western coast and much of the eastern coast of Africa. Most of these posts were manned by only a handful of Europeans. Actual European settlements were few and small; the main settlements were the Portuguese colonies in Angola and Mozambique, and the Dutch colony at the Cape. Few Europeans had ever penetrated the interior, and little was known of the inland peoples of Africa. Yet at the same time, the European presence in Africa had produced far-reaching effects on the lives of all Africans through the slave trade and through the introduction of New World food crops.

Slaves were acquired through raiding and warfare, usually in exchange for guns supplied by the Europeans. In Africa, the gun trade and the slave trade were inextricably linked. By the early eighteenth century, about 180,000 guns were being traded annually, and by the end of the century that figure had climbed to between 300,000 and 400,000.

The slave-for-gun trade shifted trade networks and disrupted the existing balance of power among African societies. Some groups, primarily coastal peoples in contact with Europeans, faced the choice of becoming slave raiders and acquiring guns or falling victim to those who opted for raiding. As slave-related warfare escalated, new states sprang up, and there was a concurrent decline in many older states. In West Africa, there was a decline in the power and influence of the old states of Sudan. The Songhai Empire disintegrated, and Kanem-Bornu weakened considerably. At the same time, along the coast of West Africa, many small kingdoms and city-states—such as Oyo, Aboney, Ashanti, and Benin—were undergoing rapid expansion traced to the slave traffic. In west-central Africa the Kongo kingdom refused to be involved in the slave trade and disintegrated because the Portuguese supported and encouraged the development of slave-raiding states. Lunda was the largest and most important of these new states.

At the same time that Africa was undergoing this dramatic escalation in warfare, New World crops brought to the continent by Europeans dramatically changed African farming. During the early 1500s, the Portuguese introduced corn, manioc, sweet potatoes, pineapples, peanuts, papayas, and some lesser crops. The introduction of these new crops, particularly corn and manioc, greatly increased the productivity of farming in Africa. In the savannas and grasslands, corn produced higher yields than native cereal crops, and in the tropical forest regions, manioc was superior to existing starchy crops. In portions of West Africa, central Angola, and the northern and southern extremes of the Congo basin, as well as in portions of eastern Africa, corn became the dominant staple in the diet. Some researchers have suggested that the introduction of corn resulted in a population explosion that minimized the demographic impact of the slave trade.

Thus the Europeans' quest for slaves caused an escalation in warfare that resulted in major losses in population and significant restructuring of African political power. However, the Europeans also introduced new crops that increased and expanded African farming. Although we cannot describe exactly what happened, we can say with certainty that the population of Africa underwent major changes. Basil Davidson (1969, 235) provides an excellent summary of the situation in Africa at the end of the eighteenth century: "By 1800 or soon after there were few regions where many polities, large or small, old or new, had not clearly felt and reacted to strong pressures of transition. Widely varying in form and power though it certainly was, the impact of change had been constantly and pervasively at work."

Europeans in Asia. The Portuguese were the first Europeans to reach Asia by sea. In 1498, Vasco da Gama landed on the coast of India. The Europeans soon learned that Asia offered a situation quite different from what confronted them in the Americas and Africa. The population of Asia far surpassed that of Europe, and Asia was divided into numerous highly developed and militarily powerful states. In economic terms Asia was a self-sufficient region with only limited interest in outside trade. Although Asia offered such desirable goods as silk, cotton textiles, spices, coffee, tea, porcelain, and so forth for trade, the Europeans had little to offer in exchange other than gold and silver bullion. The Europeans had only one major advantage: in naval warfare, European technology was superior to that of Asia.

Da Gama encountered difficulty trading Portuguese goods in India, but he managed to trade his cargo and returned home. From the outset, the Portuguese realized that the only significant role they could play in the Asian trade was as middlemen in the inter-Asian trade, particularly between the Far East (China) and India. During the early and mid-1500s they established a series of fortified trading ports from India to China. Asian goods flowed through these ports to Europe in exchange for silver and gold coming from the Americas. This trade was extremely limited; during the 1500s, the trade between Europe and Asia averaged only 10 ships annually. Of greater economic importance was the fact that an ever-increasing percentage

▶ The introduction of New World crops greatly changed the lives of many of Africa's farming peoples.

of the lucrative trade between Asian peoples themselves was being carried by Portuguese merchant ships.

The same treaty that gave Portugal a portion of the Americas (Brazil) gave Spain a portion of Asia (the Philippines). In 1564 the Spanish founded Manila (Philippines). Unlike the Portuguese trade that flowed westward around Africa, Spanish ships sailed between Manila and Acapulco, Mexico. From Acapulco goods were transported over land to Vera Cruz, and from there shipped to Spain.

It was not until after 1600 that other European powers began to compete for the trade with Asia. The earliest of these new competitors were the Dutch, who in 1602 organized the Dutch East India Company. By the mid-1600s the Dutch had established bases in the East Indies (modern-day Indonesia) and Ceylon (modern-day Sri Lanka). With fewer ships and less capital, the English were at a disadvantage relative to the Dutch during the first half of the seventeenth century. Early English attempts to establish trading bases in Asia failed. Their first success came in India (Madras) in 1639. By 1665 they had Bombay, and in 1691, Calcutta.

While Western European maritime powers were active on the southern and eastern coasts of Asia, Russia was expanding by land across northern Asia. Ivan the Terrible fused the Russians into a single centralized state during the 1550s, which allowed them to challenge the powerful Tartar groups to the east. Russian frontier people, the Cossacks, were able to sweep eastward quickly and conquer the small nomadic tribal groups of Siberia. By 1637 the Russians had reached the Pacific Coast of Asia and by the 1690s were trading with China.

On the whole, the initial European influence on Asian society was not significant. European territorial holdings and populations under their direct control were small, usually little more than port cities. Europeans had little effect on Asian economic life; they were little more than a small, parasitic group attached to an Asian economic system. The most significant influence on the Asian economy during this period was the introduction of New World crops, the most important of which were corn and sweet potatoes.

The World and the Industrial Revolution

The Industrial Revolution began during the waning decades of the eighteenth century with the production of machine-woven cotton textiles in England. By the early nineteenth century, industrialization included steel production and was spreading to other European countries and the former English colonies in North America, now the United States. The Industrial Revolution dramatically changed the relationship between European peoples and the other peoples of the world. The technological advances that were associated with industrialization rapidly elevated European peoples to a position of military, political, and economic dominance in the world.

As a result, European peoples redrew the political map and restructured the world economy to meet the needs of their new industrial economy. This new European economic system required overseas sources of raw materials, as well as markets for finished goods. Technological advancements resulted in the construction of larger and faster ships, which meant that maritime commerce was no longer limited to high-cost luxury goods. The development of railroads opened the interiors of the continents by lowering the cost of transporting goods to the coastal ports.

During the sixteenth, seventeenth, and eighteenth centuries, global trade and cultural exchange had developed. The nineteenth century saw the beginning of a global economy based on regional economic specialization and the production of commodities for export. As in the earlier period, the effects of this change varied from one portion of the world to another.

The Americas. The Americas were the first region to experience this changed relationship because the Americas were more closely tied politically and economically to Europe. Just as the Industrial Revolution was beginning in Europe, a political revolution was starting in the Americas. From the English-speaking colonies this revolution spread to the Spanish-speaking portions of the Americas. By the third decade of the nineteenth century, most areas of mainland America were independent of European political domination. These independence movements did not change the status of Native Americans because the new countries were dominated by Euro-Americans, or, in the case of Haiti, African Americans.

Although these new countries had achieved political independence, they maintained strong economic ties to Europe and quickly became the major sources of raw materials as well as markets for industrializing Europe. The West Indies and the United States supplied cotton for the textile mills of England, and the Americas—both the English- and the Spanish-speaking countries—served as the earliest major market for finished cotton textiles. The growing European need for raw materials stimulated economic development and territorial expansion of Euro-American and African American settlements throughout the Americas.

With the initial emphasis of the Industrial Revolution on the production of plantation crops, such as cotton and sugar, the African slave trade escalated to unprecedented proportions. Of the estimated 10 million-plus African slaves brought to the Americas, the vast majority came between 1750 and 1850. As industrial centers developed in the northeastern United States and as mining, grain farming, and ranching expanded throughout the Americas during the nineteenth century, the need for slave labor declined. In 1833 slavery was abolished in the British West Indies, and by the 1880s slavery had been abolished throughout the Americas. As the importation of African slaves declined, the migration of Europeans to the Americas increased. In 1835 there were about 18.6 million individuals of European ancestry in the Americas, compared with 9.8 million people of African ancestry. By 1935 the population of Euro-Americans had jumped to 172 million, whereas the number of African Americans had risen to only 36.5 million.

In 1775 the area of Euro-American and African American settlement in North America was, for the most part, limited to the region east of the Appalachian Mountains. Within a century, however, the territorial limits of these settlements had been pushed across the continent to the Pacific Ocean. During the period of expansion, Native American populations had been quickly defeated militarily and confined to small reservations. A similar pattern of territorial expansion occurred in South America. The grasslands of Argentina initially attracted few European settlers. In 1880 the territorial limits of Euro-American settlements were about the same as they had been in 1590. In the late 1800s, however, Euro-American ranchers swept through the pampas and Patagonia, virtually eliminating the Indian population. By the early 1900s, autonomous or semiautonomous Native American societies were found only in the Amazon basin and in a few scattered and isolated pockets in other portions of the Americas.

Sub-Saharan Africa. The initial impact of European industrialization on Africa was an intensification of the slave trade. During the mid-nineteenth century, as the slave trade declined, European economic interest in Africa changed. Africa had potential as both a supplier of raw materials for industrial Europe and a market for finished goods. This economic potential could not be realized under existing conditions because the slave trade and resulting warfare had destroyed the political stability of the entire region. If the economic potential of Africa was to be realized, political stability had to be reestablished, transportation systems developed, and the economies restructured to meet European needs. These goals were accomplished through direct military and political intervention by European countries, primarily England, France, Germany, Belgium, and Portugal, who proceeded unilaterally to divide up the peoples and resources of Africa. As late as 1879, European powers claimed only small portions of Africa. The Portuguese had the coastal areas of Angola, Mozambique, and Guinea. The British had Cape Colony, Lagos, Gold Coast, Sierra Leone, and Gambia. The French had only Gabon, Senegal, and a few coastal ports. Twenty years later, virtually all of sub-Saharan Africa, with the exception of Liberia and Ethiopia, was under direct European rule.

With Africa divided, the European countries concentrated on bringing the peoples of their new territories under political control. Colonial administrations supported by European soldiers and native troops soon established their authority. With some exceptions, the imposition of colonial control was accomplished with relatively little bloodshed.

As colonial authority was established, the usual policy was to institute a tax system. Taxation of native populations served a dual purpose. The revenues generated were frequently sufficient to cover the cost of the colonial administration and troops. In addition, native populations were forced either to produce marketable exports or to work for European-owned plantations or mines to raise the money for taxes. Thus, taxation forced Africans into the European economic network.

Although exploitation of native populations characterized all the European colonies in Africa, it reached its height in the Congo basin. In 1885, King Leopold of Belgium claimed the Congo as "Crown lands" and organized it as the Congo Free State. He then sold concessions to companies, which received sole rights to all land and labor within given tracts. These companies were able to ruthlessly exploit the resources and native populations within their concessions. Africans were forcibly conscripted to work on the plantations and in the mines under armed guards. The labor conditions in the Congo were some of the most brutal and exploitative in world history. Any resistance was crushed. Murder and mutilation were common. Between 1885 and 1908, when protests from other European powers caused the Belgian government to assume control, as many as 8 million Africans were killed, or about half the total population of Congo.

By the early part of the twentieth century, the authority of Europeans had been established throughout Africa. The economy of the region was being developed and integrated into the European system. Gold, silver, copper, diamonds, palm oil, rubber, cacao, and other raw materials were flowing back to Europe, while Africa became an expanding market for European manufactured goods. Few Europeans immigrated to Africa, and in most regions, the presence of Europeans was limited to a handful of government administrators, soldiers, missionaries, and entrepreneurs.

Asia. The basic pattern of European political and economic expansion in Asia was similar to that in Africa. However, the magnitude of the population and the presence of an already highly developed economic system tempered much of the European impact. The Industrial Revolution had resulted in major advances in European military technology, which shifted the balance of power in favor of the Europeans. For the first time they could successfully challenge even the largest and most powerful Asian states. This change became evident during the mid-1800s. China had successfully resisted making trade concessions to European powers. In the Opium War (1839–1842) with England, and in a second war with England and France between 1856 and 1858, China saw its navy and army badly defeated and was forced to make humiliating land and trading concessions. During the late 1700s and early 1800s, the British East India Company steadily expanded its territorial control in India through manipulation of internal political rivalries and limited localized wars. The crushing of the Sepoy Mutiny (1857–1858) ended any question about English political dominance of India.

By the end of the nineteenth century, most of Asia had been brought under the control of European colonial governments. England had India, Burma, Malaya, Sarawak, Hong Kong, and Ceylon. The French held Indochina, and the Dutch had extended their control over the Dutch East Indies. Although still politically independent, China, Nepal, Afghanistan, Thailand, Persia (Iran), and most of the Middle Eastern countries were so strongly dominated by various European powers that some historians have called them *semicolonial regions*. Japan stood alone as the only Asian state that truly retained its autonomy.

During the late nineteenth century, as European political control spread over Asia, the economy of the area was steadily modified by various means to meet the needs of industrial Europe. Although Europeans owned and operated plantations, mines, and various industries in some areas, the principal instruments for changing the existing economies were taxes and duties. Taxation encouraged the production of cash crops for export, whereas import and export duties encouraged the production of some goods and commodities and discouraged the production of others. Native industries that would directly compete with European goods were discouraged.

The degree to which the local economy was changed differed greatly from region to region. In some regions there were large-scale developments for the production of critical cash crops, and massive relocations of populations to supply labor often were associated with these developments. Such changes were most characteristic of, but not limited to, territories within the British empire.

Ceylon became a tea-producing colony, whereas Malaya focused on rubber, Burma on rice, and Bengal (India) on jute (hemp for rope). To increase production, additional labor was frequently needed. Indians and Chinese were recruited to work on the rubber plantations in Malaya. Tamil speakers from southern India provided the labor on the tea plantations of Ceylon. Rubber, tea, and hemp flowed to Europe, and Indian immigrants in Burma increased rice production ninefold, a surplus that was in turn shipped to India, Malaya, Ceylon, and other plantation regions within the empire to feed the workers.

These changes in the political and economic life of Asia were accomplished despite the relatively small number of Europeans in Asia. For example, in India during the mid-1920s, Europeans numbered only about 200,000 administrators, soldiers, and civilians, as opposed to a native population of about 320 million—a ratio of 1:1,500.

Oceania. During the latter half of the eighteenth century, French, Russian, and English naval expeditions explored the Pacific, charting and describing the major islands and island groups. These men were soon followed by merchants, colonists, and whalers. In one way, the history of Oceania during the nineteenth century parallels the history of the Americas during the first three centuries after European discovery. The total population of Melanesia, Micronesia, Polynesia, and Australia was estimated at several million at the time of contact. Disease and warfare quickly reduced the population of much of Oceania during the nineteenth century.

In 1785 the English established a penal colony in Australia and laid the foundation for the Europeanization of portions of Oceania. The pattern of white settlement expansion in Australia and New Zealand during this period closely followed that of European settlement and occupation of the United States and Canada. Native populations declined because of disease and warfare, whereas European settlements expanded, occupying an ever-increasing portion of the land. Surviving native populations were eventually limited to small reserve areas. During the nineteenth century the population of native Australians declined from about 300,000 to only 60,000. In New Zealand the native Maori were only slightly more successful in resisting. Numbering only about 100,000 in 1800, by the 1840s the surviving 40,000 Maori were a minority population confined on small reserves.

Aside from Australia, Polynesia (including New Zealand) was the region most affected by Europeans. During the nineteenth century, the indigenous population of these islands declined from 1,100,000 to only 180,000. In

1779 the native population of Hawaii numbered between 300,000 and 400,000. By 1857, only 70,000 native Hawaiians remained. Missionary-entrepreneurs from the United States were able to secure lands for plantations, and as the native population declined, they began importing laborers from Asia to work the fields. This influx of Europeans and Asians reduced the native Hawaiians to a minority population before the end of the nineteenth century. There were major exceptions to these patterns. Although the native populations of Samoa and Tonga declined, there was no significant influx of Europeans, and the native populations of these islands eventually recovered.

The islands of Micronesia also suffered from a population drop during the nineteenth century, declining from about 200,000 to about 83,000. However, these small, scattered islands had little to attract large numbers of Europeans. For the most part, Europeans contented themselves with asserting their political dominance and claiming these islands as possessions. Micronesians were mostly left on their own.

The pattern of contact differed significantly from island to island in Melanesia. Although the Germans, English, and Dutch politically divided New Guinea and established plantations along the coast, the indigenous population of the island was too vast to be displaced by Europeans. The same was not true in Fiji and New Caledonia. The native population of Fiji decreased from 300,000 to 85,000, and New Caledonia's native population declined from 100,000 to a low of 27,000. In Fiji, English entrepreneurs secured land for sugar plantations and began importing laborers from India, until by the twentieth century the Indians constituted a majority of the population.

In the 400 years following 1492, the world was dramatically changed. By 1900 European political domination was complete and the global trade network well established. Global trade allowed for the exchange of technologies, including domesticated plants and animals, between the various peoples of the world. It also exposed the world's peoples to different ideas, beliefs, and cultural practices. However, except for the peoples of the Americas and Oceania, the changes did not erode the basic economic, cultural, and social autonomy of most of the world's peoples. Although many societies became extinct, many new societies had come into existence. New technologies, ideas, beliefs, and practices had, for the most part, been adapted and integrated into preexisting economies and cultures. Global trade had dramatically changed the lives of most of the world's peoples, but it had not signficantly lessened social and cultural diversity. There had been migrations of peoples, both voluntary and forced, but direct contact between peoples was minimal in comparison with contemporary standards.

The Emergence of the Global Economy

Over the past 50 years the process of globalization has entered a new and different phase. A global economy has started to evolve. In its essence the global economy is simple: the creation of a global market and the integration of peoples and communities into this market. Global trade involved the exchange of goods between regional markets. In the global economy all labor, goods, and services are bought and sold on the global market.

We can readily see some effects of the global economy. The price we pay for a sack of flour in Kansas or a gallon of gasoline in Texas is already determined in large part by the world price for wheat and oil. Similarly the price we pay for a Ford is no longer solely influenced by competition from General Motors, but by overseas auto manufacturers as well. Foreign imports not only place American companies in competition with foreign companies but also put American workers in direct competition with their foreign counterparts. American farmers, oil producers, businesspeople, and workers are now finding that they have to compete on a global market for the prices they can charge for their goods, services, and labor. This has both good and bad points. It has resulted in cheaper prices in the United States for many manufactured goods and services. However, it has also meant the loss of jobs as companies, in order to compete, have closed their domestic manufacturing plants and offices, laid off their relatively high-paid American workers, and outsourced their jobs overseas. As a result many American companies are no longer producing the products or services they market in the United States.

Many scholars argue that the global economy differs qualitatively from global trade in that implicit in the global economy is an underlying and unifying ideology, capitalism, and a single objective, the production of wealth. Capitalism is an ideology based on Western (European) cultural beliefs and values. To survive, let alone prosper, in the new emerging global economy, a people has to adopt Western cultural ideas. Thus the global economy is not merely resulting in the restructuring of the world economic system, it is having far-ranging cultural and social consequences for the peoples of the world as well. In earlier chapters we highlighted in boxes many of the potential cultural implications of the global economy. In the last part of this chapter we will discuss the development of the global economy and some of the associated social and economic problems.

The world today, at the beginning of the twenty-first century, is a far different place from what it was when your grandparents were young. The past 50 years have seen vast changes in the lives of virtually all of the peoples of the world. The Second World War was a major watershed in human history. As we have seen, before World War II the world economic system was dominated by European-controlled colonial empires. The British, French, and Soviet (or Russian) empires were the largest. However, the Netherlands, Belgium, Spain, Portugal, and Italy also had overseas possessions. Even the United States had the Philippines, Guam, Samoa, and Puerto Rico. Global trade existed, but there was no integrated global economy. These empires had been created for only one reason: the economic enrichment of the "home country" or colonial power. The colonial powers were primarily interested in politically controlling the peoples of their colonies while economically exploiting their resources. Colonies were the economic monopolies of the home country. Thus India, South Africa, Kenya, and the other British colonies served as monopolized sources of raw materials for English factories, as well as protected markets for English manufactured goods. Economic development within the English colonies was limited to increasing the production of raw materials needed by English factories and the elimination of goods produced locally, which would compete with goods made in England. Trade between the colonial possessions of the empire and other countries was highly controlled and regulated from London. A similar relationship existed between the home country and the colonies of other colonial powers.

Even if political barriers had not inhibited trade, there were still the problems of geography and distance. International telephone service was extremely limited and most communications had to be sent by mail. International air travel was in its infancy. The vast majority of international travelers went by train or ship. As for moving raw materials and manufactured goods, compared to today, shipping was slow, expensive, and frequently difficult. Thus markets were protected by not only trade barriers, but also geography. As a result, even within the colonial empires, regions were usually self-sufficient in their basic economic needs. The people raised the food they ate, built and furnished the houses they lived in from locally produced goods, and tailored the clothes they wore from locally produced materials. Imports were usually limited to goods or products that could not be made or found locally, while exports usually consisted of goods or products not needed for local use or consumption. The development of the global economy thus required both changes in political structures as well as new technological innovation.

Three major changes have occurred since the end of World War II that have profoundly altered the course of human history and made the developing global economy possible. The most basic of these changes was the disintegration of the colonial empires and the elimination of many of the political barriers to trade. Although the precise number varies depending on how one defines an "independent" or "autonomous" country, at the beginning of World War II there were at best only about 60 politically independent countries in the world. Following the war the colonial empires began to disintegrate. Independence movements had already started in many colonial areas prior to the war, and the war had devastated the economies of many of the colonial powers such as England, France, and the Netherlands. Needing to rebuild their home economies, they lacked the resources to suppress the independence movements in their colonies.

The war also resulted in the United States emerging as the strongest economic and military power in the world. After the war the United States began pressuring its European allies to grant independence to their colonies. There were two reasons behind the actions of the United States. First, the United States was ideologically opposed to colonialism, granting independence to the Philippines immediately following the war. Second, U.S. companies wanted direct access to the resources and markets of colonial Africa and Asia. As a result, between 1946 and 1980, 88 new countries were carved out of the old colonial empires and given political independence. The collapse of the Soviet Union and Yugoslavia during the 1990s resulted in the creation of 18 additional countries. Today there are about 200 independent countries, more than three times the number that existed prior to World War II.

With the end of colonialism, the peoples of Africa and Asia had the freedom to manage their own economic affairs. These "new" countries could now sell their raw materials and products on the global market and purchase imported goods from any country they wished. Even more importantly, these former colonies could now establish local industries to compete with those of the industrialized powers of western Europe and North America.

The second critical change was in the development of new technologies, associated with production, transportation, and communications. Today we can extract more raw materials and produce more manufactured goods and food using only a fraction of the physical labor required prior to World War II. Technology has greatly improved labor efficiency, allowing people to produce a greater surplus of goods. At the same time the cost of shipping raw materials, food, and manufactured goods, as well as the time in transit, has been dramatically reduced.

▶ Container shipping has greatly lowered the cost of shipping of manufactured goods and has played a key role in the development of the global economy over the past 30 years.

© Chuck Place Photography

Oceangoing cargo ships are still the primary means of international transport. However, ships and shipping have changed dramatically. During World War II the standard military supply ship built by the U.S. government was 440 feet long and capable of carrying 9,000 tons of cargo. In contrast, modern cargo ships are commonly 700 feet long and carry about 25,000 tons of cargo. Even larger are the supertankers, which may be as long as 1,200 feet and can carry 500,000 tons of oil.

The important difference is not just the relative size of the ships but also the speed with which ships can be loaded and unloaded. Fifty years ago cargo was loaded and unloaded piecemeal. Starting in the late 1950s some shippers began loading cargo in 20- and 40-foot boxes, or containers. The containers were loaded at the factory, sent via truck or train to the port, and loaded directly onto the ship by cranes. This greatly increased the speed of loading and unloading. By the late 1960s and early 1970s container shipping became the norm and new cargo ships were being designed and constructed to carry standardized containers. A ship that took 10 days to load or unload piecemeal can now be loaded or unloaded in less than a day. Container shipping not only dramatically increased the speed with which goods could be shipped, it also drastically reduced labor costs. Container ships require smaller crews and many fewer dockworkers. The development of container shipping has been one of the key elements in the growth of international trade and thus the global economy.

Just as container shipping has reduced the time and cost of moving goods, airline travel has greatly reduced the time and cost of moving people. Business trips are a critical aspect of international trade. Trips that took days, weeks, and even months in the 1940s and 1950s have been reduced to hours and days.

The past 20 years have been a time of rapid change in information and communications technology. Communications satellites, personal computers, cell phones, and other new technologies have revolutionized our communications systems and our abilities to store, access, and analyze information. Today letters, messages, photos, music, videos, and even whole databases can be sent or accessed, while products can be bought or sold and money transferred 24 hours a day, instantaneously, to or from any part of the world via the Internet. In terms of communication it does not make any difference if the other company or branch of the company is on the other side of town or the other side of the world. In fact, small companies advertise their merchandise on Web pages and sell to customers throughout the world via e-mail. Today one can literally create and operate a global business from a home office. Effective communication is a key element in business, and without the Internet, an integrated global economy could not exist. Technological advancement in transportation and communications has not merely made the world smaller; for many purposes it has made geography irrelevant.

A third factor has been the emergence of international finance. Prior to World War II the international flow of

During the Middle Ages in Europe, the canon courts of the Catholic Church declared usury, or charging interest on loans, to be un-Christian. Thus Christians were prohibited from charging interest, and banking in medieval Europe was in the hands of Jews. During the late Middle Ages, Italian Catholics began founding banking houses and by clever semantics were able to circumvent the church laws against usury. An individual would be loaned money, interest free, for an unrealistically short period. When the loan was not repaid within this stated time, which it seldom was, the bankers charged "damages."

The Islamic religion also prohibits usury. However, Islam differs in a number of significant ways from Christianity. The Koran is not merely a book of religious teachings but also a codified legal system called the *sharia*. Courts in traditional Islamic countries use the Koran as the basis for legal rulings, functioning as what are sometimes called *Islamic courts*.

The law courts in much of the Arab world—Saudi Arabia, Kuwait, Bahrain, and the United Arab Emirates—are Islamic courts. Thirty years ago, this fact had little international significance. Relatively poor, these countries had little need for financial transactions and banking institutions. With the discovery of oil and the rapid development of this region starting in the 1960s, a need for such institutions quickly developed. A number of European and American banking houses, such as Citibank and Chase Manhattan, opened Middle Eastern branches. Not only did they manage the vast flow of dollars changing hands through the sale of oil and the purchase of imports, but they also began loaning money to local Arab entrepreneurs who organized companies to profit from this economic boom.

Like the medieval Italian bankers, they developed semantic ways of circumventing the Islamic prohibition against usury.

The word *interest* was never used in loaning money. Instead, these banks charged Islamic borrowers "administrative fees" or "loan initiation discounts." By 1986 it was estimated that the various world banks had between $8 and $9 billion in loans to Saudi Arabian companies alone. This system worked well as long as oil income kept rising and all parties made handsome profits. In the 1980s the price of oil began to decline, and in early 1986 the price collapsed, falling from $28 a barrel to (at one point) less than $10 a barrel.

As their income from oil plunged, governments began to slow payments to local contractors and suppliers. Arab companies with a cash flow problem quickly fell behind on loan payments to banks. Many Arab businessmen suddenly rediscovered their religion. A flood of Arab companies and individuals quickly took the banks to court, charging them with usury. These courts correctly found the banks guilty of usury under Islamic law.

In the summer of 1986, a number of international banks cut back on their Middle Eastern operations. Citibank reduced its offices in Bahrain and the United Arab Emirates; Chase Manhattan closed its Jordanian branch. International and Middle Eastern bankers quickly proved themselves to be as adaptive as the medieval Italians. There was a rapid growth of "Islamic banks." Initially most Islamic banks were local, some were branches of large international banks, while others were associated with international banking houses. By scrupulously avoiding charging *riba,* or interest, and operating as *modarebs,* or "money managers," Islamic banks were able to provide profits for their investors while meeting the banking needs of the region. The recovery of the oil industry in the late 1980s stimulated the growth of Islamic banks. By 2000 there were over 250 Islamic banks and financial institutions worldwide, managing over $200 billion in funds.

capital was extremely limited. Foreign investment was highly risky, particularly in underdeveloped poorer countries. Whether the loan was to a foreign government or a foreign company, there was always the question of repayment. As long as the empires existed, banks and companies would make investments in colonial possessions, knowing that they would have legal protection. However, with the end of colonialism and the emergence of new countries the problem became greater. Most of the peoples in the world today live in underdeveloped countries. The economic growth of these countries requires the development of their infrastructures: communications systems, transportation systems, and even education systems to train workers in skills. The development of infrastructure requires capital, which many of these countries do

not have. Similarly, companies in these underdeveloped countries find it difficult to secure sufficent local investment capital for their needs.

In 1945 the World Bank and the International Monetary Fund (IMF) were created to help war-ravaged Europe and Japan reestablish their industrial base. These two institutions have played a pivotal role in the creation of the global economy. The World Bank has been the major conduit for economic development loans to underdeveloped nations. The role of the World Bank is now supplemented by numerous European, American, and Japanese banking houses that have become international financiers.

Loans provided to these capital-poor countries have allowed them to more quickly adopt high-cost technology and increase their economic productivity. With these funds, underdeveloped countries have constructed irrigation systems, expanded transportation and communication systems, expanded port facilities, and developed local industries. In the past decade alone these loans have amounted to hundreds of billions of dollars. An unappreciated consequence of these loans is the stimulation of exports of developed countries, because most of these funds are used to purchase needed technology and equipment from the United States, Europe, and Japan. At the same time most of the economic development projects funded by these loans have focused on increasing the production of goods and raw materials needed by these industrialized countries, which in turn lowers the global market prices of these items.

In the global economy money flows both ways across international boundaries in search of greater profits. U.S. banks, companies, and individuals have more than $4 trillion invested in other countries. Conversely, foreign banks, companies, and individuals have similar amounts invested in the United States. Of the $3.5 trillion in U.S. government debt, 38 percent is owed to foreign individuals or banks, with the largest share owned by Japanese. Japanese banks in turn have made more than $290 billion in loans to other Asian countries.

Globalization: The Continuing Process

While the global economy is already dramatically affecting the lives of virtually everyone, it is still in the process of developing (see Figure 16.2). Some issues remain to be resolved and some new economic institutions are starting to evolve. The process of globalizing the world market is far from complete.

Although we have a global economy, we still lack free trade. Every one of the 200 or so countries in the world still has regulations concerning imports and exports, as well as its own labor laws, environmental laws, and other business regulations. In addition, almost every country still has its own currency, currency regulations, and laws concerning banking and other financial concerns. Regulation of the economy is one of the primary concerns of government. However, in a fully integrated and operative global economy there can be no local or national differences. The World Trade Organization is in the process of attempting to negotiate the elimination of all import and export laws or controls as well as any other laws that inhibit the free flow of goods or services between countries. The result will be free trade, a world in which companies and individuals may buy and sell any legal goods or services, at any price agreed upon, in any country in the world, with-

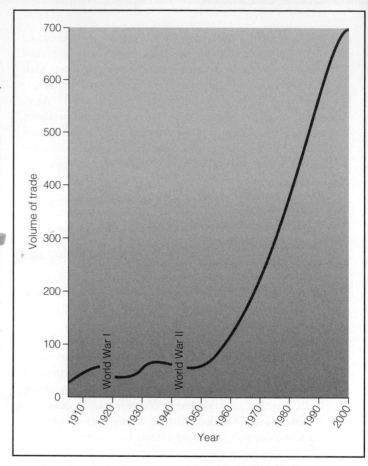

▲ **Figure 16.2** A Growth of World Trade: 1905–2000. Between 1990 and 1999 world trade grew at a rate of 6.5 percent per year.

out government regulation. In all disputes, the World Trade Organization, not the governments involved, would be the final judge. As we discussed in the Globalization box in Chapter 12, some scholars see the World Trade Organization evolving into a de facto world government.

The global economy also requires international control of currencies, banking, and other financial transactions. The International Monetary Fund is assuming the role as regulator of international monetary transactions. Most countries have their own currencies. Exchange rates for currencies are complex and volatile. In international financial transfers, varying exchange rates are an added expense. Recognizing that the use of different currencies makes integrating economies more difficult, most of the countries of the European Union changed to a single currency, the Euro, in January 2002. Some have suggested that a fully integrated global economy will require a single global monetary unit and the elimination of all national currencies.

Religion and Politics: Globalization and the Rise of "Fundamentalism"

When we speak of militant religious fundamentalism we invariably think of Islamic fundamentalism, and of Al-Qaeda and the attack of September 11, 2001. The so-called war on terrorism is a war against Islamic fundamentalists. Is Islamic fundamentalism the only source of religiously motivated "terrorism" in the world? What about Christian and Hindu terrorists? Have we forgotten that in the 1990s there were a series of attacks on abortion clinics in the United States, and doctors associated with abortion clinics were murdered in Florida and New York? The so-called Army of God, allegedly Eric Rudolph, in 1997–98, bombed the Atlanta Olympics, a gay and lesbian nightclub, and several abortion clinics. These, and numerous other acts of violence, were those of militant Christian fundamentalists. Even Timothy McVeigh, who bombed the Murrah Federal Building in Oklahoma City, though an agnostic, had links to extremist Christian groups. In India there have also been numerous similar acts of violence by militant Hindu extremists against Muslims and Christians. Hindu extremists have attacked mosques and churches throughout India and even destroyed the sixteenth-century mosque at Ayodhya. Hindu extremists have assaulted, and even killed, Indian Muslims and Christians. In 1999 Hindu extremists burned to death a Christian missionary and his two sons and in 2002 killed between 1,000 and 2,000 Muslims in Gujarat.

Historically in the United States there has always been a separation between religion and state. For 200 years the vast majority of Americans, including politicians and religious leaders, have strongly adhered to this principle. In a sermon given in 1965, Jerry Falwell summarized the position of most Christian church leaders in America when he said, "As far as the relationship of the church to the world, it can be expressed as . . . 'preach the word.' . . . Nowhere are we commissioned to reform the externals. We are not told to wage wars against bootleggers, liquor stores, gamblers, murderers, prostitutes, racketeers, prejudiced persons or institutions, or any other existing evil as such" (quoted in Harding 2000, 22). By 1976 he had repudiated this position, stating instead, "This idea of 'religion and politics don't mix' was invented by the devil to keep Christians from running their own country." In 1979 he organized the Moral Majority, a Christian political action group.

During the 1980s and 1990s Falwell and other like-minded religious leaders encouraged their followers to take an active role in politics, not just by voting for "Christian" candidates but by donating money, participating in their campaigns, and even running for political office themselves. Through radio and television talk shows, newsletters, and local churches, Christians were increasingly mobilized for political action. By the late 1990s an estimated 50 to 70 million Americans were associated with Christian political action groups; and the so-called Christian Right had emerged as the single most powerful political action group in the country.

Although modern India is predominantly a Hindu country, there is a large Muslim minority (about 120 million), as well as smaller populations of Sikhs, Buddhists, and Christians. The National Congress Party that evolved under Gandhi and led the fight for independence in 1948 was a secular nationalist movement that included Hindus and Muslims as well as members of other religious groups. In spite of attempts by leaders of the Congress Party to keep the country united, India was partitioned into India (predominantly Hindu) and

◄ Hindu fundamentalists in India have become increasingly intolerant of the Muslim minority in the country. Here Hindu militants gather in Ayodhya before destroying the Muslim mosque in the background.

© Reuters/Bettmann/Corbis

Pakistan (predominantly Muslim). In Chapter 17, the partitioning of India will be discussed in more detail.

The Congress Party, which assumed power over the newly independent and democratic India, emphasizes secularism in government. Following the assassination of Gandhi in early 1948 by a Hindu extremist opposed to the partitioning of India, Hindu nationalist parties were outlawed for over 20 years. In spite of this, many unofficial "parties" were formed, the largest being the Bharatiya Jan Sangh in 1951. In 1973 this party assumed the name Bharatiya Janata Party (the BJP) and together with numerous smaller nationalist parties became increasingly active. After 50 years of rule by the Congress Party, in 1998, the BJP under the leadership of Atal Behari Vajpayee was able to gain control of the government and become the Prime Minister. Although in the national elections of 2004 the BJP lost power to the Congress Party, the BJP and other Hindu nationalist parties remain a powerful political force in India.

Both in the United States and in India, religiously based political movements have grown rapidly in strength and influence over the past quarter century. To understand why, one has first to examine the political concerns they have raised.

Christian fundamentalists in the United States tend to view the country as heading in the direction of moral collapse. They see the primary causes of this moral crisis as being internal, the result of the government and the federal courts being controlled by overly permissive secular individuals that they usually label as "liberals." They oppose the Supreme Court's interpretation of free speech, which has allowed for the producing and marketing of sexually explicit magazines, movies, and television programs, as well as the Court's interpretation of the separation of church and state, which has removed prayer and religious activities from the public schools, while allowing evolution and sex education to be taught. At the same time, "liberal" politicians have enacted legislation supporting and encouraging women's rights, the feminist movement, and multiculturalism. The result has been increasing pornography, sexual promiscuity, homosexuality, gay marriage, and abortion, not to mention drug usage, crime, and the disintegration of the traditional family. The basic Christian American values are under attack. Christian fundamentalists feel that only by taking direct control of the political, judicial, and educational systems—by the election of Christian legislators, the appointment of Christian judges to the courts, and the election of Christian school board members—can American society be saved.

To the BJP and other Hindu nationalist groups, the ultimate source of the problems of India is the presence of what they term "Semitic monotheistic intolerance," the Western world. To them "the West" includes both Christians and Muslims. To understand the position of the Hindu nationalists, one first has to look at the history of India. Muslim armies first invaded India in the tenth century. Between then and 1948, the Hindu peoples of India were under the domination of first Muslims and later British Christians. Many Hindus converted to Islam. While only a relatively small number converted to Christianity, larger numbers of Hindus adopted Western cultural values and practices. This was particularly true of the educated elite, who cooperated with the British and, after independence in 1948, dominated Indian economic, social, and political life. They frequently spoke English at home; they dressed like the British, modeled much of their social behavior after the British, and even took up playing cricket. Some have said that Westernized Indians are more British than the British. This Westernized elite, through the Congress Party, dominated Indian politics from independence until 1998. The new India that they created was modeled after England. The governmental system, as well as the judicial and educational systems, was based on British models. Adopting a secular ideology, they attempted to accommodate religious and cultural differences within India, allowing, for example, a separate civil code for Muslims. They also outlawed discrimination based on caste, religion, or gender.

In 1998 BJP came to power advocating the policy of what they term *Hindutva*, or "Hinduness," by which they mean the restructuring of the country based on Hindu, not Western, ideology. Under the concept of *Hindutva* there are both general ideas and specific policies. Pakistanis, though Muslims, are really Indians and Pakistan should be part of India. After the BJP took power they tested the first Indian nuclear bomb. There should be no separate constitution for the disputed state of Kashmir, which is predominantly Muslim. Neither should there be a separate civil code for Indian Muslims.

Economic policies should focus on the development of India for the benefit of Indians, not Western corporations. The BJP also defines as one of its major concerns the corruption of Indian family life, with particular emphasis on women. To them the im-

Traditionally we have thought of corporations, like individuals, as having national identities. Ford, General Motors, and General Electric are "American" companies. These companies are incorporated in the United States, their stock is traded on the New York Stock Exchange, and their corporate headquarters are in the United States. However, companies such as these are increasingly becoming international, manufacturing and selling products throughout the world. Globalization is eroding the link between corporations and their countries of origin. This results in the emergence of what are now being termed transnational corporations. For

moral Western feminist movement is infecting India, undermining family life by propagating sexual promiscuity, lesbianism, and artificial insemination. Western consumerist culture is resulting in the exploitation of women in Indian society through the sale of pornographic materials. This is leading to a secularization of young people who no longer have any moral values. According to the BJP the family structure has already collapsed in Western society, and India has become infected. These corrupting Western influences have to be stopped. Some have even proposed that "forced" conversions by Datil caste ("untouchable") members to Islam, Christianity, and Buddhism be made illegal.

What is surprising is that the underlying ideas fueling the growth of Muslim, Christian, and Hindu fundamentalism are basically the same. All three groups see their societies as morally collapsing. All three cite the same basic concerns: pornography, sexual promiscuity, the changing role of women, immorality, and the erosion of the family. All three think that direct political action is necessary to protect and restore their traditional norms and values. The major difference between these groups is what they define as the source of these morally corrupting influences and how best to deal with them. To the Christian fundamentalists in the United States, the source is internal. While there have been isolated acts of terrorism, the vast majority of Christian fundamentalists feel that they can successfully work within the democratic political system to change the society. To the Hindus in India, the ultimate source of social corruption is external, the West, the Islamic and Christian world. However, there are individuals within India who are now Muslims and Christians, as well as many Hindus who have adopted Western cultural practices. As a result their struggle is primarily an internal one. Because of its religious mix, India is far more volatile and acts of religious terrorism are far more numerous than in the United States. Nonetheless the vast majority of Hindu fundamentalists feel that they can work within the democratic framework of India to uphold their cultural traditions. To Islamic fundamentalists, the West, by which they mean the United States and western Europe, is the source of the moral corruption and collapse of their societies. Scattered over numerous countries, they are politically controlled and dominated by undemocratic leaders, who are economically and militarily supported by Western governments and corporations. Lacking the democratic political options, armed revolution, in the form of terrorist acts, is the only recourse open to them to institute social change. Not surprisingly, terrorist acts are directed toward both their existing governments and those countries supporting them. Why these movements differ in their political actions is situational and understandable. The important question is, Why are their basic concerns and issues so similar?

In his recent book, *Runaway World,* Anthony Giddens (2000, 22) states, "The battleground of the twenty-first century will pit fundamentalism against cosmopolitan tolerance." By fundamentalists Giddens means those who are adherents of traditional (non-Western) cultural traditions, values, and practices. In contrast, cosmopolitan peoples are those who have embraced the cultural values and practices of globalization—in other words, people who have or have adopted a Western cultural tradition. Thus fundamentalism is a response to the rapid changes brought on by globalization—changes that the fundamentalists find disturbing and even dangerous. To Giddens (2000, 67) "Fundamentalism is beleaguered tradition. . . . Fundamentalism isn't about what people believe but, like tradition more generally, about why they believe it and how they justify it. It isn't confined to religion." Thus Giddens sees fundamentalism not as a true religious political movement but, rather, as a response to the social and cultural changes associated with globalization and which non-Western people view as synonymous with the West.

Critical Thinking Questions

1. Giddens's ideas seem to apply to what is occurring in the Islamic and Hindu worlds. Was he unaware of or did he simply overlook the growth of Christian fundamentalism in the United States? Or is the Christian Right qualitatively different from the others?

2. Are the fundamentalist political movements in the United States, India, and the Islamic world the products of social changes resulting from globalization? Is globalization resulting in profound cultural and social changes that are threatening traditional cultures in both the Western and non-Western world? Should Giddens have stated that the conflicts in the twenty-first century will pit cosmopolitan tolerance against traditional intolerance, and dropped the "non-Western"?

centuries, if not longer, some companies have produced goods for export and had overseas offices and operations. Thus the distinction between traditional national corporations and transnational corporations is not precise. A **transnational corporation** is one that has most of its employees, produces and sells most of its products or services, and generates most of its gross revenues outside the national boundaries of its "home" country.

Nokia, a Finnish company known primarily for its cellular phones, is an example of a transnational corporation. Just prior to the collapse of tech stocks in 2000,

Nokia had the highest capitalization value (the total value of its stock) of any company in Europe.

Originally a paper manufacturer, Nokia was founded in 1865. In 1967 Nokia merged with the Finnish Rubber Works and Finnish Cable Works, the latter producing telephone wire and cable. The new Nokia quickly focused on telecommunications, producing first radio telephones and later data modems. By the 1980s Nokia was becoming a major producer of computers, monitors, and TV sets. In 1987 Nokia produced the original handheld portable telephone. The 1990s was a period of rapid growth for the company as it maintained its position as the major producer of cellular phones in the world. Today Nokia markets products in more than 130 countries, has research and development projects and programs in 15 different countries (including the United States, Canada, Australia, Singapore, Japan, South Korea, Spain, Germany, and England), and produces components and assembled products in 10 different countries (United States, Mexico, Brazil, Malaysia, China, South Korea, Japan, Hungary, Germany, and England).

The production of components and assembled products shows the problem of determining the national origin of goods in the global economy. Nokia has six major suppliers: Philips Electronics, a Dutch company, produces their speakers in Austria and display screens in China; Sanyo Electric, a Japanese company, produces their barrier (a component of a phone) in Mexico; Hitachi makes its power amplification modules in Japan; Infineon Technologies makes its semiconductor chips in Germany; and R.F. Micro Devices and Texas Instruments produce their radio frequency integrated circuits and digital signal processors in the United States. Today most Nokia products are designed by non-Finnish engineers and technicians, manufactured and assembled in countries other than Finland, and sold in 130 countries in the world, in order to produce wealth and profits shared by investors from all parts of the world. Its corporate headquarters may still be located in Finland and its major management decisions are still made in Finland, but is Nokia still a Finnish company? or is it a global company with its main offices in Helsinki?

As the global economy continues to evolve all major corporations, in order to economically compete, will have to become transnational corporations. The result will be a change in the relationship between a country and "its" corporations. It used to be said that "what is good for General Motors is good for America." There was truth in this saying in that the economic health of one could not be separated from that of the other. With transnational corporations the same cannot be said. What is economically good for a transnational corporation may adversely affect the economy of its "home" country. We are already experiencing some of this as American companies close their domestic plants and offices and shift their production or outsource the work to Mexico, India, China, or some other country with lower labor costs.

Population Growth and Inequalities in the Global Economy

Probably the least controversial aspect of globalization has been the improvement in health of the world's peoples. At the end of World War II the World Health Organization (WHO) was created as part of the United Nations to address global health concerns. Working with private and government health organizations and agencies, WHO defined issues and attempted to direct resources to particular health problems. Of particular concern were infant mortality rates in most of the underdeveloped countries of the world. By improving sanitation systems, nutritional standards, and health care delivery systems in underdeveloped countries, WHO has helped to drastically lower infant mortality rates.

In addition, WHO has developed programs for the eradication of epidemic diseases. In 1946 malaria was a major health concern throughout most of the Americas, Africa, Asia, and the Pacific. In India alone it was estimated that 800,000 people a year died from the disease, while globally several million people died annually. Malaria is an insect-borne disease spread from one infected human to another by anopheles mosquitoes. Lacking vaccines, the only way to eliminate the disease was to destroy the mosquito populations that spread it. Using DDT, in 1948 WHO launched a program to eliminate malaria. By the 1960s widespread use of DDT had dramatically reduced the death rate from malaria. In the mid-1960s, India reported no deaths from the disease. At one point it was thought that malaria might be eliminated altogether. However, the discovery that DDT had numerous environmentally destructive side effects led to limitations on its use as a pesticide. This, together with the evolution of a new DDT-resistant anopheles mosquito, ended the hope of eliminating malaria. Even though the malaria program was not totally successful, tens of millions of lives were saved.

Smallpox has been a major health problem since ancient times. This virus, spread by human hosts, either through the air or by touch, can kill up to 40 percent of an infected population. In the 1960s there were on average between 10 and 15 million cases a year, and 2 million deaths from smallpox. In 1967 WHO launched a vaccination campaign designed to eliminate smallpox and within 10 years had eliminated the virus. In 1980, after 3 years during which no new cases were reported from anywhere in the world, WHO was able to announce that the smallpox virus had been eliminated.

In addition to the malaria and smallpox programs, WHO continues to work to improve health conditions by assisting in the development of health care delivery systems throughout the world. As a result infant mortality rates have declined dramatically and life expectancies have increased in virtually every part of the globe. In the past 50 years the world's population has jumped from 2.5 billion to more than 6 billion people. WHO's efforts have been the primary factor in this rapid growth.

Although health conditions among all peoples have improved, birth rates differ widely. As a result some regions of the world have seen their populations grow rapidly. The most striking differences are between the developed and undeveloped world. The birth rates of the developed countries of western Europe, North America, and Japan have dropped dramatically. In the most extreme cases some of these countries now have negative growth rates. In Italy, for example, if the present trend continues, the population will decline from 57 million (2000), to 45 million by 2050. Japan also has a negative growth rate, which if it continues at its present rate will result in its population declining from 126 million to 101 million by 2050.

In sharp contrast are the birth rates of the people of sub-Saharan Africa, Latin America, and most of Asia. The populations of these regions are increasing at a rate averaging almost 2 percent per year or more. In the next half century it is projected that the population of India will increase by more than 500 million, while that of neighboring Pakistan will jump by almost 200 million. In 1950, Nigeria, the largest country of sub-Saharan Africa, had a population of only 31 million; by 2000 that population had grown to 123 million. Even given a projected decline in the birth rate, it is still estimated that by the year 2050, Nigeria will be home to more than 300 million people.

The regional differences in growth rates are rapidly changing the geographical distribution of the world population. If we compare population changes by regions and by percentages, and limit it to only the period from 1950 to 2025, we can see quickly how significant the change will be (see Table 16.1).

By 2025, the population of the developed countries of the world will constitute only about one-sixth of the world's population. The rapidly growing majority of the world population is both impoverished and non-Western in cultural heritage.

There is no doubt that the emergence of the global economy has greatly benefited the developed world, and the United States in particular. In terms of tangible material wealth alone Americans can see a vast change in their

Table 16.1 Population Changes

	1950 (%)	2025 (%)
Developed countries	33.1	15.9
Undeveloped countries	66.9	84.1

Source: Adapted from Robbins 1999, 148.

lifestyle. In the past 50 years the size of the average new American home has more than doubled, from 900 square feet to more than 2,000 square feet. The quantity of our material possessions has grown proportionally to fill the new space. Fifty years ago the typical American family owned only a single automobile; today that same family owns two or more. Today we also eat out more and travel more and farther. The developed countries of western Europe and Japan have seen similar increases in relative wealth. In contrast, most of the underdeveloped countries of Latin America, Africa, and Asia have not participated in this new prosperity. The result has been increasing inequalities in the distribution of wealth in the world. In 1960 it was estimated that the richest 20 percent of the world's population had 30 times more income than the poorest 20 percent. By 1999 this ratio had risen to 74 to 1 and was still increasing. It is not just that many people in the world are not sharing in this new wealth; their standards of living are actually declining. Since 1980 per capita incomes in more than a third of the countries of the world have declined. Today 1.2 billion people, one-fifth of the world's population, are attempting to exist on incomes of less than $1 per day. The distribution of the world's wealth has become so skewed that the total assets of the three richest individuals in the world exceed the annual income of the poorest 600 million, while the richest 200 individuals in the world have wealth that exceeds the annual income of the poorest 2.4 billion people.

The problem is not just that a significant wealth gap exists between the rich and poor of the world, but that the gap is rapidly increasing and there appears to be no way to reverse the trend. It is not merely a question of half or more of the world's population left behind by the global economy; they are being left out of participation. In the new global economy these people do not play a significant role either as producers or as consumers. A people's ability to participate in, let alone prosper from, the evolving global economy is directly linked to its access to information and communications technology. In most countries in the world only a small minority of the population has access to telephones, let alone state of the art information and communications technology. What some have termed a digital divide now separates the world's peoples into those who have access to this new technology and those whose access is limited or nonexistent.

The new technology is expensive and the countries that lack it are poor. Presently 41 countries in Africa, Asia, and Latin America are termed "heavily indebted nations," meaning that they cannot even make the interest payments on their existing foreign loans. They are not just poor and indebted, their debts are increasing. Since 1980 the combined debts of these countries have risen $55 billion to more than $200 billion. Not only do the people of these countries lack this new technology, they lack the capital to acquire it and the educational skills to use it if they had it. They are caught in a cycle of increasing poverty from which there appears to be no escape.

If we look at the world as a whole, we find that both the global economy and human populations are growing rapidly. However, if we begin to examine this issue country by country or region by region, we quickly discover that there is an inverse correlation between economic growth and population growth. Generally speaking, countries and regions with high economic growth usually have low population growth rates, while countries with rapid population growth most commonly have slow or even negative economic growth rates.

Sub-Saharan Africa in many ways typifies the problems of the underdeveloped regions of the world. The people of this region are basically dependent upon agriculture. Relative to their population, they have limited marketable natural resources and little industry. Not only do these countries have poorly developed educational and transportation systems and a lack of information and communications technology, they do not have the financial resources available to acquire or develop them. With the highest birth rate in the world, sub-Saharan Africa has already reached the crisis point. For the past two decades the populations of these countries have grown much faster than their economies. Increasing populations have resulted in an overuse of agricultural resources and a deterioration of the land base. Since the early 1960s per capita food production has dropped by 16 percent. As a result, today the people of this region are more than 20 percent poorer in economic terms than they were in the mid-1970s.

With more than 500 million people sub-Saharan Africa is already overpopulated. It is estimated that about 40 percent of the region's population live on less than $1 per day and are chronically undernourished. In the next 50 years it is estimated that this population will grow by an additional 1 billion people. The countries of sub-Saharan Africa face the virtually impossible task of developing their economies to meet the needs of this expanding population. Economic conditions are only going to become worse as an ever-increasing percentage of the population

goes hungry. Similar, although not as severe, conditions exist in much of Latin America and Asia. Economic development cannot keep pace with population growth and already impoverished people are becoming even poorer.

There are two possible solutions to the growing economic problems of the underdeveloped world. One answer would be to create massive economic development programs to increase agricultural and industrial production, linked to programs to reduce the population growth rates. However, such programs would cost trillions of dollars and would have to be financed by the developed countries of the world. The only other solution is for a mass migration of people from the underdeveloped to the developed countries of the world. This migration has already started.

The greatest movement of people in human history is already under way. This migration is taking two forms. First is rural to urban migration, which is occurring in every country in the world. Second is the migration of people from poorer countries to wealthier countries. Just before World War II, about 50 percent of the total population of the United States and Europe was urban, compared with only about 8 to 10 percent for Africa and Asia and 25 percent for Latin America. Today, about 75 percent of Americans and 70 percent of Europeans are city dwellers. However, the urban populations of Asia and Africa have jumped to between 25 and 30 percent, and in Latin America the urban population has increased to more than 60 percent. The growth rate of urbanization has thus been highest outside Europe and North America. In fact, the world's most rapidly growing cities are located in underdeveloped nations: Bandung (Indonesia), Lagos (Nigeria), Karachi (Pakistan), Baghdad (Iraq), and Bogotá (Colombia). In some of these cities the growth rate has been phenomenal. In the 1950s, Bogotá had a population of only about 650,000; by 1995 its population was more than 5 million. Similar increases are common in many Latin American, Asian, and African nations. Most cities in the underdeveloped world lack the large industrial complexes capable of employing the great masses of people migrating into them, but their small-scale industries, transportation services, and government jobs, although limited, offer greater economic opportunities than do the increasingly overcrowded rural regions.

Whereas most migration has been within countries, the growing trend is toward international migration. The United Nations estimates that 150 million people, or almost 3 percent of the world's population, now live in a country other than the one in which they were born. Many argue that this is a conservative figure. The main difficulty in discussing international migration is that it takes so many forms. There are legal immigrants who are in the process of becoming citizens of another country;

however, not all countries allow such immigrants. There are other immigrants who have temporary legal status to live in another country: guest workers, students, and refugees. Then there are illegal immigrants, individuals who have illegally taken up residence in another country. The distinction between these categories is often blurred. In many cases individuals who come as "students" and "refugees" are in reality coming in search of jobs.

As their industrial economies expanded during the 1950s and 1960s, many western European countries began experiencing labor shortages. West Germany initiated a "guest-worker" program to actively recruit foreign laborers, first in southern Europe, Italy, and Spain, and later in Yugoslavia and Turkey. Concurrently, French factories began recruiting Arab workers from their then North African colonies, particularly Algeria. In the 1950s, England began experiencing an influx of West Indians from its possessions in the Caribbean. In the 1960s, a wave of Pakistani and Indian immigrants also settled in England. Other western European countries experienced a similar phenomenon, although usually on a smaller scale.

By the early 1970s, when the economic growth of western Europe began to slow, large non-European communities were well established in most of the major cities. When West Germany ended its guest-worker program in 1974, it had hosted 2.5 million foreign workers, a number equal to more than 10 percent of its total labor force. Through various means the West German government tried to repatriate these guest workers and their families, but failed. France, England, and other western European countries have considered stricter immigration laws to stop the continuing influx of African and Asian workers, but the number of new immigrants is increasing despite tighter controls. By 1990 almost 10 percent of the population of western Europe were recent immigrants.

The United States has always allowed relatively large numbers of legal immigrants. Since World War II, about 25 percent of American population growth has been the result of immigration. However, migration patterns to the United States have changed dramatically in the postwar period. In the 1950s, well over one-half of the immigrants to the United States were still coming from Europe; the second-largest group, about one-third, were coming from Latin America. In the 1960s, the flood of immigrants began to increase. From only about 300,000 persons per year in the 1960s, the number of immigrants jumped to more than 400,000 per year in the 1970s and to more than 700,000 per year in the 1980s and 1990s. As the number of immigrants increased, their origins shifted markedly. Proportionally, the number of Latin American immigrants remained about the same, while European immigration declined. The major change was in the number of Asian

arrivals, from less than 10 percent of all immigrants in 1950 to more than 30 percent by the 1990s. As a result, between 1980 and 2000 the number of Asian Americans almost tripled, from 3.5 million (1.5 percent) to more than 10.2 million (3.6 percent), whereas the number of Latin Americans more than doubled, from 14.5 million (6.4 percent) to more than 35 million (12.5 percent).

Although Europe and North America have been the primary destinations for most international migrants, other regions with high income, labor shortages, or both have experienced major influxes of immigrants. Many of the oil-rich Arab countries—Libya, Saudi Arabia, Kuwait, Qatar, Oman, and the United Arab Emirates—have recruited foreign workers from India, Pakistan, Bangladesh, and Egypt, and from among Palestinian refugees. Indeed, in some of the smaller of these countries foreign workers outnumber native Arabs. For example, foreign workers constitute almost 60 percent of the population of Kuwait.

Over the past 20 years international immigration patterns have changed. While the main objective of most immigrants is still to reach either the United States or western Europe, any wealthier country can be the destination. Whereas in the past most immigrants to the developed countries were from Latin America, East Asia, or South Asia, the numbers of immigrants from Africa, the Middle East, and the former republics of the Soviet Union are growing. Although in recent decades the United States and the countries of western Europe have increased their legal immigration quotas in all categories, the numbers of individuals wanting to immigrate have increased far more rapidly. The reasons why the ranks of immigrants are growing so dramatically are simple. Every part of the world, thanks in large part to satellite dishes, has television; most of the programs are American or western European. On television people see life in the developed countries and realize that there is an alternative to the desperate poverty around them, if only they can get there.

The borders of the developed countries of the world are being overwhelmed by increasing waves of illegal immigrants who will take any risk to escape from their world of hopeless poverty. Illegals from Mexico cross the deserts of the Southwest on foot with no water. Migrants from Nigeria, Ghana, and other West African countries travel across the Sahara on foot, on camels, and in old trucks to try to reach the Mediterranean coast where, if they are lucky, they might find a small boat that will take them to Spain and Europe. Some individuals have literally walked most of the way from Afghanistan to Germany. Chinese families mortgage everything they own to pay a smuggler to take one of their family members to the United States or Europe. Individuals with no property place themselves in debt bondage to criminal gangs of

© Nathan Benn/Stock Boston

▲ Illegal immigrants frequently take great personal risks in order to escape the poverty of their homelands. These Haitian refugees are attempting to reach the coast of Florida by sailing a small overcrowded boat across the open sea.

smugglers, working their debt off in illegal sweatshops or brothels in New York City, Rome, or some other city in the developed world. For many of these people, no personal expense is too great, no danger too frightening to stop them from attempting to reach their objective.

Most of the estimated 9 million illegal immigrants in the United States are from Latin America; however, they come from all parts of the world. The actual number is unknown. The only reliable figure we have is that 1.6 million illegals were deported in 2000.

The problem with illegals in western Europe is not as great as in the United States, but it is growing rapidly. It is estimated that there are already between 3 and 3.5 million illegal immigrants. This number is growing by an additional 500,000 a year.

Other developed countries are also facing the problem of growing populations of illegal workers. Japan estimates that about 250,000 Koreans, Filipinos, Chinese, and Thais are illegally living and working in Japan. Ko-

rea estimates its number of illegals at about 200,000, and Australia estimates that it has an illegal population of about 60,000. However, the country with proportionally the greatest problem is South Africa, which in spite of a high unemployment rate has an estimated 4 million illegals out of a total population of 43 million. The economy of South Africa may not be good by American or western European standards, but compared to those of the war-torn countries of central Africa, it is a paradise.

Already many people in the United States and western Europe are complaining of the growing numbers of immigrants. The same is true in other countries that feel themselves inundated by foreigners. In Libya there have been riots in which immigrants have been killed, and in South Africa some of the illegals have been murdered. If people think the problem is bad today, they need only wait for tomorrow. If the economic inequalities of the global economy are not corrected, and the economies of the underdeveloped countries are not dramatically improved, the rate of immigration will only increase. There are hundreds of millions more only waiting for the opportunity to move.

Consequences of Globalization and the Global Economy

Globalization is multifaceted and its effects and consequences are far reaching. The global economy is creating an increasing economic interdependence of the world's people, not just in technology, manufactured goods, and clothing, but in food as well. The global economy is producing tremendous new wealth, while at the same time producing poverty and an increasingly skewed distribution in wealth. The global economy is resulting in the greatest migration in human history, which is changing the ethnic mix of all the world's cities, especially the cities of western Europe and the United States. In western Europe today one sees increasing numbers of people from Africa, the Middle East, and all parts of Asia. In the United States one sees not only increasing numbers of peoples from Africa, the Middle East, and Asia, but Latin America as well. The global media is a marketing tool that is attempting to sell to the world not only material goods, but Western (primarily American) lifestyles, values, and beliefs. Some argue that, whether intended or not, the global media now serve as a means of Western cultural propaganda that is threatening and eroding the cultural traditions of the non-Western peoples of the world.

Globalization has made the world smaller and geography no longer relevant. The oceans of the world no longer separate us or protect us. The problems of one region of the world quickly become the problems

◄ Many recent immigrants to North America from Vietnam, Korea, India, and elsewhere have started small businesses that employ the entire family.

© David Young Wolff/Photo Edit

of another, and the problems of the Middle East have become the problems of America.

Recent events have raised numerous questions concerning globalization. Is the Western world, led by the United States, attempting, through its control of the global economy and world media, to impose its cultural values, norms, and beliefs on the other peoples of the world? How widespread is the resentment of Western domination, not just in the Middle East, but in other regions of the world? If this is a growing problem, what can or should be done about it? In the next chapter we'll examine the question of increasing ethnic conflict.

Summary

1. The past 500 years have been a period of tremendous change for the peoples of the world. This chapter has discussed globalization, the history of its development, and the recent emergence of the global economy.

2. Globalization started 500 years ago with Columbus. The earliest stage was that of global trade. The first phase, the time of European expansion and exploration, lasted from about 1500 to 1800. The second phase, during which European empires were created in Africa, Asia, and Oceania, began about 1800 and lasted until the end of World War II.

3. The age of European expansion and exploration began with the discovery of the Americas by Columbus in 1492. During the three centuries that followed, Europe dramatically changed the world. The Spanish and later the Portuguese, English, French, and Dutch invaded the Americas, conquering or displacing most of the native peoples and gaining control of most of the land and resources. At the same time these same European peoples were establishing a global maritime trade network that soon brought all of the peoples of the world into contact with one another, directly or indirectly. This global trade network resulted in the exchange of technology, food crops, domesticated animals, diseases, and even people. By the late 1700s, the culture of virtually every people in the world had been affected by this exchange.

4. The Industrial Revolution, starting about 1800, changed the nature of European contact with non-Western peoples from trade to colonialism and political domination. The nineteenth century was a time of European imperial expansion as the countries of Europe began claiming the lands and peoples of Africa, Asia, and Oceania. By 1900 the European powers began restructuring the economies of their colonial possessions to meet European needs. The period of Europe's ever-increasing political and economic control continued until World War II.

5. The most recent and current stage of globalization is the global economy. This stage began to develop about 50 years ago, at the end of World War II. The post–World War II period has been a time of continued economic, political, demographic, and sociocultural growth and change. The important feature of this period is the emergence of an increasingly integrated and interdependent global economic system.

6. Three major factors were involved in the emergence of the global economy. First, the collapse of the existing colonial empires allowed the countries of the world to trade directly with one another. Second, developments in technology have made geography irrelevant. New technologies in transportation and shipping make it possible to move goods and people faster and at greatly reduced cost, while new information and communication technologies have revolutionized communication with people in different parts of the world. The third factor is international finance and the globalization of world capital.

7. The global economy is still in the process of developing. Two controversial issues are free trade and transnational corporations. The governments of all countries still regulate trade. Pressure is growing to eliminate all government regulations, allowing for free trade, meaning that any company may buy or sell anything in any country, without import or export duties.

8. The population of the world is growing rapidly, in large part due to the efforts of the World Health Organization. In the last 50 years world population has jumped from 2.5 billion to more than 6 billion. The population growth of the developed countries has stabilized and in many cases started to decline. However, in the underdeveloped countries it continues to grow rapidly.

9. While the global economy has greatly benefited the developed countries, many of the countries of Asia, Africa, and Latin America have seen their economies decline. There is an ever-increasing skewing of wealth, not just between individuals, but between countries and regions of the world. The rich are getting richer and the poor are getting poorer. Globally, there is an inverse correlation between economic development and population growth.

10. Throughout the world there is a massive movement of people from rural agricultural areas to urban centers. There is also a massive migration of people from underdeveloped countries to more developed countries.

11. Globalization has resulted in increasing contact among peoples and increasing exposure of non-Western peoples to Western cultural traditions. In many parts of the non-Western world there is a growing resentment of Western economic dominance and cultural influences.

Key Terms

globalization	global economy	refugees
global trade	transnational corporations	localization

InfoTrac College Edition Terms

globalization	global economy	refugees
global trade	transnational corporations	

Suggested Readings

There are numerous excellent studies of world history since 1500. The following list includes only studies of more general interest.

Crosby, Alfred W. *The Columbian Exchange.* Westport, Conn.: Greenwood, 1972.

An important and readable study by a historian, discusses some of the cultural and demographic effects of contact between the Old World and New World. The study emphasizes the exchange of food plants, animals, and diseases.

Stavrianos, Leften. *The World Since 1500: A Global History.* 8th ed. Englewood Cliffs, N.J.: Prentice-Hall, 1998.

A history textbook that is the best and most readable general description available on world history over the past 500 years.

Wolf, Eric. *Europe and the People Without History.* Berkeley: University of California Press, 1982.

The first major attempt by an anthropologist to describe and analyze global history since 1400. It is one of the classical studies in anthropology.

Over the past few years numerous books and articles have been published on globalization. Here we list works that reflect various perspectives on the issues.

Chomsky, Noam. "Control of Our Lives." Lecture, February 26, 2000, Albuquerque, N.M. Also at http://www.zmag.org/chomskyalbag.htm.

In this attack on the global economy, Chomsky focuses on the issue of sovereignty and concentration of global economic, military, and political power.

Giddens, Anthony. *Runaway World: How Globalization Is Reshaping Our Lives.* New York: Routledge, 2000.

Seeing globalization as a powerful cultural force reordering societies, Giddens notes an emerging conflict between what he terms fundamentalism and cosmopolitan tolerance.

Hines, Colin. *Localization: A Global Manifesto.* London: Earthscan Publishing, 2000.

*Noting many of the negative social, economic, and environmental effects of globalization, Hines argues that globalization as presently conceived (international competitiveness) is not inevitable. He proposes an economic alternative, which he terms **localization**.*

Hutton, Will, and Anthony Giddens, eds. *Global Capitalism.* New York: New Press, 2000.

Bringing together a diverse array of academics and nonacademics (including Paul Volcker and George Soros), this edited work addresses both the potential promise of global capitalism and many of its dangers.

Klein, Naomi. *No Logo.* New York: Picador, 1999.

A popular account by a journalist of corporate marketing practices and the growing consumer and anticorporate activism that is emerging in much of the world.

Robbins, Richard H. *Global Problems and the Culture of Capitalism.* Boston: Allyn & Bacon, 1999.

Written by an anthropologist, this work is by far the best general introduction to the history of the development of capitalism and the current related issues and problems of globalization.

Companion Website for This Book

The Wadsworth Anthropology Resource Center
http://anthropology.wadsworth.com

The companion website that accompanies *Humanity: An Introduction to Cultural Anthropology,* Seventh Edition, includes a rich array of material, including online anthropological video clips, to help you in the study of cultural anthropology and the specific topics covered in this chapter. Begin by clicking on Student Resources. Next, click on Cultural Anthropology, and then on the cover image for this book. You have now arrived at the Student Resources home page and have the option of choosing one of several chapter resources.

Applying Anthropology. Begin your study of cultural anthropology by clicking on Applying Anthropology. Here you will find useful information on careers, graduate school programs in applied anthropology, and internships you might wish to pursue. You will also find real-world examples of working anthropologists applying the skills and methods of anthropology to help solve serious world problems.

Research Online. Click here to find a wealth of Web links that will facilitate your study of anthropology. Divided into different fields of study, specific websites are starting points for Internet research. You will be guided to rich anthropology websites that will help you prepare for class, complete course assignments, and actually do research on the Web.

InfoTrac College Edition Exercises. From the pull-down menu, select the chapter you are presently studying. Select InfoTrac College Edition Exercises from the list of resources. These exercises utilize InfoTrac College Edition's vast database of articles and help you explore the numerous uses of the search word, *culture.*

Study Aids for This Chapter. Improve your knowledge of key terms by using flash cards and study the learning objectives. Take the practice quiz, receive your results, and e-mail them to your instructor. Access these resources from the chapter and resource pull-down menus.

Chapter Seventeen

ETHNICITY AND ETHNIC CONFLICT

Ethnic Groups

Situational Nature of Ethnic Identity

Attributes of Ethnic Groups

Fluidity of Ethnic Groups

Types of Ethnic Groups

The Problem of Stateless Nationalities

Resolving Ethnic Conflict

Homogenization

Segregation

Accommodation

Resolution

© Barry D. Kass/Images of Anthropology

A city sacred to Jews, Muslims, and Christians, Jerusalem has been and is a major source of ethnic/religious conflict in the world.

WITH THE COLLAPSE OF THE SOVIET UNION and the end of the Cold War, many people thought we had entered a new, safer, and more peaceful era. Instead, we have found that ideological conflicts (capitalist vs. communist) have been replaced by ethnic conflicts and the world is a far more dangerous place. As the people of the United States discovered with the attacks on the World Trade Center and the Pentagon, no place is immune. It is not that ethnic conflicts are something new in human affairs; far from it. Ethnic hostilities and hatreds are the oldest and most basic source of conflicts among peoples. It is simply that ideological rivalries between the superpowers obscured and suppressed these differences.

SO INSTEAD OF LIVING IN PEACE, we now find ourselves in a time of growing ethnic conflicts, which are becoming ever more violent and destructive. In the past few years, more than a million people have fallen victim to genocidal wars, while tens of millions more have joined the ranks of refugees. Central governments exist in name only in parts of Africa, Asia, and even Latin America. Large regions of many of these countries are under the control of rebel armies and outlaw groups. Concerns increase about nuclear proliferation and biological warfare. Concerns are also increasing about ethnic terrorist groups and their increasing capabilities for destruction. New phrases like "ethnic cleansing," "failed state," and "rogue state" have become part of our vocabulary. It is not just that ethnic conflict is a problem, it is a problem that is growing. The differences lie only in the groups involved and their methods and objectives.

As we discussed in Chapter 16, the emergence of the global economy has resulted in an ever-increasing economic interdependence among the peoples of the world. At the same time, ethnic conflicts have escalated and seem likely to increase. Ethnic identity is the most potent political force in the modern world. It threatens not only the political stability of many nations but possibly the global economy as well. In this chapter we address several questions: (1) What is an ethnic group? (2) Why is ethnicity such a powerful political force in the modern world? (3) What has been and can be done to try to resolve ethnic conflicts?

Ethnic Groups

Over the past few decades, the terms *ethnic* and *ethnicity* have become part of our everyday vocabulary, as have the terms *ethnic food, ethnic vote, ethnic conflict, ethnic clothes, ethnic neighborhood,* and *ethnic studies.* In the 1960s, anthropologists began studying ethnicity as a distinct social phenomenon, and since that time literature on ethnicity has proliferated. Part of the increased scholarly interest in ethnic groups came as a result of Nathan Glazer and Daniel Moynihan's study of ethnic groups in New York City. They found that "in the third generation, the descendants of the immigrants confronted each other, and knew they were both Americans, in the same dress, with the same language, using the same artifacts, troubled by the same thing, but they voted differently, had different ideas about education and sex, and were still, in many essential ways, as different from one another as their grandfathers had been" (1963, 13). These findings contradicted the idea of the American melting pot. Ethnic differences were far more resilient and significant than had been believed.

What is an ethnic group? First, it is necessary to realize that all peoples, not just minority populations, have an ethnic group identity. In essence, an **ethnic group** is a named social category of people based on perceptions of shared social experience or ancestry. Members of the ethnic group see themselves as sharing cultural traditions and history that distinguish them from other groups. Ethnic group identity has a strong psychological or emotional component that divides the people of the world into the categories of "us" and "them." In contrast to social stratification (discussed in Chapter 13), which divides and unifies people along a series of horizontal axes on the basis of socioeconomic factors, ethnic identities divide and unify people along a series of vertical axes. Thus ethnic groups, at least theoretically, cross-cut socioeconomic class differences, drawing members from all strata of the population.

Before discussing the significance of ethnic differences and conflicts in the modern world, we need to examine the varying dimensions of ethnic group identity, including (1) the situational nature of ethnic group identity, (2) the attributes of ethnic groups, (3) the fluidity of ethnic group identity, and (4) the types of ethnic groups.

Situational Nature of Ethnic Identity

One of the more complicating aspects of ethnicity is that an individual's ethnic group identity is seldom absolute. A person may assume a number of different ethnic identities, depending on the social situation. For example, in the United States an individual may simultaneously be an American, a Euro-American, an Italian American, and a Sicilian American. The particular ethnic identity chosen varies with the social context. When in Europe or among Europeans, the person would assume the identity of American, in contrast to German, French, or Italian. In the United States the same individual might assume the identity of Euro-American, as opposed to African American or Native American. Among Euro-Americans, the person might take the ethnic identity of Italian American, as opposed to Irish American or Polish American. When among Italian Americans, the individual might be identified as Sicilian American, as opposed to an Italian American whose family came from Rome, Naples, or some other region of Italy.

The situational nature of ethnic identity demonstrates what some have called the **hierarchical nesting** quality of identity. A particular ethnic group forms part of a larger collection of ethnic groups of like social magnitude. In turn, these ethnic groups may collectively form still another, higher level of ethnic identity, which may be nested in yet another, higher level. Thus ethnic identity does not simply divide the world into categories of "us" and "them" but into varying, hierarchically ranked categories of "us" and "them."

Attributes of Ethnic Groups

Two main attributes help to define and identify an ethnic group: an origin myth or history, and various ethnic boundary markers.

Origin Myth. Each ethnic group is the product of a unique set of social and historical events. The common or shared historical experiences that serve to unite and distinguish the group from other groups and give it a distinct social identity constitute the group's **origin myth.** By *myth* we do not mean to imply that the historical events did not really happen, or that the group is not what it claims to be. We mean only that these particular experiences serve as the ideological charter for the group's common identity and provide the members with a sense of being different from other people. Origin myths play an integral part in creating and maintaining ethnic group identity: they define and describe the origin and collective historical experiences of the group.

Not all historical events are equally important; origin myths make selective references. Wars and conflicts are frequently emphasized, since they clearly distinguish "us" from "them." The origin myth imbues the group's members with feelings of distinctiveness and, often, superiority in relation to other groups. What makes an origin myth so powerful is that mythic themes and concepts are embedded in virtually every aspect of the people's popular culture: stories (written and oral), songs, dances, games, music, theater, film, and art. So pervasive are these mythic images in everyday life that they are learned passively rather than consciously. Thus all members of the group are well versed in the basic tenets of the group myth, and in the minds of most, these ideas become an unquestioned "truth." In larger, more sophisticated groups, the origin myth also takes the form of a written, purportedly objective history that is formally taught in schools. American history as taught in elementary and high school is not merely the objective, factual history of a geographical region; it is also the story of the American people. Thus it serves as the officially sanctioned origin myth of the American ethnic group. Similarly, English, French, Japanese, and Russian history as taught in their schools is the "authorized" origin myth of those groups.

When you realize that history as taught in schools is in fact the collective origin myth of the group, then you realize the significance of including or excluding a particular subgroup of the population. Using American history as an example, we can see how historical events play a critical role in the emergence and definition of a distinctively American ethnic identity. Among these events are the landing of the *Mayflower,* the American Revolution, the Civil War, the westward expansion, and the world wars. Certain historical groups, such as cowboys and cavalry, are used as embodiments of American ideals and identity. Americans are the descendants of the various peoples who collectively participated in these and other group-defining events. Thus it is not surprising that every American subgroup is sensitive to its portrayal in these events. To African Americans, it is important that American history, as taught in the public schools, acknowledge that the first man to die in the American Revolution was an African American; that African Americans fought as soldiers in the Revolutionary and Civil Wars; that a high percentage of cowboys were African Americans; and that African American cavalrymen played an important part in winning the West. Similarly, public acknowledgment and recognition that their groups were active participants in some, if not all, of the major events of American history are equally important for Polish Americans, Italian Americans, Irish Americans, Chinese Americans, and other immigrants in a nation of immigrants. It is inclusion in the collective origin myth that truly legitimates a people's status as members of the group.

Ethnic Boundary Markers. Every ethnic group has a way of determining or expressing membership. Overt factors used to demonstrate or denote group membership are called **ethnic boundary markers.** Ethnic boundary markers are important not only to identify the members to one another, but also to demonstrate identity to and distinctiveness from nonmembers. Because they serve to distinguish members from all other groups, a single boundary marker is seldom sufficient. A marker that might distinguish one ethnic group from a second group may not distinguish it from a third group. Thus, combinations of markers are commonly used. Differences in language, religion, physical appearance, or particular cultural traits serve as ethnic boundary markers.

As we saw at the end of Chapter 3, speech style and language are symbols of personal identity: We send covert messages about the kind of person we are by how we speak. Language, therefore, frequently serves as an ethnic boundary marker. A person's native language is the primary indicator of ethnic group identity in many areas of the world. In the southwestern United States, Hopi and Navajo members are readily distinguished by their language alone. However, just because two populations share a common language does not mean they share a common identity, any more than the fact that two populations speak different languages means that they have two distinct identities. For example, the Serbs and Croats of what was Yugoslavia speak Serbo-Croatian. They are, however, distinct and historically antagonistic ethnic groups. Conversely, a person may be Irish and speak either Gaelic or English as a native language. The German government grants automatic citizenship to all ethnic German refugees from Eastern Europe. A difficulty in assimilating these refugees is that many speak only Polish or Russian. Thus, one does not have to speak German to be an ethnic German.

Like language, religion may serve as an ethnic boundary marker. The major world religions such as Christianity, Islam, and Buddhism encompass numerous distinct ethnic groups, so that religious affiliation does not always indicate ethnic affiliation. But in many cases religion and ethnic group more or less correspond. The Jews may be categorized as either a religious or an ethnic group. Similarly, the Sikhs in India constitute both a religious and an ethnic group. In still other situations, religious differences may be the most important marker of ethnic identity. As we mentioned earlier, the Serbs and Croats speak the same language; the most important distinction between these two groups is that the Serbs are Eastern Orthodox and the Croats are Catholic. Conversely, the Chinese ethnic identity transcends religious differences: A person is still Chinese whether he or she is a Muslim, Christian, Taoist, Buddhist, or Marxist atheist.

Physical characteristics, or phenotypes, can sometimes indicate ethnic identity. It is impossible to identify Germans, Dutch, Danes, and other northern European ethnic groups by their physical characteristics. A similar situation is found in those regions of the world in which populations have been in long association with one another. Thus, physical characteristics do not distinguish a Zulu from a Swazi, a Chinese from a Korean, or a Choctaw from a Chickasaw. However, with the massive movements of people, particularly over the past few hundred years, physical characteristics have increasingly emerged as a marker of ethnic identity. Members of the three major ethnic groups in Malaysia—Malays, East Indians, and Chinese—are readily distinguishable by their physical appearance. The significance or lack of significance of physical characteristics in ethnic identity may also vary with the level of ethnic identity. The American identity includes almost the full range of human physical types. However, at a lower level of identity—Euro-American, African American, and Native American—physical characteristics do serve as one marker of ethnic identity. Yet within these groups, physical characteristics alone cannot be the only marker. Some Native Americans physically appear to be Euro-Americans or African Americans, and some African Americans would be identified as Euro-Americans or Native Americans on the basis of physical appearance alone.

A wide variety of cultural traits, clothing, house types, personal adornment, food, technology, economic activities, or general lifestyle may also serve as ethnic boundary markers. Over the past 100 years, a rapid homogenization of world material culture, food habits, and technology has erased many of the more overt cultural markers. Today you do not have to be Mexican to enjoy tacos, Italian to eat pizza, or Japanese to have sushi for lunch. Similarly, you can dine on hamburgers, the all-American food, in Japan, Oman, Russia, Mexico, and most other countries. Cultural traits remain, however, the most important, diverse, and complex category of ethnic boundary markers. For the sake of brevity, we will limit our discussion to one trait—clothing (see Chapter 15).

Clothing styles have historically served as the most overt single indicator of ethnic identity. In the not too distant past, almost every ethnic group had its own unique style of dress. Even today, a Scottish American who wants to overtly indicate his ethnic identity wears a kilt, and a German American may wear his *lederhosen*. Similarly, on special occasions Native Americans wear "Indian clothes" decorated with beadwork and ribbonwork. These are not everyday garments, and they are worn only in social situations in

▲ The dress of this woman not only identifies her as a Maya Indian, but also that she is from the town of Nabaj, in Guatemala.

which people want to emphasize their ethnic identity. In many regions of the world, however, ethnic clothes are still worn every day. In highland Guatemala, clothing, particularly women's clothing, serves to readily identify the ethnic affiliation of the wearer. Guatemalan clothing styles actually indicate two levels of ethnic identity. If a woman wears a *huipil,* a loose-fitting blouse that slips over the head, she is a Native American. Non–Native American women, called *Ladinas,* dress in Western-style clothes. The style, colors, and designs on the huipil further identify the particular Native American ethnic group the woman is from: Nahuala, Chichicastenango, Solola, or one of the other hundred or so Native American groups in highland Guatemala.

Fluidity of Ethnic Groups

Ethnic groups are not stable groupings. Ethnic groups vanish, people move between ethnic groups, and new ethnic groups come into existence.

During the past 500 years, numerous ethnic groups have vanished. Massachusetts, Erie, Susquehannock, and Biloxi were not originally place names but the names of now extinct Native American ethnic groups. Still other ethnic groups in Asia, Africa, Oceania, Europe, and the Americas have vanished as well. Extinction of an ethnic group seldom means biological extinction, though. In most cases, the members of one group are merely absorbed into the population of a larger group. The Tasmanians of Australia are typical of what happened to many smaller ethnic groups. Numbering at most 5,000 when the British began colonizing the island of Tasmania in 1802, the population was so ravaged by wars and massacres that only a handful existed by 1850; the Tasmanians as a viable ethnic group had ceased to exist. In 1869 the last full-blooded Tasmanian man died, and in 1888 the last full-blooded Tasmanian woman died. However, even today, mixed-blood descendants of the Tasmanians can be found among the Australian population.

Both individuals and communities can move between ethnic groups. During the sixteenth and seventeenth centuries French Protestants, called *Huguenots,* fled persecution in France and settled in large numbers in England and the English colonies in North America. These people quickly became absorbed into the English population. Over the past 200 years, Americans have absorbed numerous immigrant populations.

Ethnogenesis refers to the emergence of a new ethnic group. Ethnogenesis usually occurs in one of two ways: (1) a portion of an existing ethnic group splits away and forms a new ethnic group, or (2) members of two or more existing ethnic groups fuse, forming a new ethnic group.

Probably the most common cause of ethnogenesis is the division of an existing ethnic group. At one time, the Osage, Kansa, Omaha, Ponca, and Quapaw Indians of the central United States were a single ethnic group. The origin myths of these peoples tell how at different times portions broke away, until there were five distinct groups. In the 1700s, small groups of Creek Indians began moving south into Florida, where they eventually developed a distinct identity as the Seminole. Similarly, as Bantu-speaking peoples spread through central and southern Africa, they became separated, and new ethnic groups formed. As the Spanish empire in the Americas disintegrated during the early 1800s, new regional ethnic identities (such as Mexican, Guatemalan, Peruvian, and Chilean) began emerging among the Spanish-speaking peoples in that region. In 1652, the Dutch began settling near the Cape of Good Hope in southern Africa. These people eventually developed their own distinctive dialect of Dutch, called *Afrikaans,* and their own identity, Boers.

In other cases, members of two or more ethnic groups fuse and a new ethnic identity emerges. In England, the Angles, the Saxons, and the Jutes fused and became known as the English. The original Euro-American ethnic group was not the result of a split among the English people, but rather of a fusion of English, Dutch, German, Scots, Irish, French Huguenots, Scotch-Irish, and other European settlers residing on the coast of North America. Most African American groups in the Americas are the result of the fusion of numerous distinct African groups. Intermarriage between French traders and Native Americans in Canada resulted in the emergence of the Metis. Similarly, in South Africa the Cape Coloured, people of mixed Dutch and Khoikhoi ancestry, are socially and politically distinct from both whites and Africans.

Types of Ethnic Groups

From our discussion and examples so far, it should be apparent that the term *ethnic group* covers a range of social groupings. In general, ethnic groups fall into two main categories: national and subnational.

A **nationality** is an ethnic group with a feeling of **homeland,** a geographical region over which they have exclusive rights. Implicit in this concept is the assumption of an inherent right to political autonomy and self-determination. In contrast, **subnationalities** lack a concept of a distinct and separate homeland and the associated rights to separate political sovereignty and self-determination. A subnational group sees itself as a dependent and politically subordinate subset of a nationality.

Levels of Ethnic Identity

Civilizations	Groupings of two or more distinct nationalities on the basis of a shared or common cultural historical tradition. In most cases this shared cultural tradition takes the form of religion
Nationalities	Ethnic groups who collectively own, or feel that they own, a specific geographical region, or homeland, in which they have exclusive rights
Subnational groups	Ethnic groups whose identities are nested within that of a larger national identity
Transnational groups	Ethnic communities that are geographically separated from their homeland and live among members of another nationality

Although it is easy to define the difference between ethnic nationalities and subnationalities, sometimes it is far more difficult to classify particular groups. The ethnic groups in the United States demonstrate some of the difficulties in classification. With some ethnic groups there is no doubt: Italian Americans, German Americans, Polish Americans, Scottish Americans, and Irish Americans are all subnational groups. At a higher level of identity, the same is true for African Americans. None of these groups has a concept of a distinct and separate geographical homeland within the United States. Hence, they are subnational groups who, together with many other groups, collectively constitute the American ethnic nationality.

There are other ethnic groups within the United States whose status is not as clear. What is the status of Native American groups such as the Navajo, the Hopi, the Crow, the Cheyenne, the Cherokee, and the Osage, to name only a few? These groups have a concept of homelands within the United States. They also have histories quite distinct from those of other Americans. In recent years they have been asserting increased political sovereignty and self-determination within their reservations (homelands). Although there is disagreement, many Native American individuals and groups still see themselves as distinct nationalities. The U.S. government recognizes most American Indian groups as national groups with collective legal and political rights. No other ethnic groups in the United States have officially recognized governments and limited rights of self-determination. There is also some question about the ethnic status of Spanish-speaking people in the southwestern United States. Until the mid-nineteenth century, Texas, New Mexico, Arizona, and California were part of Mexico. The United States acquired this region through military conquest. Most of the native Spanish-speaking people in this region think of themselves as Mexican American or Spanish American, a subnational group. There is, however, a small group who see themselves as "Mexicans" living in a land that is rightfully part of Mexico, a region they call Atzlan.

The distinction between nationality and subnational ethnic group is important because of their different political implications. As we shall see, the demands of subnational groups for equal rights and treatment have long been a source of conflict. But the demands of nationalities for independence and sovereignty in a region carved out of an existing country create a political time bomb.

Globalization has increased our awareness of two additional levels of ethnic identity. Today more than 150 million people live in a country that they were not born in. Among these immigrants are a special category: transnationals. Transnationals are members of an ethnic community located outside their country of origin and homeland. What distinguishes transnational communities from other immigrant communities is that they feel that their true home is still where they came from and that their residence in another country is only temporary. Many transnationals are war refugees; others have come as guest workers, some legally and many illegally. In many cases they have moved as immigrants and are even citizens of the new country. While there have always been such communities, eventually most either disintegrated or their members returned home. Today, thanks to improvements in transportation and communications technology, these geographically separated groups can remain in contact with their home communities. With the Internet, e-mail, and long-distance phone service they can remain in close, even daily, contact with family and friends at home and be well aware of events at home. Air travel means that they can return home quickly if necessary in case of illness or for family weddings and other important social events. Marriages are even arranged between transnationals and spouses in their home countries. Many transnationals not only own homes in two countries, when possible many acquire dual citizenship and even take an active role in the politics of both countries. There are countless numbers of such communities in the world today, such as the communities of Pakistanis and Indians in Oman, the United Arab Emirates, Kuwait, England, Canada, the United States, and elsewhere; and the Afghani communities in Pakistan, Australia, Iran, England, and the United States. Most of these transnational communities are found in the developed countries of western Europe and North America, but almost every country in the world has some.

Globalization and the increasing contact and conflict between different peoples have also resulted in the growing significance of a level of identity that transcends nationality, civilization. A **civilization** is a grouping of a number of different nationalities on the basis of a shared cultural historical heritage that collectively distinguishes them from other like groups. Thus we speak of Western civilization, as opposed to Islamic, Hindu, or Chinese civilization. By Western, we mean those nationalities that are the inheritors of the Judeo-Christian cultural traditions of Europe. Today Western peoples are found in almost every region of the world. The Globalization box in this chapter has a discussion of civilizations.

The Problem of Stateless Nationalities

It is difficult for most Americans to understand the causes and bitterness of ethnic conflict in other parts of the world. We think of *nationality* and *nation* as being one and the same. An American is any person who is a citizen of the United States. Most of us think of ourselves as Americans first and secondarily as Irish, Italian, or Chinese Americans. This mind-set about the meaning and significance of ethnicity is due mainly to our history as a nation of immigrants—with the exception of Native Americans, immigrants renounced their claims to their national homelands when they came to the New World. For the most part, the ethnic groups in the United States are subnationalities, not nationalities. Thus, from our common perception, a Russian is a person from Russia, a Nigerian is a citizen from Nigeria, and so forth. Falsely equating country of origin with ethnic nationality, we view ethnic conflicts in other regions of the world as comparable to conflicts between subnational groups within the United States. Ethnic problems within a country are thought to be the result of social or economic discrimination—resolvable and reparable by reforms—and their political significance is minimized. However, the ethnic conflicts in most countries are not between subnational groups but between distinct nationalities.

The ethnic conflicts in Northern Ireland and in Israel and Palestine have proved particularly bitter. In 1922, after several centuries of British colonial domination and periodic rebellions by the native Irish, the Irish Free State (now the Republic of Ireland) was established. However, not all of Ireland was given independence. In the seventeenth cen-

tury, to control the Irish, the British evicted Irish farmers from the northernmost portion of the island and colonized the region with Scottish Presbyterians, who became known as the Ulster-Scots, or *Scotch-Irish* in the United States. The Ulster-Scots did not identify themselves as Irish and had no desire to become part of an independent Ireland. Recognizing the wishes of the Ulster-Scots, at independence the British partitioned the island. The northern six counties became Northern Ireland and remained part of the United Kingdom. Many Irish did not and do not accept the legality of this partitioning of Ireland. To them, Northern Ireland is part of the Irish homeland and thus should be part of the Republic of Ireland. Since 1968, the Irish Republican Army, a secretive guerrilla army that is illegal in the Republic of Ireland, has been actively waging a war with the object of reuniting Northern Ireland with the Republic of Ireland. Bombings, ambushes, and assassinations have claimed more than 2,200 lives. The news media frequently report the problems in Northern Ireland as conflict between the British and the Irish or between Catholics and Protestants; in reality, it is neither. The root of the problem is the conflicting claims of two rival and hostile nationalities: the Irish and the Ulster-Scots. The Ulster-Scots have emerged over the past 400 years as a distinct nationality who claim the northern part of Ireland as their homeland. In contrast, the Irish see the area as an integral and inalienable part of the Irish homeland.

After an absence of almost 2,000 years, the Jews began returning to their historic homeland in Palestine in 1882. During the early twentieth century Jewish settlements in Palestine grew, and in 1948 the state of Israel was proclaimed by the Jewish settlers. For the past 50 years, conflict between Israelis and Palestinians has been constant, varying only in the intensity and form of violence. The problem is similar to that in Northern Ireland: two nationalities—Israelis and Palestinians—claim the same geographical region as their legitimate homeland. Although some progress has been made recently toward peaceful settlements of the conflicts in Northern Ireland and between Israelis and Palestinians, such agreements are tenuous. These situations remain extremely volatile. In Israel and Northern Ireland, it is impossible to resolve the conflict to the total satisfaction of both nationalities.

These two conflicts vividly illustrate the strength of nationalist sentiments. In both cases we see groups of educated, rational human beings who are willing to sacrifice their lives and economic well-being in unending conflicts for what they consider to be their nationality's legitimate rights.

Such conflict is more common in the modern world than most of us realize. The world is divided into fewer

In late September 2001, as the U.S. military prepared to enter Afghanistan in search of Osama bin Laden, Silvio Berlusconi, the prime minister of Italy, remarked in a speech to his parliament that he hoped "the West will continue to conquer peoples, like it conquered communism." The Arab League demanded an apology. Just 3 days earlier on BBC television, Dr. Ghazi Algosaibi, the Saudi Arabian ambassador to the United Kingdom, had warned, "We are worried that this has turned from a war against terrorism, which we support wholeheartedly and with no reservation, into a war of America or the West against Islam." The recent invasion and occupation of Iraq has only added to these fears.

In 1996, Samuel P. Huntington, one of America's foremost political scientists, published his widely read book, *The Clash of Civilizations and the Remaking of World Order.* In this study he argues against the position held by many Western and non-Western scholars and writers that the global economy and Westernization go hand-in-hand and that Western civilization is, as V. S. Naipaul once asserted, the "universal civilization." Huntington suggests that the "Westernization" of the world's people is for the most part superficial. Although other peoples may have adopted many of the overt trappings of Western culture, in their core beliefs and values non-Western peoples have not changed. Thus, in terms of cultural traditions, people have been and still are highly differentiated.

Significant conflicts in recent world history have been what Huntington terms "Western civil wars," wars between competing Western rulers, nation-states, and ideologies. The Cold War, a conflict of Western ideologies, was the last of these "civil wars." According to Huntington, the Western world, by which he means western (Protestant and Catholic) Europe together with the United States and Canada, is now at the height of its political, economic, and military power in the world. Even though the old colonial empires are gone, the West still collectively exercises political and economic control over the world's peoples through the United Nations Security Council and the International Monetary Fund (IMF). In global political affairs, "world community" has become a euphemism to give legitimacy to the actions, frequently military, of the West. Through the control of the IMF and other similar institutions, the West still controls and manipulates global economic growth and development for its own benefit. Relative to the non-Western world, the IMF has been compared by Georgi Arbatov to "neo-Bolsheviks who love expropriating other people's money, imposing undemocratic and alien rules of economic and political conduct and stifling economic freedom" (Huntington, 184). With the United States as the only remaining military superpower, the West has aggressively pursued a policy of limiting the development of advanced military technology, particularly nuclear weapons, in the non-Western world.

The world has become divided between the West and the rest. Huntington argues that increasing contact between peoples is not serving to lessen cultural differences, but rather to make people more acutely aware of those cultural factors that divide them. People will increasingly identify with others of like cultural heritage. The result will be, according to Huntington, a "political" realignment based on cultural heritage, or "civilizations" as he calls them. The process of de-Westernization is beginning as non-Western peoples try to rid themselves of Western cultural influences. Although de-Westernization is most apparent in the fundamentalist religious movements in Iran, Algeria, and other portions of the Islamic world, it is taking root in many other parts of the non-Western world as well. To Huntington, religious traditions indicate fundamental cultural differences between peoples, and religion forms the cultural core of what he terms "civilizations." He sees the world coalescing into seven or eight "civilizations," which he identifies as Western (Protestant–Catholic), Slavic–Orthodox (Christians), Confucian, Japanese, Islamic, Hindu, Latin American, and possibly African.

Huntington does not see the coalescence of civilizations as replacing existing ethnic identities or ending internal conflicts. He does, however, see these various civilizations increasingly competing with one another, and the boundaries separating these civilizations becoming the "fault lines" along which future conflicts will occur. The intensity of the wars in Bosnia was thus not the result of mere competition between three rival ethnic groups, but rather the result of conflict between three competing civilizations: Western (the Croats), Slavic–Orthodox (the Serbs), and Islamic (the Bosnian Muslims). Ethnic and ideological wars will be superseded by wars between civilizations, and Huntington sees the most imminent of these clashes as one between Western and Islamic civilizations.

Critical Thinking Questions

Huntington's proposal is highly speculative, and many of his assertions can be questioned. He does, however, present some alarming ideas concerning the nature of future conflicts in the world. Is this present time of rising nationalism and political fragmentation only the prelude to a global political realignment of people based on opposing cultural traditions?

1. Will new supra-ethnic identities emerge as the most potent political forces in the world?

2. Will the attacks on the World Trade Center and the Pentagon and the retaliatory invasions by the United States of Afghanistan and Iraq prove to be isolated events in human history, or will they be the prelude to a clash between Western and Islamic civilizations?

than 200 countries and between 3,000 and 5,000 distinct ethnic nationalities. As a result, the populations of most countries encompass a number of distinct nationalities. China officially recognizes 56 distinct nationalities. Some estimates are as high as 300 ethnic nationalities in Indonesia. Ethiopia has at least 70 nationalities. Only a handful of countries are peopled by members of a single nationality and are thus ethnically homogeneous.

The ethnic nationality problem is further complicated because current political boundaries frequently divide members of a nationality and their historic homeland. For example, Hungarians are found not only in Hungary but also in the adjacent portions of Romania and Serbia. Somalis live not only in Somalia but also in the adjacent Ogaden portion of Ethiopia. Large numbers of Albanians live in adjoining portions of Kosovo (Serbia) and Macedonia. Thus the world is filled with ethnic groups who do not fully recognize the legitimacy of "their" central government and who aspire or may potentially aspire to have political autonomy (see Figure 17.1).

For the most part, nationality problems were not created by the nationalities themselves. The current political boundaries for most of the world are legacies of European colonialism and expansion. In 1884–1885 at the Berlin Conference, European leaders sat at a table and with pens and pencils drew lines on a map of Africa, dividing the resources and peoples of that continent among themselves. Through this agreement, the English, French, Germans, Belgians, Portuguese, and other European powers assumed sovereignty over lands they had never traveled and over peoples who had never seen a white man. Nor was Africa the only continent to have boundaries imposed by Europeans. The national boundaries of most of the world were drawn by Europeans for their own interests, with little regard for the interest of any indigenous peoples or the boundaries of the ethnic groups affected. As a result, most European colonial possessions were a polyglot of ethnic groups, many of whom had long histories of hostilities toward one another. Sometimes the land and people of an ethnic group were divided between two or more European colonies. To make matters worse, colonial powers frequently moved people from one colony to another to supply labor, introducing groups to new areas. For example, the British settled Indian laborers in Burma (Myanmar), Malaya (Malaysia), Fiji, Sri Lanka, Kenya, Uganda, South Africa, Trinidad, and British Guiana.

The end of the colonial period did not end the ethnic conflicts in the world. As European powers granted independence to their colonies, they made little attempt to redefine political boundaries. In most cases these newly independent countries had precisely the same boundaries and ethnic composition as the former colonies. Because these political divisions were imposed by European military power, some scholars have termed the former colonies **artificial countries** (see Figure 17.2). In most cases the basic colonial administrative and governmental structure was maintained after independence; the major departure from the colonial period was that native officials replaced European officials. However, not all ethnic groups were equally represented in these new governments, and most former colonies quickly came under the domination of one or two of the more powerful ethnic groups. Thus, in many instances European domination was replaced by domination by one or another "native" ethnic group. With this in mind, the political problems

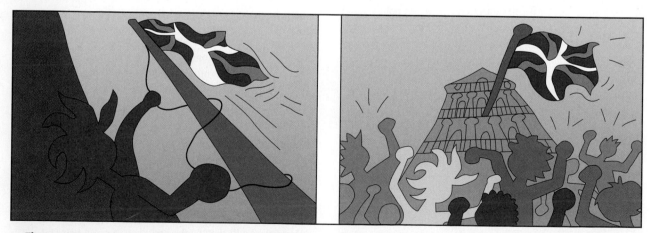

▲ **Figure 17.1** Nationalist organizations use various means to communicate their message of separation. These cartoon panels showing the Basque flag are from a small booklet distributed by Basque separatists in northern Spain.

endemic in much of the former colonial world become more comprehensible (see A Closer Look).

India is a prime example of ethnic problems in the postcolonial period. Consisting of several hundred distinct ethnic groups as well as major religious divisions, India did not exist—and never existed—as a unified country before British domination. As independence approached in the 1940s, hostilities between rival Muslim and Hindu factions became so intense that British officials decided that a unified, independent India was an impossibility. They decided that India had to be divided into two countries: India (predominantly Hindu) and Pakistan (predominantly Muslim). The borders of these new countries were drawn by the British. The problem was the lack of clear geographical boundaries separating these groups; in many regions the populations were mixed Hindu and Muslim. An East Pakistan and a West Pakistan were carved out on either side, separated by 1,000 miles of what was to be India. After the official announcement of the boundaries, massive migrations began as millions of Muslims and Hindus found themselves on the wrong sides. These migrations were stimulated by fanatics on both sides, who massacred Muslims living in what was to become India and Hindus in what was to be Pakistan. Some estimate that as many as 1 million people were killed in these riots. The grant of actual independence to the two countries in 1947 made the situation worse because neither side was satisfied with its geographical boundaries. The new Indian army occupied the largely Muslim region of Kashmir, and war quickly broke out. The first India–Pakistan war ended in 1949, with Kashmir occupied by India.

The creation of two separate states out of British India addressed—but did not solve—only one of the region's problems. Immediately after independence, the Naga people in India's easternmost Assam province revolted and demanded an independent Nagaland. This Naga secessionist movement is still active, and for more than 50 years periodic bloody clashes have occurred between Naga rebels and Indian authorities. More recently a Sikh separatist movement emerged, demanding an independent homeland in Punjab. The violent tactics of the Sikh nationalists resulted in the Indian army's attacking the holiest Sikh religious shrine, the Golden Temple in Amritsar, in 1984. Later that year, two Sikhs assassinated Indira Gandhi, the prime minister of India, causing more violence between Sikhs and Hindus. In 1990, violence again broke out in Kashmir and continues today. Muslim leaders are demanding either a separate nation or unification with Pakistan. As if India's problems with its religious–ethnic minorities were not sufficient, the Hindu majority is becoming increasingly hostile to non-Hindu minorities (see the Globalization box in Chapter 16).

Pakistan has also experienced ethnic difficulties. Although both parts of Pakistan were Muslim, there were major ethnic differences between the two. East Pakistanis were predominantly Bengalis; West Pakistan was more heterogeneous ethnically but dominated by Urdu-speaking peoples. Although West Pakistan had a smaller population, the capital was located there after independence in 1947, and the Urdu peoples gained dominance in the government and the military. In West Pakistan, a separatist movement emerged among the Baluchi, who sought an independent Baluchistan. However, it was with the Bengalis in East Pakistan that the major conflict emerged. Although the Bengalis were economically exploited and discriminated against by the Urdu, it was not until the government attempted to impose the Urdu language in the schools of East Pakistan that the situation came to a head. In 1971 the East Pakistanis revolted and, after a short but bloody war aided by India, succeeded in establishing the state of Bangladesh.

Bangladesh is experiencing its own internal ethnic problems. Even before independence from Pakistan, Bengali settlers had begun occupying land in the Chittagong hills, displacing the indigenous tribal peoples. After independence, with official encouragement, the flow of Bengali settlers increased, causing the tribal peoples to rebel and demand local autonomy. The government has refused to halt the settlements, and periodic killings and massacres are continuing. In the realm of ethnic conflict today's victims can quickly become tomorrow's villains.

Similar secessionist movements have occurred and are still occurring throughout the old colonial world: nationalist separatist movements are active in southern Sudan, the island of Mindanao in the Philippines, Sri Lanka, Burma, Burundi, Congo, and Indonesia—just to name a few. Certainly, it is facile to lay all the blame on colonialism for these and other conflicts in the postcolonial era. But it is undeniable that violence between ethnic nationalities, each believing its political and territorial claims are legitimate, is one of colonialism's most unfortunate and long-lasting legacies.

Not all ethnic conflicts are confined to the old colonial world. For example, the Kurds (who live in the mountainous regions of Turkey, Iraq, Iran, and Syria) have had an active separatist movement since the 1960s. At different times they have fought the Turks, the Iraqis, and the Iranians (see A Closer Look). In 1950 China invaded and occupied Tibet, a region that the Chinese consider part of China. A Tibetan revolt in 1959 was crushed, but

The conflict in present-day Iraq can only be understood within the history of the region. Although the Tigris and Euphrates valleys, ancient Mesopotamia, is one of the ancient "cradles" of civilization, it is also a region that has had an extremely turbulent political history. In the third millennium B.C. it was the center of Sumerian civilization, and during the second millennium B.C. the ancient city of Babylon dominated the region. Later it was at times part of the Assyrian, Persian, Seleucid, Roman, Parthian, Sassanid, Umayyad, and Ottoman Empires to name only some. In spite of the long history of the region, modern-day Iraq is a recent creation, established by the British following World War I out of three provinces or *wilayat* of the defeated Ottoman (Turkish) Empire. Like many regions long dominated by outside forces, and whose modern political boundaries others have drawn, Iraq lacks any meaningful sociopolitical cohesion uniting its population. Modern Iraq is an "artificial country."

The native population of Iraq is divided into three main ethnic/religious groups: Kurds, Sunni Arabs, and Shiite Arabs. Of the three groups the Shiite Arabs are by far the largest, constituting about 60 percent of the total population. The Kurds and Sunni Arabs each number about 20 percent. In addition, there are some smaller ethnic/religious groups: Assyrians, Turkmen, and Arab Christians. There were about 120,000 Jews in Iraq until following the war of Israeli independence when most immigrated to Israel.

Speaking an Indo-European language, the Kurds are one of the ancient indigenous peoples of the region. Distinguished by dialect differences and highly fractionalized into numerous localized tribal groups, they live primarily in mountain agricultural communities. Kurdish communities are found in Iraq, Iran, Turkey, Syria, Azerbaijan, and Armenia. Numbering between 22 and 25 million people, the Kurds are the largest stateless nationality in the world. Although predominantly Sunni Muslims, there are some tribes that are Shiite, and a few who still practice Yazdani, the pre-Islamic Kurdish religion. Occupying the more mountainous northeastern portion of Iraq, the 3.5 million Iraqi Kurds identify more strongly with Kurdish populations living in adjacent countries than with Arab Iraqis.

Although the Arabic-speaking population of Iraq total about 80 percent of the population, they are far from a unified group. The Arab population of southern Iraq is overwhelmingly Shiite, while the region of central Iraq around Baghdad is predominantly Sunni. The Sunni and Shiite represent the two major divisions in the Islamic world.

In A.D. 632 the Prophet Muhammad died with no clearly defined manner in which a new successor could be chosen. Some Muslims believed that the Prophet's successor should be chosen from the family of the Prophet. Ali ibn Abu Talib, usually referred to simply as Ali, the cousin of Muhammad and the husband of his only surviving child, Fatima, was the choice of this group. However, most leaders of the new religion thought that the position should be open to others and Abu Bakr was selected by them to be the first caliph. In the decades that followed Abu Bakr's selection, by conquest and proselytizing, Islam spread rapidly out of the Arabian peninsula, west into Egypt and North Africa and north into Syria and Iraq. Disputes began to emerge between the various leaders over the control of the lands being conquered. In A.D. 656, Uthman, the third caliph, was murdered, by the son of the first caliph, Abu Bakr. A crisis quickly developed when fractional leaders were unable to agree on a successor to Uthman. Many supported Ali who was now governor of Iraq, while others supported Muawiyah, a cousin of Uthman and governor of Syria. Among the supporters of Muawiyah was Aisha, a widow of the Prophet Muhammad.

The armies of Ali and Muawiyah met on the Plains of Siffin, in what is today Iraq. The battle was indecisive and Ali attempted to arbitrate their differences peacefully. In 661 Ali was murdered while at prayer in the mosque Al Kufah (Kufah) and buried in nearby Najaf. Muawiyah was able to convince Ali's oldest son, Hassan, to give up any claim to the caliphate, and Muawiyah was declared caliph and established what was to be called the Umayyad Dynasty, with its capital at Damascus (Syria). Shortly after Hassan had renounced his claim he died. Some say that he died of natural cause, others that he was poisoned. The death of Ali and then Hassan served to strengthen the opposition of Ali's supporters against Muawiyah.

In 680 Muawiyah died and was succeeded as caliph by his son Yazid. Hussain, the second son of Ali, refusing to recognize Yazid, led a revolt. Yazid sent an army against them. On October 10, 680, Hussain and 200 of his followers were killed at Karbala (Iraq) and Hussain's head was sent to Yazid.

The killing of Hussain and his followers created a schism in the Islamic religious community that has lasted until today. The followers of Ali and Hussain became known as the Shiite, with their main shrines at Karbala and Najaf in Iraq. The followers of Yazid became known as the Sunni. Today only about 16 percent of the Islamic peoples in the world are Shiite and only in Iraq, Iran, and Bahrain do they constitute the majority of the population. The vast majority, about 83 percent, of the Islamic peoples are Sunni.

There are important theological differences between Shiites and Sunnis. Possibly the most significant concerns spiritual leadership and the concept of Imam, or religious leader. Among the Sunni any righteous and knowledgeable Muslim can act as an Imam, leading prayers and interpreting the Holy Koran. Even the most ranking of Imams are not and cannot be considered divinely inspired. To suggest such would be considered

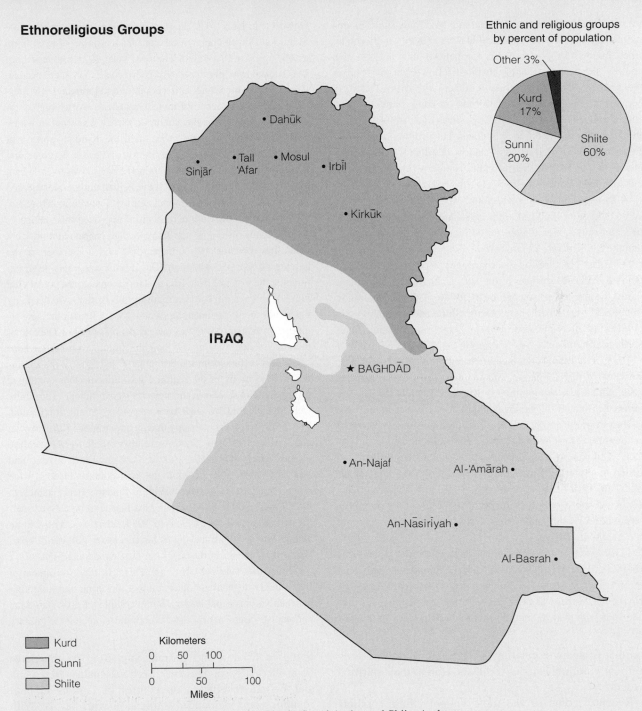

Ethnoreligious Groups

Ethnic and religious groups
by percent of population

Other 3%
Kurd 17%
Sunni 20%
Shiite 60%

• Dahūk
• Tall 'Afar
• Mosul
• Irbīl
• Sinjār
• Kirkūk

IRAQ

★ BAGHDĀD

• An-Najaf
Al-'Amārah •
An-Nāsiriyah •
Al-Basrah •

Kurd
Sunni
Shiite

Kilometers
0 50 100

0 50 100
Miles

▲ **Figure 17.2** The regions of Iraq occupied by the Kurds, Sunni Arabs, and Shiite Arabs.

heresy. For important senior leadership positions, Sunni Imams are usually appointed by political leaders and are not chosen by other Imams. In contrast, Shiites believe that the "Twelve Imams," the earliest divinely inspired followers of the Prophet Mohammed, stay in spiritual contact with their followers through the living Imams. The most ranking of these Shiite Imams are called Ayatollahs. The position of Ayatollah is based on agreement of the other Ayatollahs. They further believe that the Ayatollahs (which means "shadow of Allah") receive guidance from the Twelve Imams and thus their actions in temporal and spirituals matters are divinely inspired.

Although Arab Shiites and Sunnis speak the same language, follow the same cultural traditions, and frequently reside in the same cities and towns, they always live in two socially distinct and separate communities. Conversions from one sect to the other are rare, as are marriages between members of the two sects. Marriage, birth, and death rituals take place within the framework of one or the other of the communities. Frequently, the division between the Shiite and the Sunni communities assumes the same level of sociopolitical significance as ethnic differences.

Under Ottoman Turkish rule the region now known as Iraq consisted of three separate *wilayat* or provinces: Mosul in the north, which was predominantly Kurdish; Baghdad in the central area in which the Sunni population was concentrated: and Al-Basrah in the south, where mainly Shiites resided. Soon after the outbreak of World War I, Turkey allied itself with Germany. Quickly moving forces out of India, the British succeeded in capturing Basra and by the fall of 1915 most of the south. In 1917 they took Baghdad and the following year Mosul. At the peace conference of 1919 the three provinces were made British mandate territories under the supervision of the League of Nations.

At first Iraq, under the British, was to consist of only the provinces of Baghdad and Al-Basrah, the Sunni and Shiite Arab regions. In accordance with the 1920 Treaty of Sevres, the province of Mosul was to be part of a new autonomous Kurdish state that was also to include the Kurdish portion of Turkey.

However, in May 1920, fearing continued British control, the Sunni and Shiite communities and leaders joined forces in an armed uprising that failed. The next year, 1921, the new Iraqi government was organized. An individual from Saudi Arabia, Faisal, was named king, and a constitutional monarchy was established with a council of ministers under a British high commissioner. Meanwhile the Sultan of Turkey was overthrown by Turkish nationalists, who reoccupied the Kurdish portion of eastern Turkey, scrapping the Treaty of Sevres. Recognizing that the area around Mosul contained large oil reserves, which they desired to control, in 1923, the British unilaterally merged the Kurdish province of Mosul with the new Iraq Kingdom. Two years later the League of Nations approved this change.

The status of Iraq as a British mandate continued until 1932 when Iraq became fully independent and a member of the League of Nations. Although King Faisal was a pan-Arab nationalist, he was not from Iraq and most local Arabs considered him a foreigner imposed on them by the British. Neither King Faisal nor the government as created by the British had any legitimacy in the minds of the various peoples of Iraq. The Sunni, though smaller in numbers than the Shiite, were better educated. Under the Ottomans, Sunni had filled most of the administrative positions in the regional government. This continued under the British and in the new Iraq government. The Shiite were not pleased by what they viewed as Sunni domination. The Kurds were also unhappy that an autonomous Kurdish state had not been created. There were also problems between the various Arab tribal leaders, as well as between pan-Arab and Iraqi nationalists. In addition the new country faced a wide range of economic problems. With full independence achieved, King Faisal died in 1933, leaving his throne to his 21-year-old, Western-educated son, Ghazi. In 1939, Ghazi was killed in an automobile accident, leaving as his successor a 3-year-old son, Faisal II. A cousin of the new king was named as regent.

Under the "rule" of Ghazi and Faisal II, the government of Iraq quickly degenerated into political bickering and infighting between various tribal leaders, Sunnis, Shiites, Kurds, pan-Arab nationalists, Iraqi nationalists, communists, socialists, military

conflict is again escalating as Tibetan Buddhists seek political autonomy under the Dalai Lama, their spiritual leader.

Recently some of the most violent ethnic conflicts have been in Europe and the former Soviet Union. In the early 1990s, Yugoslavia disintegrated as the republics of Slovenia, Croatia, Bosnia, and Macedonia proclaimed their independence. Yugoslavia was reduced to only two of the former six republics: Serbia and Montenegro. Hundreds of thousands of ethnic Serbs found themselves

living in Croatia and Bosnia. Supported by the Serb-controlled Yugoslavian army, Serb nationalists in Croatia and Bosnia rebelled, took control of regions in both republics, and demanded unification with Serbia. With more than 100,000 dead and more than 1 million homeless, the war in Bosnia has been the bloodiest and most destructive war in Europe since World War II. In 1995 an agreement was reached between the Bosnian Muslims, Croats, and Serbs. Fighting stopped, and NATO troops occupied zones between the warring factions.

officers, and others. In 1948 Iraq joined the other Arab countries in sending troops to fight against Israel. The defeat of the Arab League and the continued pro-British and pro-Western position of Faisal II and his ministers resulted in a coalescence of the various anti-Western factions in Iraq. As a result, in 1958, a military coup took place, Faisal II was killed, and a republic proclaimed.

The coup and the creation of a republic did not succeed in bringing political stability to the country. During the 1960s and 1970s there were still more military coups and rapid changes in political leadership. The only consistency during this period was that the different leaders were all anti-West and pro–Soviet Union. In 1961, Mustafa al-Barzani, with backing from Iran, initiated a Kurdish separatist rebellion. This period of fighting would last until 1977 when the Iraqi government agreed to give the Kurds greater local autonomy and recognized Kurdish as an official language. The 1960s and 1970s were also a period of growing oil production and revenue, as well as increasing dependence upon civilian and military technology from the Soviet Union.

In 1979 two significant events occurred in the region: Saddam Hussein became president of Iraq, and the Shah of Iran was overthrown and the Islamic Republic of Iran was created under the control of Shiite clerics. The following year the Iran–Iraq War started with the Iraqi invasion of southern Iran. There appear to have been several reasons why Hussein ordered the invasion. There were some important border disputes that Hussein wished to settle. There was also a fear that the success of the Shiite clerics in Iran would encourage the Shiite majority in Iraq to attempt a similar revolution. Finally, by using the long-standing antipathies between Arabs and Iranians (Persians), the war could be used to help solidify Hussein's control over Iraq. The 8 years of often-bloody warfare that followed almost bankrupted the two countries while accomplishing little in resolving the border disputes. However, the Shiite Arabs in Iraq did support the national war effort and the war allowed Hussein to gain a virtually dictatorial control of the country through the military.

During the war with Iran, with weapons supplied by Iran, the Kurds in the north once again revolted. After the war with Iran ended in 1988, Hussein moved against the Kurdish-controlled areas in the north. Nerve gas and mustard gas were dropped on the Kurdish-held cities. Altogether an estimated 200,000 Kurds died in these attacks, but Kurdish guerrillas were able to hold out in some areas.

Iraqi leaders had long claimed that Kuwait should be part of Iraq. In August 1990, the Iraqi army invaded and quickly occupied the country. The United Nations condemned the occupation of Kuwait and ordered the Iraqi army to withdraw by January 15, 1991. When they did not, an allied army led by the United States militarily drove the Iraqis out of Kuwait. The allied army however did not attempt to invade and occupy Iraq. Instead, a ceasefire was announced in February, and in April the United Nations imposed restrictions on Iraq.

Hoping to remove Hussein, then U.S. president George Bush encouraged both the Kurds and the Shiite Arabs to revolt. Responding to Bush's call, in 1991 the Kurdish separatists launched a major attack against the Iraqi-held towns, while almost simultaneously Shiites revolted in the cities and towns of the south. The Iraqi army responded quickly with counterattacks both in the north and in the south. Lacking any meaningful military support from the United States, Shiite irregulars in the south were routed with tens of thousands either killed or executed. Similarly in the north the Kurds were also routed with almost a million refugees fleeing to Turkey. Only the imposition of a "no fly" zone in the north by the United States saved the Kurdish separatists from destruction and allowed them to maintain an autonomous region in the mountainous north.

With the defeat of the Iraqi army and the occupation of Iraq primarily by American forces in 2003, the United States finds itself in almost the very same situation as Britain in 1919. The constitutional monarchy established by the British certainly did not work. The only "stable" government Iraq has had over the past 85 years was that headed by Saddam Hussein. Hussein was only able to accomplish this by keeping Iraq on a war footing and using his army to impose draconian measures to suppress any internal dissension. The oil reserves of Iraq are far too important to the global economy to allow Iraq to descend into anarchy and the present situation is unsustainable.

Ethnic conflict spread to the Kosovo province of Serbia in 1998, when the Albanian majority in the province organized the Albanian Liberation Army and called for an independent Kosovo. Attempts by the Serbs to crush the rebellion resulted in armed intervention by NATO forces in 1999 and the military occupation of the province. In 2000 ethnic conflict spread to Macedonia as Albanian nationalists rebelled against Macedonian control of their regions of the country. NATO peacekeepers are now in Macedonia. The question remains whether workable political solutions can be found for the ethnic problems in Bosnia, Kosovo, and Macedonia. Will foreign peacekeeping troops have to stay in these areas indefinitely?

This is only a sampling of armed nationalist conflicts. Nationalist movements are difficult to defuse. In most cases the recognized national governments lack the military resources to defeat them. Even when a government has overwhelming resources, such as the British in Northern Ireland, guerrilla wars are difficult to win decisively. As a result, few separatist movements have been extinguished. In some cases, the central governments have either disintegrated or lost control over most of the country. In other cases, the central governments have adopted policies of geographical containment and lessening of direct conflict. A graphic example of this approach is in Western Sahara, formerly Spanish Sahara. In the early 1970s, Spain committed itself to a policy of independence and self-determination for its colony. However, in 1976, before independence was achieved Morocco occupied the northern portion of the region, claiming it was historically part of Morocco. In 1979, Morocco occupied the southern portion of the region. The Spanish did not resist the Moroccan occupation. But the local Sahrawi population rejected Moroccan domination, formed the Polisaria Front, and initiated a guerrilla war. Unable to defeat the guerrillas but unwilling to withdraw, the Moroccan government partitioned the region with a 2,500-kilometer-long sand "wall" equipped with electronic devices to detect movements; the purpose of the wall was to separate the portion Morocco controlled from the area it did not control. In 1989 the Moroccan government agreed to a referendum sponsored by the United Nations, but as of 2004 the status of Western Sahara has yet to be resolved.

Almost yearly the number of unresolved ethnic conflicts increases and the number of peoples and regions affected widens. There are about 150 ongoing armed conflicts in the world today, and 80 to 90 percent of these conflicts would be classified as nationalist movements. Central governments as a whole have been unsuccessful in achieving complete military victories over separatist groups, but nationalist separatist groups themselves seldom have been successful in achieving political victories.

Bangladesh was recognized by the United Nations only because it was a fait accompli, backed by the overwhelming military support of India. In contrast, the United Nations was extremely slow to extend recognition to Slovenia and Croatia. Only when it appeared that Yugoslavia might militarily intervene did the United Nations act, and then only in hopes of preventing a war. The recent problems of chaos and starvation in Somalia have been limited to the southern portion of the country. When the central government of Somalia disintegrated in 1991, the leaders in the north declared their independence and established their state of Somaliland. Although Somaliland is politically stable, it has yet to be granted recognition by any country. The United Nations and the Organization of African Unity have taken the position that northern and southern Somalia will "remain" united, and act as if no government exists in the north.

One may well ask why separatist movements are seldom extended official recognition. In Chapter 1, Article 1, of the Charter of the United Nations, the right of a people to self-determination is recognized. The United Nations, however, also recognizes the sovereignty and territorial integrity of existing states. Thus recognition of a secessionist group would be considered intervention in the affairs of a sovereign state. Other governments have also pledged themselves not to recognize separatist states. In 1964 the Organization of African Unity adopted the policy that "the borders of African States on the day of independence constitute a tangible reality," and thus they firmly oppose any changes in the political boundaries of Africa. The real, unstated reason is that almost every country in the world has one or more minority nationalities that either have or potentially may develop an independence movement. Thus both formal and informal agreements are made among the existing countries to maintain the current political status quo.

Resolving Ethnic Conflict

How can such deep-rooted conflicts be resolved? The most obvious solution is to divide the country, giving the members of the dissatisfied nationality their land and independence and allowing them to establish their own country or merge with another country. However, central governments have always been highly reluctant to surrender their territorial claims. As Burma, Sudan, and many other countries have shown, they would rather fight a long, destructive, and inclusive war than officially recognize the independence of a rebellious nationality. This stance is taken partly because governments fear setting a precedent. As a result, most ethnic conflicts have been resolved—and future solutions will probably have to be sought—within the existing political structure. Historically, such internal solutions to ethnic issues have taken two forms: (1) ethnic homogenization of the population through the elimination of rival ethnic groups, and (2) the political accommodation of ethnic groups.

Homogenization

Ethnic homogenization is the process by which one ethnic group attempts to eliminate rival ethnic groups within a particular region or country. Historically, ethnic homogenization has taken one of two main forms: ethnic cleansing or assimilation. The term *ethnic cleansing* entered our vocabulary in reference to the warfare in the republics of what was formerly Yugoslavia. **Ethnic cleansing** is the physical elimination of an unwanted ethnic group or groups from particular geographical areas. It involves genocide and/or relocation.

Genocide is the deliberate and systematic attempt to physically destroy the members of the rival population. The objective may be the total destruction of the group, the reduction of their numbers, or a stimulus for the surviving members of the group to migrate. The process is the same: the indiscriminate slaughter of men, women, and children of the targeted ethnic group. Today, when we think of genocide, we think of the recent events in Bosnia or Rwanda or the killing of millions of Jews and Gypsies by the Germans during World War II, but genocide has been a recurrent event in human history. Only the magnitude of the killing has varied. In the late 1970s and early 1980s, thousands of Native Americans were massacred by the Guatemalan army. The Turks instituted a policy of systematic killing of Armenians during the early years of this century. During the colonial period, the English, Dutch, French, Spanish, Portuguese, Belgians, and Germans were periodically guilty of genocide. Incidents of genocide are found even in American history, beginning with the slaughter of the Pequots in Connecticut in 1637 and ending with the massacre of more than 150 Sioux at Wounded Knee, South Dakota, in 1890. Genocide has been and still is a far too common response to ethnic conflict and rivalry.

Relocation is the forced resettlement of an unwanted ethnic group in a new geographical location. The forced relocation of the target population may be in conjunction with genocide, as in Bosnia, or separate from it. Sometimes the unwanted group is forced outside the boundaries of the country, becoming what today we term *refugees.* In other cases, an ethnic group is forcibly moved to a new area within the boundaries of the state, where it is assumed that they will pose less of a problem.

At the outbreak of World War II, the Soviet Union was home to several million ethnic Germans who had settled in Russia at the invitation of Empress Catherine the Great in the 1760s. In 1924, a separate German autonomous republic within Russia was established along the Volga River for the so-called Volga Germans. When Germany attacked the Soviet Union in 1941, Stalin, fearing that the ethnic Germans might join the invaders, ordered all of them moved from Russia and Ukraine to Kazakhstan, Siberia, and other remote areas.

After World War II, the boundaries of much of Eastern Europe were redrawn. That portion of Germany located east of the Oder River was given to Poland, and 7 million German residents were forcibly evicted. At the same time, Czechoslovakia evicted almost 3 million resident Germans from their homes. After independence, many East African countries expelled many East Indians who had settled there during the colonial period. In American history, Native Americans were regularly relocated as the frontier moved west, thus "solving" the Indian problem for white settlers and the U.S. government. The largest and best known of these relocations occurred in the 1830s, when the Five Civilized Tribes were forced to move (along the so-called Trail of Tears) from their homes in the southeastern states to what is today Oklahoma. Most indigenous tribes of the United States experienced similar resettlement programs. In Bosnia and Croatia the main objective of all the combatants had been the relocation of the other ethnic populations. The killings, rapes, and destruction were the tactics used to cause them to abandon their homes.

Assimilation is the social absorption of one ethnic group by another, dominant one. Assimilation may be total, in which the ethnic identity of one group is lost, or partial, in which one ethnic group assumes a subordinate identity. Assimilation may be either forced or passive. **Forced assimilation** occurs when the government adopts policies designed to deliberately and systematically destroy or change the ethnic identity of a particular group. The ultimate objective is usually the total absorption of the group into the dominant ethnic group. A key target of forced assimilation policy is the elimination of ethnic boundary markers: language, religion, modes of dress, and any cultural institution that readily distinguishes the population. If these boundary markers are destroyed, the group loses much of its social cohesiveness. For example, until recently the Bulgarian government pursued a policy designed to assimilate its Turkish population. Turks were not free to practice their Islamic religion, and they were forced to speak Bulgarian in public and adopt Bulgarian names.

One of the best examples of forced assimilation was the United States' Indian policy in the latter part of the nineteenth and early twentieth centuries. Federal policy attacked Native American ethnic identity from several directions. Reservation lands, which were owned communally, were broken up, and the land was allotted (deeded) to individual members of the tribe to destroy community or village life. Many ceremonies such as the Sun Dance and the peyote religion were made illegal. Traditional or hereditary tribal leaders were not recognized, and tribal governments were either dissolved or reorganized along an American political model. People who worked for the government were commonly forced to cut their hair and wear "citizen's" (Western-style) clothes. Native American children were taken from their families and placed in boarding schools, where they were forbidden to speak their native language, had their hair cut, were made to dress in citizen's clothes, were taught Euro-American technical skills, and were indoctrinated with Euro-American Christian values and attitudes. As the head of the Carlisle Indian School said, "You have to destroy the Indian to save the man."

Assimilation need not be the result of a conscious official policy to solve an "ethnic problem" by incorporating the population into the cultural mainstream. Another form, called **passive assimilation,** occurs without any formal planning or political coercion. Unless strong social barriers prevent assimilation, social and economic forces frequently result in more dominant ethnic groups absorbing members of less powerful groups with whom they are in contact. The dominant ethnic group does not necessarily have to be the largest, but it must be the most socially prestigious and economically powerful group. Many of the governments in Latin America have historically followed a laissez-faire policy toward Native American groups. Guatemala has not had a policy of forced assimilation. In Guatemala the primary differences between Ladinos and Native Americans are not biological but social and cultural, and people who are technically identified as Native Americans are socially and economically discriminated against. As a result, more ambitious and educated Native Americans frequently have abandoned their native languages, dress, and lifestyles (ethnic boundary markers) and reidentified themselves as Ladinos. During the past 100 years, the Native American population in Guatemala has decreased from about 75 percent of the total population to less than 50 percent; passive assimilation is the primary cause of this decrease.

History shows us that there are other ways of managing ethnic differences. People do not have to resort to ethnic homogenization; they can either segregate or accommodate other ethnic groups.

Segregation

The political, social, and economic **segregation** of different ethnic groups has a long history in human society. In these situations the dominant ethnic group does not attempt to eliminate the group, but rather places legal restrictions on the actions of the members of the group. In most cases they have no political rights. They may not be permitted to own land, or if they can, only in certain restricted areas. Marriage between them and members of the dominant group may be prohibited. They may also be restricted to certain economic occupations. Not only is there no attempt to assimilate them into the dominant ethnic groups, legal restrictions maintain their ethnic identities.

There are two major reasons why such ethnic relationships develop: (1) The dependent ethnic group fills a needed economic service, or (2) the dependent ethnic group is so powerless that they present no threat, economic or political, to the dominant society. The Jews and Gypsies in Europe are examples of groups that survived as segregated ethnic groups. At one time the Catholic Church prohibited Christians from being bankers, and Jews filled this important role. Jews were merchants and craftspeople at a time when most Christian Europeans were farmers. Thus the dominant society was dependent on them. Gypsies, on the other hand, were a small powerless group, which presented no threat to the dominant society.

African Americans were a critical source of agricultural labor in the American South. After the Civil War and the end of slavery, the Southern states passed so-called Jim Crow laws, which placed political, social, and economic restraints on African Americans. These new laws kept African Americans from threatening the continued political and economic dominance of Euro-Americans, while allowing Euro-American farmers and landowners the continued use of their labor. In contrast, government officials segregated Native Americans from the general population by placing them on reservations where their actions could be controlled. It was not until 1924 that U.S. citizenship was extended to all Native Americans, and not until 1948 that Native Americans living on reservations were allowed to vote in state and local elections in Arizona and New Mexico.

Accommodation

An alternative to ethnic homogenization or segregation is some form of political **accommodation** that formally recognizes and supports the ethnic and cultural differences of the population. A number of multinational countries have adopted this strategy of formalized ethnic pluralism. For instance, Canada has two main nationalities: Anglo-Canadians (English speaking) and French Canadians (French speaking). Both English and French are formally acknowledged as official languages. Although Quebec is the only province in which French Canadians are the majority, French speakers are found throughout the other, predominantly Anglo-Canadian provinces. Belgium also has two major national groups: the Flemish (Dutch speakers) and the Walloons (French speakers). Both Flemish and Walloon are official languages of Belgium, and although internal political boundaries closely correspond to ethnic boundaries, neither group is recognized politically. Spain has four main linguistic ethnic groups: Spanish, Gallego, Catalan, and Basque. Although Spanish is still the official language of Spain, since 1980 both the Basques and the Catalonians have had local political autonomy.

In the cases of Canada, Belgium, and Spain, the number of distinct nationalities is limited. Other countries have confronted far more complex ethnic mixes. Yugoslavia had eight major nationalities: Serbs, Croats, Muslims, Slovenians, Montenegrins, Macedonians, Hungarians, and Albanians. Separate republics were established for the Serbs, Croats, Montenegrins, and Macedonians. Although no separate republic was created for the Muslims, they were the largest group in the ethnically mixed republic of Bosnia. The Albanians and Hungarians were given autonomous provinces within the republic of Serbia. Yugoslavia was organized as a confederacy, and a great deal of local autonomy was given each of the republics.

Resolution

Having looked at the various means by which people have attempted to resolve ethnic differences, we can now examine the results. What are the results of ethnic cleansing? No American can deny that ethnic cleansing does not work. You need only look about you. How many Native American faces do you see? Yet America was once entirely Native American. American Indian peoples were massacred and the defeated survivors driven steadily westward to lands considered less desirable. Today, most Native Americans survive in small, scattered communities in the western states.

Setting aside the moral issues, ethnic cleansing is seldom a permanent solution. Except for very small groups, rarely has one ethnic nationality been successful in destroying another. Even though it may be greatly reduced in number, the targeted group usually survives. The history of genocidal attacks by the other group becomes an integral part of the origin myth of the victimized group and thus serves to strengthen—not weaken—their identity. Genocide also creates hatred and distrust between groups that can persist for generations after the actual event and make future political cooperation difficult, if not impossible.

Relocation also produces mixed results. As in the case of genocide, the forced removal of a people becomes part of their origin myth and strengthens their cohesion and identity. Among the Cherokee of both North Carolina and Oklahoma, the Indian Removal of the 1830s has become a defining element of their ethnic identity. Removal of a people from their homeland in no way negates their claims to the lands they lost. Four hundred years after the Irish were evicted from Northern Ireland, the Irish Republican Army is fighting to reclaim this portion of the lost Irish homeland. The Jews were expelled from Jerusalem in the first century A.D. and dispersed over Europe, North Africa, and the Middle East. Yet the past century has seen their return to Israel and the reclaiming of their homeland. The collective memory of a nationality is long. Old wrongs are seldom forgotten, and lost homelands are never truly relinquished.

Assimilation—whether passive or forced—is not always effective. There is no question that throughout his-

tory, smaller groups have been absorbed by larger groups, but assimilation is usually a slow and uncertain process. As we discussed, in Guatemala, Native Americans have slowly declined over the past 100 years as a percentage of the total population. We might therefore assume that passive assimilation has proved effective in this case. However, considering absolute rather than relative population, we find that the Native American population actually increased from 1 million to about 4 million during the same period. The main problem with passive assimilation, then, is that population growth often creates new members as fast as or faster than former members become assimilated.

Another problem is that many people do not want to give up their ethnic identity; if they did, forced assimilation would not be necessary. The forced assimilation policies in the United States were equally unsuccessful in regard to Native Americans. Loss of language, material culture, and other cultural institutions that functioned as ethnic boundary markers did not destroy ethnic identity or group cohesiveness because new cultural institutions and ethnic boundary markers soon emerged to replace the old. From a population of only about 250,000 in 1890, the Native American population of the United States has risen to more than 2 million today, and their major political demands are for greater tribal sovereignty and self-determination. So genocide, relocation, and forced or passive assimilation may be effective to a greater or lesser degree, but none of these practices, under most circumstances, truly resolves ethnic problems. More often they postpone the formulation of workable policies and are even counterproductive—they worsen rather than alleviate conflicts. Besides these "pragmatic" considerations, genocide and forced assimilation are so morally abhorrent that few modern governments would admit to pursuing such policies. Relocation, likewise, poses ethical dilemmas; most groups are moved against their will, and some other nationality must be relocated to make room for the migrants. In the modern world, there is nowhere to relocate to without violating some other group's rights. Finally, as we have seen, passive assimilation is usually slow and its result is uncertain.

Political accommodation is the only practical and morally acceptable solution. But how well does it work, and what are the problems in maintaining a multinational state? Although the vast majority of countries encompass two or more national groups, few have attempted to politically accommodate multiple nationalities. Most countries are controlled by a single nationality that politically and economically dominates the other nationalities and holds the country together by force or the implied threat of force.

In an effort to understand the problems of political accommodation, we are going to examine the recent history

Ethnic homogenization	The elimination of ethnic difference within a region or country
Ethnic cleansing	The physical elimination of an unwanted ethnic group or groups
Genocide	The elimination of an unwanted ethnic group or groups by killing the members of the group or groups
Relocation	The elimination of an unwanted ethnic group or groups by physically moving them outside the boundaries of the region or country
Assimilation	The elimination of an unwanted ethnic group or groups through the process of destroying their social identity
Forced	The process of destroying the social identity of an ethnic group by the elimination of their ethnic boundary markers
Passive	The process of destroying the social identity of an ethnic group through conscious or unconscious social and economic discrimination and "voluntary" elimination of ethnic boundary markers
Segregation	The physical separation of an ethnic group and the imposition of social and economic restraints that limit their contact with other ethnic groups
Accommodation	The creation of a balanced political relationship between two or more ethnic groups, allowing each to maintain its own social identity and cultural traditions

of three such states: Canada, Czechoslovakia, and Yugoslavia. Canada remains a united country as the leaders of both English- and French-speaking Canadians struggle to find a political solution to their ethnic problem. Czechoslovakia peacefully split into the Czech Republic and Slovakia in January 1993. The disintegration of Yugoslavia into six republics in 1991 and 1992 has resulted in a series of bloody ethnic wars. Each of these three cases tells us something about the volatility and problems inherent in multinational states.

Canada was originally settled by French colonists during the seventeenth century. The British gained control of portions of eastern Canada in 1713 after Queen Anne's War. French settlers were expelled and replaced by British colonists. In 1763, after the French and Indian War, the British took control of the rest of French Canada. Under the Quebec Act of 1774, French settlers were granted the right to have their own language, religion, and civil laws. After the American Revolution, large numbers of American loyalists settled in Canada, which greatly increased the resident English-speaking population. In 1867, the Dominion of Canada was created and the policy of accommodation continued, with both French and English being recognized as official languages.

In the 1960s, a separatist movement emerged among the French Canadians in Quebec. The main catalyst for this movement was demographic changes. Originally a small minority, the English-speaking population in Canada grew rapidly during the nineteenth century. The twentieth cen-

tury has seen an acceleration of this trend. Most immigrants to Canada during the twentieth century chose to adopt English, not French, as their language, thus adding to the English Canadian population. At the same time, the birthrate of French Canadians has declined. Thus the French Canadians see themselves as constituting an ever-smaller percentage of the total population. French Canadian separatism is not the result of personal animosity toward English Canadians, but rather the collective fear of being overwhelmed by the sheer number of English speakers, the loss of their language, and the erosion of their cultural distinctiveness. In the 1976 elections, the Parti Québecois, the separatist party, won control of the government of Quebec and the next year made French the official language of the province. However, in a 1980 referendum in Quebec, voters rejected separation from Canada. Although 60 percent of the people in Quebec voted against separation in 1980, the issue was not resolved.

Although opposing separation from Canada, the majority of French Canadians remained concerned about the potential loss of French culture and identity. In 1987, the Meech Lake Agreement was negotiated. This agreement would have given Quebec constitutional rights that could be used to preserve the French language and culture. The agreement had to receive the unanimous approval of all the provinces. Two English-speaking provinces rejected the agreement in 1990. In another attempt at reaching a political compromise, a new agreement, called the Charlottetown Accord, was reached in 1992. This new agreement would have weakened the powers of the central government and recognized Quebec as a "distinct society." It also would have permanently given Quebec 25 percent of the members of the House of Commons. Submitted to a national referendum in October 1992, the Charlottetown Accord was soundly rejected, even by the people of Quebec. As a result, in 1995 another referendum was held on Quebec separation, and this time it failed by less than 1 percent. Will there be a third referendum? Will Quebec become a separate country? The early 1990s saw the demise of two multinational states: Czechoslovakia and Yugoslavia. Both had similar histories: they had been created by the Allied powers after World War I; they had attempted political accommodation for their different nationalities and had been controlled by Communists since the end of World War II; they disintegrated once democratic institutions evolved.

Czechoslovakia was created in 1919 out of a portion of what had been the Austro-Hungarian empire. It was a two-nationality state that combined both the Czech ethnic regions of Bohemia and Moravia and the Slovak ethnic region of Slovakia. Linguistically, culturally, and socially, the Czechs and Slovaks are closely related peoples. Although rivalry exists, there was no history of any major hostilities or wars between them. Yet, in January of 1993, by mutual agreement, the country peacefully split into the Czech Republic and the Republic of Slovakia. It was the smaller nationality, the Slovaks, who initiated the division, despite the fact that separation would be to their economic disadvantage; the industrial heart of Czechoslovakia had always been in Bohemia. In terms of political and economic power as well as education, the Czechs had always dominated the country. Not surprisingly, many Slovaks thought that the Czechs treated them like poor country cousins. It was ethnic pride, not ethnic hostility, that led to the breakup of the country.

In the dismantling of the Austro-Hungarian empire after World War I, a new country was also created in the Balkans. Yugoslavia was to be the most ethnically diverse of the central European countries, including within its boundaries Slovenians, Croats, Serbs, Bosnian Muslims, Macedonians, Montenegrins, Hungarians, and Albanians. Unlike other European countries, Yugoslavia had no ethnic majority group. Originally a kingdom, the country was overrun by the Germans during World War II. The local Communist partisan forces under Marshal Tito were able to liberate the country with little direct outside assistance. After the war, Tito created a new political structure for the country in which every ethnic group would have at least some local autonomy. The country was divided into six republics: Slovenia, Croatia, Serbia, Bosnia, Montenegro,

and Macedonia. Within the republic of Serbia, two autonomous provinces were created: Kosovo, in which the majority of people were Albanians, and Vojvodina, which had a large Hungarian population. The national capital, Belgrade, was also the capital of Serbia. The army was also dominated by Serbs. With 36 percent of the total population, the Serbs were the largest national group, followed by the Croats (20 percent), the Bosnian Muslims (9 percent), the Slovenes (8 percent), the Albanians (8 percent), the Macedonians (6 percent), the Montenegrins (3 percent), the Hungarians (2 percent), and "others" (8 percent). Members of the other ethnic groups complained that the Serbs acted as if Yugoslavia was "their" country. After Tito's death in 1980, the office of president rotated among the presidents of the six republics (see Figure 17.3).

The history of the Balkans is a history of long and bloody wars between the various ethnic groups. A particularly deep hatred exists between the Croats (Catholics), the Serbs (Eastern Orthodox), and the Bosnian Muslims. Genocide has been common, and at one time or another each has massacred members of the other group. During World War II almost 2 million Yugoslavians died, and more were killed by members of rival ethnic groups than by Germans.

In June 1991, Slovenia and Croatia declared their independence, with Slovenia leading the way. The wealth-

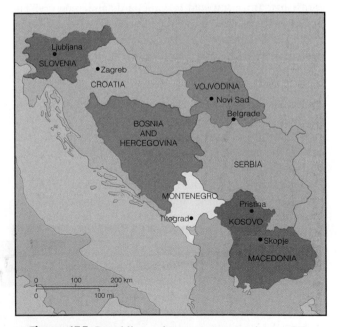

▲ **Figure 17.3** Republics and autonomous provinces of Yugoslavia. The individual republics and autonomous provinces more or less correspond with the territories of major ethnic groups.

iest and best educated of the nationalities, the Slovenians believed that the poorer republics of the country were inhibiting their economic development. The Croats seceded for both economic and nationalistic reasons. With Slovenia and Croatia gone, the ethnic balance in the remainder of Yugoslavia shifted. Serbs now constituted a majority in what remained of Yugoslavia—the country was now a de facto Serb state. In the fall of 1991 Macedonia declared independence, and in early 1992 the Bosnians voted for independence.

The collapse of Yugoslavia did not solve the problem of ethnic conflict, but only made it worse. Croatia, Bosnia, Macedonia, and the Kosovo province of Serbia had large minority populations. Eighteen percent of the population of Croatia was Serbian. Unable to tolerate political domination by the Croats, the Croatian Serbs rebelled, demanding that the areas in which they lived be politically joined to Serbia. The situation in Bosnia was different. With a population consisting of 43 percent Muslims, 31 percent Serbs, and 17 percent Croats, Bosnia had no ethnic majority. The resident Serbs rebelled. Historic hatreds aside, there were two main reasons for the rebellion of the Bosnian Serbs. The Bosnian Muslims as a group were more prosperous than the local Serbs, creating economic jealousy. In addition, the birthrate of the Muslims is higher than that of the Serbs. Thus there was the expectation that in the future the Bosnian Muslims would become the majority, and Bosnia would become an Islamic country. The war quickly became a three-sided conflict as the Bosnian Croats joined the conflict, fighting both the local Serbs and Muslims. Kosovo is the historic homeland of the Serb people. Although 80 percent or more of the population was Albanian (predominantly Muslim), it was politically controlled and economically dominated by the Serb minority. Albanian nationalists rebelled, wanting either an independent republic or unification with Albania. Twenty-two percent of the population of Macedonia is Albanian Muslims. Politically dominated by the Macedonian (Christian Orthodox) majority, Albanian separatists rebelled.

By examining these three cases we can see some of the problems that exist in multinational states, even under the best of conditions. The very presence of two or more nationalities within a country creates the potential for political volatility. Historic hatreds between groups increase the potential for conflict and political division. To be suc-

cessful, political accommodation requires the creation and maintenance of a social, political, and economic balance between the groups. Members of all groups have to feel a collective social equality with members of other groups. They cannot think that their language or cultural institutions are being threatened or eroded by those of another group. Politically, they have to believe that their collective political rights are secure. Finally, no group can feel that their collective economic well-being is inhibited or that they are collectively being exploited by other groups. No country has ever existed with a perfect social, political, and economic balance between nationalities. Some differences and inequalities between nationalities always exist. However, these differences and inequalities must not be of such magnitude as to threaten any particular ethnic group, and all must believe that political unity is to their mutual benefit. The problems faced by multinational countries are not in their initial creation but in their maintenance over time.

The two factors that most seriously threaten the political stability of multinational countries are differential rates of population growth and relative differences in economic development between the constituent nationalities. If the population of one nationality grows more rapidly than that of another, it threatens the existing social and political balance of the country. The nationality or nationalities whose relative populations are declining may think that their social and cultural institutions are being threatened. They may also think that their collective political influence will decline. Regional differences in resources may result in significant changes in the relative economic status of the different nationalities. Changes in relative economic power can be translated into shifts in relative political power. Attempts to redistribute or divide the new wealth of one nationality among the other nationalities within the country can result in a feeling of exploitation.

The evolving global economy requires close cooperation between countries and nationalities. Rising nationalism directly threatens the global economy. Although we cannot change our basic human feelings, we can more clearly understand those factors that serve to unleash ethnic emotions and attempt to minimize them. In the next chapter we discuss the critical issues of population growth, world hunger, and the rights of indigenous peoples.

Summary

1. Every individual, not just members of minority populations, belongs to an ethnic group and has an ethnic identity.

2. An ethnic group is a named social grouping of people based on what is perceived as shared ancestry, cultural traditions, and history. Ethnic group identity divides the world into categories of "us" and "them."

3. An individual's ethnic group identity is seldom absolute, but changes with social context. An individual may assume various hierarchically ranked identities. This characteristic is called the hierarchical nesting quality of identity.

4. The two main attributes of an ethnic group are origin myths and ethnic boundary markers. The origin myth or history describes the common or shared historical experiences that define the social boundaries of the group. Ethnic boundary markers consist of those overt characteristics that make its members identifiable. Ethnic boundary markers may include language, religion, physical characteristics, and other cultural traits such as clothing, house types, personal adornment, food, and so on.

5. There are two distinct levels of ethnic group identity. An ethnic nationality is an ethnic group with a feeling of homeland and the inherent right to political autonomy. A subnational group is an identity nested in a larger national identity. A subnational group does not claim a separate homeland, nor rights to political autonomy.

6. Some scholars argue that a new level of ethnic identity is now emerging: civilizations. A civilization is a grouping of two or more distinct nationalities on the basis of a shared or common cultural historical tradition, generally religion.

7. Globalization has resulted in the creation of ethnic communities that have become geographically separated from their homelands. These groups are termed transnational groups.

8. Much of the conflict in the world today is between ethnic nationalities. There are between 3,000 and 5,000 ethnic nationalities in the world, but only about 200 separate countries. Most countries are multinational countries, and much conflict is the result of nationalities wanting to establish their own independent countries.

9. There is no simple or easy solution to ethnic conflict. Genocide, relocation, and forced assimilation are not only immoral, but history shows that they seldom solve ethnic problems.

10. Passive assimilation is a slow and uncertain process. Segregation reinforces ethnic identities and perpetuates conflict. Attempts by governments of multinational states to accommodate cultural differences and nationalistic aspirations are rarely successful because of differing rates of population growth and regional differences in economic development.

Key Terms

ethnic group	subnationalities	relocation
hierarchical nesting	transnationals	assimilation
origin myth	civilization	forced assimilation
ethnic boundary markers	artificial countries	passive assimilation
ethnogenesis	ethnic homogenization	segregation
nationality	ethnic cleansing	accommodation
homeland	genocide	

InfoTrac College Edition Terms

stateless nations	genocide	transnationals
ethnic cleansing	social assimilation	

Suggested Readings

Bodley, John. *Victims of Progress.* 4th ed. Palo Alto, Calif.: Mayfield Publishing, 1998.

A very readable book that is a good overview of tribal peoples in the modern world, with emphasis on how they are being destroyed by industrial civilization.

Burger, Julian. *Report from the Frontier: The State of the World's Indigenous Peoples.* Cambridge, Mass.: Cultural Survival, 1987.

A general survey of the plight of indigenous peoples of the world.

Carmack, Robert, ed. *Harvest of Violence.* Norman: University of Oklahoma Press, 1988.

This collection of 12 original essays is concerned with the war in Guatemala during the late 1970s and early 1980s, and how the war affected and involved the native Maya communities.

Danforth, Loring M. *The Macedonian Conflict: Ethnic Nationalism in a Transnational World.* Princeton: Princeton University Press, 1995.

An interesting look at one of the most critical countries in the Balkans. This study provides an excellent background for understanding and interpreting the events that have occurred in Macedonia since the book was published.

Eicher, Joanne B., ed. *Dress and Ethnicity: Changes Across Space and Time.* Oxford: Berg, 1995.

In this edited volume, dress and changes in dress are examined in a series of case studies of different peoples from throughout the world.

Ember, Melvin, and Carol R. Ember, eds. *Countries and Their Cultures,* 4 volumes. New York: Macmillan Reference USA, 2001.

This multivolume set, written primarily by anthropologists, is by far the best introduction to the contemporary peoples and ethnic conflicts in the world. Each country is discussed separately with every contributor covering the same topics. Focusing on culture and social identity, topics covered include demography, languages, political history, national identity, and ethnic relations.

Garroutte, Eva Marie. *Real Indians: Identity and the Survival of Native America.* Berkeley: University of California Press, 2003.

This important study addresses the extremely complex issue of Native American ethnic and legal identity in the United States. Who is an "Indian"? There is no single accepted definition. The book discusses various ways in which biological ancestry, sociocultural heritage, and legal statuses have been and are being manipulated by individuals, tribal officials, and the federal government to gain or deny political, social, and/or economic benefits.

Horowitz, Donald L. *Ethnic Groups in Conflict.* 2nd ed. Berkeley: University of California Press, 2000.

The best and most comprehensive study of global ethnic conflict. Originally published in 1985, it has recently been updated.

Huntington, Samuel. *The Clash of Civilizations and the Remaking of World Order.* New York: Simon & Schuster, 1996.

A provocative study that suggests there will be a political realignment of the countries of the world on the basis of civilizations. One of the major fault lines of conflict will be between Western civilization and Islamic civilization.

Moynihan, Daniel Patrick. *Pandaemonium: Ethnicity in International Politics.* New York: Oxford University Press, 1993.

A good introduction to the problem of increasing nationalism and conflict.

Companion Website for This Book

The Wadsworth Anthropology Resource Center
http://anthropology.wadsworth.com

The companion website that accompanies *Humanity: An Introduction to Cultural Anthropology,* Seventh Edition, includes a rich array of material, including online anthropological video clips, to help you in the study of cultural anthropology and the specific topics covered in this chapter. Begin by clicking on Student Resources. Next, click on Cultural Anthropology, and then on the cover image for this book. You have now arrived at the Student Resources home page and have the option of choosing one of several chapter resources.

Applying Anthropology. Begin your study of cultural anthropology by clicking on Applying Anthropology. Here you will find useful information on careers, graduate school programs in applied anthropology, and internships you might wish to pursue. You will also find real-world examples of working anthropologists applying the skills and methods of anthropology to help solve serious world problems.

Research Online. Click here to find a wealth of Web links that will facilitate your study of anthropology. Divided into different fields of study, specific websites are starting points for Internet research. You will be guided to rich anthropology websites that will help you prepare for class, complete course assignments, and actually do research on the Web.

InfoTrac College Edition Exercises. From the pull-down menu, select the chapter you are presently studying. Select InfoTrac College Edition Exercises from the list of resources. These exercises utilize InfoTrac College Edition's vast database of articles and help you explore the numerous uses of the search word, *culture*.

Study Aids for This Chapter. Improve your knowledge of key terms by using flash cards and study the learning objectives. Take the practice quiz, receive your results, and e-mail them to your instructor. Access these resources from the chapter and resource pull-down menus.

Chapter Eighteen

WORLD PROBLEMS AND THE PRACTICE OF ANTHROPOLOGY

Applied Anthropology

Population Growth

Anthropological Perspectives on Population Growth

Costs and Benefits of Children in North America

Costs and Benefits of Children in the LDCs

World Hunger

Scarcity or Inequality?

Is Technology Transfer the Answer?

Agricultural Alternatives

Anthropologists as Advocates

Indigenous Peoples Today

Vanishing Knowledge

Medicines We Have Learned

Adaptive Wisdom

Cultural Alternatives

© Bruce Bander/Photo Researchers, Inc.

Because of anthropology's emphasis on fieldwork, ethnographers often become intimately involved with people they work among, which makes them more likely than most outsiders to listen to local voices.

THIS TEXT HAS BEEN CONCERNED with describing and explaining cultural diversity. Why is it important to study and try to understand cultural differences? In this chapter we are going to try to answer this question.

INCREASING NUMBERS of anthropologists today are using their training to help solve human problems. In the private sector, for example, anthropologists work in a variety of roles, from training international businesspeople to become culturally sensitive when dealing with people from other countries to observing how humans interact with machines. Government agencies and international organizations employ anthropological expertise in problems connected to development, health, education, social services, and ethnic relations. In the first part of this chapter we show some of the specific contributions anthropologists have made to understanding the problems of population growth and hunger. We refer to this as applied anthropology. In the second part of this chapter we discuss the anthropologist as advocate.

Applied Anthropology

Applied anthropology is most simply defined as the application of anthropological perspectives, theory, empirical knowledge of cultures, and methods to help assess and solve human problems. The subfield has grown dramatically since the early 1970s, partly because the number of new PhDs has outstripped the number of academic jobs available, and partly because larger numbers of anthropologists want to use their expertise to help people and organizations.

What special talents or insights do applied anthropologists bring to problem solving? What unique contributions can anthropologists make to programs and agencies? One way to answer this question is to think of cultural anthropologists as sharing a certain worldview (see Chapter 2), which differs somewhat from that of other professional people. This worldview includes how we think about people and groups: the assumptions we share, the categories we use to describe and analyze ideas and behavior, the kinds of information we think it is important to collect to understand a human group, how we believe this information can best be collected, and so forth. Anthropologists learn this worldview through our graduate training, our fieldwork and other experiences involving members of other cultures, our interactions with one another, our readings of ethnographies and theoretical studies, and so forth. Not all ethnologists share this worldview, of course, and (like all worldviews) this one changes over time. Nonetheless, its basic features are well engrained in most anthropologists, and the uniquely and distinctively anthropological contributions to problem solving come out of this worldview more than anything else. For applied work, five consequences of this worldview are most relevant.

Attention to small-scale communities. Ethnologists pay attention to peoples and cultures too often ignored or—what is sometimes worse—known to others mainly by inaccurate or simplistic stereotypes. In applied work, an anthropologist who has worked in a particular small-scale community is often the only outsider who knows enough to provide information about it. Commonly, because of our training in fieldwork methodologies, we are the professionals most qualified to acquire new information relevant to some project about some local community. Through field research, anthropologists provide outside agencies and organizations with information about specific people and cultures.

Insistence on prior detailed knowledge. Because of anthropology's long-standing emphasis on firsthand fieldwork, we believe it is important to devote time and resources, prior to planning a project or program, to determine what the people affected are doing and thinking. Whatever their goals, almost all projects introduce some kind of change to a group, and prior knowledge of the culture is essential to plan and implement the changes. Many projects fail because those who design them know too little about the "target population" (those whose lives will be affected by the project).

Sensitivity to cultural differences. Anthropologists try to make themselves aware of the customs and beliefs of a community, to interact with members of the community in culturally appropriate ways, and to treat community traditions with respect. This cultural sensitivity derives partly from anthropology's relativistic, anti-ethnocentric perspective (see Chapter 1).

Appreciation of alternatives. Anthropologists believe that no one culture's experts know all the answers and solutions. Different people with different histories and traditions have worked out varying solutions to similar problems. What works well in one place and time and among one group may not work well elsewhere. Indeed, local people themselves often know the solutions to their problems but do not have the resources to implement them. More than most other professionals, anthropologists listen to local voices.

Recognition of systematic complexity. Even the smallest and most homogeneous human groups are enormously complicated. But this complexity is ordered and patterned, and ethnographers have long recognized the importance of trying to determine how the parts of a complex system relate to one another and to the whole. A recognition of systematic complexity allows applied anthropologists to realize that changes introduced into a community may have unforeseen, unintended, and often undesirable consequences. Sometimes making small modifications in a program can avoid some of the potential negative impacts.

In the remainder of this chapter, we describe some examples of how these five emphases of anthropological thinking lead to new insights on human problems. Two of our cases deal with major global problems: population growth and world hunger. We show how anthropological work has contributed new insights on these problems. We hope to challenge your conceptions of population growth and hunger and to lead you to think about them in new ways or—at the very least—to question much of what you read and hear in the popular media. We also hope you will think about alternative solutions to these problems.

Quite often, applied anthropologists work in the lesser developed countries (LDCs), which are often collectively known as the Third World. Terms such as *developed, less developed, First World,* and *Third World* imply a certain level of prejudice resulting from a Western view (e.g.,

Third World to whom?). However, because they are familiar terms we continue to use them as shorthand descriptions of major world regions.

Population Growth

As we discussed in Chapter 16, one of the consequences and problems of globalization is the phenomenal increase in the earth's population. In the last 50 years world population has more than doubled, jumping from 2.5 billion to more than 6 billion. Most of this growth is occurring in the poorer countries of the world, creating a wide range of problems. Whereas the standard of living in the developed countries of North America, Europe, and Japan is increasing, the standard of living for most of the rest of the world's people is declining, and differences in population growth rates are the primary factor. In addition, overpopulation in Latin America, Africa, and parts of Asia is resulting in increasing ethnic and social conflict, environmental degradation, and massive migrations of people from the underdeveloped to the more developed countries of the world. Why are the poorest peoples of the world continuing to have large families, while the wealthier peoples are having fewer and fewer children? Why this inverse correlation?

Anthropological Perspectives on Population Growth

Anthropological insight on this issue is twofold. First, anthropologists study human reproductive behavior—including the choices couples make about how many children to have—holistically, meaning in terms of the total system in which people live their everyday lives. By understanding the overall context of behavior, we can understand how the birthrates of a region result from local conditions—especially economic conditions faced by many rural poor. Second, anthropologists have conducted detailed fieldwork in local communities to uncover the major causes of high birthrates in Third World settings.

There is an apparent paradox about the comparatively high birthrates of many underdeveloped countries. An average North American family is able to afford more children than an average Nigerian family. Canadians and Americans have more money to house, feed, clothe, educate, and otherwise provide for their children. Yet they have only two or three, whereas the Nigerian family averages six or seven. And this is the most puzzling thing about high fertility: it continues despite its adverse consequences for those very nations that are experiencing it and whose citizens are causing it—the LDCs.

Why do these people continue to have so many children? Are Indians, Nigerians, and El Salvadorans too ignorant to realize that they cannot afford to support so many children? Can't they see the strain that all these children put on their nations' educational, health, and agricultural systems? Isn't the refusal of couples in these countries to practice birth control even when condoms and pills are available a perfect example of their backwardness and ignorance?

Not at all.

Costs and Benefits of Children in North America

The March 30, 1998, cover story of the weekly newsmagazine *U.S. News & World Report* was titled "Cost of Children." The article reported on the high monetary expenses of raising an American child born in 1997. Middle-income parents (defined in the article as couples who earn between $35,000 and $60,000 a year) can anticipate paying around $300,000 for their child's day care and education, food and clothing, housing, transportation, health care, and other expenses, between birth and age 18. If parents also finance their child's college degree (not including graduate school), the cost of caring for and educating each new member of a middle-income family rises to around $460,000—close to a half-million dollars! Canadians, Japanese, Americans, Europeans, and parents living in other modernized, highly urbanized, industrial, or postindustrial nations are well aware of these monetary costs. Of course, parents in such societies do not have children because we expect our children to bring us future material rewards. For the most part, we do not have children because we expect them to help with chores around the house and yard, or that they will share their income with us when they (finally) get jobs, or that our kids will support us in our old age. Most of us realize all too well that children are an *economic* liability—however *emotionally* gratifying they might be.

Children certainly do cost a lot of money to wage-earning working-class and middle-class couples of an urbanized, industrialized, developed country. Bills for food, housing, doctors, clothing, insurance, and transportation are higher with children—not to mention the costs of day care, baby-sitting, and education. Nor do most children contribute much economically to their parents as they grow older—retirement plans, Social Security, 401(K)s, and IRAs provide most of the income of the elderly. No wonder that when a young couple read in a newsmagazine that it costs a half-million dollars to raise a child and finance a college education, they decide that one or two are quite enough.

◄ Population growth contributes to social problems in the Third World, including unemployment and overcrowding in urban areas. This is a portion of Iquitos, Peru.

© Barry D. Kass/Images of Anthropology

The dollar costs of children are not the only factor that leads North American couples to limit their family sizes. Among the other relevant factors are:

- *Cultural norms and social expectations about desirable family sizes.* Not all couples feel that one or two or three children are enough, but the majority do agree that seven or eight are too many. Enculturated norms and expectations of friends and families certainly affect how many children we have. Note, however, that these norms and expectations themselves respond to other kinds of societal and economic conditions, so they alone do not explain low (or high) fertility rates.
- *Occupational and spatial mobility.* Many young couples do not know where they will be or how they will be earning a living in the next few years. They want children someday but are too unsettled and lack the income to start their family right away. If most couples postpone pregnancy until their mid-twenties or thirties, a lower completed average family size results than if most women begin childbearing earlier.
- *Women's employment.* Many women want a career and perceive that numerous children will interfere with this goal. The limited time and energy of two-earner households lead to lowered fertility rates.
- *Social burdens of children.* Modern society offers numerous social and recreational outlets, which serve as alternatives to devoting one's time and energy to children. A couple may know some friends who have hardly left their house since their baby was born, and they have no desire to be so tied down.

None of this implies that North American couples always have the number of children they choose. Some wind up with more children than they want or with a child sooner than they had planned. And the preceding considerations, to some extent, are class and race biased—they apply more to well-educated, middle-income whites than to blacks and Hispanics, for example. But we do make reproductive choices, and the result of them—barring infertility and so forth—is that we have about the number of children we desire.

There are other factors that North American couples consider, of course. But notice the main overall feature of the considerations just listed: they are all things that will affect the deciding couple personally. People consider the benefits and costs to *themselves* of having or not having children, or of having so many and not more. They do not worry much about whether their children will increase the burden on the American educational system, increase the unemployment rate 20 years in the future, contribute to society's expenditures on public waters and sewers, or overload the nation's farmlands. That is, for the most part they do not concern themselves with the *social consequences* of their reproductive decisions. They do what they think is best for themselves.

Costs and Benefits of Children in the LDCs

Curiously, although most North Americans do not weigh heavily the future societal consequences when they decide to limit their family size, many of them expect people in the LDCs to be more altruistic by reducing their fertility. Too often, when we learn that rural people in parts of the Third World average six, seven, or more children per couple, we think this is economically irrational. They must be having large families for other noneconomic reasons. Probably "children are highly valued in their traditional culture." Or maybe "men have higher prestige if they have lots of children." Perhaps "they are not educated enough to recognize the effects of having such large families." It could be that "they don't know how to prevent pregnancy."

Part of our error comes from our failure to put ourselves in their shoes—to grasp the conditions of their lives that lead them to bear more children than we do. Just because children are an economic liability in a highly mobile, industrialized, urbanized, monetarized society does not mean that they are a liability everywhere. Many demographers argue that rural people in the LDCs have high fertility not simply because of cultural preferences but because children are economically useful. Village-level ethnographic studies suggest that children do indeed offer a variety of material benefits to their parents in the LDCs.

One such study was done in the Punjab region of northern India by anthropologist Mahmood Mamdani. He researched a family planning project that aimed to reduce the birthrate in seven villages. Mamdani found that in the village of Manupur, people accepted the birth control pills and condoms offered by the staff of the program, but most refused to use them. The reaction of the project's administrators was like that of many outsiders when local people do not behave in ways they seemingly ought to behave: They blamed the "ignorance" and "conservatism" of the villagers. To the staff, the benefits of having fewer children seemed obvious. The amount of land available to most people was barely adequate, so by reducing family size people could stop the fragmentation of land that was contributing to their poverty.

However, the village's parents interpreted their economic circumstances differently. They believed that children—especially sons—were economically beneficial, not harmful. Villagers of all castes and all economic levels reported that children were helpful to a household in many ways. They helped with everyday tasks such as washing, gathering animal dung to use as fertilizer, weeding fields, collecting firewood, and caring for livestock. Even young children supplemented family income by doing small jobs for neighbors. When they grew up,

sons were the major source of support for their elderly parents, since one or more of them usually continued to live with their parents and farm the land or work in other occupations. Adult sons often went to cities, where part of the money they earned from their jobs was sent back to help their parents and siblings.

In short, Mamdani argued, the residents of Manupur recognized that the benefits of children exceeded their costs to the parents. Outsiders did not recognize this fact because they did not fully grasp the economic circumstances under which people were actually living.

But, like people everywhere, the people of this region of India proved capable of altering their behavior as their circumstances changed. In 1982, 10 years after Mamdani's study, the village of Manupur was restudied by Moni Nag and Neeraj Kak. They found that couples had changed their attitudes about desirable family size: About half of all couples were now using contraception or had accepted sterilization after they had two sons. The reason was that changing economic conditions in the region had made children less valuable to families. Parents did not need as much children's labor as before. The introduction of new crops and farming methods had almost eliminated grazing land in the region, so boys were no longer useful in tending cattle. Increasing reliance on purchased chemical fertilizers reduced the value of children's labor in collecting cattle dung to spread on fields. Chemical weedkillers reduced the amount of hand work necessary for weeding. A new crop, rice, did not take as much work to grow as the old staples.

The increased value of formal education also led people to have fewer children. Because more outside skilled jobs were available than previously, parents became more interested in providing a secondary education that would increase their children's ability to acquire high-paying jobs. Opportunities for women increased, and secondary school enrollment rates for girls more than doubled between 1970 and 1982. Sending more children to secondary school raised the costs of child rearing. Parents had to pay for clothing and textbooks for their children who attended school, which was a significant expense for poorer families. Accordingly, they wanted and had fewer children.

Finally, most couples believed that having lots of sons was not as necessary as it had been 10 years earlier. People still desired sons for old age support, but many believed that sons were not as dependable as they used to be. Many sons no longer brought their wives with them to live on the family land, but instead left the village to live on their own. One elderly man said:

> Children are of no use any more in old age of parents. They also do not do any work while going to school. My son in

the military does not keep any connection with me. My son living with me has two sons and one daughter. I have advised him to get a vasectomy. (Nag and Kak 1984, 666)

All these and other changes increased the economic costs and decreased the benefits of having large families, and couples reacted to these changes by having fewer children. In this region of northern India, then, ideas and attitudes about desirable family sizes were not fixed by tradition but changed as people adapted their family sizes to changing circumstances.

Researchers in other parts of the world also report that children offer many economic benefits to their parents, explaining why high fertility persists in most LDCs. On the densely populated Indonesian island of Java, rural parents do not have to wait for their children to grow up to acquire the benefits of their labor. Children aged 6 to 8 spend 3 to 4 hours daily in tending livestock, gathering firewood, and caring for their younger siblings. By the time they are 14, girls work almost 9 hours a day in child care, food preparation, household chores, handicrafts, and other activities. Most of the labor of children does not contribute directly to their family's cash income or food supply, so it is easy to see how outsiders might conclude that children are unproductive. However, children accomplish many household-maintenance tasks that require little experience and skill, which frees the labor of adult family members for activities that do bring in money or food. Ethnographer Benjamin White suggests that large families are more successful economically than small families in Java.

Similar findings have been reported by ethnographers working in rural Nepal, Bangladesh, Samoa, and the Philippines. Unlike suburban and urban North Americans, farming families in the LDCs use much of the time of even young children productively. As children grow older they are used to diversify the economic activities of a household, earning cash themselves or performing subsistence work that frees their parents for wage labor.

In many countries, the grown children of rural people migrate to a city within their own country or to a developed country. They acquire jobs—which are well paid relative to what they could earn in their own villages—and send much of the cash back to their families. Such remittances contribute half or more of the family income in Western Samoa, Tonga, and some other small nations of the Pacific, both because migrants feel a continuing sense of obligation to their parents and siblings back home and because many of them hope to return to their islands someday. Remittances are also a major source of family income (and, as a by-product, of national income)

in West African countries like Nigeria and Ghana, Pakistan, India, Mexico, Central America, and parts of the Middle East.

In most parts of the world, children also serve as the major source of economic support in their parents' old age because rural villagers lack pension plans and Social Security. As Stanley Freed and Ruth Freed have pointed out, in many parts of India parents prefer to bear two or three sons to ensure themselves of having one adult son to live with them, in case one son dies or moves elsewhere.

In addition to the value of children's labor, remittances, and old age security, many other factors encourage rural families in the LDCs to have many children, including:

- Relatively high rates of infant mortality, which encourage parents to have "extra" children to cover possible deaths of their offspring
- Extended families, which spread out the burden of child care among other household members, thus reducing it to individual parents
- Low monetary cost of children compared with children in developed countries, partly because many necessities (such as housing and food) are produced by family labor rather than purchased
- The fact that the tasks women are commonly assigned are not as incompatible with child care as wage employment (see Chapter 11).

Such factors mean that children are perceived (in most cases, correctly) as both more valuable and less costly than most citizens of the developed world perceive them. We should not assume that couples in the LDCs are too ignorant to understand the costs of having many children or to appreciate the benefits of small families. Nor should we think that they are prisoners of their "traditional cultural values," which have not changed fast enough to keep up with changing conditions. We should rather assume that they make reproductive decisions just as we do. Then we can begin to understand the economic and other conditions of their lives that often lead them to want more children than affluent couples in urbanized, industrialized countries want. We can also see why birthrates are falling in so many LDCs today. It is not simply the increased education due to family planning and the recent availability of contraceptive devices. Lowered fertility is also a response to the increased urbanization of most nations, to the growth in wage employment over subsistence farming, to the rising emphasis placed on education for both girls and boys, and other factors that have changed the circumstances of family lives.

As we have seen, rising human numbers contribute to the resource shortages faced by LDCs today. One of the resources in shortest supply is one of the things people cannot do without: food. Most North Americans see malnutrition and overpopulation as two sides of the same coin. In the popular view, the "fact" that there are "too many people" in the world is the major reason that there is "too little food to go around." And the solution to world hunger is "more food," that is, increased production by the application of modern agricultural technologies. In the next section we try to convince you that neither the problem (too many people) nor the solution (more production through better technology) is this simple.

World Hunger

The famine in Somalia in the early 1990s is only the most recent reminder of hunger in the world today. Hunger is endemic in much of the world today. The World Food Programme of the United Nations estimates that 800 million people go to bed hungry every night, and that 24,000 people per day die of hunger or hunger-related causes. Hunger afflicts poor people in parts of southern Sudan, Mozambique, Ethiopia, Chad, Bolivia, Peru, Bangladesh, Pakistan, and India. Even in countries considered "moderately developed" or "rapidly developing," there are regions of extreme poverty and hunger, as in Indonesia, Egypt, Brazil, and Mexico. Women and children constitute the vast majority of the malnourished. Children are especially at risk; if malnutrition does not kill them, it frequently results in lifelong mental and physical disabilities. In this section we discuss the conditions that contribute to hunger in the Third World. Our focus is on chronic malnutrition or undernutrition on a worldwide scale, not on short-term famine in particular countries or regions. (The reason we focus on *chronic* hunger is that the immediate causes of famine are more likely to be political upheavals and conflicts that disrupt food production or distribution than economic or demographic forces.) First we discuss two alternative explanations for hunger. Then we cover attempts to increase food supply by modern technological methods, showing why such attempts are so often unsuccessful and counterproductive. Throughout, we suggest anthropological insights on the problem.

Scarcity or Inequality?

What causes hunger? In any given region, people are hungry for a variety of reasons. On a worldwide basis, however, two explanations for hunger are most commonly offered. The first, which we call the **scarcity explanation of hunger,** is that the major cause of wide-

spread hunger in the LDCs is *overpopulation:* in the twentieth century, populations have grown so large that available land and technology cannot produce enough food to feed them. The second, which we call the **inequality explanation of hunger,** holds that the *unequal distribution of resources* is largely responsible for chronic hunger on a worldwide basis: so many people are hungry today because they lack access to the resources (especially land) needed to produce food.

The scarcity explanation holds that there are not enough food-producing resources to provide the poor with adequate nutrition. In countries like India, Bangladesh, El Salvador, Kenya, and Ethiopia, populations have grown so large in the last century or two that there is not enough land to feed everyone. This argument holds that food-producing resources like land, water, fertilizers, and technology are absolutely scarce, meaning that there are not enough resources for the size of the population. In brief, the scarcity explanation holds that hunger is caused by too many people.

Although not our focus here, the scarcity explanation accounts for starvation by saying that chronic hunger turns into outright famine when some sort of disaster strikes. With so many people chronically undernourished, anything that disrupts food production (e.g., droughts, floods, plant diseases, insect infestations, or political disturbances) will reduce food supplies enough to make hungry people into starving people.

The inequality explanation arose, in part, as a reaction to the excesses of the scarcity explanation, which (some believe) blames the victims of hunger by saying that their own (reproductive) behavior causes their hunger. The inequality explanation holds that resources are not absolutely scarce. In fact, there is enough productive capacity in the land of practically every nation to feed its people an adequate diet, if only this productive capacity were used to meet the needs of the poor. But instead, too many productive resources are used to increase the profits of wealthy landowners and to fulfill the wants of the more affluent citizens of the world.

The inequality explanation says that poor people are hungry because of the way both the international economy and their national economies allocate productive resources. The international (global) economy allocates resources on the basis of ability to pay, not on need. For example, if affluent North American consumers want coffee and sugar, wealthy and politically powerful landowners in Central America will devote their land to coffee and sugar plantations for export, because this is how they can make the most money. If North Americans want tomatoes and other vegetables during the winter, large landowners in northwest Mexico will produce them, rather than the beans and corn that are major staples for Mexican peasants. The national economies of countries with hungry people work in a similar way. Urban elites have the money to buy luxuries, and urban middle- and working-class families pressure governments to keep food prices low. As a result, too much land is used to produce crops sold to city dwellers at prices made so low by government policy that the rural poor cannot feed themselves. In brief, according to the inequality explanation hunger is caused mainly by the use of and unequal access to resources.

Which explanation is correct? As is often the case, the two are not mutually exclusive. Both are correct to a certain degree, depending on time and place. The scarcity explanation is correct: all else being equal, the amount of land available per person has been and is being reduced by population growth. Moreover, as population grows, land of increasingly poorer quality has to be cultivated, reducing its productivity. And as families grow poorer, they have less money to acquire new land or to buy fertilizer or other products that will raise the productivity of their land. These arguments are the kind we encounter regularly in the popular news media. It is hard to see how such conclusions can be wrong.

But they could be right and still tell only part of the story. The explanation for hunger is more complex than "too many people" combined with "low farm productivity." Hunger is created by human institutions as much as by population increase and unproductive technologies and farming methods. For example, at a growth rate of 3 per-

cent a year a population will double in less than 25 years. Does this mean that in 25 years everybody will have only half the amount of food? Of course not. Land that formerly was underused will be brought into fuller production; more labor-intensive methods of cultivation can bring higher yields per acre; people can change their diets and eat less meat; and so on. People will adjust their cultivation methods, work patterns, eating habits, and other behaviors to the new conditions rather than tolerate hunger.

Or rather, they will adjust if they have access to the resources they need to do so. And this is a large part of the problem in many LDCs: it is not just that there are too few resources but that too few people own or control the resources available. In their books *Food First* and *World Hunger: Twelve Myths,* Frances Moore Lappé and Joseph Collins question what they call "the myth of scarcity." They claim that every nation could provide an adequate diet for its citizens if its productive resources were more equitably distributed.

A discussion of the evidence that inequality is as important as scarcity in explaining hunger around the world cannot be fully attempted here. There are several excellent contemporary studies by anthropologists of the relationship between population, resource distribution, and hunger. However, here we have chosen to discuss a well-known historical example because it personally affected the ancestors of so many North Americans—the Irish potato famine of 1845–1850.

Ireland was in the early nineteenth century an agriculturally diverse country in which large landowners

◀ Increasingly, lesser developed countries allocate food-producing resources for the production of export cash crops.

© Barry D. Kass/Images of Anthropology

controlled most of the land. Politically and economically the island was controlled by England. Starting in the last decades of the eighteenth century, large landowners had begun increasingly allotting their land to the production of cash crops for export to England where the industrial revolution was transforming the economy. Irish wool and flax were needed by English mills in their production of textiles, while Irish wheat, meat, butter, and other food products were needed to help feed the increasing numbers of factory workers. The export of wool in particular had resulted in a significant reduction of land available for farming as many wealthy landowners had evicted their tenant farmers to turn their land into sheep pastures. Still other large landowners focused on raising wheat, flax, and other exportable grains. Only a small portion of the population of Ireland worked on the large estates or in the towns or cities. The vast majority of the population survived as small subsistence farmers. Their land holdings, either owned or rented, were so small, usually less than 5 acres, that they had to plant a crop that yielded the most in terms of subsistence value. Thus they planted potatoes, which, in a normal year would yield sufficient food to feed their family, with a small surplus that might be sold. The sale of a few potatoes and some irregular wage work produced the only cash income most families had. Malnutrition was common in rural Ireland during the early nineteenth century.

In 1845 the potato blight struck, destroying between a third and half of the potato crop. The severity of the blight varied from one part of the country to another. However, in every region small farmers quickly found themselves short of food, with little if any cash, little in the way of property to sell, and little chance of finding wage labor. Many families were quickly reduced to starvation. As the blight continued in 1846 and 1847, conditions became increasingly difficult. Several million starving people began wandering the countryside in a desperate search for food or jobs or anything to keep them alive. Many simply abandoned their farms, while others were evicted for nonpayment of rent. Hundreds of thousands gathered in the port cities, where, ironically, a few found work loading ships with wool, flax, wheat, meat, butter, and other agricultural products for shipment to England. Starvation in Ireland was not the result of a lack of agricultural resources, but rather that the people of Ireland did not have money to purchase the food being grown and exported. One estimate found that, during the famine, Ireland was exporting to England food sufficient to support 18 million people. In 1845 the population of Ireland had been about 8.5 million. When the famine ended in 1850, only about 6.5 million remained. An estimated 1 million people had died of starvation or

related causes, while another 1 million had emigrated to North America, England, or Australia.

The economic relationship between agricultural Ireland and industrialized England that existed during the early nineteenth century is being seen on a global scale today. Poorer, primarily agricultural, countries are increasingly allocating their resources to the production of products to export to wealthier, more developed countries, while at the same time their populations are growing rapidly.

There is no denying that population growth contributes to hunger and poverty. But neither should we conclude that "too many people" is *the* problem, or that the scarcity explanation is sufficient. Population growth always occurs within a political and economic context, and this context greatly influences the degree to which poor people can adjust to it. In a similar vein, it is fascinating that many economists recognize that famines do not result mainly from an absolute scarcity of food, but from the inability of some groups—usually the poorest groups—to gain access to food. There is also increasing recognition that development ought to be measured by more than "income" and ought to mean more than material affluence.

The combination of population growth and increasing land concentration is doubly devastating. Even if they manage to hang on to their land, the poor will get poorer if their numbers grow. If their increased poverty makes it necessary for them to borrow from the wealthy, to sell part of their land to raise cash, or to work for low wages to make ends meet, they are likely to grow poorer still. This "double crunch" is precisely the experience of the rural poor in many LDCs.

Is Technology Transfer the Answer?

One commonly proposed solution for world hunger is to apply modern scientific know-how and technology to areas in which agriculture is still technologically underdeveloped. This solution seems simple: thanks to agricultural machinery, plant breeding, modern fertilizers, pest control methods, advances in irrigation technology, genetic engineering, and so on, the developed countries have solved the nutrition problem for most of their people. We have developed science and technology and applied it to agriculture. The LDCs need only adopt our know-how and technology to solve their hunger problems. In this view, the main thing hungry countries need is a transfer of our food production technology.

There are many problems with the **technology transfer solution.** We can touch on only a few. First, many of the methods developed for application in temperate climates fail miserably when transported to the tropics, where most hungry people live. This is largely because of the profound differences between tropical and temperate soils and climates.

Second, many experts doubt that so-called high-tech solutions to food problems are appropriate to economic conditions in the LDCs. Labor is much more available than capital in these nations, so to substitute technology (machinery, herbicides, artificial fertilizers, etc.) for labor is to waste a plentiful factor of production in favor of a scarce one. Besides, those who need to increase production the most—the poorest farmers—are those who can least afford new technology. And borrowing money for new investments involves risks because many small farmers who borrow from rich landowners lose their land if they default.

Third, new technologies often come as a package deal. For instance, new crop varieties usually require large amounts of water, pesticides, and fertilizers to do well. Small farmers must adopt the whole expensive package for success. The expense, combined with the logistics of long-term supply of each element of the package in countries with uncertain transportation and political regimes, makes many farmers wary of innovations. Further, many new high-yielding varieties of crops are hybrids, which means that farmers cannot select next year's seeds from this year's harvest. Rather, they must purchase their seeds every year from large companies, many of which operate internationally. Is it a good idea to make the world's farmers dependent on a few suppliers of genetic material for their crops?

Fourth, agricultural experts from the developed world often report problems of "resistance" by peasant farmers. Sometimes peasants cling tenaciously to their traditional crops, varieties, and methods of cultivation even when genuine improvements are made available to them. This famed cultural conservatism of peasants seems downright irrational to many technical experts.

But some anthropologists who have conducted village-level fieldwork offer an alternative interpretation of peasant resistance to change. Living in intimate contact with local people, fieldworkers are sometimes able to perceive problems the way peasants do. Subsistence farmers barely feeding their families cannot afford to drop below the minimum level of food production it takes to survive. Traditional crops and varieties give some yield even when uncontrollable environmental forces are unfavorable because over the generations they have adapted to local fluctuations of climate, disease, and pests. The new ones might not fare as well. Because the consequences of crop failure are severer for poor subsistence farmers than for well-off commercial farmers, they minimize risks by using tried and true crop varieties and

methods. Peasant cultural conservatism thus may be a sound strategy, given the conditions of peasant lives.

Finally, the technology that some believe it wise to transfer to other parts of the world may not be as effective or as efficient as they think. Modern mechanized agriculture requires a large amount of energy to produce its high yields. Studies done in the 1970s suggest that on modern commercial farms in the United States, on average about 1 calorie of energy is required to produce about 2 calories of food. The "energy subsidy" to agriculture goes into producing and running tractors, harvesters, irrigation facilities, chemical fertilizers, herbicides, pesticides, and other inputs. The payoff for this energy subsidy is enormously high yields, in terms of both yields per acre and yields per farm worker. But in traditional agricultural systems, for every calorie of energy expended in agricultural production, about 15 to 50 calories of food energy are returned (the amount depends, of course, on local conditions, cultivation methods, crop type, and a multitude of other factors). The main reason why traditional agriculture is so much more efficient in terms of energy is that human labor energy, supplemented by the muscle energy of draft animals, is the major energy input.

Many questions follow from this difference in energy subsidy. Is there enough energy for modern mechanized agricultural methods to be widely adopted around the world? If there is, can the rural poor of the Third World afford them? What will happen if the rural poor have to compete on a local level with the well-off farmers who can afford to purchase and maintain the new technologies? What will be the local and global environmental consequences of agricultural mechanization on such a large scale? The worldwide price of oil was high in the year 2004, but what will happen to it if tens or hundreds of millions of additional farmers mechanize their operations? Can such methods be used indefinitely—are they ecologically sustainable?

We raise such questions not because the answers are obvious. Some experts—mainly economists—believe that the new problems new technologies create will be solved by even newer technologies. Others say it is too risky to count on a future of uncertain technological salvation, and the consequences of being wrong are too severe to do so. Some believe that whatever future scarcities of energy or other resources occur will stimulate the search for alternative sources, so that the free market will save us. Others claim that we are near the limits of our planet's ability to produce affordable food and other products.

To point out that technology transfers are not economically or ecologically feasible for many regions is not to say that modern food-producing methods are always

388 ▼ Part IV ANTHROPOLOGY IN THE GLOBAL COMMUNITY

harmful or should not even be considered as solutions for world hunger. It merely points out that mechanized technologies have problems of their own and that "experts" do not have all the answers. Are there other solutions that avoid or minimize some of the problems with transfers of technology? Some agricultural scientists, anthropologists, and other scholars are researching alternative methods of boosting food production—methods that are productive and sustainable, yet avoid some of the high energy requirements and the problems associated with mechanized agriculture.

Agricultural Alternatives

Since the early 1980s, increasing numbers of agricultural scientists have been taking another look at traditional farming practices, that is, methods of cultivating the soil that have been used for decades or centuries by the people living in a particular region. In the past, technical experts in agricultural development often scorned traditional farming methods, which they viewed as inefficient and overly labor intensive. But today there is increasing awareness of the benefits of traditional methods.

This awareness stems partly from the failure of so many agricultural development programs for the Third World. It also stems from the environmental movement that began in the developed countries in the 1970s, which called attention to the negative environmental impacts of mechanized agriculture. In addition to the high energy requirements of mechanized agriculture previously discussed, some farming practices commonly used in the developed countries cause environmental problems. Such problems include water pollution from fertilizer runoff, poisoning of farm workers and wildlife from agricultural chemicals, soil erosion from failure to rotate crops, and increasing resistance of insects because of exclusive reliance on pesticides.

In addition to negative environmental impacts, technologies such as machinery, pesticides, herbicides, and fungicides are too expensive for many traditional farmers. Sometimes they are inappropriate or uneconomic to use on the small plots that are characteristic of farms in many parts of the world. They may be unfamiliar to local people, who understandably are reluctant to abandon proven cultivation methods for alternatives they perceive to be riskier.

Considerations such as these led some agricultural scientists in the 1980s to ask, Are there *viable* alternatives to mechanized agricultural technologies and practices? Some experts believe that there are. The main goals of such alternatives are minimization of negative environmental impacts, affordability to small farmers, reliance on technologies and resources that are locally available, adaptation to local environmental conditions, and long-term sustainability.

Over the centuries, traditional farming systems have evolved that meet many of these goals. Increasingly, agricultural scientists and development agencies look at traditional agriculture not as a system that should be replaced but as a set of farming techniques that they can learn from. Much research on this topic is ongoing; here we can present brief descriptions of only two traditional methods: intercropping and resource management.

Intercropping. One method used by traditional farmers in many parts of the world (in the tropics especially) is intercropping, also known as multiple cropping or polyculture. In contrast to monoculture, intercropping involves the intermingling of numerous crops in a single plot or field. It has been practiced for centuries by shifting cultivators, whose plots usually contain dozens of crops and varieties.

Although intercropped fields look untidy, this method offers several benefits, stemming from the diversity of crops growing together in a relatively small space. Many plant diseases and pests attack only one or a few crops, so if there is a diversity of crops, yields may still be good despite an outbreak. In regions where water supply is a problem and rainfall is erratic, some crops suffer during droughts but others will still produce a harvest. The varying growth patterns and root structures of diverse crops have useful ecological benefits: Erosion is low because more of the soil is covered, and sun-loving weeds are suppressed by the shade of the crops themselves.

Traditional farmers in some parts of the world have learned over the centuries that many crops grow better when planted together. Leguminous crops, such as beans, peas, and peanuts, take nitrogen (a necessary plant nutrient) from the air and store it in their roots. Intercropping legumes with crops that need lots of nitrogen can increase yields. This is done in Mexico and Central America, where traditional farmers have long intercropped corn, beans, and squash. The stout corn plants provide support for the bean vines to climb, and the ground-hugging squash plants keep the soil covered. African farmers intercrop sorghum with peanuts and millet with cowpea with similar benefits.

Traditional Resource Management Practices. In many parts of the world, traditional farmers actively take steps to control the plant species growing in areas that, to outsiders, look "wild" or "abandoned." They are, in other words, managing their resources so they can continue to use them indefinitely. Two brief examples illustrate these management practices.

The Kayapó of the Xingu River basin of Brazil farm in the forest by shifting cultivation. According to anthropologist Darrell Posey, who has worked among the Kayapó for years, the Kayapó manage the forest carefully. One of their traditional practices is the creation of "islands" of forest in deforested areas. They move composted soil made from termite and ant nests and vegetation into open areas and transplant crops and other useful plants. The created and managed environment provides plant foods, medicines, and building materials and attracts some of the animals hunted by the Kayapó.

The Lacandon Maya of the state of Chiapas in southern Mexico practice slash-and-burn. Although the staple crop is corn, many other crops are planted in the cleared fields, including several tree species that yield fruits. Lacandon farmers clear and plant new plots frequently, but they do not simply abandon a plot once its main crops are harvested. Rather, they return to it for many years to harvest the long-lived fruit trees and other species they planted. Even while the natural forest is regrowing, the Lacandon continue to use the land. They manage their fallowing fields and thus integrate their exploitation of the land with the natural process of forest regeneration.

We have presented some of the reasons many scientists and others concerned with agricultural development are reconsidering traditional agriculture. It is all too easy to romanticize traditional farmers, to think that they really have had the answers all along and that only recently have so-called experts been forced to pay attention. This view, too, is simplistic: in all likelihood, solutions to the food crisis will require a mixture of traditional and modern technologies. It is, however, encouraging that the knowledge and methods embedded in traditional agricultural adaptations are being taken seriously by the World Bank and other institutions in a position to make critical decisions.

Anthropologists as Advocates

Anthropologists do not merely define problems. From the earliest origins, anthropologists as individuals have been politically active, using the information gained from their research to voice their concerns about a wide range of public policy issues. Franz Boas (see Chapter 5) took an active role in attacking racist stereotypes during the first decades of the twentieth century and publicly opposed U.S. immigration laws based on racist ideas. Margaret Mead (see Chapter 5) was certainly the best-known advocate for women's rights in the United States during the

mid-twentieth century. As individuals, anthropologists have been and still are activists concerned with a wide range of particular and global issues. However, no single issue has concerned anthropologists as a group more than the rights of indigenous peoples.

This should not be surprising. Much of anthropological research has focused on the study of these peoples, and field research is a highly personal experience. As a result, not only do anthropologists as a group more clearly understand the problems of these peoples than other outsiders, collectively we know them and value them not just as individuals but friends as well. In the late nineteenth century American anthropologists were engaged in advocating the rights of American Indian peoples. As members of the Lake Mohonk Conference and other Indian rights organizations they lobbied Congress for changes in the laws concerning American Indian tribes. Throughout the twentieth century and today, at the beginning of the twenty-first century, anthropologists continue to fight for the rights of indigenous peoples. Thus it is fitting that we end this book by advocating the rights of indigenous peoples to preserve their cultural systems—assuming, of course, that is their choice.

Indigenous Peoples Today

Indigenous may be used to refer to any people who have resided in a region for many centuries. By this definition, the Germans of Germany and the Irish of Ireland are indigenous. However, as **indigenous peoples** is usually used today, the phrase refers to "culturally distinct groups that have occupied a region longer than other immigrant or colonist groups" (*Cultural Survival Quarterly,* Spring 1992, 73). Generally, indigenous peoples are small-scale societies who make their living by foraging, farming, and/or herding, live in roughly the same region as their ancestors, and are fairly remote from the economic and political centers of the countries that include their territory. Sometimes they are termed tribal peoples, or more recently Fourth World peoples. Often their territories cross modern national boundaries.

Indigenous peoples most often survive as ethnic enclaves within a larger nation. The government controlled by the dominant ethnic group of these countries usually claims to have ultimate control over the land and other resources of the indigenous people who live within the officially recognized national borders. For many indigenous peoples, in effect, the colonial world still exists. Lacking effective political autonomy and being too few to make physical resistance successful, their remaining lands are constantly threatened by the wider society. Too

When the earliest Europeans first encountered the An-ishinaabeg (also known as the Chippewa or Ojibwa), in the Upper Great Lakes region, they found that an important staple in their diet was wild rice. Wild rice is a native wild grass found in ponds and lakes throughout much of the eastern United States and Canada, although it is most abundant in the lake area of Minnesota, Wisconsin, Manitoba, and Ontario. Although called rice it is not a close relative of domestic rice and is readily distinguishable by both its shape and its color. Like most wild grain crops it is difficult to harvest. When the grains mature, which takes place over a period of 9 to 14 days, the Anishinaabeg would take their canoes into the stands of wild rice in the ponds and edges of the lakes. The long blades of rice would be bent over the sides of the canoes and wooden clubs would be used to beat the mature grains loose into the bottom of the canoe. Working in the sun on the open water to harvest rice was a long, hard, and hot job. Because of the long period of mat-uration, even under the best of conditions, half or more of the crop would not be harvested, instead dropping into the ponds or lakes. This loss was critical, because wild rice is an annual, not a perennial, and lost grains would insure the next year's crop.

Euro-Americans settled Minnesota and Wisconsin in the mid-nineteenth century. The northern portions of these states were not well suited to farming. As a result the Anishinaabeg did not face the severe land pressure as did the tribes farther south, and a series of scattered reservations were created. Even in the areas not designated as reservations the interest of the new settlers was usually limited to timber, game, and fish. While many of the settlers developed a taste for wild rice, few made any attempt to compete with the Anishinaabeg in harvest-ing it. The work was hard and difficult and as a result they pre-ferred purchasing it from the Anishinaabeg. Because of its dis-tinctive taste, during the twentieth century wild rice became considered a gourmet food. Thus not only did the Anishinaabeg continue to harvest wild rice for their own domestic consump-tion, it also became a source of cash income, being marketed throughout the United States and Canada.

As early as the 1950s the growing demand for and the rela-tively high value of wild rice had attracted the attention of com-mercial growers, and the first unsuccessful attempts were made to domesticate wild rice. In 1977 the State of Minnesota pro-claimed wild rice as its "state grain," and with funding from the state, local universities began to attempt to develop a strain of wild rice, which could be commercially grown in paddies, like domestic rice. Researchers focused on developing a strain with uniform maturation, not over a 9 to 14 day period, and one that was easier to harvest. They were successful in their attempts and a commercial paddy–grown wild rice agribusiness started developing in Minnesota.

By the 1980s, however, the commercially grown wild rice agribusiness moved to California. The U.S. Department of Agriculture had begun paying California domestic rice growers to limit the planting of domestic rice. These growers quickly shifted to the planting of paddies of "domesticated" wild rice. In 1998 and 1999, the Nor-Cal Wild Rice Company was able to patent two sterile, geneticaly engineered varieties of "wild rice." As a result both traditional Anishinaabeg wild rice har-vesters and Minnesota wild rice planters have seen their market devastated. More than 95% of the grains marketed as wild rice are grown in commercial rice paddies in California. The success of commercially grown wild rice is simply based on the fact that it looks like real wild rice, but it doesn't taste like wild rice.

To the Anishinaabeg the commercialization of wild rice pro-duction represents far more than just the loss of a source of cash income. To them the harvesting and consumption of wild rice is a critical part of their cultural heritage and community life. Many of their songs and ancient stories are concerned with wild rice. Their identity is in part associated with wild rice. Over the past century they have witnessed a steady decline in the abun-dance of wild rice due to the development of lakes and ponds for recreation purposes: boating and fishing. Now they have an added fear: if sterile varieties of "wild rice" are planted in Minnesota, they might contaminate the native wild rice and thus result in its extinction.

In 1989, Winona LaDuke, a local Anishinaabeg, helped es-tablish the White Earth Land Recovery Project (WELRP), on the White Earth Reservation in Minnesota. WELRP has several purposes, the main focus being the protection of wild rice, which they consider "uniquely" theirs. WELRP markets tradi-tionally harvested and processed wild rice. It also attempts to combat what it considers biopiracy and is opposed to scientific research on wild rice. To them wild rice is a sacred gift to hu-manity and the people who use it. The genetic altering of the plant and the patenting of the modified form are not only a sac-rilege, they are a legal claim on something that belongs to everyone. Not only is the research of companies like Nor-Cal immoral, citing what has happened with corn in parts of Mex-ico, genetically engineered crops threaten biodiversity and thus future human survival. So far their successes have been limited but important. A division of the Anheuser-Bush Company was marketing California grown "wild rice" in a package showing Indians in a canoe, inferring that this was a traditionally har-vested product. The company settled out of court by removing the picture. In Minnesota, WELRP convinced the legislature to pass a law requiring commercial rice producers in Minnesota to add the word "paddy" in their marketing.

Sources: LaDuke (2003) and Kummer (2004).

often their ways of life are destroyed because more numerous and powerful ethnic groups consider indigenous cultures barriers to national progress and development.

Altogether, there are perhaps 600 million indigenous peoples in the modern world. Among them are the Native American peoples of North, Central, and South America; the aboriginal peoples of Australia and other islands of the Pacific; the Sami (formerly known as the Lapps) and other reindeer-herding peoples of northern Europe and Asia; hundreds of "tribal" cultures of east Asia, southeast Asia, and south Asia; and numerous ethnic groups of Africa.

The legal rights of indigenous peoples became an issue with Columbus's landfall in the Americas. Questions of whether the native peoples of the Americas—or for that matter any indigenous people—had any inherent rights to their land, resources, or political autonomy were debated in Spain. Although legal particulars differed from one colonial power to another as well as over time, a basic consensus was reached early in the colonial period: an indigenous people did have some rights based on prior occupancy. However, more "civilized" peoples could unilaterally claim jurisdiction over them and make use of any land and resources that were either not utilized or underutilized. Civilized peoples had both a right and an obligation to uplift indigenous peoples and act in their "best interest." This responsibility came to be called the "white man's burden." Civilized peoples also had the right to travel and trade wherever they wanted without interference from indigenous peoples. Finally, if an indigenous people resisted, then the civilized people had the right to use military force against them. Racism, ethnocentrism, and social Darwinist ideas about the inevitability and desirability of progress provided the moral justification for the treatment of indigenous peoples.

Such attitudes and policies affected the governing of most indigenous peoples in the colonial possession of European nations. When independence came to Asian and African countries in the twentieth century, the leaders and dominant ethnic groups of many of the new nations adopted similar attitudes and policies. As discussed in Chapters 16 and 17, the modern boundaries of most existing countries are legacies of European colonization in the sixteenth through the early twentieth centuries. In many cases, the political and legal systems of these countries are also Western-derived or heavily Western-influenced. Such attitudes, governmental policies, and legal concepts are often the basis for the treatment of indigenous peoples and other ethnic groups within a Third World nation itself. In fact, to understand what is happening to most remaining indigenous peoples in the world today, one can start by reexamining American Indian policy during the nineteenth and early twentieth centuries. In Brazil, Indonesia, Sudan, and elsewhere, the same introduction of new diseases, genocide, relocation, forced assimilation, and appropriation of land and resources of smaller indigenous groups by politically dominant ethnic groups is taking place.

Modern governments in parts of Latin America, Africa, and Asia face serious economic, political, and social problems. Many governments—including those democratically elected—are under pressure from their dominant ethnic group to pursue policies that lead to the displacement or assimilation of the indigenous peoples

◀ The physical and cultural survival of the Yąnomamö and other Amazonian peoples is threatened by opening up their traditional lands to mining, logging, ranching, and other extractive industries.

© Victor Englebert/Photo Researchers, Inc.

whose territories lie within their national boundaries. In many countries aspiring to modernization, indigenous people living in remote, "undeveloped" regions are forced to move aside in the interest of what the dominant ethnic group sees as the "greater good" of their nation.

Sometimes this greater good consists of opening up undeveloped areas to settlers. For example, Indonesia resettles peasants from overpopulated Java onto its outer islands (such as Sumatra, Irian Jaya, and Kalimantan), now claimed to be "underpopulated." Although often considered a modernized nation, Brazil has some of the poorest people in the world living in its northeastern area. It is also one of the few countries left with a frontier—the vast tropical rain forest of Amazonia. In the 1970s, Brazil constructed highways intended to open up Amazonia to resettlement and to mineral, timber, grazing, and agricultural exploitation. One-third of Brazil's Native American tribes have disappeared since 1900, and many others have lost most of their lands to outsiders.

One people who are threatened by the opening up of Brazil's Amazonian frontier is the Yąnomamö, mentioned in Chapters 2, 6, and 9. Until the early 1970s, most of the approximately 20,000 Yąnomamö were relatively isolated from outside influences. In 1974, the Brazilian government constructed a road through the southern part of Yąnomamö territory. Workers involved in forest clearing and road building introduced new diseases such as influenza and measles, and in some regions as many as half the Yąnomamö died during epidemics. Dirt airstrips constructed during the 1980s also made Indian territory accessible to Brazilian gold prospectors. In the late 1980s thousands of gold seekers—most of them impoverished—poured into the area in search of wealth. By early 1990, as many as 45,000 prospectors had invaded traditional Yąnomamö lands and extracted gold worth an estimated $1 billion.

The government's National Indian Foundation is charged with protecting Brazil's Native American peoples and territories from invasion and plunder, but it has been unable to control violence against the Yąnomamö and other indigenous groups. In 1990, Brazil's former president ordered the landing strips destroyed to reduce future access and in 1992 the Yąnomomö territory was demarcated and ratified by the government. However, by 1996 miners had illegally returned to Yąnomamö lands and political pressure is growing to open more areas to mining and timber interests. The Yąnomamö have already lost rights to two-thirds of their Brazilian territory, and deaths caused by violence and disease are likely to continue.

Another common justification for the neglect of the territorial rights of indigenous peoples is the desire to improve a country's balance of trade. The Philippines, Indonesia, and other countries earn foreign exchange by leasing rights to harvest timber from their tropical hardwood forests to multinational companies, although much of the "unexploited" forest is needed as fallow by indigenous shifting cultivators. Debts owed to foreign banks and international lending agencies encourage some nations to open up their hinterlands to resource development, pushing their indigenous inhabitants aside. In countries such as Brazil and Mexico, minerals, cattle, timber, vegetables, coffee, and other exports are sold to Europe and North America to earn foreign exchange to help pay off international debts.

Many indigenous communities are affected adversely by the efforts of well-meaning people to promote environmental causes such as habitat preservation or animal conservation. For some, preservation and conservation of biological resources are interpreted to mean "no resource exploitation" or, in extreme cases, even "no people." Governments of nations with large indigenous populations sometimes react to such concerns by resettling people out of areas they have lived in for centuries. (An irony is worth pointing out here: often the areas deemed appropriate for conservation or preservation efforts are those that are recognized as relatively undisturbed—partly because it is mainly the indigenous peoples who have been using them all along.)

Within the southern African nation of Botswana lies the Central Kalahari Game Reserve (CKGR), which is the second largest game reserve in all Africa. The CKGR was established in 1961, partly to provide the indigenous hunter-gatherers of the region—the San (see Chapter 7 for information on the !Kung, one of several local San groups)—with adequate resources for their subsistence needs. In the 1960s and 1970s, local groups of San used the territory for subsistence foraging, sometimes on horseback. In the 1980s, some environmentalists tried to persuade the European Union to pressure Botswana officials to remove the people from the CKGR and declare the area a game reserve. By the 1990s, the remaining San were encouraged to move outside the reserve by various methods, including failure to repair a needed well, intimidation by selective enforcement of game laws, and (allegedly) severe physical punishments of accused "poachers."

Then, in 1997, the government of Botswana resettled several hundred San outside the boundaries of the reserve, placing them in an environment with few trees and wild plant foods and offering them very little compensation. This action was taken partly in the name of conservation. But San argued that increasing numbers of tourists in four-wheel-drive vehicles were destroying the land and that more cattle were on the reserve. According to an article by Robert Hitchcock (1999, 54) in the journal *Cultural Survival Quarterly,* the San "expressed that the reason they were being removed was so that well-to-do private citizens could set up lucrative safari camps in the reserve." Perhaps environmentalists in North America and western Europe should also give more consideration to impacts on the welfare of indigenous peoples when they propose to save wildlife or preserve ecosystems. In 1996 the governments of South Africa, Botswana, Namibia, Zambia, and Zimbabwe together created the Working Group of Indigenous Minorities in Southern Africa (WIMSA). The purpose of WIMSA, a nongovernmental organization, is to act as the collective advocate for, and voice of, the 100,000 San people scattered among the five countries. So far WIMSA appears to have had little meaningful influence.

As these and numerous other cases show, many still consider it legitimate to take land from those who have lived on it for centuries. Racism and social Darwinism are not as fashionable as official justifications as they once were. But new rationalizations exist for the forced removal and exploitation of the territories of indigenous peoples: developing natural resources for the benefit of the country; solving "national problems" by providing lands to peasants and making payments on debts owed to foreign banks and international lending institutions; making the country's products competitive in international markets; and even preserving animal habitats and ecosystems.

The indigenous peoples who remain in cultural communities are learning to protect themselves through political action. In increasing numbers, indigenous peoples around the world are fighting attempts to dispossess them of their traditional territories and resources. Many are resisting efforts to assimilate them into the cultural mainstream of their nations. They are publicly objecting to racist and ethnocentric attitudes about their beliefs and customs.

One people who are resisting are the Kayapó. In the 1980s, the government of Brazil sought World Bank funding for the construction of two enormous hydroelectric dams on Amazon River tributaries. Eighty-five percent of the land that would have been flooded belongs to one or another indigenous Indian population. Organized by leaders of the Kayapó tribe, members of 29 Brazilian Indian groups protested the dams. In early 1988, two Kayapó leaders traveled to Washington with anthropologist Darrell Posey to speak against the project to officials of the World Bank and to U.S. congressional authorities. When the World Bank deferred action on the loans, Brazil brought charges against the three protesters under a law that forbids "foreigners" from engaging in political activity harmful to the nation. The courage and sophistication of the Kayapó and other members of threatened communities illustrate how indigenous peoples are organizing themselves to acquire the political power to fight various developments. However, the pressures for the development of indigenous lands are relentless. In 2001 the Brazilian government announced new plans to build three hydroelectric dams on the Xingu River, this time using private and Brazilian governmental funding. The Kayapó and other indigenous leaders held a meeting in the summer of 2004 to resist these new dams.

Outside of Great Britain the entire English-speaking world was once populated by preindustrial peoples who died from disease and violence, were displaced, or became assimilated by colonists. In the past couple of decades, indigenous peoples in Australia, New Zealand, Canada, and the United States have asserted claims for territories and resources lost to Anglo settlers. In 1996, a New Zealand tribunal found in favor of the claim of the indigenous Maori that a sacred volcano was illegally taken by the British in the last century. Canada's First Nations are pressing their claims for lands and for compensation for lands illegally taken. The Nisga'a of British Columbia are one of 44 native groups negotiating with the provincial and national governments for return of territories and compensation for past injustices. Native Americans in Alaska, Washington, and Oregon are involved in disputes with government agencies over whaling and salmon fishing rights. Indigenous peoples in many regions are also attempting to reclaim their cultural and intellectual properties (see Globalization box in Chapter 5).

Vanishing Knowledge

Despite the increased political sophistication of indigenous peoples around the world and the protests of concerned citizens in many countries, there is no doubt that many preindustrial cultures are in danger of extinction. Even if the people themselves survive the onslaughts of lumbering, mining, damming, grazing, farming, and building, their way of life is liable to disappear. Most people would agree that genocide is a crime of the highest degree. But destruction or alteration of a culture is another matter—is it not possible that indigenous people themselves would be better off if they joined the cultural mainstream of their nations?

Yes, many peoples do want to acquire formal education, get jobs, improve their living standards, and generally "modernize" their societies. For many peoples and for many individuals within an indigenous culture, contact with the wider world offers new opportunities and new choices. Young people are especially attracted by the material goods, entertainments, new experiences, and sheer variety of activities found in towns and cities. They should have these opportunities and these choices. But indigenous peoples and their ways of life are often overwhelmed by forces over which they have no control. It is not that most indigenous peoples are given the opportunity to carefully weigh the options available to them, so that they make informed choices about whether it is best for them to preserve or to modernize their ways of life. Today, as in the past, their traditions are disappearing more often because powerful national governments want to open up their territory or because private entrepreneurs or corporations want to exploit their resources.

Anthropologists are especially concerned with the rights of indigenous peoples for several reasons. First, because of our interest in cultural diversity, we are more aware of what has happened to non-Western cultures in the past several centuries than are most people. Second, we identify with indigenous peoples partly because so many of us have worked among them. Third, our professional training gives us a relativistic outlook on the many ways of being human, so we can appreciate other peoples' customs and beliefs as viable alternatives to our own. Finally, the fieldwork experience often affects our attitudes about our own societies—deep immersion into other cultural traditions leaves some of us not so sure about our commitment to our own.

Whether one is an anthropologist or not, one can appreciate the rights of any group of people to have their lives, property, and resources secure from domination by powerful outsiders. The most important factors in considering the rights of indigenous peoples to be left alone are ethical ones. Do not people everywhere have the right to live their lives free from the unwanted interference of those more powerful and wealthy than themselves? Does any government, regardless of its "problems," have the right to dispossess people from land they have lived on and used for centuries? Is the demand of citizens in Japan, Europe, North America, or anywhere else for wood, minerals, meat, electricity, or other products a sufficient justification for relocating a people or taking land away from them? (Readers who follow politicians' statements about human rights violations in Iran, Iraq, China, Bosnia, Kosovo, and other countries might wonder why they have so little to say about the rights of indigenous peoples.)

Surely, most of us agree on the answers to such questions. Ethical concerns for the human rights of indigenous peoples, combined with a respect for their cultural traditions, are the primary reasons for granting their rights to survive as living communities.

But if the ethical arguments alone (based on shared values about human rights) are not compelling, there are other arguments (based on practical concerns, and even on the self-interest of the dominant majority). The long-term welfare of all humanity may be jeopardized by the loss of cultural diversity on our planet. Think about the cultural heritage of humanity as a whole. Consider *all* the knowledge accumulated by *all* humanity over hundreds of generations. Imagine, in other words, human culture—here defined as the sum of all knowledge stored in the cultural traditions of all humans alive today.

Some of the knowledge in present-day human culture has been widely disseminated in the past few centuries by means of written language. We may call it *global knowledge* (not meaning to imply that it is "true" or "universally known"). Although some global knowledge will be lost or replaced, much of the knowledge stored in writing (or, more recently, on computer disks) will be preserved and added to over the coming decades and centuries. Other knowledge comprising human culture is *local knowledge*—it is stored only in the heads of members of particular cultures, many of which are endangered. Most local knowledge will disappear if those cultural traditions disappear—even if the people themselves survive.

How much of this local knowledge is knowledge that may (today, tomorrow, someday) prove useful to all humanity? Of course, no one knows. But no one can doubt that the rest of the world has much to learn from indigenous cultures. (Incidentally, anthropologists have always understood the importance of learning *about* other cultures; recently, there has been increasing emphasis placed on learning *from* them.) In fact, much of what had been only the local knowledge of some indigenous culture has been incorporated into global knowledge, as a consequence of contact with the West and other colonizing peoples. We conclude this book with a small sample of some of the medical and adaptive wisdom of indigenous peoples, whose local knowledge has already contributed so much to the world.

Medicines We Have Learned

"The Medicine Man Will See You Now," proclaimed a headline in a 1993 edition of *Business Week*. The accompanying article described a California pharmaceutical company that sends ethnobotanists and other scientists into rain forests to learn from indigenous shamans. Companies as well as scholars are beginning to understand that the traditional remedies long used by preindustrial peoples often have genuine medical value. In fact, many of the important drugs in use today were derived from indigenous knowledge (see Globalization box in Chapter 5). Here we can provide only a few examples of the medicines originally discovered by indigenous peoples that now have worldwide significance. An enjoyable source of more examples is the 1993 book, *Tales of a Shaman's Apprentice,* by Mark Plotkin.

Malaria remains a debilitating, although usually not fatal, sickness in tropical and subtropical regions. Its main treatment is quinine, a component of the bark of the cinchona tree. Europeans in the seventeenth century learned of the value of quinine from Peruvian Indians.

The Madagascar periwinkle has long been used in folk medicine to treat diabetes. Researchers first became interested in the plant as a substitute for oral insulin, but it seems to have little value for this purpose. However, during the course of their investigation, scientists discovered that extracts from periwinkle yielded dramatic successes in treating childhood leukemia, Hodgkin's disease, and some other cancers. Drugs based on the plant—notably vincristine and vinblastine—remain the major treatments for these otherwise fatal diseases.

Muscle relaxants are important drugs to surgeons. A popular one is curare, made from the chondodendron tree. Taken in large amounts, curare can paralyze the respiratory organs and lead to death. This property was recognized by South American Indians, who used it as arrow poison for hunting birds, monkeys, and other game, and from whom medical science learned of the drug's value.

The ancient Greeks and several North American Indian tribes used the bark of willows for relief from pain and fever. In the nineteenth century, scientists succeeded in artificially synthesizing this compound that today we call *aspirin.*

There is no way of knowing how many plants used by surviving indigenous peoples could prove to be medically effective. The potential is great. According to pharmacologist Norman Farnsworth, about one-fourth of all prescribed drugs in the United States contain active ingredients extracted from higher plants. The world contains more than 250,000 species of higher plants. Although as many as 40,000 of these plants may have medical or nutritional values that are undiscovered by science, only about 1,100 of these have been well studied. Botanists and medical researchers are coming to realize that indigenous peoples already have discovered, through centuries of trial and error, that certain plants are effective remedies for local diseases. The future value of their medical wisdom to all of humanity is largely unknown, but probably great.

▲ Indigenous peoples, such as these Indonesian "medicine men," commonly have an extensive and potentially important knowledge of the curative powers of plants. How much medical knowledge of healers in indigenous cultures will be lost?

Adaptive Wisdom

Many preindustrial peoples have lived in and exploited their natural environments for centuries. Earlier in this chapter we discussed the problems of technology in attempting to overcome hunger, and some of the important traditional agricultural alternatives presented to us by indigenous peoples such as the Kalapó and Lacandon Maya. They have learned to control insect pests and diseases that attack the plants on which they depend, and to do so without the need for expensive and often dangerous artificial chemicals. They have often learned how to make nature work for them with minimum deterioration of their environments. They have, in short, incorporated much adaptive wisdom into their cultural traditions. Following are a few possible benefits that all humanity might gain by preserving the ecological knowledge of indigenous peoples.

Preservation of Crop Varieties. In all cultivation systems, natural selection operates in the farmers' fields. Like wild plants, crops are subject to drought, disease, insects, and other natural elements, which select for the survival of individual plants best adapted to withstand these hazards. In addition, crops are subject to human selection. For example, crop varieties most susceptible to drought or local diseases are harvested in smaller quantities than drought- and disease-resistant varieties. Perhaps without knowing it, the cultivator replants mainly those varieties best adapted to survive the onslaughts of drought and local diseases. This tuning of plant varieties to the local environment, with all its hazards and fluctuations, goes on automatically so long as the crops harvested from the fields are replanted in the same area. Thanks to the unintentional and intentional selection by hundreds of generations of indigenous cultivators around the world, each species of crop (e.g., beans, potatoes, wheat) evolved a large number of *land races,* or distinct varieties adapted to local conditions.

Over the course of human history, several thousand species of plants have been used for food but less than a hundred of these were ever domesticated. Of all the plants that have been domesticated, today only a handful provide significant amounts of food for the world's people. In fact, a mere four crops—wheat, rice, maize, and potato—provide almost half of the world's total consumption of food.

Since around 1950, plant geneticists and agricultural scientists have developed new varieties of wheat, corn, rice, and potatoes that are capable of giving higher yields if they receive proper amounts of water and fertilizers. These new strains were developed by crossing and recrossing native land races collected from all over the world. The aim was to achieve a "green revolution" that would end world hunger by increasing production. Many new varieties are hybrids, which means that farmers must receive a new supply of seeds yearly from government or private sources.

Ironically, having been bred from the genetic material present in their diverse ancestors, the new strains now threaten to drive their ancestors to extinction. As the seeds of artificially bred varieties are planted by farmers in Asia, Africa, and the Americas, the traditional varieties—the land races that are the product of generations of natural and human selection—fall into disuse and many have disappeared.

Why should we care? Increasingly, agricultural experts are realizing the dangers of dependence on a few varieties. If crops that are nearly identical genetically are planted in the same area year after year, a new variety of pest or disease will eventually evolve to attack them. The famous Irish potato famine of the 1840s was directly related to the genetic uniformity of the potato because all the potatoes in Ireland were apparently descended from only a few plants. More than a million people died as a result of the potato blight, and a million more immigrated to North America. The United States has also suffered serious economic losses: the corn blight of 1970 destroyed about 15 percent of the American crop. Losses would have been less severe had most American farmers not planted a single variety of corn.

Many plant breeders are alarmed at the prospect of losing much of the genetic diversity of domesticated plants. Today they are searching remote regions for surviving land races that contain genes that one day might prove valuable. (The seeds are stored in seed banks for future study.) They have been well rewarded—although no one knows how much of the genetic diversity of crops such as wheat and corn has already disappeared.

The knowledge of indigenous peoples is an important resource in the effort to preserve land races. In many parts of the world—the Andes, Central America, Amazonia, the Middle East, and elsewhere—cultivators still grow ancient varieties of crops. They know where these varieties yield best, how to plant and care for them, how to prepare them for eating, and so on. In the Andes, for instance, hundreds of potato varieties survive among the Quechua Indians as a legacy of the Inca civilization. Many have specific ecological requirements, and some are even unique to a single valley. Research is now under way to determine how well specific land races will grow in other areas to help solve food supply problems elsewhere. It is important to preserve the genetic information encoded in these varieties for future generations.

Indigenous peoples who still retain the hard-won knowledge of their ancestors and who still use the often-maligned "traditional crop varieties" are important informational resources in the effort to save the genetic diversity of crops on which humanity depends.

"Undiscovered" Useful Species. In addition to their familiarity with local crop varieties with potential worldwide significance, many indigenous peoples cultivate or use crop species that are currently unimportant to the rest of the world. One example is amaranth, a grain native to the Americas that was of great importance to the Indians in prehistoric times. The great Mesoamerican civilizations made extensive use of the plant in their religious rituals. This led the Spanish conquerors, in their anxiety to root out heathenism, to burn fields of amaranth and prohibit its consumption. Otherwise, it—like maize, potatoes, beans, squash, and other American crops—might have diffused to other continents. Amaranth remains an important food to some indigenous peoples of highland Latin America, who retain knowledge of its properties and requirements. Its unusually high protein content might someday make it valuable to the rest of the world.

Other plants used by native peoples have the potential to become important elsewhere. Quinoa, now grown mainly in Peruvian valleys, has twice the protein content of corn and has long been recognized as a domesticate with great potential. The tepary bean, now grown mainly by the O'odham of the American Southwest, can survive and yield well under conditions of extreme drought, which might make it cultivatable in other arid regions of the world. Another legume, the winged bean, has long been cultivated by the native peoples of Papua New Guinea, and it has helped nourish people in 50 other tropical countries.

Humans use plants for more than food. Indigenous peoples have discovered many other uses for the plants found in their habitats. Scientific researchers today are attesting to the validity of much native knowledge about the use of plants as sources of fuel, oils, medicines, and other beneficial substances, including poisons. Forest peoples of Southeast Asia use the toxic roots of a local woody climbing plant as a fish poison. The root is so powerful that a mixture of 1 part root to 300,000 parts water will kill fish. From the indigenous tribes, scientists learned of the toxicity of these roots, which allowed them to isolate the rotenoid that now is used as an insecticide spray for plants and as dips and dusting powders for livestock.

Scientists no doubt will rediscover many other useful plants that today they know nothing about—if the tropical forests in which most endangered plant species are found last long enough. Their task will be easier if the original discoverers—indigenous peoples—are around to teach them what their ancestors learned.

Cultural Alternatives

There is another kind of practical lesson we might learn from surviving indigenous peoples. Industrialized humans have developed technologies that discover, extract, and transform natural resources on a scale undreamed of a century ago. To North Americans and to many other citizens of the developed world, *progress* is almost synonymous with "having more things." Yet whether our economies can continue to produce ever-increasing supplies of goods is questionable. Many of us are frightened by the thought that economic growth might not continue. The fear that we will be forced to accept a stagnation or even a decline in our levels of material consumption no doubt contributes to the interest today's undergraduates have in careers that they believe are most likely to earn high incomes for themselves and their future families.

On the other hand, some individuals and groups in the affluent, developed world have questioned the value of what most of their fellow citizens call "economic progress." They feel that the environmental and familial costs of the unceasing drive to accumulate and to succeed in a highly competitive environment are not worth the benefits. Some of them believe that material affluence cannot bring happiness because it is gained at the high cost of the emotional gratifications that spring from community relationships, from supportive family and friendship ties, and adherence to what some call spiritual values (see Globalization box).

Most readers of this book are the beneficiaries of economic progress. At the same time, we should be careful not to become the victims of the mentality of progress—of that unceasing desire to earn more, to have more, to succeed more. If the industrial bubble does not burst in our lifetime, most of us who live in the developed world will spend our lives in continuous effort to increase our consumption of goods. We will do so despite the fact that we can never catch up with the Joneses because there will always be other Joneses whom we have not yet caught. We will do so despite the fact that our efforts will never be sufficient to get us all we want because no one can consume goods as fast as companies can turn them out and advertisers can create new desires for them. We will do so despite the fact that many of our marriages and families will be torn apart by the effort and many of us will suffer psychologically and physically from stress-related disorders. Sadly, most of us pursue our dollars and goods unthinkingly because we remain ignorant of any alternative way of living.

The world's remaining indigenous peoples provide us with such alternatives. They do not and did not live in a primitive paradise. Subjugation of neighboring peoples, exploitation by the wealthy and powerful, degradation of women, warfare, and other ideas and practices many of us find abhorrent existed among some preindustrial peoples, just as they do today. Yet we also find other cultural conditions that some of us long to recover: closer family ties, greater self-sufficiency, smaller communities, more personal and enduring social relations, and "more humane," "more moral" values. No anthropologist can tell you whether life is better or worse in preindustrial communities; indeed, we cannot agree on the meaning of *better.* We do know that humanity is diverse. We know that this diversity means that human beings—ourselves included—have many alternative ways of living meaningful and satisfying lives. In the end, it is these cultural alternatives provided by indigenous peoples that might have the greatest value to humankind.

Perhaps a people themselves are the only ones qualified to judge the quality of their lives, to decide what it will take to lend meaning and dignity to their existence. We hope to have convinced you that there are many ways of being human, and that you have learned to appreciate some of the alternative ways of living experienced by various human populations. We hope you will agree that some of these alternatives are worth preserving, both in their own right and for the long-term well-being of all humanity.

When we think of development, we almost invariably think in terms of economic development. To us, economic development of a country, a state, or a region is easily measured; it is a matter of dollars and cents. We need only to look at the gross national product (GNP) or the per capita incomes. If we compare countries in terms of their growth of GNP, then we can determine which are the most economically successful. However, are the gross production figures the only—or even the best—measure of development? Are per capita incomes the best measure of the standard of living of the society?

The Nobel Prize–winning economist Amartya Sen argues that growth in the GNP alone is not a particularly good indicator of development. As a child in India he lived through the great famine of 1943, during which 3 million people died. Perhaps not surprisingly, one of his interests as an economist is in famines. In his study of famines he discovered that famines were not solely or even primarily the result of food shortages. What he discovered was that famines are frequently the result of market forces that increase the cost of food while depressing incomes to the point that families can no longer purchase adequate food. Just as famines are not necessarily the result of food shortages, the growth in the GNP of a country does not in itself result in increased prosperity. The GNP of a country might be growing, with little economic benefit to many if not most of the people.

Sen also questions how we measure standard of living. Is it merely a question of relative income? The Indian state of Kerala is an excellent example that per capita income figures alone are not always the best measure of quality of life. Covering only 24,000 square miles along the southwest coast of India, Kerala is home to 33 million people. Depending primarily upon agriculture, Kerala is a poor state, even by Indian standards. In terms of gross domestic product (GDP), Kerala averages only about $1,000 per capita, $200 less than India as a whole, and only one-twenty-sixth of that of the United States. By such economic measures alone, residents of Kerala would appear to have a very poor standard of living. However, if we look at Kerala in terms of health, education, and other social issues, Kerala presents a far different picture.

In terms of health, the people of Kerala are better off than most other peoples in India and in countries with far higher incomes. Their infant mortality rate is among the lowest in the developing world. Their life expectancy is 72 years, 11 years longer than the average for India, and only 4 years shorter than the United States.

Even more impressive are their achievements in education. Well-maintained schools are scattered throughout the state, and education is virtually universal. As a result, 90 percent of the people are literate—an achievement that places Kerala on the same level as the far more prosperous peoples of Spain and Singapore.

Social discrimination is less of a problem than in other parts of India and most of the world. Protests against the caste system began in Kerala in the middle of the nineteenth century, and in no other part of India has this system been so expunged from social consciousness. Although there are sizable Muslim and Christian minorities in the state, there have not been the religious conflicts that have beset most of India.

However, possibly the major factor that distinguishes Kerala from other parts of India and most parts of the world is its relative equality in income and opportunity. In the 1960s the state government abolished landlordism, and redistributed the land to 1.5 million tenant families. Kerala also has a relatively high minimum wage. This wage has discouraged industrial development and as a result Kerala has an unemployment rate of 25 percent. However, since most families have land on which they can garden, they are shielded from destitution.

Critical Thinking Questions

1. What do we mean by "standard of living"? Can the standard of living of a people be measured in monetary terms alone?

2. Should development take into account not only incomes but the relative distribution of wealth, educational levels, health standards, and the level of social discrimination as well?

3. Do the people of Kerala serve as an example of more balanced development? Are they, as Akash Kapur has said, "poor but prosperous"?

4. What do we value more—money? or people?

Sources: Sen (1984, 1987) and Kapur (1998).

Summary

1. Anthropological expertise is useful for the solution of human problems because the way anthropologists look at people and cultures (our worldview) differs somewhat from that of other professionals. Applied anthropologists have done research relevant to both global and local-level problems.

2. Two global problems are population growth and world hunger. Today's high rates of worldwide population growth are caused mainly by advances in medicine and vaccines and by widespread improvements in public health facilities. These advances have reduced death rates and increased life spans in most countries, but in underdeveloped regions birthrates are still relatively high.

3. Population growth has many unfavorable consequences. It contributes to serious environmental problems, low economic productivity, urban sprawl and shantytowns, political conflicts, and even war. This is the main paradox of population growth: the high fertility of a country's citizens is mainly responsible for it, yet their high fertility contributes to many of their nation's problems.

4. Having many children is not a simple product of ignorance or irrational cultural conservatism. The fertility rate is a response to the overall economic conditions in a region or country. This is shown by how North American couples choose how many children to have. Our low fertility is a rational response of couples to the conditions of their personal lives. In deciding how many children they want, most modern couples consider the personal, not the societal, costs and benefits of children.

5. High fertility in the LDCs is likewise a consequence of the overall economic and social environment that constrains reproductive behavior. Ethnographic studies suggest that children are a net economic asset rather than a liability in the rural areas of the Third World. Children are productive family members at a young age. They seek jobs with local people, supplementing the family income. When older, they go to the cities or to foreign countries and send money back home. They provide old-age security for their parents. Under such conditions, high fertility exists because large families are beneficial.

6. Population growth is often believed to be the major cause of world hunger. This is the scarcity explanation of hunger, which holds that overpopulation results in chronic malnutrition and periodic massive starvation.

7. The alternative is the inequality explanation. It holds that land and other food-producing resources are in fact sufficient to provide an adequate diet for the whole world. Hunger is caused by the way local and world economies allocate resources.

8. These two explanations of hunger are compatible: population growth contributes to hunger by increasing the scarcity of food production resources, yet prevalent inequalities in access to productive resources aggravate the scarcity and prevent people from adjusting to it.

9. Technology transfer is a viable solution to hunger in the LDCs, according to many. But there are numerous problems with this solution. Temperate agricultural methods often do not work well in tropical climates and soils. New technologies sometimes harm rather than help the poorest families. Peasants often do not adopt new technologies and crop varieties because they perceive them not worth the costs, or because they cannot afford to assume the risks of failure. Mechanized agriculture requires so much energy to produce food that it may not be affordable to Third World farmers and may not be sustainable in the long run.

10. For such reasons, agricultural scientists, anthropologists, and others have been researching alternative methods that have long been used by the traditional farmers of the world. Traditional methods such as intercropping and resource management hold promise for increasing food production sustainably. It is likely that a combination of solutions will be necessary to alleviate problems of hunger and poverty.

11. Globalization and the global economy are threatening many of the smaller groups of indigenous peoples of the world.

12. Ethical considerations alone are a sufficient reason these peoples should be allowed to remain in their communities, on their traditional lands, living in the ways of their ancestors, if that is their choice. Pragmatic considerations are also important because these people still retain a vast body of knowledge—knowledge that is of great potential value to all humanity.

13. Science has already adapted several important medicines and treatments from indigenous peoples. Many other plants with medical value will probably be discovered, if the tropical forests and the cultural knowledge of their indigenous inhabitants last long enough.

14. Adaptive wisdom is also to be found in the traditions of indigenous peoples. Land races of important crops still survive and might contain genetic materials from which useful foods might someday be bred. Crops that today are used primarily by indigenous peoples—such as amaranth, quinoa, tepary bean, and the winged bean—might eventually have worldwide significance. Nonfood plants are also important as insecticides, oils, fibers, and other products.

15. Finally, indigenous people provide us with alternative cultural models that should reduce our anxieties about the likelihood of eventual decline in our material living standards. The diversity of the human species shows that we can live meaningful and wholly satisfying lives without the technologies and huge quantities of consumer goods we consider necessary to our economic welfare. The remaining preindustrial cultures allow us to see that there is more than one narrow road to personal fulfillment, cultural health, and national dignity and prestige.

Key Terms

applied anthropology
scarcity explanation
  of hunger

inequality explanation
  of hunger

technology transfer
  solution
indigenous peoples

InfoTrac College Edition Terms

applied anthropology
ethnobotany

famine
indigenous people

indigenous rights

Suggested Readings

Applied anthropology:

Bodley, John H. *Anthropology and Contemporary Human Problems.* 3rd ed. Mountain View, Calif.: Mayfield, 1996.

A good place to start in glimpsing the relevance of anthropology to modern problems. Provides insights on war, poverty and hunger, population, and environmental destruction.

Durham, William H. *Scarcity and Survival in Central America.* Stanford, Calif.: Stanford University Press. 1979.

This study of El Salvador is one of the most convincing analyses of the scarcity and inequality approaches to hunger and poverty.

Harris, Marvin, and Eric B. Ross. *Death, Sex, and Fertility: Population Regulation in Preindustrial and Developing Societies.* New York: Columbia, 1987.

Two noted anthropologists argue that fertility and other population characteristics of human groups result from material forces. At various times in history people have successfully controlled (regulated) their numbers. An excellent place to start for an overview of the relation between population, adaptation, and culture.

Lappé, Frances Moore, Joseph Collins, and Peter Rosset. *World Hunger: Twelve Myths.* 2nd ed. New York: Grove, 1998.

Argues against the scarcity explanation of hunger and provides evidence and analysis in favor of the inequality explanation.

Podolefsky, Aaron, and Peter J. Brown. *Applying Cultural Anthropology: An Introductory Reader.* 4th ed. Mountain View, Calif.: Mayfield, 1999.

Contains 41 articles on the applications of cultural anthropology. A good source of case studies for students.

Indigenous peoples:

Bodley, John. *Victims of Progress.* 4th ed. Palo Alto, Calif.: Mayfield, 1999.

A good overview of tribal peoples in the modern world and how they are being destroyed by industrial civilization.

Cultural Survival. *State of the Peoples: A Global Human Rights Report on Societies in Danger.* Boston: Beacon Press, 1993.

Together with other publications of the Cultural Survival organization, an excellent source on the threats to indigenous people around the world.

Davis, Shelton H. *Victims of the Miracle: Development and the Indians of Brazil.* Cambridge: Cambridge University Press, 1977.

A study discussing economic development in Brazil and the resulting destruction of Indian communities.

Denslow, Julie Sloan, and Christine Padoch, eds. *People of the Tropical Rain Forest.* Berkeley: University of California Press, 1988.

Written for the general public, this edited work is a broad introduction to both indigenous and recent peoples living in the tropical rain forests of Latin America, Asia, and Africa. Some articles discuss what can be learned from indigenous peoples about developing the forest in a sustainable manner.

Plotkin, Mark J. *Tales of a Shaman's Apprentice.* New York: Penguin, 1993.

In part an adventure story of an ethnobotanist, this book describes the author's experiences in the Amazon forest while searching for useful medicines. An interesting place to start for an overview of the medical knowledge of indigenous peoples.

Companion Website for This Book

The Wadsworth Anthropology Resource Center
http://anthropology.wadsworth.com

The companion website that accompanies *Humanity: An Introduction to Cultural Anthropology,* Seventh Edition, includes a rich array of material, including online anthropological video clips, to help you in the study of cultural anthropology and the specific topics covered in this chapter. Begin by clicking on Student Resources. Next, click on Cultural Anthropology, and then on the cover image for this book. You have now arrived at the Student Resources home page and have the option of choosing one of several chapter resources.

Applying Anthropology. Begin your study of cultural anthropology by clicking on Applying Anthropology. Here you will find useful information on careers, graduate school programs in applied anthropology, and internships you might wish to pursue. You will also find real-world examples of working anthropologists applying the skills and methods of anthropology to help solve serious world problems.

Research Online. Click here to find a wealth of Web links that will facilitate your study of anthropology. Divided into different fields of study, specific websites are starting points for Internet research. You will be guided to rich anthropology websites that will help you prepare for class, complete course assignments, and actually do research on the Web.

InfoTrac College Edition Exercises. From the pull-down menu, select the chapter you are presently studying. Select InfoTrac College Edition Exercises from the list of resources. These exercises utilize InfoTrac College Edition's vast database of articles and help you explore the numerous uses of the search word, *culture.*

Study Aids for This Chapter. Improve your knowledge of key terms by using flash cards and study the learning objectives. Take the practice quiz, receive your results, and e-mail them to your instructor. Access these resources from the chapter and resource pull-down menus.

GLOSSARY

accommodation The creation of social and political systems that provide for and support ethnic group differences.

acculturation The cultural changes that occur whenever members of two cultural traditions come into contact.

adaptation Process by which organisms develop physical and behavioral characteristics allowing them to survive and reproduce in their habitats.

aesthetic Qualities that make objects, actions, or language more beautiful or pleasurable, according to culturally relative and variable standards.

affines In-laws, or people related by marriage.

agriculture Intentional planting, cultivation, care, and harvest of domesticated food plants (crops).

ambilocal residence Residence form in which couples choose whether to live with the wife's or the husband's family.

ancestral cults A type of communal cult centered around rituals performed to worship or please a kin group's ancestors.

animism Belief in spiritual beings.

anthropological linguistics Subfield that focuses on the inter-relationships between language and other aspects of a people's culture.

anthropology The academic discipline that studies all of humanity from a broad perspective.

applied anthropology Subfield whose practitioners use anthropological methods, theories, and concepts to solve practical, real-world problems; practitioners are often employed by a government agency or private organization.

archaeology The investigation of past cultures through excavation of material remains.

art Any human action that modifies the utilitarian nature of something for the primary purpose of enhancing its aesthetic qualities; or actions or words that are valued largely for their aesthetic pleasure or symbolic communication.

artificial countries Multinationality countries created by external powers; usually applied to former colonies.

assimilation The merging of the members of one ethnic group into another, with the consequent abandonment of the former group's identity.

authority The recognized right of an individual to command another to act in a particular way; legitimate power.

avunculocal residence Couples live with or near the mother's brother of the husband.

balanced reciprocity The exchange of goods considered to have roughly equal value; social purposes usually motivate the exchange.

band A small foraging group with flexible composition that migrates seasonally.

big men Political leaders who do not occupy formal offices and whose leadership is based on influence, not authority.

bilateral kinship Kinship system in which individuals trace their kinship relations equally through both parents.

bilocal residence Postmarital residence in which couples move between the households of both sets of parents.

biological determinism The idea that biologically (genetically) inherited differences between populations are important influences on cultural differences between them.

biological/physical anthropology Major subfield that studies the biological dimensions of humans and other primates.

body arts Artificial artistic enhancement or beautification of the human body by painting, tattooing, scarification, or other means.

bound morpheme A morpheme attached to a free morpheme to alter its meaning.

brideservice Custom in which a man spends a period of time working for the family of his wife.

bridewealth Custom in which a prospective groom and his relatives are required to transfer goods to the relatives of the bride to validate the marriage.

cargo cults Melanesian revitalization movements in which prophets claimed to know secret rituals that would bring wealth (cargo).

caste Stratification system in which membership in a stratum is in theory hereditary, strata are endogamous, and contact or relations between members of different strata are governed by explicit laws, norms, or prohibitions.

chiefdoms Centralized political systems with authority vested in formal, usually hereditary, offices or titles.

civilization A form of complex society in which many people live in cities.

clan A named unilineal descent group, some of whose members are unable to trace how they are related, but who still believe themselves to be kinfolk.

class System of stratification in which membership in a stratum can theoretically be altered and intermarriage between strata is allowed.

classifications of reality Ways in which the members of a culture divide up the natural and social world into named categories.

cognatic descent Form of descent in which relationships may be traced through both females and males.

cognatic descent group A group of relatives created by the tracing of relationships through both females and males.

communal cults Cults in which the members of a group cooperate in the performance of rituals intended to benefit all.

comparative methods Methods that test hypotheses by systematically comparing elements from many cultures.

comparative perspective The insistence by anthropologists that valid hypotheses and theories about humanity be tested with information from a wide range of cultures.

composite bands Autonomous (independent) political units consisting of several extended families that live together for most or all of the year.

configurationalism Theoretical idea that each culture historically develops its own unique thematic patterns around which beliefs, values, and behaviors are oriented.

conflict theory of inequality Theory holding that stratification benefits mainly the upper stratum and is the cause of most social unrest and other conflicts in human societies.

consanguines "Blood" relatives, or people related by birth.

consultant (informant) A member of a society who provides information to a fieldworker, often through formal interviews or surveys.

controlled historical comparisons A methodology for testing a hypothesis using historic changes in societies.

court legal systems Systems in which authority for settling disputes and punishing crimes is formally vested in a single individual or group.

courts of mediation Court systems in which the judges attempt to reach compromise solutions, based on the cultural norms and values of the parties involved, which will restore the social cohesion of the community.

courts of regulation Court systems that use codified laws, with formally prescribed rights, duties, and sanctions.

cross-cultural comparisons A methodology for testing a hypothesis using a sample of societies drawn from around the world.

cultivation Planting, caring for, and harvesting domesticated plants.

cultural anthropology (ethnology) The subfield that studies the way of life of contemporary and historically recent human populations.

cultural construction of gender The idea that the characteristics a people attribute to males and females are culturally, not biologically, determined.

cultural construction of kinship The idea that the kinship relationships a given people recognize do not perfectly reflect biological relationships; reflected in the kinship terminology.

cultural construction of reality *See* **classifications of reality.**

cultural determinism Notion that the beliefs and behaviors of individuals are largely programmed by their culture.

cultural identity The cultural tradition a group of people recognize as their own; the shared customs and beliefs that define how a group sees itself as distinctive.

cultural integration The interrelationships between the various components (elements, subsystems) of a cultural system.

cultural knowledge Information, skills, attitudes, conceptions, beliefs, values, and other mental components of culture that people socially learn during enculturation.

cultural materialism Theoretical orientation holding that the main influences on cultural differences and similarities are technology, environment, and how people produce and distribute resources.

cultural relativism The notion that one should not judge the behavior of other peoples using the standards of one's own culture.

cultural universals Elements of culture that exist in all known human groups or societies.

culture (as used in this text) The socially transmitted knowledge and behavior shared by some group of people.

culture shock The feeling of uncertainty and anxiety an individual experiences when placed in a strange cultural setting.

descent group A group whose members believe themselves to be descended from a common ancestor.

diffusionists Early-twentieth-century ethnologists who studied the distribution of cultural traits between cultures, with the goal of describing their origin and historical spread.

domestication The process by which people control the distribution, abundance, and biological features of certain plants and animals in order to increase their usefulness to humans.

dowry Custom in which the family of a woman transfers property or wealth to her and/or her husband's family upon her marriage.

ecclesiastical cults Highly organized cults in which a full-time priesthood performs rituals believed to benefit believers or the whole society; occur in complex societies.

egalitarian society Form of society in which there is little inequality in access to culturally valued rewards.

enculturation (socialization) The transmission (by means of social learning) of cultural knowledge to the next generation.

endogamous rules Marriage rules requiring individuals to marry some member of their own social group or category.

Eskimo terminology Kinship terminology system in which no nuclear family kin term is extended to more distant relatives; nuclear family members have unique terms.

ethnic boundary markers Any overt characteristics that can be used to indicate ethnic group membership.

ethnic cleansing The elimination or removal of an unwanted ethnic group or groups from a country or a particular geographical region. Usually involves genocide and/or relocation of the population.

ethnic group A named social group based on perceptions of shared ancestry, cultural traditions, and common history that culturally distinguish that group from other groups.

ethnic homogenization The attempt to create a single ethnic group in a particular geographical region.

ethnocentrism The attitude or opinion that the morals, values, and customs of one's own culture are superior to those of other peoples.

ethnogenesis The creation of a new ethnic group identity.

ethnographic fieldwork Collection of information from living people about their way of life; *see also* **fieldwork.**

ethnographic methods Research methodologies used to describe a contemporary or historically recent culture.

ethnography A written description of the way of life of some human population.

ethnohistoric research The study of past cultures using written accounts and other documents.

ethnohistory *See* **ethnohistoric research.**

ethnology The study of human cultures from a comparative perspective; often used as a synonym for cultural anthropology.

evolutionary psychology *See* **sociobiology.**

exogamous rules Marriage rules prohibiting individuals to marry a member of their own social group or category.

extended family A group of related nuclear families.

feud A method of dispute settlement in self-help legal systems involving multiple but balanced killings between members of two or more kin groups.

fictive kinship Condition in which people who are not biologically related behave as if they are relatives of a certain type.

fieldwork Ethnographic research that involves observing and interviewing the members of a culture to describe their contemporary way of life.

foraging Adaptations based on the harvest of wild (undomesticated) plants and animals.

forced assimilation The social absorption of one ethnic group by another ethnic group through the use of force.

forensic anthropologists Physical anthropologists who identify and analyze human skeletal remains; usually work for or consult with law enforcement agencies.

form of descent How a people trace their descent from previous generations.

free morpheme A morpheme that can be used alone.

functional theory of inequality Theory holding that stratification is a way to reward individuals who contribute most to society's well-being.

functionalism Theoretical orientation that analyzes cultural elements in terms of their useful effects to individuals or to the persistence of the whole society.

gender crossing Custom by which one sex is allowed to adopt the roles and behavior of the opposite sex, with little or no stigma or punishment.

gender (or sex) roles The rights and duties individuals have because of their perceived identities as males, females, or another gender category.

gender stratification The degree to which males and females are unequal in dimensions such as status, power or influence, access to valued resources, eligibility for social positions, and ability to make decisions about their own lives.

generalized reciprocity The giving of goods without expectation of a return of equal value at any definite future time.

genocide The deliberate attempt to eliminate the members of an ethnic category or cultural tradition.

global economy The buying and selling of goods and services in an integrated global market.

global trade The direct or indirect exchange of goods and products between peoples from all regions of the world.

globalization The process of integrating the world peoples economically, socially, politically, and culturally into a single world system or community.

grammar Total system of linguistic knowledge that allows the speakers of a language to send meaningful messages that hearers can understand.

group marriage Several women and several men are married to one another simultaneously.

Hawaiian Kin terminology system in which only sex and generation are relevant in defining labeled categories of relatives.

herding Adaptations based on tending, breeding, and harvesting the products of domesticated animals (livestock).

hierarchical nesting Occurs when an ethnic group is part of a larger collection of ethnic groups, which together constitute a higher level of ethnic identity.

historic archaeology Field that investigates the past of literate peoples through excavation of sites and analysis of artifacts and other material remains.

historical particularism The theoretical orientation emphasizing that each culture is the unique product of all the influences to which it was subjected in its past, making cross-cultural generalizations questionable.

holistic perspective The assumption that any aspect of a culture is integrated with other aspects, so that no dimension of culture can be understood in isolation.

homeland A geographical region over which a particular ethnic group feels it has exclusive rights.

horticulture A method of cultivation in which hand tools powered by human muscles are used and in which land use is extensive.

household Dwelling or compound whose composition is culturally variable, but lived in by people, usually relatives or fictive kin, who cooperate for some purposes and share some resources.

human variation Refers to physical differences between human populations; an interest of physical anthropologists.

humanistic approach Theoretical orientation that rejects attempts to explain culture in general in favor of achieving an empathetic understanding of particular cultures.

hunting and gathering *See* **foraging.**

ideology (narrow meaning of the term) Ideas and beliefs that legitimize and thus reinforce inequalities in stratified societies.

incest taboo Prohibition against sexual intercourse between certain kinds of relatives.

incipient courts Court systems in which judicial authorities met, frequently informally, in private to discuss issues and determine solutions to be imposed. Evidence is not formally collected and the parties involved in these cases are not formally consulted.

indigenous peoples Culturally distinct peoples who have occupied a region longer than peoples who have colonized or immigrated to the region.

individualistic cults Cults based on personal relations between specific individuals and specific supernatural powers.

inequality Degree to which individuals, groups, and categories differ in their access to rewards.

inequality explanation of hunger Notion that hunger is not caused by absolute scarcity but by the unequal distribution of resources and how these resources are used.

influence The ability to convince people they should act as you suggest.

initiation rite A rite held to mark the sexual maturity of an individual or a group of individuals of the same sex.

innovation The creation of a new cultural trait by combining two or more existing traits.

intellectual/cognitive approach The notion that religious beliefs provide explanations for puzzling things and events.

intensive agriculture A system of cultivation in which plots are planted annually or semiannually; usually uses irrigation, natural fertilizers, and (in the Old World) plows powered by animals.

interpretive anthropology The contemporary theoretical orientation that analyzes cultural elements by explicating their meanings to people and understanding them in their local context.

interviewing Collection of cultural data by systematic questioning; may be structured (using questionnaires) or unstructured (open-ended).

Iroquois terminology Kinship terminology system in which Ego calls parallel cousins the same terms as siblings, calls father's brother the same as father, calls mother's sister the same as mother, and uses unique terms for the children of father's sister and mother's brother.

key consultant (informant) A member of a society who is especially knowledgeable about some subject, and who supplies information to a fieldworker.

kin group A group of people who culturally conceive themselves to be relatives, cooperate in certain activities, and share a sense of identity as kinfolk.

kin terms The words (labels) that an individual uses to refer to his or her relatives of various kinds.

kindred All the bilateral relatives of an individual.

kinship terminology The logically consistent system by which people classify their relatives into labeled categories, or into "kinds of relatives."

law A kind of social control characterized by the presence of authority, intention of universal application, obligation, and sanction.

levirate Custom whereby a widow marries a male relative (usually a brother) of her deceased husband.

lexicon The words that occur in a language.

life cycle The changes in expected activities, roles, rights and obligations, and social relations individuals experience as they move through culturally defined age categories.

limited-purpose money Money that may be used to purchase only a few kinds of goods.

lineage A unilineal descent group larger than an extended family whose members can actually trace how they are related.

market Exchange by means of buying and selling, using money.

marriage alliances The relationships created between families or kin groups by intermarriage.

matrifocal family Family group consisting of a mother and her children, with a male only loosely attached or not present at all.

matrilineal descent Form of descent in which individuals trace their primary kinship relationships through their mothers.

matrilocal residence Couples live with or near the wife's parents.

monogamy Each individual is allowed to have only one spouse at a time.

morpheme A combination of phonemes that communicates a standardized meaning.

morphology The study of the units of meaning in language.

multiple gender identities Definitions of sexual identities beyond the female and male duality, including third and fourth genders such as man–woman or woman–man.

myths Stories that recount the deeds of supernatural powers and cultural heroes in the past.

nationality An ethnic group that claims a right to a discrete homeland and to political autonomy and self-determination.

negative reciprocity Exchange motivated by the desire to obtain goods, in which the parties try to gain all the material goods they can.

neolocal residence Couples establish a separate household apart from both the husband's and the wife's parents.

nomadism Seasonal mobility, often involving migration to high-altitude areas during the hottest and driest parts of the year.

norm Shared ideals and/or expectations about how certain people ought to act in given situations.

nuclear family Family group consisting of a married couple and their offspring.

Omaha terminology Kinship terminology system associated with patrilineal descent in which Ego's mother's relatives are distinguished only by their sex.

origin myth The collective history of an ethnic group that defines which subgroups are part of it and its relationship to other ethnic groups.

paleoanthropologists Physical anthropologists who specialize in the investigation of the biological evolution of the human species.

participant observation The main technique used in conducting ethnographic fieldwork, involving living among a people and participating in their daily activities.

passive assimilation The voluntary social absorption of one ethnic group by another ethnic group.

pastoralism Adaptation in which needs of livestock for naturally occurring pasture and water greatly influence the movements of groups.

patrilineal descent Form of descent in which individuals trace their most important kinship relationships through their fathers.

patrilocal residence Couples live with or near the husband's parents.

patterns of behavior Within a single culture, the behavior that most people perform when they are in certain culturally defined situations.

peasants Rural people who are integrated into a larger society politically and economically.

performance arts Forms of art such as music, percussion, song, dance, and theater/drama that involve sound and/or stylized body movements.

phoneme The smallest unit of sound that speakers unconsciously recognize as distinctive from other sounds; when one phoneme is substituted for another in a morpheme, the meaning of the morpheme alters.

phonology The study of the sound system of language.

polyandry One woman is allowed to have multiple husbands.

polygamy Multiple spouses.

polygyny One man is allowed to have multiple wives.

postmarital residence pattern Where the majority of newly married couples locate residence after their marriage.

postmodernism Philosophical viewpoint emphasizing the relativity of all knowledge, including that of science; focuses on how the knowledge of a particular time and place is constructed, especially on how power relations affect the creation and spread of ideas and beliefs.

prehistoric archaeology Field that uses excavation of sites and analysis of material remains to investigate cultures that existed before the development of writing.

priest A kind of religious specialist, often full-time, who officiates at rituals.

primatologists Those who study primates, including monkeys and apes; subfield of biological anthropology.

procedural law The structured manner in which a breach of the law is adjudicated or resolved.

psychological approach Notion that the emotional or affective satisfactions people gain from religion are primary.

reasonable person model A model used in legal reasoning that basically asks how a reasonable individual should have acted under these circumstances.

reciprocity The transfer of goods for goods between two or more individuals or groups.

redistribution The collection of goods or money from a group, followed by a reallocation to the group by a central authority.

refugees Individuals and families who temporarily take up residence in another region or country to escape famine, warfare, or some other life-threatening event.

relocation The forced removal of the members of a particular ethnic group from one geographical region to another.

revitalization movement A religious movement explicitly intended to create a new way of life for a society or group.

rite of passage A public ceremony or ritual recognizing and making a transition from one group or status to another.

ritual Organized, stereotyped symbolic behaviors intended to influence supernatural powers.

role Rights and duties that individuals assume because of their perceived personal identity or membership in a social group. Also, the social and/or economic position a field researcher defines for him- or herself in the community being studied.

Sapir-Whorf hypothesis The idea that language profoundly shapes the perceptions and worldview of its speakers.

scarcity explanation of hunger Holds that there is not enough land, water, and other resources to feed all the people of a country or region an adequate diet, given current technology.

scientific approach Theoretical notion that human cultural differences and similarities can be explained in the same sense as biologists explain life and its evolution.

secular ideology An ideology that does not rely on the will of supernatural powers but justifies inequality on the basis of its societywide benefits.

self-help legal systems Informal legal systems in societies without centralized political systems, in which authorities who settle disputes are defined by circumstances of the case.

semantic domain A class of things or properties that are perceived as alike in some fundamental respect; hierarchically organized.

sexual division of labor The kinds of productive activities (tasks) that are assigned to women versus men in a culture.

shaman (medicine man) Part-time religious specialist who uses his special relation to supernatural powers for curing members of his group and harming members of other groups.

shamanistic cults Cults in which certain individuals (shamans) have relationships with supernatural powers that ordinary people lack.

simple bands Autonomous or independent political units, often consisting of little more than an extended family, with informal leadership vested in one of the older family members.

social anthropology *See* **cultural anthropology (ethnology).**

social control Mechanisms by which behavior is constrained and directed into acceptable channels, thus maintaining conformity.

social distance The degree to which cultural norms specify that two individuals or groups should be helpful to, intimate with, or emotionally attached to one another.

socialization The process of social learning of culture by children.

society A territorially distinct and largely self-perpetuating group whose members have a sense of collective identity and who share a common language and culture.

sociobiology Scientific approach emphasizing that humans are animals and so are subject to similar evolutionary forces as other animals; often associated with the hypothesis that behavior patterns enhance inclusive fitness.

sociocultural anthropology *See* **cultural anthropology (ethnology).**

sociolinguistics Specialty within cultural anthropology that studies how language is related to culture and the social uses of speech.

sociological approach The effects of religion on maintaining the institutions of society as a whole by instilling common values, creating solidarity, controlling behavior, and so forth.

sodalities Formal institutions that cross-cut communities and serve to unite geographically scattered groups; may be based on kin groups (clans or lineages) or on non-kin-based groups (age grades or warrior societies).

sorcery The performance of rites and spells for the purpose of causing harm to others by supernatural means.

sororate Custom whereby a widower marries a female relative of his deceased wife.

state A centralized, multilevel political unit characterized by the presence of a bureaucracy that acts on behalf of the ruling elite.

stereotyping Having preconceived mental images of a group that bias the way one perceives group members and interprets their behavior.

stratified society Society with marked and largely or partly heritable differences in access to wealth, power, and prestige; inequality is based mainly on unequal access to productive and valued resources.

subculture Cultural differences characteristic of members of various ethnic groups, regions, religions, and so forth within a single society or country.

subnationalities A subgroup within a larger nationality, which lacks the concept of a separate homeland and makes no claim to any inherent right to political autonomy and self-determination.

substantive law Refers to the actual types of behavior that are categorized as illegal, together with the appropriate sanctions imposed.

surplus The amount of food (or other goods) a worker produces in excess of the consumption of herself or himself and her or his dependents.

symbols Objects, behaviors, sound combinations, and other phenomena whose culturally defined meanings have no necessary relation to their inherent physical qualities.

technology-transfer solution Notion that developing nations can best solve their hunger problems by adopting the technology and production methods of modern mechanized agriculture.

tone languages Languages in which changing voice pitch within a word alters the entire meaning of the word.

totemism A form of communal cult in which all members of a kin group have mystical relations with one or more natural objects from which they believe they are descended.

transnational corporation A company that produces and sells most of its products or services outside its "home" country.

transnationals Members of an ethnic community living outside of their country of origin.

tribe Autonomous political unit encompassing a number of distinct, geographically dispersed communities that are held together by sodalities.

tribute The rendering of goods (typically including food) to an authority such as a chief.

unilineal descent Descent through "one line," including patrilineal and matrilineal descent.

unilineal descent group A group of relatives all of whom are related through only one sex.

unilineal evolution The nineteenth-century theoretical orientation that held that all human ways of life pass through a similar sequence of stages in their development.

unilineally extended families Family grouping formed by tracing kinship relationships through only one sex, either female or male but not both.

values Shared ideas or standards about the worthwhileness of goals and lifestyles.

vision quest The attempt to enlist the aid of supernatural powers by intentionally seeking a dream or vision.

visual arts Arts that are produced in a material or tangible form, including basketry, pottery, textiles, paintings, drawings, sculptures, masks, carvings, and the like.

witchcraft The use of psychic powers to harm others by supernatural means.

worldview The way people interpret reality and events, including how they see themselves relating to the world around them.

NOTES

CHAPTER 1—THE STUDY OF HUMANITY

Subfields of Anthropology

Clyde Snow (1995) describes his forensic work in Argentina and northern Iraq; additional material is in McDonald (1995).

Cultural Anthropology Today

The article titled "The Virtual Nuclear Weapons Laboratory in the New World Order" is by Gusterson (2001).

CHAPTER 2—CULTURE

Tylor's definition of culture is from Tylor (1871, 1).

Defining Culture

The distinction between trial and error and social learning is from Boyd and Richerson (1985) and Pulliam and Dunford (1980), who also discuss the advantages of social learning. The material on the Yąnomamö and Semai is drawn from Chagnon (1983) and Dentan (1968), respectively.

Cultural Knowledge

Edward Hall's two early books (1959, 1966) were among the first to systematically discuss the importance of nonverbal communication in everyday social interaction. The Hanunóo plant classification example is taken from Conklin (1957). Information on Navajo witchcraft comes from Kluckhohn (1967). Reichel-Dolmatoff (1971) describes shamanism among the Tukano. A wonderful book describing how some cultures experience and measure the passage of time is Aveni (1995).

Biology and Cultural Differences

Extended coverage of cultural universals is provided in D. Brown (1991).

CHAPTER 3—CULTURE AND LANGUAGE

Some Properties of Language

Information on the five distinguishing features of human language is from Hockett's (1960) seminal discussion.

How Language Works

The examples on Thai aspiration and Nupe tones are taken from Fromkin and Rodman's (1988) textbook. The author's (J. P.) own knowledge is the basis for the discussion of the Kosraen language.

Language and Culture

Berlin and Kay (1969) conducted the cross-cultural research on color terms. A concise description and discussion of the Sapir-Whorf hypothesis is in D. Brown (1991). See Farb (1974) and Trudgill (1983) on male and female speech and on Javanese "levels" of speech. Chagnon (1983) discusses the Yąnomamö name taboo. We thank Kathryn Meyer and Gary deCoker for help with the example of Japanese honorifics.

CHAPTER 4—THE DEVELOPMENT OF ANTHROPOLOGICAL THOUGHT

Nineteenth Century: Origins

Unilineal evolutionary theory is best known from the works of Tylor (1865, 1871) and Morgan (1877). The times and places of the founding of the first anthropology programs in the United States are from Black (1991).

Early Twentieth Century: Development

The best single source of writings on Boas is a collection of his articles (1966). The critique of historical particularist assumptions is taken from Harris (1968). Malinowski's ideas about the functions of institutions, behaviors, and beliefs were first presented in a 1944 book, reprinted as Malinowski (1960). Good sources on structural-functionalism are Radcliffe-Brown (1922, 1965) and Nadel (1951).

Midcentury Evolutionary Approaches (ca. 1940–1970)

See Leslie White (1949, 1959). Steward's most influential articles appear in two volumes (1955, 1977).

Anthropological Thought Today: Divisions

Most coverage of the scientific/humanistic division is from our general knowledge. Dawkins (1976) and E. O. Wilson (1975, 1978) were instrumental works popularizing sociobiology. Books by the late Marvin Harris (1977, 1979, 1985) were influential in the development of modern materialist thought. More recent, and more technical, sources on cultural evolution and adaptation are Johnson and Earle (1987) and Smith and Winterhalder (1992). On interpretive anthropology, good sources are early works by Geertz (1973, 1980). Harris's last book (1999) is an introduction to his own variety of materialist theory.

CHAPTER 5—METHODS OF INVESTIGATION

Ethnographic Methods

The discussion of how to evaluate a particular historical account was influenced by Naroll (1962). See also Hickerson (1970) on ethnohistoric methods. See Fogelson (1989) for a discussion of interpretation of historical events. The discussion of suicide in the Trobriand Islands is derived form Malinowski (1926). The problems of collecting genealogies among the Yąnomamö are recounted by Chagnon (1983). Statement on ethics taken from the Code of Ethics of the American Anthropological Association on website www. aaanet.org/committee/ethics/ethcode.htm

Comparative Methods

The cross-cultural test of the sorcery and social control hypothesis is from B. Whiting (1950). See Adams (1982, 1988) for an excellent example of what can be done with historical data. Data on matrilineal and patrilineal societies are from Bailey (1989). For the box on Captain Cook, see Sahlins (1981 and 1995) and Obeyesekere (1992). For box "Who Owns Culture?" a range of sources were used. General data on U.S. and international repatriation and issues were drawn from the National NAGPRA website (www.cr.nps.gov/nagpra) and Brown (2003). Data on the San issue in general as well as the Hoodia succulent issue are taken from the WIMSA website (www.san.org). Additional data on these and other issues are taken from BBC News (www.news.bbc.co.uk) and Time (www.time.com) websites. Data on the Hindu issue are taken from Vedantam (2004).

CHAPTER 6—ADAPTATION: ENVIRONMENT AND CULTURES

Foraging

Dobyns (1983) provided most of the information on the distribution of foragers in North America used in Figure 6.1. Denevan (1992) discusses the use of fire to provide habitat for game animals among prehistoric Native Americans. Information on specific foragers is taken from the following sources: BaMbuti (Turnbull 1962), Hadza (Woodburn 1968), Netsilik (Balikci 1970), Western Shoshone (Steward 1938, 1955), !Kung (Lee 1969, 1979, 1993), Northwest Coast (Ferguson 1984; Piddocke 1965; Suttles 1960, 1962, 1968).

Intensive Agriculture

On the benefits and costs of agriculture, see M. Cohen (1977). A readable book covering the origins of farming in various world regions is B. Smith (1995). Comparative information on foraging working hours are from Sahlins (1972) and M. Cohen (1977). M. Cohen (1989) provides an overview of evidence about the health of prehistoric foragers. Sources used to draw the North American portion of the map on the distribution of horticulture are Dobyns (1983) and Doolittle (1992). Material on shifting cultivation is from Conklin (1957), Freeman (1970), and Ruddle (1974). See Bradfield (1971) on dry-land gardening among the Pueblo (mainly, Hopi). Differences between extensive and intensive agriculture are set forth in Boserup (1965) and Grigg (1974). Material on intensive agriculture in the New World is drawn from our general knowledge and from Donkin (1979). E. Wolf (1966) is a good source on peasants. On peasant revolts, see E. Wolf (1969).

Pastoralism

Porter (1965) discusses the subsistence risk reduction benefit of pastoralism. Schneider (1981) shows the negative relation between the distribution of the tsetse fly and cattle pastoralism in Africa. A short source on the Karimojong is Dyson-Hudson and Dyson-Hudson (1969).

CHAPTER 7—EXCHANGE IN ECONOMIC SYSTEMS

Sahlins (1965) first distinguished the three forms of exchange.

Reciprocity

Malinowski (1922) describes Trobriand *wasi*. The Maring discussion is from Rappaport (1968) and Peoples (1982). Lee (1979, 1993) describes !Kung sharing, which he sees as the key to their ability to keep their work levels low and their nutritional status high. Kelly (1995) generalizes some of Lee's points to other foragers in his excellent large-scale synthesis of the foraging adaptation.

Redistribution

Alkire (1977), Sahlins (1958), and D. Oliver (1989) describe tribute in Micronesia and Polynesia.

Market Exchange

See Neale (1976) on money. Schneider (1981) describes some African monies. Pospisil (1978) discusses the multiple uses of money among Kapauku. Bohannan (1955) describes Tiv exchange spheres. On Philippine *suki,* see W. Davis (1973).

CHAPTER 8—MARRIAGE AND FAMILIES

Marriage

The material on Nayar "marriage" is from Gough (1959). Hart, Pilling, and Goodale (1988) describe Tiwi marriage and other aspects of Tiwi culture. Information on the Na is from Hua (2001).

Marriage in Comparative Perspective

Goldstein (1987) describes Tibetan polyandry and its advantages to husbands and the wife. Chagnon (1983) discusses the importance of marriage alliances among the Yanomamö. We do not believe the challenges of Tierney (2000) alter Chagnon's conclusions about marriage alliances. Kuper (1963) describes Swazi bridewealth. See Lee (1979, 240–42) on !Kung brideservice. See Goody and Tambiah (1973) and Harrell and Dickey (1985) on dowry. Material on Indian "dowry deaths" is from our general knowledge and a report in the *Columbus Dispatch* (July 25, 2004, p. A13).

Postmarital Residence Patterns

The frequencies of different residence patterns are as reported in Pasternak (1976, 44). Among those who have discussed the influences on residence patterns are Ember and Ember (1971, 1972) and Pasternak (1976).

Family and Household Forms

Murdock (1949) showed how forms of postmarital residence produce various forms of the family and household. Pasternak, Ember, and Ember (1976) suggest an economic hypothesis for why extended families exist.

CHAPTER 9—KINSHIP AND DESCENT

Unilineal Descent

Data on the frequencies of patrilineal and matrilineal descent are from Divale and Harris (1976). Firth (1936, 1965) describes the functions of Tikopian lineages and clans. See Eggan (1950) on Hopi matrilineal descent.

Cognatic Descent

Cognatic descent in Polynesia is discussed in Firth (1968), Howard and Kirkpatrick (1989), and D. Oliver (1989). The Samoan *'aiga* is described in M. Ember (1959), Holmes and Holmes (1992), and D. Oliver (1989).

Bilateral Kinship

Material on the Iban kindred is from Freeman (1968, 1970).

Influences on Kinship Systems

Sources for this discussion are Aberle (1961), Divale (1974), Divale and Harris (1976), C. Ember (1974), Ember and Ember (1971), and Ember, Ember, and Pasternak (1974).

Classifying Relatives: Kinship Terminologies

Aberle (1961) and Pasternak (1976) provide statistical data on the general, but imperfect, correlation between forms of descent and terminological systems.

CHAPTER 10—ENCULTURATION AND THE LIFE CYCLE

Growing Up

Information on Ju/'hoansi breastfeeding is from Shostak (1983). Howard and Millard (1997) report on the Chagga, a Tanzanian people who believe that a child will be harmed if the mother becomes pregnant while another child is nursing. Among others, Dozier (1970, 179) reports the Hopi use of "ogre" kachinas to frighten misbehaving children.

Two African Examples

The description of the Aka is based on Hewlett (1992). Information about the Gusii is from LeVine et al. (1994). The comparisons of the two are our own.

Life Cycle

The stages of a Gusii female's life are given in LeVine et al. (1994, 81–82). The Cheyenne concept of abortion is from Llewellyn and Hoebel (1941). See Jenness (1932) and Hoebel (1954) for a discussion of Eskimo infanticide. The description of the Osage child-naming rite is based on LaFlesche (1928). The material on whether Samoan young women do or do not experience all the stresses and strains typical of American adolescents is based on Mead (1928) and Freeman (1983). Information on drunkenness by young men from Chuuk, Micronesia, is from Marshall (1979), and personal observations by J.P. Cheyenne adolescence is mentioned in Hoebel (1978). The analysis of the phases known as separation, liminality, and incorporation is from Turner (1967). The general information on New Guinea beliefs about feminine pollution and male initiation rituals is synthesized from the case studies of Herdt (1987), Meggitt (1970), Meigs (1988), and Wormsley (1993). Detailed material on the Awa is from Newman and Boyd (1982). On the Apache girls' ceremony, see Farrer (1996). Wallace and Hoebel (1952) provided information on the treatment of the elderly among the Comanche. On the Inuit treatment of the elderly, see Hoebel (1954). Data on abandonment and patricide among subarctic peoples are drawn from Vanstone (1974) and Jenness (1932).

CHAPTER 11—GENDER IN COMPARATIVE PERSPECTIVE

Cultural Construction of Gender

The Hua material is from Meigs (1988, 1990). An excellent reader on masculinity is Cohen (2000).

Gender Crossing and Multiple Gender Identities

The primary source of information consulted on Native American peoples is Roscoe (2000). Nanda (2000) is a source of some of the conceptual discussion. Information on the Zuni is from Roscoe (1991). Hoebel (1978) discussed the Cheyenne *berdache*.

The Sexual Division of Labor

Table 11.1 was constructed from data in Murdock and Provost (1973). On female hunting among BaMbuti Pygmies and Agta, see Turnbull (1962) and Estioko-Griffin (1986), respectively. On the possibility that strenuous exercise inhibits ovulation, see Graham (1985). The influence of female child-care responsibilities on the sexual division of labor was first made forcibly by Judith Brown (1970a). The discussion of why female contributions to subsistence tend to decline with intensification uses information in C. Ember (1983), Martin and Voorhies (1975), Boserup (1970), Burton and White (1984), and White, Burton, and Dow (1981). The Kofyar material is from Stone, Stone, and McC. Netting (1995).

Gender Stratification

The general discussion in this section relies on material in di Leonardo (1991), Leacock (1978), Morgen (1989), Rosaldo and Lamphere (1974), Quinn (1977), and Sacks (1982). The information about Andalusia is from Gilmore (1980, 1990). The suggestion that women's status improves with age in many cultures is from J. Brown (1988). Information on the Iroquois is from Albers (1989), Stockard (2002), and J. Brown (1970b). On BaMbuti and Aka sexual egalitarianism, see Turnbull (1962) and Hewlett (1992). The idea that women's control over key resources frequently leads to high overall status is discussed in Sanday (1973, 1981). Friedl (1975, 1978) was

one of the first to argue that women's status in hunting and gathering cultures is positively related to the importance of women's labor in food production and to ability to control the distribution of the products they produce. Yoruba material is from Barnes (1990). Schlegel (1972) and Whyte (1978) discuss why matrilineality and matrilocality tend to give women high status, all else being equal. Information on Chinese wives is from M. Wolf (1972) and our general knowledge.

CHAPTER 12—THE ORGANIZATION OF POLITICAL LIFE

Forms of Political Organization

The definitions and ideas concerning political structure were influenced by Steward (1955), Service (1962), Cohen and Service (1978), Krader (1968), and Fried (1967). Ethnographic examples were taken from the following sources: Comanche from Hoebel (1940) and Wallace and Hoebel (1952), Tahiti from Goldman (1970), and Inca from D'Altroy (1987), Julien (1988), LaLone and LaLone (1987), LeVine (1987), and Metraux (1969).

Social Control and Law

For the basic definition of law as well as many of the concepts about legal systems, we relied upon Hoebel (1954), Pospisil (1958), Fallers (1969), Bohannan (1968), Newman (1983), and Gluckman (1972, 1973). Ethnographic examples were taken from the following sources: Comanche from Hoebel (1940); Cheyenne from Llewellyn and Hoebel (1941); Nuer from Evans-Pritchard (1940); Jívaro from Harner (1973a); and Barotse from Gluckman (1972, 1973). The data on global government and the World Trade Organization were taken from Chomsky (2000); "The MAI Shell Game: The World Trade Organization (WTO)" from the Public Citizen Global Trade Watch website (www.tradewatch.org); "The WTO in brief" from the World Trade Organization website (www.wto.org); and "Is Globalization Shifting Power from Nation States to Undemocratic Organizations?" from the Globalization Guide website (www.globalizationguide.org).

CHAPTER 13—SOCIAL INEQUALITY AND STRATIFICATION

Systems of Equality and Inequality

The classification of societies into egalitarian, ranked, and stratified was proposed by Fried (1967). Woodburn (1982) discusses the reasons for egalitarianism among foragers. The material on Tikopia is from Firth (1936). Berreman (1959) noted the similarity of race relations in the American South to a caste system.

Castes in Traditional India

The Indian caste system and its relationship to Hinduism are discussed in Dumont (1980), Hiebert (1971), Mandelbaum (1970), and Tyler (1973).

Classes in Industrial Societies: The United States

Data on the distribution of income for 2003 and previous years are taken from DeNavas-Walt, Proctor, and Mills (2004). Mishel, Bernstein, and Allegretto (2005) provided the statistical information on the distribution of wealth in the United States and the cross-national data on the compensation of chief executive officers.

Maintaining Inequality

The Hawaiian religion is described in Valeri (1985).

Theories of Inequality

Davis and Moore (1945) originated the functionalist theory. Conflict theory goes back to Marx (1967, original 1867). Dahrendorf (1959) was important in formulating the modern version of conflict theory in sociology. Lenski (1966) is an excellent source comparing and evaluating the functionalist and conflict theories.

CHAPTER 14—RELIGION AND WORLDVIEW

Defining Religion

Tylor (1871) defined religion as animism. An excellent summary of *mana* is Shore (1989). The idea that Judeo-Christian mythology helps inculcate a worldview conducive to environmental destruction is taken from Lynn White (1967). The Hopi information is from Frigout (1979) and our general knowledge.

Theories of Religion

The Trobriand magic example is from Malinowski (1954). Frazer's intellectual theory is from Frazer (1963). Geertz (1965) argues that religion provides meaning. The anthropomorphic theory is that of Guthrie (1993). Malinowski (1954) argues that magic and religion serve to alleviate anxieties during times of stress and uncertainty. Dobu beliefs about the fate of the dead are discussed in Fortune (1932, 179–188). Kwaio pollution is described in Keesing (1982). The theory that ritual behavior creates social solidarity goes back to Durkheim (1915).

Supernatural Explanations of Misfortune

The distinction between imitative and contagious magic is taken from Frazer (1963). Fortune (1932) describes Dobu sorcery. The witchcraft examples are from Kluckhohn (1967; Navajo), Wilson (1951; Nyakyusa), Evans-Pritchard (1976; Zande), Offiong (1983; Ibibio), and Middleton (1965; Lugbara). Kluckhohn (1967) hypothesizes that Navajo witchcraft beliefs reduce overt, socially disruptive hostilities.

Varieties of Religious Organization

Wallace (1966) formulated and named the kinds of cults. The vision quest material is from Lowie (1954, 1956) and our general knowledge. Harner (1973b) describes Jívaro shamanism. Middleton (1965) describes the Lugbara ancestral cult. Victor Turner (1967) describes women's fertility rituals among the Ndembu.

Revitalization Movements

A general description of cargo cults is in Worsley (1968). Lawrence (1964) describes several Garia movements. On Handsome Lake's movement among the Seneca, see Wallace (1969). Stewart (1980) and Anderson (1996) describe peyotism among Native Americans.

CHAPTER 15—ART AND THE AESTHETIC

Many of the ideas for this chapter came from Hunter and Whitten (1975) and Anderson (1989). On Shaker art, we consulted the classic study by Andrews and Andrews (1937) and a more recent study by Kirk (1997). For changes in Chinese art, we consulted the Nelson Gallery (1975). Other sources of general information used in this chapter include Lipman and Winchester (1974), Hobson (1987), and Harvey (1937). Specific information on art in particular cultures is drawn from Colton (1959; Hopi) and Connelly (1979; Hopi), Hoebel (1978; Cheyenne), Kalb (1994; New Mexican santos), and Hail (1983; Plains Indians).

Forms of Artistic Expression

The general discussion of body arts is based primarily on Brain (1979). Information on Polynesian tattooing is from Gell (1993), Hage et al. (1995), and Simmons (1983). A 1998 research paper by undergraduate Maureen McCardel of Ohio Wesleyan University also was helpful on Polynesian tattooing.

Close (1989) provides a good summary of the archaeological debate over style versus function. Material on Northwest Coast art is from our general knowledge, with specific points drawn from Anderson (1989), Boas (1955), Furst and Furst (1982), and Holm (1965, 1972). The comparative information on style in visual arts is from Fischer (1961).

We drew from the studies of Kaeppler (1978) and Lomax (1962, 1968). Good sources on *voudon* are Metraux (1972) and Wade Davis's (1985) controversial book. We drew information on !Kung healing from Lee (1993) and Shostak (1983) and on Tumbuka healing from Friedson (1998). A source of case studies on various performances and healing is Laderman and Roseman, eds. (1996). An informative and heavily illustrated source for students on Native American dance is Heth (1993). For a discussion of the individual in art see Warner (1986).

Art and Culture

Information on the use of sandpaintings and song/chants in Navajo curing ceremonials is taken from Sandner (1991) and Reichard (1950, 1977). BaMbuti *molimo* is described in Turnbull (1962). Information on the development of the ethnic arts and the Southwest was taken from Anderson (1989), Phillips (1998), Howard and Pardue (1996), Cohodas (1997), and Sheffield (1997).

CHAPTER 16—GLOBALIZATION

Globalization

The most important single source is Stavrianos (1998). Secondary information is drawn from E. Wolf (1982), Crosby (1972), and—for the period from the fifteenth through the eighteenth centuries—Braudel (1979a, 1979b). Data on the demographic effects of contact on Native American peoples are from Thornton (1987) and Dobyns (1976). Specific information on historic changes among Native Americans is from Leacock and Lurie (1971), and Kehoe (1992). Historical data on Africa and the African slave trade are from Davidson (1961, 1969), Oliver and Fage (1962), and Mintz (1986). Data on the effects of New World cultigens on Africa are primarily from Miracle (1966, 1967). Statistics on the number of Europeans in India during the 1920s are from Mayo (1927).

The Emergence of the Global Economy

For information on the global economy we have drawn from a number of studies: Chomsky (2000), Giddens (2000), Hines (2000), Hutton and Giddens (2000), Klein (1999), and Robbins (1999). Information on container ships is from an article in the *Washington Post National Weekly Edition* (September 3–9, 2001).

Population Growth and Inequalities in the Global Economy

Most of the twentieth-century general economic and population data were drawn from Hepner and McKee (1992), Jackson and Hudman (1990a, 1990b), the World Bank (1999), Robbins (1999), and the U.S. Census Bureau, International Data Base (www.census.gov). Data on the changing magnitude of world trade were obtained from Rostow (1978), supplemented with later data from the World Bank (1999), and the World Trade Organization website (www.wto.org). Data on Nokia are drawn from an article in the *Washington Post National Weekly Edition* (July 23–29, 2001) and from the Nokia website (www.nokia.com).

The data on malaria and smallpox are from Gladwell (2001). For data on wealth distribution see Wealth Distribution Statistics 1999 compiled by the United Nations (www.geocities.com), World Council of Churches (2000), and the Institute for Policy Studies, "Top 200: The Rise of Corporate Global Power" (www.ips.org).

Globalization: The Continuing Process

For data on immigration issues we drew heavily from the Migration News (www.migration.ucdavis.edu), the U.S. Immigration and Naturalization Service website (www.ins.usdoj.gov), and the U.S. Census website (www.census.gov). Additional current data on economic, social, migration, and other issues have been taken from news reports in the *Washington Post, Christian Science Monitor,* the BBC News website (www.news.bbc.co.uk), and television and radio news reports. For data on fundamentalism we drew on news accounts as well as Harding (2000), the official website of the BJP (www.bjp.org), and Giddens (2000).

CHAPTER 17—ETHNICITY AND ETHNIC CONFLICT

There is a vast body of literature in anthropology and sociology on ethnicity and related issues. Since the entire chapter draws on the sources given here, we have not divided these notes into sections. Our ideas on the nature and significance of ethnicity have been most strongly influenced by the studies of Fredrik Barth (1958, 1969), Joan Vincent (1974), Bud B. Khlief (1979), Nathan Glazer and Daniel Moynihan (1963, 1975), John Bennett (1975), Joseph Himes (1974), George DeVos and Lola Romanusci-Ross (1975), Ronald Cohen (1978), Sol Tax (1967), Bernard Nietschmann (1988), Donald Horowitz (1985), and Richard Jackson and Lloyd Hudman (1990a, 1990b). For discussions of international legal and political issues, see Gudmundur Alfredsson (1989) and Lee Swepton (1989).

For additional data concerning particular ethnic groups and historical events, we have drawn on a number of sources: Ember and Ember (2001), Gerner (1994), Hajda and Beissinger (1990), Charles Foster (1980), John Bodley (1999), Eric Wolf (1982), L. S. Stavrianos (1998), Basil Davidson (1969), Robert Carmack (1988), Alice B. Kehoe (1992), John T. McAlister (1973), Richard Handler (1988), and Richard Price (1979), as well as basic reference sources and discussions with colleagues and students from Saudi Arabia, Oman, Bangladesh, Indonesia, and Malaysia.

In addition, one of the authors spent the summer of 1988 in Yugoslavia and the summer of 1989 in Guatemala collecting data on ethnic identity and conflict. For information on current ethnic conflicts, including the events of September 11, we have had to rely upon current news reports from the *Washington Post, Christian Science Monitor,* and BBC News (www.news.bbc.co.uk), as well as television and radio news reports. Materials for the box on Iraq were taken from news accounts, as well as from Marr (1985), Tripp (2000), Izady (1992), and Houston (2001).

CHAPTER 18—WORLD PROBLEMS AND THE PRACTICE OF ANTHROPOLOGY

Applied Anthropology

The ideas about the unique contributions of anthropology to problem solving are our own. The economic interpretation of high birthrates in the Punjabi villages was presented by Mamdani (1973). The 1982 study of the same area is reported in Nag and Kak (1984). Data on large Javanese and Nepalese families appear in B. White (1973) and

Nag, White, and Peet (1978). Nardi (1981, 1983), Shankman (1976), and Small (1997) discuss the importance of remittances in Samoa and Tonga. Freed and Freed (1985) discuss why Indian couples feel they need more than one son.

World Hunger

The inequality explanation of hunger is stated and defended in lay terms in Lappé and Collins (1977, 1986). Data on the Irish famine are from O'Grada (1989), Kinealy (1995), and Woodham-Smith (1991). The discussion of the effects of the "green revolution" on Javanese peasants is from Franke (1974). Johnson (1971) discusses risk minimization among peasants. The quantitative data on the energetic efficiency of various food systems are compiled from information given in Pimentel et al. (1973, 1975), and Pimentel and Pimentel (1979).

The potential value of traditional farming methods for the modern world is described in volumes by Altieri (1987) and Wilken (1987). The advantages of intercropping and other traditional methods are covered in Innis (1980), Gliessman and Grantham (1990), and Harrison (1987). Traditional resource management is covered by Alcorn (1981) and Posey (1983, 1984, 1985). Nations and Nigh (1980) discuss the potential of Lacandon Maya shifting cultivation.

Anthropologists as Advocates

The anthropologist as advocate is best discussed by Peterson (1974). The early roles of anthropologists in American Indian rights issues are discussed in Mark (1987). For Boas and the issue of racism see Stocking (1974) and for Mead see Mark (1999).

For the best general discussion of the evolution of European attitudes to indigenous peoples, see Berkhofer (1978). Germany's policies toward the Herero are discussed in Bodley (1999). S. Davis (1977) discusses the impact on indigenous tribes of Brazil's efforts to develop the Amazon Basin. Specific material on the plight of the Yanomamö is from *Newsweek* (April 9, 1990, 34) and from the Commission for the Creation of the Yanomamö Park (1989a, 1989b), published in *Cultural Survival Quarterly.* On San relocation, see Hitchcock (1999). The Kayapó materials are from T. Turner (1989) and Goodale (2003).The Maori claim was reported in the June 15, 1996, edition of the *Columbus Dispatch.* The July 22, 1995, issue of the *Economist* reported the claims of Canada's Nisga'a. The *Business Week* issue referred to is from March 1, 1993. The examples of medicines learned about from indigenous peoples are taken from Lewis and Elvin-Lewis (1977). Farnsworth (1984) argues that many more plants will be discovered to have medical uses. A good discussion of the insights of "traditional medicine" is in Fabrega (1975). The discussion of the erosion of the genetic diversity of major food crops is from our general knowledge and Harlan (1975). The material on amaranth is from Sokolov (1986).

BIBLIOGRAPHY

Aberle, David F.

1961 "Matrilineal Descent in Cross-Cultural Perspective." In *Matrilineal Kinship,* edited by David M. Schneider and Kathleen Gough, pp. 655–727. Berkeley: University of California Press.

Adams, Richard N.

1982 *Paradoxical Harvest.* Cambridge: Cambridge University Press.
1988 "Energy and the Regulation of Nation States." *Cultural Dynamics* 1:46–61.

Albers, Patricia C.

1989 "From Illusion to Illumination: Anthropological Studies of American Indian Women." In *Gender and Anthropology: Critical Reviews for Research and Teaching,* edited by Sandra Morgen, pp. 132–170. Washington, D.C.: American Anthropological Association.

Alcorn, Janice

1981 "Huastec Non-Crop Resource Management." *Human Ecology* 9:395–417.

Alfredsson, Gudmundur

1989 "The United Nations and the Rights of Indigenous Peoples." *Current Anthropology* 30:255–259.

Alkire, William H.

1977 *An Introduction to the Peoples and Cultures of Micronesia.* 2nd ed. Menlo Park, Calif.: Cummings.

Allen, Michael

1984 "Elders, Chiefs, and Big Men: Authority Legitimation and Political Evolution in Melanesia." *American Ethnologist* 11:20–41.

Altieri, Miguel A.

1987 *Agroecology: The Scientific Basis of Alternative Agriculture.* Boulder, Colo.: Westview Press.

American Anthropological Association

1995 *The AAA Guide, 1995–96.* Arlington, Va.: American Anthropological Association.

Anderson, Edward F.

1996 *Peyote: The Divine Cactus.* 2nd ed. Tucson: University of Arizona.

Anderson, Richard L.

1989 *Art in Small-Scale Societies.* 2nd ed. Englewood Cliffs, N.J.: Prentice-Hall.

Andrews, Edward Deming, and Faith Andrews

1937 *Shaker Furniture: The Craftsmanship of American Communal Sects.* New Haven, Conn.: Yale University Press.

Aveni, Anthony

1995 *Empires of Time.* New York: Kodansha America.

Avery, Robert B., Gregory E. Elliehausen, and Arthur B. Kennickell

1987 "Measuring Wealth with Survey Data: An Evaluation of the 1983 Survey of Consumer Finances." Paper presented at the 20th Congress of the International Association for Research on Income and Wealth, Rocca di Papa, Italy.

Bailey, Garrick

1989 "Descent and Social Survival of Native Horticultural Societies of the Eastern United States." Paper presented at the American Anthropological Association meetings, Washington, D.C.
1995 *The Osage and the Invisible World: From the Works of Francis LaFlesche.* Norman: University of Oklahoma Press.

Bailey, Garrick, Daniel Swan, John Nunley, and E. Sean StandingBear

2004 *Art of the Osage.* Seattle: St. Louis Art Museum and Washington University Press.

Balikci, Asen

1970 *The Netsilik Eskimo.* Garden City, N.Y.: Natural History Press.

Barnes, Sandra T.

1990 "Women, Property, and Power." In *Beyond the Second Sex,* edited by Peggy Reeves Sanday and Ruth Gallagher Goodenough, pp. 253–280. Philadelphia: University of Pennsylvania Press.

Barth, Fredrik

1958 "Ecological Relationships of Ethnic Groups in Swat, North Pakistan." *American Anthropologist* 60:1079–1089.
1969 *Ethnic Groups and Boundaries.* Boston: Little, Brown and Company.

Begun, David R.

2004 "The Earliest Hominids—Is Less More?" *Science* 303: 1478–1480.

Benedict, Ruth

1934 *Patterns of Culture.* Boston: Houghton Mifflin.

Bennett, John, ed.

1975 "The New Ethnicity: Perspectives from Ethnology." *1973 Proceedings of the American Ethnological Society.* St. Paul, Minn.: West.

Berch, Bettina

1982 *The Endless Days: The Political Economy of Women and Work.* San Diego: Harcourt, Brace, Jovanovich.

Berkhofer, Robert F., Jr.

1978 *The White Man's Indian: Images of the American Indian from Columbus to the Present.* New York: Knopf.

Berlin, Brent, and Paul Kay

1969 *Basic Color Terms—Their Universality and Evolution.* Berkeley: University of California Press.

Berreman, Gerald D.

1959 "Caste in India and the United States." *American Journal of Sociology* 66:120–127.

Bertelsen, Judy S., ed.

1977 *Nonstate Nations in International Politics: Comparative System Analyses.* New York: Praeger.

Black, Nancy Johnson

1991 "What Is Anthropology?" In *Introduction to Library Research in Anthropology,* edited by John Weeks, pp. 1–5. Boulder, Colo.: Westview Press.

Boas, Franz

1955 *Primitive Art.* New York: Dover Publications.
1966 *Race, Language and Culture.* New York: Free Press (original 1940).

Bodley, John H.

1999 *Victims of Progress.* 4th ed. Palo Alto, Calif.: Mayfield.

Bohannan, Paul

1955 "Some Principles of Exchange and Investment Among the Tiv." *American Anthropologist* 57:60–70.
1968 *Justice and Judgement Among the Tiv.* London: Oxford University Press.

Boserup, Ester

1965 *The Conditions of Agricultural Growth.* Chicago: Aldine.
1970 *Women's Role in Economic Development.* New York: St. Martin's.

Boyd, Robert, and Peter J. Richerson

1985 *Culture and the Evolutionary Process.* Chicago: University of Chicago Press.

Bradfield, Maitland

1971 "The Changing Pattern of Hopi Agriculture." Royal Anthropological Institute of Great Britain and Ireland Occasional Paper, no. 30. London: Royal Anthropological Institute.

Brain, Robert

1979 *The Decorated Body.* New York: Harper & Row.

Braudel, Fernand

1979a *The Structures of Everyday Life. Civilization & Capitalism 15th–18th Century,* vol. 1. New York: Harper & Row.
1979b *The Wheels of Commerce. Civilization & Capitalism 15th–18th Century,* vol. 2. New York: Harper & Row.

Brown, Donald E.

1991 *Human Universals.* New York: McGraw-Hill.

Brown, Judith K.

1970a "A Note on the Division of Labor by Sex." *American Anthropologist* 72:1073–1078.
1970b "Economic Organization and the Position of Women Among the Iroquois." *Ethnohistory* 17:131–167.
1988 "Cross-Cultural Perspectives on Middle-Aged Women." In *Cultural Constructions of 'Woman,'* edited by Pauline Kolenda, pp. 73–100. Salem, Wisc.: Sheffield.

Brown, Michael F.

2003 *Who Owns Native Culture?* Cambridge: Harvard University Press.

Burger, Julian

1987 *Report from the Frontier: The State of the World's Indigenous Peoples.* Cambridge, Mass.: Cultural Survival.
1990 *The GAIA Atlas of First Peoples.* New York: Anchor Books.

Burton, Michael L., and Douglas R. White

1984 "Sexual Division of Labor in Agriculture." *American Anthropologist* 86:568–583.

Callender, Charles, and Lee M. Kochems

1983 "The North American Berdache." *Current Anthropology* 24:443–490.

Carmack, Robert, ed.

1988 *Harvest of Violence.* Norman: University of Oklahoma Press.

Casal, Father Gabriel, Regalado Trota Jose, Eric Casino, George Ellis, and Wilhelm Solheim II

1981 *The People and Art of the Philippines.* Los Angeles: Museum of Cultural History, University of California.

Chagnon, Napoleon A.

1983 *Yąnomamö: The Fierce People.* 3rd ed. New York: Holt, Rinehart and Winston.
1991 *Yąnomamö: The Last Days of Eden.* San Diego: Harcourt Brace.

Chomsky, Noam

2000 "Control of Our Lives." Lecture, February 26, 2000, Albuquerque, N.M. (www.zmag.org).

Close, Angela E.

1989 "Identifying Style in Stone Artifacts: A Case Study from the Nile Valley." In Donald Henry and George Odell, eds. "Alternative Approaches to Lithic Analysis." *Archaeological Papers of the American Anthropological Association,* no. 1, pp. 3–26.

Cohen, Mark Nathan

1977 *The Food Crisis in Prehistory.* New Haven and London: Yale University Press.
1989 *Health and the Rise of Civilization.* New Haven, Conn.: Yale University Press.

Cohen, Ronald

1978 "Ethnicity: Problem and Focus in Anthropology." In *Annual Review of Anthropology,* vol. 7, edited by Bernard Siegal. Palo Alto, Calif.: Annual Reviews.

Cohen, Ronald, and John Middleton, eds.

1970 *From Tribe to Nation in Africa.* Scranton, Pa.: Chandler Publishing Company.

Cohen, Ronald, and Elman Service

1978 *Origins of the State: The Anthropology of Political Evolution.* Philadelphia: Institute for the Study of Human Issues.

Cohen, Theodore F.

1987 "Remaking Men." *Journal of Family Issues* 8:57–77.
2000 *Men and Masculinity: A Text Reader.* Belmont, Calif.: Wadsworth.

Cohodas, Marvin

1997 *Basket Weavers for the California Curio Trade: Elizabeth and Louise Hickox.* Tucson: University of Arizona Press.

Colton, Harold S.

1959 *Hopi Kachina Dolls.* Albuquerque: University of New Mexico Press.

Commission for the Creation of Yąnomami Park (CCPY)

1989a "The Threatened Yąnomami." *Cultural Survival Quarterly* 13:45–46.
1989b "Brazilian Government Reduces Yąnomami Territory by 70 Percent." *Cultural Survival Quarterly* 13:47.

Cong, Dachang

1992 "Amish Factionalism and Technological Change: A Case Study of Kerosene Refrigerators and Conservatism." *Ethnology* 31:205–218.

Conklin, Harold C.

1957 "Hanunóo Agriculture." FAO Forestry Development Paper, no. 12. Rome: Food and Agriculture Organization of the United Nations.

Connelly, John C.

1979 "Hopi Social Organization." In *Handbook of North American Indians,* vol. 9, edited by William Sturtevant, pp. 539–553.

Coombes, Annie E.

1994 *Reinventing Africa: Museum, Material Culture, and Popular Imagination in Late Victorian and Edwardian England.* New Haven, Conn.: Yale University Press.

Crosby, Alfred W.

1972 *The Colombian Exchange.* Westport, Conn.: Greenwood.
1986 *Ecological Imperialism: The Biological Expansion of Europe, 900–1900.* Cambridge: Cambridge University Press.

D'Altroy, Terence N.

1987 "Transitions in Power: Centralization of Wanka Political Organization Under Inka Rule." *Ethnohistory* 34:78–102.

Dahrendorf, Ralf

1959 *Class and Class Conflict in Industrial Society.* Berkeley: University of California Press.

Davidson, Basil

1961 *The African Slave Trade: Precolonial History 1450–1850.* Boston: Atlantic-Little Brown.
1969 *Africa in History.* New York: Macmillan.

Davis, Kingsley, and Wilbert E. Moore

1945 "Some Principles of Stratification." *American Sociological Review* 10:242–249.

Davis, Shelton H.

1977 *Victims of the Miracle.* Cambridge: Cambridge University Press.

Davis, Wade

1985 *The Serpent and the Rainbow.* New York: Warner Books.

Davis, William G.

1973 *Social Relations in a Philippine Market.* Berkeley: University of California Press.

DeMallie, Raymond J.

1983 "Male and Female in Traditional Lakota Culture." In *The Hidden Half: Studies of Plains Indian Women,* edited by Patricia Albers and Beatrice Medicine, pp. 237–265. Lanham, Md.: University Press of America.

DeNavas-Walt, Carmen, Bernadette D. Proctor, and Robert J. Mills

2004 *Income, Poverty, and Health Insurance Coverage in the United States: 2003.* (U.S. Census Bureau Current Population Reports P60–226). Washington, D.C.: U.S. Government Printing Office.

Denevan, William M.

1992 "The Pristine Myth: The Landscape of the Americas in 1492." *Annals of the Association of American Geographers* 82:369–385.

Denig, Edwin Thompson

1961 *Five Indian Tribes of the Upper Missouri,* edited by John Ewers. Norman: University of Oklahoma Press.

Dentan, Robert Knox

1968 *The Semai: A Nonviolent People of Malaya.* New York: Holt, Rinehart and Winston.

DeVos, George, and Lola Romanusci-Ross, eds.

1975 *Ethnic Identity: Cultural Continuities and Change.* Palo Alto, Calif.: Mayfield.

di Leonardo, Micaela, ed.

1991 *Gender at the Crossroads of Knowledge.* Berkeley: University of California Press.

Diamond, Jared

1997 *Guns, Germs, and Steel.* New York: Norton.

Divale, William T.

1974 "Migration, External Warfare, and Matrilocal Residence." *Behavior Science Research* 9:75–133.

Divale, William T., and Marvin Harris

1976 "Population, Warfare, and the Male Supremacist Complex." *American Anthropologist* 78:521–538.

Dobyns, Henry F.

1976 *Native American Historical Demography: A Critical Bibliography.* Bloomington: Indiana University Press.
1983 *Their Numbers Become Thinned.* Knoxville: University of Tennessee Press.

Domhoff, G. William

1983 *Who Rules America Now?* Englewood Cliffs, N.J.: Prentice-Hall.

Donkin, Robin

1979 *Agricultural Terracing in the Aboriginal New World.* Tucson: University of Arizona Press.

Doolittle, William E.

1992 "Agriculture in North America on the Eve of Contact: A Reassessment." *Annals of the Association of American Geographers* 82:386–401.

Douglas, Mary

1966 *Purity and Danger.* Middlesex, England: Penguin.

Dozier, Edward P.

1970 *The Pueblo Indians of North America.* Prospect Heights, Ill.: Waveland Press (reissued 1983).

DuBois, Cora

1944 *The People of Alor.* Minneapolis: University of Minnesota Press.

Dumont, Louis

1980 *Homo Hierarchicus: The Caste System and Its Implications.* Chicago and London: University of Chicago Press.

Durkheim, Émile

1915 *The Elementary Forms of the Religious Life.* London: George Allen and Unwin.

Dyson-Hudson, Rada, and Eric Alden Smith

1978 "Human Territoriality: An Ecological Reassessment." *American Anthropologist* 80:21–41.

Dyson-Hudson, Rada, and Neville Dyson-Hudson

1969 "Subsistence Herding in Uganda." *Scientific American* 220:76–89.

Eggan, Fred

1950 *Social Organization of the Western Pueblos.* Chicago: University of Chicago Press.

Ember, Carol

1974 "An Evaluation of Alternative Theories of Matrilocal Versus Patrilocal Residence." *Behavior Science Research* 9:135–149.
1983 "The Relative Decline in Women's Contribution to Agriculture With Intensification." *American Anthropologist* 85:285–304.

Ember, Melvin

1959 "The Nonunilinear Descent Groups of Samoa." *American Anthropologist* 61:573–577.

Ember, Melvin, and Carol R. Ember

1971 "The Conditions Favoring Matrilocal Versus Patrilocal Residence." *American Anthropologist* 73:571–594.
1972 "The Conditions Favoring Multilocal Residence." *Southwestern Journal of Anthropology* 28:382–400.

Ember, Melvin, and Carol R. Ember, eds.

2001 *Countries and Their Cultures,* 4 vols. New York: Macmillan Reference USA.

Ember, Melvin, Carol R. Ember, and Burton Pasternak

1974 "On the Development of Unilineal Descent." *Journal of Anthropological Research* 30:69–94.

Estioko-Griffin, Agnes

1986 "Daughters of the Forest." *Natural History* 95:36–43.

Evans-Pritchard, E. E.

1940 *The Nuer.* Oxford: Clarendon.
1976 *Witchcraft, Oracles, and Magic Among the Azande.* Abridged ed. Oxford: Clarendon Press.

Ewers, John

1955 "The Horse in Blackfoot Indian Culture." Bureau of American Ethnology, Bulletin 159. Washington, D.C.: U.S. Government Printing Office.

Fabrega, H., Jr.

1975 "The Need for an Ethnomedical Science." *Science* 189:969–975.

Fagan, Brian M.

1986 *People of the Earth.* Boston: Little, Brown.

Fallers, Lloyd A.

1969 *Law Without Precedent.* Chicago: University of Chicago Press.

Farb, Peter

1974 *Word Play.* New York: Alfred A. Knopf.

Farnsworth, Norman R.

1984 "How Can the Well Be Dry When It Is Filled With Water?" *Economic Botany* 38:4–13.

Farrer, Claire F.

1996 *Thunder Rides a Black Horse.* 2nd ed. Prospect Heights, Ill.: Waveland Press.

Faulkner, Gretchen Fearon, Nancy T. Prince, and Jennifer Sapiel Neptune

1998 "Beautifully Beaded: Northeastern Native American Beadwork." *American Indian Art* 24(1):32–41.

Ferguson, R. Brian

1984 "A Reexamination of the Causes of Northwest Coast Warfare." In *Warfare, Culture, and Environment,* edited by R. Brian Ferguson, pp. 267–328. Orlando, Fla.: Academic Press.

Firth, Raymond

1936 *We, the Tikopia.* Boston: Beacon Press.
1959 *Economics of the New Zealand Maori.* 2nd ed. Wellington: Government Printer.
1965 *Primitive Polynesian Economy.* New York: Norton.
1968 "A Note on Descent Groups in Polynesia." In *Kinship and Social Organization,* edited by Paul Bohannan and John Middleton, pp. 213–223. Garden City, N.Y.: The Natural History Press.

Fischer, John

1961 "Art Styles as Cultural Cognitive Maps." *American Anthropologist* 63:80–84.

Fogelson, Raymond D.

1989 "The Ethnohistory of Events and Nonevents." *Ethnohistory* 36:133–147.

Fortune, Reo

1932 *Sorcerers of Dobu.* New York: E. P. Dutton.

Foster, Charles R., ed.

1980 *Nations Without a State: Ethnic Minorities of Western Europe.* New York: Praeger.

Franke, Richard W.

1974 "Miracle Seeds and Shattered Dreams in Java." *Natural History* 83:10–18, 84–88.

Frazer, Sir James George

1963 *The Golden Bough.* Abridged ed. Toronto: Macmillan (original 1911–1915).

Freed, Stanley A., and Ruth S. Freed

1985 "One Son Is No Sons." *Natural History* 94:10–15.

Freeman, Derek

1968 "On the Concept of the Kindred." In *Kinship and Social Organization,* edited by Paul Bohannan and John Middleton, pp. 255–272. Garden City, N.Y.: The Natural History Press.
1970 "The Iban of Western Borneo." In *Cultures of the Pacific,* edited by Thomas G. Harding and Ben J. Wallace, pp. 180–200. New York: Free Press.
1983 *Margaret Mead and Samoa.* Cambridge, Mass.: Harvard University Press.

Fried, Morton

1967 *The Evolution of Political Society.* New York: Random House.

Friedl, Ernestine

1975 *Women and Men: An Anthropologist's View.* New York: Holt, Rinehart and Winston.
1978 "Society and Sex Roles." In *Anthropology 98/99,* edited by Elvio Angeloni, pp. 122–126. Guilford, Conn.: Dushkin.

Friedson, Steven

1998 "Tumbuka Healing." In *The Garland Encyclopedia of World Music,* vol. 1, edited by Ruth M. Stone, pp. 271–284. New York: Garland Publishing, Inc.

Frigout, Arlette

1979 "Hopi Ceremonial Organization." In *Southwest,* edited by Alfonso Ortiz, pp. 564–576. *Handbook of North American Indians,* vol. 9. Washington, D.C.: Smithsonian Institution.

Fromkin, Victoria, and Robert Rodman

1988 *An Introduction to Language.* 4th ed. New York: Holt, Rinehart and Winston.

Furst, Peter T., and Jill L. Furst

1982 *North American Indian Art.* New York: Rizzoli International.

Geertz, Clifford

1963 *Agricultural Involution.* Berkeley: University of California Press.
1965 "Religion as a Cultural System." In *Anthropological Approaches to the Study of Religion,* edited by Michael Banton, pp. 1–46. Association of Social Anthropologists Monographs, no. 3. London: Tavistock Publications.
1973 *The Interpretation of Cultures.* New York: Basic Books.
1980 *Negara.* Princeton, N.J.: Princeton University Press.
1983 *Local Knowledge: Further Essays on Interpretive Anthropology.* New York: Basic Books.

Gell, Alfred

1993 *Wrapping in Images.* Oxford: Clarendon Press.

Gerner, Deborah J.

1994 *One Land, Two Peoples: The Conflict Over Palestine.* Boulder, Colo.: Westview Press.

Giddens, Anthony

2000 *Runaway World: How Globalization Is Reshaping Our Lives.* New York: Routledge.

Gilmore, David D.

1980 *The People of the Plain.* New York: Columbia University Press.
1990 *Manhood in the Making.* New Haven, Conn.: Yale University Press.

Gladwell, Malcolm

2001 "The Mosquito Killer." *New Yorker* (July 2) 42–51.

Glazer, Nathan, and Daniel P. Moynihan

1963 *Beyond the Melting Pot.* Cambridge: Harvard University Press.

Glazer, Nathan, and Daniel P. Moynihan, eds.

1975 *Ethnicity: Theory and Experience.* Cambridge: Harvard University Press.

Gliessman, Stephen, and Robert Grantham

1990 "Agroecology: Reshaping Agricultural Development." In *Lessons of the Rain Forest,* edited by Suzanne Head and Robert Heinzman, pp. 196–207. San Francisco: Sierra Club Books.

Globalisation Guide

n.d.

Gluckman, Max

1972 *The Ideas in Barotse Jurisprudence.* Manchester: Manchester University Press.
1973 *The Judicial Process Among the Barotse.* Manchester: Manchester University Press.

Goldman, Irving

1970 *Ancient Polynesian Society.* Chicago: University of Chicago Press.

Goldstein, Melvyn C.

1987 "When Brothers Share a Wife." *Natural History* 96(3):38–49.

Goodale, Ava Y.

2003 *The Kayapo Indians' Struggle in Brazil.* (www.actionbioscience. org/environment/goodale.html).

Goodale, Jane C.

1971 *Tiwi Wives.* Seattle: University of Washington Press.

Goodenough, Ward H.

1961 "Comment on Cultural Evolution." *Daedalus* 90:521–528.

Goody, Jack

1976 *Production and Reproduction.* Cambridge: Cambridge University Press.

Goody, Jack, and S. J. Tambiah

1973 *Bridewealth and Dowry.* Cambridge: Cambridge University Press.

Gough, E. Kathleen

1959 "The Nayars and the Definition of Marriage." *Journal of the Royal Anthropological Institute* 89:23–24.

Graburn, Nelson H. H., ed.

1976 *Ethnic and Tourist Arts: Cultural Expressions from the Fourth World.* Berkeley: University of California Press.

Graham, Susan Brandt

1985 "Running and Menstrual Dysfunction: Recent Medical Discoveries Provide New Insights into the Human Division of Labor by Sex." *American Anthropologist* 87:878–882.

Grigg, David

1974 *The Agricultural Systems of the World.* Cambridge: Cambridge University Press.

Gusterson, Hugh

2001 "The Virtual Nuclear Weapons Laboratory in the New World Order." *American Ethnologist* 28:417–437.

Guthrie, Stewart

1993 *Faces in the Clouds: A New Theory of Religion.* Oxford: Oxford University Press.

Hage, Per, Frank Harary, and Bojka Milicic

1995 "Tatooing, Gender and Social Stratification in Micro-Polynesia." *Journal of the Royal Anthropological Institute (N.S.)* 2:335–350.

Hail, Barbara A.

1983 *Hau, Kola!: The Plains Indian Collection of the Haffenrefer Museum.* Providence, R.I.: Brown University Press.

Haile-Selassie, Yohannes, Gen Suwa, and Tim D. White

2004 "Late Miocene Teeth from Middle Awash, Ethiopia, and Early Hominid Dental Evolution." *Science* 303:1503–1505.

Hajda, Lubomyr, and Mark Beissinger, ed.

1990 *The Nationalities Factor in Soviet Politics and Society.* Boulder, Colo.: Westview Press.

Hall, Edward T.

1959 *The Silent Language.* Greenwich, Conn.: Fawcett Publications.
1966 *The Hidden Dimension.* Garden City, N.Y.: Doubleday.

Hamill, James

1990 *Ethno-Logic: The Anthropology of Human Reasoning.* Urbana: University of Illinois Press.

Handler, Richard

1988 *Nationalism and the Politics of Culture in Quebec.* Madison: University of Wisconsin Press.

Hanson, Jeffery R.

1988 "Age-Set Theory and Plains Indian Age-Grading: A Critical Review and Revision." *American Ethnologist* 15:349–364.

Harding, Susan Friend

2000 *The Book of Jerry Falwell: Fundamentalist Language and Politics.* Princeton: Princeton University Press.

Harlan, Jack R.

1975 "Our Vanishing Genetic Resources." *Science* 188:618–621.

Harner, Michael J.

1973a *The Jívaro.* Garden City, N.Y.: Doubleday-Anchor.
1973b "The Sound of Rushing Water." In *Hallucinogens and Shamanism,* edited by Michael J. Harner, pp. 15–27. London: Oxford University Press.

Harrell, Stevan, and Sara A. Dickey

1985 "Dowry Systems in Complex Societies." *Ethnology* 24:105–120.

Harris, Marvin

1968 *The Rise of Anthropological Theory.* New York: Thomas Y. Crowell.
1977 *Cannibals and Kings.* New York: Random House.
1979 *Cultural Materialism.* New York: Vintage Books.
1981 *America Now.* New York: Simon & Schuster.

1985 *Good to Eat.* New York: Simon & Schuster.
1999 *Theories of Culture in Postmodern Times.* Walnut Creek, Calif.: Altamira Press.

Harrison, Paul

1987 *The Greening of Africa.* New York: Penguin.

Hart, C. W. M., and Arnold R. Pilling

1979 *The Tiwi of North Australia.* New York: Holt, Rinehart and Winston.

Hart, C. W. M., Arnold R. Pilling, and Jane C. Goodale

1988 *The Tiwi of North Australia.* Belmont, Calif.: Wadsworth.

Harvey, Paul

1937 *The Oxford Companion to Classical Literature.* Oxford: Clarendon Press.

Hassrick, Royal B.

1964 *The Sioux: Life and Customs of a Warrior Society.* Norman: University of Oklahoma Press.

Hepner, George F., and Jesse O. McKee

1992 *World Regional Geography: A Global Approach.* St. Paul, Minn.: West.

Herdt, Gilbert

1983 *The Sambia: Ritual and Gender in New Guinea.* New York: Holt, Rinehart and Winston.
1987 *The Sambia: Ritual and Gender in New Guinea.* Belmont, Calif.: Wadsworth.

Heth, Charlotte, general ed.

1993 *Native American Dance.* Washington, D.C.: Smithsonian Institution.

Hewlett, Barry S.

1992 *Intimate Fathers.* Ann Arbor: University of Michigan Press.

Hickerson, Harold

1970 *The Chippewa and Their Neighbors: A Study in Ethnohistory.* New York: Holt, Rinehart and Winston.

Hiebert, P. G.

1971 *Konduru: Structure and Integration in a Hindu Village.* Minneapolis: University of Minnesota Press.

Himes, Joseph S.

1974 *Racial and Ethnic Relations.* Dubuque, Ia.: Wm. C. Brown.

Hines, Colin

2000 *Localization: A Global Manifesto.* London: Earthscan Publications.

Hitchcock, Robert K.

1999 "Resource Rights and Resettlement Among the San of Botswana." *Cultural Survival Quarterly* 22(4):51–55.

Hobson, Christine

1987 *The World of the Pharaohs.* New York: Thames and Hudson.

Hockett, Charles F.

1960 "The Origin of Speech." *Scientific American* 203:88–96.

Hoebel, E. Adamson

1940 *The Political Organization and Law-Ways of the Comanche Indians.* American Anthropological Association, Memoir 54. Menasha, Wis.: American Anthropological Association.
1954 *The Law of Primitive Man.* Cambridge: Harvard University Press.
1978 *The Cheyennes.* 2nd ed. New York: Holt, Rinehart and Winston.

Holm, Bill

1965 *Northwest Coast Indian Art: An Analysis of Form.* Seattle: University of Washington Press.
1972 *Crooked Beak of Heaven.* Seattle: University of Washington Press.

Holmes, Lowell D., and Ellen Rhoads Holmes

1992 *Samoan Village Then and Now.* 2nd ed. Fort Worth: Harcourt Brace Jovanovich.

Horowitz, Donald L.

1985 *Ethnic Groups in Conflict.* Berkeley: University of California Press.

Hostetler, John A., and Gertrude Enders Huntington

1992 *Amish Children.* 2nd ed. Fort Worth, Tex.: Harcourt Brace Jovanovich College Publishers.

Howard, Alan, and John Kirkpatrick

1989 "Social Organization." In *Developments in Polynesian Ethnology,* edited by Alan Howard and Robert Borofsky, pp. 47–94. Honolulu: University of Hawaii Press.

Howard, Kathleen, and Diana Pardue

1996 *Inventing the Southwest: The Fred Harvey Company and Native American Art.* Flagstaff, Ariz.: Northland.

Howard, Mary, and Ann V. Millard

1997 *Hunger and Shame: Poverty and Childhood Malnutrition on Mount Kilimanjaro.* New York: Routledge.

Hua, Cai

2001 *A Society Without Fathers or Husbands: The Na of China.* New York: Zone Books. (Translated by Asti Hustvedt)

Hunter, David E., and Phillip Whitten, eds.

1975 *Encyclopedia of Anthropology.* New York: Harper & Row.

Huntington, Samuel P.

1996 *The Clash of Civilizations and the Remaking of World Order.* New York: Simon & Schuster.

Houston, Christopher

2001 *Islam, Kurds and the Turkish Nation-State.* Oxford and New York: Berg.

Hutton, Will, and Anthony Giddens, eds.

2000 *Global Capitalism.* New York: New Press.

Innis, Donald Q.

1980 "The Future of Traditional Agriculture." *Focus* 30:1–8.

Izady, Mehrdad R.

1992 *The Kurds.* Washington, D.C.: Taylor & Francis.

Jackson, Richard, and Lloyd E. Hudman

1990a *Cultural Geography: People, Places and Environment.* St. Paul, Minn.: West.
1990b *Cultural Geography: The Global Discipline.* St. Paul, Minn.: West.

Jenness, Diamond

1932 *The Indians of Canada.* Ottawa: National Museum of Canada.

Johnson, Allen W.

1971 "Security and Risk-Taking Among Poor Peasants: A Brazilian Case." In *Studies in Economic Anthropology,* edited by George Dalton, pp. 143–150. American Anthropological Association Special Publication, no. 7. Washington, D.C.: American Anthropological Association.

Johnson, Allen W., and Timothy Earle

1987 *The Evolution of Human Societies.* Stanford, Calif.: Stanford University Press.

Julien, Catherine J.

1988 "How Inca Decimal Administration Worked." *Ethnohistory* 35:257–279.

Jurmain, Robert, Harry Nelson, Lynn Kilgore, and Wenda Trevathan

2000 *Introduction to Physical Anthropology.* 8th ed. Belmont, Calif.: Wadsworth.

Kaeppler, Adrienne L.

1978 "Dance in Anthropological Perspective." In Bernard Siegel, ed. *Annual Review of Anthropology,* 7:31–49. Palo Alto, Calif.: Annual Reviews.

Kahn, J., et al., eds.

1979 *World Economic Development.* Boulder, Colo.: Westview.

Kalb, Laurie Beth

1994 *Crafting Devotions: Tradition in Contemporary New Mexico Santos.* Albuquerque: University of New Mexico Press.

Kammer, Jerry

1980 *The Second Long Walk: The Navajo-Hopi Land Dispute.* Albuquerque: University of New Mexico.

Kapur, Akash

1998 "The Indian State of Kerala Has Everything Against It— Except Success." *Atlantic Monthly,* Sept., 40–45.

Kardiner, Abram

1945 *The Psychological Frontiers of Society.* New York: Columbia University Press.

Keesing, Roger M.

1982 *Kwaio Religion.* New York: Columbia University Press.

Kehoe, Alice B.

1989 *The Ghost Dance.* New York: Holt, Rinehart and Winston.
1992 *North American Indians: A Comprehensive Account.* 2nd ed. Englewood Cliffs, N.J.: Prentice-Hall.

Kelly, Robert L.

1995 *The Foraging Spectrum: Diversity in Hunter-Gatherer Lifeways.* Washington, D.C.: Smithsonian Institution.

Kennickell, Arthur B.

2001 "An Examination of the Changes in the Distribution of Wealth from 1989 to 1998: Evidence from the Survey of Consumer Finances." Paper prepared for the Conference on Saving, Intergenerational Transfers, and the Distribution of Wealth, Jerome Levy Economics Institute, Bard College, June 7–9, 2000.

Khlief, Bud B.

1979 "Language as Identity: Toward an Ethnography of Welsh Nationalism." *Ethnicity* 6(4):346–357.

Kinealy, Christine

1995 *This Great Calamity: The Irish Famine 1845–52.* Boulder, Colo.: Roberts Rinehart.

Kirk, John T.

1997 *The Shaker World: Art, Life, Belief.* New York: Harry N. Abrams.

Klein, Naomi

1999 *No Logo.* New York: Picador.

Kluckhohn, Clyde

1967 *Navajo Witchcraft.* Boston: Beacon Press.

Kottak, Conrad

1992 *Assault on Paradise: Social Change in a Brazilian Village.* 2nd ed. New York: McGraw-Hill.

Krader, Lawrence

1968 *Formation of the State.* Englewood Cliffs, N.J.: Prentice-Hall.

Kraybill, Donald B.

1989 *The Riddle of Amish Culture.* Baltimore, Md.: Johns Hopkins University Press.
1990 *The Puzzles of Amish Life.* Intercourse, Pa.: Good Books.

Kummer, Corby

2004 "Going with the Grain." *Atlantic,* April, 145–148.

Kuper, Hilda

1963 *The Swazi: A South African Kingdom.* New York: Holt, Rinehart and Winston.

Laderman, Carol, and Marina Roseman, eds.

1996 *The Performance of Healing.* New York: Routledge.

LaDuke, Winona

2003 "Manoomin Wild Rice, Biodiversity and Bio Piracy" (www.foodroutes.org/doclib/192/Manoomin+Wild+Rice.doc).

LaFlesche, Francis

1905 *Who Was the Medicine Man?* Hampton, Va.: Hampton Institute Press.
1925 "The Osage Tribe: Rite of Vigil." In *39th Annual Report of the Bureau of American Ethnology (1917–18),* pp. 523–833. Washington, D.C.: Government Printing Office.
1928 "The Osage Tribe: Two Versions of the Child-Naming Rite." In *43rd Annual Report of the Bureau of American Ethnology (1925–1926),* pp. 23–164. Washington, D.C.: Government Printing Office.

LaLone, Mary B., and Darrell E. LaLone

1987 "The Inka State in the Southern Highlands: State Administrative and Production Enclaves." *Ethnohistory* 34:47–62.

Lappé, Frances Moore, and Joseph Collins

1977 *Food First.* New York: Ballantine Books.
1986 *World Hunger: Twelve Myths.* New York: Grove Press.

Lawrence, Peter

1964 *Road Belong Cargo.* Manchester: Manchester University Press.

Leach, E. R.

1968 "The Sinhalese of the Dry Zone of Northern Ceylon." In *Economic Anthropology,* edited by Edward E. LeClair, Jr., and Harold K. Schneider, pp. 395–403. New York: Holt, Rinehart and Winston (original 1960).

Leacock, Eleanor

1978 "Women's Status in Egalitarian Society: Implications for Social Evolution." *Current Anthropology* 19:247–275.

Leacock, Eleanor, and Nancy Lurie, eds.

1971 *North American Indians in Historical Perspective.* New York: Random House.

Lee, Richard B.

1968 "What Hunters Do for a Living, or, How to Make Out on Scarce Resources." In *Man the Hunter,* edited by Richard B. Lee and Irven DeVore, pp. 30–48. Chicago: Aldine.
1969 "!Kung Bushman Subsistence: An Input–Output Analysis." In *Environment and Social Behavior,* edited by Andrew P. Vayda, pp. 47–79. Garden City, N.Y.: Natural History Press.
1979 *The !Kung San.* Cambridge: Cambridge University Press.
1993 *The Dobe Ju/'hoansi.* 2nd ed. Fort Worth, Tex.: Harcourt Brace Jovanovich.

Lefkowitz, Mary

1995 *Not Out of Africa: How Afrocentrism Became an Excuse to Teach Myth as History.* New York: Basic Books.

Lenski, Gerhard E.

1966 *Power and Privilege.* New York: McGraw-Hill.

LeVine, Robert A., Suzanne Dixon, et al.,

1994 *Child Care and Culture: Lessons from Africa.* Cambridge: Cambridge University Press.

LeVine, Terry Yarov

1987 "Inka Labor Service at the Regional Level: The Functional Reality." *Ethnohistory* 34:14–46.

Lewis, Oscar

1941 "Manly-Hearted Women Among the South Piegan." *American Anthropologist* 43:173–187.

Lewis, Walter H., and Memory P. F. Elvin-Lewis

1977 *Medical Botany.* New York: John Wiley and Sons.

Linton, Ralph

1937 "The One Hundred Percent American." *American Mercury* 40:427–429.

Lipman, Jean, and Alice Winchester

1974 *The Flowering of American Folk Art.* New York: Viking Press.

Llewellyn, Karl, and E. Adamson Hoebel

1941 *The Cheyenne Way.* Norman: University of Oklahoma.

Lomax, Alan

1962 "Song Structure and Social Structure." *Ethnology* 1:425–451.
1968 "Folk Song Style and Culture." American Association for the Advancement of Science Publication, no. 88. Washington, D.C.: American Association for Advancement of Science.

Lowie, Robert H.

1954 *Indians of the Plains*. Garden City, N.Y.: American Museum of Natural History.
1956 *The Crow Indians*. New York: Holt, Rinehart and Winston (original 1935).

Malinowski, Bronislaw

1922 *Argonauts of the Western Pacific*. New York: E. P. Dutton.
1926 *Crime and Custom in Savage Society*. London: Routledge and Kegan Paul.
1954 *Magic, Science and Religion*. Garden City, N.Y.: Doubleday.
1960 *A Scientific Theory of Culture and Other Essays*. New York: Oxford University Press (original 1944).

Mamdani, Mahmood

1973 *The Myth of Population Control: Family, Caste, and Class in an Indian Village*. New York: Monthly Review Press.

Mandelbaum, David G.

1970 *Society in India*. 2 vols. Berkeley: University of California Press.

Mark, Joan

1987 *A Stranger in Her Native Land: Alice Fletcher and the American Indians*. Lincoln: University of Nebraska Press.
1999 *Margaret Mead: Coming of Age in America*. New York: Oxford University Press.

Marr, Phebe

1985 *The Modern History of Iraq*. Boulder, Colo.: Westview Press.

Martin, M. Kay, and Barbara Voorhies

1975 *Female of the Species*. New York: Columbia University Press.

Marx, Karl

1967 *Capital,* vol. 1. New York: International Publishers (original 1867).
1970 *A Contribution to the Critique of Political Economy*. New York: International Publishers (original 1859).

Mayo, Katherine

1927 *Mother India*. New York: Harcourt, Brace.

McAlister, John T., ed.

1973 *Southeast Asia: The Politics of National Integration*. New York: Random House.

McDonald, Kim

1995 "Unearthing Sins of the Past." *Chronicle of Higher Education,* Oct. 6, A12, 20.

McNickle, D'Arcy

1971 "Americans Called Indians." In *North American Indians in Historical Perspective,* edited by Eleanor Burke Leacock and Nancy Oestrich Lurie, pp. 29–63. New York: Random House.

Mead, Margaret

1928 *Coming of Age in Samoa*. New York: Morrow.

Mead, Sidney Moko, ed.

1984 *Te Maori: Maori Art From New Zealand Collections*. New York: Harry N. Abrams.

Medicine, Beatrice

1983 "Warrior Women: Sex Role Alternatives for Plains Indian Women." In *The Hidden Half: Studies of Plains Indian Women,* edited by Patricia Albers and Beatrice Medicine, pp. 267–275. Lanham, Md.: University Press of America.

Meggitt, Mervyn

1970 "Male–Female Relationships in the Highlands of Australian New Guinea." In *Cultures of the Pacific,* edited by Thomas G. Harding and Ben J. Wallace, pp. 125–143. New York: Free Press.

Meigs, Anna S.

1988 *Food, Sex, and Pollution: A New Guinea Religion*. New Brunswick, N.J.: Rutgers University Press.
1990 "Multiple Gender Ideologies and Statuses." In *Beyond the Second Sex,* edited by Peggy Reeves Sanday and Ruth Gallagher Goodenough, pp. 99–112. Philadelphia: University of Pennsylvania Press.

Metraux, Alfred

1969 *The History of the Incas*. New York: Pantheon Books.
1972 *Voodoo in Haiti*. New York: Schocken Books.

Middleton, John

1965 *The Lugbara of Uganda*. New York: Holt, Rinehart and Winston.

Mintz, Sidney W.

1986 *Sweetness and Power: The Place of Sugar in Modern History*. New York: Penguin Books.

Miracle, Marvin P.

1966 *Maize in Tropical Africa*. Madison: University of Wisconsin Press.
1967 *Agriculture in the Congo Basin*. Madison: University of Wisconsin Press.

Mishel, Lawrence, Jared Bernstein, and Sylvia Allegretto

2005 *The State of Working America 2004–5*. Ithaca, N.Y.: Cornell University Press.

Moore, Omar Khayyam

1957 "Divination—A New Perspective." *American Anthropologist* 59:69–74.

Morgan, Lewis Henry

1877 *Ancient Society*. New York: World.

Morgen, Sandra, ed.

1989 *Gender and Anthropology: Critical Reviews for Research and Teaching*. Washington, D.C.: American Anthropological Association.

Murdock, George P., and Caterina Provost

1973 "Factors in the Division of Labor by Sex: A Cross-Cultural Analysis." *Ethnology* 12:203–225.

Murdock, George Peter

1949 *Social Structure*. New York: The Free Press.
1967 *Ethnographic Atlas*. Pittsburgh: University of Pittsburgh Press.

Nadel, S. F.

1951 *The Foundations of Social Anthropology.* London: Cohen & West.

Nag, Moni, and Neeraj Kak

1984 "Demographic Transition in a Punjab Village." *Population and Development Review* 10:661–678.

Nag, Moni, Benjamin N. F. White, and R. Creighton Peet

1978 "An Anthropological Approach to the Study of the Economic Value of Children in Java and Nepal." *Current Anthropology* 19:293–306.

Nanda, Serena

2000 *Gender Diversity: Cross-Cultural Variations.* Prospect Heights, Ill.: Waveland Press.

Nardi, Bonnie

1981 "Modes of Explanation in Anthropological Population Theory." *American Anthropologist* 83:28–56.
1983 "Goals in Reproductive Decision Making." *American Ethnologist* 10:697–714.

Naroll, Raoul

1962 *Data Quality Control—A New Research Technique.* New York: Free Press.

Nations, James, and Robert Nigh

1980 "The Evolutionary Potential of Lacandon Maya Sustained-Yield Tropical Forest Agriculture." *Journal of Anthropological Research* 36:1–30.

Neale, Walter C.

1976 *Monies in Societies.* San Francisco: Chandler and Sharp.

Nelson Gallery

1975 *The Chinese Exhibition: The Exhibition of Archaeological Finds of the People's Republic of China.* Kansas City: The Nelson Gallery-Atkins Museum.

Nestor, Sandy

2003 *Indian Placenames in America: Volume 1: Cities, Towns and Villages.* London: McFarland & Company.

Newman, Katherine S.

1983 *Law and Economic Organization: A Comparative Study of Pre-industrial Societies.* Cambridge: Cambridge University Press.

Newman, Philip L., and David J. Boyd

1982 "The Making of Men: Ritual and Meaning in Awa Male Initiation." In *Rituals of Manhood: Male Initiation in Papua New Guinea,* edited by Gilbert Herdt, pp. 239–285. Berkeley and Los Angeles: University of California Press.

Nietschmann, Bernard

1988 "Third World War: The Global Conflict Over the Rights of Indigenous Nations." *Utne Reader,* Nov./Dec., 84–91.

Nimuendaju, Curt

1948 "The Tucuna." In *Handbook of South American Indians,* vol. 3, edited by Julian Steward, pp. 713–725. *Handbook of South American Indians: The Tropical Forest Tribes.* Bureau of American Ethnology Bulletin 143. Washington, D.C.: U.S. Government Printing Office.

O'Grada, Cormac

1989 *Ireland Before and After the Famine: Explorations in Economic History 1800–1925.* Manchester: University of Manchester Press.

Obeyesekere, Gananath

1992 *The Apotheosis of Captain Cook: European Mythmaking in the Pacific.* Princeton, N.J.: Princeton University Press.

Offiong, Daniel

1983 "Witchcraft Among the Ibibio of Nigeria." *African Studies Review* 26:107–124.

Oliver, Douglas L.

1989 *Oceania: The Native Cultures of Australia and the Pacific Islands.* Honolulu: University of Hawaii Press.

Oliver, Roland, and J. D. Fage

1962 *A Short History of Africa.* Baltimore: Penguin.

Oliver, Symmes C.

1962 "Ecology and Cultural Continuity as Contributing Factors in the Social Organization of the Plains Indians." University of California Publications in American Archaeology and Ethnology 48(1). Berkeley: University of Calfornia Press.

Pasternak, Burton

1976 *Introduction to Kinship and Social Organization.* Englewood Cliffs, N.J.: Prentice-Hall.

Pasternak, Burton, Carol R. Ember, and Melvin Ember

1976 "On the Conditions Favoring Extended Family Households." *Journal of Anthropological Research* 32:109–123.

Peoples, James G.

1982 "Individual or Group Advantage? A Reinterpretation of the Maring Ritual Cycle." *Current Anthropology* 23:291–309.
1985 *Island in Trust.* Boulder, Colo.: Westview Press.

Peterson, John

1974 "The Anthropologist as Advocate." *Human Organization* 33:311–318.

Phillips, Ruth B.

1998 *Trading Identities: The Souvenir in Native North American Art from the Northeast, 1700–1900.* Seattle: University of Washington Press, and Montreal: McGill-Queens University Press.

Piddocke, Stuart

1965 "The Potlatch System of the Southern Kwakiutl: A New Perspective." *Southwestern Journal of Anthropology* 21:244–264.

Pieterse, Jan Nederveen

1992 *White on Black: Images of Africa and Blacks in Western Popular Culture.* New Haven, Conn.: Yale University Press.

Pimentel, David, et al.

1973 "Food Production and the Energy Crisis." *Science* 182:443–449.
1975 "Energy and Land Constraints in Food Protein Production." *Science* 190:754–761.

Pimentel, David, and Marcia Pimentel

1979 *Food, Energy and Society.* New York: John Wiley and Sons.

Plotkin, Mark

1993 *Tales of a Shaman's Apprentice.* New York: Viking.

Pope, Kevin O., Mary E. D. Pohl et al.

2001 "Origin and Environmental Setting of Ancient Agriculture in the Lowlands of Mesoamerica." *Science* 292:1370–1373.

Porter, Philip W.

1965 "Environmental Potentials and Economic Opportunities—A Background for Cultural Adaptation." *American Anthropologist* 67:409–420.

Posey, Darrell

1983 "Indigenous Ecological Knowledge and Development of the Amazon." In *The Dilemma of Amazonian Development,* edited by Emilio Moran, pp. 225–257. Boulder, Colo.: Westview Press.
1984 "A Preliminary Report on Diversified Management of Tropical Forest by the Kayapó Indians of the Brazilian Amazon." *Advances in Economic Botany* 1:112–126.
1985 "Indigenous Management of Tropical Forest Ecosystems: The Case of the Kayapó Indians of the Brazilian Amazon." *Agroforestry Systems* 3:139–158.

Pospisil, Leopold

1958 *Kapauku Papuans and Their Law.* Yale University Publications in Anthropology, no. 54. New Haven, Conn.: Yale University Press.
1978 *The Kapauku Papuans of West New Guinea.* 2nd ed. New York: Holt, Rinehart and Winston.

Price, Richard, ed.

1979 *Maroon Societies: Rebel Slave Communities in the Americas.* Baltimore: Johns Hopkins University Press.

Public Citizen

n.d.

Pulliam, H. Ronald, and Christopher Dunford

1980 *Programmed to Learn.* New York: Columbia University Press.

Quinn, Naomi

1977 "Anthropological Studies on Women's Status." *Annual Review of Anthropology* 6:181–225.

Radcliffe-Brown, A. R.

1922 *The Andaman Islanders.* Cambridge: Cambridge University Press.
1965 *Structure and Function in Primitive Societies.* New York: Free Press.

Rappaport, Roy

1968 *Pigs for the Ancestors.* New Haven, Conn.: Yale University Press.

Rasmussen, Knud

1979 "A Shaman's Journey to the Sea Spirit." In *Reader in Comparative Religion,* edited by William A. Lessa and Evon Z. Vogt, pp. 308–311. New York: Harper & Row.

Reichard, Gladys A.

1950 *Navaho Religion.* Princeton, N.J.: Princeton University Press.
1977 *Navajo Medicine Man Sandpaintings.* New York: Dover.

Reichel-Dolmatoff, Gerardo

1971 *Amazonian Cosmos.* Chicago: University of Chicago Press.

Robbins, Richard H.

1999 *Global Problems and the Culture of Capitalism.* Boston: Allyn and Bacon.

Rosaldo, Michelle Z., and Louise Lamphere, eds.

1974 *Women, Culture, and Society.* Stanford, Calif.: Stanford University Press.

Roscoe, Will

1991 *The Zuni Man-Woman.* Albuquerque: University of New Mexico Press.
2000 *Changing Ones: Third and Fourth Genders in Native North America.*

Rostow, W. W.

1978 *The World Economy: History and Prospect.* Austin: University of Texas Press.

Ruddle, Kenneth

1974 *The Yukpa Autosubsistence System: A Study of Shifting Cultivation and Ancillary Activities in Colombia and Venezuela.* Berkeley: University of California Press.

Sacks, Karen

1982 *Sisters and Wives.* Urbana: University of Illinois Press.

Sahlins, Marshall

1958 *Social Stratification in Polynesia.* Seattle: University of Washington Press.
1965 "On the Sociology of Primitive Exchange." In *The Relevance of Models for Social Anthropology,* edited by Michael Banton, pp. 139–236. London: Tavistock.
1972 *Stone Age Economics.* New York: Aldine.
1981 *Historical Metaphors and Mythical Realities: Structure in the Early History of the Sandwich Island Kingdom.* Ann Arbor: University of Michigan Press.
1995 *How "Natives" Think: About Captain Cook, for Example.* Chicago: University of Chicago Press.

Said, Edward

1978 *Orientalism.* New York: Vintage Books.

Sampat, Payal

2001 "Last Words." *World Watch Institute,* May/June, 34–40.

Sanday, Peggy R.

1973 "Toward a Theory of the Status of Women." *American Anthropologist* 75:1682–1700.
1981 *Female Power and Male Dominance.* Cambridge: Cambridge University Press.

Sanday, Peggy Reeves, and Ruth Gallagher Goodenough, eds.

1990 *Beyond the Second Sex.* Philadelphia: University of Pennsylvania Press.

Sanderson, Stephen K.

1999 *Social Transformations.* Expanded ed. New York: Rowman & Littlefield Publishers, Inc.

Sandner, Donald

1991 *Navajo Symbols of Healing.* Rochester, Vt.: Healing Arts Press.

Sapir, Edward

1964 "The Status of Linguistics as a Science." In *Edward Sapir,* edited by David G. Mandelbaum, pp. 65–77. Berkeley: University of California Press (original 1929).

Sassen, Scokia

1996 *Losing Control: Sovereignty in an Age of Globalization.* New York: Columbia University Press.

Schlegel, Alice

1972 *Male Dominance and Female Autonomy.* New Haven, Conn.: HRAF Press.
1991 "Status, Property, and the Value on Virginity." *American Ethnologist* 18:719–734.

Schneider, Harold K.

1981 *The Africans.* Englewood Cliffs, N.J.: Prentice-Hall.

Scudder, Thayer

1982 *No Place to Go: Effects of Compulsory Relocation on Navajos.* Philadelphia: ISHI.

Sen, Amartya

1984 *Resources, Values and Development.* Cambridge, Mass.: Harvard University Press.
1987 *The Standard of Living.* Cambridge: Cambridge University Press.

Service, Elman

1962 *Primitive Social Organization: An Evolutionary Perspective.* New York: Random House.

Shankman, Paul

1976 *Migration and Underdevelopment: The Case of Western Samoa.* Boulder, Colo.: Westview Press.

Sheffield, Gail K.

1997 *The Arbitrary Indian: The Indian Arts & Crafts Act of 1990.* Norman: University of Oklahoma Press.

Sheper-Hughes, Nancy

1992 *Death Without Weeping: The Violence of Everyday Life in Brazil.* Berkeley: University of California Press.

Shore, Bradd

1989 "Mana and Tapu." In *Developments in Polynesian Ethnology,* edited by Alan Howard and Robert Borofsky, pp. 137–173. Honolulu: University of Hawaii Press.

Shostak, Marjorie

1983 *Nisa: The Life and Words of a !Kung Woman.* New York: Vintage.

Simmons, Dave

1983 "Moko." In *Art and Artists of Oceania,* pp. 226–243. Palmerston North, New Zealand: Dunmore Press.

Small, Cathy

1997 *Voyages.* Ithaca and London: Cornell University Press.

Smith, Bruce

1995 *The Emergence of Agriculture.* New York: Scientific American Library.

Smith, Eric Alden, and Bruce Winterhalder, eds.

1992 *Evolutionary Ecology and Human Behavior.* New York: Aldine de Gruyter.

Snow, Clyde

1995 "Murder Most Foul." *Science,* May/June, 16–20.

Sokolov, Raymond

1986 "The Good Seed." *Natural History* 95:102–105.

Stavrianos, Leften S.

1998 *The World Since 1500: A Global History.* 8th ed. Englewood Cliffs, N.J.: Prentice-Hall.

Steward, Julian H.

1938 *Basin-Plateau Sociopolitical Groups.* Bureau of American Ethnology Bulletin 120. Washington, D.C.: U.S. Government Printing Office.
1955 *Theory of Culture Change.* Urbana: University of Illinois Press.
1977 *Evolution and Ecology: Essays on Social Transformation,* edited by Jane C. Steward and Robert F. Murphy. Urbana: University of Illinois Press.

Stewart, Omer C.

1980 "The Native American Church." In *Anthropology on the Great Plains,* edited by W. Raymond Wood and Margot Liberty, pp. 188–196. Lincoln: University of Nebraska Press.

Stockard, Janice E.

2002 *Marriage in Culture.* Fort Worth, Tex.: Harcourt.

Stocking, George W., Jr.

1974 *The Shaping of American Anthropology, 1883–1911.* New York: Basic Books.

Stone, M. Priscilla, Glenn Davis Stone, and Robert McC. Netting

1995 "The Sexual Division of Labor in Kofyar Agriculture." *American Ethnologist* 22:165–186.

Suttles, Wayne

1960 "Affinal Ties, Subsistence, and Prestige Among the Coast Salish." *American Anthropologist* 62:296–305.
1962 "Variations in Habitat and Culture on the Northwest Coast." In *Man in Adaptation: The Cultural Present,* edited by Yehudi A. Cohen, pp. 128–141. Chicago: Aldine.
1968 "Coping with Abundance: Subsistence on the Northwest Coast." In *Man the Hunter,* edited by Richard B. Lee and Irven DeVore, pp. 56–68. Chicago: Aldine.

Swanson, Guy

1960 *The Birth of the Gods.* Ann Arbor: University of Michigan Press.

Swepton, Lee

1989 "Indigenous and Tribal Peoples and International Law: Recent Developments." *Current Anthropology* 30:259–264.

Tax, Sol, ed.

1967 *Acculturation in the Americas.* New York: Cooper Square.

Thornton, Russell

1987 *American Indian Holocaust and Survival: A Population History Since 1492.* Norman: University of Oklahoma Press.

Tierney, Patrick

2000 *Darkness in El Dorado.* New York: Norton.

Tischer, Henry L.

1990 *Introduction to Sociology.* 3rd ed. Fort Worth, Tex.: Holt, Rinehart and Winston.

Tripp, Charles

2000 *A History of Iraq.* Cambridge: Cambridge University Press.

Trudgill, Peter

1983 *Sociolinguistics.* Middlesex, England: Penguin.

Turnbull, Colin M.

1962 *The Forest People.* New York: Simon & Schuster.

Turner, Terence

1989 "Kayapo Plan Meeting to Discuss Dams." *Cultural Survival Quarterly* 13:20–22.

Turner, Victor

1967 *The Forest of Symbols.* Ithaca, N.Y.: Cornell University Press.

Tyler, Stephen A.

1973 *India: An Anthropological Perspective.* Pacific Palisades, Calif.: Goodyear.

Tyler, Stephen A., ed.

1969 *Cognitive Anthropology.* New York: Holt, Rinehart and Winston.

Tylor, Edward B.

1865 *Researches into the Early History of Mankind and the Development of Civilization.* London: J. Murray.
1871 *Primitive Culture.* London: J. Murray.

United Nations Development Programme

1995 *Human Development Report 1995.* New York: Oxford University Press.

United States Department of the Interior

1993 *Federal Historic Preservation Laws.* Washington, D.C.: U.S. Government Printing Office.

Urban, Greg, and Joel Sherzer, eds.

1992 *Nation-States and Indians in Latin America.* Austin: University of Texas.

Valeri, Valerio

1985 *Kingship and Sacrifice: Ritual and Society in Ancient Hawaii.* Chicago and London: University of Chicago Press.

Van den Berghe, Pierre

1979 *Human Family Systems.* New York: Elsevier.

Vanstone, James W.

1974 *Athapaskan Adaptations: Hunters and Fishermen of the Subarctic Forest.* Chicago: Aldine.

Vedantam, Shankar

2004 "Wrath Over a Hindu God." *Washington Post National Weekly Edition,* April 19–25, 18.

Vincent, Joan

1974 "The Structuring of Ethnicity." *Human Organization* 33:375–379.

Wallace, Anthony F. C.

1966 *Religion: An Anthropological View.* New York: Random House.
1969 *The Death and Rebirth of the Seneca.* New York: Vintage Books.

Wallace, Ernest, and E. Adamson Hoebel

1952 *The Comanches: Lords of the South Plains.* Norman: University of Oklahoma.

Warner, John Anson

1986 "The Individual in Native American Art: A Sociological View." In *The Arts of the North American Indian: Native Traditions in Evolution,* edited by Edwin L. Wade, pp. 171–202. New York: Hudson Hills Press.

Weatherford, Jack

1991 *Native Roots: How the Indians Enriched America.* New York: Fawcett Columbine.

Weigle, Marta, and Barbara A. Babcock, eds.

1996 *The Great Southwest of the Fred Harvey Company and the Santa Fe Railway.* Phoenix: The Heard Museum.

Weyler, Rey

1982 *Blood of the Land.* New York: Vintage Books.

White, Benjamin N. F.

1973 "Demand for Labor and Population Growth in Colonial Java." *Human Ecology* 1:217–236.

White, Douglas R., Michael L. Burton, and Malcolm M. Dow

1981 "Sexual Division of Labor in African Agriculture: A Network Autocorrelation Analysis." *American Anthropologist* 83:824–849.

White, Leslie

1949 *The Science of Culture.* New York: Grove Press.
1959 *The Evolution of Culture.* New York: McGraw-Hill.

White, Lynn

1967 "The Historical Roots of Our Ecological Crisis." *Science* 155:1203–1207.

Whiting, Beatrice

1950 *Paiute Sorcery.* Viking Fund Publications in Anthropology 15. New York: Viking.

Whiting, John W. M.

1977 "A Model for Psychocultural Research." In *Culture and Infancy,* edited by P. Herbert Leiderman, S. R. Tulkin, and A. Rosenfield, pp. 29–49. New York: Academic Press.

Whitworth, John McKelvie

1975 *God's Blueprints: A Sociological Study of Three Utopian Sects.* Boston: Routledge and Kegan Paul.

Whyte, Martin King

1978 *The Status of Women in Preindustrial Societies.* Princeton, N.J.: Princeton University Press.

Wilken, Gene C.

1987 *Good Farmers: Traditional Resource Management in Mexico and Central America.* Berkeley: University of California Press.

Wilson, Monica

1951 *Good Company.* Oxford: Oxford University Press.

Winterhalder, Bruce, and Eric Alden Smith, eds.

1981 *Hunter-Gatherer Foraging Strategies.* Chicago: University of Chicago Press.

Winthrop, Robert H.

1991 *Dictionary of Concepts in Cultural Anthropology.* New York: Greenwood Press.

Wolf, Eric

1966 *Peasants.* Englewood Cliffs, N.J.: Prentice-Hall.
1969 *Peasant Wars of the Twentieth Century.* New York: Harper and Row.
1982 *Europe and the People Without History.* Berkeley: University of California Press.

Wolf, Margery

1972 *Women and the Family in Rural Taiwan.* Stanford, Calif.: Stanford University Press.

Wood, Bernard

2002 "Hominid Revelations from Chad." *Nature* 418(11 July 2002):133–135.

Wood, Bernard, and Brian G. Richmond

2002 "Human Evolution: Taxonomy and Paleobiology." *Journal of Anatomy* 196:19–60.

Woodburn, James

1968 "An Introduction to Hadza Ecology." In *Man the Hunter,* edited by Richard B. Lee and Irven DeVore, pp. 49–55. Chicago: Aldine.
1982 "Egalitarian Societies." *Man* 17:431–451.

Woodham-Smith, Cecil

1991 *The Great Hunger; Ireland 1845–1849.* London: Penguin Books.

World Bank

1999 *World Development Report 1998/9.* New York: Oxford.

World Council of Churches

2000 "There Are Alternatives to Globalization." Dossier prepared by the Justice, Peace and Creation team.

World Trade Organization

n.d.

Wormsley, William E.

1993 *The White Man Will Eat You!* Fort Worth, Tex.: Harcourt Brace Jovanovich.

Worsley, Peter

1968 *The Trumpet Shall Sound.* New York: Schocken.

PHOTO CREDITS

CHAPTER 1
p 1 © James L. Stanfield/National Geographic Society
p 3 © Robert Brenner/Photo Edit
p 4 © Michael K. Nichols/National Geographic Society
p 10 © Reuters/Corbis
p 11 © Markus Matzel/Peter Arnold
p 12 © Brian Vikander/Corbis

CHAPTER 2
p 20 © D. H. Hessell/Stock Boston
p 23 © Steve Raymer/Corbis
p 24 © Michael McCoy/Photo Researchers, Inc.
p 28 © Anders Ryman/Corbis
p 37 © Jeff Greenberg/The Image Works
p 38 © Bruce Connolly/Corbis

CHAPTER 3
p 41 © Pablo Corral V/Corbis
p 42 © H. S. Terrace/Animals Animals
p 48 © Michael S. Yamashita/Corbis
p 49 © Steve Raymer/Corbis
p 51 © Erika Stone/Peter Arnold, Inc.
p 52 © Roger Wood/Corbis
p 59 © Nick Clements/FPG/Getty Images

CHAPTER 4
p 63 © Paul Chesley/Stone/Getty Images
p 65 © Scala Art Resource 1988
p 67 Courtesy The American Philosophical Society
p 69 © Ken Heyman/Woodfin Camp & Associates
p 75 © Rick Friedman/Corbis
p 78 © Sylvia Howe/Anthro-Photo File
p 80 © Randall Hagadorn/Courtesy of Clifford Geertz

CHAPTER 5
p 87 © Documentary Educational Resources
p 93 © National Anthropological Archives/Smithsonian Institution
p 99 © Gideon Mendel/Corbis

CHAPTER 6
p 104 © Michael S. Yamashita/Corbis
p 106 © Charles Hughes/Documentary Educational Resources
p 109 © Washburn/Anthro-Photo File
p 120 © David Austen/Stock Boston
p 122 © Sergio Dorantes/Corbis
p 125 © Barry D. Kass/Images of Anthropology

CHAPTER 7
p 131 © Sean Gallup/Getty Images
p 134 © William Bacon/Photo Researchers, Inc.
p 139 © Spencer Platt/Getty Images
p 141 © Paul Chesley/National Geographic Society
p 145 © Barry D. Kass/Images of Anthropology
p 147 © Barry D. Kass/Images of Anthropology

CHAPTER 8
p 150 © Jon Riley/Stone/Getty Images
p 154 © Halpern/Anthro-Photo File
p 158 © Emil Muench/Photo Researchers, Inc.
p 161 © Israel Talby/Woodfin Camp & Associates

CHAPTER 9
p 172 © Mark Segal/Stone/Getty Images
p 176 © Jeffrey L. Rotman/Peter Arnold, Inc.
p 180 © Bettmann/Corbis

CHAPTER 10
p 192 © Jeff Greenberg/Photo Edit
p 194 © Nancy Sheehan/Photo Edit
p 195 © Ian Griffiths/Robert Harding World Imagery
p 199 © JJ Travel/Robert Harding World Imagery
p 200 © Noboro Komine/Photo Researchers, Inc.
p 203 © James Peoples
p 205 © David Boyd
p 207 © Paul Chesley/Stone/Getty Images
p 209 © Noboro Komine/Photo Researchers, Inc.

CHAPTER 11
p 212 © Malcolm S. Kark/Peter Arnold, Inc.
p 216 © Lawrence Migdale/Photo Researchers, Inc.
p 219 Courtesy National Anthropological Archive, Smithsonian Institution
p 223 © Stan Wayman/Photo Researchers, Inc.
p 224 © Barry D. Kass/Images of Anthropology
p 226 © Barry D. Kass/Images of Anthropology
p 231 © Stock Montage
p 233 © R. Krubner/H. Armstrong Roberts
p 234 © David Wells/The Image Works

CHAPTER 12
p 239 © Garrick Bailey
p 246 © Mirelle Vautier/Woodfin Camp & Associates
p 249 © Garrick Bailey

CHAPTER 13
p 259 © Darkslide Productions/Corbis
p 262 © Anthony Bannister/Gallo Images/AfriPics.com
p 264 © Bernard Wolfe/Photo Researchers, Inc.
p 266 © Viviane Moos/Corbis
p 268 © Wartenberg/Picture Press/Corbis
p 270 © Matthias Clamer/Stone/Getty Images
p 275 © William Taufic/Corbis

CHAPTER 14
p 280 © Giampero Sposito/Reuters/Landov
p 283 Lucas Cranach the Elder, "The Fall from Grace," 1533, SMPK, Gemaldegalerie, Berlin. Photo © akg-images, London)
p 284 © Barry D. Kass/Images of Anthropology
p 287 © Stephanie Sinclair/Corbis
p 288 © BIOS (A. Compost)/Peter Arnold, Inc.
p 293 © Catherine Karnow/Corbis
p 296 © Bryan & Cherry Alexander Photography
p 299 © EPA/Alessia Paradisi/Landov
p 301 © Lamont Lindstrom

CHAPTER 15
p 306 © Kevin R. Morris/Corbis
p 308 © Barry D. Kass/Images of Anthropology
p 310 © Barry D. Kass/Images of Anthropology
p 312 © Paula Bronstein/Getty Images
p 314 Courtesy Thomas Gilcrease Museum, Tulsa
p 316 © Sean Sprague/Panos Pictures
p 317 © Chlaus Lotscher/Peter Arnold, Inc.
p 324 © Garrick Bailey

CHAPTER 16
p 328 © Paul Chesley/Network Aspen
p 332 © Garrick Bailey
p 334 © Ian Murphy/Stone/Getty Images
p 340 © Chuck Place Photography
p 343 © Reuters/Bettmann/Corbis
p 350 © Nathan Benn/Stock Boston
p 351 © David Young Wolff/Photo Edit

CHAPTER 17
p 354 © Barry D. Kass/Images of Anthropology
p 357 © Garrick Bailey

CHAPTER 18
p 378 © Bruce Bander/Photo Researchers, Inc.
p 381 © Barry D. Kass/Images of Anthropology
p 385 © Barry D. Kass/Images of Anthropology
p 391 © Victor Englebert/Photo Researchers, Inc.
p 395 © Bryan and Cherry Alexander Photography

Peoples and Cultures Index

Note: Page numbers in *italics* indicate illustrations. Letters *f* and *t* indicate figures and tables, respectively.

A

Aboney, 333
Aborigines. *See* Australian aborigines
Afghanistan, religion in, 299
Africa
    agriculture in, 333–334, *334*
    art of, *308,* 321
    band organization in, 109–110
    body arts in, 309–310, *310,* 312
    bridewealth in, 162
    child mortality in, 198
    communal houses in, 153
    cultural groupings in, 36
    ethnic groups in, 358, 362, 367–368, 369
    European contact, effects of, 332–333, 336
    evidence of evolution in, 64
    globalization and, 336
    hairstyle in, 309
    herding societies in, *125,* 125–126
    hominids in, 8, 9
    hunting in, 108
    legal system in, 254
    marriage in, 153, 161
    money in, 140–142
    net fishers in, *106*
    performance arts in, 318–319
    polygyny in, *158*
    population trends in, 347, 348
    problems of, 348
    quality of life in, 113
    racial classifications in, 30
    reciprocal sharing in, 110
    religion in, 290, 291, 297, 298
    right to resources in, 110–111
    rites of passage in, 204
    sexual division of labor in, 224, *224, 226,* 228
    slave trade in, 331, 333, 335–336
    social stratification in, 270, 271
    socialization in, 193, 194–199, *195, 199*
    threats to indigenous people in, 392–393
    tone languages in, 48
    two-generational households in, 167
    women's contributions in, 232–233
    See also specific countries

African Americans
    in American history, 356
    dialects of, 45–46
    as ethnic group, 358, 359
    racial pride among, 31, 53, 58
    segregation of, 370
    two-generational households of, 167
Agta (Philippines), sexual division of labor among, 224
Aka (Africa)
    egalitarianism among, 260
    socialization of, 194–196, *195,* 197, 198
    women's contributions among, 232
Alaska, art in, *317*
Albanians, 362, 367, 370, 373, 374
Amazon. *See* Yąnomamö (Amazon)
American Indians. *See* Native Americans
Amish, 57, 282, 309
Andean civilizations, 309, 396
Angles, 358
Angola, 334, 336
Anishinaabeg, 390
Apache, 91
    female initiation rituals of, 206, *207*
    religion of, 302
Armenia, 364, 369
Ashanti, 333
Asia
    agriculture in, 2, 227
    communal houses in, 153
    globalization and, 337
    languages in, 58
    old age in, 208–209, *209*
    racial classifications in, 30
    religion in, 295, 299
    sexual division of labor in, 227, 229
    trade with Europe, 334–335
    See also specific countries
Athabaskan tribes, elderly in, 208
Atzlan, 359
Australia
    cross-generational marriage in, 155–156
    ethnic groups in, 358. *See also* Australian aborigines
    European contact, effects of, 337
    immigrants in, 350
    marriage in, 155–156
    postmarital residence patterns in, 166
Australian aborigines
    Fijian culture vs., 66

    language of, 57
    religion of, 293, 298
Awa (New Guinea)
    gender stratification among, 230
    male initiation rituals of, 204–206, *205*
Azande (Sudan), religion of, 290, 291
Azerbaijan, 364
Aztecs
    agriculture of, 121
    inequality among, 269
    population of, 329
    religion of, 298
    Spanish conquest of, 330, 331

B

Baggara, child care of, *199*
Baghdad, Iraq, 348
Bali
    agriculture in, *122*
    fieldwork in, *69*
Balkans, 373
Baluchi peoples, 367
BaMbuti (Zaire), 108, 321
    egalitarianism among, 260
    sexual division of labor among, 224
    women's contributions among, 232
Bandung, Indonesia, 348
Bangladesh, 367, 368, 383
Bantu (Africa), 30
Barotse (southern Africa), 254
Basque separatists, *362,* 370
Belgium, 370
Bengal, 337, 367
Benin, 333
Boers, 358
Bogotá, Colombia, 348
Bohemia, 373
Bolivia, 32
Borneo, bilateral kinship in, 183
Bosnia, 367, 368, 369, 370, 373, 374
Botswana, threats to indigenous people in, 392–393
Brazil
    agriculture in, 389
    languages in, 57
    as Portuguese colony, 330–331, 335
    racial classifications in, 30
    threats to indigenous people in, *391,* 392, 393
Bretons, 310

Britain. *See* England
Bulgaria, 369
Bunyoro, 270, 271
Burakamin (Japan), 30
Burma, 337, 367, 368
Burundi, separatist movements in, 367

C

California, land ownership in, 131–132
Canada
    birthrate in, 380
    ethnic groups in, 370, 371–372
    threats to indigenous people in, 393
Cape Colony (Africa), 336
Caribbean, 293, 318
Catalonians, 370
Ceylon, 335, 337
Cherokee, 371
Cheyenne
    art of, 322
    children of, 201, 203
    cultural system of, 99
    gender identity among, 220
    hunting by, 111
    legal system of, 252, 253
    political organization of, 242–243
    studies of, 87
China
    agriculture in, 2, *104,* 119
    art of, 309
    bridewealth and dowry in, 163
    defeat in Opium War, 337
    diverse population in, 240
    elderly in, 208–209, *209*
    enculturation in, *192*
    ethnic groups in, 362
    families in, *150*
    foot binding in, 309
    foreign investment in, 144
    inequality in, 269, *270,* 271
    invasion of Tibet by, 367
    languages of, 57
    marriage in, 153–154
    music in, *38*
    Peking Man in, 9
    religion in, 299, 357
    sexual division of labor in, 229
    tone languages in, 48
    two-generational households in, 166
    women in, 235
Chinooks, 309
Chippewa, 390
Chuukese (Micronesia), young men of, 203
Colombia, urban centers in, 348
Comanche
    elderly of, 208
    legal system of, 250
    political organization among, 240, 242
    religion of, 302
Congo, 334, 336, 367
Creek Indians, 358

Croats, 357, 367, 368, 369, 370, 373–374
Crow
    gender identity among, 220
    gender roles among, 218
    kinship terminology of, 189
    religion of, 294
Czech Republic, 371, 373
Czechoslovakia, 369, 371, 373

D

Dakota tribe, 112
Delaware tribe, 302
Dobu (Melanesia), 286, 289
Dutch. *See* Netherlands

E

Ecuador
    legal system in, 251–252
    religion in, 295–296
Egypt
    agriculture in, 121
    art of, 320
    body arts in, 309, 310
    complex culture in, 72
    political organization in, 245
    religion in, 299
El Salvador, *10*
Elites
    control of resources by, 274
    functions of, 276–277
England
    African colonies of, 333, 339
    American colonies of, 332
    ethnic groups in, 358
    India as colony of, 339
    Irish independence from, 360
    legal system in, *239*
    as model for India, 344
    West Indians in, 349
Eskimo. *See* Inuit
Ethiopia, ethnic groups in, 362
Europe
    effects of contact with, 107, 331–339
    kinship ties in, 173
    See also specific countries

F

Fijians
    Australian aborigine culture vs., 66
    European contact, effects of, 338
Finland, 345–346
France
    African colonies of, 333
    American colonies of, 332
    cultural characteristics of French, 69
    diverse population in, 240
French Huguenots, 358

G

Gabon, 336
Gambia, 336

Garia (Papua New Guinea), religion of,
    300–301, 303
Germany
    fossils found in, 8, 64
    guest workers in, 349
    languages spoken in, 357
    in World War II, 369
Gold Coast (Africa), 336
Great Britain. *See* England
Greece, art of, 320
Guatemala
    art in, 322, *324*
    clothing in, *357,* 358
    ethnic problems in, 369, 370, 371
    global economy and, 248
Guinea (Africa), 336
Gusii (Africa), child care of, 196–199
Gypsies, 368, 370

H

Hadza people (Tanzania)
    egalitarianism among, 260
    seasonal mobility of, 108
Haiti, religion in, 293
Ham, language of, 57
Han (China), 235
Hanunóo (Philippines), 29
Harsous people, *1*
Hasidic Jews, 309
Hawaiians
    beliefs of, 96–97
    cognatic descent among, 182
    European contact, effects of, 338
    kinship terminology of, 186, 186f, 188
    social stratification of, 271–272
    tribute payments by, 138–139
Himalayas, polyandry in, 160
Hispanics
    art of, 321
    racial pride among, 53
Hispaniola, 331
Hmong, relocation of, 13, 57
Honduras, agriculture in, *145*
Hopi
    art of, *180,* 309, 321, 322
    children of, 194
    gender stratification among, 229, 231, 232
    hairstyles of, *180,* 309
    horticultural methods of, 116–117
    language of, 55, 356–357
    matrilineal society of, 179–181, *180*
    religion of, 283
Hua (Papua New Guinea)
    gender among, 214–216
    gender stratification among, 230
Huguenots, 358
Hungary, *161,* 362, 370, 373
Huron, matrilineal culture of, 184

I

Iban, bilateral kinship among, 183
Ibibio (Nigeria), religion of, 290

Incas
  agriculture of, 121, 396
  inequality among, 269
  political organization of, 245–246, *246*
  religion of, 298
India
  British model used in, 344
  castes in, 263–265, *264*, 271
  conflict with Pakistan, 366–367
  costs and benefits of children in, 382
  diverse population in, 240
  dowry deaths in, 163
  endogamy in, 157
  ethnic problems in, 363, 366–367, 368
  European contact, effects of, 337, 338, 339
  famine in, 398
  Hindu civilization in, 91, 157
  Hindu fundamentalism in, *343,* 343–345
  income in, 398
  malaria in, 346
  marriage in, 155, 156
  matrilineal culture in, 184
  population of, 347
  Sepoy Mutiny in, 337
  women in, *234*
Indians. *See* Native Americans
Indonesia
  agriculture in, *120, 122*
  diverse population in, 240
  ethnic groups in, 362
  Java Man in, 9
  knowledge of indigenous people in, *395*
  language in, 59
  religion in, *288, 296*
  separatist movements in, 367
  threats to indigenous people in, 392
Indus River valley, 121
Inuit
  body arts of, 312
  elderly of, 208
  fieldwork among, 68
  generalized reciprocity among, *134*
  kinship terminology of, 185–186, 186*f,* 188, 189
  matrilineal culture of, 184
  postmarital residence patterns of, 166
  religion of, 282, 293
Iran, 366, 367
  religion in, 299
Iraq
  ethnoreligious groups in, 364–367, 365*f*
  invasion of Kuwait by, 366
  Kurds in, 5
  occupation of, 361
  urban centers in, 348
Ireland
  independence of, 360
  potato famine in, 385–386
Irish
  cultural characteristics of, 69
  emigration of, 386

ethnic conflicts among, 360, 367, 371
languages of, 357
in United States, 30–31
Iroquois
  gender stratification among, 229, 230–231, *231*
  kinship terminology of, 186–187, 187*f,* 188
  matrilineal culture of, 184
  religion of, 301–302
Israel
  ethnic conflicts in, 360, 371
  Jewish migration to, 364
  religion in, *284*
Italy
  cultural characteristics of Italians, 69
  population of, 347

J
Jamaica, women in, *233*
Japan
  "authoritarian" personalities in, 69
  autonomy of, 337
  differences in culture of, 21
  elderly in, 208
  globalization and, *328*
  honorifics in, *59,* 59–60
  immigrants in, 350
  language in, *48*
  marriage in, 153
  politeness in, 29, *59*
  population of, 347
  racial classifications in, 30
  religion in, 299
  sexual division of labor in, 229
Java (Indonesia), 59
Jerusalem, *284, 354,* 371
Jews
  beards of, 309
  classifying, 357
  ethnic conflict with Palestinians, 360
  expulsion from Jerusalem, 371
  genocide against, 368
  in Iraq, 364
  as racial group, 31
  segregation of, 370
Jívaro (Ecuador)
  legal system of, 251–252
  religion of, 295–296
Ju/'hoansi. *See* !Kung
Jutes, 358

K
Kanem-Bornu, 333
Kansa, 358
Kapauku (Papua New Guinea)
  legal sanctions in, 249
  use of money by, 140
Karachi, Pakistan, 348
Karimojong (East Africa), 125–126
Kashmir, 366
Kayapó (Brazil), 389, 393, 395

Kazakhstan, 369
Kenya, 125
  child care in, 196–199
  marriage practices in, 153
Kerala, India, 398
Ketchikan, Alaska, *317*
Khoisan peoples (Africa), 30
Kikuyu (East Africa), 37, *310*
Kiowa, religion of, 302
Kofyar (Nigeria), sexual division of labor among, 228
Kongo kingdom, effects of European contact, 333
Korea
  elderly in, 208
  female touching in, 29
  marriage in, 153, *200*
  religion in, 293, *293,* 299
  sexual division of labor in, 229
  See also South Korea
Kosovo, 366, 367, 374
Kosrae (Micronesia), 131
Kuna (Panama), 323
!Kung, *109*
  band organization of, 109–110
  brideservice among, 162
  egalitarianism among, 260, *262*
  family among, 143
  generalized reciprocity among, 134
  gift exchange custom of, 136
  hoodia plant and, 92
  modesty among, 135
  performance arts of, 318
  quality of life among, 113
  religion of, 293
  resource sharing (reciprocity) among, 110
  rights to resources among, 110–111
  threats to, 392
  values of, 143
  women's contributions among, 232
  work of, 142–143
Kurds, 5, 364, 365*f,* 366–367
Kuwait, 349, 366
Kwaio (Solomon Islands), 286
Kwakiutl, fieldwork among, 68, 69

L
Ladinos, 370
Lagos, Nigeria, 336, 348
Lakota, gender identity among, 220
Laos, function of marriage in, *154*
Libya, 350
Lipan-Apache, 302
Lugbara (Uganda), religion of, 290, 297
Lunda, 333

M
Maasai, 125, *158, 308*
Macedonia, 367, 370, 373, 374
Madagascar, knowledge of indigenous people in, 395

Maine, *172*
Malaitans, religion of, 303
Malawi, 318
Malaysia
  bilateral kinship in, 183
  ethnic groups in, 357
  Muslims in, *23, 99*
  patterns of behavior in, 25
Manus, religion of, 303
Maori
  body arts of, 311, *312*
  cognatic descent among, 182
  threats to, 393
Maring (Papua New Guinea), 136
Marquesans, body arts of, 311–312
Mayans
  agriculture of, 121, 122, 389
  art of, *322, 324*
  clothing of, *357*
  knowledge of, 395
  religion of, 298
Melanesia
  communal houses in, 153
  European contact, effects of, 337, 338
  political organization in, 244
  religion in, 286, 289, 300–301, 303
Mennonites, 309
Mentawai (Indonesia), *296*
Mescalero Apache, female initiation rituals of, *206, 207*
Mesoamerica, 330, 331
  agriculture in, 121, 122, 396
  inequality in, 269
  religion in, 286, 298
Mesopotamia, 121, 364
Metis, 358
Mexican Americans, 359
Mexico
  agriculture in, 119, 389
  consequences of European contact with, 331
  marketplace in, *147*
Micronesia
  children in, 194, 203, *203*
  European contact, effects of, 337, 338
  land ownership in, 131
  money in, 140, 141
  political organization in, 244
  respect language in, 59
  tribute payments in, 138–139
Middle East
  agriculture in, 2
  kinship in, *176*
  religion in, 99
  resentment of U.S. in, 351
  See also specific countries
Mindoro (Philippines), 29
Mohave
  gender roles among, 219
  same-sex relations among, 220
Montenegro, 367, 371, 373
Morocco, *28,* 367–368

Mozambique, 336
Muslims, *23*
  art of, 309, 321
  banking of, 341
  clashes with West, 361
  ethnic problems among, 363, *365f,* 366, 367, 370
  fundamentalism and, 343–345
  Shiites vs. Sunnis, 364–367, *365f*

N
Na (China), marriages of, 153–154
Naga people (India), 366
Nandi (Kenya), marriage practices of, 153
Native Americans
  agriculture of, 390
  art of, 313–314, 316, 320–321, 323 324
  body arts of, 309, 310, 312, 315
  children of, 194, 201, 202
  clothing of, *357,* 357–358
  Council of Forty-Four of, 243, 252, 253
  descent groups of, 179–181, *180*
  enslavement of, 331
  ethnic problems of, 369–370, 371
  European contact, effects of, 107, 331–332, 336
  extinct groups of, 358
  families of, 108–109
  female initiation rituals of, 206, *207*
  gender roles among, 218–220, *219*
  gender stratification among, 229, 230–231, *231,* 232
  genocide against, 369, 371
  knowledge of, 395
  languages of, 50, 55, 57, 58–59, 356–357
  legal systems of, 250, 252, 253, 255
  matrilineal and patrilineal societies of, 100, 179–181, *180,* 184
  performance arts of, 318
  political organization among, 240, 242–243
  ranked societies of, 261
  religions of, 283, 290, 291–292, 293, 294–295, 296–297, 301–303
  relocation of, 369, 371
  same-sex relations among, 220
  segregation of, 370
  sexual division of labor among, 227
  threats to, 393
  transvestism among, 220
  See also specific groups
Navajo
  accuracy of data collected from, 93–94
  art of, 320–321, 323–324
  children of, 202
  gender identity among, 218, 219, 220
  language of, 356–357
  religion of, 32, 290, 291–292
Nayar (South India), 155, 156, 184
Ndembu (Zambia)
  religion of, 297
  rites of passage of, 204

Nepal, 383
Netherlands, 309
  African colonies of, 333
  African settlers from, 358
  American colonies of, 332
New Caledonia, 338
New Guinea, 2
  balanced reciprocity in, 134–135
  male initiation rituals in, 204–206, *205*
  racial classifications in, 30
  sexual division of labor among, 227
New Zealand
  body arts in, 311, *312*
  cognatic descent in, 182
  European contact, effects of, 337
  threats to indigenous people in, 393
Nigeria
  birthrate in, 380
  money in, 141–142
  performance arts in, 319
  population of, 347
  religion in, 290
  sexual division of labor in, 228
  urban centers in, 348
  women's contributions in, 232–233
Nisga'a (Canada), 393
North Americans
  costs and benefits of children of, 380–381
  ethnicity of, 357, 358
  families of, 151, 152, 166–167, 193, 196, 380–381
  female genital mutilation and, 15–16
  food needs of, 384–385
  gender crossing among, 217
  gender roles of, *216,* 216–217
  generalized reciprocity among, 133–134, 137
  inequality of, 265–268, *266,* 267t, 270, 272–274, 275–276
  kinship ties of, 173
  languages of, 57
  marital exchanges between, 161–162
  racial classifications among, 30–31
  religions of, 282, 293–294
  rites of passage of, 201
  same-sex relations among, 221
  sexual division of labor among, 229
  social inequality among, 260, 263
  touching by, 52
  view of polygyny, 159
  women, 233–234
Northwest Coast peoples, 91–92
  art of, 316–317, *317,* 323
  foraging by, 107
  ranked societies of, 261
  rights to resources among, 111
Nuer (Sudan)
  body arts of, 312
  legal system of, 250–251, 252
  marriage practices in, 153
Nyakyusa (Tanzania), religion of, 290

O

Oceania, 244
  European contact, effects of, 337–338
  See also Melanesia; Micronesia; Polynesia
Ojibwa, 390
Omaha, 358
  children of, 309
  kinship terminology of, 187, 187*f*, 188, 189
Oman, *1*
Osage, 358
  art of, 310, 313–314
  children of, 202
  humorous deception by, 94
  performance arts of, 318
  religion of, 302
Ottoman Empire, 364, 366, 367
Oyo, 333

P

Pakistan
  conflict with India, 366–367
  ethnic problems in, 367
  population of, 347
  urban centers in, 348
Palestine, ethnic conflicts in, 360
Panama, art in, 323
Papua New Guinea
  agriculture in, 397
  art of, 321–322
  balanced reciprocity in, 136
  body arts in, 310
  gender in, 214–216
  legal sanctions in, 249
  money in, 140
  religion in, 300–301, 303
  trade in, 137
  women in, *212,* 214–216
Patagonia, 336
Pequots, 369
Peru, 323, 331, *381,* 396. *See also* Incas
Philippines
  diverse population in, 240
  large vs. small families in, 383
  marketplace in, 147
  separatist movements in, 367
  sexual division of labor in, 224
  shifting cultivation in, 29
  threats to indigenous people in, 392
Plains Indians, 111–113
  art of, 321
  body arts of, 312
  children of, 201, 202, 203
  religions of, 293–294
  transvestism among, 220
  See also specific groups
Poland, 369
Polynesia
  body arts in, 311–312
  children in, 194
  cognatic descent in, 182
  European contact, effects of, 337–338
  political organization in, 244–245
  ranked societies in, 261
  religion in, 281, 298
  respect language in, 59
  tribute payments in, 138–139
Ponca, 358
Portugal
  African colonies of, 332–333, 334
  American colonies of, 330–331
  trade with Asia, 334–335
Pueblo peoples, horticultural methods of, 116–117
Punjab, 363
Pygmies (Africa), 30
  art of, 310, 321
  sexual division of labor among, 224, *226*
  socialization of, 194–196, *195,* 197, 198
  women's contributions among, 232

Q

Quapaw, 302, 358
Quebec, Canada, 370, 372
Quechua Indians, 396

R

Romans
  art of, 320
  body arts of, 310
Russia, 369
  diverse population in, 240
  expansion of, 335
  See also Soviet Union
Rwanda, 368

S

Samoa, 68
  body arts of, 311
  cognatic descent in, 182
  European contact, effects of, 338
  large vs. small families in, 383
San, 91
  hoodia plant and, 92
  threats to, 392
  See also !Kung
Saxons, 358
Scot(s), 322, 360
Scotch-Irish, 360
Scythians, 310
Semai (Malaysia), 25
Seminole Indians, 358
Seneca (New York), religion of, 301–302
Senegal, 336
Serb(s), 357, 367, 370, 374
Serbo-Croatian language, 357
Shakers, *306,* 307
Shiite Muslims, 364–367, 365*f*
Shipibo (Peru), 323
Shoshone
  bands of, 107, 108–109
  food sources of, 108–109
Siberia, 369
Sierra Leone, 336
Sikh nationalists, 366
Sioux
  gender roles among, 219, 220
  massacre at Wounded Knee, 369
Slovakia, 371, 373
Slovenia, 367, 368, 370, 373
Solomon Islands, *24,* 286
Somalia, 368, 384
Songhai Empire, 333
South Africa
  ethnic groups in, 358
  immigrants in, 350
  language taboos in, 60
  Muslims in, *99*
  social stratification in, *259*
South Korea, *20*
  female touching in, 29
  marriage in, *200*
  religion in, 293, *293*
  See also Korea
Soviet Union
  ethnic conflict in, 367
  Germans in, 369
  in World War II, 369
Spain
  colonialism of, 330–331, 367–368
  ethnic conflict in, 370
  ethnic groups in, *362*
  sexual division of labor in, 229
Sri Lanka, 335, 367
Sudan
  body arts in, 312
  child care in, *199*
  European contact, effects of, 333
  legal system in, 250–251, 252
  marriage practices in, 153
  religion in, 290, 291
  separatist movements in, 367, 368
Sunni Muslims, 364–367, 365*f*
Swazi (southern Africa), marriage of, 162
Swiss, cultural characteristics of, 69
Syria, 364

T

Tahiti
  body arts in, 311
  cognatic descent in, 182
  political organization in, 244–245
  tribute payments in, 138–139
Tannese, religion of, 303
Tanzania, 125
  egalitarianism in, 260
  religion in, 290
  seasonal mobility in, 108
Tasmanians, 358
Thailand
  art of, *316*
  Buddhists in, *63*

Thracians, 310
Tibet, 367
Tikopia
    art of, 307
    patrilineal society of, 178–179
    ranked society in, 262
Tiv (Nigeria), money of, 141–142
Tiwi (Australia)
    marriage among, 155–156
    postmarital residence patterns of, 166
Tlingit, *317*
Tokyo, Japan, *328*
Toltecs, 121
Tonga
    art of, 311
    European contact, effects of, 338
    large vs. small families in, 383
Trobriand Islands, 89
    balanced reciprocity in, 134–135
    religion in, 283–284
Tukano people (Bolivia), 32
Tumbuka, performance arts of, 318–319
Tungus (northeast Asia), 295
Turkey
    Kurds in, 364, 367
    Ottoman Empire in, 364, 366, 367
    in World War I, 366

U
Uganda, religion in, 290, 297
Ukraine, 369
Ulster-Scots, 360
United States
    agricultural losses in, 396
    art in, 313–314, 316, 320–321, 323
    birthrate in, 380
    chief executive officers (CEOs) in, 273–274
    colonialism and, 339
    costs and benefits of children in, 380–381
    diverse population in, 240
    divorce in, 160
    ethnic groups in, 355, 356, 359, 360. *See also specific groups*
    immigration to, 349–350, *351*
    Indian policy of, 369, 371
    laws in, 247, 248, 255
    marriage amendment in, 164
    multiracial culture in, *37*
    racial classifications in, 30–31
    redistribution in, 138
    religion in, 282, 293–294
    relocation of Hmong in, 13, 57
    resentment of, 351
    secular ideologies in, 272–273
    social classes in, 265–268, *266,* 267*t,* 270, 272–274, 275
    two-generational households in, 167
    women in, 233–234
    See also North Americans
Urdu peoples (Pakistan), 367

V
Vanuatu, *301*
Vietnam, tone language in, *49*
Volga Germans, 369

W
Wales, language of, 58
West Germany, guest workers in, 349
West Indies, 59, 330, 331, 336, 349
Western Sahara, 367–368

Y
Yąnomamö (Amazon)
    brideservice among, 162
    gender stratification among, 229
    intermarriage among, 160–161
    name taboo of, 60, 94
    patterns of behavior of, 25
    religion of, 293
    roles among, 25, 26
    threats to, *391,* 392
Yap (Micronesia), 140, 141
Yoruba (Nigeria), women's contributions among, 232–233
Yugoslavia
    disintegration of, 367, 368, 373*f,* 373–374
    ethnic groups in, 370, 371, 373
    language of, 357

Z
Zaire, 108, 321
    egalitarianism in, 260
    sexual division of labor in, 224
    women's contributions in, 232
Zambia, 204, 297
Zulu (South Africa)
    language taboos of, 60
    marriage among, 161
Zuni
    cultural characteristics of, 69
    gender roles among, *219,* 219–220
    horticultural methods of, 116–117
    religion of, 296–297

Name Index

Note: Page numbers in *italics* indicate illustrations.

A
Algosaibi, Ghazi, 361
Ali (Ali ibn Abu Talib), 364
Allen, Michael, 100
Anderson, Richard, 307
Arbatov, Georgi, 361

B
Barnes, Sandra, 232
Barzani, Mustafa al-, 367
Benedict, Ruth, 16, 68–69
Berlin, Brent, 54
Berlusconi, Silvio, 361
bin Laden, Osama, 361

Boas, Franz, 16, 67, *67,* 68, 71, 307, 389
Bohannan, Paul, 141
Boyd, David, 205
Brain, Robert, 311
Brown, Judith, 226
Bush, George H. W., 367
Bush, George W., 145, 164

C
Catherine the Great, empress of Russia, 369
Chagnon, Napoleon, 94
Chatty, Dawn, *1*
Cohen, Theodore, 234
Collins, Joseph, 385
Columbus, Christopher, 329, 330
Cook, Captain James, 96–97

D
da Gama, Vasco, 334
Darwin, Charles, 6, 64
Davidson, Basil, 334
Davis, William, 147
Dawkins, Richard, 74, 75
de las Casas, Bartolome, 331
Dentan, Robert, 25
Dixon, Suzanne, 196
Durkheim, Émile, 287–288, *288*
Durst, John, 234
Dyson-Hudson, Neville, 125, 126
Dyson-Hudson, Rada, 125, 126

E
Ember, Carol, 184
Ember, Melvin, 184

Estioko-Griffin, Agnes, 224
Evans-Pritchard, E. E., 291

F
Faisal, king of Saudi Arabia, 366, 367
Falwell, Jerry, 343
Farnsworth, Norman, 395
Farrer, Claire, 206
Firth, Raymond, 262
Fischer, John, 317
Frazer, James, 285, 289
Freed, Ruth, 383
Freed, Stanley, 383
Freeman, Derek, 203
Fried, Morton, 260
Friedson, Steven, 319
Frum, John, *301*

G
Gandhi, Indira, 366
Geertz, Clifford, 80, *80,* 285
Gell, Alfred, 312
Giddens, Anthony, 345
Gilmore, David, 229
Glazer, Nathan, 355
Gluckman, Max, 254
Goodale, Jane, 155, 156
Goodall, Jane, 4, 6
Goodenough, Ward H., 35
Guthrie, Stewart, 285–286

H
Hall, Edward, 51
Hamilton, William, 74
Handsome Lake, 302, 303
Harris, Marvin, 77
Hart, C. W. M., 155
Hewlett, Barry, 194
Hitchcock, Robert, 393
Hockett, Charles, 43
Hoebel, E. Adamson, 249
Huntington, Samuel P., 361
Hussain, 364
Hussein, Saddam, 5, 366, 367
Hutton, James, 64

J
Johnson, Samuel, 307

K
Kaeppler, Adrienne, 318
Kay, Paul, 54
Keller, Helen, 43
Kerry, John, 145
Kluckhohn, Clyde, 291–292
Kottak, Conrad, 30
Kroeber, Alfred, 16

L
LaDuke, Winona, 390
LaFlesche, Francis, *93,* 318
Lappé, Frances Moore, 385
Leakey, Meave, *11*
Lee, Richard, 110, 113, 135
LeVine, Robert A., 196, 198
LeVine, Sara, 196
Lomax, Alan, 319
Lyell, Charles, 64

M
Malinowski, Bronislaw, 70, 71, 77, 89, 286
Mamdani, Mahmood, 382
Marshall, Mac, 203
Marx, Karl, 142, 274, *275*
Mead, Margaret, 68, *69, 87,* 203, 389
Meigs, Anna, 214, 216
Middleton, John, 297
Morgan, Lewis Henry, 65–66, 68, 185
Moynihan, Daniel, 355
Muawiyah, 364
Muhammad, Prophet, 364
Murdock, George, 98

N
Naipaul, V. S., 361
Nanda, Serena, 218–219
Newman, Philip, 205

O
Obeyesekere, Gananath, 96–97
Oboler, Regina Smith, 153

P
Parker, Enoch, 302
Pilling, Arnold, 155
Posey, Darrell, 389
Pospisil, Leopold, 249

R
Radcliffe-Brown, A. R., 70–71
Rappaport, Roy, 136
Roscoe, Will, 218
Rudolph, Eric, 343

S
Sahlins, Marshall, 96, 97
Sanday, Peggy, 232
Sapir, Edward, 55
Schlegel, Alice, 235
Sen, Amartya, 398
Sheper-Hughes, Nancy, 202
Snow, Clyde, 5
Stalin, Josef, 369
Stevenson, Matilda Cox, 219
Steward, Julian, 71, 72, 77
Swanson, Guy, 288

T
Tito, Marshal, 373
Turner, Victor, 204, 205
Tylor, E. B., 21, 66, 281

U
Uthman, 364

W
Wallace, Anthony, 292
White, Benjamin, 383
White, Leslie, 71–72, 77
Whiting, Beatrice, 98
Whorf, Benjamin, 55
Whyte, Martin, 234
Wilson, Edward O., 74, *75*
Wilson, John, 302
Woodburn, James, 260

Y
Yazid, 364

SUBJECT INDEX

Note: Page numbers in *italics* indicate illustrations. Letters *f* and *t* indicate figures and tables, respectively.

A
Accommodation, 370, 371–374, 372*t*
Adaptation, 32–34
  cultural, 72, 105
  culture and, 126, 127*t*
  defined, 105
  domestication and, 113–116
  foraging, 107–113
  genetic, 105
  kinship system, influence on, 183
  materialistic view of, 76–79, *78*
  pastoralism, 123–126, 124*f, 125*
  physiological, 105
  of preindustrial communities, 104, *104*

Ad hoc systems, 249
Adolescence, 201*t*, 202–206, *203, 205, 207*
Adulthood
  initiation into, 204–206, *205, 207,* 321–322
  in life cycle, 206–208
Advocacy, anthropology's role in, 389–397
Aesthetics, 307
Affines, 151
Afrikaans dialect, 358

Age
    categories of, 200–209
    division of labor by, 107–108, 111
Age of Reason, 81
Agriculture, 107
    in developing regions, 122–123
    horticulture, 116–118
    in industrial nations, 122
    intensive. *See* Intensive agriculture
    intercropping in, 388
    irrigation in, 119, 121
    shift from foraging to, 114–116
    shifting cultivation in, 29
    spread of crops in, 333–334, *334*
    technology transfer to LDCs and, 386–388
    traditional farming practices in, 388–389
    "undiscovered" useful species in, 396–397
    See also Food crops
All-Apache Culture Committee, 91
Altruism, 74
Ambilocal residence, 165
American Anthropological Association, 11, 90
American historical particularism. *See*
    Historical particularism
American Medical Association (AMA), 276
Ancestral cults, 297
Ancient civilizations, 121*f*
Animism, 66, 281
Anthropological linguistics, 3*t*, 10
Anthropological thought
    contemporary perspectives in, 72–83
    early twentieth-century development of,
        67–71
    emphases of, 379
    humanistic approach in, 72–74, 74*t*, 77–83
    mid-twentieth-century evolutionary
        approaches, 72–74
    nineteenth-century origins of, 64–67
    scientific approach in, 72–77, 74*t*, 81–83
Anthropologists
    involvement with communities, *378*
    moral responsibilities of, 16, 90
    training for, 71
    See also Fieldworkers
Anthropology, 3*t*
    as academic discipline, 66–67
    advocacy role of, 389–397
    applied, 3*t*, 10–12, 379–380
    archaeology. *See* Archaeology
    biases of, 97, 230
    comparative perspective of, 14, 66, 83
    corporate, 11–12
    cultural. *See* Cultural anthropology
    development, 11
    economic, 132
    educational, 11
    forensic, 5, *10*
    general principles, lack of, 82
    holistic perspective of, 14, 71
    interpretive, 79–80, *80*
    medical, 11

origins of, 63–67
paleoanthropology, 5, *11*, 64
physical/biological, 3*t*, *4*, 4–5, 73
research goals in, 88
research methods. *See* Comparative
    methods; Ethnographic methods
scope of, 1–2, 83
subfields of, 2–12
theoretical perspectives of, 13–16
value of, 16–17
Anthropomorphism, 285
Apocalyptic message, 300
*Apotheosis of Captain Cook: European
    Mythmaking in the Pacific* (Obeyesekere),
    97
Applied anthropology, 3*t*, 10–12, 379–380
Archaeological sites, 64
Archaeology, 2–4, 3*t*
    contract, 3*t*, 4
    historic, 3–4
    prehistoric, 2–3, *3*, 73
Argonauts of the Western Pacific
    (Malinowski), 71
Arranged marriages, 152–153, 161
Art(s), 26, 306–325
    body arts, 309–312
    culture and, 319–325
    defined, 307
    ethnic, 322, 323–324
    forms of, 309–319
    gender and, 321–322
    ornamentation as, 315–316
    performance arts, 317–319
    pervasiveness of, 307–309
    religion and, 313–314, 318–319, 320–321
    rock, 315
    secular and religious, 319–321
    social functions of, 322, 324–325
    status and, 324–325
    symbolism in, 314, 316
    visual arts, 312–317
    women and, 321–322
Artificial countries, 362
Assimilation, 369–370, 371, 372*t*
Australopithecines, 6–9, 7*f*
Avunculocal residence, 165, 168–169, 181

B

Balanced reciprocity, 134–136
Bands, 109–110, 240–242
    composite, 241, 241*t*
    simple, 240–241, 241*t*
Banishment, 253
Banking, Islamic, 341
Basketry, 315, 323, 324
Behavior
    choice-making process of, 34, 35
    conflicting models of, 35–36
    cultural knowledge and, 34–36
    culture and, 34–35
    gender and, 214

individual, 34–36, 193
influence of values on, 27, 34–35
interpretation of, 80
language and, 10
meanings of, 27–29
normatively expected, 110
patterns of, 22, 25–26
research on, 4
shared understandings of, 27–28, 34
symbolic content of, 80
thought and, 21–22
verbal and nonverbal, 56, 58–60, *59. See
    also* Nonverbal communication
Beliefs, 22, 32, 281
Bell Curve, The, 31
Berdaches, 218, 219, *219,* 220–221, 321
Bias
    in anthropology, 97, 230
    Eurocentric, 230
Big men, 241
Bilateral kinship, *172,* 183
Bill of Rights, 27
Bilocal residence, 165, 168
Biological anthropology, 3*t, 4,* 4–5, 73
Biological determinism, 36
Biological evolution, 5, 6–9, 7*f,* 30. *See also*
    Evolution
Biological needs, 37
Biological variation
    independence from cultural differences,
        23, 36–39, 68
    between sexes, *223,* 223–224, 225*t,* 226
Bipedalism, 6
Body arts, 309–312
    body painting, 310, *310*
    physical alterations, 309–310
    scarification, 311, 312
    tattooing, 310–312, *312*
Body language, 51–52, *52*
Body painting, 310, *310*
Bound morphemes, 50, 51
Brain, size of, 6
Brideservice, 162
Bridewealth, 159, 162, 163
British functionalism, 70–71
Buddhism, *63*
Bureaucracy, 245

C

Calendrical rituals, 283
Capital, internationalization of, 144
Capitalism, 338
Cargo cults, 290–291, *291*
Carving, 315
Case studies, 87
Caste systems, 261*t,* 263–265, *264*
Catholicism, *280,* 299, *299*
Census, 100
Ceramics, 315–316, *316*
Changing Ones (Roscoe), 218
Charlottetown Accord, 372

Chief(s), 244
  leopard-skin, 250–251
  war, 243
Chiefdoms, 240, 241*t*, 244
Child care
  labor and, compatibility of, 225*t*, 226
  women and, 154, *154*
Child Care and Culture: Lessons from Africa
  (Levine, Dixon, & LeVine), 196
Childhood, 201*t*, 202
Child mortality, 198, 383, 398
Child-rearing practices
  diversity in, 193–200
  factors affecting, 197–198
Children
  costs and benefits of, 380–384
  enculturation of. *See* Enculturation
  malnourishment of, 384
  as old age security, 382–383
Chinese civilization, 360
Christian fundamentalists, 343, 345
Christianity. *See* Judeo-Christian civilization
Civilizations, 121*f*, 121–122, 359*t*, 360
  peasantry in, *122*, 122–123, 387
  of world, 361
Civil law, 249
Clan, 178, 180. *See also* Kin groups; Kinship
  systems
*Clash of Civilizations and the Remaking of
  World Order, The* (Huntington), 361
Classifications, 33*t*
  cultural, 174, 214
  of reality, 29, 32, 214
Class systems, 261*t*, 265–268, *266*, 267*t*, *268*
Clean Air Act (U.S.), 248
Clothing
  ethnicity and, 322, *357*, 357–358
  ornamentation on, 316
Code of Hammurabi, 254
Cognatic descent, 181–182
Cognitive approaches to religion, 285–286
Cognitive interpretations of sorcery and
  witchcraft, 291
Cold War, 361
Colonialism, 329–339
Coming of Age in Samoa (Mead), 68, 203
Communal cults, 292, 294*t*, 297–298
Communication
  of abstract ideas, 43
  material means of, 307
  miscommunication, 52
  nonverbal, 27–28, *28*, 51–52, *52*, *91*
  status of individuals interacting and, 56,
    58–59
  study of. *See* Linguistics
  symbolic, *41*, 79
  of worldview, 43
  See also Language; Speech
Comparative methods, 87, 96–101, 101*t*
Comparative perspective, 14, 66, 83
Competition, 64–65

Composite bands, 241, 241*t*
Compromise, 255
Configurationalism, 68–69
Conflict, ideological, 354. *See also* Ethnic
  conflicts
Conflict theory of inequality, 273, 274–275, *275*
Consanguines, 151, 174
Consonant phonemes, 47*t*
Consultants, 93–94
Contagious principle of magic, 289
Container shipping, 340, *340*
Contract archaeology, 3*t*, 4
Controlled historical comparison, 99–101, 101*t*
Cooperation, patterns of, 106
Corporal punishment, 249
Corporate anthropology, 11–12
Corporations
  global economy and, 247
  transnational, 344–346
Council of Forty-Four (Native Americans),
  243, 252, 253
Court systems, 252, 254–255
  courts of mediation, 252, 254
  courts of regulation, 254–255
  incipient courts, 252
  Islamic, 341
Cousins, 177. *See also* Kinship systems
Crisis rituals, 283
Crops. *See* Agriculture; Food crops
Cross cousins, 177
Cross-cultural comparison, 96–99, 101*t*
  ahistorical examination methods, 99
  correlation vs. causation in, 98
  with *Ethnographic Atlas,* 98
Cross-gender roles, 219–220
Cult(s)
  ancestral, 297
  cargo, 290–291, *291*
  communal, 292, 294*t*, 297–298
  defined, 292
  ecclesiastical, 292–293, 294*t*, 298–299, *299*
  individualistic, 292, 294*t*, 294–295
  shamanistic, 292, 294*t*, 295–297, *296*
Cultivation. *See* Agriculture
Cultural anthropology, 3*t*, 5, 8–9
  objectives of, 5
  overlaps with other disciplines, 13
  present-day status of, 12–13
  science vs. humanity issue in, 72–83
Cultural barriers, 94
Cultural construction
  of gender, 213–217
  of kinship systems, 185
  of race, 30–31
Cultural diversity, 14, 37
  appreciation of, 16–17
  in child-rearing practices, 193–200
  independence from biological variation,
    23, 36–39, 68
  sensitivity to, 16–17
  in ways of thinking and behaving, 21–22

Cultural evolution, 72
Cultural identity, 22
Cultural integration, 22
Cultural knowledge, 22, 25
  commercial use of, 92
  components of, 26–29, 32, 33*t*
  individual behavior and, 34–36
  learning of, 33
  products and expressions of, 26
Cultural materialism, 76–79, *78*
Cultural nationalism, 91
Cultural progress, 65
Cultural relativism, 14–16, 68, 94
Cultural resource management, 4
Cultural systems, 22
Cultural universals, *38*, 38–39
Culture, 20–40
  adaptation and, 126, 127*t*
  appreciation of, *12*
  arts and, 319–325
  behavioral components of, 22
  behavior and, 34–35
  changes in, 36–37
  common core elements of, 72
  complexity of, 65–67, 72
  defined, 16, 21, 22–26
  fact gathering on, 68
  foraging and, 107–113
  health and, 11
  human life and, 32–34
  independence from race, 16, 36–39, *37*
  language and, 52–56
  laws of, 66
  mental components of, 22, 34
  ownership of, 91–92
  protoculture, 33
  subcultures, 23
  technology and, 71–72
  transmission of, 33. *See also* Enculturation
  unilineal evolution of, 65–66
  uniqueness of, 79–80
Culture shock, 95
Curing rituals
  arts and, 320–321
  music and, 318–319

D

Dance, 317, 318, 319
Decentralized tribal people, 197
Deception, 94
Descent
  cognatic, 181–182
  communal rituals and, 298
  form of, 174, 175*t*
  gender stratification and, 234–235
  horticulture and, 183–184
  kinship terminology and, 187–189
  See also Matrilineal descent; Patrilineal
    descent; Unilineal descent
Descent groups, 177–181
  matrilineal, 177

Descent groups (continued)
patrilineal, 177
unilineal, 177–178
Descent of Man, The (Darwin), 6
Developed nations
emigration to, 348–350, *350, 351*
health conditions in, 347
See also Industrial nations
Development anthropology, 11
Dialects, 45–46, 358
Diffusionism, 68
Disease
eradication of, 346–347
European contact and, 107, 331, 332, 337
Divination, 282–283
Division of labor, 106
by age, 107–108, 111
in foraging societies, 107–108, 111
by sex. *See* Sexual division of labor
Domestication, 107, 113–116
adaptation and, 113–116
advantages of, 113–116
in Old and New Worlds, 113, 114–115
Dowry, 162–163
Dry land gardening, 116–117
Dutch East India Company, 335

E

Ecclesiastical cults, 292–293, 294*t*, 298–299, *299*
Economic activity, 132
Economic anthropology, 132
Economic classes, 266–268, *268*
Economic development, 348, 398
Economic inequality, 266–267, 267*t*, 268
Economic Policy Institute, 268
Economic progress, 397
Economic specialization, 243
Economic systems, 132
Economy
global. *See* Global economy
market, 142–146, 147
Educational anthropology, 11
Egalitarianism, 135, 260–261, 261*t*, 262
among bands, 242
defined, 260
in tribal societies, 242
Egalitarian societies, 260–261, 261*t*, 262
Elderly, 208–209, *209*
Elites
functions of, 276–277
resource control held by, 274
social control held by, 270–271
Enculturation, 23, 32–34
defined, 192
diversity in practices of, 194–200
factors affecting, *194*
language and, 43
learning through observation or imitation, 202
roles and group expectations, transmission of, 26

Endogamous marriage rules, 157
English language, 48–51
Enlightenment period, 81
Environment
adaptation to. *See* Adaptation
classification of things in, 29, 32
determination of cultural adaptation, 72
herding environments, 107, 123–125
natural resources in, 105. *See also*
Resource(s)
objective conditions of, 79
problems posed by, 105
Equality, systems of, 260–261. *See also*
Inequality
Ethics, 90
Ethnic art, 322, 323–324
Ethnic boundary markers, 356–358
Ethnic cleansing, 368–369, 371, 372*t*
Ethnic conflicts, 354, *354,* 363–374
resolving, 368–374
from stateless nationalities, 360–368
Ethnic groups, 356–360
accommodations of, 370, 371–374, 372*t*
assimilation of, 369–370, 371, 372*t*
attributes of, 356–358
defined, 355
ethnogenesis of, 358
fluidity of, 358
homogenization of, 368–370, 372*t*
migration of, 366
relocation of, 369, 371, 372*t*
segregation of, 370, 372*t*
situational nature of group identity, 355–356
types of, 358–360
Ethnic homogenization, 368–370, 372*t*
Ethnic identity
hierarchical nesting quality of, 355–356
as political force, 355
situational nature of, 355–356
visual markers of, 322
Ethnic nationalities, 362
Ethnic pride, 31, 53, 58
Ethnocentrism, 14, 79
in ethnohistorical accounts, 95
reducing, 16
Ethnogenesis, 358
Ethnographic Atlas, 98
Ethnographic fieldwork, 88–95, 101*t*
Ethnographic methods, 87, 88–96, 101*t*
Ethnographic research, 88, 95–96, 101*t*
Ethnography, 9
Ethnohistory, 95–96, 101*t*
Ethnologue (journal), 57
Ethnology. *See* Cultural anthropology
Eurocentric bias, 230
European contact
in Africa, 332–334, *334,* 336–337
with agriculturists, 118, 119*f*
in Americas, 330–332, *332*
in Asia, 334–335
descent systems and, 100

disease and, 107, 331, 332, 337
with foraging societies, 107, 108*f*
intensive agriculture and, 121*f*
with Native Americans, 107, 330–332, *332*
in Oceania, 337–338
pastoralism and, 124*f*
political boundaries resulting from, 363, 366
European expansion, 329–335
European Union (E.U.), 248, 342
Evolution
biological, 5, 6–9, 7*f,* 30
cultural, 72
Darwin's theory of, 6, 64–65
human, 6–9, 7*f*
language and, 42–43
paleoanthropology and, 5
unilineal, 65–66
Evolutionary psychology, 74–76
Exchange, *131,* 132
marital, 161–163
peasant marketplaces for, 146–147, *147*
reciprocity, 133*f,* 133–137
redistribution, 132, 133*f,* 138–139
See also Market exchange
Exchange spheres, 141–142
Exogamous marriage rules, 157
Extended family, *150,* 152, 152*t,* 167–169, 177–178
Extended households, 167–169

F

Face painting, 310, *310*
Factors of production, 105, 106
Familial legal systems, 249–250, 255*t*
Families, 150–169
in Africa, 143
economic influences on, 143
extended, *150,* 152, 152*t,* 167–168, 177–178
in foraging societies, 108–109
forms of, 167–169
matrifocal, 167
of Native Americans, 108–109
norms concerning size of, 381, 383
nuclear, 151, 152*t*
Farming. *See* Agriculture
Fathers. *See* Child-rearing practices
Federal Reserve Board (Fed), 268
Feedback, 77
Female circumcision and genital mutilation, 15–16
Female infanticide, 159
Female initiation rites, 206, *207,* 321–322
Fertility maintenance, 225, 225*t*
Fertility rates, 197–198
Feuds, 251
Fictive kinship, 151
Fieldwork, 8–9, 13, 68
benefits of, 68
biases of, 230
consultants, identifying and interviewing, 93–94

Fieldwork (continued)
    culture shock during, 95
    ethical observations in, 90
    ethnographic, 88–95, 101t
    humanistic approach to, 72–83
    interviewing techniques in, 88–89
    methodological issues of, 73
    participant observation in, 89
    problems and issues in, 90, 92–94
    as rite of passage, 94–95
    scientific approach to, 72–83
    stereotyping resulting from, 90, 92–93
    as training for anthropologists, 71
Fieldworkers
    deception of, 94
    modification of behavior of, 94
    objectivity of, 14–15, 68, 83
    rapport with research community, 93
    role and rapport of, developing, 93
    study subjects of, 13
Five Civilized Tribes, 369
Food crops, 113
    Old and New World domesticates, 114
    preservation of varieties, 395–396
    rice, *104, 120,* 390
    spread of, 333–334, *334*
    "undiscovered" useful species, 396–397
    See also Agriculture
Food First (Lappé & Collins), 385
Food production, sexual division of labor for,
    212, 221–222, 227–228
Foraging, 107–113, 224
    cultural consequences of, 127t
    culture and, 107–113
    division of labor and, 107–108, *109,* 110, 111
    egalitarianism and, 260–261
    European contact and, 108f
    shift to agriculture from, 114–116
Forced assimilation, 369, 371, 372t
Ford Foundation, 11
Forensic anthropology, 5, *10*
Fraternal polyandry, 160
Free market, 139
Free morphemes, 50
Free trade, 144, 247–248, 342
Functionalism
    British, 70–71
    theory of inequality in, 273–274
Fundamentalism, *343,* 343–345, 361

G

Gardening, 116–117, 224
Gathering, as female activity, 224. *See also*
    Foraging
Gay marriage, 164
Gender
    arts and, 321–322
    cultural construction of, 213–217
    initiation rites and, 321–322
    kin terms and, 185
    multiple gender identities, 218–221
    sex vs., 213–214

Gender crossing, 217–218, 219–220
Gendered division of labor. *See* Sexual
    division of labor
Gender roles, *212,* 219–220, 221
Gender stratification, 228–236
    descent systems and, 234–235
    factors affecting, 228–229
    in industrial societies, 235–236
    influences on, 232–235
    postmarital residence patterns and, 234–235
    in religion, 226
    women, subordination of, 229–232
General Agreement on Tariffs and Trade
    (GATT), 247
Generalized reciprocity, 133–134, *134*
Genocide, 354, 368–369, 371, 372t. *See also*
    Ethnic conflicts
Gerber Corporation, 248
Gerontology, 208
Gift giving, 136
Global economy, 144–146, *145,* 247–248
    consequences of, 350–351
    corporations and, 247
    emergence of, 338–342, *340*
    inequality in, 269, 270, 346–350, *385*
    technology necessary for, 339–340, *340*
Globalization, 328–352
    architecture and, *328*
    art of traditional peoples and, 323–324
    continuing process of, 342–346
    cultural nationalism and, 91
    defined, 13, 329
    future of nation-states and, 247–248
    global economy and, 338–342. *See also*
        Global economy
    Industrial Revolution and, 335–338
    inequality and, 269, 270, 346–350, *385*
    language and, 57–58
    of markets, 144–146, *145*
    population growth and, 346–350
    protests against, 328
    religious fundamentalism and, *343,* 343–345
Global knowledge, 394
Global media, 350
Global trade
    development of, 329–338
    growth of, 342f
Golden Bough, The (Frazer), 285
Goods, national origin of, 346
Gossip, as form of social control, 248, *249*
Grammar, 45
    compound-word formation rules, 49–51
    sound systems and, 46–49
Gross domestic product (GDP), 398
Gross national product (GNP), 398
Group cooperation, 106, *106*
Group marriage, 157
Guardian spirit, 294

H

Handsome Lake revitalization movement,
    301–302, 303

Headmen, 261
Health and healing
    culture and, 11
    improvements in, 346–347
    medical knowledge of indigenous peoples,
        394–395, *395*
Herding, 107, 123–125
Hidden Dimension, The (Hall), 51
Hierarchical nesting quality of ethnic identity,
    355–356
Hindi language, 47–48
Hinduism, *78,* 91, 360
    caste system and, 261t, 263–265, *264*
    conflicts with Muslims, 363
    fundamentalism in, *343,* 343–345
Historical comparison, controlled, 99–101, 101t
Historical Metaphors and Mystical Realities
    (Sahlins), 96
Historical particularism, 67–70
    configurationalism, 68–69
    contributions to anthropology, 68
    diffusionism, 68
    limitations of, 69–70
Historic archaeology, 3–4
Holism, 14, 71, 80
Homelands, 358
Hominids, 7f, 9
Homo erectus, 7f, 9
Homogenization, ethnic, 368–370, 372t
Homo habilis, 7f, 9
Homo rudolfensis, 9
Homo sapiens, 5, 6, 7f, 8, 9
    evolution of, 30
    speech capabilities of, 42
    time in existence, 107
    See also Human(s)
Homosexual relations, 218, 220–221
Horse, in Americas, 112, 113
Horticulture, 116–118
    consequences of, 117–118, 127t
    descent systems associated with,
        183–184
    dry land gardening in, 116–117
    regions of, at time of European contact, 117f
    sexual division of labor in, 227–228
    shifting cultivation in, 116
Household(s), 151, 152t
    extended, 167–169
    forms of, 167–169, 168f
    residence and, 166–167
Household income, distribution of, 267t
Human(s)
    ancestors of, 7f
    biological evolution of. *See* Evolution
    biological needs of, 37, 70
    brain size of, 6
    as cultural beings, 32–34, 79
    sedentism of, 118
    self-identity of, 213
    as study subjects, 82–83
    uniqueness of, 78
    vocal tract of, 42–43

Human condition, anthropological
    contributions to, 16–17
Human evolution
    linearity vs. branching of, 7f, 8–9
    misconceptions of, 6–9
Humanistic approach, 72–74, 74t, 77–83
Humanities, 73
Human variation, 4–5
Humorous deception, 94
Hunger, 384–389, 398
    inequality explanation of, 384–386
    scarcity explanation of, 384–386
    technology transfer solution to, 386–388
Hunting
    band formation and, 241–242
    as male activity, 222–223, 224
Hunting and gathering. See Foraging

I
Ideas, 22, 43
Ideological conflicts, 354
Ideology
    defined, 271
    of inequality, 271–273
    secular, 272–273
Imitative principle of magic, 289
Incest taboo, 154–155, 157
Incipient court systems, 252
Incising, 315
Indian Arts & Crafts Act, 323
Indigenous peoples
    adaptive wisdom of, 395–397
    advocacy for, 389–397
    arts of, 323–324
    forced removal and exploitation of,
        391–393
    knowledge of, 393–397, 395
    legal rights of, 390, 391
    medical knowledge of, 394–395, 395
    modernization of, 393–394
    present situation of, 389–393
    territorial rights of, 391–393
Individual behavior, 193
    cultural knowledge and, 34–36
    variations in, 35–36
    See also Behavior
Individualistic cults, 292, 294t, 294–295
Individuality, and art, 322
Indus River valley, 121, 121f
Industrial nations
    agricultural techniques in, 122
    cultural alternatives to, 397
    gender stratification in, 235–236
    ideologies of inequality in, 272–273
    reciprocity and redistribution in, 132,
        138
    secular art in, 319–320
    social classes in, 261t, 265–268, 266,
        267t, 268
    social inequality in, 266, 266–268, 268
    See also Developed nations
Industrial Revolution, 335–338

Inequality
    beneficiaries of, 275–277
    conflict theory of, 273, 274–275, 275
    defined, 260
    economic, 266–267, 267t, 268
    egalitarian societies and, 260–261, 261t
    as explanation of hunger, 384–386
    functionalist theory of, 273–274
    in global economy, 269, 270, 346–350,
        385
    ideologies of, 271–273
    maintaining, 268–273
    between nationalities, 374
    in ranked societies, 261–262
    secular ideologies of, 272–273
    in stratified societies, 262–268
    systems of, 260–268
    theories of, 273–277, 275
Infancy, 201t, 201–202
Infant betrothal, 156
Infanticide, 159
Influence, political, 241
Informants, 93–94
Inheritance
    in matrilineal societies, 177
    in patrilineal societies, 176
Initiation rites, 204–206, 205, 207, 321–322
Intellectual approaches to religion, 285–286
Intensification, 77
Intensive agriculture, 118–123, 120
    cultural consequences of, 120–123, 127t
    in Old and New Worlds, 119
    regions of, at time of European contact,
        121f
    sexual division of labor and, 227–228
Intercropping, 388
Intermarriage, 157
International Monetary Fund (IMF), 341, 342,
    361
Interpretive anthropology, 79–80, 80
Interviewing
    limitations of, 88–89
    structured vs. unstructured, 88
    techniques for, 88–89
"Invisible hand," 142
Irish Free State, 360
Irrigation, 119, 121
Islam, 23, 360
    art of, 309, 321
    banking and, 341
    clashes with West, 361
    courts and, 341
    ethnic problems in, 363–367, 365f
    fundamentalism and, 343–345, 361
    Shiites vs. Sunnis in, 364–367, 365f

J
Java Man (Indonesia), 9
Judeo-Christian civilization, 282
    banking and, 341
    Christian fundamentalists in, 343, 345
    conversion of native peoples to, 332

music in, 318
    sociological aspects of, 287
    worldview of, 64
Judicial systems, 252, 254–255, 341

K
Key consultants and informants, 93–94
Kindreds, 183
Kinesics, 51
Kin groups, 151, 152t
    ancestor-focused, 183
    descent groups, 177–181
    ego-focused, 183
    marriage alliances between, 160–161
    multifunctional, 181
    new relationship formation in, 155
Kinship, fictive, 151
Kinship diagrams, 163, 165f
Kinship systems, 29, 39
    bilateral, 172, 183
    cultural construction of, 185
    cultural distinctions of relatives in, 54
    cultural variations in, 173–174
    influences on, 183–184
    norms of, 174
Kinship terminologies, 184–189
    Eskimo system of, 185–186, 186f, 188
    Hawaiian, 186, 186f, 188
    Iroquois, 186–187, 187f, 188
    Omaha, 187, 187, 188–189
    variations in, 187–189
Kinship ties, tracing, 173
Kin terms, 184–185
Knowledge
    cultural. See Cultural knowledge
    elderly persons' control of, 209
    global, 394
    of indigenous peoples, 393–397, 395
    local, 394
    medical, 394–395, 395
    power and, 81
    relativity of, 81
    transmission via language, 43

L
Labor, 105
    compatibility with child care, 225t, 226
    division of. See Division of labor
    internationalization of, 144
Labor shortages, 349
Land concentration, 386
Land races, 396
Language
    arbitrariness of words in, 27, 44
    behavior and, 10
    body, 51–52, 52
    culture and, 52–56
    defined, 41
    dialects of, 45–46
    discreteness of, 44
    displacement property, 44–45
    enculturation and, 43

Language (continued)
  as ethnic boundary marker, 356–357
  evolution and, 42–43
  extinction of, 57
  globalization and, 57–58
  grammar and, 45, 46–51
  humanity and, 42–43
  multimedia potential of, 43
  productivity of, 44
  properties of, 43–45
  relativity of, 46
  Romance, 56
  sign, *42,* 43
  specialized vocabularies in, 53
  study of, 10
  thought and, 43
  tone, 48–49, *49*
  withering of, 57
  words and meanings in, 49–51
  worldview and, 54–56
  See also Speech
Language taboo, 60
Law(s)
  civil, 249
  on clean air, 248
  Code of Hammurabi, 254
  on historic preservation, 4
  on Indian arts and crafts, 323
  separation from norms and values, 255
  social control and, 246–249, *249*
Legal rights of indigenous peoples, 390, 391
Legal systems, *239,* 249–255
  court systems, 252, 254–255, 341
  familial, 249–250, 255*t*
  mediator, 250–251, 255*t*
  reasonable-person model in, 254, 255
  self-help systems, 249–252, 255*t*
Leopard-skin chiefs, 250–251
Lesser developed countries (LDCs), 379–380
  costs and benefits of children in, 382–384
  economic problems of, 347–348
  health conditions in, 347
  hunger in, 384–389, 398
  migration away from, 348–350, *350, 351*
  population growth in, 380, *381,* 382–384
  technology transfer to, 386–388
Levirate, 161
Lexicon, 49, 53
Life cycle, 192, 200–209
  adolescence, 201*t,* 202–206, *203, 205, 207*
  adulthood, 206–208
  childhood, 201*t,* 202
  cultural expectations of stages, 201
  defined, 200
  infancy, 201*t,* 201–202
  initiation rites and, 204–206, *205, 207*
  old age, 208–209, *209*
  variations in, 201*t*
Limited-purpose money, 141
Lineages, 178. *See also* Kin groups; Kinship
  systems

Linguistic communities, 57
Linguistics
  anthropological, 3*t,* 10
  sociolinguistics, 56
Livestock, 112, 113
  husbandry of, 123–126, *125*
  Old and New World domesticates,
    114–115
Local knowledge, 394
"Lucy" *(Australopithecus afarensis),* 8

M
Magic
  logical principles of, 289–290
  religion and, 283–284, 285
Malaria, 346
Male dominance, 229–232
Male initiation rites, 204–206, *205,* 321–322
Maquiladores, 144
Margaret Mead in Samoa (Freeman), 203
Marital exchanges, 161–163
Market(s), *131,* 132, 133*f*
  free, 139
  globalization of, 144–146, *145*
  peasant, 146–147, *147*
Market economy, 142–146
  impersonality of, 147
  principles of, 142
Market exchange, *139,* 139–147
  market economy, 142–146, 147
  money, 140–142
  negative reciprocity vs., 137
  social distance in, 137
Marriage, defined, 152, 153
Marriage alliances, 160–161
Marriage practices, 152–156, *200*
  adult status conferred by, 207–208
  arranged marriages, 152–153, 161
  functions of, *154,* 154–155
  of gay couples, 164
  group marriage, 157
  intermarriage, 157
  monogamy, 157
  number of spouses, 157–160, *158*
  polyandry, 157, 158, 159–160
  polygamy, 157–160
  polygyny, 156, 157, *158,* 158–159, 197
  postmarital residence patterns, 164–169,
    168*f,* 234–235
  variety of forms of, 155–156
Marriage rules, 157
Materialism, 105
  cultural, 76–79, *78*
Matriarchy, 181
Matrifocal family, 167
Matrilineal descent, 100, 175, 176*f,* 176–177,
  179–181, *180*
  avunculocal residence and, 181
  among horticulturalists, 184
Matrilocal residence, 164, 166, 168, 184
Maturation, sexual vs. social, 202

Meanings
  of behavior, 27–29
  biological, 15
  in language, 49–51
Media, global, 350
Mediation, courts of, 252, 254
Mediator legal systems, 250–251, 255*t*
Medical anthropology, 11
Medical knowledge of indigenous peoples,
  394–395, *395*
Medium, 295
Meech Lake Agreement, 372
Methodological relativism, 15–16
Middle class, 265
Migration
  of ethnic groups, 366
  from undeveloped to developed nations,
    348–350, *350, 351*
Military force, and inequality, 270–271
Miscommunication, 52
Misfortune, supernatural explanations of,
  289–292
Missing link, 6
Missionaries, 95, 331, 333, 338
Money, 140–142
  limited-purpose, 141
  objects used as, 140, *141*
  symbolism of, 140
Monogamy, 157
Monotheism, 66, 99, *99*
Moral relativism, 15
Morphemes, 50–51, *51*
Morphology, 49–51
Mothers. *See* Child-rearing practices
Multicultural movement, 322, 324
Multinational countries
  political stability of, 374
  problems of, 371–374
Multiple gender identities, 218–221
Murder, and legal system, 251–252, 253
Music, 38, *38,* 317–319, 320
Myths, 281–282, *283,* 284, 285, 356

N
Name taboo, 60
Naming rites, 202
National Historic Preservation Act of
  1966, 4
National Indian Foundation (Brazil), 392
Nationalist organizations, *362*
Nationalities
  ethnic, 362
  inequality between, 374
  stateless, 360–368
  subnationalities, 358, 359*t*
  See also Ethnic groups
National Park Service, 4
Nation-states, and globalization, 247–248
Natural resources. *See* Resource(s)
Neandertals, 7*f,* 8, 9, 64
Negative reciprocity, 136–137

Neolocal residence, 165, 166
Net worth, 268, *268*
New World, 329
    conquest of, 330–332
    domestication in, 113, 114–115
    Industrial Revolution in, 335–336
    intensive agriculture in, 119
New York Stock Exchange, *139*
Nile River valley, 121, 121*f*
Nokia, 345–346
Nomadism, 123
Nonverbal communication, 27–28, *28,* 51–52, *52, 91*
Non-Western peoples, rationality of, 97. *See also* Indigenous peoples; Lesser developed countries (LDCs)
Norm(s), 26, 33*t,* 34
    ambiguity of, 35
    in child rearing, 193–194
    about family size, 381, 383
    of kinship systems, 174
    reinforcement of, 291
    separation from laws, 255
    violations of, 35, 246, 248. *See also* Social control
North American Free Trade Agreement, 144
Nuclear family, 151, 152*t*

O
Observation
    ethical, 90
    learning through, 202
    participant, 89
Old age, 208–209, *209*
Old World, 329
    domestication in, 113, 114
    intensive agriculture in, 119
On the Origin of Species (Darwin), 64
Opium War, 337
Oppression, 15
Organization, 33
    of production, 105–106, *106*
    religious, 292–299, 294*t*
    See also Political organization
Organization of African Unity, 368
Origin myths, *283,* 285, 356
Ornamentation, 315–316

P
Painting, 315
    body painting, 310, *310*
    sandpainting, 320–321
Paleoanthropology, 5, *11,* 64
Parallel cousins, 177
Parents. *See* Child-rearing practices
Participant observation, 89
Passive assimilation, 369–370, 371, 372*t*
Pastoralism, 107, 123–126, 124*f, 125*
    cultural consequences of, 127*t*
    descent systems associated with, 183–184
    herding environments, 107, 123–125

limiting factors of, 124–125
    regions of, at time of European contact, 124*f*
Patrilineal descent, 100, 175*f,* 175–176, *176,* 178–179, 197
    intergroup warfare and, 184
    among pastoralists, 183–184
    segmentation of, 178
Patrilineal principle, 177
Patrilocal residence, 164, 166, 168, 197
Patterns of behavior, 22, 25–26
Patterns of Culture (Benedict), 68
Peasant(s), *122,* 122–123
    cultural conservatism of, 387
    marketplaces for, 146–147, *147*
Peking Man (China), 9
Pentagon, attack on, 354
Performance arts, 317–319
Personal space, *28,* 28–29, 51–52, *52*
Peyote religion, 302–303
Pharmaceuticals, 92
Philips Electronics, 346
Phonemes, 46–47, 47*t, 48*
Phonological systems, 46–49
Phonology, 46–47
Physical anthropology, 3*t, 4,* 4–5, 73
Physical characteristics, as ethnic boundary marker, 357
Physical punishment, 249
Physical space, *28,* 28–29, 51–52, *52*
Physical violence, sanctioning of, 251–252
Plants
    Old and New World domesticates, 114
    use of, 396–397
    See also Agriculture; Horticulture
Political accommodation, 370, 371–374
Political authority, 241
Political boundaries vs. ethnic boundaries, 363
Political influence, 241
Political organization
    bands, 240–242, 241*t*
    chiefdoms, 240, 241*t,* 244
    forms of, 240–246
    intensive agriculture and, 120
    states, 240, 241*t,* 244–246
    tribes, 240, 241*t,* 242–243
Political power, and wealth, 267
Political stability, of multinational countries, 374
Politics, gender stratification in, 231
Polity, 240
Polyandry, 157, 158, 159–160
Polygamy, 157–160
Polygyny, 156, 157, *158,* 158–159, 197
Polytheism, 66, 99
Population growth, 380–384
    anthropological perspectives on, 380
    globalization and, 346–350
    regional differences in, 347*t*
    in Third World, 380, *381,* 382–384
Postmarital residence patterns, 164–167
    gender stratification and, 234–235
    household forms and, 167–169, 168*f*

Postmodernism, 79, 80–81
Potato famine, Irish, 385–386
Pottery, 315–316, *316,* 324
Power, 260
    knowledge and, 81
    wealth and, 267
Prehistoric archaeology, 2–3, *3,* 73
Preindustrial cultures, *104*
    adaptations of, 104, *104*
    limited-purpose money in, 141
    property rights in, 106
    tribute payments in, 138–139
Prestige, 260
Price, 139
Priests, 298
Primatology, 4, *4*
Primitive Culture (Tylor), 21
Primogeniture, 160
Private property, 139
Production, 105–106
    factors of, 105, 106
    organization of, 105–106, *106*
    as social activity, *106*
Progress
    cultural, 65
    economic, 397
    technological, 72
Property, inheritance of, 176–177
Property rights, 106, 118
Prophet, 300
Protoculture, 33
Proxemics, 51–52
Psychological approaches to religion, 286, *287*
Psychological sanctions, 249
Psychology, evolutionary, 74–76
Puberty rites. *See* Initiation rites
Pueblo, 179
Punishment, corporal, 249

R
Race
    biological meaning of, 15
    classifications of, 30
    cultural construction of, 30–31
    cultural variation vs., 36–39
    independence from culture, 16, 36–39, *37*
    traits and, 31
"Racial purity," 31
Rank, speech as reinforcer of, 56, 58–59
Ranked societies, 260, 261*t,* 261–262
Reality
    classifications of, 29, 32, 214
    cultural influence on, 33
Reasonable-person model, 254, 255
Reciprocity, 132, 133*f,* 133–137
    balanced, 134–136
    generalized, 133–134, *134*
    negative, 136–137
    of rights and duties, 25–26
    social distance and, 137
Redistribution, 132, 133*f,* 138–139, 244

Refugees, 349, *350,* 369
Reincarnation, 264
Relatives
    affinal, 151
    biological, 174
    consanguineal, 151, 174
    cultural classification of, 174. *See also*
        Kinship systems
    cultural distinctions of, 54
Relativism
    cultural, 14–16, 68, 94
    methodological, 15–16
    moral, 15
Relativistic perspective, 14–16
Religion, *63,* 99, *99,* 280, 280–304
    in Americas, 331, *332*
    animism, 66, 281
    art and, 313–314, 318–319, 320–321
    defined, 281–283
    as ethnic boundary marker, 357
    fundamentalism in, *343,* 343–345
    gender stratification in, 226
    ideological functions of, 271–272
    intellectual (cognitive) approaches to,
        285–286
    in Iraq, 364–367, 365*f*
    magic and, 283–284, 285
    monotheism, 66, 99, *99*
    music and, 318
    myths and, 281–282, *283,* 284, 285, 356
    origins and development of, 66
    peyote, 302–303
    polytheism, 66, 99
    psychological approaches to, 286, *287*
    reincarnation and, 264
    revitalization movements and, 299–303,
        301
    rituals in, 282–283
    sociological approaches to, 287–289, *288*
    spread of religious traditions, 56
    supernatural explanations of misfortune,
        289–292
    symbols of, 282–283
    theories of, 283–289
    as worldview, 32
Religious fundamentalism, *343,* 343–345, 361
Religious organization, 292–299, 294*t*
Relocation of ethnic groups, 369, 371, 372*t*
Remittance, 167
Reproductive choices, 380–384
Research, ethnographic, 88, 95–96, 101*t*
Residence patterns, postmarital, 164–169,
    168*f,* 234–235
Resource(s), 106
    allocation of, *385*
    culturally defined nature of, 79
    elite control of, 274
    knowledge of indigenous peoples as,
        393–397, *395*
    land concentration, 386
    rights to, 106, 110–111, 113, 118

sharing of, 110
surplus of, 120–121
unequal distribution of, 384–386
women's control over, 232–234, *233, 234*
Resource management
    cultural, 4
    traditional, 388–389
Revelation, 300
Revitalization movements, 299–303, *301*
Rice, *104, 120,* 390
Rights
    of indigenous peoples, 391–393
    legal, 390, 391
    property, 106, 118
    reciprocity of, 25–26
    to resources, 106, 110–111, 113, 118
Rites of passage, 71, 192
    defined, 200–201
    fieldwork as, 94–95
    gender and, 321–322
    initiation rites, 204–206, *205, 207,* 321–322
    naming rites, 202
    weddings, *200,* 207–208
Rituals, 282–283, *288*
    calendrical, 283
    communal, 298
    conscious purposes of, 282–283
    crisis, 283
    curing, 318–321
    defined, 282
    effects of, 284
    schedule of, 283
    symbolism of, 282–283
Rock art, 315
Rockefeller Foundation, 11
Roles, 25
    advocacy, 389–397
    age and, 200
    cross-gender, 219–220
    expectations, duties, and rights of, 25–26
    of fieldworkers, 93
    gender, *212,* 219–220, 221
Romance languages, 56

S

Sandpainting, 320–321
Sapir-Whorf hypothesis, 55–56
Scarcity explanation of hunger, 384–386
Scarification, 311, 312
Science, 285
Science vs. humanity issue, 72–83
Scientific approach
    in anthropological thought, 72–77, 74*t,*
        81–83
    in cultural materialism, 76–79, *78*
Seasonal congregation and dispersal, 108–109
Seasonal mobility, 108
Secessionist movements, 366–367
Secular art, 319–320
Secular ideologies of inequality, 272–273
Segmentary organization, 178

Segregation, 370, 372*t*
Self-help legal systems, 249–252, 255*t*
Self-identity, 213
Selfishness, 74–75
Semantic domains, 53–54
Semicolonial regions, 337
Sepoy Mutiny, 337
September 11, 2001, attacks, 79, 354
Settlements, size and permanence of,
    108–110, 118
Sewing, 316
Sex(es)
    biological variation between, *223,* 223–224,
        225*t,* 226
    gender vs., 213–214
    marriage and, 154
    relative strength of, *223,* 225*t,* 226, *226*
    same-sex relations, 220–221
Sex roles, *212,* 219–220, 221
Sexual division of labor, 107–108, *109,* 111,
    126, 221–228, *223, 224,* 225*t,* 226
    for food production, *212,* 221–222, 227–228
    patterns in, 222*t,* 222–226
    variability in, 227–228
Shamanism, 292, 294*t,* 295–297, *296*
Sharing. *See* Reciprocity
Shifting cultivation, 29, 116
Sign language, *42,* 43
Silent Language, The (Hall), 51
Simple bands, 240–241, 241*t*
Slavery and slave trade, 331, 332, 333
    abolishment of, 336
    in Americas, 335–336
Smallpox, 346–347
Small-scale societies. *See* Indigenous peoples;
    Preindustrial cultures
Social anthropology. *See* Cultural
    anthropology
Social birth, 201
Social control
    gossip as form of, 248, *249*
    held by elites, 270–271
    law and, 246–249, *249*
    sorcery as form of, 97–98
    supernatural sanctions as form of,
        248–249
    witchcraft as form of, 291–292
Social distance, and reciprocity, 137
Social groups, 151, 172. *See also* Kin groups;
    Marriage practices
Social identity, 25, 213, 322, 324
Social inequality
    address terms and, 56, 58–59
    functionalist theory of, 273–274
    in industrial nations, *266,* 266–268, *268*
Socialization, 23. *See also* Enculturation
Social life, cultural basis of, 33
Social mobility, 263
Social person, 201
Social reality, cultural classifications of, 214
Social relationships, 25, 79

conflict and strain in, 289–290
gift giving in, 136
reciprocity and, 137
Social rewards, 260, 262–263, 276
Social sciences, 82
Social stratification, *259,* 260, 262–268
castes, 261*t,* 263–265, *264*
in chiefdoms, 244
classes, 261*t,* 265–268, *266, 267t, 268*
conflict theories of, 273, 274–275, *275*
wealth and, 266–268, *268*
See also Inequality
Social stratum, 262
Social structure, 70
Social systems, 70
Society, 22–23
Sociobiology, 74–75, 76
Sociocultural anthropology. *See* Cultural
anthropology
Sociolinguistics, 56
Sociological approaches to religion, 287–289,
288
Sociological interpretations of sorcery and
witchcraft, 291–292
Sodalities, 242, 243
Song, 317–319, 320
Sorcery, 289–290
as form of social control, 97–98
interpretations of, 291–292
Sororal polygyny, 159
Sororate, 161
Space, personal, *28,* 28–29, 51–52, *52*
Speech, 10
context of, 56, 59
pitch and, 48
presentation of self with, 60
social uses of, 56–60, *59*
vocal tract evolution for, 42–43
See also Language
Spirit helpers, 295
Standard American English (SAE), 45, 46
State of Working America 2004/5 (Economic
Policy Institute), 268
States, 121, 240, 241*t,* 244–246
Status, 260
art and, 324–325
conferred by marriage, 207–208
of cultural anthropology, 12–13
speech as reinforcer of, 56, 58–59
of women, 228–236, *233*
Status groups, 266
Stereotypes, 69, 90, 92–93
Stratified societies, 260, 261*t,* 262–268
Structured interviewing, 88
Study communities
ethical obligations to, 90
perception of fieldworkers, 83
Subcultures, 23
Subnationalities, 358, 359*t*
Subsistence risk reduction, 123
Suicide, 253

Summer Institute of Linguistics (Monterey,
Calif.), 57
Supernatural explanations of misfortune,
289–292
Supernatural powers
alternative gender identities and, 220
beliefs about, 281
Supernatural sanctions, as form of social
control, 248–249
Superstition, 284
Supply and demand, 139
Surplus, 120–121
Survey of Consumer Finances (Federal
Reserve Board), 268
Symbolic communication, *41,* 79
Symbolism, 27–29, 33*t*
in art, 314, 316
in female-male differences, 214
of money, 140
of rituals, 282–283
in social behavior, 80
of speech, 60

T
Taboos, 60, 154–155, 157
Tattoos, 310–312, *312*
Taxation, 121, 123, 124, 138, 246, 336, 337
Taxonomy, 6
Techno-environmental determinism, 72
Technological determinism, 72
Technological progress, 72
Technology, 105
access to, 347–348
culture and, 71–72
determination of cultural adaptation, 72
global economy and, 339–340, *340*
military, 329
Technology transfer, 386–388
Textile designs, 315
Third World. *See* Lesser developed countries
(LDCs)
Thought
behavior and, 21–22
language and, 43
See also Anthropological thought
Tigris and Euphrates River valley, 121
Time, conception of, 32, 55
Tiwi Wives (Goodale), 156
Tone language, 48–49, *49*
Tools, 26
making, 6, 8
prehistoric, 64, 65
Totemic clan, 178
Totemism, 298
Touching, 52, *52*
Trade
free, 144, 247–248, 342
global, 329–338, 342*f*
inter-Asian, 334–335
in slaves. *See* Slavery and slave trade
surplus and, 120

Trade partnerships, 134–136
Traditional farming practices, 388–389
Traditional resource management, 388–389
Trail of Tears, 369
Traits, and race, 31
Trance, 295
Transnational(s), 359, 359*t*
Transnational corporations, 344–346
Transvestism, 220
Treaty of Sevres, 366
Tribal war chiefs, 243
Tribes, 240, 241*t,* 242–243
Tribute, 138–139

U
Unilineal descent, 174–181
communal rituals and, 298
matrilineal, 175, 176*f,* 176–177, 179–181,
180, 184
patrilineal, 175*f,* 175–176, *176,* 178–179,
183–184, 197
Unilineal evolution, 65–66
United Nations Development Program, 11
United Nations Security Council, 361
U.S. Agency for International Development, 11
U.S. Census Bureau, 267, 267*t*
U.S. Forest Service, 4
U.S. Supreme Court, 344
Unstructured interviewing, 88
Untouchables (India), 265

V
Values, 26–27, 33*t*
conflicts of, 35
cultural influences on, 15
economic influences on, 143, 146
gender and, 214
influence on behavior, 27, 34–35
moral relativism and, 16
separation from laws, 255
Vietnamese language, *49*
Villages, 118
Violence, sanctioning of, 251–252
Vision quests, 294–295
Visual arts, 312–317
Voudon (voodoo), 318

W
Wailing wall (Jerusalem), *284*
Warfare, 251, 252
descent systems associated with, 184
sexual division of labor and, 227–228
slave-related, 333
Warrior societies, 243
Wealth, 260
bridewealth, 159, 162, 163
distribution of, 267
power and, 267
social stratification based on, 266–268,
268
Weddings, *200,* 207–208

Western civilization, 350–351, 360, 361
Wild rice, 390
Witchcraft, 290–291
    defined, 290
    interpretations of, 291–292
Women
    art and, 321–322
    as caretakers, *216*
    child care and, 154, *154*
    control over resources, 232–234, *233, 234*
    in division of labor, 107–108, *109,* 126
    dowry deaths of, 163
    fertility maintenance and, 225, 225*t*
    as food suppliers, *212,* 221–222, 227–228, *231*
    in foraging societies, 107–108, *109,* 110
    garden work of, 227

    gender roles of, *212*
    as heads of households, 167
    labor, compatibility with child care, 225*t,* 226
    material welfare, contributions to, 232–233
    status of, 228–236, *233*
    subordination of, 229–232
    See also Gender stratification; Sex(es)
Words, 49–51
Work, 105, 142–143
Working Group of Indigenous Minorities in Southern Africa (WIMSA), 91
World Bank, 11, 341, 342
World Health Organization (WHO), 346–347
World Hunger: Twelve Myths (Lappé & Collins), 385

World Trade Center attack, 354
World Trade Organization (WTO), 247–248, 342, 346
Worldview, 32, 33*t*
    communication of, 43
    Judeo-Christian, 64
    language and, 54–56
    myths and, 281–282
    religious beliefs and, 32
World War II, 339, 340
Writing systems, 26, 43
Written records, 2, 3

Y
Yazdani religion, 364